16641

BENJAMIN FRANKLIN'S AUTOBIOGRAPHY

AN AUTHORITATIVE TEXT

BACKGROUNDS

CRITICISM

16641

BENJAMIN FRANKLIN'S AUTOBIOGRAPHY

An Authoritative Text
Backgrounds
Criticism

⇛⇚

Edited by

J. A. LEO LEMAY

H. F. DUPONT WINTERTHUR PROFESSOR
UNIVERSITY OF DELAWARE

P. M. ZALL

CALIFORNIA STATE
UNIVERSITY, LOS ANGELES

W • W • Norton & Company
New York   *London*

16641

The text of this book is composed in Electra, with display type set in Deepdene. Composition by Spartan Typographers. Manufacturing by The Murray Printing Company.

FIRST EDITION

Library of Congress Cataloging in Publication Data
Franklin, Benjamin, 1706-1790.
  Autobiography : an authoritative text.
  (A Norton critical edition)
  Bibliography: p. 361
  1. Franklin, Benjamin, 1706-1790. 2. Statesmen—
United States—Biography. I. Lemay, J. A. Leo
(Joseph A. Leo), 1935-   II. Zall, Paul M.
E302.6.F7A2 1984   973.3'092'4 [B]   84-3999
ISBN 0-393-01737-0
ISBN 0-393-95294-0 {pbk.}

W.W. Norton & Company, Inc.
500 Fifth Avenue, New York, N.Y. 10110
W.W. Norton & Company, Ltd.
10 Coptic Street, London WC1A 1PU

1234567890

For Kevin & David

COPYRIGHT ACKNOWLEDGMENTS

Contents

Acknowledgments

Since this text is based on our edition of *The Autobiography of Benjamin Franklin: A Genetic Text* (Knoxville: University of Tennessee Press, 1981), we are again indebted to those libraries that allowed us to use materials for that edition: the Henry E. Huntington Library and Art Gallery for the holograph manuscript of Franklin's autobiography, the J. Pierpont Morgan Library for the outline of the autobiography, the American Antiquarian Society for Uncle Benjamin Franklin's poems, and the Boston Public Library for Franklin's wagon advertisement.

Our greatest scholarly debt is to the splendid series, *The Papers of Benjamin Franklin* (New Haven: Yale University Press, 1959–), eds. Leonard W. Labaree, William B. Willcox, et al. Its documents and annotations are the essential source where all Franklin scholarship must now begin.

Those individuals who helped with the former volume—Virginia Rener, Jean Preston, Daniel H. Woodward, Bruce Henry, Elisabeth Zall, Dorothy W. Bridgewater, James E. Mooney, John C. Broderick, Sue Sadler Luce, Herbert Cahoon, Marion Simpson, Carla Mulford, and Hershel Parker—again have our thanks. And we have incurred new obligations. Carla Mulford, Sue Peters, and James M. Hutchisson have helped with the proofreading. Alan Gribben provided us with information concerning Mark Twain's relations with Franklin before that material appeared in his masterful *Mark Twain's Library: A Reconstruction,* 2 vols. (Boston: G. K. Hall & Co., 1980); and David Nordloh sent on references to William Dean Howells's writings on Benjamin Franklin. The staffs of the Huntington Library, the Hugh C. Morris Library at the University of Delaware, and the John F. Kennedy Library at California State University, Los Angeles, have been unfailingly helpful. And finally, at W. W. Norton & Company, we wish to thank Peter Phelps, John Benedict, and, most recently, Marian Johnson.

Introduction

Franklin's *Autobiography* is the only enduring best-seller written in America before the nineteenth century. It is the most popular autobiography ever written. No other classic of English or American literature has served as a model for the lives of so many people (or roused the ire of so many readers) as the *Autobiography*. And its audience has been world-wide. By comparison with Franklin's *Autobiography*, the writings of his great English contemporary Dr. Samuel Johnson are provincial, for their circulation and influence are comparatively small. Yet we, like all lovers of English and American literature, believe Johnson to be a major writer and a major man of letters. We also believe that Franklin is a great writer, but we know that many critics deny Franklin this distinction. The purpose of the Norton Critical Edition is to present the reader with the materials to judge for himself Franklin's major work, the *Autobiography*.

Franklin wrote his autobiography over a period of more than eighteen years. The book is usually divided into three or four parts, according to the dates of the original composition. Except for Part Four, Franklin's manuscript justifies the divisions, for his notes within the text clearly distinguish Parts One, Two and Three. The danger of speaking of the "parts" of the manuscript and of printing it in "parts" is that this distinction seemingly denies the book's unity. The outline, however, proves that the book was planned as a whole when Franklin began composing it. Although Franklin made a number of significant changes and additions, he generally followed the outline as he composed the *Autobiography*.

The actual writing was done on large folio-size pages which Franklin folded lengthways in half, and then wrote on only one half (or column) of the page, leaving the other column blank for possible additions and revisions. Two hundred of the 230 pages of the original manuscript contain additions or revisions in the columns originally left blank. The longest addition was made at the very beginning: after the third sentence (but Franklin changed its concluding period to a semi-colon and continued the sentence; see our textual notes at 1.5–2.18 and 2.19 on p. 157), he added two full columns giving his supposed reasons for writing the *Autobiography*.

Part One (87 ms. pages) was written between Tuesday, July 30, and Tuesday, August 13, 1771, while Franklin, age 65, was visiting Jonathan Shipley, Bishop of St. Asaph, at his country estate, Chilbolton, near Twyford, Hampshire, England. Part One was revised several times between 1788 and early 1790 while Franklin was writing Parts

Three and Four. Franklin also drew up the outline of the *Autobiography* in 1771—probably, as Carl Van Doren suggested, after writing the first eight pages of the manuscript (see pp. 169–72, The Outline). Franklin left the outline and the ms. of Part One in Philadelphia in 1776 when he sailed to France. By the summer of 1782 the outline and the ms. had come into the possession of his old friend Abel James, who sent Franklin a copy of the outline and urged him to complete the book. Franklin corrected the outline and brought it up to date. Sometime in 1784, during his excessively busy years in France, he spent a few days writing the twelve pages that comprise Part Two.

Part Three (119 ms. pages) was begun in August, 1788, while Franklin was at home in Philadelphia, age 82. Evidently Franklin wrote all but the final sixteen pages (and the ten inserted pages, see the textual note at 102.23 on p. 154) of this section before the end of the year. He was very ill by 1789, his handwriting increasingly shaky, but he completed the final sixteen pages of Part Three before May, 1789. And he revised Part Three (as well as Parts One and Two) several times during 1788 and 1789. Part Four (7 ms. pages) was written sometime after November 13, 1789, and before Franklin's death on April 17, 1790, at age 84. Perhaps he again read through the whole manuscript between these dates, for he made a few revisions in Part One at this time.

This is the first accurate edition of the *Autobiography* intended for the general reader. (The Lemay and Zall *Genetic Text* is intended for the scholar.) As we show in our Note on the Text (page xvii this edition) every previous editor, rather than transcribe the original manuscript, has made the procedural mistake of "correcting" a faulty edition in print, thereby perpetuating some old errors. Our textual notes record all instances in which we depart from the manuscript and all later revisions made by Franklin, as well as all the more significant cancellations and revisions. The footnotes elucidate references, allusions, and sources; define uncommon words; call attention to Franklin's errors; and locate analogues in his other writings. The biographical sketches give a brief notice (and a bibliographical reference) for all the persons mentioned in the *Autobiography*.

The section on Backgrounds includes Franklin's most important statements about the purpose of the *Autobiography*. Since his diction and tone are colloquial without being familiar (deliberately so, as his revisions demonstrate), it is interesting to compare his expressions of the same ideas in private letters. Here too we record oral versions of some anecdotes that appear in the *Autobiography*. And since Franklin's ideas about wealth, the art of virtue, and perfection have so often been misunderstood, we include a brief collection of his statements on these subjects as another context for the book.

The criticism section begins with the opinions of some of Franklin's contemporaries—in part, to show that he was widely regarded by his contemporaries as an important writer and in part, to show that his contemporaries were as divided in their opinions of his reputation and personality as modern critics are about the art of the *Autobiography*. The nineteenth-century criticism shows that hostile and favorable opinions about the values of Franklin's *Autobiography* have existed as long as the book has been in print. Of course, we have tried to select the most interesting opinions. And we include a selection of recent analytical essays on Franklin's *Autobiography*. The bibliography lists first, the most important previous editions of the *Autobiography*; second, the books and articles referred to by short title in the notes; and third, the most important twentieth-century books and essays about the *Autobiography*.

Note on the Text

The Norton Critical Edition of Franklin's *Autobiography* is a clear text (i.e., one without textual symbols that might impede reading) based on the Lemay and Zall *Genetic Text* (which contains textual symbols that attempt to reveal the process of Franklin's composition). In Franklin's day, people paid less attention to standard spellings and to "correct" punctuation than today. Writing quickly, Franklin spells *Rhode Island* as *Rhodeisland* and *Pennsylvania* sometimes as *Pensilvania*. His friend the Reverend George Whitefield appears as *Whitefiel*, *Whitfield*, and *Whitefield*. Had Franklin printed his *Autobiography*, he would have normalized his hurried manuscript spellings, just as he did for his other writings. For the Norton Critical Edition, we have decided to correct his slips of the pen and carelessnesses and to present a slightly modernized text (thus his *Sope* becomes *Soap*, *disputacious* becomes *disputatious*, etc.). But all our changes, with a few exceptions noted under "Accidentals," are listed in the textual notes. In order to preserve the eighteenth-century flavor of the text, we have kept his capitals and his apostrophes for the missing "e". And we have of course retained his eighteenth-century spellings whenever we thought a modernization might weaken its effect (thus we leave *blustring* at 24.13, though we consistently change *rendred* to *rendered*). We believe that the resulting text is easier to read—and the purist may always consult our *Genetic Text*.

Previous editions based on the holograph manuscript contain numerous errors because previous editors, rather than make a completely fresh transcription of the holograph, have merely corrected existing editions: thus John Bigelow corrected Jared Sparks's edition; Max Farrand (and his staff at the Huntington Library) corrected Bigelow's edition; and Leonard W. Labaree et al. (using a photographic facsimile of the holograph rather than the original) corrected Farrand's edition. All previous editors therefore perpetuated some errors. We have collated our edition with the best previous editions of the *Autobiography* and discovered over six hundred discrepancies in Farrand's and Labaree's editions, including more than fifty substantive passages. To give the reader an idea of these substantive differences, we list here the errors made by Farrand and Labaree in the first twenty pages of the original holograph. Farrand, 2.35, prints "the next Thing," as does Labaree, 44.2; but the holograph manuscript shows that Franklin cancelled "next" and that the text should read simply "the Thing." Farrand, 4.32, has "Reverse," as does Labaree, 45.7; but the ms. reads "Reverso." Farrand, 6.3, has "these," as does Labaree, 45.13; but the ms. has "those." Farrand 8.18, has "they," as does

Labaree, 47.2; but the ms. has "those." Farrand, 24.6, has "Opinion in," as does Labaree, 55.5; but the ms. has "Opinion on." After "Spectator," Farrand, 36.1, prints the sentence "It was the third," as does Labaree, 61.16-62.1; but the manuscript shows that Franklin cancelled the sentence in pencil. Farrand 46.37-8, has "frequently had" (although he points out, 46, n. 33, that Franklin cancelled this in pencil and inserted "began to have"), as does Labaree, 68.16 (who, however, omits the important note); and we follow, of course, Franklin's revised version, "began to have." In addition, Farrand, 8.24, correctly prints "qualify'd himself for," but Labaree, 47.7, drops the word "himself." We might also point out that Farrand makes frequent errors in his few transcriptions of cancelled passages, but Labaree simply omits most cancellations printed by Farrand.

Our text also differs from the Farrand and Labaree editions in several matters of editorial judgment. Farrand and Labaree are inconsistent regarding manuscript symbols and abbreviations. Farrand substitutes "per" for the ms. symbol (with no indication that Franklin used the symbol) but does not write out either the ampersand (except where he does so in error) or the symbol for "etc." Sometimes Farrand spells out Franklin's abbreviated words but generally he does not. Labaree spells out "per" and "and" but not the symbol for "etc." Labaree uses the abbreviated names but generally spells out abbreviated words. Our text expands all manuscript symbols and abbreviations except those commonly used in printed texts (i.e., Mr. and Dr.), and although Franklin is inconsistent about including periods after abbreviations, we always use them. We omit the clause about William Bradford (see below, 17.31 on p. 159) because Franklin added brackets around this clause and connected the brackets with a line. Thus we believe that he meant to cancel the clause. But Farrand and Labaree (following Bigelow, who followed Sparks, who followed William Temple Franklin, who followed—either directly or indirectly—Buisson) print the clause within parentheses. (Of course the cancelled passage is recorded in our textual notes.) Farrand and Labaree sometimes print Franklin's notes to himself (or to his printer or copyist) such as "(Here insert it)"—though Labaree, 56.6, omits the note before the inscription on Franklin's parents' tombstone. We believe that Franklin would not have wanted such directions to be printed, and so we only record them in our textual notes. Farrand and Labaree sometimes incorporate Franklin's footnotes in the text (e.g., that on "Mr. Matthew Adams"), but generally they print them as footnotes. We invariably print them as notes, but we distinguish them from our notes (which are numbered) by using Franklin's symbols, by separating them with rules from the text and the editor's notes, and by writing "[BF note.]" after them. These differences are all matters of editorial judgment rather than errors on the part of former editors.

Franklin himself intended at one time to include six supporting documents in the *Autobiography* (although they are not now in the original manuscript): 1, notes on the name *Franklin*; 2, poems that his Uncle Benjamin Franklin wrote to him; 3, an editorial on Massachusetts politics, October 9, 1729; 4, the letters from Abel James and Benjamin Vaughan urging him to continue the *Autobiography*; 5, the Golden Verses of Pythagoras; and 6, the advertisement for the wagons for Braddock's army. Farrand's edition omits them all. Labaree's edition omits the first, third and fifth. We print them all. And, like Bigelow, Farrand, and Labaree, we print Franklin's important outline of the *Autobiography*.

Various abbreviations are used in the annotations. See pages 362–65 for complete bibliographical references.

Franklin Enters Philadelphia, Sunday, October 6, 1723†

1. Market Street Wharf,[1] where Franklin landed "about 8 or 9 o' Clock."
2. Crooked Billet Tavern, the site of the present 35 South Front Street, where Franklin was "suspected" to "be some Runaway" and where he spent his first night in Philadelphia.
3. Thomas Denham's shop, the site of the present 39 South Front Street, where Franklin clerked after returning from England, 1726–27.
4. Andrew Bradford's office, c. 1717–24, the site of the present 12–18 South Second Street, where Franklin applied for work, Monday morning, October 7, 1723.
5. Friends' Meeting House, at the south west corner of Second and Market Streets, where Franklin "being very drowsy thro' Labour and want of Rest . . . fell fast asleep."
6. Court House, erected c. 1709.
7. Christ Church, at the north west corner of Second Street and Church Alley, where Franklin's family attended services.
8. First Presbyterian Church, where Franklin "despaired of ever meeting" with any morality from the preaching of Jedediah Andrews but where Samuel Hemphill "delivered with a good Voice, and apparently extempore, most excellent Discourses."
9. Indian King Tavern, where the Junto and the Masons sometimes met.
10. John Read's residence, the site of the present 318 Market Street, where Deborah supposedly stood and saw Franklin and "thought I made as I certainly did a most awkward ridiculous Appearance."
11. Franklin Court, where Franklin built his last home, 1764–87.
12. The New Building, erected for George Whitefield in 1740, which Franklin secured and renovated in 1749–50 for the Philadelphia Academy, now the University of Pennsylvania.
13. Christ Church Cemetery, where Franklin and his family are buried.
14. State House (now Independence Hall), designed by Franklin's patron Andrew Hamilton, with Thomas Godfrey, who was then living with Franklin, doing most of the glass work.

† Sources: Franklin's *Autobiography*; Hannah Benner Roach, "Benjamin Franklin Slept Here," *PMHB*, 84 (1960), 127–74; Grant M. Simon's map *Part of Old Philadelphia* (1951, 1952; rev. 1966), also published in *Historic Philadelphia* (Philadelphia: American Philosophical Society, 1953); and "Franklin's Philadelphia, 1723-1776," a map in *The Papers of Benjamin Franklin*, 2 (New Haven: Yale University Press, 1960), 456.

1. The indicated route does not reflect two uncertainties: as he walked west up Market Street, he detoured off on Second Street to a baker's, where he bought "three great Puffy Rolls"; and walking down Chestnut Street, he may have continued as far as Second Street before going south to Walnut Street.

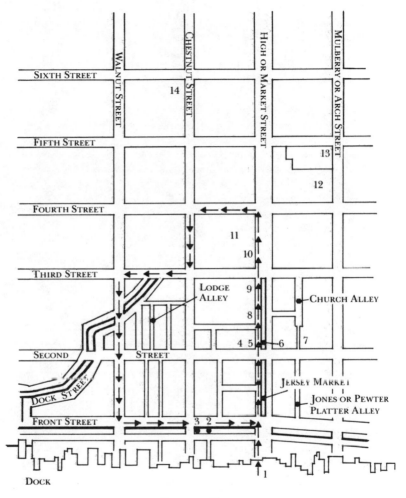

SIXTH STREET

WALNUT STREET

CHESTNUT STREET

HIGH OR MARKET STREET

MULBERRY OR ARCH STREET

14

FIFTH STREET

13

12

FOURTH STREET

11

10

THIRD STREET

LODGE
ALLEY

9

CHURCH ALLEY

8

4 5 6 7

SECOND STREET

DOCK STREET

JERSEY MARKET

JONES OR PEWTER
PLATTER ALLEY

FRONT STREET

3 2

1

DOCK

DELAWARE RIVER

The Text of the
Autobiography

The Autobiography

[Part One]

Twyford,[1] at the Bishop of St. Asaph's 1771.

Dear Son,[2]

I have ever had a Pleasure in obtaining any little Anecdotes of my Ancestors. You may remember the Enquiries I made among the Remains of my Relations when you were with me in England; and the Journey I took for that purpose.[3] Now imagining it may be equally agreeable to you to know the Circumstances of my Life, many of which you are yet unacquainted with; and expecting a Week's uninterrupted Leisure in my present Country Retirement, I sit down to write them for you. To which I have besides some other Inducements. Having emerg'd from the Poverty and Obscurity in which I was born and bred, to a State of Affluence and some Degree of Reputation in the World, and having gone so far thro' Life with a considerable Share of Felicity, the conducting Means I made use of, which, with the Blessing of God, so well succeeded, my Posterity may like to know, as they may find some of them suitable to their own Situations, and therefore fit to be imitated. That Felicity, when I reflected on it, has induc'd me sometimes to say, that were it offer'd to my Choice, I should have no Objection to a Repetition of the same Life from its Beginning, only asking the Advantage Authors have in a second Edition to correct some Faults of the first. So would I if I might, besides correcting the Faults, change some sinister Accidents and Events of it for others more favorable, but tho' this were denied, I should still accept the Offer. However, since such a Repetition is not to be expected, the Thing most like living one's Life over again, seems to be a *Recollection* of that Life; and to make that Recollection as durable as possible, the putting it down in Writing. Hereby, too, I shall indulge the Inclination so natural in old Men, to be talking of themselves and their own past Actions, and I shall indulge it, without being troublesome to others who thro' respect to Age might think themselves oblig'd to give me a Hearing, since this may be read or not as any one pleases. And lastly, (I may as well confess it, since my Denial of it will be believ'd by

1. Rural estate of Jonathan Shipley, Bishop of St. Asaph, six miles from Winchester, fifty miles south of London, where BF vacationed and wrote Part One of his *Autobiography*, July 30-August 13, 1771.
2. William Franklin, in 1771, was the forty-

year-old Governor of New Jersey.
3. In July, 1758, BF and William Franklin visited the Franklin ancestral homes at Ecton and Banbury in Northamptonshire. (P, 8: 114-21.)

no body) perhaps I shall a good deal gratify my own *Vanity*. Indeed I scarce ever heard or saw the introductory Words, *Without Vanity I may say*, etc. but some vain thing immediately follow'd. Most People dislike Vanity in others whatever Share they have of it themselves, but I give it fair Quarter wherever I meet with it, being persuaded that it is often productive of Good to the Possessor and to others that are within his Sphere of Action: And therefore in many Cases it would not be quite absurd if a Man were to thank God for his Vanity among the other Comforts of Life.

And now I speak of thanking God, I desire with all Humility to acknowledge, that I owe the mention'd Happiness of my past Life to his kind Providence, which led me to the Means I us'd and gave them Success. My Belief of This, induces me to *hope*, tho' I must not *presume*, that the same Goodness will still be exercis'd towards me in continuing that Happiness, or in enabling me to bear a fatal Reverso, [4] which I may experience as others have done, the Complexion of my future Fortune being known to him only: and in whose Power it is to bless to us even our Afflictions.

The Notes [5] one of my Uncles (who had the same kind of Curiosity in collecting Family Anecdotes) once put into my Hands, furnish'd me with several Particulars, relating to our Ancestors. From those Notes I learned that the Family had liv'd in the same Village, Ecton [6] in Northamptonshire, for 300 Years, and how much longer he knew not, (perhaps from the Time when the Name *Franklin* that before was the Name of an Order of People, was assum'd by them for a Surname, when others took Surnames all over the Kingdom)* on a Freehold of about 30 Acres, aided by the Smith's Business which had continued in the Family till his Time, the eldest Son being always bred to that Business. A Custom which he and my Father both followed as to their

---

* As a proof that FRANKLIN was anciently the common name of an order or rank in England, see Judge Fortescue, *De laudibus Legum Angliae*, written about the year 1412, in which is the following passage, to show that good juries might easily be formed in any part of England.

"Regio etiam illa, ita respersa refertaque est *possessoribus terrarum* et agrorum, quod in ea, villula tam parva reperiri non poterit, in qua non est *miles, armiger*, vel pater-familias, qualis ibidem *Franklin* vulgariter nuncupatur, magnis ditatus possessionibus, nec non libere tenentes et alii *valeci* plurimi, suis patrimoniis sufficientes ad faciendum juratam, in forma praenotata."

"Moreover, the same country is so filled and replenished with landed menne, that therein so small a Thorpe cannot be found werein dweleth not a knight, an esquire, or such a householder, as is there commonly called a *Franklin*, enriched with great possessions; and also other freeholders and many yeomen able for their livelihoods to make a jury in form aforementioned."

—*(Old Translation.)*

Chaucer too calls his Country Gentleman, a *Franklin*, and after describing his good housekeeping thus characterises him:

"This worthy Franklin bore a purse of silk,
Fix'd to his girdle, white as morning milk.
Knight of the Shire, first Justice at th' Assize,
To help the poor, the doubtful to advise.
In all employments, generous, just, he proved;
Renown'd for courtesy, by all beloved."

[BF note.]

---

4. A back-handed stroke, as in dueling with rapiers.
5. Uncle Benjamin Franklin's "A short account of the Family of Thomas Franklin of Ecton in Northamptonshire. 21 June 1717" is at the Yale University Library.
6. Five miles northeast of Northampton, fifty miles northwest of London.

eldest Sons. When I search'd the Register at Ecton, I found an Account of their Births, Marriages and Burials, from the Year 1555 only, there being no Register kept in that Parish at any time preceding. By that Register I perceiv'd that I was the youngest Son of the youngest Son for 5 Generations back.[7] My Grandfather Thomas, who was born in 1598, lived at Ecton till he grew too old to follow Business longer, when he went to live with his Son John, a Dyer at Banbury in Oxfordshire, with whom my Father serv'd an Apprenticeship. There my Grandfather died and lies buried. We saw his Gravestone in 1758. His eldest Son Thomas liv'd in the House at Ecton, and left it with the Land to his only Child, a Daughter, who with her Husband, one Fisher of Wellingborough, sold it to Mr. Isted, now Lord of the Manor there.

My Grandfather had 4 Sons that grew up, viz. Thomas, John, Benjamin and Josiah. I will give you what Account I can of them at this distance from my Papers, and if those are not lost in my Absence, you will among them find many more Particulars. Thomas was bred a Smith under his Father, but being ingenious, and encourag'd in Learning (as all his Brothers likewise were,) by an Esquire Palmer then the principal Gentleman in that Parish, he qualified himself for the Business of Scrivener,[8] became a considerable Man in the County Affairs, was a chief Mover of all public Spirited Undertakings for the County or Town of Northampton and his own Village, of which many Instances were told us at Ecton, and he was much taken Notice of and patroniz'd by the then Lord Halifax. He died in 1702, Jan. 6, old Stile,[9] just 4 Years to a Day before I was born. The Account[1] we receiv'd of his Life and Character from some old People at Ecton, I remember struck you as something extraordinary from its Similarity to what you knew of mine. Had he died on the same Day, you said once might have suppos'd a Transmigration.

John was bred a Dyer, I believe of Woollens. Benjamin was bred a Silk Dyer, serving an Apprenticeship at London. He was an ingenious Man. I remember him well, for when I was a Boy he came over to my Father in Boston, and lived in the House with us some Years. He lived to a great Age. His Grandson Samuel Franklin now lives in Boston. He left behind him two Quarto[2] Volumes, Manuscript of his own

7. When BF made this same observation on July 31, 1758, he added "whereby I find that had there originally been any Estate in the Family none could have stood a worse chance for it." (P, 8: 118.)
8. Professional penman similar to modern public stenographers.
9. Until September, 1752, England used the Julian calendar, in which the new year began on March 25. Since the Julian calendar did not have leap years, it was lagging behind, so the English skipped eleven days (September 3 to 13,

1752) when they adopted the Gregorian calendar. BF's birthday is reckoned January 6, 1705/ 6, "old style" or January 17, 1706, "new style."
1. BF reported this "account" to his wife, September 6, 1758. (P, 8: 137–38.)
2. In folio books, the sheet of paper is folded once, making four pages measuring about 38 cm x 25 cm; in octavo, the sheet is folded twice, making eight pages (each about 25 x 19); and in quarto, the sheet is folded three times, making sixteen pages (each about 19 x 12).

Poetry, consisting of little occasional Pieces address'd to his Friends and Relations, of which the following sent to me, is a Specimen.* He had form'd a Shorthand of his own, which he taught me, but never practicing it I have now forgot it. I was nam'd after this Uncle, there being a particular Affection between him and my Father. He was very pious, a great Attender of Sermons of the best Preachers, which he took down in his Shorthand and had with him many Volumes of them. He was also much of a Politician, too much perhaps for his Station. There fell lately into my Hands in London a Collection he had made of all the principal Pamphlets relating to Public Affairs from 1641 to 1717. Many of the Volumes are wanting, as appears by the Numbering, but there still remains 8 Volumes Folio, and 24 in Quarto and Octavo. A Dealer in old Books met with them, and knowing me by my sometimes buying of him, he brought them to me.[3] It seems my Uncle must have left them here when he went to America, which was above 50 Years since. There are many of his Notes in the Margins.

This obscure Family of ours was early in the Reformation, and continu'd Protestants thro' the Reign of Queen Mary,[4] when they were sometimes in Danger of Trouble on Account of their Zeal against Popery. They had got an English Bible, and to conceal and secure it, it was fastened open with Tapes under and within the Frame of a Joint Stool. When my Great Great Grandfather read in it to his Family, he turn'd up the Joint Stool upon his Knees, turning over the Leaves then under the Tapes. One of the Children stood at the Door to give Notice if he saw the Apparitor coming, who was an Officer of the

---

* Sent to My Name upon a Report
of his Inclination to Martial affaires
7 July 1710
Beleeve me Ben. It is a Dangerous Trade
The Sword has Many Marr'd as well as Made
By it doe many fall Not Many Rise
Makes Many poor few Rich and fewer Wise
Fills Towns with Ruin, fields with blood
                                        beside 5
Tis Sloths Maintainer, And the Shield of pride
Fair Citties Rich to Day, in plenty flow
War fills with want, Tomorrow, & with woe
Ruin'd Estates, The Nurse of Vice, broke limbs
                                        & scarss
Are the Effects of Desolating Warrs   10

Sent to B. F. in N. E. 15 July 1710
B   e to thy parents an Obedient Son

E   ach Day let Duty constantly be Done
N   ever give Way to sloth or lust or pride
I   f free you'd be from Thousand Ills beside
A   bove all Ills be sure Avoide the shelfe   5
M   ans Danger lyes in Satan sin and selfe
I   n vertue Learning Wisdome progress Make
N   ere shrink at Suffering for thy saviours sake

F   raud and all Falshood in thy Dealings Flee
R   eligious Always in thy station be   10
A   dore the Maker of thy Inward part
N   ow's the Accepted time, Give him thy
                                        Heart
K   eep a Good Consceince 'tis a constant Frind
L   ike Judge and Witness This Thy Acts Attend
I   n Heart with bended knee Alone Adore 15
N   one but the Three in One Forevermore.
                                  [BF note.]

---

3. BF bought these books in early July, 1771, less than a month before writing this passage, but he was mistaken in identifying the penmanship as his uncle's. (Wolf, "Reconstruction," p. 9.)

4. From 1553-58, Mary, the older sister of Elizabeth I, tried to reestablish Catholicism in England.

Spiritual Court. In that Case the Stool was turn'd down again upon its feet, when the Bible remain'd conceal'd under it as before. This Anecdote I had from my Uncle Benjamin.[5] The Family continu'd all of the Church of England till about the End of Charles the Second's Reign,[6] when some of the Ministers that had been outed for Nonconformity, holding Conventicles[7] in Northamptonshire, Benjamin and Josiah adher'd to them, and so continu'd all their Lives. The rest of the Family remain'd with the Episcopal Church.

Josiah, my Father, married young, and carried his Wife with three Children unto New England, about 1682.[8] The Conventicles having been forbidden by Law, and frequently disturbed, induced some considerable Men of his Acquaintance to remove to that Country, and he was prevail'd with to accompany them thither, where they expected to enjoy their Mode of Religion with Freedom. By the same Wife he had 4 Children more born there, and by a second Wife ten more, in all 17, of which I remember 13 sitting at one time[9] at his Table, who all grew up to be Men and Women, and married. I was the youngest Son and the youngest Child but two, and was born in Boston, New England.

My Mother the second Wife was Abiah Folger, a Daughter of Peter Folger, one of the first Settlers of New England, of whom honorable mention is made by Cotton Mather, in his Church History of that Country, (entitled Magnalia Christi Americana) as a *godly learned Englishman*,[1] if I remember the Words rightly. I have heard that he wrote sundry small occasional Pieces, but only one of them was printed which I saw now many Years since. It was written in 1675,[2] in the homespun Verse of that Time and People, and address'd to those then concern'd in the Government there. It was in favor of Liberty of Conscience, and in behalf of the Baptists, Quakers, and other Sectaries, that had been under Persecution; ascribing the Indian Wars and other Distresses that had befallen the Country to that Persecution, as so many Judgments of God, to punish so heinous an Offence; and exhorting a Repeal of those uncharitable Laws. The whole appear'd to me as written with a good deal of Decent Plainness and manly Freedom. The six last concluding Lines I remember, tho' I have forgotten the two first of the Stanza, but the Purport of them was that his Censures proceeded from *Goodwill*, and therefore he would be known as the Author,

5. BF's father wrote him this anecdote, May 26, 1739. (P, 2: 230.)
6. From 1660–85, Parliament severely restricted dissenters who would not conform to the Church of England.
7. Private meetings for worship, outlawed in 1664.
8. October, 1683.
9. At a dinner about 1715. (P, 9: 18.)
1. To be precise, "an Able Godly Englishman." (*Magnalia*, London, 1702. Book VI, Chap. vi, Sec. 2, p. 54.)
2. Though dated "April 23, 1676," Folger's *A Looking Glass for the Times* was not printed until 1725; reprinted, 1763. (Shipton-Mooney, p. 273a.)

because to be a Libeller, (says he)
I hate it with my Heart.
From *Sherburne Town where now I dwell,
My Name I do put here,
Without Offence, your real Friend,
It is Peter Folgier.

My elder Brothers were all put Apprentices to different Trades. I was put to the Grammar School at Eight Years of Age, my Father intending to devote me as the Tithe[3] of his Sons to the Service of the Church. My early Readiness in learning to read (which must have been very early, as I do not remember when I could not read)[4] and the Opinion of all his Friends that I should certainly make a good Scholar, encourag'd him in this Purpose of his. My Uncle Benjamin too approv'd of it, and propos'd to give me all his Shorthand Volumes of Sermons, I suppose as a Stock to set up with, if I would learn his Character.[5] I continu'd however at the Grammar School not quite one Year, tho' in that time I had risen gradually from the Middle of the Class of that Year to be the Head of it, and farther was remov'd into the next Class above it, in order to go with that into the third at the End of the Year. But my Father in the meantime, from a View of the Expense of a College Education which, having so large a Family, he could not well afford, and the mean Living many so educated were afterwards able to obtain, Reasons that he gave to his Friends in my Hearing, altered his first Intention, took me from the Grammar School, and sent me to a School for Writing and Arithmetic kept by a then famous Man, Mr. George Brownell, very successful in his Profession generally, and that by mild encouraging Methods. Under him I acquired fair Writing pretty soon, but I fail'd in the Arithmetic, and made no Progress in it. At Ten Years old, I was taken home to assist my Father in his Business, which was that of a Tallow Chandler and Soap-Boiler.[6] A Business he was not bred to, but had assumed on his Arrival in New England and on finding his Dying Trade would not maintain his Family, being in little Request. Accordingly I was employed in cutting Wick for the Candles, filling the Dipping Mold, and the Molds for cast Candles, attending the Shop, going of Errands, etc. I dislik'd the Trade and had a strong Inclination for the Sea; but my Father declar'd against it; however, living near the Water, I was much in and about it, learned early to swim well, and to manage Boats, and when in a Boat or Canoe with other Boys I was commonly allow'd to govern, especially in any case of Difficulty; and upon other Occasions I was

* "In the Island of Nantucket." [BF note.]

3. Tenth part of annual income, donated to the church. BF was the tenth son.
4. His sister reported that BF "read his Bible at five years old." (Dexter, 2: 375.)
5. Shorthand symbols.
6. Manufactured candles and soap from animal fats.

generally a Leader among the Boys, and sometimes led them into Scrapes, of which I will mention one Instance, as it shows an early projecting public Spirit, tho' not then justly conducted. There was a Salt Marsh that bounded part of the Mill Pond, on the Edge of which at Highwater, we us'd to stand to fish for Minnows. By much Trampling, we had made it a mere Quagmire. My Proposal was to build a Wharf there fit for us to stand upon, and I show'd my Comrades a large Heap of Stones which were intended for a new House near the Marsh, and which would very well suit our Purpose. Accordingly in the Evening when the Workmen were gone, I assembled a Number of my Playfellows, and working with them diligently like so many Emmets,[7] sometimes two or three to a Stone, we brought them all away and built our little Wharf. The next Morning the Workmen were surpris'd at Missing the Stones; which were found in our Wharf; Enquiry was made after the Removers; we were discovered and complain'd of; several of us were corrected by our Fathers; and tho' I pleaded the Usefulness of the Work, mine convinc'd me that nothing was useful which was not honest.

I think you may like to know something of his Person and Character. He had an excellent Constitution of Body, was of middle Stature, but well set and very strong. He was ingenious, could draw prettily, was skill'd a little in Music and had a clear pleasing Voice, so that when he play'd Psalm Tunes on his Violin and sung withal as he sometimes did in an Evening after the Business of the Day was over, it was extremely agreeable to hear. He had a mechanical Genius too, and on occasion was very handy in the Use of other Tradesmen's Tools. But his great Excellence lay in a sound Understanding, and solid Judgment in prudential Matters, both in private and public Affairs. In the latter indeed he was never employed, the numerous Family he had to educate and the Straitness of his Circumstances, keeping him close to his Trade, but I remember well his being frequently visited by leading People, who consulted him for his Opinion on Affairs of the Town or of the Church[8] he belong'd to and show'd a good deal of Respect for his Judgment and Advice. He was also much consulted by private Persons about their Affairs when any Difficulty occur'd, and frequently chosen an Arbitrator between contending Parties. At his Table he lik'd to have as often as he could, some sensible Friend or Neighbor, to converse with, and always took care to start some ingenious or useful Topic for Discourse, which might tend to improve the Minds of his Children. By this means he turn'd our Attention to what was good, just, and prudent in the Conduct of Life; and little or no Notice was ever taken of what related to the Victuals on the Table, whether it was well or ill drest, in or out of season, of good or bad flavor, preferable or inferior to this or that other thing of the kind; so

7. Ants.   8. Boston's Old South Church.

that I was brought up in such a perfect Inattention to those Matters as to be quite Indifferent what kind of Food was set before me; and so unobservant of it, that to this Day, if I am ask'd I can scarce tell, a few Hours after Dinner, what I din'd upon. This has been a Convenience to me in travelling, where my Companions have been sometimes very unhappy for want of a suitable Gratification of their more delicate because better instructed Tastes and Appetites.

My Mother had likewise an excellent Constitution. She suckled all her 10 Children. I never knew either my Father or Mother to have any Sickness but that of which they died, he at 89 and she at 85 Years of age. They lie buried together at Boston, where I some Years since[9] plac'd a Marble stone over their Grave with this Inscription:

Josiah Franklin
And Abiah his Wife
Lie here interred.
They lived lovingly together in Wedlock
Fifty-five Years.
Without an Estate or any gainful Employment,
By constant Labour and Industry,
With God's Blessing,
They maintained a large Family
Comfortably;
And brought up thirteen Children,
And seven Grandchildren
Reputably.
From this Instance, Reader,
Be encouraged to Diligence in thy Calling,
And distrust not Providence.
He was a pious and prudent Man,
She a discreet and virtuous Woman.
Their youngest Son,
In filial Regard to their Memory,
Places this Stone.
J.F. born 1655—Died 1744. Ætat 89
A.F. born 1667—died 1752 —— 85.

By my rambling Digressions I perceive myself to be grown old. I us'd to write more methodically. But one does not dress for private Company as for a public Ball. 'Tis perhaps only Negligence.[1]

To return. I continu'd thus employ'd in my Father's Business for two Years, that is till I was 12 Years old; and my Brother John, who was bred to that Business having left my Father, married and set up for himself at Rhode Island, there was all Appearance that I was destin'd

9. About 1753-54. (*P*, 7: 229–30.)

1. This short paragraph begins atop BF's manuscript page 9. Carl Van Doren suggested that BF composed eight pages on the first day, then on the next day drew up the outline (see pp. 169–72 of this edition) before writing this paragraph. We further suggest that Franklin added the long columnar insertion to the opening paragraph at this time (see 1.5–2.18 and 2.19 on p. 157 on this edition).

to supply his Place and be a Tallow Chandler. But my Dislike to the Trade continuing, my Father was under Apprehensions that if he did not find one for me more agreeable, I should break away and get to Sea, as his Son Josiah had done to his great Vexation. He therefore sometimes took me to walk with him, and see Joiners, Bricklayers, Turners, Braziers, etc. at their Work, that he might observe my Inclination, and endeavour to fix it on some Trade or other on Land. It has ever since been a Pleasure to me to see good Workmen handle their Tools; and it has been useful to me, having learned so much by it, as to be able to do little Jobs myself in my House, when a Workman could not readily be got; and to construct little Machines for my Experiments while the Intention of making the Experiment was fresh and warm in my Mind. My Father at last fix'd upon the Cutler's Trade, and my Uncle Benjamin's Son Samuel who was bred to that Business in London being about that time establish'd in Boston, I was sent to be with him some time on liking. But his Expectations of a Fee with me displeasing my Father, I was taken home again.

From a Child I was fond of Reading, and all the little Money that came into my Hands was ever laid out in Books. Pleas'd with the Pilgrim's Progress, my first Collection was of John Bunyan's Works, in separate little Volumes.[2] I afterwards sold them to enable me to buy R. Burton's Historical Collections;[3] they were small Chapmen's Books and cheap, 40 or 50 in all. My Father's little Library consisted chiefly of Books in polemic Divinity, most of which I read, and have since often regretted, that at a time when I had such a Thirst for Knowledge, more proper Books had not fallen in my Way, since it was now resolv'd I should not be a Clergyman. Plutarch's Lives there was, in which I read abundantly, and I still think that time spent to great Advantage.[4] There was also a Book of Defoe's called an Essay on Projects[5] and another of Dr. Mather's call'd Essays to do Good,[6] which perhaps gave me a Turn of Thinking that had an Influence on some of the principal future Events of my Life.

This Bookish Inclination at length determin'd my Father to make

2. Among them, doubtlessly, *Grace Abounding* (1666), *Life & Death of Mr. Badman* (1680), and *Holy War* (1682), all available in cheap, one shilling editions. BF's early reading is discussed by Tourtellot.

3. "R. Burton" was Nathaniel Crouch who published countless chapbooks, small enough to be carried in the backpacks of chapmen, or pedlars, yet averaging 230 pages of small type and selling for a shilling.

4. BF probably read John Dryden's translation (1683–86). In its initial purchase, the Library Company of Philadelphia bought this translation (ed. 1727) in 1732. (Wolf, "First Books," p. 62.)

5. BF twice quoted Defoe's book in the "Silence Dogood" essays, and followed its precepts in such improvement programs as hospitals and insurance companies. (*P*, 1: 20, 32–36.)

6. The running title of Cotton Mather's *Bonifacius* (1710), a book which, although spoofed by BF's early pseudonym "Silence Dogood," still provided BF with hints for such improvement programs as the Junto. BF inserted this reference to Mather at a later date (1789?), evidently echoing his letter of May 12, 1784 (Smyth, 9:208) to Cotton Mather's son. BF probably added it to emphasize his American background. The books BF mentions were selected from a very large number that he had read. In France, BF told Cabanis that, as a youth, Pascal's *Provincial Letters* "ravished" him and that he reread it many times. (Cabanis, 5: 228.)

me a Printer, tho' he had already one Son, (James) of that Profession. In 1717 my Brother James return'd from England with a Press and Letters to set up his Business in Boston. I lik'd it much better than that of my Father, but still had a Hankering for the Sea. To prevent the apprehended Effect of such an Inclination, my Father was impatient to have me bound to my Brother. I stood out some time, but at last was persuaded and signed the Indentures,[7] when I was yet but 12 Years old. I was to serve as an Apprentice till I was 21 Years of Age, only I was to be allow'd Journeyman's Wages during the last Year. In a little time I made great Proficiency in the Business, and became a useful Hand to my Brother. I now had Access to better Books. An Acquaintance with the Apprentices of Booksellers enabled me sometimes to borrow a small one, which I was careful to return soon and clean. Often I sat up in my Room reading the greatest Part of the Night,[8] when the Book was borrow'd in the Evening and to be return'd early in the Morning lest it should be miss'd or wanted. And after some time an ingenious Tradesman* who had a pretty Collection of Books, and who frequented our Printing-House, took Notice of me, invited me to his Library, and very kindly lent me such Books as I chose to read. I now took a Fancy to Poetry, and made some little Pieces. My Brother, thinking it might turn to account encourag'd me, and put me on composing two occasional Ballads. One was called the *Light House Tragedy*, and contain'd an Account of the drowning of Capt. Worthilake with his Two Daughters;[9] the other was a Sailor Song on the Taking of *Teach* or Blackbeard the Pirate.[1] They were wretched Stuff, in the Grubstreet Ballad Style,[2] and when they were printed he sent me about the Town to sell them. The first sold wonderfully, the Event being recent, having made a great Noise. This flatter'd my Vanity. But my Father discourag'd me, by ridiculing my Performances, and telling me Verse-makers were generally Beggars; so I escap'd being a Poet, most probably a very bad one. But as Prose Writing has been of great Use to me in the Course of my Life, and was a principal Means of my Advancement, I shall tell you how in such a Situation I acquir'd what little Ability I have in that Way.

There was another Bookish Lad in the Town, John Collins by Name, with whom I was intimately acquainted. We sometimes disputed, and very fond we were of Argument, and very desirous of

* "Mr. Matthew Adams" [BF note.]

7. Normally an apprentice contracted for seven years' board, room, and training.
8. His sister recalled that BF "Studied incessantly a nights when a boy" and was "Addicted to all kinds of reading." (Dexter, 2: 376.)
9. George Worthylake, keeper of Boston Harbor light, drowned with his wife and daughter (not two daughters) on November 3, 1718. (P, 1: 6.)

1. Edward Teach, *alias* Blackbeard, was killed off the Carolina coast on November 22, 1718. The account of the battle in the *Boston News Letter*, March 2, 1719, probably inspired BF's ballad.
2. Doggerel. BF's ballads probably have not survived, although claimants have been advanced. (P, 1: 6–7.)

confuting one another. Which disputatious Turn, by the way, is apt to become a very bad Habit, making People often extremely disagreeable in Company, by the Contradiction that is necessary to bring it into Practice, and thence, besides souring and spoiling the Conversation, is productive of Disgusts and perhaps Enmities where you may have occasion for Friendship. I had caught it by reading my Father's Books of Dispute about Religion. Persons of good Sense, I have since observ'd, seldom fall into it, except Lawyers, University Men, and Men of all Sorts that have been bred at Edinburgh.[3] A Question was once some how or other started between Collins and me, of the Propriety of educating the Female Sex in Learning, and their Abilities for Study. He was of Opinion that it was improper; and that they were naturally unequal to it. I took the contrary Side, perhaps a little for Dispute sake.[4] He was naturally more eloquent, had a ready Plenty of Words, and sometimes as I thought bore me down more by his Fluency than by the Strength of his Reasons. As we parted without settling the Point, and were not to see one another again for some time, I sat down to put my Arguments in Writing, which I copied fair and sent to him. He answer'd and I replied. Three or four Letters of a Side had pass'd, when my Father happen'd to find my Papers, and read them. Without entering into the Discussion, he took occasion to talk to me about the Manner of my Writing, observ'd that tho' I had the Advantage of my Antagonist in correct Spelling and pointing[5] (which I ow'd to the Printing House) I fell far short in elegance of Expression, in Method and in Perspicuity, of which he convinc'd me by several Instances. I saw the Justice of his Remarks, and thence grew more attentive to the *Manner* in Writing, and determin'd to endeavour at Improvement.

About this time I met with an odd Volume of the Spectator.[6] I had never before seen any of them. I bought it, read it over and over, and was much delighted with it. I thought the Writing excellent, and wish'd if possible to imitate it. With that View, I took some of the Papers, and making short Hints of the Sentiment in each Sentence, laid them by a few Days, and then without looking at the Book, tried to complete the Papers again, by expressing each hinted Sentiment at length and as fully as it had been express'd before, in any suitable Words that should come to hand.[7]

3. Although debating was a favorite sport at Edinburgh dinners (Nolan, p. 64), BF may simply be poking fun at that standard butt of eighteenth-century humor, the Scotsman.
4. The fifth Dogood essay (May 28, 1722) discusses the subject. (*P*, 1: 18–21.) In fact, BF argued for the natural equality of women throughout his life. See his comments on Elizabeth Timothée, below, p. 81. The feminist arguments in Defoe's *Essay Upon Projects* may have influenced BF.

5. Punctuation. Lacking accepted standards, printers relied on schoolbooks as guides to punctuation and spelling.
6. BF's Silence Dogood essay series reveals a general indebtedness to Addison and Steele's influential *Spectator*, a weekly paper which appeared 1711–12, 1714. (*P*, 1: 9, 44; Lewis.)
7. BF proposed this method of teaching composition in his "Idea of the English School" in 1751. (*P*, 4: 107.)

Then I compar'd my Spectator with the Original, discover'd some of my Faults and corrected them. But I found I wanted a Stock of Words or a Readiness in recollecting and using them, which I thought I should have acquir'd before that time, if I had gone on making Verses, since the continual Occasion for Words of the same Import but of different Length, to suit the Measure, or of different Sound for the Rhyme, would have laid me under a constant Necessity of searching for Variety, and also have tended to fix that Variety in my Mind, and make me Master of it. Therefore I took some of the Tales and turn'd them into Verse: And after a time, when I had pretty well forgotten the Prose, turn'd them back again. I also sometimes jumbled my Collections of Hints into Confusion, and after some Weeks, endeavour'd to reduce them into the best Order, before I began to form the full Sentences, and complete the Paper. This was to teach me Method in the Arrangement of Thoughts. By comparing my Work afterwards with the original, I discover'd many faults and amended them; but I sometimes had the Pleasure of Fancying that in certain Particulars of small Import, I had been lucky enough to improve the Method or the Language and this encourag'd me to think I might possibly in time come to be a tolerable English Writer, of which I was extremely ambitious.

My Time for these Exercises and for Reading, was at Night after Work, or before Work began in the Morning; or on Sundays, when I contrived to be in the Printing-House alone, evading as much as I could the common Attendance on public Worship, which my Father used to exact of me when I was under his Care: And which indeed I still thought a Duty; tho' I could not, as it seemed to me, afford the Time to practice it.

When about 16 Years of Age, I happen'd to meet with a Book written by one Tryon,[8] recommending a Vegetable Diet. I determined to go into it. My Brother being yet unmarried, did not keep House, but boarded himself and his Apprentices in another Family. My refusing to eat Flesh occasioned an Inconveniency, and I was frequently chid for my singularity. I made myself acquainted with Tryon's Manner of preparing some of his Dishes, such as Boiling Potatoes or Rice, making Hasty Pudding, and a few others, and then propos'd to my Brother, that if he would give me Weekly half the Money he paid for my Board, I would board myself. He instantly agreed to it, and I presently found that I could save half what he paid me. This was an additional Fund for buying Books: But I had another Advantage in it. My Brother and the rest going from the Printing-House to their Meals, I remain'd there alone, and dispatching pres-

8. Thomas Tryon's major self-help medical book, *The Way to Health, Wealth, and Happiness* (1682–98) had 670 pages, but BF could have read a digest such as *Wisdom's Dictates* (1691) where 150 pages of aphorisms set out the rules for diet, bathing, exercise, and taking fresh air.

ently my light Repast, (which often was no more than a Biscuit or a Slice of Bread, a Handful of Raisins or a Tart from the Pastry Cook's, and a Glass of Water) had the rest of the Time till their Return, for Study, in which I made the greater Progress from that greater Clearness of Head and quicker Apprehension which usually attend Temperance in Eating and Drinking. And now it was that being on some Occasion made asham'd of my Ignorance in Figures, which I had twice fail'd in learning when at School, I took Cocker's Book of Arithmetic,[9] and went thro' the whole by myself with great Ease. I also read Seller's and Sturmy's Books of Navigation,[1] and became acquainted with the little Geometry they contain, but never proceeded far in that Science. And I read about this Time Locke on Human Understanding[2] and the Art of Thinking by Messrs. du Port Royal.[3]

While I was intent on improving my Language, I met with an English Grammar (I think it was Greenwood's)[4] at the End of which there were two little Sketches of the Arts of Rhetoric and Logic, the latter finishing with a Specimen of a Dispute in the Socratic Method. And soon after I procur'd Xenophon's Memorable Things of Socrates,[5] wherein there are many Instances of the same Method. I was charm'd with it, adopted it, dropped my abrupt Contradiction and positive Argumentation, and put on the humble Enquirer and Doubter. And being then, from reading Shaftesbury and Collins,[6] become a real Doubter in many Points of our Religious Doctrine, I found this Method safest for myself and very embarassing to those against whom I used it, therefore I took a Delight in it, practic'd it continually and grew very artful and expert in drawing People even of superior Knowledge into Concessions the Consequences of which they did not foresee, entangling them in Difficulties out of which they could not extricate themselves, and so obtaining Victories that neither myself nor my Cause always deserved. I continu'd this Method some few Years, but gradually left it, retaining only the Habit of expressing myself in Terms of modest Diffidence, never using when I advance any thing that may possibly be disputed, the Words, *Certainly, undoubtedly,* or any others that give the Air of Positiveness to an Opinion; but rather say, *I conceive,* or *I apprehend* a Thing to be so or so, *It*

9. Edward Cocker, *Arithmetic* (1677) had 20 editions before 1700, and over 100 by 1800.
1. John Seller, *Practical Navigation* (1669; 8 eds. before 1700); Samuel Sturmy, *Mariner's Magazine* (1669; 3 eds. before 1700).
2. John Locke, *Essay Concerning Human Understanding* (1690), the basic work on philosophy and psychology for the eighteenth century, had five revised, expanded versions through 1706.
3. Jansenist monks set up a school at Port Royal, applying Cartesian inducative methods to education and emphasizing vernacular vs. classical languages. BF owned the 1717 edition of

John Ozell's translation of Antoine Arnauld and Pierre Nichole, *Logic: or the Art of Thinking* (1662). (Korty, p. 19.)
4. Actually the second edition of "John Brightland" [Charles Gildon], *A Grammar of the English Tongue* (London: John Brightland, 1712), which added "The Arts of Poetry, Rhetoric, Logic, etc." not in the first (1711) edition.
5. Translated by Edward Bysshe (1712).
6. Anthony Ashley Cooper, Third Earl of Shaftesbury, *Characteristics of Men, Manners, Opinions, Times,* 3 vols. (1711); and, among the several deistic works by Anthony Collins, perhaps *A Discourse of Free Thinking* (1713).

appears to me, or *I should think it so or so for such and such Reasons,* or *I imagine* it to be so, or *it is so* if *I am not mistaken.* This Habit I believe has been of great Advantage to me, when I have had occasion to inculcate my Opinions and persuade Men into Measures that I have been from time to time engag'd in promoting. And as the chief Ends of Conversation are to *inform,* or to be *informed,* to *please* or to *persuade,* I wish well-meaning sensible Men would not lessen their Power of doing Good by a Positive assuming Manner that seldom fails to disgust, tends to create Opposition, and to defeat every one of those Purposes for which Speech was given us, to wit, giving or receiving Information, or Pleasure: For If you would *inform,* a positive dogmatical Manner in advancing your Sentiments, may provoke Contradiction and prevent a candid Attention. If you wish Information and Improvement from the Knowledge of others and yet at the same time express yourself as firmly fix'd in your present Opinions, modest sensible Men, who do not love Disputation, will probably leave you undisturb'd in the Possession of your Error; and by such a Manner you can seldom hope to recommend yourself in *pleasing* your Hearers, or to persuade those whose Concurrence you desire. Pope says, judiciously,

> *Men should be taught as if you taught them not,*
> *And things unknown propos'd as things forgot,*

farther recommending it to us,

> *To speak tho' sure, with seeming Diffidence.*[7]

And he might have coupl'd with this Line that which he has coupled with another, I think less properly,

> *For want of Modesty is want of Sense.*

If you ask why *less properly,* I must repeat the Lines;

> "Immodest Words admit of *no* Defence;
> For Want of Modesty is Want of Sense."[8]

Now is not *Want of Sense,* (where a Man is so unfortunate as to want it) some Apology for his *Want of Modesty?* and would not the Lines stand more justly thus?

> Immodest Words admit *but this* Defence,
> That Want of Modesty is Want of Sense.

This however I should submit to better Judgments.

My Brother had in 1720 or 21, begun to print a Newspaper. It was

---

7. Evidently quoted from memory. In *Essay on Criticism* (1711), 11. 574–75 and 567, the second word is "must" and the third line begins with "And" rather than "To."

8. Again, evidently from memory. Wentworth Dillon, Earl of Roscommon, *Essay on Translated Verse* (1684) 114. The second line reads "Decency" instead of "Modesty."

the second that appear'd in America,[9] and was called *The New England Courant.* The only one before it, was *the Boston News Letter.* I remember his being dissuaded by some of his Friends from the Undertaking, as not likely to succeed, one Newspaper being in their Judgment enough for America. At this time 1771 there are not less than five and twenty. He went on however with the Undertaking, and after having work'd in composing the Types and printing off the Sheets I was employ'd to carry the Papers thro' the Streets to the Customers. He had some ingenious Men among his Friends who amus'd themselves by writing little Pieces for this Paper, which gain'd it Credit, and made it more in Demand; and these Gentlemen[1] often visited us. Hearing their Conversations, and their Accounts of the Approbation their Papers were receiv'd with, I was excited to try my Hand among them. But being still a Boy, and suspecting that my Brother would object to printing any Thing of mine in his Paper if he knew it to be mine, I contriv'd to disguise my Hand, and writing an anonymous Paper I put it in at Night under the Door of the Printing-House.

It was found in the Morning and communicated to his Writing Friends when they call'd in as Usual. They read it, commented on it in my Hearing, and I had the exquisite Pleasure, of finding it met with their Approbation, and that in their different Guesses at the Author none were named but Men of some Character among us for Learning and Ingenuity. I suppose now that I was rather lucky in my Judges: And that perhaps they were not really so very good ones as I then esteem'd them. Encourag'd however by this, I wrote and convey'd in the same Way to the Press several more Papers,[2] which were equally approv'd, and I kept my Secret till my small Fund of Sense for such Performances was pretty well exhausted, and then I discovered[3] it; when I began to be considered a little more by my Brothers' Acquaintance, and in a manner that did not quite please him, as he thought, probably with reason, that it tended to make me too vain. And perhaps this might be one Occasion of the Differences that we began to have about this Time. Tho' a Brother, he considered himself as my Master, and me as his Apprentice; and accordingly expected the same Services from me as he would from another; while I thought he demean'd me too much in some he requir'd of me, who from a Brother expected more Indulgence. Our Disputes were often brought before our Father, and I fancy I was either generally in the right, or else a better

9. Before the *Courant* appeared on August 7, 1721, there were three newspapers: *Boston News-Letter* (April 24, 1704); *Boston Gazette* (December 21, 1719), which James Franklin at first printed; and, in Philadelphia, *American Weekly Mercury* (December 22, 1719).
1. James Franklin's "Couranteers" included Matthew Adams, John Checkley, Dr. William

Douglas, Thomas Fleet, and the prolific Nathaniel Gardner. Gardner importantly influenced BF's prose style. (Lemay, "Benjamin Franklin," pp. 205–6.)
2. Fourteen "letters" from "Silence Dogood" (April 12–October 8, 1722) made up the earliest essay series in America. (P, 1: 9–45.)
3. Revealed.

Pleader, because the Judgment was generally in my favor: But my Brother was passionate and had often beaten me, which I took extremely amiss;* and thinking my Apprenticeship very tedious, I was continually wishing for some Opportunity of shortening it, which at length offered in a manner unexpected.

One of the Pieces in our Newspaper, on some political Point which I have now forgotten, gave Offence to the Assembly. He was taken up, censur'd and imprison'd for a Month by the Speaker's Warrant, I suppose because he would not discover his Author.[4] I too was taken up and examin'd before the Council; but tho' I did not give them any Satisfaction, they contented themselves with admonishing me, and dismiss'd me; considering me perhaps as an Apprentice who was bound to keep his Master's Secrets. During my Brother's Confinement, which I resented a good deal, notwithstanding our private Differences, I had the Management of the Paper, and I made bold to give our Rulers some Rubs in it,[5] which my Brother took very kindly, while others began to consider me in an unfavorable Light, as a young Genius that had a Turn for Libelling and Satire. My Brother's Discharge was accompanied with an Order of the House, (a very odd one) *that James Franklin should no longer print the Paper called the New England Courant.*[6] There was a Consultation held in our Printing-House among his Friends what he should do in this Case. Some propos'd to evade the Order by changing the Name of the Paper; but my Brother seeing Inconveniences in that, it was finally concluded on as a better Way, to let it be printed for the future under the Name of *Benjamin Franklin.* And to avoid the Censure of the Assembly that might fall on him, as still printing it by his Apprentice, the Contrivance was, that my old Indenture should be return'd to me with a full Discharge on the Back of it, to be shown on Occasion; but to secure to him the Benefit of my Service I was to sign new Indentures for the Remainder of the Term, which were to be kept private. A very flimsy Scheme it was, but however it was immediately executed, and the Paper went on accordingly under my Name for several Months. At length a fresh Difference arising between my Brother and me, I took upon me to assert my Freedom, presuming that he would not venture to produce the new Indentures. It was not fair in me to take this Advantage, and this I therefore reckon one of the first Errata of my

---

* "I fancy his harsh and tyrannical Treatment of me, might be a means of impressing me with that Aversion to arbitrary Power that has stuck to me thro' my whole life." [BF note.]

4. The *Courant* for June 11, 1722, hinted at collusion between local authorities and pirates raiding off Boston Harbor. James Franklin was promptly jailed from June 12 until July 7.
5. Perhaps the boldest was the Dogood letter of July 23, 1722, overtly satirizing ex-Governor Joseph Dudley, but covertly attacking the Mathers and Chief Justice Samuel Sewall. (P,

1: 30–32; Lemay, "Benjamin Franklin," p. 208)
6. Events are compressed: When the *Courant* for January 14, 1723, hinted at hypocrites in local government, James Franklin was ordered to submit to censorship or cease publishing. The *Courant* carried BF's name as printer from February 11, 1723 until the paper failed in 1727.

Life: But the Unfairness of it weigh'd little with me, when under the Impressions of Resentment, for the Blows his Passion too often urg'd him to bestow upon me. Tho' he was otherwise not an ill-natur'd Man: Perhaps I was too saucy and provoking.

When he found I would leave him, he took care to prevent my getting Employment in any other Printing-House of the Town, by going round and speaking to every Master, who accordingly refus'd to give me Work. I then thought of going to New York as the nearest Place where there was a Printer: and I was the rather inclin'd to leave Boston, when I reflected that I had already made myself a little obnoxious to the governing Party; and from the arbitrary Proceedings of the Assembly in my Brother's Case it was likely I might if I stay'd soon bring myself into Scrapes; and farther that my indiscreet Disputations about Religion began to make me pointed at with Horror by good People, as an Infidel or Atheist; I determin'd on the Point: but my Father now siding with my Brother, I was sensible that if I attempted to go openly, Means would be used to prevent me. My Friend Collins therefore undertook to manage a little for me. He agreed with the Captain of a New York Sloop for my Passage, under the Notion of my being a young Acquaintance of his that had got a naughty Girl with Child, whose Friends would compel me to marry her, and therefore I could not appear or come away publicly. So I sold some of my Books to raise a little Money, was taken on board privately, and as we had a fair Wind, in three Days I found myself in New York near 300 Miles from home, a Boy of but 17, without the least Recommendation to or Knowledge of any Person in the Place, and with very little Money in my Pocket.

My Inclinations for the Sea, were by this time worn out, or I might now have gratified them. But having a Trade, and supposing myself a pretty good Workman, I offer'd my Service to the Printer of the Place, old Mr. William Bradford. He could give me no Employment, having little to do, and Help enough already: But, says he, my Son at Philadelphia has lately lost his principal Hand, Aquila Rose, by Death. If you go thither I believe he may employ you. Philadelphia was 100 Miles farther. I set out, however, in a Boat for Amboy;[7] leaving my Chest and Things to follow me round by Sea. In crossing the Bay we met with a Squall that tore our rotten Sails to pieces, prevented our getting into the Kill,[8] and drove us upon Long Island. In our Way a drunken Dutchman, who was a Passenger too, fell overboard; when he was sinking I reach'd thro' the Water to his shock Pate[9] and drew him up so that we got him in again. His Ducking

---

7. Perth Amboy, then capital of East Jersey, is just across Arthur Kill from Staten Island, New York. See "Franklin's Journey from Boston to Philadelphia, 1723," pp. 166–68, below.

8. Dutch for "channel," this is the Kill van Kull, a channel northwest of Staten Island, New York Harbor.

9. Shaggy head.

sober'd him a little, and he went to sleep, taking first out of his Pocket a Book which he desir'd I would dry for him. It prov'd to be my old favorite Author Bunyan's Pilgrim's Progress in Dutch, finely printed on good Paper with copper Cuts,[1] a Dress better than I had ever seen it wear in its own Language. I have since found that it has been translated into most of the Languages of Europe, and suppose it has been more generally read than any other Book except perhaps the Bible. Honest John was the first that I know of who mix'd Narration and Dialogue, a Method of Writing very engaging to the Reader, who in the most interesting Parts finds himself as it were brought into the Company, and present at the Discourse. Defoe in his Cruso, his Moll Flanders, Religious Courtship, Family Instructor, and other Pieces, has imitated it with Success. And Richardson has done the same in his Pamela, etc.[2]

When we drew near the Island we found it was at a Place where there could be no Landing, there being a great Surf on the stony Beach. So we dropped Anchor and swung round towards the Shore. Some People came down to the Water Edge and hallow'd to us, as we did to them. But the Wind was so high and the Surf so loud, that we could not hear so as to understand each other. There were Canoes on the Shore, and we made Signs and hallow'd that they should fetch us, but they either did not understand us, or thought it impracticable. So they went away, and Night coming on, we had no Remedy but to wait till the Wind should abate, and in the mean time the Boatman and I concluded to sleep if we could, and so crowded into the Scuttle with the Dutchman who was still wet, and the Spray beating over the Head of our Boat, leak'd thro' to us, so that we were soon almost as wet as he. In this Manner we lay all Night with very little Rest. But the Wind abating the next Day, we made a Shift to reach Amboy before Night, having been 30 Hours on the Water without Victuals, or any Drink but a Bottle of filthy Rum: The Water we sail'd on being salt.

In the Evening I found myself very feverish, and went ill to Bed. But having read somewhere that cold Water drank plentifully was good for a Fever,[3] I follow'd the Prescription, sweat plentifully most of the Night, my Fever left me, and in the Morning crossing the Ferry, proceeded on my Journey, on foot, having 50 Miles to Burlington,[4] where I was told I should find Boats that would carry me the rest of the Way to Philadelphia.

It rain'd very hard all the Day, I was thoroughly soak'd, and by Noon a good deal tir'd, so I stopped at a poor Inn, where I stayed all

---

1. The first Dutch edition (1682) had eleven small copperplate engravings.
2. *Robinson Crusoe* (1719), *Moll Flanders* (1722), *Religious Courtship* (1722), and *Family Instructor* (1715). Samuel Richardson's *Pamela* (1740) became the first novel printed in

America when BF reprinted it from the fourth London edition in 1742 and 1743.
3. Prescribed in Cotton Mather, *Manuductio ad Ministerium* (Boston, 1726), p. 132.
4. Then capital of West Jersey, about eighteen miles above Philadelphia.

Night, beginning now to wish I had never left home. I cut so miserable a Figure too, that I found by the Questions ask'd me I was suspected to be some runaway Servant, and in danger of being taken up on that Suspicion. However I proceeded the next Day, and got in the Evening to an Inn within 8 or 10 Miles of Burlington,[5] kept by one Dr. Browne.

He entered into Conversation with me while I took some Refreshment, and finding I had read a little, became very sociable and friendly. Our Acquaintance continu'd as long as he liv'd. He had been, I imagine, an itinerant Doctor, for there was no Town in England, or Country in Europe, of which he could not give a very particular Account. He had some Letters, and was ingenious, but much of an Unbeliever, and wickedly undertook some Years after to travesty the Bible in doggerel Verse as Cotton had done Virgil.[6] By this means he set many of the Facts in a very ridiculous Light, and might have hurt weak minds if his Work had been publish'd: but it never was. At his House I lay that Night, and the next Morning reach'd Burlington.—But had the Mortification to find that the regular Boats were gone a little before my coming, and no other expected to go till Tuesday, this being Saturday. Wherefore I return'd to an old Woman in the Town of whom I had bought Gingerbread to eat on the Water, and ask'd her Advice; she invited me to lodge at her House till a Passage by Water should offer; and being tired with my foot Travelling, I accepted the Invitation. She understanding I was a Printer, would have had me stay at that Town and follow my Business, being ignorant of the Stock necessary to begin with. She was very hospitable, gave me a Dinner of Ox Cheek with great Goodwill, accepting only of a Pot of Ale in return. And I thought myself fix'd till Tuesday should come. However walking in the Evening by the Side of the River a Boat came by, which I found was going towards Philadelphia, with several People in her. They took me in, and as there was no Wind, we row'd all the Way; and about Midnight not having yet seen the City, some of the Company were confident we must have pass'd it, and would row no farther, the others knew not where we were, so we put towards the Shore, got into a Creek, landed near an old Fence with the Rails of which we made a Fire, the Night being cold, in October, and there we remain'd till Daylight. Then one of the Company knew the Place to be Cooper's Creek a little above Philadelphia,[7] which we saw as soon as we got out of the Creek, and arriv'd there about 8 or 9 o'Clock, on the

5. Dr. John Browne's inn (later known as Washington House) was located at the northwest intersection of Main (or Farnsworth Street) and Crosswick Street, Bordentown, New Jersey. (Charles S. Boyer, *Old Inns and Taverns in West Jersey* [Camden, N.J., 1962], p. 39, and map facing p. 38.)

6. Charles Cotton, *Scarronides* (1664–65) travestied the first and fourth books of the *Aeneid* in this fashion: "I sing the Man (read it who list, / A Trojan true as ever pist)."

7. Site of present Camden, New Jersey, across the Delaware River from Philadelphia.

Sunday morning,[8] and landed at the Market Street Wharf.[9]
I have been the more particular in this Description of my Journey, and shall be so of my first Entry into that City, that you may in your Mind compare such unlikely Beginning with the Figure I have since made there.[1] I was in my working Dress, my best Clothes being to come round by Sea. I was dirty from my Journey; my Pockets were stuff'd out with Shirts and Stockings; I knew no Soul, nor where to look for Lodging. I was fatigu'd with Travelling, Rowing and Want of Rest. I was very hungry, and my whole Stock of Cash consisted of a Dutch Dollar and about a Shilling in Copper. The latter I gave the People of the Boat for my Passage, who at first refus'd it on Account of my Rowing; but I insisted on their taking it, a Man being sometimes more generous when he has but a little Money than when he has plenty, perhaps thro' Fear of being thought to have but little. Then I walk'd up the Street, gazing about, till near the Market House I met a Boy with Bread. I had made many a Meal on Bread, and inquiring where he got it, I went immediately to the Baker's he directed me to in Second Street; and ask'd for Biscuit, intending such as we had in Boston, but they it seems were not made in Philadelphia, then I ask'd for a three-penny Loaf, and was told they had none such: so not considering or knowing the Difference of Money and the greater Cheapness nor the Names of his Bread, I bad him give me three pennyworth of any sort. He gave me accordingly three great Puffy Rolls. I was surpris'd at the Quantity, but took it, and having no Room in my Pockets, walk'd off, with a Roll under each Arm, and eating the other. Thus I went up Market Street as far as Fourth Street, passing by the Door of Mr. Read, my future Wife's Father, when she standing at the Door saw me, and thought I made as I certainly did a most awkward ridiculous Appearance. Then I turn'd and went down Chestnut Street and part of Walnut Street, eating my Roll all the Way, and coming round found myself again at Market Street Wharf, near the Boat I came in, to which I went for a Draught of the River Water, and being fill'd with one of my Rolls, gave the other two to a Woman and her Child that came down the River in the Boat with us and were waiting to go farther. Thus refresh'd I walk'd again up the Street, which by this time had many clean dress'd People in it who were all walking the same Way; I join'd them, and thereby was led into the great Meeting House of the Quakers[2] near the Market. I sat down among them, and after looking round a while and hearing nothing

---

8. Franklin arrived in Philadelphia on Sunday morning, October 6, 1723. See pp. 166–68 of this edition.
9. No. 1 in the map of Philadelphia. Other places mentioned are also located on the map. See pp. xx–xxi of this edition.
1. When BF left Philadelphia for England on November 7, 1764, 300 people accompanied

him to Chester, where he was greeted by cannon salute and by a song that adapted "God Save the King." (P, 11: 447–48.) BF wryly reports two other times when he made a "Figure" in Philadelphia. (See notes 4 and 7 on pp. 128 and 129.)
2. Quakers (originally a derogatory name) are members of the Religious Society of Friends.

said, being very drowsy thro' Labour and want of Rest the preceding Night, I fell fast asleep, and continu'd so till the Meeting broke up, when one was kind enough to rouse me. This was therefore the first House I was in or slept in, in Philadelphia.[3]

Walking again down towards the River, and looking in the Faces of People, I met a young Quaker Man whose Countenance I lik'd, and accosting him requested he would tell me where a Stranger could get Lodging. We were then near the Sign of the Three Mariners. Here, says he, is one Place that entertains Strangers, but it is not a reputable House; if thee wilt walk with me, I'll show thee a better. He brought me to the Crooked Billet in Water Street. Here I got a Dinner. And while I was eating it, several sly Questions were ask'd me, as it seem'd to be suspected from my youth and Appearance, that I might be some Runaway. After Dinner my Sleepiness return'd: and being shown to a Bed, I lay down without undressing, and slept till Six in the Evening; was call'd to Supper; went to Bed again very early and slept soundly till the next Morning. Then I made myself as tidy as I could, and went to Andrew Bradford the Printer's. I found in the Shop the old Man his Father, whom I had seen at New York, and who travelling on horse back had got to Philadelphia before me. He introduc'd me to his Son, who receiv'd me civilly, gave me a Breakfast, but told me he did not at present want a Hand, being lately supplied with one. But there was another Printer in town lately set up, one Keimer, who perhaps might employ me; if not, I should be welcome to lodge at his House, and he would give me a little Work to do now and then till fuller Business should offer.

The old Gentleman said, he would go with me to the new Printer: And when we found him, Neighbor, says Bradford, I have brought to see you a young Man of your Business, perhaps you may want such a One. He ask'd me a few Questions, put a Composing Stick[4] in my Hand to see how I work'd, and then said he would employ me soon, tho' he had just then nothing for me to do. And taking old Bradford whom he had never seen before, to be one of the Townspeople that had a Goodwill for him, enter'd into a Conversation on his present Undertaking and Prospects; while Bradford not discovering that he was the other Printer's Father; on Keimer's Saying he expected soon to get the greatest Part of the Business into his own Hands, drew him on by artful Questions and starting little Doubts, to explain all his Views, what Interest he relied on, and in what manner he intended to proceed. I who stood by and heard all, saw immediately that one of them was a crafty old Sophister, and the other a mere Novice. Bradford left me with Keimer, who was greatly surpris'd when I told him who the old Man was.

Keimer's Printing-House I found, consisted of an old shatter'd Press

---

3. For another version of this episode, see "Backgrounds," pp. 207–8 of this edition.

4. Compositors set type on a small, adjustable tray (or "stick") held in one hand.

and one small worn-out Fount of English,[5] which he was then using himself, compising in it an Elegy on Aquila Rose before-mentioned, an ingenious young Man of excellent Character much respected in the Town, Clerk of the Assembly, and a pretty Poet. Keimer made Verses, too, but very indifferently. He could not be said to write them, for his Manner was to compose them in the Types directly out of his Head; so there being no Copy, but one Pair of Cases,[6] and the Elegy likely to require all the Letter, no one could help him. I endeavour'd to put his Press (which he had not yet us'd, and of which he understood nothing) into Order fit to be work'd with; and promising to come and print off his Elegy as soon as he should have got it ready, I return'd to Bradford's who gave me a little Job to do for the present, and there I lodged and dieted. A few Days after Keimer sent for me to print off the Elegy.[7] And now he had got another Pair of Cases, and a Pamphlet[8] to reprint, on which he set me to work.

These two Printers I found poorly qualified for their Business. Bradford had not been bred to it, and was very illiterate; and Keimer tho' something of a Scholar, was a mere Compositor, knowing nothing of Presswork.[9] He had been one of the French Prophets and could act their enthusiastic Agitations.[1] At this time he did not profess any particular Religion, but something of all on occasion; was very ignorant of the World, and had, as I afterwards found, a good deal of the Knave in his Composition. He did not like my Lodging at Bradford's while I work'd with him. He had a House indeed, but without Furniture, so he could not lodge me: But he got me a Lodging at Mr. Read's before-mentioned, who was the Owner of his House. And my Chest and Clothes being come by this time, I made rather a more respectable Appearance in the Eyes of Miss Read, than I had done when she first happen'd to see me eating my Roll in the Street.

I began now to have some Acquaintance among the young People of the Town, that were Lovers of Reading with whom I spent my Evenings very pleasantly and gaining Money by my Industry and Frugality, I lived very agreeably, forgetting Boston as much as I could,

5. A font, or complete set of letters and numbers, in the size called "English," one size larger than pica and thus too large for newspapers or most books.
6. Two shallow trays divided into small partitions or boxes which held the types. Cases are commonly in pairs: one for capitals and one for lower-case letters.
7. Printed on a single leaf, *An Elegy on the much Lamented Death of the Ingenious and Well-Beloved Aquila Rose* . . . appeared in 1723 (Evans 2436), containing such doggerel as: "In sable Characters the News is read, / Our Rose is withered, and our Eagle's fled, / In that our dear Aquila Rose is dead."
8. The third edition of Thomas Chalkley,

Letter to a Friend in Ireland (1723), perhaps commissioned by Philadelphia followers of this Quaker leader. (Evans 2416.)
9. The compositor set the type. Printing it off was called "presswork."
1. In 1701, the French Prophets (or Camisards) in London became the nucleus for an English sect preaching doomsday, speaking in tongues, and swooning into fits. Outlawed in 1709, the sect dissolved. Descriptions of its fanatic excesses were featured in the 1740s as propaganda against the emotionalism of the Great Awakening. (*The Wonderful Narrative: or a Faithful Account of the French Prophets* [Boston, 1742]; Evans 4915.)

and not desiring that any there should know where I resided except my Friend Collins who was in my Secret, and kept it when I wrote to him. At length an Incident happened that sent me back again much sooner than I had intended.

I had a Brother-in-law, Robert Holmes,[2] Master of a Sloop that traded between Boston and Delaware. He being at New Castle 40 Miles below Philadelphia, heard there of me, and wrote me a Letter, mentioning the Concern of my Friends in Boston at my abrupt Departure, assuring me of their Goodwill to me, and that everything would be accommodated to my Mind if I would return, to which he exhorted me very earnestly. I wrote an Answer to his Letter, thank'd him for his Advice, but stated my Reasons for quitting Boston fully, and in such a Light as to convince him I was not so wrong as he had apprehended. Sir William Keith[3] Governor of the Province, was then at New Castle, and Captain Homes happening to be in Company with him when my Letter came to hand, spoke to him of me, and show'd him the Letter. The Governor read it, and seem'd surpris'd when he was told my Age. He said I appear'd a young Man of promising Parts, and therefore should be encouraged: The Printers at Philadelphia were wretched ones, and if I would set up there, he made no doubt I should succeed; for his Part, he would procure me the public Business, and do me every other Service in his Power. This my Brother-in-Law afterwards told me in Boston. But I knew as yet nothing of it; when one Day Keimer and I being at Work together near the Window, we saw the Governor and another Gentleman (which prov'd to be Colonel French, of New Castle) finely dress'd, come directly across the Street to our House, and heard them at the Door.

Keimer ran down immediately, thinking it a Visit to him. But the Governor enquir'd for me, came up, and with a Condescension and Politeness I had been quite unus'd to, made me many Compliments, desired to be acquainted with me, blam'd me kindly for not having made myself known to him when I first came to the Place, and would have me away with him to the Tavern where he was going with Colonel French to taste as he said some excellent Madeira. I was not a little surpris'd, and Keimer star'd like a Pig poison'd. I went however with the Governor and Colonel French, to a Tavern the Corner of Third Street, and over the Madeira he propos'd my Setting up my Business, laid before me the Probabilities of Success, and both he and Colonel French assur'd me I should have their Interest and Influence in procuring the Public-Business of both Governments. On my doubting whether my Father would assist me in it, Sir William said he would give me a Letter to him, in which he would state the Advantages, and he did not doubt of prevailing with him. So it was con-

2. Robert Homes.
3. Keith was governor of both Pennsylvania and Delaware, where New Castle was capital.

Colonel French was the Speaker of the Delaware assembly.

cluded I should return to Boston in the first Vessel with the Governor's Letter recommending me to my Father.

In the meantime the Intention was to be kept secret, and I went on working with Keimer as usual, the Governor sending for me now and then to dine with him, a very great Honor I thought it, and conversing with me in the most affable, familiar, and friendly manner imaginable. About the End of April 1724, a little Vessel offer'd for Boston. I took Leave of Keimer as going to see my Friends. The Governor gave me an ample Letter, saying many flattering things of me to my Father, and strongly recommending the Project of my setting up at Philadelphia, as a Thing that must make my Fortune. We struck on a Shoal in going down the Bay and sprung a Leak, we had a blustring time at Sea, and were oblig'd to pump almost continually, at which I took my Turn. We arriv'd safe however at Boston in about a Fortnight. I had been absent Seven Months and my Friends had heard nothing of me, for my Brother Homes was not yet return'd; and had not written about me. My unexpected Appearance surpris'd the Family; all were however very glad to see me and made me Welcome, except my Brother.

I went to see him at his Printing-House: I was better dress'd than ever while in his Service, having a genteel new Suit from Head to foot, a Watch, and my Pockets lin'd with near Five Pounds Sterling in Silver. He receiv'd me not very frankly, look'd me all over, and turn'd to his Work again. The Journeymen were inquisitive where I had been, what sort of a Country it was, and how I lik'd it? I prais'd it much, and the happy Life I led in it; expressing strongly my Intention of returning to it; and one of them asking what kind of Money we had there, I produc'd a handful of Silver and spread it before them, which was a kind of Raree-Show[4] they had not been us'd to, Paper being the Money of Boston.[5] Then I took an Opportunity of letting them see my Watch: and lastly, (my Brother still grum and sullen) I gave them a Piece of Eight to drink and took my Leave. This Visit of mine offended him extremely. For when my Mother some time after spoke to him of a Reconciliation, and of her Wishes to see us on good Terms together, and that we might live for the future as Brothers, he said, I had insulted him in such a Manner before his People that he could never forget or forgive it. In this however he was mistaken.

My Father receiv'd the Governor's Letter with some apparent Surprise; but said little of it to me for some Days; when Captain Homes returning, he show'd it to him, ask'd if he knew Keith, and what kind of a Man he was: Adding his Opinion that he must be of small Discretion, to think of setting a Boy up in Business who wanted yet 3

4. A sidewalk peepshow or puppet show, usually carried in a box.
5. Silver coins, rare in the colonies, were especially so in Boston where they were rigidly regulated by law at a fixed low value and were thus bought up by speculators for sale in other colonies, at higher prices.

Years of being at Man's Estate. Homes said what he could in favor of the Project; but my Father was clear in the Impropriety of it; and at last gave a flat Denial to it. Then he wrote a civil Letter to Sir William thanking him for the Patronage he had so kindly offered me, but declining to assist me as yet in Setting up, I being in his Opinion too young to be trusted with the Management of a Business so important; and for which the Preparation must be so expensive.

My Friend and Companion Collins, who was a Clerk at the Post-Office, pleas'd with the Account I gave him of my new Country, determin'd to go thither also: And while I waited for my Father's Determination, he set out before me by Land to Rhode Island, leaving his Books which were a pretty Collection of Mathematics and Natural Philosophy, to come with mine and me to New York where he propos'd to wait for me. My Father, tho' he did not approve Sir William's Proposition, was yet pleas'd that I had been able to obtain so advantageous a Character from a Person of such Note where I had resided, and that I had been so industrious and careful as to equip myself so handsomely in so short a time: therefore seeing no Prospect of an Accommodation between my Brother and me, he gave his Consent to my Returning again to Philadelphia, advis'd me to behave respectfully to the People there, endeavour to obtain the general Esteem, and avoid lampooning and libelling to which he thought I had too much Inclination; telling me, that by steady Industry and a prudent Parsimony, I might save enough by the time I was One and Twenty to set me up, and that if I came near the Matter he would help me out with the Rest. This was all I could obtain, except some small Gifts as Tokens of his and my Mother's Love, when I embark'd again for New York, now with their Approbation and their Blessing.

The Sloop putting in at Newport, Rhode Island, I visited my Brother John, who had been married and settled there some Years. He received me very affectionately, for he always lov'd me. A Friend of his, one Vernon, having some Money due to him in Pennsylvania, about 35 Pounds Currency, desired I would receive it for him, and keep it till I had his Directions what to remit it in. Accordingly he gave me an Order. This afterwards occasion'd me a good deal of Uneasiness. At Newport we took in a Number of Passengers for New York: Among which were two young Women, Companions, and a grave, sensible Matron-like Quaker-Woman with her Attendants. I had shown an obliging Readiness to do her some little Services which impress'd her I suppose with a degree of Goodwill towards me. Therefore when she saw a daily growing Familiarity between me and the two Young Women, which they appear'd to encourage, she took me aside and said, Young Man, I am concern'd for thee, as thou has no Friend with thee, and seems not to know much of the World, or of the Snares Youth is expos'd to; depend upon it those are very bad Women, I can see it in all their Actions, and if thee art not upon thy

Guard, they will draw thee into some Danger: they are Strangers to thee, and I advise thee in a friendly Concern for thy Welfare, to have no Acquaintance with them. As I seem'd at first not to think so ill of them as she did, she mention'd some Things she had observ'd and heard that had escap'd my Notice; but now convinc'd me she was right. I thank'd her for her kind Advice, and promis'd to follow it. When we arriv'd at New York, they told me where they liv'd, and invited me to come and see them: but I avoided it. And it was well I did:·For the next Day, the Captain miss'd a Silver Spoon and some other Things that had been taken out of his Cabin, and knowing that these were a Couple of Strumpets, he got a Warrant to search their Lodgings, found the stolen Goods, and had the Thieves punish'd. So tho' we had escap'd a sunken Rock which we scrap'd upon in the Passage, I thought this Escape of rather more Importance to me.

At New York I found my Friend Collins, who had arriv'd there some Time before me. We had been intimate from Children, and had read the same Books together. But he had the Advantage of more time for Reading, and Studying and a wonderful Genius for Mathematical Learning in which he far outstripped me. While I liv'd in Boston most of my Hours of Leisure for Conversation were spent with him, and he continu'd a sober as well as an industrious Lad; was much respected for his Learning by several of the Clergy and other Gentlemen, and seem'd to promise making a good Figure in Life: but during my Absence he had acquir'd a Habit of Sotting with Brandy; and I found by his own Account and what I heard from others, that he had been drunk every day since his Arrival at New York, and behav'd very oddly. He had gam'd too and lost his Money, so that I was oblig'd to discharge his Lodgings, and defray his Expences to and at Philadelphia: Which prov'd extremely inconvenient to me. The then Governor of New York, Burnet, Son of Bishop Burnet, hearing from the Captain that a young Man, one of his Passengers, had a great many Books, desired he would bring me to see him. I waited upon him accordingly, and should have taken Collins with me but that he was not sober. The Governor treated me with great Civility, show'd me his Library, which was a very large one, and we had a good deal of Conversation about Books and Authors. This was the second Governor who had done me the Honor to take Notice of me, which to a poor Boy like me was very pleasing.

We proceeded to Philadelphia. I received on the Way Vernon's Money, without which we could hardly have finish'd our Journey. Collins wish'd to be employ'd in some Counting House; but whether they discover'd his Dramming by his Breath, or by his Behaviour, tho' he had some Recommendations, he met with no Success in any Application, and continu'd Lodging and Boarding at the same House with me and at my Expense. Knowing I had that Money of Vernon's he was continually borrowing of me, still promising Repayment as soon as he should be in Business. At length he had got so much of it, that I was distress'd to think what I should do, in case of being call'd on to remit it. His Drinking continu'd, about which we sometimes quarrel'd, for when a little intoxicated he was very fractious. Once in a Boat on the Delaware with some other young Men, he refused to row in his Turn: I will be row'd home, says he. We will not row you, says I. You must, says he, or stay all Night on the Water, just as you please. The others said, Let us row; What signifies it? But my Mind being soured with his other Conduct, I continu'd to refuse. So he swore he would make me row, or throw me overboard; and coming along stepping on the Thwarts towards me, when he came up and struck at me, I clapped my Hand under his Crotch, and rising, pitch'd him head-foremost into the River. I knew he was a good Swimmer, and so was under little Concern about him; but before he could get round to lay hold of the Boat, we had with a few Strokes pull'd her out of his Reach. And ever when he drew near the Boat, we ask'd if he would row, striking a few Strokes to slide her away from him. He was ready to die with Vexation, and obstinately would not promise to row; however seeing him at last beginning to tire, we lifted him in; and brought him home dripping wet in the Evening. We hardly exchang'd a civil Word afterwards; and a West India Captain who had a Commission to procure a Tutor for the Sons of a Gentleman at Barbados, happening to meet with him, agreed to carry him thither. He left me then, promising to remit me the first Money he should receive in order to discharge the Debt. But I never heard of him after.

The Breaking into this Money of Vernon's was one of the first great Errata of my Life. And this Affair show'd that my Father was not much out in his Judgment when he suppos'd me too Young to manage Business of Importance. But Sir William, on reading his Letter, said he was too prudent. There was great Difference in Persons, and Discretion did not always accompany Years, nor was Youth always without it. And since he will not set you up, says he, I will do it myself. Give me an Inventory of the Things necessary to be had from England, and I will send for them. You shall repay me when you are able; I am resolv'd to have a good Printer here, and I am sure you must succeed. This was spoken with such an Appearance of Cordiality, that I had not the least doubt of his meaning what he said. I had hitherto kept the Proposition of my Setting up a Secret in Philadelphia, and I still kept it. Had it been known that I depended on the Governor, probably some Friend that knew him better would have advis'd me not to rely on him, as I afterwards heard it as his known Character to be liberal of Promises which he never meant to keep. Yet unsolicited as he was by me, how could I think his generous Offers insincere? I believ'd him one of the best Men in the World.

I presented him an Inventory of a little Printing House, amounting by my Computation to about 100 Pounds Sterling. He lik'd it, but ask'd me if my being on the Spot in England to choose the Types and see that everything was good of the kind, might not be of some Advantage. Then, says he, when there, you may make Acquaintances and establish Correspondences in the Bookselling, and Stationery Way. I agreed that this might be advantageous. Then says he, get yourself ready to go with Annis;[6] which was the annual Ship, and the only one at that Time usually passing between London and Philadelphia. But it would be some Months before Annis sail'd, so I continu'd working with Keimer, fretting about the Money Collins had got from me, and in daily Apprehensions of being call'd upon by Vernon, which however did not happen for some Years after.

I believe I have omitted mentioning that in my first Voyage from Boston, being becalm'd off Block Island, our People set about catching Cod and haul'd up a great many. Hitherto I had stuck to my Resolution of not eating animal Food; and on this Occasion, I consider'd with my Master Tryon,[7] the taking every Fish as a kind of unprovok'd Murder, since none of them had or ever could do us any Injury that might justify the Slaughter. All this seem'd very reasonable. But I had formerly been a great Lover of Fish, and when this came hot out of the Frying Pan, it smelt admirably well. I balanc'd some time between Principle and Inclination: till I recollected, that when the Fish were opened, I saw smaller Fish taken out of their Stomachs: Then, thought I, if you eat one another, I don't see why we mayn't eat you. So I din'd upon Cod very heartily and continu'd to eat with other People, returning only now and then occasionally to a vegetable Diet. So convenient a thing it is to be a *reasonable Creature*, since it enables one to find or make a Reason for everything one has a mind to do.

Keimer and I liv'd on a pretty good familiar Footing and agreed tolerably well: for he suspected nothing of my Setting up. He retain'd a great deal of his old Enthusiasms, and lov'd an Argumentation. We therefore had many Disputations. I us'd to work him so with my Socratic Method, and had trapann'd[8] him so often by Questions apparently so distant from any Point we had in hand, and yet by degrees led to the Point, and brought him into Difficulties and Contradictions, that at last he grew ridiculously cautious, and would hardly answer me the most common Question, without asking first, *What do you intend to infer from that?* However it gave him so high an Opinion of my Abilities in the Confuting Way, that he seriously propos'd my being his Colleague in a Project he had of setting up a new Sect. He was to preach the Doctrines, and I was to confound all

---

6. Thomas Annis, captain of the annual mail packet, the *London Hope*. Because of European wars and the constant danger from pirates, transatlantic sailing was usually done in a large convoy, protected by the English navy.

7. "Flesh and Fish cannot be eaten without Violence, and doing that which a man would not be done unto." (Thomas Tryon, *Way to Health* [1683], p. 343.)

8. Snared.

Opponents. When he came to explain with me upon the Doctrines, I found several Conundrums which I objected to, unless I might have my Way a little too, and introduce some of mine. Keimer wore his Beard at full Length, because somewhere in the Mosaic Law it is said, *thou shalt not mar the Corners of thy Beard.*[9] He likewise kept the seventh-day Sabbath; and these two Points were Essentials with him. I dislik'd both, but agreed to admit them upon Condition of his adopting the Doctrine of using no animal Food. I doubt, says he, my Constitution will not bear that. I assur'd him it would, and that he would be the better for it. He was usually a great Glutton, and I promis'd myself some Diversion in half-starving him. He agreed to try the Practice if I would keep him Company. I did so and we held it for three Months. We had our Victuals dress'd and brought to us regularly by a Woman in the Neighborhood, who had from me a List of 40 Dishes to be prepar'd for us at different times, in all which there was neither Fish Flesh nor Fowl, and the Whim suited me the better at this time from the Cheapness of it, not costing us above 18 Pence Sterling each, per Week. I have since kept several Lents most strictly, leaving the common Diet for that, and that for the common, abruptly, without the least Inconvenience: So that I think there is little in the Advice of making those Changes by easy Gradations. I went on pleasantly, but Poor Keimer suffer'd grievously, tir'd of the Project, long'd for the Flesh Pots of Egypt,[1] and order'd a roast Pig; He invited me and two Women Friends to dine with him, but it being brought too soon upon table, he could not resist the Temptation, and ate it all up before we came.

I had made some Courtship during this time to Miss Read. I had a great Respect and Affection for her, and had some Reason to believe she had the same for me: but as I was about to take a long Voyage, and we were both very young, only a little above 18, it was thought most prudent by her Mother to prevent our going too far at present, as a Marriage if it was to take place would be more convenient after my Return, when I should be as I expected set up in my Business. Perhaps too she thought my Expectations not so well founded as I imagined them to be.

My chief Acquaintances at this time were, Charles Osborne, Joseph Watson, and James Ralph; All Lovers of Reading. The two first were Clerks to an eminent Scrivener or Conveyancer in the Town, Charles Brockden; the other was Clerk to a Merchant. Watson was a pious sensible young Man, of great Integrity. The others rather more lax in their Principles of Religion, particularly Ralph, who as well as Collins had been unsettled by me, for which they both made me suffer.

9. He probably also had long hair, since *Leviticus* 19: 27 reads, "Ye shall not round the corners of your heads, neither shalt thou mar the corners of thy beard."

1. Forbidden by Moses to eat flesh in the wilderness, the Israelites yearned for the pots of meat they had left behind in Egypt (*Exodus* 16: 2–3).

Obsorne was sensible, candid, frank, sincere, and affectionate to his Friends; but in literary Matters too fond of Criticizing. Ralph, was ingenious, genteel in his Manners, and extremely eloquent; I think I never knew a prettier Talker. Both of them great Admirers of Poetry, and began to try their Hands in little Pieces. Many pleasant Walks we four had together, on Sundays into the Woods near Skuylkill, where we read to one another and conferr'd on what we read. Ralph was inclin'd to pursue the Study of Poetry, not doubting but he might become eminent in it and make his Fortune by it, alledging that the best Poets must when they first began to write, make as many Faults as he did. Osborne dissuaded him, assur'd him he had no Genius for Poetry, and advis'd him to think of nothing beyond the Business he was bred to; that in the mercantile way tho' he had no Stock, he might by his Diligence and Punctuality recommend himself to Employment as a Factor, and in time acquire wherewith to trade on his own Account. I approv'd the amusing oneself with Poetry now and then, so far as to improve one's Language, but no farther. On this it was propos'd that we should each of us at our next Meeting produce a Piece of our own Composing, in order to improve by our mutual Observations, Criticisms and Corrections. As Language and Expression was what we had in View, we excluded all Considerations of Invention, by agreeing that the Task should be a Version of the 18th Psalm, which describes the Descent of a Deity. When the Time of our Meeting drew nigh, Ralph call'd on me first, and let me know his Piece was ready. I told him I had been busy, and having little Inclination had done nothing. He then show'd me his Piece for my Opinion; and I much approv'd it, as it appear'd to me to have great Merit. Now, says he, Osborne never will allow the least Merit in any thing of mine, but makes 1000 Criticisms out of mere Envy. He is not so jealous of you. I wish therefore you would take this Piece, and produce it as yours. I will pretend not to have had time, and so produce nothing: We shall then see what he will say to it. It was agreed, and I immediately transcrib'd it that it might appear in my own hand. We met.

Watson's Performance was read: there were some Beauties in it: but many Defects. Osborne's was read: It was much better. Ralph did it Justice, remark'd some Faults, but applauded the Beauties. He himself had nothing to produce. I was backward, seem'd desirous of being excus'd, had not had sufficient Time to correct; etc. but no Excuse could be admitted, produce I must. It was read and repeated; Watson and Osborne gave up the Contest; and join'd in applauding it immoderately. Ralph only made some Criticisms and propos'd some Amendments, but I defended my Text. Osborne was against Ralph, and told him he was no better a Critic than Poet; so he dropped the Argument. As they two went home together, Osborne express'd himself still more strongly in favor of what he thought my Production, having restrain'd himself before as he said, lest I should think it

Flattery. But who would have imagin'd, says he, that Franklin had been capable of such a Performance; such Painting, such Force! such Fire! He has even improv'd the Original! In his common Conversation, he seems to have no Choice of Words; he hesitates and blunders; and yet, good God, how he writes!

When we next met, Ralph discover'd the Trick we had played him, and Osborne was a little laughed at. This Transaction fix'd Ralph in his Resolution of becoming a Poet. I did all I could to dissuade him from it, but he continu'd scribbling Verses, till *Pope* cur'd him.[2] He became however a pretty good Prose Writer. More of him hereafter. But as I may not have occasion again to mention the other two, I shall just remark here, that Watson died in my Arms a few Years after, much lamented, being the best of our Set. Osborne went to the West Indies, where he became an eminent Lawyer and made Money, but died young. He and I had made a serious Agreement, that the one who happen'd first to die, should if possible make a friendly Visit to the other, and acquaint him how he found things in that separate State. But he never fulfill'd his Promise.

The Governor, seeming to like my Company, had me frequently to his House; and his Setting me up was always mention'd as a fix'd thing. I was to take with me Letters recommendatory to a Number of his Friends, besides the Letter of Credit to furnish me with the necessary Money for purchasing the Press and Types, Paper, etc. For these Letters I was appointed to call at different times, when they were to be ready, but a future time was still named. Thus we went on till the Ship whose Departure too had been several times postponed was on the Point of sailing. Then when I call'd to take my Leave and receive the Letters, his Secretary, Dr. Bard, came out to me and said the Governor was extremely busy, in writing, but would be down at New Castle before the Ship, and there the Letters would be delivered to me.

Ralph, tho' married and having one Child, had determined to accompany me in this Voyage. It was thought he intended to establish a Correspondence, and obtain Goods to sell on Commission. But I found afterwards, that thro' some Discontent with his Wife's Relations, he purposed to leave her on their Hands, and never return again. Having taken leave of my Friends, and interchang'd some Promises with Miss Read, I left Philadelphia in the Ship, which anchor'd at New Castle. The Governor was there. But when I went to his Lodging, the Secretary came to me from him with the civillest Message in the World, that he could not then see me being engag'd in Business of the utmost Importance, but should send the Letters to me

2. After Ralph attacked Pope in his poem *Sawney* (1728), Pope, alluding to Ralph's *Night* (also 1728), wrote him into the second edition of the *Dunciad* (1728): "Silence, ye Wolves! while Ralph to Cynthia howls, / And makes Night hideous—Answer him ye Owls!" (Book 3, 11. 159–60.) In the 1742 *Dunciad*, Pope also introduced Ralph into the first Book: "And see! The very Gazeteers give o'er, / Ev'n Ralph repents. . . ." (I, 215–16.) (James Sutherland, ed., *The Dunciad* [London: Methuen, 1953], pp. 165, 285.)

on board, wish'd me heartily a good Voyage and a speedy Return, etc. I return'd on board, a little puzzled, but still not doubting.

Mr. Andrew Hamilton, a famous Lawyer of Philadelphia, had taken Passage in the same Ship for himself and Son: and with Mr. Denham a Quaker Merchant, and Messrs. Onion and Russel Masters of an Iron Work in Maryland, had engag'd the Great Cabin; so that Ralph and I were forc'd to take up with a Berth in the Steerage: And none on board knowing us, were considered as ordinary Persons. But Mr. Hamilton and his Son (it was James, since Governor) return'd from New Castle to Philadelphia, the Father being recall'd by a great Fee to plead for a seized Ship.[3] And just before we sail'd Colonel French coming on board, and showing me great Respect, I was more taken Notice of, and with my Friend Ralph invited by the other Gentlemen to come into the Cabin, there being now Room. Accordingly we remov'd thither.

Understanding that Colonel French had brought on board the Governor's Dispatches, I ask'd the Captain for those Letters that were to be under my Care. He said all were put into the Bag together; and he could not then come at them; but before we landed in England, I should have an Opportunity of picking them out. So I was satisfied for the present, and we proceeded on our Voyage. We had a sociable Company in the Cabin, and lived uncommonly well, having the Addition of all Mr. Hamilton's Stores, who had laid in plentifully. In this Passage Mr. Denham contracted a Friendship for me that continued during his Life. The Voyage was otherwise not a pleasant one, as we had a great deal of bad Weather.

When we came into the Channel, the Captain kept his Word with me, and gave me an Opportunity of examining the Bag for the Governor's Letters. I found none upon which my Name was put, as under my Care; I pick'd out 6 or 7 that by the Handwriting I thought might be the promis'd Letters, especially as one of them was directed to Basket the King's Printer, and another to some Stationer. We arriv'd in London the 24th of December, 1724. I waited upon the Stationer who came first in my Way, delivering the Letter as from Governor Keith. I don't know such a Person, says he: but opening the Letter, O, this is from Riddlesden; I have lately found him to be a complete Rascal, and I will have nothing to do with him, nor receive any Letters from him. So putting the Letter into my Hand, he turn'd on his Heel and left me to serve some Customer. I was surprised to find these were not the Governor's Letters. And after recollecting and comparing Circumstances, I began to doubt his Sincerity. I found my Friend Denham, and opened the whole Affair to him. He let me into Keith's Character, told me there was not the least Probability that he had

---

3. The *American Weekly Mercury* for November 5, 1724, reported Hamilton had set out on November 2, but had been called back. The "great Fee" was £300.

written any Letters for me, that no one who knew him had the smallest
Dependence on him, and he laughed at the Notion of the Governor's
giving me a Letter of Credit, having as he said no Credit to give. On
my expressing some Concern about what I should do: He advis'd me to
endeavour getting some Employment in the Way of my Business.
Among the Printers here, says he, you will improve yourself; and
when you return to America, you will set up to greater Advantage.
We both of us happen'd to know, as well as the Stationer, that
Riddlesden the Attorney, was a very Knave. He had half ruin'd Miss
Read's Father by drawing him in to be bound for him. By his Letter it
appear'd, there was a secret Scheme on foot to the Prejudice of
Hamilton, (Suppos'd to be then coming over with us,) and that Keith
was concern'd in it with Riddlesden. Denham, who was a Friend of
Hamilton's, thought he ought to be acquainted with it. So when he
arriv'd in England, which was soon after, partly from Resentment and
Ill-Will to Keith and Riddlesden, and partly from Goodwill to him: I
waited on him, and gave him the Letter. He thank'd me cordially, the
Information being of Importance to him. And from that time he
became my Friend, greatly to my Advantage afterwards on many
Occasions.

But what shall we think of a Governor's playing such pitiful Tricks,
and imposing so grossly on a poor ignorant Boy! It was a Habit he had
acquired. He wish'd to please everybody; and having little to give, he
gave Expectations. He was otherwise an ingenious sensible Man, a
pretty good Writer, and a good Governor for the People, tho' not for
his Constituents the Proprietaries, whose Instructions he sometimes
disregarded. Several of our best Laws were of his Planning, and pass'd
during his Administration.

Ralph and I were inseparable Companions. We took Lodgings
together in Little Britain[4] at 3 shillings 6 pence per Week, as much as
we could then afford. He found some Relations, but they were poor
and unable to assist him. He now let me know his Intentions of
remaining in London, and that he never meant to return to Philadelphia. He had brought no Money with him, the whole he could muster
having been expended in paying his Passage. I had 15 Pistoles. So he
borrowed occasionally of me, to subsist while he was looking out for
Business. He first endeavoured to get into the Playhouse, believing
himself qualified for an Actor; but Wilkes,[5] to whom he applied,
advis'd him candidly not to think of that Employment, as it was
impossible he should succeed in it. Then he propos'd to Roberts, a
Publisher in Paternoster Row, to write for him a Weekly Paper like the
Spectator, on certain Conditions, which Roberts did not approve.
Then he endeavour'd to get Employment as a Hackney Writer to copy

4. Alley in midtown London, north of St.   5. Robert Wilks.
Paul's.

for the Stationers and Lawyers about the Temple:[6] but could find no Vacancy.

I immediately got into Work at Palmer's, then a famous Printing-House in Bartholomew Close;[7] and here I continu'd near a Year. I was pretty diligent; but spent with Ralph a good deal of my Earnings in going to Plays and other Places of Amusement.[8] We had together consum'd all my Pistoles, and now just rubb'd on from hand to mouth. He seem'd quite to forget his Wife and Child, and I by degrees my Engagements with Miss Read, to whom I never wrote more than one Letter, and that was to let her know I was not likely soon to return. This was another of the great Errata of my Life, which I should wish to correct if I were to live it over again. In fact, by our Expenses, I was constantly kept unable to pay my Passage.

At Palmer's I was employ'd in Composing for the second Edition of Wollaston's Religion of Nature.[9] Some of his Reasonings not appearing to me well-founded, I wrote a little metaphysical Piece, in which I made Remarks on them. It was entitled, A Dissertation on Liberty and Necessity, Pleasure and Pain.[1] I inscrib'd it to my Friend Ralph. I printed a small Number. It occasion'd my being more consider'd by Mr. Palmer, as a young Man of some Ingenuity, tho' he seriously expostulated with me upon the Principles of my Pamphlet which to him appear'd abominable. My printing this Pamphlet was another Erratum.

While I lodg'd in Little Britain I made an Acquaintance with one Wilcox a Bookseller, whose Shop was at the next Door. He had an immense Collection of second-hand Books. Circulating Libraries were not then in Use; but we agreed that on certain reasonable Terms which I have now forgotten, I might take, read and return any of his Books. This I esteem'd a great Advantage, and I made as much Use of it as I could.

My Pamphlet by some means falling into the Hands of one Lyons, a Surgeon, Author of a Book entitled The Infallibility of Human Judgment, it occasioned an Acquaintance between us; he took great Notice of me, call'd on me often, to converse on these Subjects, carried me to the Horns a pale Ale-House in [blank] Lane, Cheapside,[2] and introduc'd me to Dr. Mandeville, Author of the Fable of the Bees[3] who had

6. One of the Inns of Court, location of law offices.
7. Just off Little Britain, it was the remains of an ancient monastery attached to the church of St. Bartholomew the Great. Palmer's shop occupied the top floor at 54 Bartholomew Close and the type foundry of Thomas and John James was evidently downstairs. (Webb, 2: 80.)
8. Four years later Ralph published The Touch-stone (1729), a guide to London amusement centers.
9. BF set the type for the third edition of William Wollaston's Religion of Nature Delineated

(London: Samuel Palmer, 1725) in January or February, for it was advertised for sale by the end of February, 1725 (Monthly Catalogue for February, 1724/5, p. 21).
1. P, 1: 58–71.
2. Possibly a "Horns Tavern" in Gutter Lane, Cheapside. (See Lillywhite, London Signs, nos. 8911 and 8885.)
3. Published in 1714, it expanded an earlier poem, The Grumbling Hive (1705). Just before BF's coming to London, the grand jury had declared the book "a public nuisance."

a Club there, of which he was the Soul, being a most facetious entertaining Companion. Lyons too introduc'd me to Dr. Pemberton, at Batson's Coffee House,[4] who promis'd to give me an Opportunity some time or other of seeing Sir Isaac Newton, of which I was extremely desirous; but this never happened.

I had brought over a few Curiosities among which the principal was a Purse made of the Asbestos, which purifies by Fire. Sir Hans Sloane heard of it,[5] came to see me, and invited me to his House in Bloomsbury Square; where he show'd me all his Curiosities, and persuaded me to let him add that to the Number, for which he paid me handsomely.

In our House there lodg'd a young Woman, a Millener, who I think had a Shop in the Cloisters.[6] She had been genteelly bred, was sensible and lively, and of most pleasing Conversation. Ralph read Plays to her in the Evenings, they grew intimate, she took another Lodging, and he follow'd her. They liv'd together some time, but he being still out of Business, and her Income not sufficient to maintain them with her Child, he took a Resolution of going from London, to try for a Country School, which he thought himself well qualified to undertake, as he wrote an excellent Hand, and was a Master of Arithmetic and Accounts. This however he deem'd a Business below him, and confident of future better Fortune when he should be unwilling to have it known that he once was so meanly employ'd, he chang'd his Name, and did me the Honor to assume mine. For I soon after had a Letter from him, acquainting me, that he was settled in a small Village in Berkshire, I think it was, where he taught reading and writing to 10 or a dozen Boys at 6 pence each per Week, recommending Mrs. T. to my Care, and desiring me to write to him directing for Mr. Franklin Schoolmaster at such a Place. He continu'd to write frequently, sending me large Specimens of an Epic Poem,[7] which he was then composing, and desiring my Remarks and Corrections. These I gave him from time to time, but endeavour'd rather to discourage his Proceeding. One of Young's Satires was then just publish'd. I copied and sent him a great Part of it, which set in a strong Light the Folly of pursuing the Muses with any Hope of Advancement by them.[8] All was in vain. Sheets of the Poem continu'd to come by every Post. In the mean time Mrs. T. having on his Account lost her Friends and Business, was often in Distresses, and us'd to send for me, and borrow what I could spare to help her out of them. I grew fond of

---

4. A rendezvous for physicians at No. 17, Cornhill, "against the Royal Exchange." (Lillywhite, *London Coffee Houses*, no. 90.)

5. From BF himself in a letter (June 2, 1725) offering to show or sell these curiosities. (*P*, 1: 54.)

6. The ancient monastic cloisters of St. Bartholomew's had been converted to commercial use, including a tavern. (Webb, 2: 137.)

7. Perhaps Ralph's *Sawney* (1728), "an heroic poem."

8. Satires i-iv of Edward Young's *The Universal Passion* were published in 1725. Satire ii contains such pertinent lines as: "Fame and Fortune both are made of Prose."

her Company, and being at this time under no Religious Restraints, and presuming on my Importance to her, I attempted Familiarities, (another Erratum) which she repuls'd with a proper Resentment, and acquainted him with my Behaviour. This made a Breach between us, and when he return'd again to London, he let me know he thought I had cancel'd all the Obligations he had been under to me. So I found I was never to expect his Repaying me what I lent to him or advanc'd for him. This was however not then of much Consequence, as he was totally unable. And in the Loss of his Friendship I found myself reliev'd from a Burden. I now began to think of getting a little Money beforehand; and expecting better Work, I left Palmer's to work at Watts's near Lincoln's Inn Fields,[9] a still greater Printing-House.[1] Here I continu'd all the rest of my Stay in London.

At my first Admission into this Printing-House, I took to working at Press, imagining I felt a Want of the Bodily Exercise I had been us'd to in America, where Presswork is mix'd with Composing. I drank only Water; the other Workmen, near 50 in Number, were great Guzzlers of Beer. On occasion I carried up and down Stairs a large Form of Types in each hand, when others carried but one in both Hands. They wonder'd to see from this and several Instances that the Water-American as they call'd me was *stronger* than themselves who drunk *strong* Beer. We had an Alehouse Boy who attended always in the House to supply the Workmen. My Companion at the Press drank every day a Pint before Breakfast, a Pint at Breakfast with his Bread and Cheese; a Pint between Breakfast and Dinner; a Pint at Dinner; a Pint in the Afternoon about Six o'clock, and another when he had done his Day's Work. I thought it a detestable Custom. But it was necessary, he suppos'd, to drink *strong* Beer that he might be *strong* to labour. I endeavour'd to convince him that the Bodily Strength afforded by Beer could only be in proportion to the Grain or Flour of the Barley dissolved in the Water of which it was made; that there was more Flour in a Penny-worth of Bread, and therefore if he would eat that with a Pint of Water, it would give him more Strength than a Quart of Beer. He drank on however, and had 4 or 5 Shillings to pay out of his Wages every Saturday Night for that muddling Liquor; an Expense I was free from. And thus these poor Devils keep themselves always under.

Watts after some Weeks desiring to have me in the Composing-Room, I left the Pressmen. A new *Bienvenu*[2] or Sum for Drink, being 5 Shillings, was demanded of me by the Compositors. I thought it an Imposition, as I had paid below. The Master thought so too, and forbad my Paying it. I stood out two or three Weeks, was accordingly considered as an Excommunicate, and had so many little Pieces of

9. The largest park in mid-London.
1. Relative size may be judged from Palmer having two apprentices while Watts had fifteen. (Ellic Howe, *The London Compositor* [London:

Bibliographical Society, 1947] , p. 37.)
2. Traditional initiation fee was five shillings for those who had not yet finished their apprenticeship. (Howe, p. 32.)

private Mischief done me, by mixing my Sorts, transposing my Pages, breaking my Matter,[3] etc. etc. if I were ever so little out of the Room, and all ascrib'd to the Chapel Ghost, which they said ever haunted those not regularly admitted, that notwithstanding the Master's Protection, I found myself oblig'd to comply and pay the Money; convinc'd of the Folly of being on ill Terms with those one is to live with continually. I was now on a fair Footing with them, and soon acquir'd considerable Influence. I propos'd some reasonable Alterations in their Chapel* Laws, and carried them against all Opposition. From my Example a great Part of them, left their muddling Breakfast of Beer and Bread and Cheese, finding they could with me be supplied from a neighboring House with a large Porringer of hot Water-gruel, sprinkled with Pepper, crumb'd with Bread, and a Bit of Butter in it, for the Price of a Pint of Beer, viz, three halfpence. This was a more comfortable as well as cheaper Breakfast, and kept their Heads clearer. Those who continu'd sotting with Beer all day, were often, by not paying, out of Credit at the Alehouse, and us'd to make Interest with me to get Beer, *their Light*, as they phras'd it, *being out*. I watch'd the Pay table on Saturday Night, and collected what I stood engag'd for them, having to pay some times near Thirty Shillings a Week on their Accounts. This, and my being esteem'd a pretty good Riggite, that is a jocular verbal Satirist, supported my Consequence in the Society. My constant Attendance, (I never making a St. Monday),[4] recommended me to the Master; and my uncommon Quickness at Composing, occasion'd my being put upon all Work of Dispatch, which was generally better paid. So I went on now very agreeably.

My Lodging in Little Britain being too remote, I found another in Duke Street opposite to the Romish Chapel.[5] It was two pair of Stairs backwards at an Italian Warehouse. A Widow Lady kept the House; she had a Daughter and a Maid Servant, and a Journeyman who attended the Warehouse, but lodg'd abroad. After sending to enquire my Character at the House where I last lodg'd, she agreed to take me in at the same Rate, 3 Shillings 6 Pence per Week, cheaper as she said from the Protection she expected in having a Man lodge in the House. She was a Widow, an elderly Woman, had been bred a Protestant, being a Clergyman's Daughter, but was converted to the Catholic Religion by her Husband, whose Memory she much revered, had lived much among People of Distinction, and knew a 1000 Anecdotes

---

* "A Printing House is always called a Chappel by the Workmen.—" [BF note.] The word referred both to the shop as a place of work and to the workmen as a self-governing group who set local customs, practices, fines, etc.

3. By putting the types in the wrong boxes, mixing up the pages of the manuscript he was setting in type, and breaking up the columns of type he had already set.
4. Taking Monday off because of a hangover from Sunday carousing.
5. Now Sardinia Street. About one mile closer than Little Britain, it was only two blocks south of Watts's shop on Wild Court.

of them as far back as the Times of Charles the second.[6] She was lame in her Knees with the Gout, and therefore seldom stirr'd out of her Room, so sometimes wanted Company; and hers was so highly amusing to me that I was sure to spend an Evening with her whenever she desired it. Our Supper was only half an Anchovy each, on a very little Strip of Bread and Butter, and half a Pint of Ale between us. But the Entertainment was in her Conversation. My always keeping good Hours, and giving little Trouble in the Family, made her unwilling to part with me; so that when I talk'd of a Lodging I had heard of, nearer my Business, for 2 Shillings a Week, which, intent as I now was on saving Money, made some Difference; she bid me not think of it, for she would abate me two Shillings a Week for the future, so I remain'd with her at 1 Shilling 6 Pence as long as I stayed in London.

In a Garret of her House there lived a Maiden Lady of 70 in the most retired Manner, of whom my Landlady gave me this Account, that she was a Roman Catholic, had been sent abroad when young and lodg'd in a Nunnery with an Intent of becoming a Nun: but the Country not agreeing with her, she return'd to England, where there being no Nunnery, she had vow'd to lead the Life of a Nun as near as might be done in those Circumstances: Accordingly She had given all her Estate to charitable Uses, reserving only Twelve Pounds a Year to live on, and out of this Sum she still gave a great deal in Charity, living herself on Watergruel only, and using no Fire but to boil it. She had lived many Years in that Garret, being permitted to remain there gratis by successive catholic Tenants of the House below, as they deem'd it a Blessing to have her there. A Priest visited her, to confess her every Day. I have ask'd her, says my Landlady, how she, as she liv'd, could possibly find so much Employment for a Confessor? O, says she, it is impossible to avoid *vain Thoughts*. I was permitted once to visit her: She was cheerful and polite, and convers'd pleasantly. The Room was clean, but had no other Furniture than a Mattress, a Table with a Crucifix and Book, a Stool, which she gave me to sit on, and a Picture over the Chimney of St. *Veronica*, displaying her Handkerchief with the miraculous Figure of Christ's bleeding Face on it, which she explain'd to me with great Seriousness. She look'd pale, but was never sick, and I give it as another Instance on how small an Income Life and Health may be supported.

At Watts's Printing-House I contracted an Acquaintance with an ingenious young Man, one Wygate, who having wealthy Relations, had been better educated than most Printers, was a tolerable Latinist, spoke French, and lov'd Reading. I taught him, and a Friend of his, to swim at twice going into the River, and they soon became good Swimmers. They introduc'd me to some Gentlemen from the Coun-

6. Forty to sixty-five years earlier, i.e., 1660–85.

try who went to Chelsea by Water to see the College[7] and Don Saltero's Curiosities.[8] In our Return, at the Request of the Company, whose Curiosity Wygate had excited, I stripped and leaped into the River, and swam from near Chelsea to Blackfriars,[9] performing on the Way many Feats of Activity both upon and under Water, that surpris'd and pleas'd those to whom they were Novelties. I had from a Child been ever delighted with this Exercise, had studied and practic'd all Thevenot's Motions and Positions,[1] added some of my own, aiming at the graceful and easy, as well as the Useful. All these I took this Occasion of exhibiting to the Company, and was much flatter'd by their Admiration. And Wygate, who was desirous of becoming a Master, grew more and more attach'd to me on that account, as well as from the Similarity of our Studies. He at length propos'd to me travelling all over Europe together, supporting ourselves every where by working at our Business. I was once inclin'd to it. But mentioning it to my good Friend Mr. Denham, with whom I often spent an Hour when I had Leisure, he dissuaded me from it; advising me to think only of returning to Pennsylvania, which he was now about to do.

I must record one Trait of this good Man's Character. He had formerly been in Business at Bristol, but fail'd in Debt to a Number of People, compounded and went to America. There, by a close Application to Business as a Merchant, he acquir'd a plentiful Fortune in a few Years. Returning to England in the Ship with me, He invited his old Creditors to an Entertainment, at which he thank'd them for the easy Composition they had favor'd him with, and when they expected nothing but the Treat, every Man at the first Remove found under his Plate an Order on a Banker for the full Amount of the unpaid Remainder with Interest.[2]

He now told me he was about to return to Philadelphia, and should carry over a great Quantity of Goods in order to open a Store there: He propos'd to take me over as his Clerk, to keep his Books (in which he would instruct me), copy his Letters, and attend the Store. He added, that as soon as I should be acquainted with mercantile Business he would promote me by sending me with a Cargo of Flour and Bread etc. to the West Indies, and procure me Commissions from others; which would be profitable, and if I manag'd well, would establish me

7. On the site of a former college, Chelsea Hospital, now a home for old soldiers, had lovely Dutch gardens and an avenue of elms sloping down to the river.
8. A former barber of Sir Hans Sloane who gave him cast-off curios, James Salter (dubbed Don Saltero by the *Tatler*, no. 34, June 28, 1709) kept a coffee house exhibiting such marvels as Job's tears, pieces of the Holy Cross, and "Pontius Pilate's wife's chambermaid's sister's hat." Lillywhite, *London Coffee Houses*, no.

352.)
9. Well over three miles.
1. World traveler and librarian of the King of France, Melchisédech Thévenot wrote *L'Art de Nager* (1696; tr. as *The Art of Swimming*, 1699), a small, 60-page book with 39 plates demonstrating various strokes and positions.
2. This sounds like a popular oral anecdote, and records show that Denham paid his creditors in 1721 or 1722, well before returning to England in 1724 with BF. (Tolles, p. 249n.)

handsomely. The Thing pleas'd me, for I was grown tired of London, remember'd with Pleasure the happy Months I had spent in Pennsylvania, and wish'd again to see it. Therefore I immediately agreed, on the Terms of Fifty Pounds a Year, Pennsylvania Money; less indeed than my then Gettings as a Compositor, but affording a better Prospect.

I now took Leave of Printing, as I thought for ever, and was daily employ'd in my new Business; going about with Mr. Denham among the Tradesmen, to purchase various Articles, and see them pack'd up, doing Errands, calling upon Workmen to dispatch, etc. and when all was on board, I had a few Days' Leisure. On one of these Days I was to my Surprise sent for by a great Man I knew only by Name, a Sir William Wyndham and I waited upon him. He had heard by some means or other of my Swimming from Chelsey to Blackfriars, and of my teaching Wygate and another young Man to swim in a few Hours. He had two Sons about to set out on their Travels; he wish'd to have them first taught Swimming; and propos'd to gratify me handsomely if I would teach them. They were not yet come to Town and my Stay was uncertain, so I could not undertake it. But from this Incident I thought it likely, that if I were to remain in England and open a Swimming School, I might get a good deal of Money. And it struck me so strongly, that had the Overture been sooner made me, probably I should not so soon have returned to America. After Many Years, you and I had something of more Importance to do with one of these Sons of Sir William Wyndham, become Earl of Egremont, which I shall mention in its Place.[3]

Thus I spent about 18 Months in London. Most Part of the Time, I work'd hard at my Business, and spent but little upon myself except in seeing Plays, and in Books. My Friend Ralph had kept me poor. He owed me about 27 Pounds; which I was now never likely to receive; a great Sum out of my small Earnings. I lov'd him notwithstanding, for he had many amiable Qualities. Tho' I had by no means improv'd my Fortune, I had pick'd up some very ingenious Acquaintance whose Conversation was of great Advantage to me, and I had read considerably.

We sail'd from Gravesend on the 23d of July 1726. For The Incidents of the Voyage, I refer you to my Journal, where you will find them all minutely related. Perhaps the most important Part of that Journal is the *Plan*[4] to be found in it which I formed at Sea for regulating my future Conduct in Life. It is the more remarkable, as being form'd when I was so young, and yet being pretty faithfully adhered to quite thro' to old Age. We landed in Philadelphia the 11th

3. BF initially hoped to have his *Autobiography* cover his life up to 1771. But, since this son of William Wyndham did not become secretary of state for the colonies until 1761, and since BF's *Autobiography* breaks off at 1757, he will not be mentioned again.
4. The full journal as well as the preamble and the outline of the "*Plan*" survive. (*P*, 1: 72–99.)

of October, where I found sundry Alterations. Keith was no longer Governor, being superseded by Major Gordon: I met him walking the Streets as a common Citizen.[5] He seem'd a little asham'd at seeing me, but pass'd without saying anything. I should have been as much asham'd at seeing Miss Read, had not her Friends despairing with Reason of my Return, after the Receipt of my Letter, persuaded her to marry another, one Rogers, a Potter, which was done in my Absence.[6] With him however she was never happy, and soon parted from him, refusing to cohabit with him, or bear his Name, It being now said that he had another Wife. He was a worthless Fellow tho' an excellent Workman which was the Temptation to her Friends. He got into Debt, and ran away in 1727 or 28, went to the West Indies, and died there. Keimer had got a better House, a Shop well supplied with Stationery, plenty of new Types, a number of Hands tho' none good, and seem'd to have a great deal of Business.

Mr. Denham took a Store in Water Street,[7] where we open'd our Goods. I attended the Business diligently, studied Accounts, and grew in a little Time expert at selling. We lodg'd and boarded together, he counsell'd me as a Father, having a sincere Regard for me: I respected and lov'd him: and we might have gone on together very happily: But in the Beginning of February 1726/7 when I had just pass'd my 21st Year, we both were taken ill.[8] My Distemper was a Pleurisy, which very nearly carried me off: I suffered a good deal, gave up the Point in my own mind, and was rather disappointed when I found myself recovering; regretting in some degree that I must now sometime or other have all that disagreeable Work to do over again. I forget what his Distemper was. It held him a long time, and at length carried him off. He left me a small Legacy in a nuncupative Will,[9] as a Token of his Kindness for me, and he left me once more to the wide World. For the Store was taken into the Care of his Executors, and my Employment under him ended: My Brother-in-law Homes, being now at Philadelphia, advis'd my Return to my Business. And Keimer tempted me with an Offer of large Wages by the Year to come and take the Management of his Printing-House that he might better attend his Stationer's Shop. I had heard a bad Character of him in London, from his Wife and her Friends, and was not fond of having any more to do

---

5. Removed in June, 1726, Keith was now popular leader of the party opposing the Proprietors.

6. Deborah Read married John Rogers in Christ Church, Philadelphia, on August 5, 1725. (*Pa. Archives*, 2nd ser., 8: 221.) Rogers absconded in December, 1727. (Roach, p. 141.)

7. Located south of the Crooked Billet, the present site of 39 South Front Street. (Roach, p. 135.)

8. Events are compressed here. BF probably worked for Denham from October 1726 until August 1727, and was ill during March and April, 1727. He evidently went back to work for Keimer in the fall of 1727, while Denham lived until July 4, 1728. (Roach, pp. 136–7; Tolles, p. 249n.)

9. The oral will was heard by three witnesses, December 29, 1726, and approved September 1, 1729. It forgave BF's debt of £10 owed Denham for the return fare from London. (Roach, p. 136.)

with him. I tried for farther Employment as a Merchant's Clerk; but not readily meeting with any, I clos'd again with Keimer.

I found in *his* House these Hands; Hugh Meredith a Welsh-Pennsylvanian, 30 Years of Age, bred to Country Work: honest, sensible, had a great deal of solid Observation, was something of a Reader, but given to drink: Stephen Potts, a young Country Man of full Age, bred to the Same, of uncommon natural Parts, and great Wit and Humor, but a little idle. These he had agreed with at extreme low Wages, per Week, to be rais'd a Shilling every 3 Months, as they would deserve by improving in their Business, and the Expectation of these high Wages to come on hereafter was what he had drawn them in with. Meredith was to work at Press, Potts at Bookbinding, which he by Agreement, was to teach them, tho' he knew neither one nor t'other. John ——— a wild Irishman brought up to no Business, whose Service for 4 Years Keimer had purchas'd[1] from the Captain of a Ship. He too was to be made a Pressman. George Webb, an Oxford Scholar, whose Time for 4 Years he had likewise bought, intending him for a Compositor: of whom more presently. And David Harry, a Country Boy, whom he had taken Apprentice. I soon perceiv'd that the Intention of engaging me at Wages so much higher than he had been us'd to give,[2] was to have these raw cheap Hands form'd thro' me, and as soon as I had instructed them, then, they being all articled to him, he should be able to do without me. I went on however, very cheerfully; put his Printing-House in Order, which had been in great Confusion, and brought his Hands by degrees to mind their Business and to do it better.

It was an odd Thing to find an Oxford Scholar in the Situation of a bought Servant. He was not more than 18 Years of Age, and gave me this Account of himself; that he was born in Gloucester, educated at a Grammar School there, had been distinguish'd among the Scholars for some apparent Superiority in performing his Part when they exhibited Plays; belong'd to the Witty Club there, and had written some Pieces in Prose and Verse which were printed in the Gloucester Newspapers. Thence he was sent to Oxford; there he continu'd about a Year, but not well-satisfied, wishing of all things to see London and become a Player. At length receiving his Quarterly Allowance of 15 Guineas, instead of discharging his Debts, he walk'd out of Town, hid his Gown in a Furz Bush, and footed it to London, where having no Friend to advise him, he fell into bad Company, soon spent his Guineas, found no means of being introduc'd among the Players, grew necessitous, pawn'd his Clothes and wanted Bread. Walking the Street very hungry, and not knowing what to do with himself, a Crimp's Bill[3] was put into his Hand, offering immediate Entertain-

---

1. Paid his passage in return for four years labor as an indentured servant.
2. Originally BF wrote "80 Pounds a Year."

3. Advertisement by a recruiter of seamen and emigrant laborers.

ment and Encouragement to such as would bind themselves to serve in America. He went directly, sign'd the Indentures, was put into the Ship and came over; never writing a Line to acquaint his Friends what was become of him. He was lively, witty, good-natur'd and a pleasant Companion, but idle, thoughtless and imprudent to the last Degree.

John the Irishman soon ran away. With the rest I began to live very agreeably; for they all respected me, the more as they found Keimer incapable of instructing them, and that from me they learned something daily. We never work'd on a Saturday, that being Keimer's Sabbath. So I had two Days for Reading. My Acquaintance with ingenious People in the Town increased. Keimer himself treated me with great Civility and apparent Regard; and nothing now made me uneasy but my Debt to Vernon, which I was yet unable to pay, being hitherto but a poor Economist. He however kindly made no Demand of it.

Our Printing-House often wanted Sorts,[4] and there was no Letter Founder in America. I had seen Types cast at James's in London,[5] but without much Attention to the Manner: However I now contriv'd a Mold, made use of the Letters we had as Puncheons, struck the Matrices in Lead,[6] and thus supplied in a pretty tolerable way all Deficiencies. I also engrav'd several Things on occasion. I made the Ink, I was Warehouse-man and everything, in short quite a Factotum.

But however serviceable I might be, I found that my Services became every Day of less Importance, as the other Hands improv'd in the Business. And when Keimer paid my second Quarter's Wages, he let me know that he felt them too heavy, and thought I should make an Abatement. He grew by degrees less civil, put on more of the Master, frequently found Fault, was captious and seem'd ready for an Outbreaking. I went on nevertheless with a good deal of Patience, thinking that his encumber'd Circumstances were partly the Cause. At length a Trifle snapped our Connection. For a great Noise happening near the Courthouse, I put my Head out of the Window to see what was the Matter.[7] Keimer being in the Street look'd up and saw me, call'd out to me in a loud Voice and angry Tone to mind my Business, adding some reproachful Words, that nettled me the more for their Publicity, all the Neighbors who were looking out on the same Occasion being Witnesses how I was treated. He came up immediately into the Printing-House, continu'd the Quarrel, high Words pass'd on both Sides, he gave me the Quarter's Warning we had stipulated, expressing a Wish that he had not been oblig'd to so long a Warning: I told him his Wish was unnecessary for I would leave him that Instant; and so taking my Hat walk'd out of Doors; desiring Meredith whom I saw

4. Duplicate types.
5. See n. 7, p. 34 of this section.
6. BF thus made the first types in America. (Wroth, *Colonial Printer*, p. 97.)

7. If this (as BF wrote and cancelled, see the textual note) was election day, then it must have been Monday, October 2, 1727.

below to take care of some Things I left, and bring them to my Lodging.

Meredith came accordingly in the Evening, when we talk'd my Affair over. He had conceiv'd a great Regard for me, and was very unwilling that I should leave the House while he remain'd in it. He dissuaded me from returning to my native Country[8] which I began to think of. He reminded me that Keimer was in debt for all he possess'd, that his Creditors began to be uneasy, that he kept his Shop miserably, sold often without Profit for ready Money, and often trusted without keeping Account. That he must therefore fail; which would make a Vacancy I might profit of. I objected my Want of Money. He then let me know, that his Father had a high Opinion of me, and from some Discourse that had pass'd between them, he was sure would advance Money to set us up, if I would enter into Partnership with him. My Time, says he, will be out with Keimer in the Spring. By that time we may have our Press and Types in from London: I am sensible I am no Workman. If you like it, Your Skill in the Business shall be set against the Stock I furnish; and we will share the Profits equally.—The Proposal was agreeable, and I consented. His Father was in Town, and approv'd of it, the more as he saw I had great Influence with his Son, had prevail'd on him to abstain long from Dramdrinking, and he hop'd might break him of that wretched Habit entirely, when we came to be so closely connected. I gave an Inventory to the Father, who carried it to a Merchant; the Things were sent for; the Secret was to be kept till they should arrive, and in the mean time I was to get Work if I could at the other Printing-House. But I found no Vacancy there, and so remain'd idle a few Days, when Keimer, on a Prospect of being employ'd to print some Paper-money, in New Jersey, which would require Cuts and various Types that I only could supply, and apprehending Bradford might engage me and get the Job from him, sent me a very civil Message, that old Friends should not part for a few Words, the Effect of sudden Passion, and wishing me to return. Meredith persuaded me to comply, as it would give more Opportunity for his Improvement under my daily Instructions. So I return'd, and we went on more smoothly than for some time before. The New Jersey Job was obtain'd. I contriv'd a Copper-Plate Press for it, the first that had been seen in the Country. I cut several Ornaments and Checks for the Bills.[9] We went together to Burlington,[1] where I executed the Whole to Satisfaction, and he received so large a Sum for the Work, as to be enabled thereby to keep his Head much longer above Water.

At Burlington I made an Acquaintance with many principal People

8. Boston.
9. BF's copperplate engravings may have been the earliest in the Middle Colonies, but Francis Dewing had made copperplate engravings in Boston in 1717. (Wroth, "Benjamin Franklin,"

pp. 158–59.)
1. In the spring of 1728. (Newman, p. 202.) While Keimer's press was at Burlington, BF and he printed the *Acts and Laws of. . . New Jersey* (Burlington: Keimer, 1725); Evans 3071.

of the Province. Several of them had been appointed by the Assembly a Committee[2] to attend the Press, and take Care that no more Bills were printed than the Law directed. They were therefore by Turns constantly with us, and generally he who attended brought with him a Friend or two for Company. My Mind having been much more improv'd by Reading than Keimer's, I suppose it was for that Reason my Conversation seem'd to be more valu'd. They had me to their Houses, introduc'd me to their Friends and show'd me much Civility, while he, tho' the Master, was a little neglected. In truth he was an odd Fish, ignorant of common Life, fond of rudely opposing receiv'd Opinions, slovenly to extreme dirtiness, enthusiastic in some Points of Religion, and a little Knavish withal. We continu'd there near 3 Months, and by that time I could reckon among my acquired Friends, Judge Allen, Samuel Bustill, the Secretary of the Province, Isaac Pearson, Joseph Cooper and several of the Smiths, Members of Assembly, and Isaac Decow the Surveyor General. The latter was a shrewd sagacious old Man, who told me that he began for himself when young by wheeling Clay for the Brickmakers, learned to write after he was of Age, carried the Chain for Surveyors, who taught him Surveying, and he had now by his Industry acquir'd a good Estate; and says he, I foresee, that you will soon work this Man out of his Business and make a Fortune in it at Philadelphia. He had not then the least Intimation of my Intention to set up there or anywhere. These Friends were afterwards of great Use to me, as I occasionally was to some of them. They all continued their Regard for me as long as they lived.

Before I enter upon my public Appearance in Business, it may be well to let you know the then State of my Mind, with regard to my Principles and Morals, that you may see how far those influenc'd the future Events of my Life. My Parents had early given me religious Impressions, and brought me through my Childhood piously in the Dissenting Way. But I was scarce 15 when, after doubting by turns of several Points as I found them disputed in the different Books I read, I began to doubt of Revelation itself. Some Books against Deism[3] fell into my Hands; they were said to be the Substance of Sermons preached at Boyle's Lectures.[4] It happened that they wrought an Effect on me quite contrary to what was intended by them: For the Arguments of the Deists which were quoted to be refuted, appeared to me much Stronger than the Refutations. In short I soon became a thorough Deist. My Arguments perverted some others, particularly

2. Two groups of inspectors, one each from East Jersey and West Jersey, oversaw printing of the £25,760, voted by the assembly the previous year. (Tanner, p. 551.)
3. Perhaps BF read the sermons of 1705 by Samuel Clarke, *Discourse Concerning . . . Natural Religion, and . . . Christian Revelation* (1706). Clarke quotes the arguments of four kinds of deists in order to refute them.

4. Pioneer chemist Robert Boyle (1627–91) endowed £50 annually for preaching eight sermons a year against "notorious Infidels," excluding controversies among Christians themselves. A list of "The Boyle Lectures 1692–1714" is given in Margaret C. Jacob, *The Newtonians and the English Revolution 1689–1720* (Ithaca: Cornell Univ. Press, 1976), pp. 273-74.

Collins and Ralph: but each of them having afterwards wrong'd me greatly without the least Compunction, and recollecting Keith's Conduct towards me, (who was another Freethinker) and my own towards Vernon and Miss Read which at Times gave me great Trouble, I began to suspect that this Doctrine tho' it might be true, was not very useful.[5] My London Pamphlet, which had for its Motto those Lines of Dryden

——Whatever is, is right
Tho' purblind Man Sees but a Part of
The Chain, the nearest Link,
His Eyes not carrying to the equal Beam,
That poizes all, above.[6]

And from the Attributes of God, his infinite Wisdom, Goodness and Power concluded that nothing could possibly be wrong in the World, and that Vice and Virtue were empty Distinctions, no such Things existing: appear'd now not so clever a Performance as I once thought it; and I doubted whether some Error had not insinuated itself unperceiv'd into my Argument, so as to infect all that follow'd, as is common in metaphysical Reasonings. I grew convinc'd that *Truth, Sincerity* and *Integrity* in Dealings between Man and Man, were of the utmost Importance to the Felicity of Life, and I form'd written Resolutions, (which still remain in my Journal Book) to practice them ever while I lived. Revelation had indeed no weight with me as such; but I entertain'd an Opinion, that tho' certain Actions might not be bad *because* they were forbidden by it, or good *because* it commanded them; yet probably those Actions might be forbidden *because* they were bad for us, or commanded *because* they were beneficial to us, in their own Natures, all the Circumstances of things considered. And this Persuasion, with the kind hand of Providence, or some guardian Angel, or accidental favorable Circumstances and Situations, or all together, preserved me (thro' this dangerous Time of Youth and the hazardous Situations I was sometimes in among Strangers, remote from the Eye and Advice of my Father) without any *willful* gross Immorality or Injustice that might have been expected from my Want of Religion. I say *willful*, because the Instances I have mentioned, had something of *Necessity* in them, from my Youth, Inexperience, and the Knavery of others. I had therefore a tolerable Character to begin the World with, I valued it properly, and determin'd to preserve it.

We had not been long return'd to Philadelphia, before the New Types arriv'd from London. We settled with Keimer, and left him by

5. BF alludes to a well-known eighteenth-century intellectual debate. John Shebbeare, for instance, argued that utility is truth. *Letters on the English Nation* (London, 1755) no. 9; compare John Adams, 1:52.
6. The pamphlet quotes more accurately from Dryden's *Oedipus* (3.i.244–48). "Whatever . . . right" is from Pope's *Essay on Man* (1: 284)—an understandable slip of memory since Dryden's line immediately before "Tho' purblind Man" reads: "Whatever is, is in its Causes just."

his Consent before he heard of it. We found a House to hire near the Market, and took it.[7] To lessen the Rent, (which was then but 24 Pounds a Year tho' I have since known it let for 70) We took in Thomas Godfrey a Glazier, and his Family, who were to pay a considerable Part of it to us, and we to board with them. We had scarce opened our Letters and put our Press in Order, before George House, an Acquaintance of mine, brought a Countryman to us; whom he had met in the Street enquiring for a Printer. All our Cash was now expended in the Variety of Particulars we had been obliged to procure, and this Countryman's Five Shillings, being our First Fruits and coming so seasonably, gave me more Pleasure than any Crown[8] I have since earn'd; and from the Gratitude I felt towards House, has made me often more ready than perhaps I should otherwise have been to assist young Beginners.

There are Croakers in every Country always boding its Ruin. Such a one then lived in Philadelphia, a Person of Note, an elderly Man, with a wise Look and very grave Manner of Speaking. His Name was Samuel Mickle. This Gentleman, a Stranger to me, stopped one Day at my Door, and ask'd me if I was the young Man who had lately opened a new Printing-House: Being answer'd in the Affirmative; He said he was sorry for me; because it was an expensive Undertaking, and the Expense would be lost, for Philadelphia was a sinking Place, the People already half Bankrupts or near being so; all Appearances of the contrary such as new Buildings and the Rise of Rents, being to his certain Knowledge fallacious, for they were in fact among the Things that would soon ruin us.[9] And he gave me such a Detail of Misfortunes now existing or that were soon to exist, that he left me half-melancholy. Had I known him before I engag'd in this Business, probably I never should have done it. This Man continu'd to live in this decaying Place, and to declaim in the same Strain, refusing for many Years to buy a House there, because all was going to Destruction, and at last I had the Pleasure of seeing him give five times as much for one as he might have bought it for when he first began his Croaking.

I should have mention'd before, that in the Autumn of the preceding Year, I had form'd most of my ingenious Acquaintance into a Club, for mutual Improvement, which we call'd the Junto.[1] We met on Friday Evenings. The Rules I drew up, requir'd that every Member

---

7. Rented from a local pewterer, it was a narrow, brick house, three stories high, on Market Street below Second Street, the site of the present 139 Market St. (Roach, p. 139.)
8. A crown is worth five shillings.
9. BF opened the new printing house in the spring of 1728, just after the city suffered a depression (October 1727 to January 1728), with severe devaluation of Pennsylvania money.

1. Inspiration for the Junto (Spanish "junta," or fraternity) may have come from a proposal for neighborhood societies in Cotton Mather, *Religious Societies* (Boston, 1724) or John Locke, "Rules of a Society which Met Once a Week for the Improvement of Useful Knowledge, and the Promoting of Truth and Charity," in *Collection of Several Pieces of Mr. John Locke . . .* (1720). BF owned the Locke. (Korty, p. 19.)

in his Turn should produce one or more Queries[2] on any Point of Morals, Politics or Natural Philosophy, to be discuss'd by the Company, and once in three Months produce and read an Essay of his own Writing on any Subject he pleased. Our Debates were to be under the Direction of a President, and to be conducted in the sincere Spirit of Enquiry after Truth, without fondness for Dispute, or Desire of Victory; and to prevent Warmth, all expressions of Positiveness in Opinion, or of direct Contradiction, were after some time made contraband and prohibited under small pecuniary Penalties. The first Members were, Joseph Breintnall, a Copier of Deeds for the Scriveners; a good-natur'd friendly middle-ag'd Man, a great Lover of Poetry, reading all he could meet with, and writing some that was tolerable; very ingenious in many little Nicknackeries, and of sensible Conversation. Thomas Godfrey, a self-taught Mathematician, great in his Way, and afterwards Inventor of what is now call'd Hadley's Quadrant.[3] But he knew little out of his way, and was not a pleasing Companion, as like most Great Mathematicians I have met with, he expected unusual Precision in everything said, or was forever denying or distinguishing upon Trifles, to the Disturbance of all Conversation. He soon left us. Nicholas Scull, a Surveyor, afterwards Surveyor-General, Who lov'd Books, and sometimes made a few Verses. William Parsons, bred a Shoemaker, but loving Reading, had acquir'd a considerable Share of Mathematics, which he first studied with a View to Astrology that he afterwards laughed at. He also became Surveyor General. William Maugridge, a Joiner, and a most exquisite Mechanic, and a solid sensible Man. Hugh Meredith, Stephen Potts, and George Webb, I have Characteris'd before. Robert Grace, a young Gentleman of some Fortune, generous, lively and witty, a Lover of Punning and of his Friends. And William Coleman, then a Merchant's Clerk, about my Age, who had the coolest clearest Head, the best Heart, and the exactest Morals, of almost any Man I ever met with. He became afterwards a Merchant of great Note, and one of our Provincial Judges: Our Friendship continued without Interruption to his Death, upwards of 40 Years. And the Club continu'd almost as long and was the best School of Philosophy, Morals and Politics that then existed in the Province; for our Queries which were read the Week preceding their Discussion, put us on reading with Attention upon the several Subjects, that we might speak more to the purpose: and here too we acquired better Habits of Conversation, everything being studied in our Rules which might prevent our disgusting each other. From hence the long Continuance of the Club, which I shall have frequent Occasion to speak farther of hereafter; But my giving

2. Examples are in *P*, 1: 255–64.
3. He perfected a quadrant in November, 1730, but James Hadley, an Englishman working independently, constructed a model in May, 1730. The Royal Society justly gave Hadley priority but awarded Godfrey £200. (Stearns, p. 514n.)

this Account of it here, is to show something of the Interest I had, everyone of these exerting themselves in recommending Business to us.

Breintnall particularly procur'd us from the Quakers, the Printing 40 Sheets[4] of their History, the rest being to be done by Keimer: and upon this we work'd exceeding hard, for the Price was low. It was a Folio, Pro Patria Size, in Pica with Long Primer Notes. I compos'd of it a Sheet a Day, and Meredith work'd it off at Press. It was often 11 at Night and sometimes later, before I had finish'd my Distribution[5] for the next day's Work: For the little Jobs sent in by our other Friends now and then put us back. But so determin'd I was to continue doing a Sheet a Day of the Folio, that one Night when having impos'd my Forms, I thought my Day's Work over, one of them by accident was broken and two Pages reduc'd to Pie,[6] I immediately distributed and compos'd it over again before I went to bed. And this Industry visible to our Neighbors began to give us Character and Credit; particularly I was told, that mention being made of the new Printing Office at the Merchants' Every-night-Club, the general Opinion was that it must fail, there being already two Printers in the Place, Keimer and Bradford; but Doctor Baird (whom you and I saw many Years[7] after at his native Place, St. Andrews in Scotland) gave a contrary Opinion; for the Industry of that Franklin, says he, is superior to anything I ever saw of the kind: I see him still at work when I go home from Club; and he is at Work again before his Neighbors are out of bed. This struck the rest, and we soon after had Offers from one of them to supply us with Stationery. But as yet we did not choose to engage in Shop Business.

I mention this Industry the more particularly and the more freely, tho' it seems to be talking in my own Praise, that those of my Posterity who shall read it, may know the Use of that Virtue, when they see its Effects in my Favor throughout this Relation.

George Webb, who had found a Friend that lent him wherewith to purchase his Time of Keimer, now came to offer himself as a Journeyman to us. We could not then employ him, but I foolishly let him know, as a Secret, that I soon intended to begin a Newspaper, and might then have Work for him. My Hopes of Success as I told him were founded on this, that the then only Newspaper, printed by Bradford was a paltry thing, wretchedly manag'd, no way entertaining; and yet was profitable to him. I therefore thought a good Paper could scarcely fail of good Encouragement. I requested Webb not to mention it, but he told it to Keimer, who immediately, to be beforehand

4. Keimer printed the first 532 pages, BF the remaining 178 plus title page, of William Sewel, *History of the . . . Quakers*, 3rd ed. (Philadelphia: Samuel Keimer, 1728). Keimer received £300 for the edition of 500 copies, and probably paid BF a proportionate share. (Mil-

ler, no. 1.)
5. After printing he distributed the letters back to their cases, ready for the next day's composing.
6. A confused pile of type.
7. In early October, 1759. (P, 8: 431.)

with me, published Proposals[8] for Printing one himself, on which Webb was to be employ'd. I resented this, and to counteract them, as I could not yet begin our Paper, I wrote several Pieces of Entertainment for Bradford's Paper,[9] under the Title of the Busy Body which Breintnall continu'd some Months.[1] By this means the Attention of the Public was fix'd on that Paper, and Keimer's Proposals which we burlesqu'd and ridicul'd, were disregarded. He began his Paper however, and after carrying it on three Quarters of a Year, with at most only 90 Subscribers, he offer'd it to me for a Trifle, and I having been ready some time to go on with it, took it in hand directly, and it prov'd in a few Years extremely profitable to me.[2]

I perceive that I am apt to speak in the singular Number, though our Partnership still continu'd. The Reason may be, that in fact the whole Management of the Business lay upon me. Meredith was no Compositor, a poor Pressman, and seldom sober. My Friends lamented my Connection with him, but I was to make the best of it.

Our first Papers made a quite different Appearance from any before in the Province, a better Type and better printed: but some spirited Remarks* of my Writing on the Dispute then going on between

---

* [BF wrote, "Insert these Remarks in a Note." Here follows his editorial from the *Pennsylvania Gazette*, October 9, 1729, p. 3:]

His Excellency Governor *Burnet* died unexpectedly about two Days after the Date of this Reply to his last Message: And it was thought the Dispute would have ended with him, or at least have lain dormant till the Arrival of a new Governor from *England*, who possibly might, or might not be inclin'd to enter too rigorously into the Measures of his Predecessor. But our last Advices by the Post acquaint us, that his Honour the Lieutenant Governour (on whom the Government immediately devolves upon the Death or Absence of the Commander in Chief) has vigorously renew'd the Struggle on his own Account; of which the Particulars will be seen in our Next.

Perhaps some of our Readers may not fully understand the Original or Ground of this warm Contest between the Governour and Assembly.—It seems, that People have for these Hundred Years past, enjoyed the Privilege of Rewarding the Governour for the Time being,

according to *their Sense* of his Merit and Services; and few or none of their Governors have hitherto complain'd, or had Reason to complain, of a too scanty Allowance. But the late Gov. *Burnet* brought with him Instructions to demand a *settled Salary* of 1000 £. *per Annum*, Sterling, on him and all his Successors, and the Assembly were required to fix it immediately. He insisted on it strenuously to the last, and they as constantly refused it. It appears by their Votes and Proceedings, that they thought it an Imposition, contrary to their own Charter, and to *Magna Charta*; and they judg'd that by the Dictates of Reason there should be a mutual Dependence between the *Governor* and the *Governed*, and that to make any Governour independent of his People, would be dangerous, and destructive of their Liberties, and the ready Way to establish Tyranny: They thought likewise, that the Province was not the less dependent on the Crown of *Great-Britain*, by the Governour's depending immediately on them and his own good Conduct for an ample Support, because all Acts and Laws which he might

---

8. Dated October 1, 1728, Keimer's proposal promised publication of the *Universal Instructor in All Arts & Sciences: and Pennsylvania Gazette* about "the latter end of November," but the first issue was dated December 24, 1728.
9. *American Weekly Mercury*.
1. Periodically from February 4, 1728, through September 25, 1729, BF wrote the first four and parts of the fifth and eighth. (*P*, 1: 113–39; Lemay, "Franklin's Suppressed Busy-

Body.")
2. In no. 39, September 25, 1729, Keimer announced he had sold the paper to BF, who issued no. 40 for October 2. (*P*, 1: 157–61.) After 1730, BF made an estimated £750 (Pennsylvania money) a year from the paper with a circulation of about 1500 copies weekly. Total income from printing was about £800 a year. (Wroth, "Benjamin Franklin," pp. 163–64.)

Governor Burnet and the Massachusetts Assembly, struck the principal People, occasion'd the Paper and the Manager of it to be much talk'd of, and in a few Weeks brought them all to be our Subscribers. Their Example was follow'd by many, and our Number went on growing continually. This was one of the first good Effects of my having learned a little to scribble. Another was, that the leading Men, seeing a Newspaper now in the hands of one who could also handle a Pen, thought it convenient to oblige and encourage me. Bradford still printed the Votes and Laws and other Public Business. He had printed an Address of the House to the Governor in a coarse blundering manner; We reprinted it elegantly and correctly, and sent one to every Member.[3] They were sensible of the Difference, it strengthen'd the Hands of our Friends in the House, and they voted us their Printers for the Year ensuing.[4]

Among my Friends in the House I must not forget Mr. Hamilton before-mentioned, who was then returned from England and had a Seat in it.[5] He interested himself for me strongly in that Instance, as he did in many others afterwards, continuing his Patronage till his Death.* Mr. Vernon about this time put me in mind of the Debt I ow'd him: but did not press me. I wrote him an ingenuous Letter of Acknowledgments, crav'd his Forbearance a little longer which he allow'd me, and as soon as I was able I paid the Principal with Interest and many Thanks. So that *Erratum* was in some degree corrected.

---

be induc'd to pass, must nevertheless be constantly sent Home for Approbation in Order to continue in Force. Many other Reasons were given and Arguments us'd in the Course of the Controversy, needless to particularize here, because all the material Papers relating to it, have been inserted already in our Public News.

Much deserved Praise has the deceas'd Governour received, for his steady Integrity in adhering to his Instructions, notwithstanding the great Difficulty and Opposition he met with, and the strong Temptations offer'd from time to time to induce him to give up the Point.—And yet perhaps something is due to the *Assembly* (as the Love and Zeal of that Country for the present Establishment is too well known to suffer any Suspicion of Want of Loyalty) who continue thus resolutely to Abide by what *they Think* their Right, and that of the People they represent, maugre all the Arts and Menaces of a Governour fam'd for his Cunning and Politicks, back'd with Instructions from

Home, and powerfully aided by the great Advantage such an Officer always has of engaging the principal Men of a Place in his Party, by conferring where he pleases so many Posts of Profit and Honour. Their happy Mother Country will perhaps observe with Pleasure, that tho' her gallant Cocks and matchless Dogs abate their native Fire and Intrepidity when transported to a Foreign Clime (as the common Notion is) yet her S O N S in the remotest Part of the Earth, and even to the third and fourth Descent, still retain that ardent Spirit of Liberty, and that undaunted Courage in the Defence of it, which has in every Age so gloriously distinguished B R I T O N S and E N G L I S H M E N from all the Rest of Mankind.

* "I got his Son once 500£." [BF note.] In February 1754, Governor James Hamilton was feuding with the Pennsylvania assembly but—conceivably through BF's influence—the legislators nevertheless voted him his salary of £500. (*Pa. Archives*, 8th ser., 5:3635.)

---

3. The address of March 29, 1729, asked the Governor to implement the riot act against "great Numbers of dissolute and disorderly Persons" who had been disturbing the peace. BF's separate reprint has not been found, but he later reprinted it as part of Pennsylvania's *Votes and Proceedings* (1754). (*Pa. Archives*, 8th ser., 3:

1939–40; Miller, nos. 9, 596.)
4. BF served as the colony's official printer from January, 1730, until September, 1766.
5. Elected Speaker of the Pennsylvania assembly, October 14, 1729, Hamilton held the same post in Delaware's assembly.

But now another Difficulty came upon me, which I had never the least Reason to expect. Mr. Meredith's Father, who was to have paid for our Printing-House according to the Expectations given me, was able to advance only one Hundred Pounds, Currency, which had been paid, and a Hundred more was due to the Merchant; who grew impatient and su'd us all. We gave Bail, but saw that if the Money could not be rais'd in time, the Suit must come to a Judgment and Execution, and our hopeful Prospects must with us be ruined, as the Press and Letters must be sold for Payment, perhaps at half-Price. In this Distress two true Friends whose Kindness I have never forgotten nor ever shall forget while I can remember anything, came to me separately unknown to each other, and without any Application from me, offering each of them to advance me all the Money that should be necessary to enable me to take the whole Business upon myself if that should be practicable, but they did not like my continuing the Partnership with Meredith, who as they said was often seen drunk in the Streets, and playing at low Games in Alehouses, much to our Discredit. These two Friends were *William Coleman* and *Robert Grace*.

I told them I could not propose a Separation while any Prospect remain'd of the Merediths fulfilling their Part of our Agreement. Because I thought myself under great Obligations to them for what they had done and would do if they could. But if they finally fail'd in their Performance, and our Partnership must be dissolv'd, I should then think myself at Liberty to accept the Assistance of my Friends. Thus the matter rested for some time. When I said to my Partner, perhaps your Father is dissatisfied at the Part you have undertaken in this Affair of ours, and is unwilling to advance for you and me what he would for you alone: If that is the Case, tell me, and I will resign the whole to you and go about my Business. No—says he, my Father has really been disappointed and is really unable; and I am unwilling to distress him farther. I see this is a Business I am not fit for. I was bred a Farmer, and it was a Folly in me to come to Town and put myself at 30 Years of Age an Apprentice to learn a new Trade. Many of our Welsh People are going to settle in North Carolina where Land is cheap: I am inclin'd to go with them, and follow my old Employment. You may find Friends to assist you. If you will take the Debts of the Company upon you, return to my Father the hundred Pound he has advanc'd, pay my little personal Debts, and give me Thirty Pounds and a new Saddle, I will relinquish the Partnership and leave the whole in your Hands. I agreed to this Proposal. It was drawn up in Writing, sign'd and seal'd immediately.[6] I gave him what he demanded and he went soon after to Carolina; from whence he sent me next Year two long Letters, containing the best Account that had been given of that Country, the Climate, Soil, Husbandry, etc. for in those Matters he

6. July 14, 1730. (P, 1: 175.)

was very judicious. I printed them in the Papers, and they gave great Satisfaction to the Public. [7]

As soon as he was gone, I recurr'd to my two Friends; and because I would not give an unkind Preference to either, I took half what each had offered and I wanted, of one, and half of the other; paid off the Company Debts, and went on with the Business in my own Name, advertising that the Partnership was dissolved. I think this was in or about the Year 1729.

About this Time there was a Cry among the People for more Paper-Money, only 15,000 Pounds being extant in the Province and that soon to be sunk. [8] The wealthy Inhabitants oppos'd any Addition, being against all Paper Currency, from an Apprehension that it would depreciate as it had done in New England to the Prejudice of all Creditors. We had discuss'd this Point in our Junto, where I was on the Side of an Addition, being persuaded that the first small Sum struck in 1723 had done much good, by increasing the Trade, Employment, and Number of Inhabitants in the Province, since I now saw all the old Houses inhabited, and many new ones building, where as I remember'd well, that when I first walk'd about the Streets of Philadelphia, eating my Roll, I saw most of the Houses in Walnut Street between Second and Front Streets with Bills on their Doors, to be let; and many likewise in Chestnut Street, and other Streets; which made me then think the Inhabitants of the City were one after another deserting it. Our Debates possess'd me so fully of the Subject, that I wrote and printed an anonymous Pamphlet on it, entitled, *The Nature and Necessity of a Paper Currency.* [9] It was well receiv'd by the common People in general; but the Rich Men dislik'd it; for it increas'd and strengthen'd the Clamor for more Money; and they happening to have no Writers among them that were able to answer it, their Opposition slacken'd, and the Point was carried by a Majority in the House. My Friends there, who conceiv'd I had been of some Service, thought fit to reward me, by employing me in printing the Money, a very profitable Job, and a great Help to me. [1] This was another Advantage gain'd by my being able to write. The Utility of this Currency became by Time and Experience so evident, as never afterwards to be much disputed, so that it grew soon to 55,000 Pounds,

7. In the *Pennsylvania Gazette*, May 6 and 13, 1731, as by a correspondent "lately" a resident of North Carolina.
8. In 1723, paper money had become so scarce that the assembly issued £45,000 secured by real estate mortgages. When the mortgages were paid off, the bills would be "sunk," i.e., destroyed. But by 1726, the value of the bills had dipped so low that they were recalled, even though only about £5000 had been sunk, and the assembly voted new currency based on new mortgage loans. Again, in May 1729, the as-

sembly would vote another issue of £30,000. (Bezanson, pp. 10–11, 320.)
9. Dated April 3, 1729. (*P*, 1: 139–57; Miller, no. 4.)
1. Andrew Bradford printed the Pennsylvania money voted in May, 1729; but BF may have printed the corresponding Delaware issue. (Newman, pp. 237 and 77; Miller, no. 3.) BF did print Pennsylvania's additional £40,000 (for which he earned £100), voted February 6, 1731. (Miller, no. 42) Newman, p. 238.)

and in 1739 to 80,000 Pounds, since which it arose during War to upwards of 350,000 Pounds—Trade, Building and Inhabitants all the while increasing. Tho' I now think there are Limits beyond which the Quantity may be hurtful.

I soon after obtain'd, thro' my Friend Hamilton, the Printing of the New Castle Paper Money, another profitable Job,[2] as I then thought it; small Things appearing great to those in small Circumstances. And these to me were really great Advantages, as they were great Encouragements. He procured me also the Printing of the Laws and Votes of that Government[3] which continu'd in my Hands as long as I follow'd the Business.

I now open'd a little Stationer's Shop. I had in it Blanks of all Sorts the correctest that ever appear'd among us,[4] being assisted in that by my Friend Breintnall; I had also Paper, Parchment, Chapmen's Books,[5] etc. One Whitmarsh a Compositor I had known in London, an excellent Workman now came to me and work'd with me constantly and diligently, and I took an Apprentice the Son of Aquila Rose.[6] I began now gradually to pay off the Debt I was under for the Printing-House. In order to secure my Credit and Character as a Tradesman, I took care not only to be in *Reality* Industrious and frugal, but to avoid all *Appearances* of the Contrary. I dressed plainly; I was seen at no Places of idle Diversion; I never went out a-fishing or shooting; a Book, indeed, sometimes debauch'd me from my Work; but that was seldom, snug, and gave no Scandal: and to show that I was not above my Business, I sometimes brought home the Paper I purchas'd at the Stores, thro' the Streets on a Wheelbarrow. Thus being esteem'd an industrious thriving young Man, and paying duly for what I bought, the Merchants who imported Stationery solicited my Custom, others propos'd supplying me with Books, and I went on swimmingly. In the mean time Keimer's Credit and Business declining daily, he was at last forc'd to sell his Printing-House to satisfy his Creditors. He went to Barbados, and there lived some Years, in very poor Circumstances.

His Apprentice David Harry, whom I had instructed while I work'd with him, set up in his Place at Philadelphia, having bought his Materials. I was at first apprehensive of a powerful Rival in Harry, as his Friends were very able, and had a good deal of Interest. I therefore propos'd a Partnership to him; which he, fortunately for me, rejected with Scorn. He was very proud, dress'd like a Gentleman, liv'd expensively, took much Diversion and Pleasure abroad, ran in debt, and neglected his Business, upon which all Business left him; and

2. Delaware's assembly voted an issue of £12,000 in 1729, another in 1735, and £6,000 in 1739. (Miller, nos. 3, 83, and 161.)
3. BF first printed the Delaware laws in 1734. (Miller, no. 82.)
4. For examples of these blank forms, see Miller nos. 10, 18, 30, etc.; for a discussion, see Eddy, 1:33–35.
5. See n. 3, p. 9 of this section.
6. Thomas Whitmarsh joined him before April 1730, about the same time that Joseph Rose became apprentice. (Eddy, 1: 14–16.)

finding nothing to do, he follow'd Keimer to Barbados; taking the Printing-House with him. There this Apprentice employ'd his former Master as a Journeyman. They quarrel'd often. Harry went continually behind-hand, and at length was forc'd to sell his Types, and return to his Country Work[7] in Pennsylvania. The Person that bought them employ'd Keimer to use them, but in a few years he died. There remain'd now no Competitor with me at Philadelphia, but the old one, Bradford, who was rich and easy, did a little Printing now and then by straggling Hands, but was not very anxious about the Business. However, as he kept the Post Office, it was imagined he had better Opportunities of obtaining News, his Paper was thought a better Distributer of Advertisements than mine, and therefore had many more, which was a profitable thing to him and a Disadvantage to me. For tho' I did indeed receive and send Papers by the Post, yet the public Opinion was otherwise; for what I did send was by Bribing the Riders who took them privately: Bradford being unkind enough to forbid it: which occasion'd some Resentment on my Part; and I thought so meanly of him for it, that when I afterwards came into his Situation,[8] I took care never to imitate it.

I had hitherto continu'd to board with Godfrey who lived in Part of my House with his Wife and Children, and had one Side of the Shop for his Glazier's Business, tho' he work'd little, being always absorb'd in his Mathematics. Mrs. Godfrey projected a Match for me with a Relation's Daughter, took Opportunities of bringing us often together, till a serious Courtship on my Part ensu'd, the Girl being in herself very deserving. The old Folks encourag'd me by continual Invitations to Supper, and by leaving us together, till at length it was time to explain. Mrs. Godfrey manag'd our little Treaty. I let her know that I expected as much Money with their Daughter as would pay off my Remaining Debt for the Printing-House, which I believe was not then above a Hundred Pounds. She brought me Word they had no such Sum to spare. I said they might mortgage their House in the Loan Office.[9] The Answer to this after some Days was, that they did not approve the Match; that on Enquiry of Bradford they had been inform'd the Printing Business was not a profitable one, the Types would soon be worn out and more wanted, that S. Keimer and D. Harry had fail'd one after the other, and I should probably soon follow them; and therefore I was forbidden the House, and the Daughter shut up.

Whether this was a real Change of Sentiment, or only Artifice, on a Supposition of our being too far engag'd in Affection to retract, and therefore that we should steal a Marriage, which would leave them at Liberty to give or withhold what they pleas'd, I know not: But I

7. Farming.
8. BF replaced Bradford as postmaster of Philadelphia in October 1737.
9. The office that disbursed paper money as loans secured by real estate. See above, n. 8, p. 53 of this section.

suspected the latter, resented it, and went no more. Mrs. Godfrey brought me afterwards some more favorable Accounts of their Disposition, and would have drawn me on again: But I declared absolutely my Resolution to have nothing more to do with that Family.[1] This was resented by the Godfreys, we differ'd, and they removed, leaving me the whole House,[2] and I resolved to take no more Inmates. But this Affair having turn'd my Thoughts to Marriage, I look'd round me, and made Overtures of Acquaintance in other Places; but soon found that the Business of a Printer being generally thought a poor one, I was not to expect Money with a Wife unless with such a one, as I should not otherwise think agreeable. In the mean time, that hard-to-be-govern'd Passion of Youth, had hurried me frequently into Intrigues with low Women that fell in my Way, which were attended with some Expense and great Inconvenience, besides a continual Risk to my Health by a Distemper which of all Things I dreaded, tho' by great good Luck I escaped it.

A friendly Correspondence as Neighbors and old Acquaintances, had continued between me and Mrs. Read's Family who all had a Regard for me from the time of my first Lodging in their House.[3] I was often invited there and consulted in their Affairs, wherein I sometimes was of Service. I pitied poor Miss Read's unfortunate Situation, who was generally dejected, seldom cheerful, and avoided Company. I consider'd my Giddiness and Inconstancy when in London as in a great degree the Cause of her Unhappiness; tho' the Mother was good enough to think the Fault more her own than mine, as she had prevented our Marrying before I went thither, and persuaded the other Match in my Absence. Our mutual Affection was revived, but there were now great Objections to our Union. That Match was indeed look'd upon as invalid, a preceding Wife being said to be living in England; but this could not easily be prov'd,[4] because of the Distance, etc. And tho' there was a Report of his Death, it was not certain. Then, tho' it should be true, he had left many Debts which his Successor might be call'd upon to pay. We ventured however, over all these Difficulties, and I took her to Wife Sept. 1, 1730. None of the Inconveniencies happened that we had apprehended, she prov'd a good and faithful Helpmate, assisted me much by attending the Shop, we throve together, and have ever mutually endeavour'd to make each other happy. Thus I corrected that great *Erratum* as well as I could.

1. Still chaffing at the family's "artifice" several years later, BF recounted the story in his "Anthony Afterwit" newspaper skit. (P, 1: 237–40; Lemay, "Benjamin Franklin," pp. 211–12.)
2. The Godfreys lived with BF from May, 1728, to mid-April, 1730. (Roach, p. 141.)
3. BF lived with the Reads from 1723 to 1724. (Roach, p. 131.)
4. Without proof of Rogers's bigamy, Deborah's marriage could not be annulled. If BF and Deborah had officially married, they would have become liable to a charge of bigamy and could have been sentenced to 39 lashes, plus life imprisonment at hard labor. Thus common-law marriage was a sensible solution. (Thomas R. Meehan, "Evolution of Divorce in Early Pennsylvania," *PMHB*, 92 [1968], 442–43.)

About this Time our Club meeting, not at a Tavern, but in a little Room of Mr. Grace's set apart for that Purpose; a Proposition was made by me, that since our Books were often referr'd to in our Disquisitions upon the Queries, it might be convenient to us to have them all together where we met, that upon Occasion they might be consulted; and by thus clubbing our Books to a common Library, we should, while we lik'd to keep them together, have each of us the Advantage of using the Books of all the other Members, which would be nearly as beneficial as if each owned the whole. It was lik'd and agreed to, and we fill'd one End of the Room with such Books as we could best spare. The Number was not so great as we expected; and tho' they had been of great Use, yet some Inconveniencies occurring for want of due Care of them, the Collection after about a Year was separated, and each took his Books home again.

And now I set on foot my first Project of a public Nature, that for a Subscription Library.[5] I drew up the Proposals, got them put into Form by our great Scrivener Brockden, and by the help of my Friends in the Junto, procur'd Fifty Subscribers of 40 Shillings each to begin with and 10 Shillings a Year for 50 Years, the Term our Company was to continue. We afterwards obtain'd a Charter, the Company being increas'd to 100. This was the Mother of all the North American Subscription Libraries now so numerous. It is become a great thing itself, and continually increasing. These Libraries have improv'd the general Conversation of the Americans, made the common Tradesmen and Farmers as intelligent as most Gentlemen from other Countries, and perhaps have contributed in some degree to the Stand so generally made throughout the Colonies in Defense of their Privileges.*

Memo.

Thus far was written with the Intention express'd in the Beginning and therefore contains several little family Anecdotes of no Importance to others. What follows was written many Years after in compliance with the Advice contain'd in these Letters, and accordingly intended for the Public. The Affairs of the Revolution occasion'd the Interruption.

---

* "My Manner of acting to engage People in this and future Undertakings." [BF note.] When he stopped writing in 1771, BF added this reminder to himself for his next topic.

---

5. America's first circulating library open to public subscription was the Library Company of Philadelphia. The "Instrument of Association" was dated July 1, 1731, and the charter, March 25, 1742. (P, 1: 208–10; 2: 345–48.)

[*Part Two*]

LETTER FROM MR. ABEL JAMES, WITH NOTES[6] ON MY LIFE,
(*RECEIVED IN PARIS.*)

My dear and honored Friend.

I have often been desirous of writing to thee, but could not be
reconciled to the Thought that the Letter might fall into the Hands
of the British, lest some Printer or busy Body should publish some
Part of the Contents and give our Friends Pain and myself Censure.

Some Time since there fell into my Hands to my great Joy about
23 Sheets in thy own handwriting containing an Account of the
Parentage and Life of thyself, directed to thy Son ending in the Year
1730 with which there were Notes likewise in thy writing, a Copy of
which I enclose in Hopes it may be a means if thou continuedst it up
to a later period, that the first and latter part may be put together;
and if it is not yet continued, I hope thou wilt not delay it. Life is
uncertain as the Preacher tells us, and what will the World say if
kind, humane and benevolent Ben Franklin should leave his
Friends and the World deprived of so pleasing and profitable a
Work, a Work which would be useful and entertaining not only to a
few, but to millions.

The Influence Writings under that Class have on the Minds of
Youth is very great, and has no where appeared so plain as in our
public Friends' Journals. It almost insensibly leads the Youth into
the Resolution of endeavouring to become as good and as eminent
as the Journalist. Should thine for Instance when published, and I
think it could not fail of it, lead the Youth to equal the Industry and
Temperance of thy early Youth, what a Blessing with that Class
would such a Work be. I know of no Character living nor many of
them put together, who has so much in his Power as Thyself to
promote a greater Spirit of Industry and early Attention to Business,
Frugality and Temperance with the American Youth. Not that I
think the Work would have no other Merit and Use in the World,
far from it, but the first is of such vast Importance, that I know
nothing that can equal it.

The foregoing letter and the minutes accompanying it being shown
to a friend, I received from him the following:

LETTER FROM MR. BENJAMIN VAUGHAN

MY DEAREST SIR,   *Paris, January 31, 1783.*

When I had read over your sheets of minutes of the principal
incidents of your life, recovered for you by your Quaker acquaintance; I told you I would send you a letter expressing my reasons why
I thought it would be useful to complete and publish it as he desired.

---

6. James probably wrote this letter in the spring or summer of 1782. The "Notes" that James
enclosed were BF's topics (in effect, an outline) for the *Autobiography*. See pp. 169–72 of this
edition.

Various concerns have for some time past prevented this letter being written, and I do not know whether it was worth any expectation: happening to be at leisure however at present, I shall by writing at least interest and instruct myself; but as the terms I am inclined to use may tend to offend a person of your manners, I shall only tell you how I would address any other person, who was as good and as great as yourself, but less diffident. I would say to him, Sir, I *solicit* the history of your life from the following motives.

Your history is so remarkable, that if you do not give it, somebody else will certainly give it; and perhaps so as nearly to do as much harm, as your own management of the thing might do good.

It will moreover present a table of the internal circumstances of your country, which will very much tend to invite to it settlers of virtuous and manly minds. And considering the eagerness with which such information is sought by them, and the extent of your reputation, I do not know of a more efficacious advertisement than your Biography would give.

All that has happened to you is also connected with the detail of the manners and situation of *a rising* people; and in this respect I do not think that the writings of Caesar and Tacitus can be more interesting to a true judge of human nature and society.

But these, Sir, are small reasons in my opinion, compared with the chance which your life will give for the forming of future great men; and in conjunction with your *Art of Virtue*, (which you design to publish)[7] of improving the features of private character, and consequently of aiding all happiness both public and domestic.

The two works I allude to, Sir, will in particular give a noble rule and example of *self-education*. School and other education constantly proceed upon false principles, and show a clumsy apparatus pointed at a false mark; but your apparatus is simple, and the mark a true one; and while parents and young persons are left destitute of other just means of estimating and becoming prepared for a reasonable course in life, your discovery that the thing is in many a man's private power, will be invaluable!

Influence upon the private character late in life, is not only an influence late in life, but a weak influence. It is in *youth* that we plant our chief habits and prejudices; it is in youth that we take our party as to profession, pursuits, and matrimony. In youth therefore the turn is given; in youth the education even of the next generation is given; in youth the private and public character is determined; and the term of life extending from youth to age, life ought to begin well from youth; and more especially *before* we take our party as to our principal objects.

But your Biography will not merely teach self-education, but the education of *a wise man*; and the wisest man will receive lights and improve his progress, by seeing detailed the conduct of another wise

---

7. Vaughan refers to BF's long-projected scheme to write "a little Work for the Benefit of Youth, to be call'd *The Art of Virtue*" (BF to Lord Kames, May 3, 1760; P, 9: 104.) Except for its beginning, Part Two of the *Autobiography* presents BF's Art of Virtue, perhaps partially because of Vaughan's reminder.

man. And why are weaker men to be deprived of such helps, when we see our race has been blundering on in the dark, almost without a guide in this particular, from the farthest trace of time. Show then, Sir, how much is to be done, *both to sons and fathers*; and invite all wise men to become like yourself; and other men to become wise.

When we see how cruel statesmen and warriors can be to the humble race, and how absurd distinguished men can be to their acquaintance, it will be instructive to observe the instances multiply of pacific acquiescing manners; and to find how compatible it is to be great and *domestic*; enviable and yet *good-humored*.

The little private incidents which you will also have to relate, will have considerable use, as we want above all things, *rules of prudence in ordinary affairs*; and it will be curious to see how you have acted in these. It will be so far a sort of key to life, and explain many things that all men ought to have once explained to them, to give them a chance of becoming wise by foresight.

The nearest thing to having experience of one's own, is to have other people's affairs brought before us in a shape that is interesting; this is sure to happen from your pen. Your affairs and management will have an air of simplicity or importance that will not fail to strike; and I am convinced you have conducted them with as much originality as if you had been conducting discussions in politics or philosophy; and what more worthy of experiments and system, (its importance and its errors considered) than human life!

Some men have been virtuous blindly, others have speculated fantastically, and others have been shrewd to bad purposes; but you, Sir, I am sure, will give under your hand, nothing but what is at the same moment, wise, practical, and good.

Your account of yourself (for I suppose the parallel I am drawing for Dr. Franklin, will hold not only in point of character but of private history), will show that you are ashamed of no origin; a thing the more important, as you prove how little necessary all origin is to happiness, virtue, or greatness.

As no end likewise happens without a means, so we shall find, Sir, that even you yourself framed a plan by which you became considerable; but at the same time we may see that though the event is flattering, the means are as simple as wisdom could make them; that is, depending upon nature, virtue, thought, and habit.

Another thing demonstrated will be the propriety of every man's waiting for his time for appearing upon the stage of the world. Our sensations being very much fixed to the moment, we are apt to forget that more moments are to follow the first, and consequently that man should arrange his conduct so as to suit the *whole* of a life. Your attribution appears to have been applied to your *life*, and the passing moments of it have been enlivened with content and enjoyment, instead of being tormented with foolish impatience or regrets. Such a conduct is easy for those who make virtue and themselves their standard, and who try to keep themselves in countenance by examples of other truly great men, of whom patience is so often the characteristic.

Your Quaker correspondent, Sir (for here again I will suppose the subject of my letter resembling Dr. Franklin,) praised your frugality, diligence, and temperance, which he considered as a pattern for all youth: but it is singular that he should have forgotten your modesty, and your disinterestedness, without which you never could have waited for your advancement, or found your situation in the mean time comfortable; which is a strong lesson to show the poverty of glory, and the importance of regulating our minds.

If this correspondent had known the nature of your reputation as well as I do, he would have said; your former writings and measures would secure attention to your Biography, and Art of Virtue; and your Biography and Art of Virtue, in return, would secure attention to them. This is an advantage attendant upon a various character, and which brings all that belongs to it into greater play; and it is the more useful, as perhaps more persons are at a loss for the *means* of improving their minds and characters, than they are for the time or the inclination to do it.

But there is one concluding reflection, Sir, that will show the use of your life as a mere piece of biography. This style of writing seems a little gone out of vogue, and yet it is a very useful one; and your specimen of it may be particularly serviceable, as it will make a subject of comparison with the lives of various public cut-throats and intriguers, and with absurd monastic self-tormentors, or vain literary triflers. If it encourages more writings of the same kind with your own, and induces more men to spend lives fit to be written; it will be worth all Plutarch's Lives put together.

But being tired of figuring to myself a character of which every feature suits only one man in the world, without giving him the praise of it; I shall end my letter, my dear Dr. Franklin, with a personal application to your proper self.

I am earnestly desirous then, my dear Sir, that you should let the world into the traits of your genuine character, as civil broils may otherwise tend to disguise or traduce it. Considering your great age, the caution of your character, and your peculiar style of thinking, it is not likely that any one besides yourself can be sufficiently master of the facts of your life, or the intentions of your mind.

Besides all this, the immense revolution of the present period, will necessarily turn our attention towards the author of it; and when virtuous principles have been pretended in it, it will be highly important to show that such have really influenced; and, as your own character will be the principal one to receive a scrutiny, it is proper (even for its effects upon your vast and rising country, as well as upon England and upon Europe), that it should stand respectable and eternal. For the furtherance of human happiness, I have always maintained that it is necessary to prove that man is not even at present a vicious and detestable animal; and still more to prove that good management may greatly amend him; and it is for much the same reason, that I am anxious to see the opinion established, that there are fair characters existing among the individuals of the race;

for the moment that all men, without exception, shall be conceived abandoned, good people will cease efforts deemed to be hopeless, and perhaps think of taking their share in the scramble of life, or at least of making it comfortable principally for themselves.

Take then, my dear Sir, this work most speedily into hand: show yourself good as you are good, temperate as you are temperate; and above all things, prove yourself as one who from your infancy have loved justice, liberty, and concord, in a way that has made it natural and consistent for you to have acted, as we have seen you act in the last seventeen years of your life. Let Englishmen be made not only to respect, but even to love you. When they think well of individuals in your native country, they will go nearer to thinking well of your country; and when your countrymen see themselves well thought of by Englishmen, they will go nearer to thinking well of England. Extend your views even further; do not stop at those who speak the English tongue, but after having settled so many points in nature and politics, think of bettering the whole race of men.

As I have not read any part of the life in question, but know only the character that lived it, I write somewhat at hazard. I am sure however, that the life, and the treatise I allude to (on the *Art of Virtue*), will necessarily fulfil the chief of my expectations; and still more so if you take up the measure of suiting these performances to the several views above stated. Should they even prove unsuccessful in all that a sanguine admirer of yours hopes from them, you will at least have framed pieces to interest the human mind; and whoever gives a feeling of pleasure that is innocent to man, has added so much to the fair side of a life otherwise too much darkened by anxiety, and too much injured by pain.

In the hope therefore that you will listen to the prayer addressed to you in this letter, I beg to subscribe myself, my dearest Sir, etc. etc.

Signed   BENJ. VAUGHAN.

Continuation of the Account of my Life.
Begun at Passy, 1784.[8]

It is some time since I receiv'd the above Letters, but I have been too busy till now to think of complying with the Request they contain. It might too be much better done if I were at home among my Papers, which would aid my Memory, and help to ascertain Dates. But my Return being uncertain, and having just now a little Leisure, I will endeavour to recollect and write what I can; if I live to get home, it may there be corrected and improv'd.

Not having any Copy here of what is already written, I know not whether an Account is given of the means I used to establish the Philadelphia public Library, which from a small Beginning is now

8. Franklin wrote Part Two of the *Autobiography* at his French residence, the lovely Hotel de Valentenois in Passy, which was then a Pari- sian suburb. The peace treaty with Britain was signed on September 3, 1783, but BF remained in France until July, 1785.

become so considerable, though I remember to have come down to near the Time of that Transaction, 1730. I will therefore begin here, with an Account of it, which may be struck out if found to have been already given.

At the time I establish'd myself in Pennsylvania, there was not a good Bookseller's Shop in any of the Colonies to the Southward of Boston. In New York and Philadelphia the Printers were indeed Stationers, they sold only Paper, etc., Almanacs, Ballads, and a few common School Books. Those who lov'd Reading were oblig'd to send for their Books from England. The Members of the Junto had each a few. We had left the Alehouse where we first met, and hired a Room to hold our Club in. I propos'd that we should all of us bring our Books to that Room, where they would not only be ready to consult in our Conferences, but become a common Benefit, each of us being at Liberty to borrow such as he wish'd to read at home. This was accordingly done, and for some time contented us. Finding the Advantage of this little Collection, I propos'd to render the Benefit from Books more common by commencing a Public Subscription Library. I drew a Sketch of the Plan and Rules that would be necessary, and got a skillful Conveyancer Mr. Charles Brockden to put the whole in Form of Articles of Agreement to be subscribed, by which each Subscriber engag'd to pay a certain Sum down for the first Purchase of Books and an annual Contribution for increasing them. So few were the Readers at that time in Philadelphia, and the Majority of us so poor, that I was not able with great Industry to find more than Fifty Persons, mostly young Tradesmen, willing to pay down for this purpose Forty shillings each, and Ten Shillings per Annum. On this little Fund we began. The Books were imported.[9] The Library was open one Day in the Week for lending them to the Subscribers, on their Promissory Notes to pay Double the Value if not duly returned. The Institution soon manifested its Utility, was imitated by other Towns and in other Provinces, the Libraries were augmented by Donations, Reading became fashionable, and our People having no public Amusements to divert their Attention from Study became better acquainted with Books, and in a few Years were observ'd by Strangers to be better instructed and more intelligent than People of the same Rank generally are in other Countries.

When we were about to sign the above-mentioned Articles, which were to be binding on us, our Heirs, etc. for fifty Years, Mr. Brockden, the Scrivener, said to us, "You are young Men, but it is scarce probable that any of you will live to see the Expiration of the Term fix'd in this Instrument." A Number of us, however, are yet living: But the Instrument was after a few Years rendered null by a Charter that incorporated and gave Perpetuity to the Company.

---

9. Wolf, "First Books," lists the books received, as well as (p. 46, n. 5) the additional ones ordered.

The Objections, and Reluctances I met with in Soliciting the Subscriptions, made me soon feel the Impropriety of presenting oneself as the Proposer of any useful Project that might be suppos'd to raise one's Reputation in the smallest degree above that of one's Neighbors, when one has need of their Assistance to accomplish that Project. I therefore put myself as much as I could out of sight, and stated it as a Scheme of *a Number of Friends*, who had requested me to go about and propose it to such as they thought Lovers of Reading. In this way my Affair went on more smoothly, and I ever after practic'd it on such Occasions; and from my frequent Successes, can heartily recommend it. The present little Sacrifice of your Vanity will afterwards be amply repaid. If it remains a while uncertain to whom the Merit belongs, someone more vain than yourself will be encourag'd to claim it, and then even Envy will be dispos'd to do you Justice, by plucking those assum'd Feathers, and restoring them to their right Owner.[1]

This Library afforded me the Means of Improvement by constant Study, for which I set apart an Hour or two each Day; and thus repair'd in some Degree the Loss of the Learned Education my Father once intended for me. Reading was the only Amusement I allow'd myself. I spent no time in Taverns, Games, or Frolics of any kind. And my Industry in my Business continu'd as indefatigable as it was necessary. I was in debt for my Printing-House, I had a young Family coming on to be educated, and I had to contend with for Business two Printers who were establish'd in the Place before me. My Circumstances however grew daily easier: my original Habits of Frugality continuing. And My Father having among his Instructions to me when a Boy, frequently repeated a Proverb of Solomon, *"Seest thou a Man diligent in his Calling, he shall stand before Kings, he shall not stand before mean Men."*[2] I from thence consider'd Industry as a Means of obtaining Wealth and Distinction, which encourag'd me: tho' I did not think that I should ever literally stand before Kings, which however has since happened; for I have stood before five,[3] and even had the honor of sitting down with one, the King of Denmark, to Dinner.[4]

We have an English Proverb that says,

He that would thrive
Must ask his Wife,[5]

it was lucky for me that I had one as much dispos'd to Industry and Frugality as myself. She assisted me cheerfully in my Business, folding

1. John Bigelow suggested BF alluded to Descartes' motto, derived from Ovid's cynical precept, "Credi mihi, bene qui latuit bene vixit," *Let me Tell Thee, he who hides well his life, lives well* (Ovid, *Tristia*, III, iv, 25). (Bigelow, p. 209.)

2. *Proverbs* 22: 29, with "Calling" in place of the scriptural "Business."

3. Louis XV and Louis XVI of France, George II and George III of England, and Christian VI of Denmark.

4. BF's letter of October 5, 1768 includes a sketch of the seating arrangement. (P, 15: 224–27.)

5. "He that will thrive must ask leave of his wife." (Wilson, p. 819.)

and stitching Pamphlets, tending Shop, purchasing old Linen Rags for the Paper-makers, etc., etc. We kept no idle Servants, our Table was plain and simple, our Furniture of the cheapest. For instance my Breakfast was a long time Bread and Milk, (no Tea,) and I ate it out of a twopenny earthen Porringer with a Pewter Spoon. But mark how Luxury will enter Families, and make a Progress, in Spite of Principle. Being Call'd one Morning to Breakfast, I found it in a China Bowl with a Spoon of Silver. They had been bought for me without my Knowledge by my Wife, and had cost her the enormous Sum of three and twenty Shillings, for which she had no other Excuse or Apology to make, but that she thought *her* Husband deserv'd a Silver Spoon and China Bowl as well as any of his Neighbors. This was the first Appearance of Plate and China in our House, which afterwards in a Course of Years as our Wealth increas'd, augmented gradually to several Hundred Pounds in Value.

I had been religiously educated as a Presbyterian;[6] and tho' some of the Dogmas of that Persuasion, such as the Eternal Decrees of God, Election, Reprobation, etc. appear'd to me unintelligible, others doubtful, and I early absented myself from the Public Assemblies of the Sect, Sunday being my Studying-Day, I never was without some religious Principles; I never doubted, for instance, the Existence of the Deity, that he made the World, and govern'd it by his Providence; that the most acceptable Service of God was the doing Good to Man; that our Souls are immortal; and that all Crime will be punished and Virtue rewarded either here or hereafter; these I esteem'd the Essentials of every Religion, and being to be found in all the Religions we had in our Country I respected them all, tho' with different degrees of Respect as I found them more or less mix'd with other Articles which without any Tendency to inspire, promote or confirm Morality, serv'd principally to divide us and make us unfriendly to one another. This Respect to all, with an Opinion that the worst had some good Effects, induc'd me to avoid all Discourse that might tend to lessen the good Opinion another might have of his own Religion; and as our Province increas'd in People and new Places of worship were continually wanted, and generally erected by voluntary Contribution, my Mite for such purpose, whatever might be the Sect, was never refused.

Tho' I seldom attended any Public Worship, I had still an Opinion of its Propriety, and of its Utility when rightly conducted, and I regularly paid my annual Subscription for the Support of the only Presbyterian Minister[7] or Meeting we had in Philadelphia. He us'd to visit me sometimes as a Friend, and admonish me to attend his

6. BF's parents were pillars of Boston's Old South Church, which was Congregational. Presbyterianism, however, was closely related to Congregationalism; and in Philadelphia, BF ostensibly belonged to the Presbyterian church. Deborah, however, belonged to the Anglican Christ Church. Both children (Sarah and Francis Folger) were baptised at Christ Church; Franklin paid for three seats there and supported it generously; and he is buried there, beside Deborah.

7. Jedediah Andrews.

Administrations, and I was now and then prevail'd on to do so, once for five Sundays successively. Had he been, *in my Opinion*, a good Preacher perhaps I might have continued, notwithstanding the occasion I had for the Sunday's Leisure in my Course of Study: But his Discourses were chiefly either polemic Arguments, or Explications of the peculiar Doctrines of our Sect, and were all to me very dry, uninteresting and unedifying, since not a single moral Principle was inculcated or enforc'd, their Aim seeming to be rather to make us Presbyterians than good Citizens. At length he took for his Text that Verse of the 4th Chapter of Philippians, *Finally, Brethren, Whatsoever Things are true, honest, just, pure, lovely, or of good report, if there be any virtue, or any praise, think on these Things;*[8] and I imagin'd in a Sermon on such a Text, we could not miss of having some Morality: But he confin'd himself to five Points only as meant by the Apostle, viz. 1. Keeping holy the Sabbath Day. 2. Being diligent in Reading the Holy Scriptures. 3. Attending duly the Public Worship. 4. Partaking of the Sacrament. 5. Paying a due Respect to God's Ministers.—These might be all good Things, but as they were not the kind of good Things that I expected from that Text, I despaired of ever meeting with them from any other, was disgusted, and attended his Preaching no more. I had some Years before compos'd a little Liturgy or Form of Prayer for my own private Use, viz, in 1728, entitled, *Articles of Belief and Acts of Religion.*[9] I return'd to the Use of this, and went no more to the public Assemblies. My Conduct might be blameable, but I leave it without attempting farther to excuse it, my present purpose being to relate Facts, and not to make Apologies for them.

It was about this time that I conceiv'd the bold and arduous Project of arriving at moral Perfection.[1] I wish'd to live without committing any Fault at anytime; I would conquer all that either Natural Inclination, Custom, or Company might lead me into. As I knew, or thought I knew, what was right and wrong, I did not see why I might not *always* do the one and avoid the other. But I soon found I had undertaken a Task of more Difficulty than I had imagined: While my Care was employ'd in guarding against one Fault, I was often surpris'd by another. Habit took the Advantage of Inattention. Inclination was sometimes too strong for Reason. I concluded at length, that the mere speculative Conviction that it was our Interest to be completely virtuous, was not sufficient to prevent our Slipping, and that the contrary Habits must be broken and good Ones acquired and established, before we can have any Dependence on a steady uniform Rectitude of Conduct. For this purpose I therefore contriv'd the following Method.

8. The same paraphrase of *Phillipians* 4:8 is in James Foster, "Sermon XI," *Sermons* (1743), p. 250.
9. Dated November 20, 1728. (*P*, 1: 101–9.)

1. Although the tone here is ironic, BF was not entirely exempt from eighteenth-century idealism. See "Backgrounds," pp. 223–28 this edition.

In the various Enumerations of the moral Virtues I had met with in my Reading, I found the Catalogue more or less numerous, as different Writers included more or fewer Ideas under the same Name.[2] Temperance, for Example, was by some confin'd to Eating and Drinking, while by others it was extended to mean the moderating every other Pleasure, Appetite, Inclination or Passion, bodily or mental, even to our Avarice and Ambition. I propos'd to myself, for the sake of Clearness, to use rather more Names with fewer Ideas annex'd to each, than a few Names with more Ideas; and I included after Thirteen Names of Virtues all that at that time occurr'd to me as necessary or desirable, and annex'd to each a short Precept, which fully express'd the Extent I gave to its Meaning.

These Names of Virtues with their Precepts were

1. TEMPERANCE.
Eat not to Dulness. Drink not to Elevation.
2. SILENCE.
Speak not but what may benefit others or your self. Avoiding trifling Conversation.
3. ORDER.
Let all your Things have their Places. Let each Part of your Business have its Time.
4. RESOLUTION.
Resolve to perform what you ought. Perform without fail what you resolve.
5. FRUGALITY.
Make no Expense but to do good to others or yourself: i.e. Waste nothing
6. INDUSTRY.
Lose no Time. Be always employ'd in someting useful. Cut off all unnecessary Actions.
7. SINCERITY.
Use no hurtful Deceit. Think innocently and justly; and, if you speak; speak accordingly.
8. JUSTICE.
Wrong none, by doing Injuries or omitting the Benefits that are your Duty.
9. MODERATION.
Avoid Extremes. Forbear resenting Injuries so much as you think they deserve.
10. CLEANLINESS.
Tolerate no Uncleanness in Body, Clothes or Habitation.

2. About 1737, BF voiced this same complaint to James Logan, who was then writing a book "on Moral Good or Virtue." (*P*, 2: 185.)

11. TRANQUILITY.
Be not disturbed at Trifles, or at Accidents common or unavoidable.

12. CHASTITY.
Rarely use Venery but for Health or Offspring; Never to Dulness, Weakness, or the Injury of your own or another's Peace or Reputation.

13. HUMILITY.
Imitate Jesus and Socrates.

My intention being to acquire the *Habitude* of all these Virtues, I judg'd it would be well not to distract my Attention by attempting the whole at once, but to fix it on one of them at a time, and when I should be Master of that, then to proceed to another, and so on till I should have gone thro' the thirteen. And as the previous Acquisition of some might facilitate the Acquisition of certain others, I arrang'd them with that View as they stand above. *Temperance* first, as it tends to procure that Coolness and Clearness of Head, which is so necessary where constant Vigilance was to be kept up, and Guard maintained, against the unremitting Attraction of ancient Habits, and the Force of perpetual Temptations. This being acquir'd and establish'd, *Silence* would be more easy, and my Desire being to gain Knowledge at the same time that I improv'd in Virtue, and considering that in Conversation it was obtain'd rather by the Use of the Ears than of the Tongue, and therefore wishing to break a Habit I was getting into of Prattling, Punning and Joking, which only made me acceptable to trifling Company, I gave *Silence* the second Place. This, and the next, *Order*, I expected would allow me more Time for attending to my Project and my Studies; RESOLUTION once become habitual, would keep me firm in my Endeavours to obtain all the subsequent Virtues; *Frugality* and *Industry*, by freeing me from my remaining Debt, and producing Affluence and Independence would make more easy the Practice of *Sincerity* and *Justice*, etc. etc. Conceiving then that agreeable to the Advice of Pythagoras in his Golden Verses,* daily Examination would be necessary, I contriv'd the following Method for conducting that Examination.

---

* [BF wrote: "Insert those Lines that direct it in a Note." Here follow the lines from Nicholas Rowe's translation which BF used in his "Letter from Father *Abraham*," *The New England Magazine of Knowledge and Pleasure*, no. 1 (August, 1758), p. 22:]
Let not the stealing God of Sleep surprize,
Nor creep in Slumbers on thy weary Eyes,
Ere ev'ry Action of the former Day,
Strictly thou dost, and righteously survey.
With Rev'rence at thy own Tribunal stand,
And answer justly to thy own Demand.

Where have I been? In what have I transgrest?
What Good or Ill has this Day's Life exprest?
Where have I fail'd in what I ought to do?
In what to GOD, to Man, or to myself I owe?
Inquire severe whate'er from first to last,
From Morning's Dawn till Ev'nings Gloom has past.
If Evil were thy Deeds, repenting mourn,
And let thy Soul with strong Remorse be torn:
If Good, the Good with Peace of Mind repay,
And to thy secret Self with Pleasure say,
Rejoice, my Heart, for all went well to Day.

Form of the Pages

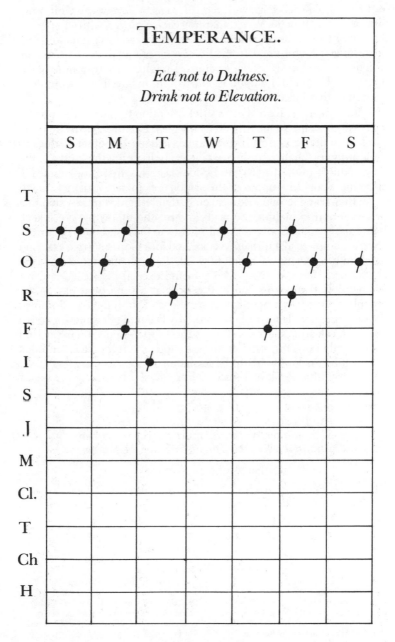

TEMPERANCE.

Eat not to Dulness.
Drink not to Elevation.

	S	M	T	W	T	F	S
T							
S	● ●	●		●		●	
O	●	●	●		●	●	●
R			●			●	
F		●			●		
I			●				
S							
J							
M							
Cl.							
T							
Ch							
H							

I made a little Book[3] in which I allotted a Page for each of the Virtues. I rul'd each Page with red Ink so as to have seven Columns, one for each Day of the Week, marking each Column with a Letter for the Day. I cross'd these Columns with thirteen red Lines, marking the Beginning of each Line with the first Letter of one of the Virtues, on which Line and in its proper Column I might mark by a little black Spot every Fault I found upon Examination, to have been committed respecting that Virtue upon that Day.

I determined to give a Week's strict Attention to each of the Virtues successively. Thus in the first Week my great Guard was to avoid every the least Offence against Temperance, leaving the other Virtues to their ordinary Chance, only marking every Evening the Faults of the Day. Thus if in the first Week I could keep my first Line marked T clear of Spots, I suppos'd the Habit of that Virtue so much strengthen'd and its opposite weaken'd, that I might venture extending my Attention to include the next, and for the following Week keep both Lines clear of Spots. Proceeding thus to the last, I could go thro' a Course complete in Thirteen Weeks, and four Courses in a Year. And like him who having a Garden to weed, does not attempt to eradicate all the bad Herbs at once, which would exceed his Reach and his Strength, but works on one of the Beds at a time, and having accomplish'd the first proceeds to a second; so I should have, (I hoped) the encouraging Pleasure of seeing on my Pages the Progress I made in Virtue, by clearing successively my Lines of their Spots, till in the End by a Number of Courses, I should be happy in viewing a clean Book after a thirteen Weeks' daily Examination.

This my little Book had for its Motto these Lines from *Addison's Cato*,

> *Here will I hold: If there is a Pow'r above us,*
> *(And that there is, all Nature cries aloud*
> *Thro' all her Works) he must delight in Virtue,*
> *And that which he delights in must be happy.* [4]

Another from *Cicero*.

O Vitæ Philosophia Dux! O Virtutum indagatrix, expultrixque vitiorum! Unus dies bene, et ex preceptis tuis actus, peccanti immortalitati est anteponendus. [5]

Another from the Proverbs of Solomon speaking of Wisdom or Virtue;

3. Cabanis testifies that BF had his "little Book" with him in France, (Cabanis, 5: 232) and William Temple Franklin, BF's grandson, had a copy dated July 1, 1733. (WTF, p. 69n.)
4. Addison's *Cato* (1713), V.i. 15–18, which BF also used as epigraph for his little book of "Articles of Belief and Acts of Religion." (P, 1: 101.)
5. *Tusculum Disputations*, V.2.5, with several lines omitted. This version was popular among liberal theologians, e.g., Samuel Clark, *Discourse of Natural Religion*, 3rd ed. (1711), p. 94. "O, Philosophy, guide of life! O teacher of virtue and corrector of vice. One day of virtue is better than an eternity of vice." Cicero's point was that virtue alone could make a happy life, without the necessity of supernatural agencies.

Length of Days is in her right hand, and in her Left Hand Riches and Honors; Her Ways are Ways of Pleasantness, and all her Paths are Peace.[6]

III, 16, 17

And conceiving God to be the Fountain of Wisdom, I thought it right and necessary to solicit his Assistance for obtaining it; to this End I form'd the following little Prayer, which was prefix'd to my Tables of Examination, for daily Use.

O Powerful Goodness! bountiful Father! merciful Guide! Increase in me that Wisdom which discovers my truest Interests; Strengthen my Resolutions to perform what that Wisdom dictates. Accept my kind Offices to thy other Children, as the only Return in my Power for thy continual Favors to me.[7]

I us'd also sometimes a little Prayer which I took from *Thomson's* Poems, viz.

> *Father of Light and Life, thou Good supreme,*
> *O teach me what is good, teach me thy self!*
> *Save me from Folly, Vanity and Vice,*
> *From every low Pursuit, and fill my Soul*
> *With Knowledge, conscious Peace, and Virtue pure,*
> *Sacred, substantial, neverfading Bliss!*[8]

The Precept of *Order* requiring that *every Part of my Business should have its allotted Time*, one Page in my little Book contain'd the following Scheme of Employment for the Twenty-four Hours of a natural Day.

I enter'd upon the Execution of this Plan for Self-examination, and continu'd it with occasional Intermissions for some time. I was surpris'd to find myself so much fuller of Faults than I had imagined, but I had the Satisfaction of seeing them diminish. To avoid the Trouble of renewing now and then my little Book, which by scraping out the Marks on the Paper of old Faults to make room for new Ones in a new Course, became full of Holes: I transferr'd my Tables and Precepts to the Ivory Leaves of a Memorandum Book,[9] on which the Lines were drawn with red Ink that made a durable Stain, and on those Lines I mark'd my Faults with a black Lead Pencil, which Marks I could easily wipe out with a wet Sponge. After a while I went thro' one Course only in a Year, and afterwards only one in several Years; till at length I omitted them entirely, being employ'd in Voyages and Business abroad with a Multiplicity of Affairs, that interfered. But I always carried my little Book with me.

6. Another favorite among liberal theologians, e.g., James Foster, "Sermon XIII," *Sermons* (1745) uses the passage as epigraph.

7. This prayer was evidently intended for BF's "Articles of Belief and Acts of Religion." (P, 1: 104n.)

8. In James Thomson's *Winter* (1726), this hymn heralds an attack against the "lying vanities" of social life.

9. William Temple Franklin had a copy of this book also. (WTF, p. 72n.)

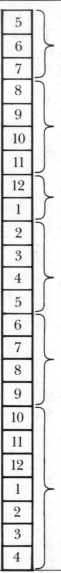

The Morning Question, What Good shall I do this Day?		Rise, wash, and address *Powerful Goodness;* contrive Day's Business and take the Resolution of the Day; prosecute the present Study: and breakfast? —
	5 6 7	
	8 9 10 11	Work.
	12 1	Read, or overlook my Accounts, and dine.
	2 3 4 5	Work.
	6 7 8	Put Things in their Places, Supper, Musick, or Diversion, or Conversation,
Evening Question, What Good have I done to day?	9 10 11 12	Examination of the Day.
	1 2 3 4	Sleep.—

My Scheme of ORDER, gave me the most Trouble, and I found, that tho' it might be practicable where a Man's Business was such as to leave him the Disposition of his Time, that of a Journeyman Printer for instance, it was not possible to be exactly observ'd by a Master, who must mix with the World, and often receive People of Business at their own Hours. *Order* too, with regard to Places for Things, Papers, etc. I found extremely difficult to acquire. I had not been early accustomed to it, and having an exceeding good Memory, I was not so sensible of the Inconvenience attending Want of Method. This Article therefore cost me so much painful Attention and my Faults in it vex'd me so much, and I made so little Progress in Amendment, and had such frequent Relapses, that I was almost ready to give up the Attempt, and content myself with a faulty Character in that respect. Like the Man who in buying an Axe of a Smith my Neighbor, desired to have the whole of its Surface as bright as the Edge; the Smith consented to grind it bright for him if he would turn the Wheel. He turn'd while the Smith press'd the broad Face of the Axe hard and heavily on the Stone, which made the Turning of it very fatiguing. The Man came every now and then from the Wheel to see how the Work went on; and at length would take his Axe as it was without farther Grinding. No, says the Smith, Turn on, turn on; we shall have it bright by and by; as yet 'tis only speckled. Yes, says the Man; but—*I think I like a speckled* Axe *best.*—And I believe this may have been the Case with many who having for want of some such Means as I employ'd found the Difficulty of obtaining good, and breaking bad Habits, in other Points of Vice and Virtue, have given up the Struggle, and concluded that *a speckled Axe was best*. For something that pretended to be Reason was every now and then suggesting to me, that such extreme Nicety as I exacted of myself might be a kind of Foppery in Morals, which if it were known would make me ridiculous; that a perfect Character might be attended with the Inconvenience of being envied and hated; and that a benevolent Man should allow a few Faults in himself, to keep his Friends in Countenance.

In Truth I found myself incorrigible with respect to *Order*; and now I am grown old, and my Memory bad, I feel very sensibly the want of it. But on the whole, tho' I never arrived at the Perfection I had been so ambitious of obtaining, but fell far short of it, yet I was by the Endeavour made a better and a happier Man than I otherwise should have been, if I had not attempted it; As those who aim at perfect Writing by imitating the engraved Copies,[1] tho' they never reach the wish'd for Excellence of those Copies, their Hand is mended by the Endeavour, and is tolerable while it continues fair and legible.

And it may be well my Posterity should be informed, that to this

---

1. Models in penmanship books. BF here deliberately echoes the simile used in *The Advancement of Learning*, Bk. 7, Chap. 1, para. 1, where Bacon discusses the "science" of virtue or "moral knowledge."

little Artifice, with the Blessing of God, their Ancestor ow'd the constant Felicity of his Life down to his 79th Year in which this is written. What Reverses may attend the Remainder is in the Hand of Providence: But if they arrive, the Reflection on past Happiness enjoy'd ought to help his Bearing them with more Resignation. To *Temperance* he ascribes his long-continu'd Health, and what is still left to him of a good Constitution. To *Industry* and *Frugality* the early Easiness of his Circumstances, and Acquisition of his Fortune, with all that Knowledge which enabled him to be an useful Citizen, and obtain'd for him some Degree of Reputation among the Learned. To *Sincerity* and *Justice* the Confidence of his Country, and the honorable Employs it conferr'd upon him. And to the joint Influence of the whole Mass of the Virtues, even in their imperfect State he was able to acquire them, all that Evenness of Temper, and that Cheerfulness in Conversation which makes his Company still sought for, and agreeable even to his younger Acquaintance. I hope therefore that some of my Descendants may follow the Example and reap the Benefit.

It will be remark'd that, tho' my Scheme was not wholly without Religion there was in it no Mark of any of the distinguishing Tenets of any particular Sect. I had purposely avoided them; for being fully persuaded of the Utility and Excellency of my Method, and that it might be serviceable to People in all Religions, and intending some time or other to publish it, I would not have anything in it that should prejudice anyone of any Sect against it. I purposed writing a little Comment on each Virtue, in which I would have shown the Advantages of possessing it,* and the Mischiefs attending its opposite Vice; and I should have called my Book the ART *of Virtue*,[2] because it would have shown the *Means and Manner* of obtaining Virtue; which would have distinguish'd it from the mere Exhortation to be good, that does not instruct and indicate the Means; but is like the Apostle's Man of verbal Charity, who only, without showing to the Naked and the Hungry *how* or where they might get Clothes or Victuals, exhorted them to be fed and clothed. *James* II, 15, 16.[3]

But it so happened that my Intention of writing and publishing this Comment was never fulfilled. I did indeed, from time to time put down short Hints of the Sentiments, Reasonings, etc. to be made use of in it; some of which I have still by me: But the necessary close Attention to private Business in the earlier part of Life, and public Business since, have occasioned my postponing it. For it being connected in my Mind with a *great and extensive Project* that required the whole Man to execute, and which an unforeseen Succession of

---

* "Nothing so likely to make a Man's Fortune as Virtue." [BF memo.]

2. See n. 7, p. 59 of this section.
3. "If a brother or sister be naked, and destitute of daily food, and one of you say unto them, Depart in peace, be ye warmed and filled; notwithstanding ye give them not those things which are needful to the body; what doth it profit?"

Employs prevented my attending to, it has hitherto remain'd unfinish'd.

In this Piece it was my Design to explain and enforce this Doctrine, that vicious Actions are not hurtful because they are forbidden, but forbidden because they are hurtful, the Nature of Man alone consider'd: That it was therefore every one's Interest to be virtuous, who wish'd to be happy even in this World.[4] And I should from this Circumstance (there being always in the World a Number of rich Merchants, Nobility, States and Princes, who have need of honest Instruments for the Management of their Affairs, and such being so rare) have endeavoured to convince young Persons, that no Qualities were so likely to make a poor Man's Fortune as those of Probity and Integrity.

My List of Virtues contain'd at first but twelve: But a Quaker Friend having kindly inform'd me that I was generally thought proud; that my Pride show'd itself frequently in Conversation; that I was not content with being in the right when discussing any Point, but was overbearing and rather insolent; of which he convinc'd me by mentioning several Instances; I determined endeavouring to cure myself if I could of this Vice or Folly among the rest, and I added *Humility* to my List, giving an extensive Meaning to the Word. I cannot boast of much Success in acquiring the *Reality* of this Virtue; but I had a good deal with regard to the *Appearance* of it. I made it a Rule to forbear all direct Contradiction to the Sentiments of others, and all positive Assertion of my own. I even forbid myself, agreeable to the old Laws of our Junto, the Use of every Word or Expression in the Language that imported a fix'd Opinion; such as *certainly*, *undoubtedly*, etc. and I adopted instead of them, I *conceive*, I *apprehend*, or I *imagine* a thing to be so or so, or it so appears to me at present. When another asserted something that I thought an Error, I denied myself the Pleasure of contradicting him abruptly, and of showing immediately some Absurdity in his Proposition; and in answering I began by observing that in certain Cases or Circumstances his Opinion would be right, but that in the present case there *appear'd* or *seem'd* to me some Difference, etc. I soon found the Advantage of this Change in my Manners. The Conversations I engag'd in went on more pleasantly. The modest way in which I propos'd my Opinions, procur'd them a readier Reception and less Contradiction; I had less Mortification when I was found to be in the wrong, and I more easily prevail'd with others to give up their Mistakes and join with me when I happen'd to be in the right. And this Mode, which I at first put on, with some violence to natural Inclination, became at length so easy and so habitual to me, that perhaps for these

4. BF thus attempts to prove that virtue is necessary for any man who wishes to lead a happy life, even one who denies religious systems of rewards and punishments. BF had attempted to promulgate this doctrine as early as 1739: "Sin is not hurtful because it is forbidden but it is forbidden because it's hurtful." (*Poor Richard*, Oct., 1739; *P*, 2: 224.)

Fifty Years past no one has ever heard a dogmatical Expression escape me. And to this Habit (after my Character of Integrity) I think it principally owing, that I had early so much Weight with my Fellow Citizens, when I proposed new Institutions, or Alterations in the old; and so much Influence in public Councils when I became a Member. For I was but a bad Speaker, never eloquent, subject to much Hesitation in my choice of Words, hardly correct in Language, and yet I generally carried my Points.

In reality there is perhaps no one of our natural Passions so hard to subdue as *Pride*. Disguise it, struggle with it, beat it down, stifle it, mortify it as much as one pleases, it is still alive, and will every now and then peep out and show itself. You will see it perhaps often in this History. For even if I could conceive that I had completely overcome it, I should probably be proud of my Humility.[5]

Thus far written at Passy, 1784.

5. BF echoes a well-known religious paradox. For example, one of the Couranteers whom BF knew and read as a boy, wrote "There is none so proud as the *proud-humble man*, who *is proud of his Humility!*" (John Checkley, *Choice Dialogues* [Boston, 1720], p. 18; Evans 2100.) See also Jonathan Edwards, *Works*, ed. Sereno E. Dwight, 10 vols. (New York: Carvell, 1830), 1: 151.

[*Part Three*]

I am now about to write at home, August 1788, but cannot have the help expected from my Papers, many of them being lost in the War. [6] *I have however found the following.*

Having mentioned *a great and extensive Project* which I had conceiv'd, it seems proper that some Account should be here given of that Project and its Object. Its first Rise in my Mind appears in the following little Paper, accidentally preserv'd, viz.

OBSERVATIONS on my Reading
History in Library, May 9, 1731.

"That the great Affairs of the World, the Wars, Revolutions, etc. are carried on and effected by Parties.

"That the View of these Parties is their present general Interest, or what they take to be such.

"That the different Views of these different Parties, occasion all Confusion.

"That while a Party is carrying on a general Design, each Man has his particular private Interest in View.

"That as soon as a Party has gain'd its general Point, each Member becomes intent upon his particular Interest, which thwarting others, breaks that Party into Divisions, and occasions more Confusion.

"That few in Public Affairs act from a mere View of the Good of their Country, whatever they may pretend; and tho' their Actings bring real Good to their Country, yet Men primarily consider'd that their own and their Country's Interest was united, and did not act from a Principle of Benevolence.

"That fewer still in public Affairs act with a View to the Good of Mankind.

"There seems to me at present to be great Occasion for raising an united Party for Virtue, by forming the Virtuous and good Men of all Nations into a regular Body, to be govern'd by suitable good and wise Rules, which good and wise Men may probably be more unanimous in their Obedience to, than common People are to common Laws.

"I at present think, that whoever attempts this aright, and is well qualified, cannot fail of pleasing God, and of meeting with Success.
B.F."

Revolving this Project in my Mind, as to be undertaken hereafter when my Circumstances should afford me the necessary Leisure, I put down from time to time on Pieces of Paper such Thoughts as occur'd to me respecting it. Most of these are lost; but I find one purporting to be the Substance of an intended Creed, containing as I thought the

6. Left for safekeeping with Joseph Galloway in urban Philadelphia, BF's papers were pillaged by marauding troops in 1778.

Essentials of every known Religion, and being free of everything that might shock the Professors of any Religion. It is express'd in these Words, viz.

"That there is one God who made all things.

"That he governs the World by his Providence.

"That he ought to be worshipped by Adoration, Prayer and Thanksgiving.

"But that the most acceptable Service of God is doing Good to Man.[7]

"That the Soul is immortal.

"And that God will certainly reward Virtue and punish Vice either here or hereafter."

My Ideas at that time were, that the Sect should be begun and spread at first among young and single Men only; that each Person to be initiated should not only declare his Assent to such Creed, but should have exercis'd himself with the Thirteen Weeks' Examination and Practice of the Virtues as in the before-mention'd Model; that the Existence of such a Society should be kept a Secret till it was become considerable, to prevent Solicitations for the Admission of improper Persons; but that the Members should each of them search among his Acquaintance for ingenuous well-disposed Youths, to whom with prudent Caution the Scheme should be gradually communicated: That the Members should engage to afford their Advice, Assistance and Support to each other in promoting one another's Interest, Business and Advancement in Life: That for Distinction we should be call'd the Society of the *Free and Easy*; Free, as being by the general Practice and Habit of the Virtues, free from the Dominion of Vice, and particularly by the Practice of Industry and Frugality, free from Debt, which exposes a Man to Confinement and a Species of Slavery to his Creditors. This is as much as I can now recollect of the Project, except that I communicated it in part to two young Men, who adopted it with some Enthusiasm. But my then narrow Circumstances, and the Necessity I was under of sticking close to my Business, occasion'd my Postponing the farther Prosecution of it at that time, and my multifarious Occupations public and private induc'd me to continue postponing, so that it has been omitted till I have no longer Strength or Activity left sufficient for such an Enterprise: Tho I am still of Opinion that it was a practicable Scheme, and might have been very useful, by forming a great Number of good Citizens: And I was not discourag'd by the seeming Magnitude of the Undertaking, as I have always thought that one Man of tolerable Abilities may work great Changes, and accomplish great Affairs among Mankind, if he first forms a good

7. The version in BF's *Proposals Relating to the Education of Youth* (1749) has "*Doing Good to Men* is the *only Service of God* in our Power." P, 3: 419.)

Plan, and, cutting off all Amusements or other Employments that would divert his Attention, makes the Execution of that same Plan his sole Study and Business.

In 1732 I first published my Almanac, under the Name of *Richard Saunders;*[8] it was continu'd by me about 25 Years, commonly call'd *Poor Richard's* Almanac.[9] I endeavour'd to make it both entertaining and useful, and it accordingly came to be in such Demand that I reap'd considerable Profit from it, vending annually near ten Thousand.[1] And observing that it was generally read, scarce any Neighborhood in the Province being without it, I consider'd it as a proper Vehicle for conveying Instruction among the common People, who bought scarce any other Books. I therefore filled all the little Spaces that occur'd between the Remarkable Days in the Calendar, with Proverbial Sentences, chiefly such as inculcated Industry and Frugality, as the Means of procuring Wealth and thereby securing Virtue, it being more difficult for a Man in Want to act always honestly, as (to use here one of those Proverbs) *it is hard for an empty Sack to stand upright.*[2] These Proverbs, which contained the Wisdom of many Ages and Nations, I assembled[3] and form'd into a connected Discourse prefix'd to the Almanac of 1757,[4] as the Harangue of a wise old Man to the People attending an Auction. The bringing all these scatter'd Counsels thus into a Focus, enabled them to make greater Impression. The Piece being universally approved was copied in all the Newspapers of the Continent, reprinted in Britain on a Broadside to be stuck up in Houses, two Translations were made of it in French, and great Numbers bought by the Clergy and Gentry to distribute gratis among their poor Parishioners and Tenants. In Pennsylvania, as it discouraged useless Expense in foreign Superfluities, some thought it had its share of Influence in producing that growing Plenty of Money which was observable for several Years after its Publication.

8. Name of an actual London almanac maker (1613?–1687?) whose *Apollo Anglicanae, or English Apollo* was a best seller from 1664. It was continued after his death by another Richard Saunder (no "s"), a dull, pedantic mathematician. (Wing A2325–2370, and Huntington Library Collections.)

9. The title combined Saunders' name with the title of another best-selling London almanac, *Poor Robin* (1661–1776), a comic, often bawdy parody of both astrological and astronomical almanacs. James Franklin's *Rhode Island Almanac* (1728–41) also used the pseudonym "Poor Robin."

1. During 1748–60, Philadelphia's population climbed from 17,000 to 24,000, and BF's almanac sold a little over 10,000 a year, at four pence apiece. BF's total profit was roughly £5,000. (Wroth, "Benjamin Franklin," pp. 163, 173.)

2. In 1740, "An empty Bag cannot stand upright"; in 1750, "An empty Sack can hardly stand upright"; and in 1758, " 'Tis hard for an empty Bag to stand upright." (P, 2: 248; 3: 446; 7: 348.)

3. About two-thirds of the proverbs have been traced to some half-dozen earlier collections, but BF often refashioned them for brevity or comic effect; e.g., "A penny saved by wise provision availeth two" becomes "A penny saved is a penny earned." (P, 1: 281–82. Frances M. Barbour, *Concordance to . . . Poor Richard* [1974].)

4. Composed in 1757 for the 1758 *Poor Richard*, the prefatory "Harangue," later called "The Way to Wealth," was BF's most widely reprinted work—at least 145 editions before 1800. (P, 7: 340–50.)

I consider'd my Newspaper[5] also as another Means of communicating Instruction, and in that View frequently reprinted in it Extracts from the Spectator and other moral Writers, and sometimes publish'd little Pieces of my own which had been first compos'd for Reading in our Junto. Of these are a Socratic Dialogue tending to prove, that, whatever might be his Parts and Abilities, a vicious Man could not properly be called a Man of Sense. And a Discourse on Self-denial, showing that Virtue was not Secure, till its Practice became a Habitude, and was free from the Opposition of contrary Inclinations. These may be found in the Papers about the beginning of 1735.[6] In the Conduct of my Newspaper I carefully excluded all Libelling and Personal Abuse, which is of late Years become so disgraceful to our Country.[7] Whenever I was solicited to insert anything of that kind, and the Writers pleaded as they generally did, the Liberty of the Press, and that a Newspaper was like a Stage Coach in which any one who would pay had a Right to a Place, my Answer was, that I would print the Piece separately if desired, and the Author might have as many Copies as he pleased to distribute himself, but that I would not take upon me to spread his Detraction, and that having contracted with my Subscribers to furnish them with what might be either useful or entertaining, I could not fill their Papers with private Altercation in which they had no Concern without doing them manifest Injustice.[8] Now many of our Printers make no scruple of gratifying the Malice of Individuals by false Accusations of the fairest Characters[9] among ourselves, augmenting Animosity even to the producing of Duels, and are moreover so indiscrete as to print scurrilous Reflections on the Government of neighboring States, and even on the Conduct of our best national Allies, which may be attended with the most pernicious Consequences.[1] These Things I mention as a Caution to young Printers, and that they may be encouraged not to pollute their Presses and disgrace their Profession by such infamous Practices, but refuse steadily; as they may see by my Example, that such a Course of Conduct will not on the whole be injurious to their Interests.

5. With weekly circulation averaging about 1500 copies, the *Pennsylvania Gazette* accounted for about sixty-one percent of BF's business, 1748–65. (Wroth, "Benjamin Franklin," pp. 163, 173.)
6. *Pennsylvania Gazette* for February 11 and 18, 1735. (*P*, 2: 15–21.)
7. Writing from Paris in 1782, BF said he was afraid to lend newspapers from home to Frenchmen "until I have examined and laid aside such as would disgrace us." (Smyth, 8: 647.)
8. In the *Pennsylvania Gazette* for June 10, 1731, BF wrote of having fallen into the ill graces of many men "for refusing absolutely to print any of their Party or Personal Reflections." (*P*, 1: 196.) On December 24, 1782, he wrote

Francis Hopkinson: "If People will print their Abuses of one another, let them do it in little Pamphlets, and distribute them where they think proper." (Smyth, 8: 648.)
9. On April 6, 1788, BF's friend Francis Hopkinson wrote Thomas Jefferson: "Our public News Papers have announced General Washington to be a Fool influenced and lead by that Knave Dr. Franklin who is a public Defaulter for Millions of Dollars . . . and that they are to cover their frauds by this new Government [the fledgling USA]." (Boyd, 13: 39.)
1. In 1784, America's first newspaper in French, *Le Courier de l'Amerique*, strained Franco-American relations by its unremitting attacks on France's government. (Zall, pp. 17–18.)

In 1733, I sent one of my Journeymen to Charleston South Carolina where a Printer was wanting.[2] I furnish'd him with a Press and Letters, on an Agreement of Partnership, by which I was to receive One Third of the Profits of the Business, paying One Third of the Expense. He was a Man of Learning and honest, but ignorant in Matters of Account; and tho' he sometimes made me Remittances, I could get no Account from him, nor any satisfactory State of our Partnership while he lived. On his Decease, the Business was continued by his Widow, who being born and bred in Holland, where as I have been inform'd the Knowledge of Accounts makes a Part of Female Education, she not only sent me as clear a State as she could find of the Transactions past, but continu'd to account with the greatest Regularity and Exactitude every Quarter afterwards; and manag'd the Business with such Success that she not only brought up reputably a Family of Children, but at the Expiration of the Term was able to purchase of me the Printing-House and establish her Son in it. I mention this Affair chiefly for the Sake of recommending that Branch of Education for our young Females, as likely to be of more Use to them and their Children in Case of Widowhood than either Music or Dancing, by preserving them from Losses by Imposition of crafty Men, and enabling them to continue perhaps a profitable mercantile House with establish'd Correspondence till a Son is grown up fit to undertake and go on with it, to the lasting Advantage and enriching of the Family.

About the Year 1734, there arrived among us from Ireland, a young Presbyterian Preacher named Hemphill, who delivered with a good Voice, and apparently extempore, most excellent Discourses, which drew together considerable Numbers of different Persuasions, who join'd in admiring them. Among the rest I became one of his constant Hearers, his Sermons pleasing me as they had little of the dogmatical kind, but inculcated strongly the Practice of Virtue, or what in the religious Style are called Good Works. Those however, of our Congregation, who considered themselves as orthodox Presbyterians, disapprov'd his Doctrine, and were join'd by most of the old Clergy, who arraign'd him of Heterodoxy before the Synod, in order to have him silenc'd. I became his zealous Partisan, and contributed all I could to raise a Party in his Favor; and we combated for him a while with some Hopes of Success. There was much Scribbling pro and con upon the Occasion; and finding that tho' an elegant Preacher he was but a poor Writer, I lent him my Pen and wrote for him two or three Pamphlets, and one Piece in the Gazette of April 1735. Those Pamphlets, as is generally the Case with controversial Writings, tho' eagerly read at the

2. BF had sponsored Thomas Whitmarsh (d. 1733) in South Carolina in 1731, and in November 1733 sent Louis Timothée to suc- ceed him. Elizabeth Timothée succeeded her husband at his death in 1738. (*P*, 1: 205–8, 339–42.)

time, were soon out of Vogue, and I question whether a single Copy of them now exists.[3]

During the Contest an unlucky Occurrence hurt his Cause exceedingly. One of our Adversaries having heard him preach a Sermon that was much admired, thought he had somewhere read that Sermon before, or at least a part of it. On Search he found that Part quoted at length in one of the British Reviews, from a Discourse of Dr. Forster's.[4] This Detection gave many of our Party Disgust, who accordingly abandoned his Cause, and occasion'd our more speedy Discomfiture in the Synod. I stuck by him, however, as I rather approv'd his giving us good Sermons compos'd by others, than bad ones of his own Manufacture; tho' the latter was the Practice of our common Teachers. He afterwards acknowledg'd to me that none of those he preach'd were his own; adding that his Memory was such as enabled him to retain and repeat any Sermon after one Reading only. On our Defeat he left us, in search elsewhere of better Fortune, and I quitted the Congregation, never joining it after, tho' I continu'd many Years my Subscription for the Support of its Ministers.

I had begun in 1733 to study Languages. I soon made myself so much a Master of the French as to be able to read the Books with Ease. I then undertook the Italian. An Acquaintance who was also learning it, us'd often to tempt me to play Chess with him. Finding this took up too much of the Time I had to spare for Study, I at length refus'd to play anymore, unless on this Condition, that the Victor in every Game, should have a Right to impose a Task, either in Parts of the Grammar to be got by heart, or in Translation, etc., which Tasks the Vanquish'd was to perform upon Honor before our next Meeting. As we play'd pretty equally we thus beat one another into that Language. I afterwards with a little Pains-taking acquir'd as much of the Spanish as to read their Books also.

I have already mention'd that I had only one Year's Instruction in a Latin School, and that when very young, after which I neglected that Language entirely.—But when I had attained an Acquaintance with the French, Italian and Spanish, I was surpris'd to find, on looking over a Latin Testament, that I understood so much more of that Language than I had imagined; which encouraged me to apply myself again to the Study of it, and I met with the more Success, as those preceding Languages had greatly smooth'd my Way. From these Circumstances I have thought, that there is some Inconsistency in our common Mode of Teaching Languages. We are told that it is proper to begin first with the Latin, and having acquir'd that, it will be more easy to attain those modern Languages which are deriv'd from it; and yet we

3. The *Gazette* piece appeared on April 10, 1735. At least two copies of each of BF's three pamphlets are extant. (Miller, nos. 101, 102, and 105 [2nd ed., 106]; *P*, 2: 27–33, 37–126.)

4. James Foster, a leading liberal preacher. Hemphill was found guilty by the Synod of preaching "Unsound and Dangerous" doctrine. (*P*, 2: 37.)

do not begin with the Greek in order more easily to acquire the Latin. It is true, that if you can clamber and get to the Top of a Staircase without using the Steps, you will more easily gain them in descending: but certainly if you begin with the lowest you will with more Ease ascend to the Top. And I would therefore offer it to the Consideration of those who superintend the Educating of our Youth, whether, since many of those who begin with the Latin, quit the same after spending some Years, without having made any great Proficiency, and what they have learned becomes almost useless, so that their time has been lost, it would not have been better to have begun them with the French, proceeding to the Italian etc., for tho' after spending the same time they should quit the Study of Languages, and never arrive at the Latin, they would however have acquir'd another Tongue or two that being in modern Use might be serviceable to them in common Life.[5]

After ten Years' Absence from Boston, and having become more easy in my Circumstances, I made a Journey[6] thither to visit my Relations, which I could not sooner well afford. In returning I call'd at Newport, to see my Brother then settled there with his Printing-House. Our former Differences were forgotten, and our Meeting was very cordial and affectionate. He was fast declining in his Health, and requested of me that in case of his Death which he apprehended not far distant, I would take home his Son, then but 10 Years of Age, and bring him up[7] to the Printing Business. This I accordingly perform'd, sending him a few Years to School before I took him into the Office. His Mother carried on the Business till he was grown up, when I assisted him with an Assortment of new Types, those of his Father being in a Manner worn out.—Thus it was that I made my Brother ample Amends for the Service I had depriv'd him of by leaving him so early.

In 1736 I lost one of my Sons, a fine Boy of 4 Years old, by the Smallpox taken in the common way. I long regretted bitterly and still regret that I had not given it to him by Inoculation.[8] This I mention for the Sake of Parents, who omit that Operation on the Supposition that they should never forgive themselves if a Child died under it; my Example showing that the Regret may be the same either way, and that therefore the safer should be chosen.

Our Club, the Junto, was found so useful, and afforded such Satisfaction to the Members, that several were desirous of introducing

5. BF may echo John Locke's *Some Thoughts Concerning Education* (1693): French should be learned before Latin, both should be taught through conversation, and grammar should be taught only to those who can already speak the language. (Axtell, pp. 266–67, 273.)

6. Of "near seven Weeks" in September and early October, 1733. (*P*, 1: 346.)

7. After James died, February 4, 1735, his son came to live with BF while attending school, then served as apprentice, 1740–47, sometimes vexing BF with his conduct. (*P*, 2: 261–62, 388.)

8. After Francis Folger Franklin died in November, 1736, BF printed a notice in his paper scotching rumors that the child had died of inoculation. (*P*, 2: 154.)

their Friends, which could not well be done without exceeding what we had settled as a convenient Number, viz. Twelve. We had from the Beginning made it a Rule to keep our Institution a Secret, which was pretty well observ'd. The Intention was, to avoid Applications of improper Persons for Admittance, some of whom perhaps we might find it difficult to refuse. I was one of those who were against any Addition to our Number, but instead of it made in Writing a Proposal, that every Member separately should endeavour to form a subordinate Club, with the same Rules respecting Queries, etc. and without informing them of the Connection with the Junto. The Advantages propos'd were the Improvement of so many more young Citizens by the Use of our Institutions; Our better Acquaintance with the general Sentiments of the Inhabitants on any Occasion, as the Junto-Member might propose what Queries we should desire, and was to report to Junto what pass'd in his separate Club; the Promotion of our particular Interests in Business by more extensive Recommendations; and the Increase of our Influence in public Affairs and our Power of doing Good by spreading thro' the several Clubs the Sentiments of the Junto. The Project was approv'd, and every Member undertook to form his Club: but they did not all succeed. Five or six only were completed, which were call'd by different Names, as the Vine, the Union, the Band, etc. They were useful to themselves, and afforded us a good deal of Amusement, Information, and Instruction, besides answering in some considerable Degree our Views of influencing the public Opinion on particular Occasions, of which I shall give some Instances in course of time as they happened.

My first Promotion was my being chosen in 1736 Clerk of the General Assembly. The Choice was made that Year without Opposition;[9] but the Year following when I was again propos'd (the Choice, like that of the Members being annual) a new Member made a long Speech against me in order to favor some other Candidate.[1] I was however chosen; which was the more agreeable to me, as besides the Pay for immediate Service as Clerk, the Place gave me a better Opportunity of keeping up an Interest among the Members, which secur'd to me the Business of Printing the Votes, Laws, Paper Money, and other occasional Jobs for the Public, that on the whole were very profitable.[2] I therefore did not like the Opposition of this new Member, who was a Gentleman of Fortune, and Education, with Talents that were likely to give him in time great Influence in the

9. BF was chosen clerk on October 15, 1736, after the former clerk was defeated for the position. (*Pa. Archives*, 8th ser., 3: 2373.)
1. Evidently Issac Norris (1701–1766), a new member fitting BF's description. The Norris family disliked BF both because of his advocacy of a paper currency (Isaac Norris Sr. was one of the "Rich Men" who "dislik'd" BF's pamphlet) and because BF's newspaper supported Andrew Hamilton (Katherine D. Carter, "Isaac Norris II's Attack on Andrew Hamilton," *PMHB*, 104 (1980), 139–61.)
2. BF's combined salary as clerk and printer for the assembly grew from £24.9.6 in 1736–37 to £113.2.0 in 1739–40. (*Pa. Archives*, 8th ser., 3: 2402, 2662.)

House, which indeed afterwards happened. I did not however aim at gaining his Favor by paying any servile Respect to him, but after some time took this other Method. Having heard that he had in his Library a certain very scarce and curious Book, I wrote a Note to him expressing my Desire of perusing that Book, and requesting he would do me the Favor of lending it to me for a few Days. He sent it immediately; and I return'd it in about a Week, with another Note expressing strongly my Sense of the Favor. When we next met in the House he spoke to me, (which he had never done before) and with great Civility. And he ever afterwards manifested a Readiness to serve me on all Occasions, so that we became great Friends, and our Friendship continu'd to his Death. This is another Instance of the Truth of an old Maxim I had learned, which says, *He that has once done you a Kindness will be more ready to do you another, than he whom you yourself have obliged.*[3] And it shows how much more profitable it is prudently to remove, than to resent, return and continue inimical Proceedings.

In 1737, Colonel Spotswood, late Governor of Virginia, and then Postmaster General, being dissatisfied with the Conduct of his Deputy at Philadelphia, respecting some Negligence in rendering, and Inexactitude of his Accounts, took from him the Commission and offered it to me.[4] I accepted it readily, and found it of great Advantage; for tho' the Salary was small, it facilitated the Correspondence that improv'd my Newspaper, increas'd the Number demanded, as well as the Advertisements to be inserted, so that it came to afford me a very considerable Income. My old Competitor's Newspaper declin'd proportionably,[5] and I was satisfied without retaliating his Refusal, while Postmaster, to permit my Papers being carried by the Riders.[6] Thus He suffer'd greatly from his Neglect in due Accounting; and I mention it as a Lesson to those young Men who may be employ'd in managing Affairs for others that they should always render Accounts and make Remittances with great Clearness and Punctuality. The Character of observing Such a Conduct is the most powerful of all Recommendations to new Employments and Increase of Business.

I began now to turn my Thoughts a little to public Affairs, beginning however with small Matters. The City Watch was one of the first Things that I conceiv'd to want Regulation. It was managed by the

3. BF may echo Lord Kames, *Introduction to the Art of Thinking* (Edinburgh, 1761), pp. 16–17: "You may sooner expect a favour from him who has already done you one, than from him to whom you have done it."
4. For the last three of his nine years as postmaster, Bradford did not submit accounts, and was thus succeeded in October 1737 by BF who held office until made deputy postmaster for North America in 1753. (*P*, 2: 180, 235.)
5. Although Bradford neglected his paper for ventures in real estate and mining, it did not

decline appreciably from his loss of the post office. (DeArmond, pp. 32–33.)
6. Evidently BF complained of Bradford's unfair business practice to Alexander Spotswood, deputy postmaster general for North America, for BF advertised on January 23, 1735, that "By the Indulgence" of Spotswood, he was "allow'd to send the *Gazettes* by the Post." (*P*, 2: 131.) In 1739, however, because of Bradford's still delinquent post office accounts, Spotswood forbad BF to allow Bradford's papers to be carried by the post. (*P*, 2: 235–6, 275–81.)

Constables of the respective Wards in Turn. The Constable warn'd a Number of Housekeepers to attend him for the Night. Those who chose never to attend paid him Six Shillings a Year to be excus'd, which was suppos'd to be for hiring Substitutes; but was in Reality much more than was necessary for that purpose, and made the Constableship a Place of Profit. And the Constable for a little Drink often got such Ragamuffins about him as a Watch, that reputable Housekeepers did not choose to mix with. Walking the Rounds too was often neglected, and most of the Night spent in Tippling. I thereupon wrote a Paper to be read in Junto, representing these Irregularities, but insisting more particularly on the Inequality of this Six Shilling Tax of the Constables, respecting the Circumstances of those who paid it, since a poor Widow Housekeeper, all whose Property to be guarded by the Watch did not perhaps exceed the Value of Fifty Pounds, paid as much as the wealthiest Merchant who had Thousands of Pounds worth of Goods in his Stores. On the whole I proposed as a more effectual Watch, the Hiring of proper Men to serve constantly in that Business; and as a more equitable Way of supporting the Charge, the levying a Tax that should be proportion'd to Property. This Idea being approv'd by the Junto, was communicated to the other Clubs, but as arising in each of them. And tho' the Plan was not immediately carried into Execution,[7] yet by preparing the Minds of People for the Change, it paved the Way for the Law obtain'd a few Years after, when the Members of our Clubs were grown into more Influence.

About this time I wrote a Paper, (first to be read in Junto but it was afterwards publish'd)[8] on the different Accidents and Carelessnesses by which Houses were set on fire, with Cautions against them, and Means proposed of avoiding them. This was much spoken of as a useful Piece, and gave rise to a Project, which soon followed it, of forming a Company for the more ready Extinguishing of Fires, and mutual Assistance in Removing and Securing of Goods when in Danger. Associates in this Scheme were presently found amounting to Thirty. Our Articles of Agreement[9] oblig'd every Member to keep always in good Order and fit for Use, a certain Number of Leather Buckets, with strong Bags and Baskets (for packing and transporting of Goods), which were to be brought to every Fire; and we agreed to meet once a Month and spend a social Evening together, in discoursing, and communicating such Ideas as occur'd to us upon the Subject of Fires as might be useful in our Conduct on such Occasions. The Utility of this Institution soon appear'd, and many more desiring to be admitted than we thought convenient for one Company, they were advised to form another; which was accordingly done. And this went

7. Though first proposed about 1735, the plan was not adopted until 1752. (*P*, 4: 327–32.)
8. *Pennsylvania Gazette*, February 4, 1735.

(*P*, 2: 12–15.)
9. Dated December 7, 1736. (*P*, 2: 150–53.)

on, one new Company being formed after another, till they became so numerous as to include most of the Inhabitants who were Men of Property; and now at the time of my Writing this, tho' upwards of Fifty Years since its Establishment, that which I first formed, called the Union Fire Company, still subsists and flourishes, tho' the first Members are all deceas'd but myself and one who is older[1] by a Year than I am. The small Fines that have been paid by Members for Absence at the Monthly Meetings, have been applied to the Purchase of Fire Engines, Ladders, Firehooks, and other useful Implements for each Company, so that I question whether there is a City in the World better provided with the Means of putting a Stop to beginning Conflagrations; and in fact since these Institutions, the City has never lost by Fire more than one or two Houses at a time, and the Flames have often been extinguish'd before the House in which they began has been half-consumed.

In 1739 arriv'd among us from England the Rev. Mr. Whitefield, who had made himself remarkable there as an itinerant Preacher. He was at first permitted to preach in some of our Churches; but the Clergy taking a Dislike to him, soon refus'd him their Pulpits and he was oblig'd to preach in the Fields.[2] The Multitudes of all Sects and Denominations that attended his Sermons were enormous and it was matter of Speculation to me who was one of the Number, to observe the extraordinary Influence of his Oratory on his Hearers, and how much they admir'd and respected him, notwithstanding his common Abuse of them, by assuring them they were naturally *half Beasts and half Devils*.[3] It was wonderful to see the Change soon made in the Manners of our Inhabitants; from being thoughtless or indifferent about Religion, it seem'd as if all the World were growing Religious; so that one could not walk thro' the Town in an Evening without Hearing Psalms sung in different Families of every Street.[4] And it being found inconvenient to assemble in the open Air, subject to its Inclemencies, the Building of a House to meet in was no sooner propos'd and Persons appointed to receive Contributions, but sufficient Sums were soon receiv'd to procure the Ground and erect the Building which was 100 feet long and 70 broad, about the Size of

1. Philip Syng, who had also been a member of the original Junto as well as a founder of the Library Company.
2. During his second visit to America, 1739–40, many Anglican churches excluded Whitefield but most Presbyterian churches welcomed him. Preaching in the fields was his custom in England.
3. Preaching on the parable of the Pharisee and the Publican (Luke, 18:9–14) Whitefield asked, "Would he ['this publican'] have been angry, if any one had told him, that, by nature, he was half a devil and half a beast?" (Tyerman, 1:

277). Others also objected to Whitefield's characterization. The Rev. William Cooper (a Whitefield supporter) began one sermon (c. 1742): "I know it hath given offence to some, when they have heard sinful man represented as half beast and half devil." (Huntington Library ms.: CO/267.)
4. *Pennsylvania Gazette*, June 12, 1740: "Instead of idle Songs and Ballads, the People are every where entertaining themselves with Psalms, Hymns and Spiritual Songs." (P, 2: 288.)

Westminster Hall, and the Work was carried on with such Spirit as to be finished in a much shorter time than could have been expected.[5] Both House and Ground were vested in Trustees, expressly for the Use of any Preacher of any religious Persuasion who might desire to say something to the People of Philadelphia, the Design in building not being to accommodate any particular Sect, but the Inhabitants in general, so that even if the Mufti of Constantinople were to send a Missionary to preach Mahometanism to us, he would find a Pulpit at his Service.*

Mr. Whitefield, in leaving us, went preaching all the Way thro' the Colonies to Georgia. The Settlement of that Province had lately been begun; but instead of being made with hardy industrous Husbandmen accustomed to Labor, the only People fit for such an Enterprise, it was with Families of broken Shopkeepers and other insolvent Debtors, many of indolent and idle habits, taken out of the Jails, who being set down in the Woods, unqualified for clearing Land, and unable to endure the Hardships of a new Settlement, perished in Numbers, leaving many helpless Children unprovided for. The Sight of their miserable Situation inspired the benevolent Heart of Mr. Whitefield with the Idea of building an Orphan House there, in which they might be supported and educated. Returning northward he preach'd up this Charity, and made large Collections;—for his Eloquence had a wonderful Power over the Hearts and Purses of his Hearers, of which I myself was an Instance. I did not disapprove of the Design, but as Georgia was then destitute of Materials and Workmen, and it was propos'd to send them from Philadelphia at a great Expense, I thought it would have been better to have built the House here and brought the Children to it. This I advis'd, but he was resolute in his first Project, and rejected my Counsel, and I thereupon refus'd to contribute.

I happened soon after to attend one of his Sermons, in the Course of which I perceived he intended to finish with a Collection, and I silently resolved he should get nothing from me. I had in my Pocket a Handful of Copper Money, three or four silver Dollars, and five Pistoles in Gold. As he proceeded I began to soften, and concluded to give the Coppers. Another Stroke of his Oratory made me asham'd of that, and determin'd me to give the Silver; and he finish'd so admirably, that I emptied my Pocket wholly into the Collector's Dish, Gold and all. At this Sermon there was also one of our Club, who being of my Sentiments respecting the Building in Georgia, and suspecting a Collection might be intended, had by Precaution emptied his Pockets before he came from home; towards the Conclusion of the Discourse

* "This to come in hereafter, where I shall mention my Election as one of the Trustees." [BF note.] See p. 99 of this section.

5. Except for the roof, the building was completed in six months. (Tyerman, 1: 436.)

however, he felt a strong Desire to give, and apply'd to a Neighbor who stood near him to borrow some Money for the Purpose. The Application was unfortunately to perhaps the only Man in the Company who had the firmness not to be affected by the Preacher. His Answer was, *At any other time, Friend Hopkinson, I would lend to thee freely; but not now; for thee seems to be out of thy right Senses.* [6]

Some of Mr. Whitefield's Enemies affected to suppose that he would apply these Collections to his own private Emolument; but I, who was intimately acquainted with him, (being employ'd in printing his Sermons and Journals, etc.)[7] never had the least Suspicion of his Integrity, but am to this day decidedly of Opinion that he was in all his Conduct, a perfectly *honest Man*. And methinks my Testimony in his Favor ought to have the more Weight, as we had no religious Connection. He us'd indeed sometimes to pray for my Conversion, but never had the Satisfaction of believing that his Prayers were heard.[8] Ours was a mere civil Friendship, sincere on both Sides, and lasted to his Death.

The following Instance will show something of the Terms on which we stood. Upon one of his Arrivals from England at Boston, he wrote to me that he should come soon to Philadelphia, but knew not where he could lodge when there, as he understood his old kind Host Mr. Benezet[9] was remov'd to Germantown. My Answer was; You know my House, if you can make shift with its scanty Accommodations you will be most heartily welcome. He replied, that if I made that kind Offer for Christ's sake, I should not miss of a Reward.—And I return'd, *Don't let me be mistaken; it was not for Christ's sake, but for your sake.* One of our common Acquaintance jocosely remark'd, that knowing it to be the Custom of the Saints, when they receiv'd any favor, to shift the Burden of the Obligation from off their own Shoulders, and place it in Heaven, I had contriv'd to fix it on Earth.

The last time I saw Mr. Whitefield was in London,[1] when he consulted me about his Orphan House Concern, and his Purpose of appropriating it to the Establishment of a College.

He had a loud and clear Voice, and articulated his Words and

6. BF's characterization of the powerful effect of Whitefield's oratory may recall Cotton Mather's condemnation of Samuel May, a religious imposter of 1699. As BF knew, the Rev. Jonathan Ashley used Mather's condemnation of May to discredit Whitefield in 1743. As rephrased by Ashley, Cotton Mather advanced "as the surest Argument of *the Power of his* [May's] *Oratory* . . . that he *open'd the People's Pockets*, as well as mov'd their Passions." (Jonathan Ashley, *A Letter from . . . Ashley to the Rev. Mr. William Cooper* [Boston, 1743], Evans 5120.) The sermon BF described probably took place on Sunday, April 20, 1740. The *Pennsylvania Gazette* for April 24, 1740,

tells of the large sum of money Whitefield collected "on *Sunday* last . . . for the Orphans in *Georgia*."
7. BF printed a large number of Whitefield's books as well as his journals in 1739–41. (Miller, nos. 180, 214–24, 269–70.)
8. Whitefield wrote BF, November 26, 1740: "I do not despair of your seeing the reasonableness of Christianity. Apply to GOD; be willing to do the divine will, and you shall know it." (*P*, 2: 270.)
9. John Stephen Benezet moved to Germantown in 1743, and Whitefield next came to Philadelphia in September 1745.
1. During the winter of 1767–68. (*P*, 15: 28.)

Sentences so perfectly that he might be heard and understood at a great Distance, especially as his Auditors, however numerous, observ'd the most exact Silence. He preach'd one Evening from the Top of the Court House Steps, which are in the Middle of Market Street, and on the West Side of Second Street which crosses it at right angles. Both Streets were fill'd with his Hearers to a considerable Distance. Being among the hindmost in Market Street, I had the Curiosity to learn how far he could be heard, by retiring backwards down the Street towards the River, and I found his Voice distinct till I came near Front Street, when some Noise in that Street, obscur'd it. Imagining then a Semicircle, of which my Distance should be the Radius, and that it were fill'd with Auditors, to each of whom I allow'd two square feet, I computed that he might well be heard by more than Thirty Thousand. This reconcil'd me to the Newspaper Accounts of his having preach'd to 25,000 People[2] in the Fields, and to the ancient Histories of Generals haranguing whole Armies, of which I had sometimes doubted.[3]

By hearing him often I came to distinguish easily between Sermons newly compos'd, and those which he had often preach'd in the Course of his Travels. His Delivery of the latter was so improv'd by frequent Repetitions, that every Accent, every Emphasis, every Modulation of Voice, was so perfectly well turn'd and well plac'd, that without being interested in the Subject, one could not help being pleas'd with the Discourse, a Pleasure of much the same kind with that receiv'd from an excellent Piece of Music. This is an Advantage itinerant Preachers have over those who are stationary: as the latter cannot well improve their Delivery of a Sermon by so many Rehearsals.

His Writing and Printing from time to time gave great Advantage to his Enemies. Unguarded Expressions and even erroneous Opinions delivered in Preaching might have been afterwards explain'd, or qualified by supposing others that might have accompanied them; or they might have been denied; but *litera scripta manet*.[4] Critics attack'd his Writings violently,[5] and with so much Appearance of Reason as to diminish the Number of his Votaries, and prevent their Increase: So that I am of Opinion, if he had never written anything he would have left behind him a much more numerous and important Sect. And his Reputation might in that case have been still growing, even after his Death; as there being nothing of his Writing on which to

2. Whitefield's own journal says he preached to 30,000. (Tyerman, 1: 268.)
3. *Poor Richard* for January 1749, evidently inspired by BF's observation of the crowds attending Whitefield, comments that 45,000 auditors could "stand in a space . . . but 100 yards square." (P, 3: 336.)
4. More completely: "Vox audita perit, littera scripta manet": *The spoken word passes away, the written word remains.* (Wilson, p. 469.)
5. The first of many such attacks came at the start of Whitefield's career, when an anonymous London pamphlet's complaint against his doctrine resulted in his being barred from Anglican churches. (Tyerman, 1: 151–52.)

found a Censure; and give him a lower Character, his Proselytes would be left at Liberty to feign for him as great a Variety of Excellencies, as their enthusiastic Admiration might wish him to have possessed.

My Business was now continually augmenting, and my Circumstances growing daily easier, my Newspaper having become very profitable,[6] as being for a time almost the only one in this and the neighboring Provinces. I experienc'd too the Truth of the Observation, that *after getting the first hundred Pound, it is more easy to get the second:* Money itself being of a prolific Nature: The Partnership at Carolina having succeeded, I was encourag'd to engage in others, and to promote several of my Workmen[7] who had behaved well, by establishing them with Printing-Houses in different Colonies, on the same Terms with that in Carolina. Most of them did well, being enabled at the End of our Term, Six Years, to purchase the Types of me; and go on working for themselves, by which means several Families were raised. Partnerships often finish in Quarrels, but I was happy in this, that mine were all carried on and ended amicably; owing I think a good deal to the Precaution of having very explicitly settled in our Articles[8] everything to be done by or expected from each Partner, so that there was nothing to dispute, which Precaution I would therefore recommend to all who enter into Partnerships, for whatever Esteem Partners may have for and Confidence in each other at the time of the Contract, little Jealousies and Disgusts may arise, with Ideas of Inequality in the Care and Burden of the Business, etc. which are attended often with Breach of Friendship and of the Connection, perhaps with Lawsuits and other disagreeable Consequences.

I had on the whole abundant Reason to be satisfied with my being established in Pennsylvania. There were however two things that I regretted: There being no Provision for Defense, nor for a complete Education of Youth. No Militia nor any College. I therefore in 1743, drew up a Proposal[9] for establishing an Academy; and at that time thinking the Rev. Mr. Peters, who was out of Employ, a fit Person to superintend such an Institution, I communicated the Project to him. But he having more profitable Views in the Service of the Proprietor, which succeeded, declin'd the Undertaking. And not knowing another at that time suitable for such a Trust, I let the Scheme lie a while dormant. I succeeded better the next Year, 1744, in proposing

---

6. BF earned about £750 a year from his newspaper, 1748–65, when about twenty-five percent of its circulation went to out-of-town subscribers. (Wroth, "Benjamin Franklin," p. 163.)
7. Thomas Smith in Antigua (1748), Benjamin Mecom to succeed Smith (1752), and Samuel Holland in Lancaster, Pennsylvania

(1753). (*P*, 3: 322n; 4: 355–56; 4: 506–7.)
8. BF's contract with Holland is in *P*, 4: 506–7.
9. Not extant. The plan apparently included using the building constructed for Whitefield. Richard Peters declined BF's offer because of the prospective Academy's association with Whitefield. (Cummings, p. 143.)

and establishing a Philosophical Society. The Paper[1] I wrote for that purpose will be found among my Writings when collected.

With respect to Defense, Spain having been several Years at War against Britain, and being at length join'd by France, which brought us into greater Danger,[2] and the laboured and long-continued Endeavours of our Governor Thomas to prevail with our Quaker Assembly to pass a Militia Law, and make other Provisions for the Security of the Province having proved abortive, I determined to try what might be done by a voluntary Association of the People. To promote this I first wrote and published a Pamphlet, entitled, PLAIN TRUTH,[3] in which I stated our defenseless Situation in strong Lights, with the Necessity of Union and Discipline for our Defense, and promis'd to propose in a few Days an Association to be generally signed for that purpose. The Pamphlet had a sudden and surprising Effect. I was call'd upon for the Instrument of Association: And having settled the Draft of it with a few Friends, I appointed a Meeting of the Citizens in the large Building before-mentioned.

The House was pretty full. I had prepared a Number of printed Copies, and provided Pens and Ink dispers'd all over the Room. I harangu'd them a little on the Subject, read the Paper and explain'd it, and then distributed the Copies which were eagerly signed, not the least Objection being made. When the Company separated, and the Papers were collected we found above Twelve hundred Hands; and other Copies being dispers'd in the Country the Subscribers amounted at length to upwards of Ten Thousand. These all furnish'd themselves as soon as they could with Arms; form'd themselves into Companies, and Regiments, chose their own Officers, and met every Week to be instructed in the manual Exercise, and other Parts of military Discipline. The Women, by Subscriptions among themselves, provided Silk Colors, which they presented to the Companies, painted with different Devices and Mottos which I supplied.[4] The Officers of the Companies composing the Philadelphia Regiment, being met, chose me for their Colonel; but conceiving myself unfit, I declin'd that Station, and recommended Mr. Lawrence,[5] a fine Person and Man of Influence, who was accordingly appointed. I then propos'd a Lottery[6] to defray the Expense of Building a Battery below the Town, and furnishing it with Cannon. It filled expeditiously and the Battery was

1. A *Proposal for Promoting Useful Knowledge among the British Plantations in America* was dated May 14, 1743. The idea was naturalist John Bartram's, modified by BF. (Miller, no. 325; *P*, 2: 380–83.)
2. The war with Spain (the War of Jenkins' Ear) began 1737 and with France (King George's War) 1744. The immediate alarm was the appearance of enemy ships in Delaware Bay, spring–summer 1747.
3. *Plain Truth; or, Serious Considerations on*
the *Present State of the City of Philadelphia, and Province of Pennsylvania*, by "a Tradesman of Philadelphia" (November 17, 1747.) (Miller, nos. 416, 417; *P*, 3: 188–204.)
4. *Pennsylvania Gazette*, January 12 and 16, 1748, describes twenty designs. (*P*, 3: 268–69.)
5. Thomas Lawrence was elected lieutenant colonel; Abraham Taylor, colonel.
6. Announced in *Pennsylvania Gazette*, December 12, 1747. (*P*, 3: 223–24.)

soon erected, the Merlons being fram'd of Logs and fill'd with Earth. We bought some old Cannon from Boston, but these not being sufficient, we wrote to England for more, soliciting at the same Time our Proprietaries for some Assistance, tho' without much Expectation of obtaining it.

Meanwhile Colonel Lawrence, William Allen, Abraham Taylor, Esquires, and myself were sent to New York by the Associators, commission'd to borrow some Cannon of Governor Clinton. He at first refus'd us peremptorily: but at a Dinner with his Council where there was great Drinking of Madeira Wine, as the Custom at that Place then was, he soften'd by degrees, and said he would lend us Six. After a few more Bumpers he advanc'd to Ten. And at length he very good-naturedly conceded Eighteen.[7] They were fine Cannon, 18 pounders, with their Carriages, which we soon transported and mounted on our Battery, where the Associators kept a nightly Guard while the War lasted: And among the rest I regularly took my Turn of Duty there as a common Soldier.

My Activity in these Operations was agreeable to the Governor and Council; they took me into Confidence, and I was consulted by them in every Measure wherein their Concurrence was thought useful to the Association. Calling in the Aid of Religion, I propos'd to them the Proclaiming a Fast, to promote Reformation, and implore the Blessing of Heaven on our Undertaking. They embrac'd the Motion, but as it was the first Fast ever thought of in the Province, the Secretary had no Precedent from which to draw the Proclamation. My Education in New England, where a Fast is proclaim'd every Year, was here of some Advantage. I drew it in the accustomed Style, it was translated into German, printed in both Languages and divulg'd thro' the Province.[8] This gave the Clergy of the different Sects an Opportunity of Influencing their Congregations to join in the Association; and it would probably have been general among all but Quakers if the Peace had not soon interven'd.

It was thought by some of my Friends that by my Activity in these Affairs, I should offend that Sect, and thereby lose my Interest in the Assembly where they were a great Majority. A young Gentleman[9] who had likewise some Friends in the House, and wish'd to succeed me as their Clerk, acquainted me that it was decided to displace me at the next Election, and he therefore in goodwill advis'd me to resign, as more consistent with my Honor than being turn'd out. My Answer to him was, that I had read or heard of some Public Man, who made it a Rule never to ask for an Office, and never to refuse one when offer'd to him. I approve, says I, of his Rule, and will practice it with a small

7. New York gave twelve 12-pounders and two 18-pounders. They arrived in April 1748. (*P*, 3: 222.)
8. The proclamation of December 9, 1747, set

January 7, 1748, as the fasting day. (Miller, no. 431; *P*, 3: 226–29.)
9. James Read opposed BF as Clerk in 1747. (*P*, 3: 39n, 329–30.)

Addition; I shall never *ask*, never *refuse*, nor ever *resign* an Office.[1] If they will have my Office of Clerk to dispose of to another, they shall take it from me. I will not by giving it up, lose my Right of some time or other making Reprisals on my Adversaries. I heard however no more of this. I was chosen again, unanimously as usual, at the next Election. Possibly as they dislik'd my late Intimacy with the Members of Council, who had join'd the Governors in all the Disputes about military Preparations with which the House had long been harass'd, they might have been pleas'd if I would voluntarily have left them; but they did not care to displace me on Account merely of my Zeal for the Association; and they could not well give another Reason.

Indeed I had some Cause to believe, that the Defense of the Country was not disagreeable to any of them, provided they were not requir'd to assist in it. And I found that a much greater Number of them than I could have imagined, tho' against offensive War, were clearly for the defensive. Many Pamphlets *pro and con* were publish'd on the Subject, and some by good Quakers in favor of Defense,[2] which I believe convinc'd most of their younger People. A Transaction in our Fire Company gave me some Insight into their prevailing Sentiments. It had been propos'd that we should encourage the Scheme for building a Battery by laying out the present Stock, then about Sixty Pounds, in Tickets of the Lottery. By our Rules no Money could be dispos'd of but at the next Meeting after the Proposal. The Company consisted of Thirty Members,[3] of which Twenty-two were Quakers, and Eight only of other Persuasions. We eight punctually attended the Meeting; but tho' we thought that some of the Quakers would join us, we were by no means sure of a Majority. Only one Quaker, Mr. James Morris, appear'd to oppose the Measure:[4] He express'd much Sorrow that it had ever been propos'd, as he said *Friends* were all against it, and it would create such Discord as might break up the Company. We told him, that we saw no Reason for that; we were the Minority, and if *Friends* were against the Measure and outvoted us, we must and should, agreeable to the Usage of all Societies, submit.

When the Hour for Business arriv'd, it was mov'd to put the Vote. He allow'd we might then do it by the Rules, but as he could assure us that a Number of Members intended to be present for the purpose of opposing it, it would be but candid to allow a little time for their

---

1. BF repeats a letter of 1770, commenting on rumors that enemies were trying to have him fired as deputy postmaster-general. (*P*, 17: 314.) In fact, he had actively sought that post as well as his first post as assembly clerk. BF may echo Sir William Temple, who wrote "a good and wise man may not refuse [public office]. . .yet he will seldom or never seek it." (Samuel Holt Monk, ed., *Five Miscellaneous Essays by Sir William Temple* [Ann Arbor: Univ. of Michi-

gan Press, 1963], p.3.)
2. BF offered to print such arguments either in his newspaper or as pamphlets at no charge. (*P*, 3: 216.)
3. Besides BF, three others were from the original Junto. (*P*, 2: 376.)
4. For another version of this episode, see the excerpt from John Jay's journal, p. 211 of this edition.

appearing. While we were disputing this, a Waiter came to tell me two Gentlemen below desir'd to speak with me. I went down, and found they were two of our Quaker Members. They told me there were eight of them assembled at a Tavern just by; that they were determin'd to come and vote with us if there should be occasion, which they hop'd would not be the Case; and desir'd we would not call for their Assistance if we could do without it, as their Voting for such a Measure might embroil them with their Elders and Friends. Being thus secure of a Majority, I went up, and after a little seeming Hesitation, agreed to a Delay of another Hour. This Mr. Morris allow'd to be extremely fair. Not one of his opposing Friends appear'd, at which he express'd great Surprise; and at the Expiration of the Hour, we carried the Resolution Eight to one; And as of the 22 Quakers, Eight were ready to vote with us and, Thirteen by their Absence manifested that they were not inclin'd to oppose the Measure, I afterwards estimated the Proportion of Quakers sincerely against Defense as one to twenty-one only. For these were all regular Members of that Society, and in good Reputation among them, and had due Notice of what was propos'd at that Meeting.

The honorable and learned Mr. Logan, who had always been of that Sect, was one who wrote an Address[5] to them, declaring his Approbation of defensive War, and supporting his Opinion by many strong Arguments: He put into my Hands Sixty Pounds,[6] to be laid out in Lottery Tickets for the Battery, with Directions to apply what Prizes might be drawn wholly to that Service. He told me the following Anecdote of his old Master William Penn respecting Defense. He came over from England, when a young Man, with that Proprietary, and as his Secretary. It was War Time, and their Ship was chas'd by an armed Vessel suppos'd to be an Enemy. Their Captain prepar'd for Defense, but told William Penn and his Company of Quakers, that he did not expect their Assistance, and they might retire into the Cabin; which they did, except James Logan, who chose to stay upon Deck, and was quarter'd to a Gun. The suppos'd Enemy prov'd a Friend; so there was no Fighting. But when the Secretary went down to communicate the Intelligence, William Penn rebuk'd him severely for staying upon Deck and undertaking to assist in defending the Vessel, contrary to the Principles of *Friends*, especially as it had not been required by the Captain. This Reproof being before all the Company, piqu'd the Secretary, who answer'd, *I being thy Servant, why did thee not order me to come down: but thee was willing enough that I should stay and help to fight the Ship when thee thought there was Danger*.[7]

5. Printed by BF as a four-page pamphlet, dated September 22, 1741: *To Robert Jordan, and other Friends of the Yearly Meeting.* James Logan withheld the thirty copies (all that were printed) from circulation, "For we are most unhappily divided and if I cannot heal I would do nothing to widen." (Miller, no. 249.)

6. Actually £50. (P, 3: 220n., 274n.)

7. This occurred in the fall of 1699. (Tolles, *James Logan*, pp. 13–14.)

My being many Years in the Assembly, the Majority of which were constantly Quakers, gave me frequent Opportunties of seeing the Embarrassment given them by their Principle against War, whenever Application was made to them by Order of the Crown to grant Aids for military Purposes. They were unwilling to offend Government on the one hand, by a direct Refusal, and their Friends the Body of Quakers on the other, by a Compliance contrary to their Principles. Hence a Variety of Evasions to avoid Complying, and Modes of disguising the Compliance when it became unavoidable. The common Mode at last was to grant Money under the Phrase of its being *for the King's Use*, and never to enquire how it was applied. But if the Demand was not directly from the Crown, that Phrase was found not so proper, and some other was to be invented. As when Powder was wanting, (I think it was for the Garrison at Louisburg,) and the Government of New England solicited a Grant of some from Pennsylvania, which was much urg'd on the House by Governor Thomas, they could not grant Money to buy Powder, because that was an Ingredient of War, but they voted an Aid to New England, of Three Thousand Pounds, to be put into the hands of the Governor, and appropriated it for the Purchasing of Bread, Flour, Wheat, *or other Grain.* Some of the Council desirous of giving the House still farther Embarrassment, advis'd the Governor not to accept Provision, as not being the Thing he had demanded. But he replied, "I shall take the Money, for I understand very well their Meaning; *Other Grain,* is Gunpowder;" which he accordingly bought; and they never objected to it.*

It was in Allusion to this Fact, that when in our Fire Company we feared the Success of our Proposal in favor of the Lottery, and I had said to my friend Mr. Syng, one of our Members, if we fail, let us move the Purchase of a Fire Engine with the Money; the Quakers can have no Objection to that: and then if you nominate me, and I you, as a Committee for that purpose, we will buy a great Gun, which is certainly a *Fire-Engine*: I see, says he, you have improv'd by being so long in the Assembly; your equivocal Project would be just a Match for their Wheat *or other grain.*

These Embarrassments that the Quakers suffer'd from having established'd and publish'd it as one of their Principles, that no kind of War was lawful, and which being once published, they could not afterwards, however they might change their minds, easily get rid of, reminds me of what I think a more prudent Conduct in another Sect among us; that of the Dunkers.[8] I was acquainted with one of its

---

* "See the Votes" [BF note.] On July 25, 1745, the assembly voted £4000 "to the King's Use . . . to be laid out . . . in the purchase of Bread, Beef, Pork, Flour, Wheat or other Grain." (*Pa. Archives*, 8th ser., 4: 3042.)

8. So-called from the rite of baptizing through immersion ("Dunkards"), the sect settled in Pennsylvania, 1729–33, and in the 1740s num- bered about forty families at Ephrata. They became the Church of the Brethren.

Founders, Michael Welfare, soon after it appear'd. He complain'd to me that they were grievously calumniated by the Zealots of other Persuasions, and charg'd with abominable Principles and Practices to which they were utter Strangers. I told him this had always been the case with new Sects; and that to put a Stop to such Abuse, I imagin'd it might be well to publish the Articles of their Belief and the Rules of their Discipline. He said that it had been propos'd among them, but not agreed to, for this Reason; "When we were first drawn together as a Society, says he, it had pleased God to enlighten our Minds so far, as to see that some Doctrines which we once esteemed Truths were Errors, and that others which we had esteemed Errors were real Truths. From time to time he has been pleased to afford us farther Light, and our Principles have been improving, and our Errors diminishing. Now we are not sure that we are arriv'd at the End of this Progression, and at the Perfection of Spiritual or Theological Knowledge; and we fear that if we should once print our Confession of Faith, we should feel ourselves as if bound and confin'd by it, and perhaps be unwilling to receive farther Improvement; and our Successors still more so, as conceiving what we their Elders and Founders had done, to be something sacred, never to be departed from."

This Modesty in a Sect is perhaps a singular Instance in the History of Mankind, every other Sect supposing itself in Possession of all Truth, and that those who differ are so far in the Wrong:[9] Like a Man travelling in foggy Weather: Those at some Distance before him on the Road he sees wrapped up in the Fog, as well as those behind him, and also the People in the Fields on each side; but near him all appears clear.—Tho' in truth he is as much in the Fog as any of them. To avoid this kind of Embarrassment the Quakers have of late Years been gradually declining the public Service in the Assembly and in the Magistracy.[1] Choosing rather to quit their Power than their Principle.

In Order of Time I should have mentioned before, that having in 1742 invented an open Stove, for the better warming of Rooms and at the same time saving Fuel,[2] as the fresh Air admitted was warmed in Entering, I made a Present of the Model to Mr. Robert Grace, one of my early Friends, who having an Iron Furnace, found the Casting of the Plates for these Stoves a profitable Thing, as they were growing in Demand. To promote that Demand I wrote and published a Pamphlet

9. Speaking to the Constitutional Convention, September 17, 1787, BF said: "Most men, indeed, as well as most sects in religion, think themselves in possession of all truth, and that wherever others differ from them, it is so far error." (Symth 9: 607.)
1. After June 15, 1756, twenty-three of thirty-five Quakers in the assembly resigned, partly from conscience but also as scapegoats for Braddock's defeat—when the British government sought to exclude all Quakers from the assembly but came to accept the resignations of the most conservative, or, as BF called them, "All the Stiffrumps" (P, 6: 456; Hanna, pp. 96–103.)
2. BF wrote that his "common Room . . . is made twice as warm as it used to be, with a quarter of the Wood I formerly consum'd there." (P, 2: 437.) An early conservationist, BF hoped that "by the Help of this saving Invention, our Wood may grow as fast as we consume it, and our Posterity may warm themselves at a moderate Rate." (P, 2: 422 and 441.)

Entitled, An Account of the New-Invented PENNSYLVANIA FIRE PLACES: Wherein their Construction and manner of Operation is particularly explained; their Advantages above every other Method of warming Rooms demonstrated; and all Objections that have been raised against the Use of them answered and obviated, etc.[3] This Pamphlet had a good Effect. Governor Thomas was so pleas'd with the Construction of this Stove, as describ'd in it, that he offer'd to give me a Patent for the sole Vending of them for a Term of Years; but I declin'd it from a Principle which has ever weigh'd with me on such Occasions, viz. That as we enjoy great Advantages from the Inventions of Others, we should be glad of an Opportunity to serve others by any Invention of ours, and this we should do freely and generously. An Ironmonger in London, however, after assuming a good deal of my Pamphlet and working it up into his own, and making some small Changes in the Machine, which rather hurt its Operation, got a Patent for it there, and made as I was told a little Fortune by it.[4] And this is not the only Instance of Patents taken out for my Inventions[5] by others, tho' not always with the same success: which I never contested, as having no Desire of profiting by Patents myself, and hating Disputes. The Use of these Fireplaces in very many Houses both of this and the neighboring Colonies, has been and is a great Saving of Wood to the Inhabitants.

Peace being concluded, and the Association Business therefore at an End, I turn'd my Thoughts again to the Affair of establishing an Academy. The first Step I took was to associate in the Design a Number of active Friends, of whom the Junto furnished a good Part; the next was to write and publish a Pamphlet entitled, Proposals relating to the Education of Youth in Pennsylvania.[6] This I distributed among the principal Inhabitants gratis; and as soon as I could suppose their Minds a little prepared by the Perusal of it, I set on foot a Subscription for Opening and Supporting an Academy; it was to be paid in Quotas yearly for Five Years; by so dividing it I judg'd the Subscription might be larger, and I believe it was so, amounting to no less (if I remember right) than Five thousand Pounds.[7] In the Intro-

3. He printed his pamphlet in 1744 at the expense of Robert Grace who was then manufacturing the stoves. (Miller, no. 349.)

4. Probably James Sharp, who took out his patent in 1781. (J. A. Woods, "James Sharp: Common Councillor of London," in A. Whiteman, et al., Statesmen, Scholars & Merchants [1973], p. 280.)

5. BF may have had in mind Joseph Jacob's patents (of July 13, 1769, and February 1, 1783) for wheel carriages (P, 20: 157), as well as a patent for the application of copper-plate engravings to tiles and other earthen ware (P, 20: 459). Besides the stove and lightning rod, BF invented the armonica, the "long-arm" for taking down objects from high shelves, a chair that

converts to a step-ladder, a rocking chair with a fan that cools by the action of the rocker, a lamp with three wicks yielding the light of six candles, an umbrella-shaped anchor, a laundry mangle, and bifocal glasses.

6. BF's 32-page pamphlet (published in the early fall of 1749) featured an "English School" of equal importance with the more conventional, classical curriculum. This feature, BF later claimed, attracted "most of the original Benefactors" (Smyth, 10: 10) but was later subverted by the trustees. (Miller, no. 470; P, 3: 385–88; 395–421.)

7. Actually £2000, to which BF contributed the annual sum of £10. (P, 3: 429.)

duction to these Proposals, I stated their Publication not as an Act of mine, but of some *public-spirited Gentlemen*,[8] avoiding as much as I could, according to my usual Rule, the presenting myself to the Public as the Author of any Scheme for their Benefit.

The Subscribers, to carry the Project into immediate Execution chose out of their Number Twenty-four Trustees, and appointed Mr. Francis, then Attorney General, and myself, to draw up Constitutions for the Government of the Academy, which being done and signed, an House was hired, Masters engag'd and the Schools opened I think in the same Year 1749.[9] The Scholars increasing fast, the House was soon found too small, and we were looking out for a Piece of Ground properly situated, with Intention to build, when Providence threw into our way a large House ready built, which with a few Alterations might well serve our purpose, this was the Building before-mentioned erected by the Hearers of Mr. Whitefield, and was obtain'd for us in the following Manner.

It is to be noted, that the Contributions to this Building being made by People of different Sects, Care was taken in the Nomination of Trustees, in whom the Building and Ground was to be vested, that a Predominancy should not be given to any Sect, lest in time that Predominancy might be a means of appropriating the whole to the Use of such Sect, contrary to the original Intention; it was therefore that one of each Sect was appointed, viz. one Church-of-England-man, one Presbyterian, one Baptist, one Moravian, etc. Those in case of Vacancy by Death were to fill it by Election from among the Contributors. The Moravian happen'd not to please his Colleagues, and on his Death, they resolved to have no other of that Sect. The Difficulty then was, how to avoid having two of some other Sect, by means of the new Choice. Several Persons were named and for that Reason not agreed to. At length one mention'd me, with the Observation that I was merely an honest Man, and of no Sect at all; which prevail'd with them to choose me.

The Enthusiasm[1] which existed when the House was built, had long since abated, and its Trustees had not been able to procure fresh Contributions for paying the Ground Rent, and discharging some other Debts the Building had occasion'd, which embarrass'd them greatly. Being now a Member of both Sets of Trustees, that for the Building and that for the Academy, I had good Opportunity of negotiating with both, and brought them finally to an Agreement, by which the Trustees for the Building were to cede it to those of the Academy, the latter undertaking to discharge the Debt, to keep forever

8. ". . . to whom it has been privately communicated . . . they have directed a Number of Copies to be made by the Press, and properly distributed" (P, 3: 397.)

9. In fact, January 1751, and even then the remodeling was incomplete, but by September there was "above 100 Scholars, and the Number daily encreasing" (P, 4: 194.)

1. In the eighteenth century, the word *enthusiasm* implied excessive emotionalism.

open in the Building a large Hall for occasional Preachers according to the original Intention, and maintain a Free School for the Instruction of poor Children. Writings were accordingly drawn, and on paying the Debts the Trustees of the Academy were put in Possession of the Premises, and by dividing the great and lofty Hall into Stories, and different Rooms above and below for the several Schools, and purchasing some additional Ground, the whole was soon made fit for our purpose, and the Scholars remov'd into the Building. The Care and Trouble of agreeing with the Workmen, purchasing Materials, and superintending the Work fell upon me, and I went thro' it the more cheerfully, as it did not then interfere with my private Business,[2] having the Year before taken a very able, industrious and honest Partner, Mr. David Hall, with whose Character I was well acquainted, as he had work'd for me four Years. He took off my Hands all Care of the Printing-Office, paying me punctually my Share of the Profits.[3] This Partnership continued Eighteen Years, successfully for us both.

The Trustees of the Academy after a while were incorporated by a Charter from the Governor; their Funds were increas'd by Contributions in Britain, and Grants of Land from the Proprietaries, to which the Assembly has since made considerable Addition, and thus was established the present University of Philadelphia.[4] I have been continued one of its Trustees from the Beginning, now near forty Years, and have had the very great Pleasure of seeing a Number of the Youth who have receiv'd their Education in it, distinguish'd by their improv'd Abilities, serviceable in public Stations, and Ornaments to their Country.

When I disengag'd myself as above-mentioned from private Business, I flatter'd myself that, by the sufficient tho' moderate Fortune I had acquir'd, I had secur'd Leisure during the rest of my Life, for Philosophical Studies[5] and Amusements; I purchas'd all Dr. Spencer's[6] Apparatus, who had come from England to lecture here; and I proceeded in my Electrical Experiments with great Alacrity; but the Public now considering me as a Man of Leisure, laid hold of me for their Purposes; every Part of our Civil Government, and almost at the same time, imposing some Duty upon me. The Governor put me into the Commission of the Peace; the Corporation of the City chose me of the Common Council, and soon after an Alderman; and the Citizens at large chose me a Burgess to represent them in Assembly.[7]

2. Acting as a contractor did, however, take up a great deal of his time, and BF wrote, February 13, 1750: "In this Affair, as well as in other public Affairs I have been engag'd in, the Labouring Oar has lain and does lay very much upon me." (P, 3: 462.)
3. About £350 a year. The partnership with Hall began on January 21, 1748. (P, 3: 263–67.)
4. Chartered as an academy in 1743, as a college in 1755, and as the University of Pennsylvania, 1765. BF was ousted as head of the trustees in 1756, but served on the board till his death.
5. Scientific studies.
6. Archibald Spencer.
7. City Councilman, 1748; Justice of the Peace, 1749; Assemblyman, August 1751; and Alderman, October 1751.

This latter Station was the more agreeable to me, as I was at length tired with sitting there to hear Debates in which as Clerk I could take no part, and which were often so unentertaining, that I was induc'd to amuse myself with making magic Squares, or Circles, or anything to avoid Weariness.[8] And I conceiv'd my becoming a Member would enlarge my Power of doing Good. I would not however insinuate that my Ambition was not flatter'd by all these Promotions.[9] It certainly was. For considering my low Beginning they were great Things to me. And they were still more pleasing, as being so many spontaneous Testimonies of the public's good Opinion, and by me entirely unsolicited.

The Office of Justice of the Peace I tried a little, by attending a few Courts, and sitting on the Bench to hear Causes. But finding that more knowledge of the Common Law than I possess'd, was necessary to act in that Station with Credit, I gradually withdrew from it, excusing myself by my being oblig'd to attend the higher Duties of a Legislator in the Assembly. My Election to this Trust was repeated every Year for Ten Years, without my ever asking any Elector for his Vote, or signifying either directly or indirectly any Desire of Being chosen. On taking my Seat in the House, my Son was appointed their Clerk.

The Year following, a Treaty being to be held with the Indians at Carlisle, the Governor sent a Message* to the House, proposing that they should nominate some of their Members to be join'd with some Members of Council as Commissioners for that purpose. The House nam'd the Speaker (Mr. Norris) and myself; and being commission'd we went to Carlisle, and met the Indians accordingly. As those People are extremely apt to get drunk, and when so are very quarrelsome and disorderly, we strictly forbad the selling any Liquor to them; and when they complain'd of this Restriction, we told them that if they would continue sober during the Treaty, we would give them Plenty of Rum when Business was over.[1] They promis'd this; and they kept their Promise—because they could get no Liquor—and the Treaty was conducted very orderly, and concluded to mutual Satisfaction. They then claim'd and receiv'd the Rum. This was in the Afternoon. They were near 100 Men, Women and Children, and were lodg'd in

---

* "See the Votes to have this more correctly" [BF memo.] Fearing the encroaching French, some tribes asked the English to renew mutual defense treaties, asking for a conference at Carlisle, September 1753. Governor Hamilton quickly complied. He named Richard Peters; the assembly named BF and Isaac Norris. (*P*, 5: 63–64.)

8. In the squares, the sum of every row—horizontal, vertical, diagonal—is equal; in the circles, the sum of every concentric circle is equal. (Examples in *P*, 4: 397, 401.)
9. His mother reacted to news of one election: "I am glad to hear that you are so well respected in your toun for them to chuse you alderman altho I dont know what it means nor what the better you will be of it beside the honer of it." (*P*, 4: 199.)
1. The order against liquor was on September 26, 1753; the conference lasted October 1–4, and the commissioners' report was made on November 1, 1753. (*P*, 5: 65, 84–107.)

temporary Cabins built in the Form of a Square just without the Town. In the Evening, hearing a great Noise among them, the Commissioners walk'd out to see what was the Matter. We found they had made a great Bonfire in the Middle of the Square. They were all drunk, Men and Women, quarrelling and fighting. Their dark-color'd Bodies, half naked, seen only by the gloomy Light of the Bonfire, running after and beating one another with Firebrands, accompanied by their horrid Yellings, form'd a Scene the most resembling our Ideas of Hell that could well be imagin'd. There was no appeasing the Tumult, and we retired to our Lodging. At Midnight a Number of them came thundering at our Door, demanding more Rum; of which we took no Notice. The next Day, sensible they had misbehav'd in giving us that Disturbance, they sent three of their old Counsellors to make their Apology. The Orator acknowledg'd the Fault, but laid it upon the Rum; and then endeavour'd to excuse the Rum, by saying, *"The great Spirit who made all things made everything for some Use, and whatever Use he design'd anything for, that Use it should always be put to; Now, when he made Rum, he said,* LET THIS BE FOR INDIANS TO GET DRUNK WITH. *And it must be so."*—And indeed if it be the Desire of Providence to extirpate these Savages in order to make room for Cultivators of the Earth, it seems not improbable that Rum may be the appointed Means.[2] It has already annihilated all the Tribes who formerly inhabited the Seacoast.[3]

In 1751 Dr. Thomas Bond, a particular Friend of mine, conceiv'd the Idea of establishing a Hospital in Philadelphia for the Reception and Cure of poor sick Persons, whether Inhabitants of the Province or Strangers. A very beneficent Design, which has been ascrib'd to me, but was originally his. He was zealous and active in endeavouring to procure Subscriptions for it; but the Proposal being a Novelty in America, and at first not well understood, he met with small Success. At length he came to me, with the Compliment that he found there was no such thing as carrying a public-spirited Project through, without my being concern'd in it; "for, says he, I am often ask'd by those to whom I propose Subscribing, Have you consulted Franklin upon this Business? and what does he think of it? And when I tell them that I have not, (supposing it rather out of your Line,) they do not subscribe, but say they will consider of it." I enquir'd into the Nature, and probable Utility of his Scheme, and receiving from him a very satisfactory Explanation, I not only subscrib'd to it myself, but engag'd

2. BF alludes to the stage theory of civilization, which held that increasingly less *lebensraum* was necessary to support life in the four progressive "stages" (hunting, pastoral, agricultural, and manufacturing) of civilization. BF also refers ironically to the Puritan supposition that God wisely oversees all human changes by various "appointed Means."

3. In the early eighteenth century, the Virginia historian Robert Beverley and the Maryland poet Richard Lewis both lamented the vanishing of the Indian from the coastal areas. By the time that BF wrote this passage (1788), he had also read the splendid *ubi sunt* passage on the coastal Indians in chapter 4 of Crèvecoeur's *Letters of an American Farmer* (London, 1782).

heartily in the Design of Procuring Subscriptions from others. Previous however to the Solicitation, I endeavoured to prepare the Minds of the People by writing on the Subject in the Newspapers,[4] which was my usual Custom in such Cases, but which he had omitted. The Subscriptions afterwards were more free and generous, but beginning to flag, I saw they would be insufficient without some Assistance from the Assembly, and therefore propos'd to petition for it, which was done.[5] The Country Members did not at first relish the Project. They objected that it could only be serviceable to the City, and therefore the Citizens should alone be at the Expense of it; and they doubted whether the Citizens themselves generally approv'd of it: My Allegation on the contrary, that it met with such Approbation as to leave no doubt of our being able to raise 2000 Pounds by voluntary Donations, they considered as a most extravagant Supposition, and utterly impossible. On this I form'd my Plan; and asking Leave to bring in a Bill, for incorporating the Contributors, according to the Prayers of their Petition, and granting them a blank Sum of Money, which Leave was obtain'd chiefly on the Consideration that the House could throw the Bill out if they did not like it, I drew it so as to make the important Clause a conditional One, viz. "And be it enacted by the Authority aforesaid That when the said Contributors shall have met and chosen their Managers and Treasurer, *and shall have raised by their Contributions a Capital Stock of 2000 Pounds Value,* (the yearly Interest of which is to be applied to the Accommodating of the Sick Poor in the said Hospital, free of Charge for Diet, Attendance, Advice and Medicines) and *shall make the same appear to the Satisfaction of the Speaker of the Assembly* for the time being; that *then* it shall and may be lawful for the said Speaker, and he is hereby required to sign an Order on the Provincial Treasurer for the Payment of Two Thousand Pounds in two yearly Payments, to the Treasurer of the said Hospital, to be applied to the Founding, Building and Finishing of the same."—[6] This Condition carried the Bill through; for the Members who had oppos'd the Grant, and now conceiv'd they might have the Credit of being charitable without the Expense, agreed to its Passage; And then in soliciting Subscriptions among the People we urg'd the conditional Promise of the Law as an additional Motive to give, since every Man's Donation would be doubled. Thus the Clause work'd both ways. The Subscriptions accordingly soon exceeded the requisite Sum, and we claim'd and receiv'd the Public Gift, which enabled us to carry the Design into Execution. A convenient and handsome

4. *Pennsylvania Gazette* for August 8 and 15, 1751; reprinted in BF's *Some Account of the Pennsylvania Hospital* (1754). The plan leaned heavily on Defoe's plan described in *Tour thro' . . . Great Britain* (3rd ed., 1742), extracts of which are given in BF's notes. (*P*, 4: 147–54; 5: 284–330.)

5. The newspaper articles appeared six months after the petition (January 23, 1751), and even after Governor Hamilton signed the act of incorporation, May 11. (*P*, 4: 108–11.)

6. Slight differences from a contemporary copy suggest that this was written from memory. (*P*, 5: 289.)

Building[7] was soon erected, the Institution has by constant Experience been found useful, and flourishes to this Day. And I do not remember any of my political Maneuvers, the Success of which gave me at the time more Pleasure. Or that in after-thinking of it, I more easily excus'd myself for having made some Use of Cunning.

It was about this time that another Projector, the Revd. Gilbert Tennent, came to me, with a Request that I would assist him in procuring a Subscription for erecting a new Meetinghouse.[8] It was to be for the Use of a Congregation he had gathered among the Presbyterians who were originally Disciples of Mr. Whitefield. Unwilling to make myself disagreeable to my fellow Citizens, by too frequently soliciting their Contributions, I absolutely refus'd. He then desir'd I would furnish him with a List of the Names of Persons I knew by Experience to be generous and public-spirited. I thought it would be unbecoming in me, after their kind Compliance with my Solicitations, to mark them out to be worried by other Beggars, and therefore refus'd also to give such a List. He then desir'd I would at least give him my Advice. That I will readily do, said I; and, in the first Place, I advise you to apply to all those whom you know will give something; next to those whom you are uncertain whether they will give anything or not; and show them the List of those who have given: and lastly, do not neglect those who you are sure will give nothing; for in some of them you may be mistaken. He laugh'd, and thank'd me, and said he would take my Advice. He did so, for he ask'd of *everybody*; and he obtain'd a much larger Sum than he expected, with which he erected the capacious and very elegant Meetinghouse that stands in Arch Street.

Our City, tho' laid out with a beautiful Regularity, the Streets large, straight, and crossing each other at right Angles, had the Disgrace of suffering those Streets to remain long unpav'd, and in wet Weather the Wheels of heavy Carriages plough'd them into a Quagmire, so that it was difficult to cross them. And in dry Weather the Dust was offensive. I had liv'd near what was call'd the Jersey Market,[9] and saw with Pain the Inhabitants wading in Mud while purchasing their Provisions. A Strip of Ground down the middle of that Market was at length pav'd with Brick, so that being once in the Market they had firm Footing, but were often over Shoes in Dirt to get there. By talking and writing on the Subject, I was at length instrumental in getting the Street pav'd with Stone between the Market and the brick'd Foot-Pavement that was on each Side next the Houses. This for some time gave an easy Access to the Market, dry-shod. But the rest of the Street not being pav'd, whenever a Carriage came out of the Mud upon this Pavement, it shook off and left its Dirt on it, and it was soon cover'd

7. Erected in 1756 on 8th Street between Pine and Spruce. (P, 6: 61–62.)
8. His Second Presbyterian Church was organized in 1743. The new building opened in 1752 at Arch (now Mulberry) and Third Streets.
9. The Jersey Market was in the middle of Market Street, between Front and Second.

with Mire, which was not remov'd, the City as yet having no Scavengers. After some Enquiry I found a poor industrious Man, who was willing to undertake keeping the Pavement clean, by sweeping it twice a week and carrying off the Dirt from before all the Neighbors' Doors, for the Sum of Sixpence per Month, to be paid by each House. I then wrote and printed a Paper,[1] setting forth the Advantages to the Neighborhood that might be obtain'd by this small Expense; the greater Ease in keeping our Houses clean, so much Dirt not being brought in by People's Feet; the Benefit to the Shops by more Custom, as Buyers could more easily get at them, and by not having in windy Weather the Dust blown in upon their Goods, etc. etc. I sent one of these Papers to each House, and in a Day or two went round to see who would subscribe an Agreement to pay these Sixpences. It was unanimously sign'd, and for a time well executed. All the Inhabitants of the City were delighted with the Cleanliness of the Pavement that surrounded the Market; it being a Convenience to all; and this rais'd a general Desire to have all the Streets paved; and made the People more willing to submit to a Tax for that purpose.

After some time I drew a Bill for Paving[2] the City, and brought it into the Assembly. It was just before I went to England in 1757 and did not pass till I was gone, and then with an Alteration in the Mode of Assessment, which I thought not for the better, but with an additional Provision for lighting[3] as well as Paving the Streets, which was a great Improvement. It was by a private Person, the late Mr. John Clifton, his giving a Sample of the Utility of Lamps by placing one at his Door, that the People were first impress'd with the Idea of enlightening all the City. The Honor of this public Benefit has also been ascrib'd to me, but it belongs truly to that Gentleman. I did but follow his Example; and have only some Merit to claim respecting the Form of our Lamps as differing from the Globe Lamps we at first were supplied with from London. Those we found inconvenient in these respects; they admitted no Air below, the Smoke therefore did not readily go out above, but circulated in the Globe, lodg'd on its Inside, and soon obstructed the Light they were intended to afford; giving, besides, the daily Trouble of wiping them clean: and an accidental Stroke on one of them would demolish it, and render it totally useless. I therefore suggested the composing them of four flat Panes, with a long Funnel above to draw up the Smoke, and Crevices admitting Air below, to

1. No copy of this paper is known to be extant. Although not listed by Miller, it appears in William J. Campbell, *The Collection of Franklin Imprints in the Museum of the Curtis Publishing Company* (Philadelphia: Curtis Publishing Co., 1918), no. 549.
2. Since 1718, householders paved the streets with gravel voluntarily. Ordinances requiring the practice were introduced in 1736, 1739, and March 3, 1758 (probably BF's petition), but did not pass until 1762. (*Pa. Archives*, 8th ser., 6: 4743; Allinson and Penrose, pp. 29–33.)
3. An act of 1763 extended earlier ordinances for lighting (1751, 1756) and paving (1762), with funds now to come from a lottery as well as assessments, determined by a board of assessors and a board of commissioners. (Allinson and Penrose, pp. 29–33.)

facilitate the Ascent of the Smoke.[4] By this means they were kept clean, and did not grow dark in a few Hours as the London Lamps do, but continu'd bright till Morning; and an accidental Stroke would generally break but a single Pane, easily repair'd. I have sometimes wonder'd that the Londoners did not, from the Effect Holes in the Bottom of the Globe Lamps us'd at Vauxhall,[5] have in keeping them clean, learn to have such Holes in their Street Lamps. But those Holes being made for another purpose, viz. to communicate Flame more suddenly to the Wick, by a little Flax hanging down thro' them, the other Use of letting in Air seems not to have been thought of.—And therefore, after the Lamps have been lit a few Hours, the Streets of London are very poorly illuminated.

The Mention of these Improvements puts me in mind of one I propos'd when in London, to Dr. Fothergill, who was among the best Men I have known, and a great Promoter of useful Projects. I had observ'd that the Streets when dry were never swept and the light Dust carried away, but it was suffer'd to accumulate till wet Weather reduc'd it to Mud, and then after lying some Days so deep on the Pavement that there was no Crossing but in Paths kept clean by poor People with Brooms, it was with great Labour rak'd together and thrown up into Carts open above, the Sides of which suffer'd some of the Slush at every jolt on the Pavement to shake out and fall, sometimes to the Annoyance of Foot-Passengers. The Reason given for not sweeping the dusty Streets was, that the Dust would fly into the Windows of Shops and Houses. An accidental Occurrence had instructed me how much Sweeping might be done in a little Time. I found at my Door in Craven Street[6] one Morning a poor Woman sweeping my Pavement with a birch Broom.* She appeared very pale and feeble as just come out of a Fit of Sickness. I ask'd who employ'd her to sweep there. She said, "Nobody; but I am very poor and in Distress, and I sweeps before Gentlefolkeses Doors, and hopes they will give me something." I bid her sweep the whole Street clean and I would give her a Shilling. This was at 9 o'Clock. At 12 she came for the Shilling. From the Slowness I saw at first in her Working, I could scarce believe that the Work was done so soon, and sent my Servant to examine it, who reported that the whole Street was swept perfectly clean, and all the Dust plac'd in the Gutter which was in the Middle. And the next Rain wash'd it quite away, so that the Pavement and even the Kennel[7] were perfectly clean. I then judg'd that if that feeble

* "The Happiness of Man consists in small Advantages occurring every Day—" "Sleep by Sunshine" [BF's marginal notes for future topics.]

---

4. Replicas are in Independence Square, Philadelphia.
5. Fashionable London amusement park where the lamps looked like Japanese lanterns. (*Wits Magazine*, 1 [1784], 200.)

6. In 1757 to 1762 and 1764 to 1775, BF boarded in London with widow Margaret Stevenson at No. 7 Craven Street. (P, 7: 245n.)
7. Channel, gutter.

Woman could sweep such a Street in 3 Hours, a strong active Man might have done it in half the time. And here let me remark the Convenience of having but one Gutter in such a narrow Street, running down its Middle, instead of two, one on each Side near the Footway. For Where all the Rain that falls on a Street runs from the Sides and meets in the middle, it forms there a Current strong enough to wash away all the Mud it meets with: But when divided into two Channels, it is often too weak to cleanse either, and only makes the Mud it finds more fluid, so that the Wheels of Carriages and Feet of Horses throw and dash it up on the Foot Pavement which is thereby rendered foul and slippery, and sometimes splash it upon those who are walking. My Proposal communicated to the good Doctor, was as follows.

"For the more effectual cleaning and keeping clean the Streets of London and Westminister, it is proposed,

"That the several Watchmen be contracted with to have the Dust swept up in dry Seasons, and the Mud rak'd up at other Times, each in the several Streets and Lanes of his Round.

"That they be furnish'd with Brooms and other proper Instruments for these purposes, to be kept at their respective Stands, ready to furnish the poor People they may employ in the Service.

"That in the dry Summer Months the Dust be all swept up into Heaps at proper Distances, before the Shops and Windows of Houses are usually opened: when the Scavengers with close-covered Carts shall also carry it all away.

"That the Mud when rak'd up be not left in Heaps to be spread abroad again by the Wheels of Carriages and Trampling of Horses; but that the Scavengers be provided with Bodies of Carts, not plac'd high upon Wheels, but low upon Sliders; with Lattice Bottoms, which being cover'd with Straw, will retain the Mud thrown into them, and permit the Water to drain from it, whereby it will become much lighter, Water making the greatest Part of its Weight. These Bodies of Carts to be plac'd at convenient Distances, and the Mud brought to them in Wheelbarrows, they remaining where plac'd till the Mud is drain'd, and then Horses brought to draw them away."

I have since had Doubts of the Practicability of the latter Part of this Proposal, on Account of the Narrowness of some Streets, and the Difficulty of placing the Draining Sleds so as not to encumber too much the Passage: But I am still of Opinion that the former, requiring the Dust to be swept up and carried away before the Shops are open, is very practicable in the Summer, when the Days are long. For in walking thro' the Strand and Fleet Street one Morning at 7 o'Clock I observ'd there was not one shop open tho' it had been Daylight and the Sun up above three Hours. The Inhabitants of London choosing voluntarily to live much by Candle Light, and sleep by Sunshine; and yet often complain, a little absurdly, of the Duty on Candles and the high Price of Tallow.[8]

Some may think these trifling Matters not worth minding or relating. But when they consider, that tho' Dust blown into the Eyes of a single Person or into a single Shop on a windy Day, is but of small Importance, yet the great Number of the Instances in a populous City, and its frequent Repetitions give it Weight and Consequence; perhaps they will not censure very severely those who bestow some of Attention to Affairs of this seemingly low Nature. Human Felicity is produc'd not so much by great Pieces of good Fortune that seldom happen, as by little Advantages that occur every Day. Thus if you teach a poor young Man to shave himself and keep his Razor in order, you may contribute more to the Happiness of his Life than in giving him a 1000 Guineas. The Money may be soon spent, and the Regret only remaining of having foolishly consum'd it. But in the other Case he escapes the frequent Vexation of waiting for Barbers, and of their sometimes, dirty Fingers, offensive Breaths and dull Razors. He shaves when most convenient to him, and enjoys daily the Pleasure of its being done with a good Instrument.[9]—With these Sentiments I have hazarded the few preceding Pages, hoping they may afford Hints which some time or other may be useful to a City I love, having lived many Years in it very happily, and perhaps to some of our Towns in America.

Having been for some time employed by the Postmaster General of America, as his Comptroller, in regulating the several Offices, and bringing the Officers to account, I was upon his Death in 1753 appointed jointly with Mr. William Hunter to succeed him by a Commission from the Postmaster General in England. The American Office had never hitherto paid anything to that of Britain. We were to have 600 Pounds a Year between us if we could make that Sum out of the Profits of the Office. To do this, a Variety of Improvements were necessary; some of these were inevitably at first expensive; so that in the first four Years the Office became above 900 Pounds in debt to us. But it soon after began to repay us, and before I was displac'd, by a Freak[1] of the Minister's, of which I shall speak hereafter, we had brought it to yield *three times* as much clear Revenue[2] to the Crown as the Post-Office of Ireland. Since that imprudent Transaction, they have receiv'd from it,—Not one Farthing.

8. BF's bagatelle ("An Economical Project") in *Journal de Paris*, April 26, 1784, humorously calculated the expense of burning candles in the evening and proposed daylight savings time. (Smyth 9: 183–89.)
9. An echo of BF's letter, February 28, 1768, to Lord Kames: "Happiness consists more in small Conveniencies or Pleasures that occur every day, than in great Pieces of good Fortune that happen but seldom to a Man in the Course of his Life. Thus I reckon it among my Felicities that I can set my own Razor and shave my self perfectly well, in which I have a daily Pleasure, and avoid the Uneasiness one is otherwise oblig'd sometimes to suffer from dull Razors, and the dirty Fingers or bad Breath of a slovenly Barber." (P, 15: 60–61.)
1. Because of his political writings, acts, outspoken identification with America, and his role in the Hutchinson letters affair, BF was fired on January 30, 1774, the day after his public humiliation in the Cockpit. (See pp. 232–35 of this edition.)
2. Almost £3000 a year.

The Business of the Post-Office occasion'd my taking a Journey this Year to New England, where the College of Cambridge of their own Motion, presented me with the Degree of Master of Arts. Yale College in Connecticut, had before made me a similar Compliment.[3] Thus without studying in any College I came to partake of their Honors. They were confer'd in Consideration of my Improvements and Discoveries in the electric Branch of Natural Philosophy.

In 1754, War with France being again apprehended, a Congress of Commissioners from the different Colonies, was by an Order of the Lords of Trade, to be assembled at Albany, there to confer with the Chiefs of the Six Nations,[4] concerning the Means of defending both their Country and ours. Governor Hamilton, having receiv'd this Order, acquainted the House with it, requesting they would furnish proper Presents for the Indians to be given on this Occasion; and naming the Speaker (Mr. Norris) and myself, to join Mr. Thomas Penn[5] and Mr. Secretary Peters, as Commissioners to act for Pennsylvania. The House approv'd the Nomination, and provided the Goods for the Present[6], tho' they did not much like treating out of the Province, and we met the other Commissioners and met at Albany about the Middle of June. In our Way thither, I projected and drew up a Plan[7] for the Union of all the Colonies, under one Government so far as might be necessary for Defense, and other important general Purposes. As we pass'd thro' New York, I had there shown my Project to Mr. James Alexander and Mr. Kennedy, two Gentlemen of great Knowledge in public Affairs, and being fortified by their Approbation I ventur'd to lay it before the Congress. It then appear'd that several of the Commissioners had form'd Plans of the same kind. A previous Question was first taken whether a Union should be established, which pass'd in the Affirmative unanimously. A Committee was then appointed, One Member from each Colony, to consider the several Plans and report. Mine happen'd to be prefer'd, and with a few Amendments was accordingly reported.

By this Plan, the general Government was to be administered by a President General appointed and supported by the Crown, and a Grand Council to be chosen by the Representatives of the People of the several Colonies met in their respective Assemblies. The Debates

3. Actually Harvard's degree came on July 27 and Yale's on September 12, 1753. (*P*, 5: 16–17, 58.)
4. The Six Nations (or Iroquois Indians) were a confederacy (formed c. 1570) of Seneca, Cayuga, Onondaga, Oneida, Mohawk, and (in 1715) Tuscarora Indians. The colonists organized the Albany Congress because they feared that the Iroquois, exploited by New York traders, would defect to the French.
5. Not Thomas, but John Penn, according to the commissions signed by Governor James

Hamilton, May 13, 1754. (*P*, 5: 275–80.)
6. Custom dictated that presents be given the Indians.
7. The complete plan, along with James Alexander's response, is in *P*, 5: 335–38. Archibald Kennedy's manuscript of *Importance of Gaining and Preserving the Friendship of the Indians* (New York, 1751) inspired BF's thoughts on colonial union (March 20, 1751), which appeared as an appendix to that pamphlet, pp. 27–31. (*P*, 4: 117–21.)

upon it in Congress went on daily hand in hand with the Indian Business. Many Objections and Difficulties were started, but at length they were all overcome, and the Plan was unanimously agreed to, and Copies ordered to be transmitted to the Board of Trade and to the Assemblies of the several Provinces. Its Fate was singular. The Assemblies did not adopt it, as they all thought there was too much *Prerogative* in it; and in England it was judg'd to have too much of the *Democratic:*[8] The Board of Trade therefore did not approve of it; nor recommend it for the Approbation of his Majesty; but another Scheme was form'd (suppos'd better to answer the same Purpose) whereby the Governors of the Provinces with some Members of their respective Councils were to meet and order the raising of Troops, building of Forts, etc. etc. to draw on the Treasury of Great Britain for the Expense, which was afterwards to be refunded by an Act of Parliament laying a Tax on America. My Plan, with my Reasons in support of it, is to be found among my political Papers that are printed.[9]

Being the Winter following in Boston, I had much Conversation with Governor Shirley upon both the Plans. Part of what pass'd between us on the Occasion may also be seen among those Papers.[1] The different and contrary Reasons of dislike to my Plan, makes me suspect that it was really the true Medium; and I am still of Opinion it would have been happy for both Sides the Water if it had been adopted. The Colonies so united would have been sufficiently strong to have defended themselves; there would then have been no need of Troops from England; of course the subsequent Pretense for Taxing America, and the bloody Contest it occasioned, would have been avoided. But such Mistakes are not new; History is full of the Errors of States and Princes.

> "Look round the habitable World, how few
> Know their own Good, or knowing it pursue."[2]

Those who govern, having much Business on their hands, do not generally like to take the Trouble of considering and carrying into Execution new Projects. The best public Measures are therefore seldom *adopted from previous Wisdom*, but *forc'd by the Occasion*.

The Governor[3] of Pennsylvania in sending it down to the Assembly, express'd his Approbation of the Plan "as appearing to him to be drawn up with great Clearness and Strength of Judgment, and therefore recommended it as well worthy their closest and most serious

8. For the fate of the plan of union, see Gipson, 5: 143–66. Also see n. 6, p. 114 of this section.

9. [Benjamin Vaughan, ed.,] *Political, Miscellaneous, and Philosophical Pieces . . .* (1779), pp. 85–143.

1. BF's letters to Shirley, dated December 3, 4, and 22, 1754 (P, 5: 441–51), were widely reprinted, appearing first in the *London Chronicle*, February 8, 1766.

2. From Dryden's translation of Juvenal's "Satire X" (1693), ll. 1–2, showing the folly of pursuing wealth when virtue and health were enough for happiness.

3. James Hamilton.

Attention."[4] The House however, by the Management of a certain Member,[5] took it up when I happen'd to be absent, which I thought not very fair, and reprobated it without paying any Attention to it at all, to my no small Mortification.

In my Journey to Boston this Year I met at New York with our new Governor, Mr. Morris, just arriv'd there from England, with whom I had been before intimately acquainted. He brought a Commission to supersede Mr. Hamilton, who, tir'd with the Disputes his Proprietary Instructions subjected him to, had resigned. Mr. Morris ask'd me, if I thought he must expect as uncomfortable an Administration.[6] I said, No; you may on the contrary have a very comfortable one, if you will only take care not to enter into any Dispute with the Assembly; "My dear Friend, says he, pleasantly, how can you advise my avoiding Disputes. You know I love Disputing; it is one of my greatest Pleasures: However, to show the Regard I have for your Counsel, I promise you I will if possible avoid them." He had some Reason for loving to dispute, being eloquent, an acute Sophister, and therefore generally successful in argumentative Conversation. He had been brought up to it from a Boy, his Father (as I have heard) accustoming his Children to dispute with one another for his Diversion while sitting at Table after Dinner. But I think the Practice was not wise, for in the Course of my Observation, these disputing, contradicting and confuting People are generally unfortunate in their Affairs. They get Victory sometimes, but they never get Good Will, which would be of more use to them. We parted, he going to Philadelphia, and I to Boston. In returning, I met at New York with the Votes of the Assembly,[7] by which it appear'd that notwithstanding his Promise to me, he and the House were already in high Contention, and it was a continual Battle between them, as long as he retain'd the Government.

I had my Share of it; for as soon as I got back to my Seat in the Assembly, I was put on every Committee for answering his Speeches and Messages, and by the Committees always desired to make the

4. Evidently BF relied upon his memory. Actually Governor Hamilton, on August 7, 1754, speaking to the Assembly about both the "Representation of the present State of the Colonies" drawn up by the Albany commissioners and the "general Plan" for a union of the colonies "for their mutual Defense," said: "And as both those Papers appear to me to contain Matters of the utmost Consequence to the Welfare of the Colonies in general, and to have been digested and drawn up with great Clearness and Strength of Judgment, I cannot but express my Approbation of them, and do, therefore, recommend them to you as well worthy of your closest and most serious Attention." (Pa. Col. Records, v. 6 [for 1754–1756]: 135.)
5. Most likely BF's friend, Isaac Norris,

Speaker of the assembly. BF's plan would have diluted the assembly's control of finances. Thus Hamilton favored it and Norris opposed it. The House took it up on August 17, 1754. (P, 5: 376, 427n.)
6. For another version of this episode, see John Jay's journal, p. 209 of this edition. BF, on a postal inspection tour, missed two months of the legislative session, winter 1754–55, when Morris first tangled with the assembly.
7. BF was in New York in February, 1755, on his way back to Philadelphia. Since the relevant Votes and Proceedings of the House were not printed until April, 1755 (Miller, no. 595), BF probably saw the exchanges in the newspapers, perhaps those in the Pennsylvania Gazette, January 7 and 14, 1755.

Drafts. Our Answers as well as his Messages were often tart, and sometimes indecently abusive.[8] And as he knew I wrote for the Assembly, one might have imagined that when we met we could hardly avoid cutting Throats. But he was so good-natur'd a Man, that no personal Difference between him and me was occasion'd by the Contest, and we often din'd together. One Afternoon in the height of this public Quarrel, we met in the Street. "Franklin, says he, you must go home with me and spend the Evening. I am to have some Company that you will like;" and taking me by the Arm he led me to his House. In gay Conversation over our Wine after Supper he told us Jokingly that he much admir'd the Idea of Sancho Panza, who when it was propos'd to give him a Government, requested it might be a Government of *Blacks*, as then, if he could not agree with his People he might sell them.[9] One of his Friends who sat next me, says, "Franklin, why do you continue to side with these damn'd Quakers? had not you better sell them? the Proprietor would give you a good Price." The Governor, says I, had not yet *black'd* them enough. He had indeed labour'd hard to blacken the Assembly in all his Messages, but they wip'd off his Coloring as fast as he laid it on, and plac'd it in return thick upon his own Face; so that finding he was likely to be negrified himself, he as well as Mr. Hamilton, grew tir'd of the Contest, and quitted the Government.*

These public Quarrels were all at bottom owing to the Proprietaries, our hereditary Governors; who when any Expense was to be incurr'd for the Defense of their Province, with incredible Meanness instructed their Deputies to pass no Act for levying the necessary Taxes, unless their vast Estates were in the same Act expressly excused; and they had even taken Bonds of those Deputies to observe such Instructions. The Assemblies for three Years[1] held out against this Injustice, Tho' constrain'd to bend at last. At length Captain Denny, who was Governor Morris's Successor, ventur'd to disobey those Instructions; how that was brought about I shall show hereafter.†

But I am got forward too fast with my Story; there are still some Transactions to be mentioned that happened during the Administration of Governor Morris.

---

* "My Acts in Morris's time—military etc." [BF memo.]   † "Lord Loudon etc." [BF memo.]

---

8. When the Assembly replied to Governor Morris on May 17, 1755, it was no doubt Franklin who implicitly condemned him for his "Joy in Disputation" and characterized him as an enemy to Pennsylvania. (P, 6: 49.)
9. Probably a distortion of *Don Quixote*, Part One, Chapter 29, where Sancho, instead of requesting a government of blacks, grieves at the idea of governing blacks until realizing he can sell them. BF may also recall Chapter 31, where the subject is not obedience but the climate: "If the Air does not agree with me, I may transport my Black Slaves, make a Profit of them, and go live somewhere else." (Tr. by Peter Motteux, 2 vols. [1700–12], 1: 381.)
1. The conflict lasted 1751–59, but the assembly first tried to tax the proprietary estates in 1755.

War being, in a manner, commenced with France, the Government of Massachusetts Bay projected an Attack upon Crown Point,[2] and sent Mr. Quincy to Pennsylvania, and Mr. Pownall, afterwards Governor Pownall, to New York to solicit Assistance. As I was in the Assembly, knew its Temper, and was Mr. Quincy's Countryman,[3] he applied to me for my Influence and Assistance. I dictated his Address to them which was well receiv'd. They voted an Aid of Ten Thousand Pounds, to be laid out in Provisions. But the Governor refusing his Assent to their Bill,[4] (which included this with other Sums granted for the Use of the Crown) unless a Clause were inserted exempting the Proprietary Estate from bearing any Part of the Tax that would be necessary, the Assembly, tho' very desirous of making their Grant to New England effectual, were at a Loss how to, accomplish it. Mr. Quincy laboured hard with the Governor to obtain his Assent, but he was obstinate. I then suggested a Method of doing the Business without the Governor, by Orders on the Trustees of the Loan-Office, which by Law the Assembly had the Right of Drawing. There was indeed little or no Money at that time in the Office, and therefore I propos'd that the Orders should be payable in a Year and to bear an Interest of Five percent. With these Orders I suppos'd the Provisions might easily be purchas'd. The Assembly with very little Hesitation adopted the Proposal. The Orders were immediately printed, and I was one of the Committee directed to sign and dispose of them. The Fund for Paying them was the Interest of all the Paper Currency then extant in the Province upon Loan, together with the Revenue arising from the Excise, which being known to be more than sufficient, they obtain'd instant Credit, and were not only receiv'd in Payment for the Provisions, but many money'd People who had Cash lying by them, vested it in those Orders, which they found advantageous, as they bore Interest while upon hand, and might on any Occasion be used as Money: So that they were eagerly all bought up, and in a few Weeks none of them were to be seen. Thus this important Affair was by my means completed. Mr. Quincy return'd Thanks to the Assembly in a handsome Memorial,[5] went home highly pleas'd with the Success of his Embassy, and ever after bore for me the most cordial and affectionate Friendship.

The British Government not choosing to permit the Union of the Colonies, as propos'd at Albany, and to trust that Union with their Defense, lest they should thereby grow too military, and feel their own Strength, Suspicions and Jealousies at this time being entertain'd of

2. A fort at Crown Point on Lake Champlain protected the Southern approach to the St. Lawrence River.
3. A native of Massachusetts.
4. Although Morris supported BF's request, the assembly included it in an omnibus bill along with provisions for printing new money—which the Governor rejected.
5. Dated April 1, 1755. (P, 6: 3–5.)

them,[6] sent over General Braddock with two Regiments of Regular English Troops for that purpose. He landed at Alexandria in Virginia, and thence march'd to Frederick Town in Maryland, where he halted for Carriages. Our Assembly apprehending, from some Information, that he had conceived violent Prejudices[7] against them, as averse to the Service, wish'd me to wait upon him, not as from them, but as Postmaster General, under the guise of proposing to settle with him the Mode of conducting with most Celerity and Certainty the Dispatches between him and the Governors of the several Provinces, with whom he must necessarily have continual Correspondence, and of which they propos'd to pay the Expense. My Son accompanied me on this Journey. We found the General at Frederick Town, waiting impatiently for the Return of those he had sent thro' the back Parts of Maryland and Virginia to collect Waggons. I stayed with him several Days, Din'd with him daily, and had full Opportunity of removing all his Prejudices, by the Information of what the Assembly had before his Arrival actually done and were still willing to do to facilitate his Operations.

When I was about to depart, the Returns of Waggons to be obtain'd were brought in, by which it appear'd that they amounted only to twenty-five, and not all of those were in serviceable Condition. The General and all the Officers were surpris'd, declar'd the Expedition was then at an End, being impossible, and exclaim'd against the Ministers for ignorantly landing them in a Country destitute of the Means of conveying their Stores, Baggage, etc. not less than 150 Waggons being necessary. I happen'd to say, I thought it was pity they had not been landed rather in Pennsylvania, as in that Country almost every Farmer had his Waggon. The General eagerly laid hold of my Words, and said, "Then you, Sir, who are a Man of Interest there, can probably procure them for us; and I beg you will undertake it." I ask'd what Terms were to be offer'd the Owners of the Waggons; and I was desir'd to put on Paper the Terms that appear'd to me necessary. This I did, and they were agreed to, and a Commission and Instructions accordingly prepar'd immediately. What those Terms were will appear in the Advertisement I publish'd as soon as I arriv'd at Lancaster, which being, from the great and sudden Effect[8] it produc'd, a Piece of some Curiosity, I shall insert at length, as follows.*

---

* "(Here insert it, from the Quire Book of Letters written during this Transaction)." [BF note.] The "Quire Book" of Letters is not ex-tant, but the broadside advertisement itself survives. Our text follows the Boston Public Library copy of the broadside, Evans 40745.

---

6. On August 9, 1755, the Rev. James Maury wrote to a friend in England that "the great men on your side of the water have not thought proper to apply [the Albany Plan], from a principle [?keep the colonies divided and weak?] in politics, which we on this side of it think more obvious than wise or just." (Maury, p. 382.)

7. When Governor Morris warned him that the Quakers would not cooperate, Braddock threatened them (February 28, 1755) with "unpleasant Methods" if the assembly failed either to place an embargo on French goods or to provide his army with decent postal service. (*P*, 6: 13n, 54–55.)

8. BF secured over 150 wagons and almost 300 horses within a week.

ADVERTISEMENT.

Lancaster, April 26, 1755.
WHEREAS 150 Waggons, with 4 Horses to each Waggon, and 1500 Saddle or Pack-Horses are wanted for the Service of his Majesty's Forces now about to rendezvous at *Wills's* Creek;[9] and his Excellency General *Braddock* hath been pleased to empower me to contract for the Hire of the same; I hereby give Notice, that I shall attend for that Purpose at *Lancaster* from this Time till next *Wednesday* Evening; and at *York* from next *Thursday* Morning 'till *Friday* Evening; where I shall be ready to agree for Waggons and Teams, or single Horses, on the following Terms, *viz.*

1*st.* That there shall be paid for each Waggon with 4 good Horses and a Driver, *Fifteen Shillings* per *Diem*: And for each able Horse with a Pack-Saddle or other Saddle and Furniture, *Two Shillings* per *Diem*. And for each able Horse without a Saddle, *Eighteen Pence* per *Diem*.

2*dly*, That the Pay commence from the Time of their joining the Forces at *Wills's* Creek (which must be on or before the twentieth of *May* ensuing) and that a reasonable Allowance be made over and above for the Time necessary for their travelling to *Wills's* Creek and home again after their Discharge.

3*dly*, Each Waggon and Team, and every Saddle or Pack Horse is to be valued by indifferent Persons, chosen between me and the Owner, and in Case of the Loss of any Waggon, Team or other Horse in the Service, the Price according to such Valuation, is to be allowed and paid.

4*thly*, Seven Days' Pay is to be advanced and paid in hand by me to the Owner of each Waggon and Team, or Horse, at the Time of contracting, if required; and the Remainder to be paid by General *Braddock*, or by the Paymaster of the Army, at the Time of their Discharge, or from time to time as it shall be demanded.

5*thly*, No Drivers of Waggons, or Persons taking care of the hired Horses, are on any Account to be called upon to do the Duty of Soldiers, or be otherwise employ'd than in conducting or taking Care of their Carriages and Horses.

6*thly*, All Oats, Indian Corn or other Forage, that Waggons or Horses bring to the Camp more than is necessary for the Subsistence of the Horses, is to be taken for the Use of the Army, and a reasonable Price paid for it.

Note. My Son *William Franklin*, is empowered to enter into like Contracts with any Person in *Cumberland* County.

B. FRANKLIN.

---

9. In Western Maryland, where Wills Creek flows into the Potomac River, the site of present-day Cumberland.

To the Inhabitants of the Counties of Lancaster,
York, and Cumberland.

Friends and Countrymen,
    BEING occasionally at the Camp at *Frederick* a few Days since, I found the General and Officers of the Army extremely exasperated, on Account of their not being supplied with Horses and Carriages, which had been expected from this Province as most able to furnish them; but thro' the Dissensions between our Governor and Assembly, Money had not been provided nor any Steps taken for that Purpose.
    It was proposed to send an armed Force immediately into these Counties, to seize as many of the best Carriages and Horses as should be wanted, and compel as many Persons into the Service as would be necessary to drive and take care of them.
    I apprehended that the Progress of a Body of Soldiers thro' these Counties on such an Occasion, especially considering the Temper they are in, and their Resentment against us, would be attended with many and great Inconveniences to the Inhabitants; and therefore more willingly undertook the Trouble of trying first what might be done by fair and equitable Means.
    The People of these back Counties have lately complained to the Assembly that a sufficient Currency was wanting; you have now an Opportunity of receiving and dividing among you a very considerable Sum; for if the Service of this Expedition should continue (as it's more than probable it will) for 120 Days, the Hire of these Waggons and Horses will amount to upwards of *Thirty thousand Pounds*, which will be paid you in Silver and Gold of the King's Money.
    The Service will be light and easy, for the Army will scarce march above 12 Miles per Day, and the Waggons and Baggage Horses, as they carry those Things that are absolutely necessary to the Welfare of the Army, must march with the Army and no faster, and are, for the Army's sake, always plac'd where they can be most secure, whether on a March or in Camp.
    If you are really, as I believe you are, good and loyal Subjects to His Majesty, you may now do a most acceptable Service, and make it easy to yourselves; for three or four of such as cannot separately spare from the Business of their Plantations a Waggon and four Horses and a Driver, may do it together, one furnishing the Waggon, another one or two Horses, and another the Driver, and divide the Pay proportionably between you. But if you do not this Service to your King and Country voluntarily, when such good Pay and reasonable Terms are offered you, your Loyalty will be strongly suspected; the King's Business must be done; so many brave Troops, come so far for your Defense, must not stand idle, thro' your backwardness to do what may be reasonably expected from you; Waggons and Horses must be had; violent Measures will probably be used; and you will be to seek for a Recompense where you can find it, and your Case perhaps be little pitied or regarded.

I have no particular Interest in this Affair; as (except the Satisfaction of endeavouring to do Good and prevent Mischief) I shall have only my Labor, for my Pains. If this Method of obtaining the Waggons and Horses is not like to succeed, I am oblig'd to send Word to the General in fourteen Days; and I suppose Sir *John St. Clair* the Hussar,[1] with a Body of Soldiers, will immediately enter the Province, for the Purpose aforesaid, of which I shall be sorry to hear, because
I am,

very sincerely and truly
your Friend and Well-wisher, B. FRANKLIN

I receiv'd of the General about 800 Pounds[2] to be disburs'd in Advance-money to the Waggon-Owners etc.: but that Sum being insufficient, I advanc'd upwards of 200 Pounds more, and in two Weeks, the 150 Waggons with 259 carrying Horses were on their March for the Camp. The Advertisement promised Payment according to the Valuation, in case any Waggon or Horse should be lost. The Owners however, alledging they did not know General Braddock, or what Dependance might be had on his Promise, insisted on my Bond for the Performance, which I accordingly gave them.

While I was at the Camp, supping one Evening with the Officers of Colonel Dunbar's Regiment, he represented to me his Concern for the Subalterns, who he said were generally not in Affluence, and could ill afford in this dear[3] Country to lay in the Stores that might be necessary in so long a March thro' a Wilderness where nothing was to be purchas'd. I commiserated their Case, and resolved to endeavour procuring them some Relief. I said nothing however to him of my Intention, but wrote the next Morning to the Committee of Assembly, who had the Disposition of some public Money, warmly recommending the Case of these Officers to their Consideration, and proposing that a Present should be sent them of Necessaries and Refreshments. My Son, who had had some Experience of a Camp Life, and of its Wants, drew up a List for me, which I enclos'd in my Letter. The Committee approv'd, and used such Diligence, that conducted by my Son, the Stores arrived at the Camp as soon as the Waggons.[4] They consisted of 20 Parcels, each containing

1. BF's contemporaries considered the latter part of the Advertisement especially effective. Braddock's secretary, William Shirley, Jr., wrote: "I cannot but honour Franklin for the last clause of his advertisement" (*P*, 6: 22n.). BF's political enemy William Smith chafed under "The wicked insinuation that the Germans would perhaps be obliged sometime to plough the Lord Proprietor's Manors, as in Germany" (Hanna, p. 216, n. 22). And the *Gentleman's Magazine*, 25 (August, 1755), 378, reported: "The *Germans* having formerly lived under despotic power, knew the *Hussars* too well to doubt their serving themselves."

2. £795.15.6. (*P*, 6: 17.)

3. Costly.

4. Sixty wagons were ready to roll from Philadelphia by May 30.

6 lb. Loaf Sugar
6 lb. good Muscovado[5] Ditto
1 lb. good Green Tea
1 lb. good Bohea[6] Ditto
6 lb. good ground Coffee
6 lb. Chocolate
½ Hundredweight[7] best white Biscuit
½ lb. Pepper
1 Quart best white Wine Vinegar
1 Gloucester Cheese
1 Keg containing 20 lb. good Butter
2 Doz. old Madeira Wine
2 Gallons Jamaica Spirits[8]
1 Bottle Flour of Mustard
2 well-cur'd Hams
½ Doz. dried Tongues
6 lb. Rice
6 lb. Raisins.

These 20 Parcels well pack'd were plac'd on as many Horses, each Parcel with the Horse, being intended as a Present for one Officer. They were very thankfully receiv'd, and the Kindness acknowledg'd by Letters to me from the Colonels of both Regiments in the most grateful Terms. The General too was highly satisfied with my Conduct in procuring him the Waggons, etc. and readily paid my Account of Disbursements; thanking me repeatedly and requesting my farther Assistance in sending Provisions after him. I undertook this also, and was busily employ'd in it till we heard of his Defeat, advancing, for the Service, of my own Money, upwards of 1000 Pounds Sterling,[9] of which I sent him an Account. It came to his Hands luckily for me a few Days before the Battle, and he return'd me immediately an Order on the Paymaster for the round Sum of 1000 Pounds, leaving the Remainder to the next Account. I consider this Payment as good Luck; having never been able to obtain that Remainder; of which more hereafter.

This General was I think a brave Man, and might probably have made a Figure as a good Officer in some European War. But he had too much self-confidence, too high an Opinion of the Validity of Regular Troops, and too mean a One of both Americans and Indians.[1] George Croghan, our Indian Interpreter, join'd him on his March with 100 of those People, who might have been of great Use to his

---

5. Brown sugar.
6. Black tea.
7. BF used the abbreviation "C$^{wt.}$"
8. Rum.
9. Expenses came to £1005 even before BF advertised for wagons in Lancaster. (*P*, 6: 18.)

1. Braddock thus shared the contemptuous opinion of Americans as soldiers held by most British army officers. BF replied to such opinions at length in his "Defense of the Americans," May 9, 1759. (*P*, 8: 340–56.)

Army as Guides, Scouts, etc. if he had treated them kindly; but he slighted and neglected them, and they gradually left him.

In Conversation with him one day, he was giving me some Account of his intended Progress. "After taking Fort Duquesne,[2] says he, I am to proceed to Niagara; and having taken that, to Frontenac,[3] if the Season will allow time; and I suppose it will; for Duquesne can hardly detain me above three or four Days; and then I see nothing that can obstruct my March to Niagara."—Having before revolv'd in my Mind the long Line his Army must make in their March, by a very narrow Road to be cut for them thro' the Woods and Bushes; and also what I had read of a former Defeat of 1500 French who invaded the Iroquois Country,[4] I had conceiv'd some Doubts, and some Fears for the Event of the Campaign. But I ventur'd only to say, To be sure, Sir, if you arrive well before Duquesne, with these fine Troops so well provided with Artillery, that Place, not yet completely fortified, and as we hear with no very strong Garrison, can probably make but a short Resistance. The only Danger I apprehend of Obstruction to your March, is from Ambuscades of Indians, who by constant Practice are dextrous in laying and executing them. And the slender Line near four Miles long, which your Army must make, may expose it to be attack'd by Surprise in its Flanks, and to be cut like a Thread into several Pieces, which from their Distance cannot come up in time to support each other.

He smil'd at my Ignorance, and replied, "These Savages may indeed be a formidable Enemy to your raw American Militia; but, upon the King's regular and disciplin'd Troops, Sir, it is impossible they should make any Impression." I was conscious of an Impropriety in my Disputing with a military Man in Matters of his Profession, and said no more.—The Enemy however did not take the Advantage of his Army which I apprehended its long Line of March expos'd it to, but let it advance without Interruption till within 9 Miles of the Place; and then when more in a Body, (for it had just pass'd a River, where the Front had halted till all were come over) and in a more open Part of the Woods than any it had pass'd, attack'd its advanc'd Guard, by a heavy Fire from behind Trees and Bushes; which was the first Intelligence the General had of an Enemy's being near him.[5] This Guard being disordered, the General hurried the Troops up to their Assistance, which was done in great Confusion thro' Waggons, Baggage and Cattle; and presently the Fire came upon their Flank; the Officers being on Horseback were more easily distinguish'd, pick'd out as

2. Now Pittsburgh.
3. Now Kingston, Ontario.
4. BF may have recalled Lahontan's exaggerated report of the ambush of Marquis de Brisay de Denonville by the Iroquois in 1687: "Had you but seen, Sir, what Disorder our Troops and Militia were in amidst the thick trees, you would have joyn'd with me, in thinking that several thousands of *Europeans* are no more than a sufficient number to make head against five hundred Barbarians." (*New Voyages to North America* [London, 1703], I, 76.)
5. Actually, the British were not ambushed. Both sides were surprised. (Gipson, 6: 94–95.)

Marks, and fell very fast; and the Soldiers were crowded together in a Huddle, having or hearing no Orders, and standing to be shot at till two-thirds of them were killed, and then being seiz'd with a Panic the whole fled with Precipitation. The Waggoners took each a Horse out of his Team, and scamper'd; their Example was immediately follow'd by others, so that all the Waggons, Provisions, Artillery and Stores were left to the Enemy.

The General being wounded was brought off with Difficulty, his Secretary Mr. Shirley[6] was killed by his Side, and out of 86 Officers 63 were killed or wounded, and 714 Men killed out of 1100. These 1100 had been picked Men, from the whole Army, the Rest had been left behind with Colonel Dunbar, who was to follow with the heavier Part of the Stores, Provisions and Baggage. The Fliers, not being pursu'd, arriv'd at Dunbar's Camp, and the Panic they brought with them instantly seiz'd him and all his People. And tho' he had now above 1000 Men, and the Enemy who had beaten Braddock did not at most exceed 400,[7] Indians and French together; instead of Proceeding and endeavouring to recover some of the lost Honor, he order'd all the Stores, Ammunitions, etc. to be destroy'd, that he might have more Horses to assist his Flight towards the Settlements, and less Lumber to remove. He was there met with Requests from the Governors of Virginia, Maryland and Pennsylvania, that he would post his Troops on the Frontiers so as to afford some Protection to the Inhabitants; but he continu'd his hasty March thro' all the Country, not thinking himself safe till he arriv'd at Philadelphia, where the Inhabitants could protect him.[8] This whole Transaction gave us Americans the first Suspicion that our exalted Ideas of the Prowess of British Regulars had not been well founded.

In their first March too, from their Landing till they got beyond the Settlements, they had plundered and stripped the Inhabitants, totally ruining some poor Families, besides insulting, abusing and confining the People if they remonstrated.[9] This was enough to put us out of Conceit of such Defenders if we had really wanted any. How different was the Conduct of our French Friends in 1781, who during a March thro' the most inhabited Part of our Country, from Rhode Island to Virginia, near 700 Miles, occasion'd not the smallest Complaint, for

---

6. William Shirley, Jr., son of BF's friend, Governor Shirley of Massachusetts.

7. Closer to 800, vs. the British 1459–of whom 977 were killed or wounded. Of the French and Indians, only 25 were killed and 25 wounded. (Douglas F. Leach, *Arms for Empire*, New York, 1973, p. 367; Gipson, 6: 96.)

8. His troops spent a month at Philadelphia (August 29—October 1, 1755) on their way to New York.

9. James Maury protested that Braddock made "free with the liberties of the people and the constitutions of the several governments." (Maury, p. 383.) Dr. Alexander Hamilton reported that Braddock "treated our Country planters with great harshness & Severity, taking from them in a Rapacious manner their bought white Servants to Recruit his Army." Braddock also disgusted Hamilton by treating all colonists, even the Governors, "as if they had been infinitely his Inferiors." (Breslaw, p. 131.) And John Mercer testified that Braddock "Oppressed, Insulted and treated [the colonists] like rebells." (Davis, p. 27n.)

the Loss of a Pig, a Chicken, or even an Apple!

Captain Orme, who was one of the General's Aides de Camp, and being grievously wounded was brought off with him, and continu'd with him to his Death, which happen'd in a few Days, told me, that he was totally silent, all the first Day, and at Night only said, *Who'd have thought it?* that he was silent again the following Days, only saying at last, *We shall better know how to deal with them another time;* and died a few Minutes after.

The Secretary's Papers with all the General's Orders, Instructions and Correspondence falling into the Enemy's Hands, they selected and translated into French a Number of the Articles, which they printed to prove the hostile Intentions of the British Court before the Declaration of War. Among these I saw some Letters of the General to the Ministry speaking highly of the great Service I had rendered the Army, and recommending me to their Notice.[1] David Hume too, who was some Years after Secretary to Lord Harcourt when Minister in France, and afterwards to General Conway when Secretary of State, told me he had seen among the Papers in that Office Letters from Braddock highly recommending me. But the Expedition having been unfortunate, my Service it seems was not thought of much Value, for those Recommendations were never of any Use to me.

As to Rewards from himself, I ask'd only one, which was, that he would give Orders to his Officers not to enlist any more of our bought servants,[2] and that he would discharge such as had been already enlisted. This he readily granted, and several were accordingly re-turn'd to their Masters on my Application. Dunbar, when the Command devolv'd on him, was not so generous. He Being at Philadelphia on his Retreat, or rather Flight, I applied to him for the Discharge of the Servants of three poor Farmers of Lancaster County that he had enlisted, reminding him of the late General's Orders on that head. He promis'd me, that if the Masters would come to him at Trenton, where he should be in a few Days on his March to New York, he would there deliver their Men to them. They accordingly were at the Expense and Trouble of going to Trenton, and there he refus'd to perform his Promise, to their great Loss and Disappointment.

As soon as the Loss of the Waggons and Horses was generally known, all the Owners came upon me for the Valuation which I had given Bond to pay. Their Demands gave me a great deal of Trouble, my acquainting them that the Money was ready in the Paymaster's

---

1. Jacob Nicholas Moreau, *Mémoire* . . . (Paris, 1756; tr. New York [2 eds.] and Philadelphia, 1757; London, 1759). Braddock's commendation, dated June 5, 1755, says BF acted "with so much Goodness and Readiness, that it is almost the first Instance of Integrity, Address and Ability that I have seen in all these Provinces" (Philadelphia ed., p. 242, Evans

7897.)

2. Braddock's temporary successor, Governor (now General) Shirley, on September 19, 1755, ordered Dunbar "in the Strongest Manner" to avoid enlisting indentured servants, but the practice was allowed by a law the following year. (P, 6: 190, 227n, 474–75.)

Hands, but that Orders for paying it must first be obtained from General Shirley, and my assuring them that I had applied to that General by Letter, but he being at a Distance an Answer could not soon be receiv'd, and they must have Patience; all this was not sufficient to satisfy, and some began to sue me. General Shirley at length reliev'd me from this terrible Situation, by appointing Commissioners to examine the Claims and ordering Payment.[3] They amounted to near twenty Thousand Pound, which to pay would have ruined me.

Before we had the News of this Defeat, the two Doctors Bond[4] came to me with a Subscription Paper, for raising Money to defray the Expense of a grand Firework, which it was intended to exhibit at a Rejoicing on receipt of the News of our Taking Fort Duquesne. I looked grave and said, "it would, I thought, be time enough to prepare for the Rejoicing when we knew we should have occasion to rejoice."—They seem'd surpris'd that I did not immediately comply with their Proposal. "Why, the D—l," says one of them, "you surely don't suppose that the Fort will not be taken?" "I don't know that it will not be taken; but I know that the Events of War are subject to great Uncertainty."—I gave them the Reasons of my doubting. The Subscription was dropped, and the Projectors thereby miss'd that Mortification they would have undergone if the Firework had been prepared. Dr. Bond on some other Occasions afterwards said, that he did not like Franklin's forebodings.

Governor Morris who had continually worried the Assembly with Message after Message before the Defeat of Braddock, to beat them into the making of Acts to raise Money for the Defense of the Province without Taxing among others the Proprietary Estates, and had rejected all their Bills for not having such an exempting Clause, now redoubled his Attacks, with more hope of Success, the Danger and Necessity being greater. The Assembly however continu'd firm, believing they had Justice on their side, and that it would be giving up an essential Right, if they suffered the Governor to amend their Money-Bills. In one of the last, indeed, which was for granting 50,000 Pounds, his propos'd Amendment was only of a single Word; the Bill express'd that all Estates real and personal were to be taxed, those of the Proprietaries *not* excepted. His Amendment was; For *not* read *only*.[5] A small but very material Alteration! However, when the News of this Disaster reach'd England, our Friends there whom we had taken care to furnish with all the Assembly's Answers to the Governor's Messages, rais'd a Clamour against the Proprietaries for their Mean-

3. As Commander-in-Chief, William Shirley asked Governor Morris to name the commission, and BF was able to send warrants to the paymaster on October 16, 1755. Nevertheless, BF continued to be vexed by the unpaid account for decades. (*P*, 6: 190; 19: 73–74.)
4. Thomas and Phineas Bond.
5. Morris suggested this amendment on November 17, 1755. (*Pa. Col. Records*, 6: 702.)

ness and Injustice in giving their Governor such Instructions, some going so far as to say that by obstructing the Defense of their Province, they forfeited their Right to it. They were intimidated by this, and sent Orders to their Receiver General to add 5000 Pounds of their Money to whatever Sum might be given by the Assembly, for such Purpose.[6] This being notified to the House, was accepted in Lieu of their Share of a general Tax, and a new Bill was form'd with an exempting Clause which pass'd accordingly. By this Act I was appointed one of the Commissioners for disposing of the Money, 60,000 Pounds. I had been active[7] in modelling it, and procuring its Passage: and had at the same time drawn a Bill for establishing and disciplining a voluntary Militia, which I carried thro' the House without much Difficulty, as Care was taken in it, to leave the Quakers at their Liberty.[8]

To promote the Association necessary to form the Militia, I wrote a Dialogue,* stating and answering all the Objections I could think of to such a Militia, which was printed and had as I thought great Effect. While the several Companies in the City and Country were forming and learning their Exercise, the Governor prevail'd with me to take Charge of our Northwestern Frontier,[9] which was infested by the Enemy, and provide for the Defense of the Inhabitants by raising Troops, and building a Line of Forts. I undertook this military Business, tho' I did not conceive myself well-qualified for it. He gave me a Commission with full Powers and a Parcel of blank Commissions for Officers to be given to whom I thought fit. I had but little Difficulty in raising Men, having soon 560 under my Command. My Son who had in the preceding War been an Officer in the Army rais'd against Canada,[1] was my Aide de Camp, and of great Use to me. The Indians had burned Gnadenhut,[2] a Village settled by the Moravians,[3] and

---

* "This Dialogue and the Militia Act, are in the *Gentleman's Magazine* for February and March 1756" [BF note.] The "Dialogue between X, Y, and Z" appeared first in the *Pennsylvania* Gazette, December 18, 1755, and was reprinted in the *Gentleman's Magazine*, 26 (March, 1756), 122–26. (P, 6: 295–306.) The Militia Act appeared in the *Gentleman's Magazine* in February (26:83–84). (P, 6: 266–73.)

---

6. On November 24, 1755, Governor Morris informed the assembly of the proprietors' free gift of £5,000, which the House accepted in lieu of taxes on the proprietary lands, and so passed a tax bill of £55,000 exempting the proprietors' estates—only to learn that the proprietors' £5,000 consisted mainly of uncollectible bad debts. (Hutson, pp. 24–26; P, 6: 257n, 480–83.)

7. BF served on the commission from December 1755 through December 1756, pending his mission to England.

8. BF's bill exempted conscientious objectors, made enlistment voluntary, and minimized military discipline—and therefore was vetoed by the Ministry, July 7, 1756. (P, 6: 266–73.)

9. BF first went as one of a three-man commis-

sion (December 18–31, 1755) but was named military and civilian commander January 5, 1756, just after the Governor got word of the latest attack on Gnadenhütten. (For a chronology and map, see P, 6: 307–12.)

1. William Franklin was an ensign in a proposed expedition against Canada, 1746–47, during King George's War. He spent most of the time in bivouac at Albany. (P, 3: 89.)

2. Gnadenhütten, present-day Lehightown, Pennsylvania, had been burned November 24, 1755, and the new troops stationed there had been defeated on January 1, 1756. (P, 6: 340–52.)

3. Church of the United Brethren, immigrants from Saxony in 1735, chose Bethlehem as their North American headquarters in 1744.

massacred the Inhabitants, but the Place was thought a good Situation for one of the Forts. In order to march thither, I assembled the Companies at Bethlehem, the chief Establishment of those People. I was surprised to find it in so good a Posture of Defense. The Destruction of Gnadenhut had made them apprehend Danger. The principal Buildings were defended by a Stockade: They had purchased a Quantity of Arms and Ammunition from New York, and had even plac'd Quantities of small Paving Stones between the Windows of their high Stone Houses, for their Women to throw down upon the Heads of any Indians that should attempt to force into them. The armed Brethren too, kept Watch, and reliev'd as methodically as in any Garrison Town. In Conversation[4] with Bishop Spangenberg, I mention'd this my Surprise; for knowing they had obtain'd an Act of Parliament exempting them from military Duties in the Colonies, I had suppos'd they were conscientiously scrupulous of bearing Arms. He answer'd me, "That it was not one of their establish'd Principles; but that at the time of their obtaining that Act, it was thought to be a Principle with many of their People. On this Occasion, however, they to their Surprise found it adopted by but a few." It seems they were either deceiv'd in themselves, or deceiv'd the Parliament. But Common Sense aided by present Danger, will sometimes be too strong for whimsical Opinions.

It was the Beginning of January when we set out upon this Business of Building Forts. I sent one Detachment towards the Minisinks,[5] with Instructions to erect one for the Security of that upper Part of the Country; and another to the lower Part, with similar Instructions. And I concluded to go myself with the rest of my Force to Gnadenhut,[6] where a Fort was thought more immediately necessary. The Moravians procur'd me five Waggons for our Tools, Stores, Baggage, etc. Just before we left Bethlehem, Eleven Farmers who had been driven from their Plantations by the Indians, came to me, requesting a supply of Fire Arms, that they might go back and fetch off their Cattle. I gave them each a Gun with suitable Ammunition. We had not march'd many Miles before it began to rain, and it continu'd raining all Day. There were no Habitations on the Road, to shelter us, till we arriv'd near Night, at the House of a German, where and in his Barn we were all huddled together as wet as Water could make us. It was well we were not attack'd in our March, for Our Arms were of the most

4. December 30, 1755. (Nolan, *General Benjamin Franklin*, p. 38.)
5. The area, named after Northern Delaware Indians, was Northeastern Pennsylvania, where Fort Norris (fifteen miles northeast of Gnadenhütten, near present Kresgeville, Monroe County) was built. Franklin built Fort Allen (now Weissport, Carbon County), and the party

sent to the "lower Part" built Fort Franklin (about fifteen miles southwest of Gnadenhütten, south of Snyders, Schuylkill County) (Nolan, *General Benjamin Franklin*, map on end-papers.)
6. He had 500 men when he left Bethlehem. (Nolan, *General Benjamin Franklin*, p. 60.)

ordinary Sort, and our Men could not keep their Gunlocks[7] dry. The
Indians are dextrous in Contrivances for that purpose, which we had
not. They met that Day the eleven poor Farmers above-mentioned
and kill'd Ten of them. The one who escap'd inform'd that his and his
Companions' Guns would not go off, the Priming being wet with the
Rain.[8]

The next Day being fair, we continu'd our March and arriv'd at the
desolated Gnadenhut. There was a Saw Mill near, round which were
left several Piles of Boards, with which we soon hutted ourselves; an
Operation the more necessary at that inclement Season, as we had no
Tents. Our first Work was to bury more effectually the Dead we found
there, who had been half interr'd by the Country People. The next
Morning our Fort was plann'd and mark'd out, the Circumference
measuring 455 feet, which would require as many Palisades to be
made of Trees one with another of a Foot Diameter each. Our Axes, of
which we had 70 were immediately set to work, to cut down Trees; and
our Men being dextrous in the Use of them, great Dispatch was made.
Seeing the Trees fall so fast, I had the Curiosity to look at my Watch
when two Men began to cut at a Pine. In 6 Minutes they had it upon
the Ground; and I found it of 14 Inches Diameter. Each Pine made
three Palisades of 18 Feet long, pointed at one End. While these were
preparing, our other Men, dug a Trench all round of three feet deep in
which the Palisades were to be planted, and our Waggons, the Body
being taken off, and the fore and hind Wheels separated by taking out
the Pin which united the two Parts of the Perch,[9] we had 10 Carriages
with two Horses each, to bring the Palisades from the Woods to the
Spot.[1] When they were set up, our Carpenters built a Stage of Boards
all round within, about 6 Feet high, for the Men to stand on when to
fire thro' the Loopholes. We had one swivel Gun which we mounted
on one of the Angles; and fired it as soon as fix'd, to let the Indians
know, if any were within hearing, that we had such Pieces. And thus
our Fort, (if such a magnificent Name may be given to so miserable a

7. Firing mechanisms that required priming powder.
8. The farmers, led by Christian Bomper, were attacked on Saturday, January 17, Franklin's fiftieth birthday. Evidently Franklin had detached a few soldiers to accompany them. One soldier and one servant (John Adam Huth) survived. Huth's account in the *Pennsylvania Gazette*, January 29, 1756, testifies that at least he, his father, and Christian Bomper (as well as the Indians) were able to fire their weapons.
9. The shaft connecting front and rear axles.
1. The *Pennsylvania Gazette*, January 29, 1756, quoted BF's dispatch: "We have been here [Gnadenhütten] since Sunday Afternoon. That Day [Jan. 18] we had only Time to get up some Shelter from the Weather and the

Enemy. Yesterday [Jan. 19] all Day it rained, with so thick a Fog, that we could not see round us, so as either to chuse a Place for a Fort, or find Materials to build it. In the Night it cleared up, and this Morning [Jan. 20] we determined, marked out the Ground, and at Ten o'clock set the Men to work, and they have worked with such Spirit, that now, at Half past Three in the Afternoon, all the Logs for the Stockade are cut, to the Number of 450, being most of them more than a Foot in Diameter, and 15 Feet long. The Trench to set them in being three Feet deep, and two wide, is dug; 14 Pair of Wheels are drawing them together . . . The Fort will be about 125 Feet long, and 50 broad." (*P*, 6: 362–63; BF's sketch of fort, p. 367.)

Stockade) was finished in a Week, tho' it rain'd so hard every other Day that the Men could not work.

This gave me occasion to observe, that when Men are employ'd they are best contented. For on the Days they work'd they were good-natur'd and cheerful; and with the consciousness of having done a good Day's work they spent the Evenings jollily; but on the idle Days they were mutinous and quarrelsome, finding fault with their Pork, the Bread, etc. and in continual ill-humor: which put me in mind of a Sea-Captain, whose Rule it was to keep his Men constantly at Work; and when his Mate once told him that they had done everything, and there was nothing farther to employ them about; O, says he, *make them scour the Anchor*.

This kind of Fort, however contemptible, is a sufficient Defense against Indians who have no Cannon. Finding ourselves now posted securely, and having a Place to retreat to on Occasion, we ventur'd out in Parties to scour the adjacent Country. We met with no Indians, but we found the Places on the neighboring Hills where they had lain to watch our Proceedings. There was an Art in their Contrivance of these Places that seems worth mention. It being Winter, a Fire was necessary for them. But a common Fire on the Surface of the Ground would by its Light have discover'd their Position at a Distance. They had therefore dug Holes in the Ground about three feet Diameter, and somewhat deeper. We saw where they had with their Hatchets cut off the Charcoal from the Sides of burned Logs lying in the Woods. With these Coals they had made small Fires in the Bottom of the Holes, and we observ'd among the Weeds and Grass the Prints of their Bodies made by their laying all round with their Legs hanging down in the Holes to keep their Feet warm, which with them is an essential Point. This kind of Fire, so manag'd, could not discover them either by its Light, Flame, Sparks or even Smoke. It appear'd that their Number was not great, and it seems they saw we were too many to be attack'd by them with Prospect of Advantage.

We had for our Chaplain a zealous Presbyterian Minister, Mr. Beatty, who complain'd to me that the Men did not generally attend his Prayers and Exhortations. When they enlisted, they were prom- is'd, besides Pay and Provisions, a Gill[2] of Rum a Day, which was punctually serv'd out to them, half in the Morning and the other half in the Evening, and I observ'd they were as punctual in attending to receive it. Upon which I said to Mr. Beatty, "It is perhaps below the Dignity of your Profession to act as Steward of the Rum. But if you were to deal it out, and only just after Prayers, you would have them all about you." He lik'd the Thought, undertook the Office, and with the help of a few hands to measure out the Liquor executed it to Satisfac- tion; and never were Prayers more generally and more punctually

2. A quarter-pint.

attended. So that I thought this Method preferable to the Punishments inflicted by some military Laws for Non-Attendance on Divine Service.

I had hardly finish'd this Business, and got my Fort well stor'd with Provisions, when I receiv'd a Letter from the Governor, acquainting me that he had called[3] the Assembly, and wish'd my Attendance there, if the Posture of Affairs on the Frontiers was such that my remaining there was no longer necessary. My Friends too of the Assembly pressing me by their Letters to be if possible at the Meeting, and my three intended Forts being now completed, and the Inhabitants contented to remain on their Farms under that Protection, I resolved to return. The more willingly as a New England Officer, Colonel Clapham,[4] experienc'd in Indian War, being on a Visit to our Establishment, consented to accept the Command. I gave him a Commission, and parading the Garrison had it read before them, and introduc'd him to them as an Officer who from his Skill in Military Affairs, was much more fit to command them than myself; and giving them a little Exhortation took my Leave. I was escorted as far as Bethlehem, where I rested a few Days, to recover from the Fatigue I had undergone.[5] The first Night being in a good Bed, I could hardly sleep, it was so different from my hard Lodging on the Floor of our Hut at Gnaden, wrapped only in a Blanket or two.[6]

While at Bethlehem, I enquir'd a little into the Practices of the Moravians. Some of them had accompanied me, and all were very kind to me. I found they work'd for a common Stock, ate at common Tables, and slept in common Dormitories, great Numbers together. In the Dormitories I observ'd Loopholes at certain Distances all along just under the Ceiling, which I thought judiciously plac'd for Change of Air. I was at their Church, where I was entertain'd with good Music, the Organ being accompanied with Violins, Hautboys,[7] Flutes, Clarinets, etc. I understood that their Sermons were not usually preached to mix'd Congregations of Men, Women and Children, as is our common Practice; but that they assembled sometimes the married Men, at other times their Wives, then the Young Men, the young Women, and the little Children, each Division by itself. The Sermon I heard was to the latter, who came in and were plac'd in Rows on

3. The assembly would normally have met in March but Morris capriciously called it for February.

4. William Clapham, a captain rather than colonel, had conned the assembly out of £100 in anticipation of this appointment. He proved ineffectual and was dismissed. (Nolan, *General Benjamin Franklin*, p. 84.)

5. BF hurried back to Philadelphia, staying only the night of February 4, 1756, at Bethlehem, in order to forestall the military reception and parade planned in his honor. (P,

6: 308.) On his way to the frontier, he had stayed a week in Bethlehem and heard the Moravian music on Saturday, January 10, and attended church service the next day. (Nolan, *General BF*, pp. 63–64.) Either BF misremembered the sequence or misrepresented it because he did not want to interrupt the narrative earlier.

6. On January 25, 1756, however, he said he slept "on deal feather beds, in warm blankets" (P, 6: 365.) BF was probably recalling the march to Gnadenhütten.

7. Oboes.

Benches, the Boys under the Conduct of a young Man their Tutor, and the Girls conducted by a young Woman. The Discourse seem'd well adapted to their Capacities, and was delivered in a pleasing familiar Manner, coaxing them as it were to be good. They behav'd very orderly, but look'd pale and unhealthy, which made me suspect they were kept too much within-doors, or not allow'd sufficient Exercise. I enquir'd concerning the Moravian Marriages, whether the Report was true that they were by Lot? I was told that Lots were us'd only in particular Cases. That generally when a young Man found himself dispos'd to marry, he inform'd the Elders of his Class, who consulted the Elder Ladies that govern'd the young Women. As these Elders of the different Sexes were well acquainted with the Tempers and Dispositions of their respective Pupils, they could best judge what Matches were suitable, and their Judgments were generally acquiesc'd in. But if for example it should happen that two or three young Women were found to be *equally* proper for the young Man, the Lot was then recurr'd to. I objected, If the Matches are not made by the mutual Choice of the Parties, some of them may chance to be very unhappy. And so they may, answer'd my Informer,[8] if you let the Parties choose for themselves.—Which indeed I could not deny.

Being return'd to Philadelphia, I found the Association went on swimmingly, the Inhabitants that were not Quakers having pretty generally come into it, form'd themselves into Companies, and chosen their Captains, Lieutenants and Ensigns according to the new Law.[9] Dr. B.[1] visited me, and gave me an Account of the Pains he had taken to spread a general good Liking to the Law, and ascrib'd much to those Endeavours. I had had the Vanity to ascribe all to my Dialogue; However, not knowing but that he might be in the right, I let him enjoy his Opinion, which I take to be generally the best way in such Cases.—The Officers meeting chose me[2] to be Colonel of the Regiment; which I this time accepted. I forget how many Companies we had, but We paraded about 1200 well-looking Men,[3] with a Company of Artillery who had been furnish'd with 6 brass Field Pieces, which they had become so expert in the Use of as to fire twelve times in a Minute. The first Time[4] I review'd my Regiment, they accompanied me to my House, and would salute me with some Rounds fired before my Door, which shook down and broke several Glasses of my Electrical Apparatus. And my new Honor prov'd not much less brittle; for all

---

8. Conceivably his host at Bethlehem, Timothy Horsfield.
9. The militia elections of December 22–24 caused great excitement, even rioting, especially when Governor Morris refused to recognize the polls.
1. WTF (1818), I, 121, has "Dr. Bond." Dr. Thomas Bond led reasoned reaction to the Governor's opposition. (P, 6: 385.)
2. BF was elected Colonel on February 12, and

officially commissioned on February 24, 1756. (P, 6: 409–12.)
3. A rival said the troops numbered no more than 600 or 700 "*Men and Boys,*" while the *Pennsylvania Gazette,* March 25, 1756, reported a gala parade on March 18 of "Upwards of 1000 able-bodied effective Men, besides Officers." (P, 6: 411n.)
4. The first review was held on February 28.

our Commissions were soon after broke by a Repeal of the Law in England.[5]

During the short time of my Colonelship, being about to set out on a Journey to Virginia, the Officers of my Regiment took it into their heads that it would be proper for them to escort me out of town as far as the Lower Ferry. Just as I was getting on Horseback, they came to my door, between 30 and 40, mounted, and all in their Uniforms. I had not been previously acquainted with the Project, or I should have prevented it, being naturally averse to the assuming of State on any Occasion, and I was a good deal chagrin'd at their Appearance, as I could not avoid their accompanying me. What made it worse, was, that as soon as we began to move, they drew their Swords, and rode with them naked all the way.[6] Somebody[7] wrote an Account of this to the Proprietor, and it gave him great Offense. No such Honor had been paid him when in the Province; nor to any of his Governors; and he said it was only proper to Princes of the Blood Royal; which may be true for aught I know, who was, and still am, ignorant of the Etiquette, in such Cases. This silly Affair, however greatly increas'd his Rancour against me, which was before not a little, on account of my Conduct in the Assembly, respecting the Exemption of his Estate from Taxation, which I had always oppos'd very warmly, and not without severe Reflections on his Meanness and Injustice in contending for it. He accus'd me to the Ministry as being the great Obstacle to the King's Service, preventing by my Influence in the House the proper Forming of the Bills for raising Money; and he instanc'd this Parade with my Officers as a Proof of my having an Intention to take the Government of the Province out of his Hands by Force. He also applied[8] to Sir Everard Fawkener, then Post Master General, to deprive me of my Office. But this had no other Effect, than to procure from Sir Everard a gentle Admonition.

Notwithstanding the continual Wrangle between the Governor and the House, in which I as a Member had so large a Share, there still subsisted a civil Intercourse between that Gentleman and myself, and we never had any personal Difference.[9] I have sometimes since thought that his little or no Resentment against me for the Answers it was known I drew up to his Messages, might be the Effect of professional Habit, and that, being bred a Lawyer, he might consider us both as merely Advocates for contending Clients in a Suit, he for the

5. October 1756. (P, 6: 411n.)

6. March 19, 1756. BF said on November 5, 1756, that 20 officers and 30 men accompanied him about 3 miles to the ferry, and rode with swords drawn "to the End of the Street, which is about 200 Yards." (P, 7: 13.)

7. Richard Peters reported to Thomas Penn that the troops acted "as if he had been a member of the Royal Family or Majesty itself." (P, 7: 73.)

8. August 13, 1756. (Hanna, pp. 87, 214n.) Penn had written Richard Peters on January 10, 1756, that he would "always despise" BF. (Hutson, p. 42.)

9. In 1783 BF remembered Governor Robert Hunter Morris as "a good natured Man—had Talents & Learning but his Imagination was too strong & he was not deep in any Thing." (See p. 209 this edition.)

Proprietaries and I for the Assembly. He would therefore sometimes call in a friendly way to advise with me on difficult Points, and sometimes, tho' not often, take my Advice. We acted in Concert to supply Braddock's Army with Provisions, and When the shocking News arriv'd of his Defeat, the Governor sent in haste for me, to consult with him on Measures for preventing the Desertion of the back Counties. I forget now the Advice I gave, but I think it was, that Dunbar should be written to and prevail'd with if possible to post his Troops on the Frontiers for their Protection, till by Reinforcements from the Colonies, he might be able to proceed on the Expedition.—[1] And after my Return from the Frontier, he would have had me undertake the Conduct of such an Expedition with Provincial Troops, for the Reduction of Fort Duquesne, Dunbar and his Men being otherwise employ'd; and he propos'd to commission me as General. I had not so good an Opinion of my military Abilities as he profess'd to have; and I believe his Professions must have exceeded his real Sentiments: but probably he might think that my Popularity would facilitate the Raising of the Men, and my Influence in Assembly the Grant of Money to pay them;—and that, perhaps, without taxing the Proprietary Estate. Finding me not so forward to engage as he expected, the Project was dropped: and he soon after left the Government, being superseded by Captain Denny.[2]

Before I proceed in relating the Part I had in public Affairs under this new Governor's Administration, it may not be amiss here to give some Account of the Rise and Progress of my Philosophical Reputation.

In 1746 being at Boston, I met there with a Dr. Spencer,[3] who was lately arrived from Scotland, and show'd me some electric Experiments. They were imperfectly perform'd, as he was not very expert; but being on a Subject quite new to me, they equally surpris'd and pleas'd me. Soon after my Return to Philadelphia, our Library Company receiv'd from Mr. Peter Collinson, F.R.S. of London a Present of a Glass Tube,[4] with some Account of the Use of it in making such Experiments. I eagerly seiz'd the Opportunity of repeating what I had seen at Boston, and by much Practice acquir'd great Readiness in performing those also which we had an Account of from England, adding a Number of new Ones. I say much Practice, for my House was continually full for some time, with People who came to see these new Wonders. To divide a little this Incumbrance among my Friends, I

1. On July 28, 1755, the assembly asked the Governor to request Colonel Thomas Dunbar to post his troops on the frontier. (*P*, 6: 111–12.)
2. News of William Denny's appointment reached Philadelphia in mid-July 1756.
3. BF met Archibald Spencer in Boston in May and June 1743. When BF again visited Boston in November–December, 1746, Spencer was settled in Virginia. (Lemay, "Franklin's 'Dr. Spence,'" pp. 200, 204.)
4. Solid glass rod rubbed briskly with cloth pads to produce electrical charges. BF thanked Collinson for his "kind present of an electric tube, with directions for using it" on March 28, 1747. (*P*, 3: 118.)

caused a Number of similar Tubes to be blown at our Glass-House, with which they furnish'd themselves, so that we had at length several Performers. Among these the principal was Mr. Kinnersley,[5] an ingenious Neighbor, who being out of Business, I encouraged to undertake showing the Experiments for Money, and drew up for him two Lectures,[6] in which the Experiments were rang'd in such Order and accompanied with Explanations, in such Method, as that the foregoing should assist in Comprehending the following. He procur'd an elegant Apparatus for the purpose, in which all the little Machines that I had roughly made for myself, were nicely form'd by Instrument-makers. His Lectures were well attended and gave great Satisfaction; and after some time he went thro' the Colonies exhibiting them in every capital Town, and pick'd up some Money. In the West India Islands indeed it was with Difficulty the Experiments could be made, from the general Moisture of the Air.

Oblig'd as we were to Mr. Collinson for his Present of the Tube, etc., I thought it right he should be inform'd of our Success in using it, and wrote him several Letters containing Accounts of our Experiments.[7] He got them read in the Royal Society, where they were not at first thought worth so much Notice as to be printed in their Transactions. One Paper which I wrote for Mr. Kinnersley, on the Sameness of Lightning with Electricity,[8] I sent to Dr. Mitchel, an Acquaintance of mine, and one of the Members also of that Society; who wrote me word that it had been read but was laughed at by the Connoisseurs:[9] The Papers however being shown to Dr. Fothergill, he thought them of too much value to be stifled, and advis'd the Printing of them. Mr. Collinson then gave them to *Cave* for publication in his Gentleman's Magazine; but he chose to print them separately in a Pamphlet,[1] and Dr. Fothergill wrote the Preface. *Cave* it seems judg'd rightly for his Profit; for by the Additions that arriv'd afterwards they swell'd to a Quarto Volume, which has had five Editions, and cost him nothing for Copy-money.[2]

It was however some time before those Papers were much taken Notice of in England. A Copy of them happening to fall into the

5. Ebenezer Kinnersley gave the first public lectures on the Franklinian theory of electricity (including the hypothesis of the electrical nature of lightning) in Annapolis, May 15, 1749. (Lemay, *Ebenezer Kinnersley*, pp. 67–70.)

6. These are omitted from *P*, but may be found in Lemay, *Ebenezer Kinnersley*, pp. 68–70.

7. The earlier ones are dated May 25 and July 28, 1747, and April 29, 1749. (*P*, 3: 126–35, 156–64, 352–76.)

8. This letter is dated April 29, 1749. (See *P*, 3: 365, where the original addressee is mistakenly identified as Dr. John Mitchell.)

9. Mitchell's letter is not extant, but one in the *Gentleman's Magazine* for June, 1752 (22: 263) states that the experts at first "ridiculed" BF's theory of the electrical nature of lightning. Other aspects of his theories won immediate acceptance, with William Watson, England's foremost electrical scientist, reporting on them in a paper read to the Royal Society on January 21, 1748.

1. *Experiments and Observations on Electricity, made at Philadelphia in America* (1751), appeared in April 1751. Edward Cave's *Gentleman's Magazine* printed notices of BF's work in January and May 1750 (20: 34–35, 208; *P*, 3: 472–3; 4: 126).

2. Payment to author; royalties.

Hands of the Count de Buffon, a Philosopher deservedly of great Reputation in France, and indeed all over Europe, he prevail'd with M. Dalibard to translate them into French; and they were printed at Paris.[3] The Publication offended the Abbé Nollet, Preceptor in Natural Philosophy to the Royal Family, and an able Experimenter, who had form'd and publish'd a Theory of Electricity, which then had the general Vogue.[4] He could not at first believe that such a Work came from America, and said it must have been fabricated by his Enemies at Paris, to decry his System. Afterwards having been assur'd that there really existed such a Person as Franklin of Philadelphia, which he had doubted, he wrote and published a Volume of Letters,[5] chiefly address'd to me, defending his Theory, and denying the Verity of my Experiments and of the Positions deduc'd from them. I once purpos'd answering the Abbé, and actually began the Answer.[6] But on Consideration that my Writings contain'd only a Description of Experiments, which any one might repeat and verify, and if not to be verified could not be defended; or of Observations, offer'd as Conjectures, and not delivered dogmatically, therefore not laying me under any Obligation to defend them; and reflecting that a Dispute between two Persons writing in different Languages might be lengthened greatly by mis-translations, and thence misconceptions of one another's Meaning, much of one of the Abbé's Letters being founded on an Error in the Translation;[7] I concluded to let my Papers shift for themselves; believing it was better to spend what time I could spare from public Business in making new Experiments, than in Disputing about those already made. I therefore never answer'd M. Nollet; and the Event gave me no Cause to repent my Silence; for my Friend M. le Roy of the Royal Academy of Sciences took up my Cause and refuted him,[8] my Book was translated into the Italian, German and Latin Languages,[9] and the Doctrine it contain'd was by degrees universally adopted by the Philosophers of Europe in preference to that of the Abbé, so that he liv'd to see himself the last of his Sect:

3. *Expériences et Observations* . . . (Paris, 1752; 2nd ed. 1756). Jacques Barbeu-Dubourg made a new translation in 1773.

4. Abbé Nollet, "Conjectures sur les Causes de l'Electricite" *Historie de l'Academie Royale des Sciences (Mémoires*, 1745) pp. 107-51.

5. *Lettres sur l'Electricité* (Paris, 1753). The ensuing controversy was duly reported in the Royal Academy's *Mémoires* for 1753 (pp. 429–46, 447–74, 475–514).

6. In January, 1754, when he intended to show Nollet was guilty of falsifying experiments in order to bolster his theory. (*P*, 5: 186.) BF indirectly answered Nollet by including David Colden's "Remarks on the Abbé Nollet's Letters on Electricity" in the 1754 edition of his *Experiments and Observations*. (*P*, 5: 135–44.)

7. Where the preface of BF's *Letters* said, "He

exhibits to our consideration" the existence of electrical charges, Dalibard translated it to say that BF had "discovered" them. (*Gentleman's Magazine*, 26 [1756], 513–14.)

8. Le Roy's "Mémoire sur l'électricité," in the *Histoire de l'Académie Royale des Sciences*, 1753, pp. 447–74; and ibid., 1755, pp. 22–27 (*P*, 6: 99n). Giambatista Beccaria of Italy also replied to Nollet (*P*, 5: 395n).

9. Carlo Giuseppe Campi, tr., *Scelta di Lettere e di Opuscoli del Signor Beniamino Franklin* (Milan, 1774); Johan Carl Wilcke, tr., *Des Herrn Benjamin Franklins Esq. Briefe von der Elektricität* (Leipzig, 1758). A Latin translation, evidently by Jan Ingenhousz, was made but not printed (*P*, 4: 127n.); Peter W. van der Pas, "The Latin Translation of BF's Letters on Electricity," *Isis*, 69 (1978), 82–85.

except Mr. B——[1] his Elève and immediate Disciple.

What gave my Book the more sudden and general Celebrity, was the Success of one of its propos'd Experiments,[2] made by Messrs. Dalibard and Delor, at Marly, for drawing Lightning from the Clouds. This engag'd the public Attention everywhere. M. Delor, who had an Apparatus for experimental Philosophy, and lectur'd in that Branch of Science, undertook to repeat what he call'd the *Philadelphia Experiments*, and after they were performed before the King and Court, all the Curious of Paris flock'd to see them.[3] I will not swell this Narrative with an Account of that capital Experiment, nor of the infinite Pleasure I receiv'd in the Success of a similar one I made soon after with a Kite at Philadelphia, as both are to be found in the Histories of Electricity.[4] Dr. Wright, an English Physician then at Paris, wrote to a Friend who was of the Royal Society an Account of the high Esteem my Experiments were in among the Learned abroad, and of their Wonder that my Writings had been so little noticed in England.[5] The Society on this resum'd the Consideration of the Letters that had been read to them, and the celebrated Dr. Watson drew up a summary Account of them, and of all I had afterwards sent to England on the Subject, which he accompanied with some Praise of the Writer.[6] This Summary was then printed in their Transactions And some Members of the Society in London, particularly the very ingenious Mr. Canton, having verified the Experiment of procuring Lightning from the Clouds by a Pointed Rod,[7] and acquainting them with the Success, they soon made me more than Amends for the Slight with which they had before treated me. Without my having made any Application for that Honor, they chose me a Member, and voted that I should be excus'd the customary Payments, which would

1. Mathurin-Jaques Brisson.

2. Using the tall, pointed rods on towers that Franklin had suggested to attract lightning, Dalibard and Delor verified the electrical nature of lightning on May 10 and 18, 1752. In June, 1752, before learning of their success, BF achieved similar results in his famous kite experiment (P, 4: 302–10), thus demonstrating not only that lightning was electrical but also that electricity was a fundamental aspect of the universe, not merely an amusing phenomenon of laboratories.

3. Playful and entertaining experiments included an attempted kiss "repuls'd by the Ladies Fire" and "A Leaf of the most weighty Metals, suspended in the Air." (Lemay, *Kinnersley*, p. 69.)

4. Joseph Priestley, *History and Present State of Electricity* (1767), reports the kite experiment, pp. 179–81, evidently from BF's own statement. An earlier notice in the *Pennsylvania Gazette*, October 19, 1752, was reprinted in the London press. (P, 4: 366–69.)

5. Edward Wright's letter has not been found, but it was probably written after the successful French experiments in May, 1752.

6. BF evidently has in mind William Watson's report of the English success in verifying the electrical nature of lightning, December 21, 1752 (P, 4: 390–92). Actually, however, Watson had followed the progress of BF's experiments with great interest and reported his observations in detail to the Royal Society (e.g., January 21, 1748, January 11, 1750, and June 6, 1751; see P, 3: 135n, 457–8; 4: 136–42). Franklin probably tended to forget or downplay Watson's early reports of his experiments because Watson misleadingly stressed the similarities of BF's experiments to his own traditional ones and because Watson did not appreciate the significance of BF's radical theoretical advances. (Cohen, *Franklin and Newton*, pp. 442–52, 463–67.)

7. Canton succeeded in verifying BF's experiment on July 20, 1752. Besides Canton, John Bevis and Benjamin Wilson also made experiments in the summer of 1752. (P, 4: 390–92.)

have amounted to twenty-five Guineas, and ever since have given me their Transactions gratis. They also presented me with the Gold Medal of Sir Godfrey Copley for the Year 1753,[8] the Delivery of which was accompanied by a very handsome Speech of the President Lord Macclesfield, wherein I was highly honored.[9]

Our new Governor, Captain Denny, brought over for me the before-mentioned Medal from the Royal Society, which he presented to me at an Entertainment given him by the City. He accompanied it with very polite Expressions of his Esteem for me, having, as he said been long acquainted with my Character. After Dinner, when the Company as was customary at that time, were engag'd in Drinking, he took me aside into another Room, and acquainted me that he had been advis'd by his Friends in England to cultivate a Friendship with me, as one who was capable of giving him the best Advice, and of contributing most effectually to the making his Administration easy. That he therefore desired of all things to have a good Understanding with me; and he begg'd me to be assur'd of his Readiness on all Occasions to render me every Service that might be in his Power. He said much to me also of the Proprietor's good Dispositions towards the Province, and of the Advantage it might be to us all, and to me in particular, if the Opposition that had been so long continu'd to his Measures, were dropped, and Harmony restor'd between him and the People, in effecting which it was thought no one could be more serviceable than myself, and I might depend on adequate Acknowledgements and Recompenses, etc. etc.

The Drinkers finding we did not return immediately to the Table, sent us a Decanter of Madeira, which the Governor made liberal Use of, and in proportion became more profuse of his Solicitations and Promises. My Answers were to this purpose, that my Circumstances, Thanks to God, were such as to make Proprietary Favors unnecessary to me; and that being a Member of the Assembly I could not possibly accept of any; that however I had no personal Enmity to the Proprietary, and that whenever the public Measures he propos'd should appear to be for the Good of the People, no one should espouse and forward them more zealously than myself, my past Opposition having been founded on this, that the Measures which had been urg'd were evidently intended to serve the Proprietary Interest with great Prejudice to that of the People. That I was much obliged to him (the Governor) for his Professions of Regard to me, and that he might rely

8. BF was elected to membership in the Royal Society on April 29, 1756, three years after receiving the Copley Medal (P, 6: 375–76.)
9. Actually, the medal and speech (made November 30, 1753) were given to Collinson for delivery to BF. Collinson sent them to BF by William Smith (future Provost of the Philadel-

phia Academy and political enemy of BF) in early 1754. (P, 5: 126–34, 334.) Governor Denny did not come over until August 1756. Perhaps Denny delivered BF's diploma of membership in the Royal Society at an entertainment the City Corporation of New York held for Denny on August 22.

on everything in my Power to make his Administration as easy to him as possible, hoping at the same time that he had not brought with him the same unfortunate Instructions[1] his Predecessor had been hamper'd with. On this he did not then explain himself. But when he afterwards came to do Business with the Assembly they appear'd again, the Disputes were renewed, and I was as active as ever in the Opposition, being the Penman first of the Request to have a Communication of the Instructions, and then of the Remarks upon them, which may be found in the Votes of the Time, and in the Historical Review I afterwards publish'd;[2] but between us personally no Enmity arose; we were often together, he was a Man of Letters, had seen much of the World, and was very entertaining and pleasing in Conversation. He gave me the first Information that my old Friend James Ralph was still alive, that he was esteem'd one of the best political Writers in England, had been employ'd in the Dispute between Prince Frederick[3] and the King, and had obtain'd a Pension of Three Hundred a Year; that his Reputation was indeed small as a Poet, *Pope* having damn'd his Poetry in the Dunciad,[4] but his Prose was thought as good as any Man's.

The Assembly finally, finding the Proprietaries obstinately persisted in manacling their Deputies with Instructions inconsistent not only with the Privileges of the People, but with the Service of the Crown, resolv'd to petition the King against them, and appointed me their Agent to go over to England to present and support the Petition.[5] The House had sent up a Bill to the Governor granting a Sum of Sixty Thousand Pounds for the King's Use, (10,000 Pounds of which was subjected to the Orders of the then General Lord Loudon,) which the Governor absolutely refus'd to pass, in Compliance with his Instructions.[6] I had agreed with Captain Morris[7] of the Packet at New York for my Passage, and my Stores were put on board, when Lord Loudon arriv'd at Philadelphia, expressly, as he told me to endeavour an Accomodation between the Governor and Assembly, that his

1. As proprietor, Thomas Penn gave detailed instructions to his governors. The assembly distinguished these from instructions issued by the Ministry, which they willingly obeyed. The basic question was who would control the money appropriated by the assembly—Penn insisted on executive rather than legislative control. (Hutson, passim.)

2. The assembly requested Governor Denny's instructions on August 31, 1756 (*P*, 6: 496) and made its long remarks on them on September 23, 1756 (*P*, 6: 516). Richard Jackson wrote *Historical Review of the Constitution and Government of Pennsylvania* (1759), but it was based upon materials furnished by BF who paid for its publication on behalf of the assembly (*P*, 8: 360–61).

3. Frederic Louis, Prince of Wales (1707–51) and father of George III (1738–1820), feuded with his own father George II (1683–1760) for refusing to increase his allowance.

4. See n. 2, p. 31 of this section.

5. The assembly originally, on January 28, resolved to send "a Commission, or Commissioners," but settled on BF on February 3, perhaps partially because of his great scientific reputation abroad. (*P*, 7: 109–11.)

6. The quarrel between Governor Denny and the assembly took place September 13–16, 1756 (*P*, 6: 504–15.)

7. William Morris captained the mail boat, *Halifax*, which sailed from New York on March 15, 1757. (*P*, 7: 133n.)

Majesty's Service might not be obstructed by their Dissensions: Accordingly he desir'd the Governor and myself to meet him[8] that he might hear what was to be said on both sides.

We met and discuss'd the Business. In behalf of the Assembly I urg'd all the Arguments that may be found in the public Papers of that Time, which were of my Writing, and are printed with the Minutes of the Assembly and the Governor pleaded his Instructions, the Bond he had given to observe them, and his Ruin if he disobey'd: Yet seem'd not unwilling to hazard himself if Lord Loudon would advise it. This his Lordship did not choose to do,[9] tho' I once thought I had nearly prevail'd with him to do it; but finally he rather chose to urge the Compliance of the Assembly; and he entreated me to use my Endeavours with them for that purpose; declaring he could spare none of the King's Troops for the Defense of our Frontiers, and that if we did not continue to provide for that Defense ourselves they must remain expos'd to the Enemy. I acquainted the House with what had pass'd, and (presenting them with a Set of Resolutions I had drawn up,[1] declaring our Rights, and that we did not relinquish our Claim to those Rights but only suspended the Exercise of them on this Occasion thro' *Force*, against which we protested) they at length agreed to drop that Bill and frame another[2] conformable to the Proprietary Instructions. This of course the Governor pass'd, and I was then at Liberty to proceed on my Voyage: but in the meantime the Packet had sail'd with my Sea-Stores, which was some Loss to me, and my only Recompense was his Lordship's Thanks for my Service, all the Credit of obtaining the Accommodation falling to his Share.

He set out for New York before me; and as the Time for dispatching the Packet Boats, was in his Disposition, and there were two then remaining there, one of which he said was to sail very soon, I requested to know the precise time, that I might not miss her by any Delay of mine. His Answer was, I have given out that she is to sail on Saturday next, but I may let you know *entre nous*, that if you are there by Monday morning you will be in time, but do not delay longer. By some Accidental Hindrance at a Ferry, it was Monday Noon before I arrived, and I was much afraid she might have sailed as the Wind was fair, but I was soon made easy by the Information that she was still in the Harbor, and would not move till the next Day.

One would imagine that I was now on the very point of Departing for Europe. I thought so; but I was not then so well acquainted with his Lordship's Character, of which *Indecision* was one of the Strongest Features. I shall give some Instances. It was about the Beginning of

8. On February 20, 1757, Loudoun invited BF to help with a council of war with southern governors which met in Philadelphia, March 14. (*P*, 7: 133.)
9. In fact, Loudoun initiated, and Denny passed the bill on March 21, 1757, much to

Thomas Penn's disgust. (*P*, 7: 152–53n.) Because of the emergency, the assembly had already (February 3) exempted the proprietary estates from taxation. (*P*, 7:121–32.)
1. January 26, 1757. (*P*, 7: 106–09.)
2. March 21, 1757. (*P*, 7: 149–52.)

April that I came to New York, and I think it was near the End of June
before we sail'd.[3] There were then two of the Packet Boats which had
been long in Port, but were detain'd for the General's Letters, which
were always to be ready tomorrow. Another Packet arriv'd, and she too
was detain'd, and before we sail'd a fourth was expected. Ours was the
first to be dispatch'd, as having been there longest. Passengers were
engag'd in all, and some extremely impatient to be gone, and the
Merchants uneasy about their Letters, and the Orders they had given
for Insurance (it being War-time) and for Fall Goods. But their
Anxiety avail'd nothing; his Lordship's Letters were not ready. And yet
whoever waited on him found him always at his Desk, Pen in hand,
and concluded he must needs write abundantly.[4]

Going myself one Morning to pay my Respects, I found in his
Antechamber one Innis, a Messenger of Philadelphia, who had come
from thence express, with a Packet from Governor Denny for the
General. He deliver'd to me some Letters from my Friends there,
which occasion'd my enquiring when he was to return and where he
lodg'd, that I might send some Letters by him. He told me he was
order'd to call tomorrow at nine for the General's Answer to the
Governor, and should set off immediately. I put my Letters into his
Hands the same Day. A Fortnight after I met him again in the same
Place. So you are soon return'd, Innis! *Return'd*; No, I am not *gone*
yet.—How so?—I have call'd here by Order every Morning these two
Weeks past for his Lordship's Letter, and it is not yet ready.—Is it
possible, when he is so great a Writer, for I see him constantly at his
Scritoire. Yes, says Innis, but he is like St. George on the Signs,
always on horseback, and never rides on.[5] This Observation of the
Messenger was it seems well founded; for when in England, I understood that Mr. Pitt gave it as one Reason for Removing this General,
and sending Amherst and Wolf, *that the Ministers never heard from
him, and could not know what he was doing.*[6]

This daily Expectation of Sailing, and all the three Packets going
down Sandy hook, to join the Fleet there, the Passengers thought it
best to be on board, lest by a sudden Order the Ships should sail, and

3 BF left Philadelphia April 4, arrived at New
York April 8, and finally boarded the *General
Wall* June 5. But even then the boat anchored
off Sandy Hook until June 20, sailing with Loudoun's convoy on June 23. (P, 7: 174.) Loudoun was awaiting reinforcements from England before obeying orders to attack Quebec.
They were expected in mid-May but did not
arrive at Halifax until July 10. (Gipson, 7:
101–2.)
4. A meticulous record-keeper, he wrote detailed memoranda on conversations, meetings,
and even letters he received. (Loudoun mss.,
Huntington Library.)
5. The old proverb (Wilson, pp. 693–94) was

based on a common tavern sign that showed St.
George astride a horse with a slain dragon at its
feet. Since BF previously used the proverb in
Poor Richard, August 1738, and in a letter of
June 26, 1755 (P, 2: 195; 6: 87), he may have
made up this anecdote.
6. Said the *London Gazetteer,* December 22,
1757: "Except a written scrap of paper, no advice has been received from him since June or
July last." His London agent reported another
complaint—that he had slighted the governors
by corresponding with Franklin. (Huntington
Library ms. LO/5140.) Loudoun lost his
command December 30, 1757.

they be left behind. There if I remember right we were about Six Weeks, consuming our Sea Stores, and oblig'd to procure more. At length the Fleet sail'd, the General and all his Army on board, bound to Louisburg with Intent to besiege and take that Fortress; all the Packet Boats in Company, ordered to attend the General's Ship, ready to receive his Dispatches when those should be ready. We were out 5 Days before we got a Letter with Leave to part; and then our Ship quitted the Fleet and steered for England. The other two Packets he still detain'd, carried them with him to Halifax, where he stayed some time to exercise the Men in sham Attacks upon sham Forts, then alter'd his Mind as to besieging Louisburg, and return'd to New York with all his Troops, together with the two Packets above-mentioned and all their Passengers.[7] During his Absence the French and Savages had taken Fort George on the Frontier of that Province, and the Savages had massacred many of the Garrison after Capitulation.[8]

I saw afterwards in London, Captain Bonnell, who commanded one of those Packets. He told me, that when he had been detain'd a Month, he acquainted his Lordship that his Ship was grown foul, to a degree that must necessarily hinder her fast Sailing, a Point of consequence for a Packet Boat, and requested an Allowance of Time to heave her down and clean her Bottom. He was ask'd how long time that would require. He answer'd Three Days. The General replied, If you can do it in one Day, I give leave; otherwise not; for you must certainly sail the Day after tomorrow. So he never obtain'd leave tho' detain'd afterwards from day to day during full three Months. I saw also in London one of Bonnell's Passengers,[9] who was so enrag'd against his Lordship for deceiving and detaining him so long at New York, and then carrying him to Halifax, and back again, that he swore he would sue him for Damages. Whether he did or not I never heard; but as he represented the Injury to his Affairs it was very considerable.

On the whole I then wonder'd much, how such a Man came to be entrusted with so important a Business as the Conduct of a great Army: but having since seen more of the great World, and the means of obtaining and Motives for giving Places and Employments, my Wonder is diminished. General Shirley, on whom the Command of the Army devolved upon the Death of Braddock, would in my Opinion if continued in Place, have made a much better Campaign than that of Loudon in 1757, which was frivolous, expensive and disgraceful to our Nation beyond Conception: For tho' Shirley was not a bred

7. They arrived in New York on September 1, 1757.
8. The French had captured Fort William Henry on Lake George, August 9. General Amherst built a new fort, Fort George, near the site the following year.
9. Probably Major Charles Craven, Paymaster of the 51st Regiment, who had been detained in Bonnell's packet, the *Harriott*, from May to October, 1757. Loudoun also refused to promote Craven to lieutenant colonel, questioned his accounts, and reprimanded him. (Stanley M. Pargellis, *Lord Loudoun in North America* [New Haven: Yale University Press, 1933], pp. 315, 342.)

Soldier, he was sensible and sagacious in himself, and attentive to good Advice from others, capable of forming judicious Plans, quick and active in carrying them into Execution. Loudon, instead of defending the Colonies with his great Army, left them totally expos'd while he paraded it idly at Halifax, by which means Fort George was lost;—besides he derang'd all our mercantile Operations, and distress'd our Trade by a long Embargo[1] on the Exportation of Provisions, on pretense of keeping Supplies from being obtain'd by the Enemy, but in Reality for beating down their Price in Favor of the Contractors, in whose Profits it was said, perhaps from Suspicion only, he had a Share. And when at length the Embargo was taken off, by neglecting to send Notice of it to Charlestown, the Carolina Fleet was detain'd near three Months longer, whereby their Bottoms were so much damag'd by the Worm,[2] that a great Part of them founder'd in the Passage home. Shirley was I believe sincerely glad of being reliev'd from so burdensome a Charge as the Conduct of an Army must be to a Man unacquainted with military Business. I was at the Entertainment given by the City of New York, to Lord Loudon on his taking upon him the Command. Shirley, tho' thereby superseded, was present also. There was a great Company of Officers, Citizens and Strangers, and some Chairs having been borrowed in the Neighborhood, there was one among them very low which fell to the Lot of Mr. Shirley. Perceiving it as I sat by him, I said, they have given you, Sir, too low a Seat.—No Matter, says he; Mr. Franklin, I find *a low Seat* the easiest![3]

While I was, as afore-mention'd, detain'd at New York, I receiv'd all the Accounts of the Provisions, etc. that I had furnish'd to Braddock, some of which Accounts could not sooner be obtain'd from the different Persons I had employ'd to assist in the Business. I presented them to Lord Loudon,[4] desiring to be paid the Balance. He caus'd them to be regularly examin'd by the proper Officer, who, after comparing every Article with its Voucher, certified them to be right, and the Balance due, for which his Lordship promis'd to give me an Order on the Paymaster. This, however, was put off from time to time, and tho' I called often for it by Appointment, I did not get it. At length, just before my Departure, he told me he had on better Consideration concluded not to mix his Accounts with those of his Predecessors.[5] And you, says he, when in England, have only to exhibit your

1. From March 2 to June 27, to ensure sufficient supplies for the Louisburg campaign.
2. Wormlike mollusk that bored through ships' planks, especially in tropical waters.
3. Evidently Shirley made the remark (cf. *P*, 10: 273), but BF may have supplied its dramatic and witty setting. New York entertained Loudoun on July 23, 1756.
4. Loudoun's journal records meeting BF on

March 15, 19, 21, 26; April 9, 15, 25, 26 and 30.
5. Loudoun's journal also says about BF's bill: "The state of his Accounts surprised me, being £17–2–6 a Load for Carrying each Load of Forrage from Philadelphia to the Camp—His Answer as to this was the Country gave near as much more to persuade the People to go—" (Huntington ms. LO/1717, 2: 166–67.)

Accounts at the Treasury, and you will be paid immediately. I mention'd, but without Effect, the great and unexpected Expense I had been put to by being detain'd so long at New York, as a Reason for my desiring to be presently paid; and On my observing that it was not right I should be put to any farther Trouble or Delay in obtaining the Money I had advanc'd, as I charg'd no Commissions for my Service. O, Sir, says he, you must not think of persuading us that you are no Gainer. We understand better those Affairs, and know that every one concern'd in supplying the Army finds means in the doing it to fill his own Pockets. I assur'd him that was not my Case, and that I had not pocketed a Farthing: but he appear'd clearly not to believe me; and indeed I have since learned that immense Fortunes are often made in such Employments.—As to my Balance,[6] I am not paid it to this Day, of which more hereafter.

Our Captain[7] of the Packet had boasted much before we sail'd, of the Swiftness of his Ship. Unfortunately when we came to Sea, she proved the dullest of 96 Sail,[8] to his no small Mortification. After many Conjectures respecting the Cause, when we were near another Ship almost as dull as ours, which however gain'd upon us, the Captain order'd all hands to come aft and stand as near the Ensign Staff as possible. We were, Passengers included, about forty Persons. While we stood there the Ship mended her Pace, and soon left our Neighbor far behind, which prov'd clearly what our Captain suspected, that she was loaded too much by the Head. The Casks of Water it seems had been all plac'd forward. These he therefore order'd to be remov'd farther aft; on which the Ship recover'd her Character, and prov'd the best Sailor in the Fleet.

The Captain said she had once gone at the Rate of 13 Knots, which is accounted 13 Miles per hour.[9] We had on board as a Passenger Captain Kennedy[1] of the Navy, who contended that it was impossible, that no Ship ever sailed so fast, and that there must have been some Error in the Division of the Log-Line, or some Mistake in heaving the Log. A Wager ensu'd between the two Captains, to be decided when there should be sufficient Wind. Kennedy thereupon examin'd rigorously the Log-line, and being satisfied with that, he determin'd to throw the Log himself. Accordingly some Days after when the Wind blew very fair and fresh, and the Captain of the Packet (Lutwidge) said he believ'd she then went at the Rate of 13 Knots, Kennedy made the

6. The balance owed BF was only £17 12s. 6d., but BF had good cause to be irritated with Loudoun. BF had worked ceaselessly for the British armies for months, advancing his own funds and pledging his own credit, had charged nothing for his services, and then suffered the indignity of having his honor impugned and his small outstanding bill refused.

7. BF paid Walter Lutwidge, master of the *General Wall*, 50 guineas on May 5, 1758, fare for himself, son, and two servants. (P, 7: 234n.)

8. A good example of BF's choosing a specific detail, though not precisely true, rather than a fuzzy generalization. Loudoun's convoy had more than 100 ships. (Gipson, 7: 102.)

9. Nautical miles, or about seventeen land miles per hour.

1. Archibald Kennedy, Jr.

Experiment, and own'd his Wager lost.

The above Fact I give for the sake of the following Observation. It has been remark'd as an Imperfection in the Art of Shipbuilding, that it can never be known 'till she is tried, whether a new Ship will or will not be a good Sailer; for that the Model of a good sailing Ship has been exactly follow'd in a new One, which has prov'd on the contrary remarkably dull. I apprehend this may be partly occasion'd by the different Opinions of Seamen respecting the Modes of lading, rigging and sailing of a Ship. Each has his System. And the same Vessel laden by the Judgment and Orders of one Captain shall sail better or worse than when by the Orders of another. Besides, it scarce ever happens that a Ship is form'd, fitted for the Sea, and sail'd by the same Person. One Man builds the Hull, another rigs her, a third lades and sails her. No one of these has the Advantage of knowing all the Ideas and Experience of the others, and therefore cannot draw just Conclusions from a Combination of the whole. Even in the simple Operation of Sailing when at Sea, I have often observ'd different Judgments in the Officers who commanded the successive Watches, the Wind being the same. One would have the Sails trimm'd sharper or flatter than another, so that they seem'd to have no certain Rule to govern by. Yet I think a Set of Experiments might be instituted, first to determine the most proper Form of the Hull for swift sailing; next the best Dimensions and properest Place for the Masts; then the Form and Quantity of Sail, and their Position as the Winds may be; and lastly the Disposition of her Lading. This is the Age of Experiments; and such a Set accurately made and combin'd would be of great Use. I am therefore persuaded that ere long some ingenious Philosopher will undertake it—to whom I wish Success.

We were several times chas'd on our Passage,[2] but outsail'd everything, and in thirty Days had Sounding.[3] We had a good Observation,[4] and the Captain judg'd himself so near our Port, (Falmouth)[5] that if we made a good Run in the Night we might be off the Mouth of that Harbor in the Morning, and by running in the Night might escape the Notice of the Enemy's Privateers, who often cruis'd near the Entrance of the Channel. Accordingly all the Sail was set that we could possibly make, and the Wind being very fresh and fair, we went right before it, and made great Way. The Captain after his Observation, shap'd his Course as he thought so as to pass wide of the Scilly Isles,[6] but it seems there is sometimes a strong Indraft setting up St. George's Channel[7] which deceives Seamen, and caus'd the Loss of Sir Cloudsley Shovel's Squadron. This Indraft was probably the Cause of

2. William Franklin, writing at the time, also reported they were "several Times chac'd," apparently by French warships. (P, 7: 244.)
3. The lead-line touched bottom, showing they were near shore.

4. Could tell their location from the sun.
5. On the coast of Cornwall.
6. Group of islands and rocks 25 miles west of Land's End, southeastern tip of England.
7. Between Ireland and Wales.

what happen'd to us. We had a Watchman plac'd in the Bow to whom they often call'd, *Look well out befor'e, there*; and he as often answer'd *Aye, Aye!* But perhaps had his Eyes shut, and was half asleep at the time: they sometimes answering as is said mechanically: For he did not see a Light just before us, which had been hid by the Studding Sails from the Man at Helm and from the rest of the Watch; but by an accidental Yaw of the Ship was discover'd, and occasion'd a great Alarm, we being very near it, the light appearing to me as big as a Cart Wheel. It was Midnight, and Our Captain fast asleep. But Captain Kennedy jumping upon Deck, and seeing the Danger, ordered the Ship to wear round, all Sails standing. An Operation dangerous to the Masts, but it carried us clear, and we escap'd Shipwreck, for we were running right upon the Rocks on which the Lighthouse was erected. This Deliverance impress'd me strongly with the Utility of Light-houses, and made me resolve to encourage the building more of them in America, if I should live to return there.[8]

In the Morning it was found by the Soundings, etc. that we were near our Port, but a thick Fog hid the Land from our Sight. About 9 o'Clock the Fog began to rise, and seem'd to be lifted up from the Water like the Curtain at a Playhouse, discovering underneath the Town of Falmouth, the Vessels in its Harbor, and the Fields that surrounded it. A most pleasing Spectacle to those who had been so long without any other Prospects, than the uniform View of a vacant Ocean! And it gave us the more Pleasure, as we were now freed from the Anxieties which the State of War occasion'd.

I set out immediately with my Son for London, and we only stopped a little by the Way to view Stonehenge on Salisbury Plain, and Lord Pembroke's House and Gardens, with his very curious Antiquities at Wilton.[9]

We arriv'd in London the 27th of July 1757.[1] [*Part Four*] As soon as I was settled in a Lodging Mr. Charles had provided for me,[2] I went to visit Dr. Fothergill, to whom I was strongly recommended, and whose Counsel respecting my Proceedings I was advis'd to obtain. He was against an immediate Complaint to Government, and thought the Proprietaries should first be personally applied to, who might possibly

8. At the time, BF wrote: "Were I a Roman Catholic, perhaps I should on this occasion vow to build a chapel to some saint; but as I am not, if I were to vow at all, it should be to build a *lighthouse*" (P, 7: 243).

9. Stonehenge is about ten miles north of Salisbury. Wilton House, where Sir Philip Sidney wrote *The Arcadia*, is famed for magnificent gardens, architecture, and art. The mansion of Sir Philip Sidney's day was destroyed in England's Civil War but rebuilt in the late seventeenth century.

1. BF arrived at Falmouth on July 17, 1757, and reached London on the evening of July 26.

(P, 7: 243–45.) This sentence concludes Part Three of the *Autobiography*. It was the last sentence in the ms. copies of the *Autobiography* that BF sent to Benjamin Vaughan and to Louis Le Veillard in November, 1789, and the last sentence in the *Autobiography* as printed by William Temple Franklin in 1818.

2. BF seems actually to have stayed with Peter Collinson his first night (July 26) in London, then at the Bear Inn for three nights (July 27–29), and, beginning on July 30, with Mrs. Margaret Stevenson at No. 7 Craven Street (P, 7: 245n).

be induc'd by the Interposition and Persuasion of some private Friends to accommodate Matters amicably. I then waited on my old Friend and Correspondent Mr. Peter Collinson, who told me that John Hanbury, the great Virginia Merchant, had requested to be informed when I should arrive, that he might carry me to Lord Granville's, who was then President of the Council,[3] and wish'd to see me as soon as possible. I agreed to go with him the next Morning. Accordingly Mr. Hanbury called for me and took me in his Carriage to that Nobleman's, who receiv'd me with great Civility; and after some Questions respecting the present State of Affairs in America, and Discourse thereupon, he said to me, "You Americans have wrong Ideas of the Nature of your Constitution; you contend that the King's Instructions to his Governors are not Laws, and think yourselves at Liberty to regard or disregard them at your own Discretion. But those Instructions are not like the Pocket Instructions given to a Minister going abroad, for regulating his Conduct in some trifling Point of Ceremony. They are first drawn up by Judges learned in the Laws; they are then considered, debated and perhaps amended in Council, after which they are signed by the King. They are then so far as relates to you, the *Law of the Land*; for THE KING IS THE LEGISLATOR OF THE COLONIES."[4]

I told his Lordship this was new Doctrine to me. I had always understood from our Charters, that our Laws were to be made by our Assemblies, to be presented indeed to the King for his Royal Assent, but that being once given the King could not repeal or alter them. And as the Assemblies could not make permanent Laws without his Assent, so neither could he make a Law for them without theirs. He assur'd me I was totally mistaken. I did not think so however. And his Lordship's Conversation having a little alarm'd me as to what might be the Sentiments of the Court concerning us, I wrote it down as soon as I return'd to my Lodgings.—[5] I recollected that about 20 Years before, a Clause in a Bill brought into Parliament by the Ministry, had propos'd to make the King's Instructions Laws in the Colonies; but the Clause was thrown out by the Commons,[6] for which we ador'd them as our Friends and Friends of Liberty, till by their Conduct towards us in 1765, it seem'd that they had refus'd that Point of Sovereignty to the King, only that they might reserve it for themselves.[7]

After some Days, Dr. Fothergill having spoken to the Proprietaries, they agreed to a Meeting with me at Mr. J. Penn's[8] House in Spring

3. The Privy Council, or the King-in-Council, sometimes called the Ministry, ruled the nation in the King's name. Similar to the United States Cabinet, it had stronger executive power.
4. For other versions, see BF's letters of March 19, 1759, January 13, 1772, and April 29, 1781. (P, 8: 293; and 19: 11; and Smyth, 8: 241.)
5. BF evidently had the memo in January 1772, but it has disappeared (P, 19: 11.)
6. The 1744 bill containing this clause died

when Parliament adjourned for the summer. (Stock, 5: 187.)
7. After repealing the Stamp Act in 1766, Parliament passed the Declaratory Act asserting the right to legislate for the colonies without their consent "in all cases whatsoever."
8. Not John Penn, but Thomas Penn. The interviews at Penn's house were on August 13 and 16. (P, 7: 250n., 291.)

Garden. The Conversation at first consisted of mutual Declarations of Disposition to reasonable Accommodation; but I suppose each Party had its own Ideas of what should be meant by *reasonable*. We then went into Consideration of our several Points of Complaint which I enumerated. The Proprietaries justified their Conduct as well as they could, and I the Assembly's. We now appeared very wide, and so far from each other in our Opinions, as to discourage all Hope of Agreement. However, it was concluded that I should give them the Heads of our Complaints in Writing, and they promis'd then to consider them.—I did so soon after; but they put the Paper into the Hands of their Solicitor Ferdinando John Paris, who manag'd for them all their Law Business in their great Suit with the neighboring Proprietary of Maryland, Lord Baltimore, which had subsisted 70 Years,[9] and wrote for them all their Papers and Messages in their Dispute with the Assembly. He was a proud angry Man; and as I had occasionally in the Answers of the Assembly treated his Papers with some Severity, they being really weak in point of Argument, and haughty in Expression, he had conceiv'd a mortal Enmity to me,[1] which discovering itself whenever we met, I declin'd the Proprietary's Proposal that he and I should discuss the Heads of Complaint between our two selves, and refus'd treating with anyone but them. They then by his Advice put the Paper into the Hands of the Attorney and Solicitor General[2] for their Opinion and Counsel upon it, where it lay unanswered a Year wanting eight Days,[3] during which time I made frequent Demands of an Answer from the Proprietaries but without obtaining any other than that they had not yet receiv'd the Opinion of the Attorney and Solicitor General: What it was when they did receive it I never learned, for they did not communicate it to me, but sent a long Message to the Assembly drawn and signed by Paris reciting my Paper, complaining of its want of Formality[4] as a Rudeness on my part, and giving a flimsy Justification of their Conduct, adding that they should be willing to accommodate Matters, if the Assembly would send over *some Person of Candor* to treat with them for that purpose, intimating thereby that I was not such.[5]

9. The boundary dispute was settled by the Mason-Dixon line in 1767.

1. Governor Morris warned Paris to be wary of BF as having "nothing in view but to serve himself." (*P*, 7: 247n.)

2. Franklin did not know that the "paper" put into the hands of Charles Pratt, Attorney General, and Charles Yorke, Solicitor General, was a carefully distorted version of his "Heads of Complaint." The officials had to give answers favoring the proprietors. (Hutson, p. 43.)

3. Yorke replied January 13, 1758, but Pratt delayed until November, thus preventing Penn's replying earlier. (*P*, 7: 366.)

4. Thomas Penn called BF's complaints "a loose Paper not address'd to any body." (*P*, 7: 251–52; cf. 8: 184.)

5. Although the Proprietors did not send BF copies of the opinions of the Attorney and Solicitor General, they incorporated elements of these opinions in their answer to Franklin, dated November 27, 1758, which expressed the wish that the assembly would send over "some Persons of Candour" to treat with them. (*P*, 8: 179–83.) But the proprietors did not give him a copy of their message (November 28, 1758) to the assembly complaining of his "Disrespect." (*P*, 8: 184.)

The want of Formality or Rudeness, was probably my not having address'd the Paper to them with their assum'd Titles of true and absolute Proprietaries of the Province of Pennsylvania, which I omitted as not thinking it necessary in a Paper the Intention of which was only to reduce to a Certainty by writing what in Conversation I had delivered *vivâ voce*. But during this Delay, the Assembly having prevail'd with Governor Denny to pass an Act[6] taxing the Proprietary Estate in common with the Estates of the People, which was the grand Point in Dispute, they omitted answering the Message.

When the Act however came over, the Proprietaries counsell'd by Paris[7] determin'd to oppose its receiving the Royal Assent. Accordingly they petition'd the King in Council, and a Hearing[8] was appointed, in which two Lawyers were employ'd by them against the Act, and two by me in Support of it. They alledg'd that the Act was intended to load the Proprietary Estate in order to spare those of the People, and that if it were suffer'd to continue in force, and the Proprietaries who were in Odium with the People, left to their Mercy in proportioning the Taxes, they would inevitably be ruined. We replied that the Act had no such Intention and would have no such Effect. That the Assessors were honest and discreet Men, under an Oath to assess fairly and equitably, and that any Advantage each of them might expect in lessening his own Tax by augmenting that of the Proprietaries was too trifling to induce them to perjure themselves. This is the purport of what I remember as urg'd by both Sides, except that we insisted strongly on the mischievous Consequences that must attend a Repeal; for that the Money, 100,000 Pounds, being printed and given to the King's Use, expended in his Service, and now spread among the People, the Repeal would strike it dead in their Hands to the Ruin of many, and the total Discouragement of future Grants, and the Selfishness of the Proprietors in soliciting such a general Catastrophe, merely from a groundless Fear of their Estate being taxed too highly, was insisted on in the strongest Terms.

On this Lord Mansfield, one of the Council rose, and beckoning to me, took me into the Clerk's Chamber, while the Lawyers were pleading, and ask'd me if I was really of Opinion that no Injury would be done the Proprietary Estate in the Execution of the Act. I said, Certainly. Then says he, you can have little Objection to enter into an Engagement to assure that Point. I answer'd None, at all. He then call'd in Paris, and after some Discourse his Lordship's Proposition was accepted on both Sides; a Paper to the purpose was drawn up by the Clerk of the Council, which I sign'd with Mr. Charles, who was

6. Denny signed on June 20, 1759. (*P*, 8: 419n.)
7. Not Paris, who died on December 16, 1759, but Henry Wilmot. (*P*, 9: 126.)
8. Actually two hearings: Pratt and Yorke represented the Proprietors, and William de Grey and Richard Jackson represented the assembly before the Board of Trade (May–June) which found in favor of the Penns. BF's lawyer, Francis Eyre, then appealed in the hearing described here (August 27–28, 1760). (*P*, 8: 396n.; 9: 197.)

also an Agent of the Province for their ordinary Affairs; when Lord Mansfield return'd to the Council Chamber where finally the Law was allowed to pass. Some Changes were however recommended and we also engag'd they should be made by a subsequent Law; but the Assembly did not think them necessary. For one Year's Tax having been levied by the Act before the Order of Council arrived, they appointed a Committee to examine the Proceedings of the Assessors, and On this Committee they put several particular Friends of the Proprietaries. After a full Enquiry they unanimously sign'd a Report that they found the Tax had been assess'd with perfect Equity.

The Assembly look'd on my entering into the first Part of the Engagement as an essential Service to the Province, since it secur'd the Credit of the Paper Money then spread over all the Country; and they gave me their Thanks in form when I return'd.[9] But the Proprietaries were enrag'd at Governor Denny for having pass'd the Act, and turn'd him out, with Threats of suing him for Breach of Instructions which he had given Bond to observe. He however having done it at the Instance of the General[1] and for his Majesty's Service, and having some powerful Interest at Court, despis'd the Threats, and they were never put in Execution

9. BF arrived back in Philadelphia on November 1, 1762, and the assembly voted him their thanks on February 19, 1763. (P, 10: 153n, 196–7, 238.)

1 General Lord Jeffrey Amherst pressured both the Governor and the assembly by threatening to pull his troops out of the Pennsylvania frontier. (P, 8: 326n.)

Textual Notes

There are twelve separate textual notes. They record:

1. Substantive Emendations (p. 148)
2. Alternative Word Choices (p. 152)
3. Notes That Franklin Made Regarding the Contents (p. 153)
4. Paragraph Divisions Added to the Norton Text (p. 154)
5. Revisions Made at a Later Time (including all revisions in pencil) (p. 155)
6. The Most Significant Additions (p. 157)
7. The Most Significant Cancellations (p. 159)
8. Damage to the Holograph Text (p. 160)
9. The Division into Four Parts (p. 161)
10. Red Ink in the Chart and the Schedule (p. 161)
11. Textual Notes on Materials Added to the *Autobiography* (p. 162)
12. Notes on Accidentals, including: (a) All Capitals, Periods, and Other Accidentals Added to the Norton Text, and (b) Possibly Significant Deleted or Superseded Punctuation Marks (p. 162)

SIGLA USED IN THE TEXTUAL NOTES

The words before the closing half bracket, preceded by page and line numbers from the Norton Critical Edition, give the passage as printed in this edition. The matter following the half bracket gives the passage as found in Franklin's holograph manuscript.

~ = The wavy dash indicates that the same word or sequence is repeated exactly as found before the half bracket.

^ = The caret calls attention to the lack of punctuation.

. . . = ellipses indicate textual matter omitted in the notes.

↑ . . . ↓ = single arrows enclose interlinear additions.

↑↑ . . . ↓↓ = double arrows enclose columnar additions.

< . . . > = side-angle brackets enclose cancellations.

{ . . . } = braces enclose matter written over by the following material.

[. . .] = editorial explanations are enclosed by brackets.

BF = Benjamin Franklin

Bigelow = John Bigelow, ed. *Autobiography of Benjamin Franklin*. Philadelphia: Lippincott, 1868.

Farrand = Max Farrand, ed. *Benjamin Franklin's Memoirs: Parallel Text Edition*. Berkeley: University of California Press, 1949.

Genetic Text = J. A. Leo Lemay and P. M. Zall, eds. *The Autobiography of Benjamin Franklin: A Genetic Text*. Knoxville: University of Tennessee Press, 1981.

Le Veillard = Louis Guillaume Le Veillard, tr. "Memoires de B. Franklin traduits par M. Le Veillard." Manuscript Division (no. 215–0282), Library of Congress.

Mathew Carey = "Biographical notices of the late dr. Benjamin Franklin."
[Ed. Mathew Carey.] *American Museum*, 8 (July, 1790), 12–20;
(November), 210–12.
Van Doren = Carl Van Doren, ed. *Benjamin Franklin's Autobiographical
Writings*. New York: Viking, 1945.
WTF = William Temple Franklin, ed. *Memoirs of the Life and Writings of
Benjamin Franklin*, v. 1. London: Henry Colburn, 1818.

1. Substantive Emendations

We include here all changes in Franklin's letters, although not the changes
from upper to lower-case letters and vice versa, which are recorded in the
"Notes on Accidentals" (below, section 12). The emendations are almost
entirely corrections of Franklin's careless slips or modernizations. For the few
exceptions, see below at 40.33, 88.16, 127.25, 141.39, and 146.17–18.

The word before the half-bracket is our emendation; the word following it is
Franklin's original.

Norton
page
1.8 agreeable] agreable
1.24 favorable] favourable
1.24 denied] deny'd
2.22 learned] learnt
3.19 were] werre
3.20 qualified] qualify'd
3.22 public] publick
4.10 Public] Publick
4.22 fastened] fastned
5.21 honorable] honourable
5.28 favor] favour
6.20 Expense] Expence
6.30 Soap] Sope
6.38 learned] learnt
7.5 Minnows] Minews
7.13 Wharf] Wharff
7.13 surpris'd] surpriz'd
7.14 Wharf] Wharff
7.25 agreeable] agreable
7.28 public] publick
7.38 Neighbor]. Neighbour
7.44 flavor] flavour
8.1 brought] bro't
8.10 died] dy'd
8.36 public] publick
9.3 agreeable] agreable
9.9 learned] learnt
10.26 Style] Stile
11.1 disputatious] disputacious
11.2 extremely] extreamly
11.2 disagreeable] disagreable
11.9 Edinburgh] Edinborough
11.19 replied] reply'd
11.21 entering] entring
11.34 tried] try'd
11.35 complete] compleat
12.14 complete] compleat
12.21 extremely] extreamly

Norton
page
12.25 public] publick
12.28 practice] practise
13.1 Biscuit] Bisket
13.9 Arithmetic] Arithmetick
13.20 dropped] dropt
13.22 Shaftesbury] Shaftsbury
13.25 practic'd] practis'd
16.2-3 extremely] extreamly
16.3 amiss*] ~ ^ [BF did not key this note
(which he added in the blank column just
below "amiss") to a specific word. WTF at
11.13, runs it in at the end of the paragraph,
but both Bigelow, at 104.8, and Le Veillard,
p. 29n, print it as a footnote keyed to the last
word in the paragraph, "unexpected."]
16.17 unfavorable] unfavourable
16.18 Satire] Satyr
16.19 accompanied] accompany'd
17.13 indiscreet] indiscrete
17.22 publicly] publickly
17.28 worn] worne
17.29 gratified] gratify'd
18.3 favorite] favourite
18.16 Surf] Surff
18.17 dropped] dropt
18.19 Surf] Surff
18.40 stopped] stopt
18.40 stayed] staid
19.6 Browne] Brown
19.7 entered] entred
19.14 doggerel] doggrel
19.28 thought] tho't
19.39 o'Clock] a Clock
20.1 Wharf] Wharff
20.5 Clothes] Cloaths
20.18 Biscuit] Bisket
20.24 surpris'd] surpriz'd
20.31 Wharf] Wharff

Norton
page

21.1 drowsy] drowzy
21.22 supplied] supply'd
21.28. Neighbor] Neighbour
21.39 relied] rely'd
21.42 surpris'd] surpriz'd
22.33 agreeably] agreably
23.5 Homes] Holmes
23.15 Homes] Holmes
23.17 surpris'd] surpriz'd
23.21 public] publick
23.35 surpris'd] surpriz'd
23.38 before] beforre
23.40 Public-Business] Publick Business
24.5 Honor] Honour
24.16 Homes] Holmes
24.17 surpris'd] surpriz'd
24.33 extremely] extreamly
24.39 Surprise] Surprize
25.12 Mathematics] Mathematicks
25.32 Pennsylvania] Pensilvania
26.10 Cabin] Cabbin
26.19 outstripped] outstript
26.29 extremely] extreamly
26.37 Honor] Honour
26.45 Expense] Expence
27.12 clapped] clapt
27.12 Crotch] Crutch
27.22 Barbados] Barbadoes
28.1 choose] chuse
28.4 Correspondences] Correspondencies
28.4 Stationery] Stationary
28.14 haul'd] hawl'd
29.12 if] if . . . if
29.14 Neighborhood] Neighbourhood
29.39 Brockden] Brogden
30.2 literary] litterary
30.2 Criticizing] Criticising
30.3 extremely] extreamly
30.16 oneself] one's Self
30.43 dropped] dropt
30.45 favor] favour
31.6 played] plaid
31.7 laughed] laught
31.29 extremely] extreamly
32.20 satisfied] satisfy'd
32.36 complete] compleat
32.39 surprised] surprized
33.2 laughed] laught
33.2 Dependence] Dependance
33.38 qualified] qualify'd
33.38 applied] apply'd
34.12 Expenses] Expences
34.15 Wollaston's] Woollaston's
34.32 entitled] intituled
34.36 Mandeville] Mandevile
35.5 extremely] extreamly
35.19 qualified] qualify'd
35.24 Honor] Honour
35.34 copied] copy'd
36.7 advanc'd] advan'd
36.10 Burden] Burthen

Norton
page

36.35 Expense] Expence
36.39 Compositors] Compostors
37.11 supplied] supply'd
37.12 neighboring] neighbouring
37.22 Satirist] Satyrist
37.26 agreeably] agreably
38.30 cheerful] chearful
38.31 Mattress] Matras
39.3 stripped] stript
39.3 leaped] leapt
39.4 Blackfriars] Blackfryars
39.5 surpris'd] surpriz'd
39.7] practic'd] practis'd
39.18 Pennsylvania] Pensilvania
39.25 favor'd] favour'd
40.4 Pennsylvania] Pensylvania
40.5 Compositor] Compostor
40.12 Surprise] Surprize
40.14 Blackfriars] Blackfryars
40.33 Fortune, I] Fortune. But I
41.2 superseded] superceded
41.13 supplied] supply'd
41.14 Stationery] Stationary
41.26 disagreeable] disagreable
42.1 tried] try'd
42.4 Pennsylvania] Pensilvania
42.8 extreme] extream
42.24 cheerfully] chearfully
42.35 well-satisfied] well-satisfy'd
42.41 Clothes] Cloaths
43.7 agreeably] agreably
43.8 learned] learnt
43.14 Economist] Oeconomist
43.19 Mold] Mould
43.20 supplied] supply'd
43.30 encumber'd] incumber'd
43.31 snapped] snapt
43.31 Connection] Connexion
43.36 Neighbors] Neighbours
44.19 agreeable] agreable
44.30 Job] Jobb
44.36 Job] Jobb
45.11 extreme] extream
45.18 learned] learnt
45.19 carried] carry'd
46.30 favorable] favourable
46.33 *willful*] *wilful*
46.35 *willful*] *wilful*
47.18 stopped] stopt
47.22 Expense] Expence
48.10 Breintnall] Brientnal
48.10 Copier] Copyer
48.24 laughed] laught
49.10 Jobs] Jobbs
49.16 Neighbors] Neighbours
49.24 Neighbors] Neighbours
49.26 Stationery] Stationary
49.26 choose] chuse
49.30 Favor] Favour
49.32-33 Journeyman] Joureyman
49.33 employ] imploy

Norton
page
50.5 Breintnall] Brientnal
50.6 Public] Publick
50.11 extremely] extreamly
50.14-15 Compositor] Compostor
51.6 learned] learnt
53.1 great] grate
53.2 Public] Publick
53.22 Chestnut] Chesnut
53.25 entitled] entituled
53.28 Clamor] Clamour
53.33 Job] Jobb
54.6 Job] Jobb
54.14 Breintnall] Brientnal
54.15 Whitmarsh] Whitemarsh
54.20 Tradesman] Tradesmen
54.21 dressed] drest
54.28 Stationery] Stationary
54.32 Barbados] Barbadoes
55.1 Barbados] Barbadoes
55.5 Pennsylvania] Pensilvania
55.15 public] publick
55.43 withhold] withold
56.2 favorable] favourable
56.11 agreeable] agreable
56.13 Expense] Expence
56.14 Risk] Risque
56.17 Neighbors] Neighbours
56.21 pitied] pity'd
56.22 cheerful] chearful
57.34 Public] Publick
58.31 shown] shewn
60.3 Show] Shew
60.29 show] shew
61.. show] shew
61.17 show] shew
61.37 show] shew
62.5 show] shew
62.41 public] publick
63.5 Pennsylvania] Pensylvania
63.8 Almanacs] Almanacks
63.23 increasing] encreasing
63.30 Promissory] Promisory
63.32 Libraries] Librarys
63.34 public] publick
63.43 rendered] renderd
64.2-3 oneself] one's self
64.4 Neighbors] Neighbours
64.9 practic'd] practis'd
64.20 Frolics] Frolicks
64.32 honor] honour
64.38 cheerfully] chearfully
65.12 Neighbors] Neighbours
65.14 increas'd] encreas'd
65.21 Existence] Existance
66.16 Public] Publick
66.35 surpris'd] surpriz'd
66.38 completely] compleatly
66.41 Dependence] Dependance
67.26 Expense] Expence
67.38 Extremes] Extreams
67.41 Clothes] Cloaths

Norton
page
68.30 Independence] Independance
70.18 complete] compleat
71.2 Honors] Honours
71.13 Favors] Favours
71.27-28 surpris'd] surpriz'd
73.4 exactly] exastly
73.7 extremely] extreamly
73.14 Axe] Ax
73.14 Neighbor] Neighbour
73.17 Axe] Ax
73.20 Axe] Ax
73.22 Axe] Ax
73.27 Axe] Ax
73.28 extreme] extream
74.11-12 honorable] honourable
74.14 Cheerfulness] Chearfulness
74.15-16 agreeable] agreable
74.32 Clothes] Cloaths
75.25 agreeable] agreable
75.30 denied] deny'd
76.13 completely] compleatly
76.14 be] by
77.22 mere] meer
77.30 the] the the
77.32 wise] wiss
78.35 Occupations] Occupapations
78.37 Enterprise] Enterprize
79.4 Almanac] Almanack
79.6 Almanac] Almanack
79.10 Neighborhood] Neighbourhood
79.20 Almanac] Almanack
79.28 Expense] Expence
80.26 indiscrete] indiscreet
80.27 neighboring] neighbouring
81.5 Expense] Expence
81.10 Accounts] Accompts
81.32 Style] Stile
81.37 Favor] Favour
82.27 Honor] Honour
83.6 Educating] Eduting
83.9 learned] learnt
83.25 carried] carry'd
84.10 Connection] Connexion
84.20 completed] compleated
84.31 favor] favour
84.32 agreeable] agreable
84.36 Jobs] Jobbs
85.2 Favor] Favour
85.6 Favor] Favour
85.8 Favor] Favour
85.13 learned] learnt
85.23 increas'd] encreas'd
85.26 satisfied] satisfy'd
86.8 choose] chuse
86.39 occurr'd] occur'd
87.8 applied] apply'd
87.16 Whitefield] Whitefiel
88.10 Whitefield] Whitfield
88.16 Jails] Goals
88.27 Expense] Expence
88.41 emptied] empty'd

Norton
page
89.29 Burden] Burthen
90.2 Auditors] Auditories
90.15 ancient] antient
90.31 qualified] qualify'd
90.31 accompanied] accompany'd
90.35 Increase] Encrease
91.1 Proselytes] Proselites
91.8 neighboring] neighbouring
91.18 carried] carry'd
91.25 Burden] Burthen
91.27 disagreeable] disagreable
91.30 Defense] Defence
91.30 complete] compleat
92.3 Defense] Defence
92.11 defenseless] defenceless
92.12 Defense] Defence
92.14 surprising] surprizing
92.30 Colors] Colours
92.36 Expense] Expence
93.18 agreeable] agreable
93.27 Style] Stile
93.39 Honor] Honour
93.42 practice] practise
94.17 favor] favour
94.17 Defense] Defence
94.33 agreeable] agreable
95.10 extremely] extreamly
95.12 Surprise] Surprize
95.12 carried] carry'd
95.16 Defense] Defence
95.26 Defense] Defence
95.30 Defense] Defence
96.15 Pennsylvania] Pensilvania
96.23 replied] reply'd
96.27 favor] favour
96.35 Embarrassments] Embarassments
97.9 enlighten] inlighten
97.25 wrapped] wrapt
97.30 Choosing] Chusing
97.34 Entering] Entring
98.1 Entitled] Intitled
98.20 neighboring] neighbouring
98.26 entitled] intitled
99.2 *public-spirited*] *publick-spirited*
99.3 Public] Publick
99.10 increasing] encreasing
99.32 choose] chuse
99.39 negotiating] negociating
100.11 cheerfully] chearfully
100.31 Spencer] Spence
100.33 Public] Publick
101.1 agreeable] agreable
101.12 tried] try'd
101.16 Duties] Dutys
101.28 extremely] extreamly
102.5-6 dark-color'd] dark-colour'd
103.10 Expense] Expence
103.34 Expense] Expence
104.3 Maneuvers] Maneuvres
104.11 disagreeable] disagreable
104.17 least] leas

Norton
page
104.27 beautiful] beautifull
104.28 straight] strait
105.4 Neighbors'] Neighbours
105.7 Neighborhood] Neighbourhood
105.7 Expense] Expence
105.26 enlightening] enlightning
105.27 Honor] Honour
105.30 supplied] supply'd
105.34 obstructed the] ˜ ˜ the
106.33 o'Clock] aClock
107.11 rendered] rendred
107.40 carried] carry'd
107.42 o'Clock] aClock
107.44 choosing] chusing
109.5 Honors] Honours
109.22 Defense] Defence
109.33 administered] administred
110.14 Expense] Expence
110.25 Pretense] Pretence
112.19 Coloring] Colouring
112.21 negrified] negrify'd
112.24 Expense] Expence
112.25 Defense] Defence
112.27 expressly] expresly
113.4 solicit] sollicit
113.6 applied] apply'd
113.18 therefore] therefor
113.33 completed] compleated
113.37 choosing] chusing
113.39 Defense] Defence
114.3 Frederick] Frederic
114.11 Expense] Expence
114.12 Frederick] Frederic
114.14 stayed] staid
114.22 surpris'd] surpriz'd
115.6 empower] impower
115.37 empowered] impowered
116.4 *Frederick*] *Frederic*
116.5 extremely] extreamly
116.6 supplied] supply'd
116.18 Inconveniences] Inconveniencies
116.44 Defense] Defence
116.47 Recompense] Recompence
117.3 Labor] Labour
117.26 commiserated] commisserated
117.33 enclosed] enclos'd
118.11 Keg] Kegg
118.16 dried] dry'd
119.15 completely] compleatly
119.21 Surprise] Surprize
119.24 replied] reply'd
120.3 Panic] Pannick
120.13 Fliers] Flyers
120.14 Panic] Pannick
120.18 Honor] Honour
120.30 stripped] stript
121.2 Aides de Camp] Aid de Camps
121.8 died] dy'd
121.14 rendered] rendred
121.28 applied] apply'd
121.30 enlisted] inlisted

Norton
page

121.33 Expense] Expence
122.2 applied] apply'd
122.16 surpris'd] surpriz'd
122.21 dropped] dropt
122.27 Defense] Defence
123.20 Defense] Defence
123.27 Aide] Aid
123.28 burned] burnt
124.4 surprised] surprized
124.4 Defense] Defence
124.13 Surprise] Surprize
124.15 conscientiously] conscienciously
124.19 Surprise] Surprize
124.22 whimsical] whimsicall
124.28 thought] tho't
126.5 cheerful] chearful
126.8 ill-humor] ill-humour
126.13 Defense] Defence
126.17 neighboring] neighbouring
126.24 burned] burnt
126.30 even] evon
126.37 punctually] puctually
127.22 wrapped] wrapt
127.25 ate] eat
127.27 Dormitories] Dormitorys
127.28 Ceiling] Cieling
127.29 Music] Musick
128.20 choose] chuse
128.38 Honor] Honour
129.14 Offense] Offence
129.14 Honor] Honour
129.27 applied] apply'd
129.28 Fawkener] Fauckener
130.21 dropped] dropt
130.27 Spencer] Spence
130.30 surpris'd] surpriz'd
131.4 Neighbor] Neighbour
131.24 laughed] laught
132.17 verified] verify'd
132.18 delivered] deliverd
132.20 lengthened] lengthend
133.24 Lightning] Lightnin
133.27 Honor] Honour
134.5 honored] honoured
134.22 dropped] dropt
134.25 Recompenses] Recompences
134.30 Favors] Favours
135.15 Frederick] Frederic
135.31 expressly] expresly
136.5 public] publick
136.8 observe] observ
136.10 choose] chuse
136.12 entreated] intreated

Norton
page

136.14 Defense] Defence
136.15 Defense] Defence
136.23 Packet] Paquet
136.24 Recompense] Recompence
136.28 Packet] Pacquet
136.37 Harbor] Harbour
137.2 Packet] Pacquet
137.4 Packet] Pacquet
137.7 extremely] extreamly
137.15 Packet] Pacquet
137.26 Scritoire] Scritore
137.32 the] thr
138.4 Louisburg] Lewisburg
138.9 carried] carry'd
138.9 stayed] staid
138.22 replied] reply'd
138.26 Bonnell's] Bonell's
139.8 pretense] pretence
139.9 Favor] Favour
139.16 burdensome] burthensom
139.21 Neighborhood] Neighbourhood
139.30 Balance] Ballance
139.33 Balance] Ballance
140.2 Expense] Expence
140.12 learned] learnt
140.13 Balance] Ballance
140.15 Packet] Paquet
140.23 Neighbor] Neighbour
140.35 satisfied] satisfy'd
141.4 tried] try'd
141.13 rigs] riggs
141.33 Harbor] Harbour
141.39 Indraft] Indraught
141.41 Indraft] Indraught
142.19 o'Clock] aClock
142.21 Harbor] Harbour
142.25 occasion'd] accosion'd
142.26 stopped] stopt
142.35 applied] apply'd
143.37 they] the
144.5 justified] justify'd
144.12 neighboring] neighbouring
144.27 learned] learnt
144.30 flimsy] flimsey
144.33 *Candor*] *Candour*
145.2 Paper] Pager
145.3 Pennsylvania] Pensilvania
145.19 replied] reply'd
145.39 some] som
146.7 Proceedings] Percedings
146.11 entering] entring
146.17-18 it at] it

2. Alternative Word Choices

In eleven places, Franklin wrote an alternative (or possibly alternative) choice for a word, phrase, or clause, without cancelling the previous choice. In some cases, he may simply have forgotten to cross out the earlier choice; he may not have finally decided between the two choices; he may, after adding an alternative, have seen reason to prefer the original; or he may, in a few cases, have meant to print both. Indeed, at 3.17, where Franklin added "many" before "more Particulars" and at 53.16, where Franklin added "Employment" after "Trade," there may exist additional examples of an alternative choice; but we believe that he simply meant to add these words; and therefore we do not include them in the following list. In some instances, previous editors (we believe mistakenly) have printed both of Franklin's alternatives, sometimes by adding or changing his words. No previous editor has called attention to the alternatives.

We have chosen the alternative that Franklin added later. Whenever the William Temple Franklin text or the Bigelow text disagrees with the reading we have adopted, we print their texts as well.

5.35 six last] ↑↑<6 last>↓↓ ↑⁻⁻↓ concluding [Bigelow 84.7 prints "six concluding".]
33.14 he ought to be] he should ↑ought to↓ be
40.5 then] ↑⁻↓ present [WTF 39.31 has both "then present"; Bigelow 153.21 has "present".]
51.16 then] now ↑then↓
66.34–35 Care was employ'd] *Attention was taken up* ↑Care was employ'd↓ [1788 revision. BF underlined the first clause, evidently to indicate that it was the passage for which he was posing an alternative. WTF 67.17–18 adds a comma, adds the word "and" and deletes the second "was" in order to print both clauses: "my attention was taken up, and care employed".]
73.8 it] *Method* ↑<it> it↓ [BF underlined "*Method*," evidently to indicate that it was the word for which he was posing an alternative. WTF 72.13 has "*method*" in italics.]
102.29 for] towards ↑for↓
129.19 not a little] considerable ↑⁻⁻⁻↓ [WTF 121.30–31 has "considerable."]
132.9 decry] oppose ↑⁻↓ [WTF 124.7 has "oppose".]
136.17 presenting] ⁻[BF added "ing" above the "ed" concluding "presented," but did not cancel the "ed." Both WTF 128.3 and Bigelow 339.23 have "presenting".]
136.21 conformable] agreable ↑⁻↓

3. Notes That Franklin Made Regarding the Contents

As Franklin composed, he sometimes made notes of future topics that he intended to write about, and he often made a note of the next topic that he wanted to take up when he stopped writing for the day. These notes, like Franklin's outline of the *Autobiography*, are key sources both for Franklin's method of composition and for his principles of organization. They also may be useful in dating the stages and in some cases, even the particular times in composing the *Autobiography* (see also Textual Note 5).

We also list in this Textual Note those cancelled passages which Franklin decided to postpone to a later position in the *Autobiography*.

2.26 Kingdom ⌒.)] ⁻ (Here a Note) [BF's note on the name Franklin was printed by Mathew Carey, pp. 12–13, and translated by Le Veillard, pp. 3–4.]
4.2 Specimen.] ⁻. (Here insert it.) ↓↓ [1790. BF subsequently decided to print not one but two poems. See Le Veillard, pp. 6–8.]
8.12 Inscription:] ⁻⌐ (Here insert it) [Van Doren, pp. 209–10, suggested that BF probably concluded his first day's composition (Wednesday, July 31, 1771) with "(Here insert it)," and that when he resumed composition on August 1, he began by writing the outline of the *Autobiography* (see Appendix II this edition). We also think that this is probable. Further, we speculate that he added the long opening columnar addition (from 1.5 to 2.18) on August 1, as he read over the previous day's composition.]
10.33 Advancement] ⁻ ↑↑Arithm^k↓↓ [Topic taken up at 13.6]
18.40 Inn] ⁻ ↑↑ Keimer & his new Religion ↓↓ [Topic taken up at 28.30.]
36.13 London.] ⁻ ↑↑ Ghost ↓↓ [Topic taken up at 36.38.]

40.11 Leisure.] ˉ ↑↑ <Swimming> ↓↓ [Since this topic immediately follows, BF may have stopped
for the day after writing this remainder.]

46.35 Religion.] ˉ <Some foolish Intrigues with low Women excepted, which from the Expence
were rather more <inconvenient> prejudicial to me than to them.> [Postponed to 56.11.]

47.14 Beginners.] ˉ ↑↑Memº Samˡˡ Mickle's Discourageˢ Discourse↓↓ [Sometime after BF made
the note for this future topic, he decided to include it here, and so he added the paragraph about
the "Croaker" Samuel Mickle in the black column.]

50.19 Remarks] ˉ ↑↑Insert these Remarks f in a Note.—↓↓

57.28 Privileges.] ˉ. ↑↑My Manner of acting to engage People in this & future Undertakings.↓↓
[When BF stopped writing in 1771 (probably the date was Monday, August 12), he noted this
topic as the next to take up. But when he resumed composition in 1784, he did not have the
manuscript of Part One with him, and so he repeated (but in greater detail) the story of the
founding of the Library Company of Philadelphia, before taking up this topic at 64.1.]

68.32 Verses, *] ˉ, * ↑↑Insert those lines that direct it in a Note.——↓↓

70.26 Examination.] ˉ. [*New paragraph follows:*] <The Precept of *Order* requiring that *every Part of
my Business should have* its allotted time, I> [Postponed to 71.22.]

74.26 Vice;] ˉ; ↑↑Nothing so likely to make a Man's Fortune as Virtue.↓↓ [Topic taken up at 75.6.]

88.9 Service.] ˉ. <the Contributions being made <pro> by People of different Sects promiscuously, Care was taken in the Nomination of Trustees to avoid giving a Predominancy to any
<one> Sect, so that one of each was appointed, viz. one Church of England-man, one
Presbyterian, one Baptist, one Moravian, &c.> ↑↑ This to come in hereafter, where I shall
mention my Election as one of the Trustees.↓↓ [Postponed to 99.17.]

96.16 Thomas,] ˉ, ↑↑See the Votes↓↓

98.33 Pounds.] ˉ. ↑↑<House>↓↓ [Since BF used this topic in the following paragraph, he may
have stopped writing for the day at the end of this paragraph.]

101.25 purpose.] ˉ. ↑↑See the Votes to have this more correctly↓↓

102.23 Seacoast.] ˉ. ↑↑Here bring in an Account of my <electrical Fame>. Part in establishing the
Hospital. . . . ↓↓ [Here BF added the ten ms. pages (from 102.24–108.21) which were evidently
written after he composed the section from 108.22 to 135.18. See below, 108.21n and 135.19n.]

103.1 others.] ˉ. ↑↑<Gilbert Tenent>↓↓ [Topic taken up at 104.6.]

106.25 Houses.] ˉ. ↑↑<The Happiness of Man consists in small Advantages occurring every
Day—Sleep by Sunshine> ↓↓ [Topics taken up at 108.8 and 107.44, respectively.]

108.21 America.] ˉ. [This completes the ten ms. pages that BF composed after writing to 135.19.
Cf. 102.23n and 135.19n.]

112.22 Government.] ˉ. ↑↑My Acts in Morris's time military &c.↓↓ [Topic taken up at 113.1.]

112.32 hereafter.] ˉ. ↑↑Lord <Dunmore> ↑ Loudon ↓ &c↓↓ [Topic taken up at 135.30.]

114.37 follows.] ˉ. (Here insert it, from the Quire Book of Letters written during that Transaction).
[BF's letter-book from the period does not survive. We reprint the advertisement from the Boston
Public Library copy of the original broadside. For an examination of its text, see our *Genetic Text*,
Appendix 6.]

125.30-31 and . . . Pieces.] ↑↑ˉ. . . ˉ.↓↓ [This columnar addition is set off by a brace, with
"Qu" (Query ?) at the point.]

127.13 Colonel Clapham] ↑↑<Quʸ· the Name>↓↓ ↑, Col. Clapham,↓ [The marginal query was
evidently written before the interlined name. The cancellation is in pencil.]

135.19 Man's.] ˉ. [BF evidently wrote to this point by the fall of 1788. After a lapse of some time, he
next wrote the ten manuscript pages (102.24–108.21) that he inserted after 102.23. Later, he
continued with 135.20 ff. He also penned a columnar query:] ↑↑The ↑many↓ unanimous
Resolves of the Assembly what Date?↓↓

135.24 Petition] ˉ. ↑↑Quarters↓↓

4. Paragraph Divisions Added to the Norton Text

Franklin used comparatively few paragraphs in writing the *Autobiography*,
but he probably would have included more paragraph breaks if he had seen the
Autobiography through the press. All printed editions (including Buisson,
1791; William Temple Franklin, 1818; Bigelow, 1868; and Labaree, 1964)
that have attempted to be "reading" editions have introduced additional paragraphs (*Farrand's Parallel Text Edition*, 1949, and our own *Genetic Text* are
the only editions that have not added paragraphs).

For this edition we have added the following paragraphs: 3.14, 3.31, 6.7; 6.29, 15.19, 23.28, 24.3, 24.20, 26.15, 26.39, 27.26, 30.34, 31.6, 49.4, 52.19, 55.40, 73.1, 73.34, 82.3, 82.31, 88.31, 92.18, 93.6, 94.12, 94.35, 96.26, 97.21, 99.33, 105.19, 109.33, 110.17, 111.30, 114.19, 117.12, 119.3, 119.24, 123.14, 125.7, 134.26, 136.4, 137.13, 138.16, 138.31, 140.28, 141.2, 143.22, 145.1, 145.33, and 146.11.

5. Revisions Made at a Later Time

Most revisions were made at the approximate time (i.e., the same day or within a few days) Franklin wrote that portion of the *Autobiography*. We make no attempt to date such revisions. But we do try to date all revisions made at a later stage of composition. Thus for Parts One and Two (written in 1771 and 1784, respectively), we note all revisions made in 1788 or later. (Franklin evidently did not revise either of these Parts before 1788.) In the earlier portion of Part Three (through 135.19), we note all revisions made in 1789 or 1790 (the earlier portion of Part Three was written in the summer and fall of 1788). In the latter portion of Part Three (after 135.19), we note all revisions made after Franklin completed writing Part Three.

The dating of revisions is, to some degree, a matter of opinion. We discuss the problem at length in our *Genetic Text*. The dates represent our opinion, based upon repeated painstaking examination of the changes in handwriting and in ink (its shade of color and relative glossiness often distinguish the different times of composition) within the original holograph. We also record here all revisions in pencil (Franklin did not compose any passages of the *Autobiography* in pencil, but he did make a number of revisions in pencil), except such internal directions as carets and other proofreader's symbols. Pencilled revisions cannot be dated as well as those in ink. Therefore, when both pencil and ink revisions are present, the dates refer to the time of the ink revisions.

1.1 Twyford . . . 1771.] [Added in 1789.]
1.13 considerable] <good> ↑considerable↓ [1789]
3.17 many] ↑ ⁻↓ [1789; "many" written first in pencil and then inked over.]
3.29 on] ↑-↓ [1789]
4.2 and Relations . . . Specimen.] ↑↑ ⁻ ⁻. . . . ⁻. (Here insert it)↓↓ [1790. The ink is similar to that used at 14.10-11 and in the transposition line at 15.7–9.]
5.23 (. . .)] ↑(. . .)↓ [1789. There is a pencilled caret after "Country"; the word "entitled" and a comma following it were also written originally in pencil, but "entitled" was written over in ink, though the following comma was not.]
6.14–15 I . . . with,] ↑ ⁻. . . . ⁻,↓ [1789]
8.10 89] 8{7}9 [1789]
8.34–35 J. F. . . . 85.] ↑↑ ⁻. . . . ⁻.↓↓ [1789]
9.12 the Experiment] the {m} <se> ↑Experiment<s>↓ [1789. BF originally wrote "of making them was"; later, in pencil, he wrote "se" over the "m" in "them," added a caret and the word "Experiments"; and later still, using ink, he cancelled the "m" in "them" and also inked over the word "Experiment" but omitted inking the final "s."]
9.16 time] <days> ↑ ⁻↓ [1789; "days" is cancelled in pencil.]
9.24 polemic] ↑ ⁻<& practical>↓ [1789]
9.29–30 and . . . Good,] ↑ ⁻. . . ⁻.↓ [1789]
10.30 generally] <always> ↑ ⁻↓ [1789; insertion and cancellation in pencil, with the insertion later inked over.]
11.29 Spectator.] ⁻. <It was the third.> [Cancelled in pencil.]
12.23 before Work] before <it> ↑↑Work↓↓ [The cancellation and insertion are both in pencil.]

12.38 Board,] ˜, [The comma is in pencil.]
13.10 Seller's . . . Books] Seller↑'s↓ & Sturmy's <on>/N/Book↑s↓ [1788]
13.35–14.2 *I conceive . . . mistaken*] [Underscored in pencil.]
14.10–11 to . . . Pleasure:] ↑↑˜. . . ˜:↓↓ [1790; similar ink used at 4.2 and 15.7–9.]
15.7–9 after . . . Customers.] [BF wrote "I was employ'd to carry the Papers thro' the Streets to the Customers, after having work'd in composing the Types and printing off the Sheets." In 1790, he indicated the transposition by a heavy ink line, similar to the ink used at 4.2 and 14.10–11.]
15.33 began to have] <frequently had> ↑ ˜˜˜↓ [1789; the cancellation and insertion were both made in pencil, but the insertion was later inked over.]
18.20 hear . . . each] ˜<a Word.> ↑so as {or} to understand ˜↓ [1789]
18.40 poor] <miserable> ↑˜↓ [1789]
23.10–11 to which . . . me] ↑to↓ which . . . me <to> [1788]
23.28 immediately] <directly> ↑˜↓ [1788]
24.4 and] ↑&↓ [1788]
26.30 Son . . . Burnet] ↑˜. . .˜↓ [1789; the handwriting and ink are similar to that employed later at 40.36, 40.38–42, 41.3–4, 54.18–19, 54.35, 57.3, 68.29, 73.4, 140.23, and 142.6.]
28.20 hot] ↑↑˜↓↓ [1790]
29.10 Glutton] <Gormandizer> ↑˜↓ [1788]
30.36 applauded] appla↑u↓ded [The "u" appears to be a late interlineation, 1788(?)]
30.36–37 himself] ↑˜↓ [1788]
31.7 a little] ↑˜˜↓ [1790]
31.11 again] ↑˜↓ [1790]
35.29 Franklin] [Revised to "F———"; then, in 1789, restored.]
40.32 Qualities.] ˜. <I had improv'd my Knowledge, however, by ↑↑Reading &↓↓ Conversation, & > [1790 cancellation.]
40.36 23d] ↑˜↓ [1789 sequence; cf. 26.30n.]
40.38–42 Perhaps . . . Age] ↑↑˜. . .˜↓↓ [1789 sequence; cf. 26.30n.]
40.42 11th] ↑˜↓ [1789 sequence; cf. 26.30n.]
41.3–4 seeing me] see↑ᵍ↓↑ing↓ me [1789 sequence; cf. 26.30n.]
54.18–19 I . . . Printing-House.] < ˜. . . .˜.> ↑↑Stet↓↓ ["Stet" added in 1789 sequence; cf. 26.30n.]
54.35 at Philadelphia,] ↑ ˜˜^↓ [1789 sequence; cf. 26.30n.]
57.3 by me,] ↑˜˜, ↓ [1789 sequence; cf. 26.30n.]
57.29–35 Memo . . . Interruption.] ˜. . . .˜. [Added in 1788, perhaps when BF began writing Part Three.]
62.30 Begun . . . 1784.] ↑↑˜. . . .˜^↓↓ [1788]
63.28 The . . . imported.] ↑˜. . . .˜.↓ [1788]
66.29 moral] ↑˜↓ [1788]
66.31–32 or . . . knew,] ↑˜. . . .˜,↓ [1788]
66.34–35 Care was employ'd] *Attention was taken up* ↑Care was employ'd↓ [1788. BF did not cancel the first clause but underlined it to indicate that it was the passage for which he posed an alternative.]
67.3 fewer] <less> ↑˜↓ [1788]
68.29 my remaining] ↑↑˜ ˜↓↓ [1788 sequence; cf. 26.30n.]
73.4 exactly] ↑exastly↓ [1789 sequence; cf. 26.30n.]
75.25 agreeable . . . Junto,] ↑↑˜. . . .˜,↓↓ [1788]
76.15 Thus . . . 1784] ↑↑˜. . . ˜↓↓ [1788]
81.9–10 as . . . inform'd] ↑˜. . . .˜↓ [1789]
83.31–32 bitterly . . . regret] ↑˜. . . ˜↓ [1789]
88.15 many . . . habits,] ↑˜. . . ˜,↓ [1789]
89.6 *right*] ↑↑˜↓↓ [1789]
90.29–30 and . . . delivered] ↑↑˜. . . delᵈ↓↓ [1789]
91.37–38 a while] <dorm for some years> ↑˜˜↓ [1789]
104.32 what was call'd] ↑↑˜˜˜↓↓ [1789; the clause was originally in pencil, then inked over by BF.]
105.10 as . . . them] ↑˜. . . .˜ [Originally in pencil, then inked over later; 1789(?)]
105.37 flat] ↑↑flatt↓↓ ↑flat↓ [1789. The interlinear insertion was originally in pencil, later inked over. The columnar ink duplicate with two "t's" was not cancelled.]
112.29–30 Tho' . . . last.] ↑↑˜. . . .˜.↓↓ [In pencil.]
117.26–27 I . . . Relief.] ↑↑˜. . . .˜.↓↓ [In pencil.]
117.27 however] ↑˜↓ [In pencil.]
122.29 Franklin's] <my> ↑˜↓ [1789]
123.15 Dialogue, *] ˜, * [The asterisk and the note itself are in pencil.]

124.38–125.1 Our . . . and] ↑↑⁻. . .⁻↓↓ [BF wrote the caret and the entire insertion in pencil. He first indicated that the addition was to come interlinearly before "for," then cancelled that caret and added one after "for." WTF later inked over the last caret and the addition, but he omitted inking over the "and."]

131.19–20 at first] ↑↑⁻⁻↓↓ [1789]

133.20–21 some Praise of] <an Eulogium on> ↑⁻⁻⁻↓ [1789 sequence; cf. 39.23n.]

135.19 Man's.] ⁻. [BF evidently wrote to this point by the fall of 1788. After a break of some time, he wrote the ten pages (102.24–108.21) that he inserted after 102.24. And after that he continued with 135.20 ff. He also penned a columnar query :] ↑↑The ↑many↓ unanimous Resolves of the Assembly what Date?↓↓

137.8 Letters, and] ⁻ , ↑&↓ ["&" in pencil.]

138.34 and Employments,] ↑↑&⁻ˌ↓↓ [In pencil.]

140.23 our Captain] <he> ↑our Captain↓ [1789? Similar to the ink used in the 1789 sequence; cf. 26.30n.]

141.30 Days] ↑⁻↓ [1789 sequence; cf. 26.30n.]

142.6 and from] & ↑⁻↓ [1789 sequence; cf. 26.30n.]

6. The Most Significant Additions

Like some cancellations (see Textual Note 7), some additions seem to us of such significance that they should be recorded. But we suspect that practically no one would read through this list if we gave all the thousands of additions. Therefore we have selected those that seemed the most significant. Readers especially interested in the additions are referred to our *Genetic Text*.

1.5–2.18 and the Journey . . . even our Afflictions.] ↑↑and . . . Afflictions.↓↓ [This extremely long columnar addition was probably written when BF began his second day's composition in 1771; see below, 2.19 and 8.12.]

1.14–15 with the Blessing of God] ↑with . . . God↓

2.19 The Notes] [Originally, "The Notes" began the next sentence after "England" (at 1.5) without a paragraph break; see above 1.5–2.18.]

5.20–6.6 My . . . Folgier.] ↑↑⁻. . .⁻.↓↓

7.25–26 He . . . Tools.] ↑↑⁻. . .⁻.↓↓

7.34–36 He . . . Parties.] ↑↑⁻. . .⁻.↓↓

8.12 Inscription:] ⁻ˌ(Here insert it) [Van Doren, pp. 209–10, suggested that BF probably concluded his first day's composition (Wednesday, July 31, 1771) with "(Here insert it)," and that when he resumed composition on August 1, he began by writing the outline of the *Autobiography* (see Appendix II this edition). We also think that this is probable. Further, we speculate that he added the long opening columnar addition (from 1.5 to 2.18) on August 1, as he read over the previous day's composition.]

8.13–33 Josiah . . . Stone.] ↑↑⁻. . .⁻.↓↓

9.29–32 There . . . Life.] ↑↑⁻. . .⁻.↓↓

10.20–28 My . . . Vanity.] ↑↑⁻. . .⁻.↓↓

11.32–12.2 With . . . But] ↑↑⁻. . .⁻↓↓

12.2–3 Stock . . . them,] ↑↑⁻. . .⁻,↓↓

12.20–21 of . . . ambitious.] ↑ . . . ⁻ˌ↓

16.37–17.1 and . . . it] ↑↑⁻. . .⁻↓↓

17.9–15 and . . . but] ↑↑⁻. . .⁻↓↓

17.36 leaving . . . Sea.] ↑⁻. . .⁻.↓

19.2 too,] ⁻, ↑↑<my best Clothes being left in my Chest to go by Sea,>↓↓

19.20–29 Wherefore . . . come.] ↑↑⁻. . .⁻.↓↓

20.26–29 passing . . . Appearance.] ↑↑⁻. . .⁻.↓↓

23.1–2 except . . . him.] ↑↑⁻. . .⁻.↓↓

24.10–11 and . . . Fortune.] ↑↑⁻. . .⁻.↓↓

25.31–36 A Friend . . . Newport] ↓↓⁻⁻. . .⁻↓↓

26.32–33 and . . . sober.] ↑↑⁻. . .⁻.↓↓

27.3–21 His . . . and a] ↑↑⁻. . .⁻⁻↓↓

27.26–27 The . . . Life.] ↑↑⁻. . .⁻.↓↓

27.27–29 Father . . . But] ↑⁻. . .⁻↓

28.30–29.12 He . . . if] ↑↑˜. . .˜↓↓
29.13–18 We . . . Week.] ↑↑˜. . .˜.↓↓
29.21–26 I . . . came.] ↑. . .˜.↓
29.30 only . . . 18,] ↑˜. . .˜,↓
33.8–28 We . . . Administration.] ↑↑˜. . .˜.↓↓
34.11–12 This . . . again.] ↑↑˜. . .˜.↓↓
34.14–35.11 At . . . handsomely.] ↑↑˜. . .˜.↓↓
36.1 and . . . Restraints,] ↑↑˜. . .˜.↓↓
36.3 (another Erratum)] ↑↑(˜˜)↓↓
36.18–19 On . . . Hands.] ↑↑˜. . .˜. ↓↓
36.22–23 We . . . Workmen.] ↑↑˜. . .˜.↓↓
36.36 under.] ˜. ↑↑<the Hatches>↓↓
38.14–37 In . . . supported.] ↑↑˜. . .˜.↓↓
42.4–6 honest . . . drink:] ↑↑˜. . .˜:↓↓
42.7–8 of uncommon . . . idle.] ↑↑˜. . .˜.↓↓
42.28 was . . . and] ↑↑<was but about 18, and> ˜. . .˜↓↓
43.5 idle,] ↓↓˜,↓↓
45.34 said to be] ↑↑˜˜˜↓↓
46.2–4 and . . . Trouble,] ↑↑˜. . .˜,↓↓
47.15–34 There . . . Croaking.] ↑↑˜. . .˜.↓↓
48.16–20 But . . . us.] ↑↑˜. . .˜.↓↓
48.25–26 William . . . Man.] ↑↑˜. . .˜.↓↓
48.34–42 And . . . hereafter;] ↑↑ ˜. . .˜;↓↓
49.12–13 having . . . Forms] ↑˜. . .˜↓
49.15–16 visible . . . Neighbours] ↑↑. . .˜↓↓
50.4 Paper ‸ . . . Body,] ˜. , . . .˜‸ [Although the caret for the interlineation ("↑under the Title of the Busy Body↓") follows the comma, BF may have intended the interlineation to precede the comma.]
51.12–13 it . . . they] ↑↑˜. . .˜↓↓
51.23 So . . . corrected.] ↑˜. . .˜.↓
52.21–22 Because . . . could.] ↑↑˜. . .˜.↓↓
53.33–34 This . . . write.] ↑↑˜. . .˜. ↓↓
54.24 seldom,] ↑↑˜,↓↓
54.27–28 and . . . bought,] ↑↑˜. . .˜,↓↓
55.25–26 the . . . deserving.] ↑↑˜. . .˜.↓↓
56.21–22 who . . . Company .] ↑↑˜. . .˜↓↓.
56.27 Our . . . but] ↑↑˜. . .˜↓↓
56.38 Thus . . . could.] ↑˜. . .˜.↓ [This passage was added at the bottom of the page.]
64.1–15 The . . . Owner.] ↑↑˜. . .˜.↓↓
64.17–19 and . . . me.] ↑↑˜. . .˜.↓↓
66.11 *true,*] ↑true,↓
66.12 *or*] ↑or↓
73.43–74.17 And . . . Benefit] ↑↑˜. . .˜.↓↓
81.1–24 In . . . Family.] ↑↑˜. . .˜.↓↓
83.30–36 In . . . chosen.] ↑↑˜. . .˜.↓↓
89.18–30 The . . . Earth.] ↑↑ ˜. . .˜.↓↓
91.10–27 The . . . Consequences.] ↑↑˜. . .˜‸↓↓
97.27–30 To . . . Principle.] ↑↑˜. . .˜.↓↓
101.8 For . . . me.] ↑↑˜. . .˜.↓↓
102.27–28 A . . . his.] ↑↑˜. . .˜.↓↓
104.4–5 Or . . . Cunning.] ↑↑˜. . .˜.↓↓ ["Or" actually added in the space left blank at the end of the line.]
109.33–36 By . . . Assemblies.] ↑↑˜. . .˜.↓↓
110.29–33 *"Look* . . . Projects.] ↑↑"˜. . .˜{.}.↓↓
120.29–121.1 In . . . Apple!] ↑↑˜. . .˜!↓↓
121.22–121.35 As . . . Disappointment.] ↑↑˜. . .˜.↓↓
124.23–124.28 I . . . necessary.] ↑↑˜. . .˜.↓↓
129.3–129.30 During . . . Admonition.] ↑↑˜. . .˜.↓↓
132.11 which . . . doubted,] ↑↑˜. . .˜,↓↓
135.6–10 and . . . publish'd;] ↑↑˜. . .˜;↓↓
142.8–9 the . . . and] ↑↑˜. . .˜↓↓
145.1–6 The . . . *voce.*] ↑↑˜. . .˜.↓↓
146.5–10 For . . . Equity.] ↑↑˜. . .˜.↓↓

7. The Most Significant Cancellations

1.12 <Fame> ↑Reputation↓
1.21 <the> ↑some↓ Faults
2.11 <firmly believe> owe
2.26 <A Farm> on a <Farm> Freehold
3.16 lost <or destroy'd>
3.20 <Lord of that Manor> the principal Gentleman
5.8 <Church of England> Episcopal Church
5.31 <Judgments> Distresses
6.37 against it; <and so it seem'd that I was destin'd for a Tallow Chandler>
10.30 <always> ↑generally↓ Beggars
11.13–14 <because he left me no Choice> a little for Dispute sake
11.29 Spectator. <It was the Third.>
12.2–3 <Copia verborum> ↑↑Stock of Words . . .↓↓
14.6 Conversation ↑<seemingly>↓
14.23 recommending <as I do>
15.33 <frequently had> ↑began to have↓
16.15 <took care> ↑made bold↓
17.3 me. <when I offended>
17.31 Bradford <who had been the first Printer in Pensilvania but remov'd from thence upon the quarrel of Geo. Keith>
18.36 50 Miles <to walk to the>
18.40 <miserable> ↑poor↓
19.32 Way, <in which I bore a Share>
20.31 Way, and <drinking>
23.26 Colonel French <a principal Man>
25.2 Impropriety of it; <and ↑said↓ he had advanc'd too much already to my Brother James>
26.15 <Intimate> ↑Friend↓ Collins
26.33 <a little too drunk> not sober
26.38 pleasing. <Collins was too drunk to go with me on this Visit>
28.18–19 <was> ↑seem'd↓ very reasonable
28.41 <dispute with> confound
29.10 <Gormandizer> ↑Glutton↓
29.22 Project <and the new Sect>
30.21 Considerations of <Sentiment>
30.26 He <said Osborne was malicious an> then
30.29 <Malice & ↑or↓> Envy
31.32 Voyage. <He was not well>
33.29 Companions. <He led me about & show'd me the City, with which he had been>
33.30 ↑↑<at a Fan Shop>. in Little Britain↓↓
34.12 correct if <Living a second Edition. Living>
34.20 <Person> ↑young Man↓
35.11 handsomely. <By one means or another, I pi>
35.12 <two single> ↑a young↓ Woman
35.37 Post <, so that the Postage was a Burthen>
37.3–4 haunted those <who refus'd to comply were>
40.21 <some> ↑↑a good deal of↓↓ Money
42.20 <80 Pounds a Year> Wages
43.31 For <on the Day of the County Election>
44.21 <Spiritous Liquors> ↑Dramdrinking↓
45.17 shrewd <sensible>
45.26 Business <for my self>
46.22 <Revealed Religion> Revelation
46.34 Religion. <some foolish Intrigues with low Women excepted, which from the Expence was rather more <inconvenient> prejudicial to me than to them.>
48.13–14 Conversation. <He was much my Fa>
48.34 Years. <That death I shall ever lament.—This Club>
49.1 Interest <we> ↑I↓
49.31 Webb <was lucky enough to be taken care>
49.31 ↑<She Female>↓ Friend
49.40 told it <immediately>

50.3 <my> ↑our↓ Paper

53.32 Barbadoes, & <there died ↑after some time↓>

56.18 Family <Her youngest Daughter had married my Friend Watson (early mentioned in this <Account> ↑Relation↓) and had some Regard for me on his Account>

56.27 Absence. <on receiving my foolish Letter.>

57.12 some <Books being lost>

57.26 contributed <considerably>

57.30–31 Beginning <of gratifying the suppos'd Curiosity of my Son; ↑and others of Posterity↓ what follows being>

64.14 Justice, by <returning the Reputation thus assumed to its right owner.>

65.31 worst <was better than none>

66.5 Explications of ↑<s Attempts to explain>

66.38 <my> ↑our↓ Interest

66.39 <my> ↑our↓ Slipping

74.1 ow'd <the Fortune & the Reputation he acquir'd, with>

82.10 him <indeed to the last>

85.11 Friends ↑<mutually serving each other^>↓

88.9 Service. <The Contributions being <pro> by People of different Sects promiscuously, Care was taken in the Nomination of Trustees to avoid giving a Predominancy to any <one> Sect, so that one of each was appointed, viz. one Church of England-man, one Presbyterian, one Baptist, one Moravian, &c.>

97.10 <many> ↑some↓

99.12 <Fortune> Providence

108.8 <The Happiness of Man consists> Human

111.4 Mortification. <Governor Hutchinson, too, who was one of the Congress, lik'd it so well>

112.21 <Governor> ↑Mr. ↓ Hamilton

112.26 <Governors> ↑Deputies↓

112.28 <Governors> ↑Deputies↓

120.18 Honour, <or posting his Troops so as to guard in some Degree the Frontier,>

121.21 me. <The French General Dieskau, who was <made a> wounded afterwards and taken Prisoner in an Action <with Sir> against Sir William Johnson, on the Frontier of New York, told some Gentlemen of >

121.31 <desired me not to insist told> ↑promis'd↓

122.9 me. <The Indians near different Parts of our Frontiers, encouraged by ↑the News of↓ this Defeat>

122.39 <I> we

130.20 engaged <in the Business>

131.15 <Warmth> general Moisture

132.26 Nollet <nor any of those others>

132.27–28 M. le Roy <and others>

138.29 Damages. <and if he could not recover them, he would cut his Th>

138.36 Braddock, <tho' not bred a Soldier>

8. Damage to the Holograph Text

32.35 Keith_] ˜. [The paper is frayed at the edge. The period appears in the photograph reproduction of the ms. made in 1927. WTF 31.31 and Bigelow 138.19 both have a period.]

34.22–23 Pamphlet . . . Erratum.] [Although now completely missing from the frayed bottom of the ms. page, the tops of the ascenders in these words and most of the letters in "Erratum" were present when a photocopy was taken of the ms. in 1927. The words are corroborated by WTF 33.22 and by Bigelow 142.2–3.]

52.29 Business] [Since the bottom of ms. 77 was trimmed, only the top half of the "B," the dot for the "i," and the top of the penultimate long "s" are now present in the catchword "Business."]

55.14 the Post] [The ms. is torn through the "th" in "the." WTF 55.1 and Bigelow 189.2 have "the."]

55.41 Supposition] [We supply the "sit" in the middle of "Supposition" because the ms. is torn. WTF 55.22 and Bigelow 190.7 both have "supposition."]

56.12 had] [Part of the "h" is missing because the edge of the ms. page is frayed. WTF 55.34 has "had" but Bigelow 190.27 omits it.]

56.17 old] [The "d" is missing in "old." Ms. torn. WTF 56.3 omits the phrase "& old Acquaintances." Bigelow 191.3 corroborates "old."]

56.30 Distance] [In the original ms., following "Distance," there appears "&c.," although the
ms. is unevenly frayed. WTF 56.14 includes "etc.," but Bigelow 191.21 omits it and follows
"distance" with a semi-colon.]

56.31 Then,] [We supply the "n," here because the ms. is unevenly frayed. WTF 56.15 and
Bigelow 191.22 both corroborate the concluding "n" and the comma.]

56.32 which] [We supply the last "h" because the ms. is frayed. Both WTF 56.15 and Bigelow
191.23 corroborate "which."]

56.33 upon] [We supply "upon." Farrand 180.19 has "[on]," perhaps because only about 15
mm. were left for this word on the page, but it seems to us that BF could easily have written
"upon" in that space. WTF 56.16 and Bigelow 191.24 both corroborate "upon."]

56.33 ventured] [We supply the "ed" because the ms. is frayed. WTF 56.16 and Bigelow 191.24
both corroborate "ventured."]

56.38 Thus . . . could.] ↑˜. . . .˜.↓ [Squeezed into the bottom of the page, this passage is not
now present; however, all but the final "l" in "well" was present in 1927 when a photocopy
was made of the ms. WTF 56.20 and Bigelow 192.1–2 use the same wording, except that they
do not capitalize the "E" in "Erratum."]

57.1 this] [The ms. is torn through "this." Both WTF 56.21 and Bigelow 193.1 print "this."]

57.15 that] [The edge of the ms. is torn through "that." Both WTF 56.33 and Bigelow 194.10
corroborate "that."]

57.16 I] [The edge of the ms. is torn through "I." Both WTF 56.34 and Bigelow 194.10
corroborate "I."]

57.21 was the] [The word "was" and the "t" in "the" are now missing from the edge of the ms.,
although all but the first part of the "w" was present on the photocopy made in 1927. Both
WTF 57.3 and Bigelow 194.17 corroborate "was the."]

57.22 It] [The word "It" is in the position of a catchword on ms. 86 but is not repeated on ms.
87. Between the time of our preparation of the text and the notes for this passage in 1974 and
the repair of the ms. in April 1976, the word "It" has been lost from the edge of the page.]

91.31 Youth.] ˜. [The period is now missing from the edge of the ms. but was present in 1927
when the photographic copy was made. WTF 88.21 and Bigelow 260.5 both print a semi-
colon.]

9. The Division into Four Parts

We follow the modern practice of dividing the *Autobiography* into four
parts, but since these headings are not found in the holograph manuscript, we
print them in brackets. Franklin's own notes within the manuscript justify the
first three divisions, but not the fourth, which occurs within a paragraph. The
trouble with dividing the book into parts is that this denies its unity, for, as the
outline shows, it was planned as a whole in 1771. And even though Franklin
significantly altered the order of some entries, omitted some, and added
others, he kept the outline by him and used it in composing the book.

We have added the words "[*Part One*]," "[*Part Two*]," "[*Part Three*]," and
"[*Part Four*]," on pp. 1, 58, 77, and 142.

10. Red Ink in the Chart and Schedule

Had Franklin, as he once intended, overseen the publication of his *Autobiography*, we suspect that he might have used red ink in the chart and
schedule, just as he did in the manuscript.

On p. 69, the lines of the chart are drawn in red ink, while the dots, letters,
and words are in black ink.

On p. 72, the lines around the schedule and hours are in red ink, while the
braces, numbers, and words are in black ink.

11. Textual Notes on Materials Added to the Autobiography

2.26 The Note on the Name Franklin.

Reprinted from the Lemay-Zall *Genetic Text*, pp. 175–77, which follows William Temple Franklin's first edition, *Memoirs of the Life and Writings of Benjamin Franklin* (London: Henry Colburn, 1817–18), I, 3. There are no emendations. For a discussion showing that Franklin intended to print this note and for a comparison of the three early texts, see our *Genetic Text*, pp. 175–76.

4.2 Uncle Benjamin Franklin's Poems.

Reprinted from the Lemay-Zall *Genetic Text*, pp. 177–78, which follows Uncle Benjamin Franklin's original fair copy book of poetry in the American Antiquarian Society. There are no emendations. For a discussion showing that Franklin intended to print this note and for a comparison of the two early texts, see our *Genetic Text*, pp. 177–79.

50.19 The *Pennsylvania Gazette* Editorial, October 9, 1729.

Reprinted from the Lemay-Zall *Genetic Text*, pp. 179–81, which follows the original in the *Pennsylvania Gazette*. We have emended a preposition: in the second column on p. 50, the original reads "to make any Governour independent on his People"; we have changed "on" to "of". For a discussion showing that Franklin intended to print this note and for a comparison of the three early texts, see our *Genetic Text*, pp. 179–82.

58.1 The letters from Abel James and Benjamin Vaughan.

Reprinted from the Lemay-Zall *Genetic Text*, pp. 184–89, which follows William Short's copy of the Abel James letter and follows William Temple Franklin's first edition, *Memoirs of the Life and Writings of Benjamin Franklin* I, 59–63, for the headings, transition, and the Benjamin Vaughan letter. We emend three accidentals of the William Short copy: at 58.5 "thought" is emended to "Thought"; and at 58.20 "friends' journals" is emended to "Friends' Journals." For a discussion showing that Franklin intended to print these letters and for a comparison of the three early texts of the James letter and the two early texts of the Vaughan letter, see our *Genetic Text*, pp. 182–84, 189–90.

68.32 The Golden Verses of Pythagoras.

Reprinted from the Lemay-Zall *Genetic Text*, p. 191, which follows the text in BF's "A Letter from Father *Abraham*, to his beloved Son," *New England Magazine of Knowledge and Pleasure*, no. 1 (August, 1758), 22. There are no emendations. For a discussion suggesting that Franklin may have decided not to print this note, see our *Genetic Text*, pp. 190–91.

115.1 The Wagon Advertisement.

Reprinted from the Lemay-Zall *Genetic Text*, pp. 192–95, which follows the text of the Boston Public Library copy of the broadside advertisement. There are no emendations. For a discussion showing that Franklin intended to print this advertisement and for a comparison of the four early texts, see our *Genetic Text*, pp. 191–92, 195–96.

12. Notes on Accidentals

We include here all periods, apostrophes, and other punctuation marks added to the Norton text, except for the periods after *Mr.*, *Dr.*, *Rev.*, etc., which we have consistently added. We record all changes from lower-case letters to capitals and vice versa (with the exceptions listed at the end of this paragraph). We do not list all omitted marks of punctuation, because Franklin often did not bother to cancel such marks as he superseded them while making revisions. Although clearly superseded accidentals are not listed, we record all possibly doubtful cases below. All changes in italicization are itemized. Finally, Franklin was inconsistent regarding his treatment of certain compound words. We list all changes in spacing, hyphenation, and capitalization with the following exceptions: we print compound words beginning with *any*, *every*, *mean*, and *some* (e.g., *anything*, *everybody*, *meantime*, and *someone*) as one word; we print compounds ending with *self* or *selves* (e.g., *myself*, *ourselves*) as one word; and we print *Journeyman*, *Journeymen*, *Goodwill*, and *Newspaper* as one word; we hyphenate *Printing-House;* and we print *New Castle, New York,* and *Rhode Island* as two words.

Norton
page
1.8 Week's] Weeks
2.26 Kingdom)] ˜.ˆ
3.1 Sons.] ˜ˆ
3.12 Wellingborough,] ˜ˆ
3.19 likewise] like wise
3.22 Undertakings] ˜,
3.23 County] ˜.
3.24 Ecton,] ˜ˆ
3.25 1702,] 1702ˆ
3.25 6,] 6.
3.31 Benjamin] ˜,
3.33 Man.] ˜,
5.8 Church.]˜ˆ
5.31 Distresses] ˜,
6.14 Sermons,] ˜ˆ
8.12 Inscription:] ˜ˆ
8.23 Grandchildren] Grand Children
8.33 85.] 85ˆ
12.14 Sentences,] ˜.
14.7 well-meaning] ˜˜˜
14.23 recommending] ˜,
16.39 Life.] ˜ˆ
17.3 he] He
17.23 was] Was
17.40 overboard] over board
17.11 Defoe] De foe
20.8 Lodging.] ˜ˆ
20.18 Second] second
20.26 Fourth] fourth
20.31 Street] street
21.11 Water Street] ˜-˜
21.33 Townspeople] Towns People
24.7 1724,] 1724.
25.10 Father's] Fathers
25.15 Proposition,] ˜ˆ
26.30 Bishop Burnet,] ˜˜ˆ
27.7 must,] ˜ˆ
27.12 rising,] ˜ˆ
27.29 Importance.] ˜ˆ
29.27 Read.] ˜,
29.30 18,] 18.
31.3 He] he
31.9 he] He
31.22 Credit] ˜,
31.34 Wife's] Wifes
33.13 over] ˜,
33.39 that] ˜,
34.3 Palmer's,] ˜ˆ
34.36 Bees,] ˜ˆ
35.12 Woman,] ˜;
35.13 bred,] ˜;
35.37 Post.] ˜ˆ
36.9 Friendship] ˜.
36.23 Press] ˜,
36.27 Day's Work ˜-˜
37.25 Dispatch,] ˜
37.28 Duke Street] ˜-˜

37.33 Rate,] ˜ˆ
37.35 Woman,] ˜ˆ
37.37 revered,] ˜ˆ
38.16 Roman Catholic] ˜-˜
38.39 Wygate,] ˜.
38.42 swim] ˜,
39.12 me] ˜,
39.16 Hour] ˜,
39.17 Leisure,] ˜.
39.17 he] He
39.26 Remove] ˜,
39.32 me)] ˜),
40.3 it.] ˜ˆ
40.4 Year,] ˜ˆ
40.11 Days'] ˜ˆ
40.32 Tho'] tho'
40.39 Sea] ˜,
41.9 Name,] ˜ˆ
41.12 28,] 28.
41.14 Stationery,] ˜ˆ
41.34 House] ˜.
42.4 Work] ˜ˆ
42.7 Same,] ˜:
43.11 Town] ˜,
43.13 pay,] ˜.
44.32 Words,] ˜ˆ
45.23 up] ˜.
45.29 Parents] Parent's
46.33 Father)] ˜,)
48.35 long] ˜.
49.18 Merchants'] ˜ˆ
49.39 Encouragement.] ˜ˆ
50.10 directly,] ˜.
50.11 me.] ˜ˆ
51.16 before-mentioned] ˜˜˜
51.40 [note 9] 500 pounds.] ˜ £ˆ
53.16 Trade,] ˜ˆ
53.20 Street] street
53.21 Streets] streets
53.34 write.] ˜ˆ
53.36 55,000 Pounds,] 55000, £ˆ
54.1 80,000 Pounds,] 80,000 £ˆ
54.2 Pounds—Trade] £. ˜
54.35 Philadelphia,] ˜ˆ
55.2 him.] ˜ˆ
55.25 ensu'd,] ˜ˆ
56.21 Situation,] ˜ˆ
56.29 invalid,] ˜ˆ
57.6 by] By
57.31 Beginning] ˜.
58.9 handwriting] hand-writing
58.14 it.] ˜,
60.35 is,] ˜ˆ
61.2 Sir]˜,
62.31 Passy,] ˜ˆ
62.31 1784.] ˜ˆ
62.37 if] If

Norton
page
62.38 improv'd] ~^
63.1 considerable,] ~.
63.8 etc.,] ~.^
63.39 etc.] ~^
64.25 easier:] ~,:
64.32 happened;] ~.
65.2 etc., etc.] ~^^~.
66.11 *true*] true
66.12 *or*] or
66.22 1728,] 1728.
67.15 Dulness.] ~^
67.40 *Cleanliness.*] ~^
68.1 *Tranquility.*] ~^
70.26 Weeks'] ~^
70.26 Examination.] ~^
71.8 Examination,] ~;
71.15 Poems,] ~.
71.15 viz.] ~^
71.25 Day.] ~,
71.26 Self-examination] Self Examination
71.39 But] but
73.25 Points] ~.
74.4 arrive,] ~^
74.6 *Temperance*] ~.
74.10 Learned.] ~^
75.8 Circumstance] ~,
75.8 (there] ^~
75.11 rare)] ~^
72.25 myself,] ~^
76.15 Passy,] ~^
76.15 1784.] ~^
77.1 1788,] ~.
77.9 9,] ~.
77.32 Laws.] ~^
77.35 B. F."] ~.~.^
78.3 Words,] ~.
78.16 Weeks'] ~^
78.23 Advice,] ~^
78.24 Interest,] ~^
80.7 Self-denial] ~^~
81.25 1734.] ~.
82.26 etc.,] ~^,
82.31 Year's] Years
82.41 that,] ~^
83.2 Staircase] Stair-Case
83.11 etc.,] ~.^
83.15 Years'] ~^
83.30 Sons,] ~^
83.31 Smallpox] Small Pox
83.32 Inoculation.] ~;
84.22 They] they
84.23 Information,] ~^
85.18 Postmaster] Post-master,
86.16 Pounds' worth] Pounds-worth
87.32 meet in] ~-~
88.1 Westminster Hall] Westminster-hall
88.34 Copper] ~,
89.6 *right*] right
89.19 stood.]~.:
90.9–10 Front Street] ~-~
90.11 Semicircle] Semi-Circle

Norton
page
90.13 Thirty Thousand] ~-~
90.15 25,000] 25000
91.27 Consequences.] ~^
92.17 before-mentioned] ~-~
92.31 Mottos] Motto's
94.16 *con*] ~.
95.8 Friends.] ~;
95.16 twenty-one] ~^~
95.26 Penn] ~.
96.20 *or*] or
98.6 Effect.] ~,
98.7 it,] ~^
100.22 above-mentioned] ~^~
102.5 drunk,] ~^
102.18 *it*] it
102.19 *so.*"] ~. ^
102.24 1751] ~
102.32 public-spirited] public^Spirited
104.8 Meetinghouse] Meeting-house
104.26 Meetinghouse] Meeting-house
104.26 Street] street
105.4 Neighbors'] Neighbours^
107.43 Daylight] Day-light
107.46 complain,] ~^
108.2–3 relating.] ~.:
108.21 happily,] ~;
109.30 appointed,] ~.
110.8 *Democratic*] Democratic
110.30 pursue."] ~.^
110.34 *from*] from
111.1 Attention."] ~^"
113.26 Excise,] ~^
113.33 completed.] ~,
114.20 brought] ~,
114.25 Baggage,] ~.
115.25 Days'] ~^
117.13 etc.:] ~^;
118.31 Pounds,] ~^
119.4 Duquesne] DuQuesne
119.12 Event] ~:
120.20 Settlements,] ~.
120.21 Governors] Governor's
122.12 Firework] Fire Work
122.17 D—l,"] ~,^
122.18 taken?"] ~?^
122.20 Uncertainty."—] ~.^—
122.35 Pounds,] £^
123.24 Officers] ~.
125.5 Companions'] ~^
125.31 And] and
126.6 Day's] Days
126.11 O] O
126.30 Flame,] ~;
126.37 them,] ~^
127.2–3 Service.] ~^
127.31 etc.] ~^
127.32 Congregations] ~;
127.32 Men,] ~^
128.29 Opinion,] ~.
129.4 Regiment] ~,
130.1 Assembly.] ~,

Norton
page
130.10 Colonies,] ˜ˆ
130.19 that,] ˜˜
130.19 perhaps,] ˜ˆ
131.17 etc.,] ˜.ˆ
132.2 Europe,] ˜ˆ
132.22 another's] anothers
132.22 Abbé's] Abbe's
132.32 Sect:] ˜,;
133.1 Elève] Eleve
133.4 Marly,]˜;
134.7 before-mentioned] ˜˜˜
135.28 pass,] ˜ˆ
136.17 (presenting] ˆ˜
136.20 protested)] ˜,
136.26 Share.] ˜ˆ
137.4 tomorrow] to-morrow
137.9 Insurance] ˜.
137.9 Goods.] ˜,
137.10 Lordship's] Lordships

Norton
page
137.19 tomorrow] to-morrow
137.31 *know*] know
137.33 there,] ˜ˆ
137.33 Passengers] ˜,
138.5 Packet Boats] ˜-˜
138.24 tomorrow] to-morrow
138.34 Places] ˜,
138.34 Employments,] ˜ˆ
139.2 others,] ˜.
139.16 Charge] ˜.
139.17 Business.] ˜,
139.24 Franklin,] ˜;
139.26 afore-mention'd] aforemention'd
141.3 Shipbuilding] ˜-˜
141.19 same.] ˜,
141.23 it—] ˜.—
142.20 Playhouse] ˜-˜
144.18 me,] ˜.
146.5 necessary.] ˜,

Franklin's Journey from Boston to Philadelphia, 1723

Mrs. Claude-Anne Lopez, an editor of *The Papers of Benjamin Franklin*, deduced in the summer of 1980 that a series of dates in Franklin's handwriting referred to his first coming to Philadelphia in 1723, when he was seventeen. When Franklin wrote the notes, he was living in Passy, France, at the end of 1783, serving as Minister Plenipotentiary just after the close of the Revolutionary War. He evidently came across the date of Monday, September 23, 1723, picked up a handy piece of paper (the blank side of a business letter, dated November 29, 1783, from his Paris banker, Ferdinand Grand), and jotted down the following:

	Monday	Sept. 23	
	T ———————————	24	
	W———————————	25	
	T———————————	26	
	Fr———————————	27	
	S ———————————	28	
	Sund —————————	29	
	Monday ————————	<1>	30 <Oct>
Bay	Tues —————————	<2>	1 Oct
Amboy	Wednes ————————	2	Water
Pines	Thurd —————————	3	Amb
Brown's	Friday —————————	4	
River D	Sat———————————	5	
Philad	Sund —————————	6	

The handwriting is a hurried scribble—except for the names of the places on the left, "Bay" through "Philad," which are deliberate and quite distinct. We hypothesize that when Franklin came across the date Monday, September 23, 1723, he remembered that at approximately that time, sixty years ago, he had been about to leave Boston. But we think the only date he recalled clearly was that of his arrival in Philadelphia—the first Sunday in October, 1723. We can be reasonably certain he knew this date, because twelve years earlier, when he wrote Part One of the *Autobiography*, he described his journey in great detail, including the fact that he arrived in Philadelphia on a Sunday morning in October. And the *Autobiography* was on his mind. Just the previous fall, he had received a letter from an old Philadelphia friend, Abel James, urging him to continue the *Autobiography* and enclosing a copy of the outline. Franklin subsequently solicited Benjamin Vaughan's opinion, which Vaughan sent him on January 31, 1783—early in the same year that Franklin penned these notes. He was hoping to return to the *Autobiography*, and sometime within the coming year, 1784, he composed Part Two. When he scribbled these notes, he was probably trying to calculate where he had been on those specific dates, some sixty years ago. Perhaps he intended to include them if he had a chance to revise the manuscript of Part One.

The errors and false starts in the dates and places suggest that as he was hurriedly writing down the days and dates, he was thinking ahead to his arrival in Philadelphia and calculating back from that time to where he would have been a few days before. Thus when he got to Monday, September 30, he carelessly wrote instead "Monday ——— 1 Oct" and then "Tues ——— 2." Then he realized he had omitted the 30th of September, so he wrote "30" over "1" and crossed out "Oct." And he crossed out "2" by "Tues" and wrote "1 Oct." As he jotted the days and dates for the next two entries, he anticipated the places on his journey and incorrectly wrote "Water" and "Amb[oy]" after them. He probably perceived his error as he wrote "Friday ——— 4," and so he wrote only the day and dates down to "Sund ——— 6." Then he began writing the places where he had been on those dates, writing on the left, evidently going backwards, from the one place and time he was certain of ("Phila"), to "River D," "Brown's," "Pines," "Amboy," and, finally, "Bay." At least, this is our reconstruction of what happened, based primarily on the false starts and the appearance of the handwriting, which is obviously hurried—except for the deliberate clarity of the places written in the left column.

Even before Mrs. Lopez made her exciting discovery, we had hypothesized this chronology, based mainly on the fact that Franklin's personal file of the *New England Courant* extended only through September 16, 1723. Therefore, he left his brother's employ before the next week's paper, September 23, appeared. As he tells us in the *Autobiography*, he looked for work as a printer in Boston, but James Franklin had already spoken to all the Boston printers who, consequently, refused him work. This could not have taken Franklin more than a day or two, so by September 23, he knew that he had to leave Boston. He resolved to go to New York, "as the nearest Place where there was a Printer." According to the local papers, the only boats to leave Boston for New York between early September and late October were William Beckman's, which cleared out on September 14, and Arnout Schemerhoorn's, which cleared customs and sailed on September 25.

Franklin probably sailed with Schemerhoorn. In the September 30 *New England Courant*, James Franklin advertised for a "likely lad" as an apprentice, so it seems reasonable to assume that James Franklin knew before September 30 that Benjamin Franklin had left Boston. Franklin's jottings of dates and places tend to confirm that he sailed from Boston about September 25. He tells us in the *Autobiography* that the voyage took three days. If he sailed with Schemerhoorn, he arrived in New York on September 27, probably late that Friday afternoon. Since most people worked six days a week in the eighteenth century, Franklin probably went to see William Bradford on Saturday morning, September 28, and there he received the advice to try Andrew Bradford in Philadelphia. Of course he may not have been able to see William Bradford until Monday, the thirtieth.

At any rate, the document found by Mrs. Lopez, together with Franklin's own account in the *Autobiography*, made the itinerary and dates of the six-day journey from New York to Philadelphia perfectly clear.

Tuesday, October 1. Franklin set out in a small boat from New York to Perth Amboy, the capital of East Jersey. The voyage normally took several hours, but a squall came up as the boat was crossing Upper New York Harbor, "tore our rotten Sails to pieces," and prevented the ship from reaching the safety of the Kill van Kull, a channel separating the northern tip of Staten Island from the mainland of New Jersey. The storm drove the boat east, across Upper New York Harbor, to Long Island, where it was in danger of being

wrecked in "a great Surf on the stony Beach." The boat and its passengers
spent a miserable night off Long Island, "the Spray beating over the Head of
our Boat."

Wednesday, October 2nd. The storm abated and so the boat managed to
make Perth Amboy, New Jersey, by that afternoon, after "30 Hours on the
Water without Victuals, or any Drink but a Bottle of filthy Rum: The Water
we sail'd on being Salt." Sick with a fever, Franklin spent that night at an inn
in Perth Amboy.

Thursday, October 3rd. In the morning, Franklin took Redford's Ferry
across Raritan Bay to South Amboy, New Jersey, and set out to walk fifty miles
to Bordentown, where he believed he could get a boat to Philadelphia. Thus
he took Governor Lowrie's (the Lower) Road across New Jersey, which went
from South Amboy by Cranbury and Crosswicks, to Bordentown and to
Burlington. But Franklin did not get far. "It rain'd very hard all the Day, I was
thoroughly soak'd and by Noon a good deal tir'd, so I stopt at a poor Inn, where
I staid all night, beginning now to wish I had never left home." In his
memorandum of the dates, penned sixty years later, Franklin wrote "Pines" by
this date. Perhaps "Pines" was the name of the "poor Inn" but it is also a
generic name for the area. On April 23, 1761, Franklin characterized this
route as "chiefly" going through "a heavy loose land, very fatiguing to the
Horses [let alone to the foot-traveller]: That being thro' a barren country, it
was not well inhabited, nor the Inns well supply'd with Provisions." Perhaps
Franklin walked as far as Cranbury in the rain before spending the night at the
"poor Inn."

Friday, October 4th: He walked from the "poor Inn" to Bordentown, New
Jersey, where he spent the night at Dr. John Browne's inn (later known as
Washington House), which was located at the northwest intersection of Main
(or Farnsworth) and Crosswick Streets. There he enjoyed talking with Dr.
John Browne at dinner.

Saturday, October 5th: From Dr. John Browne's inn at Bordentown,
Franklin walked to Burlington, the capital of West Jersey, about eighteen
miles above Philadelphia, on the east side of the Delaware River. When he
reached Burlington on Saturday morning, he "had the Mortification to find
that the regular Boats were gone, a little before my coming, and no other to go
till Tuesday." He therefore intended to stay there until Tuesday, but that
evening a boat came by, "which I found was going towards Philadelphia." As
there was no wind, the people in the boat "row'd all the Way." By midnight,
"some of the Company were confident we must have pass'd" Philadelphia, so
they decided to land, "got into a Creek," and stayed the night in the open,
huddled around a fire, "the Night being cold."

Sunday, October 6th: In the light, "one of the Company" recognized the
place as "Cooper's Creek a little above Philadelphia," site of present-day
Camden, New Jersey. As soon as they rowed out of the creek into the
Delaware River, they could see Philadelphia, where Franklin arrived "about 8
or 9 o'clock, on the Sunday morning, and landed at Market Street Wharf."

The Outline of the Autobiography

As Carl Van Doren suggested in *Benjamin Franklin's Autobiographical Writing*, pp. 209–11, Franklin probably composed the outline of the *Autobiography* on the morning of his second day's stay at the Bishop of St. Asaph's August 1, 1771. Van Doren pointed out that the first eight pages of the *Autobiography* discuss Franklin's family and childhood, topics not included in the outline. When Franklin read over the first day's composition (presumably the first eight pages of the holograph manuscript), he was struck by the need for a plan, so he then drew up the outline and wrote that brief paragraph about his "rambling Digressions" (above, 8.36–38). We further believe that at the same time, Franklin added the long addition to the very beginning of the manuscript, telling his reasons for writing the *Autobiography* (see 1.5–2.18 on p. 177).

Franklin's original holograph of the outline is not extant, but the copy at the Pierpont Morgan Library, New York, which we reproduce here, was the one he had by him and used when he wrote Parts Two, Three, and Four. Abel James sent this copy to him in the late spring or summer of 1782, urging him (in the letter to Franklin printed in the *Autobiography*, above, p. 58) to continue writing the book. In Passy, France, Franklin read through this copy of the outline, interlined one word ("Armonica") in red ink on p. 3, added the instruction "verte" (over) in the position of a catchword, and wrote a continuation (on p. 4) in red ink, beginning with "Hutchinson's Letters." The continuation covers the years since the summer of 1771, when he had written the original. At a later time, Franklin again read through this copy of the outline and corrected it. Using black ink, he interlined two phrases ("and at Easton" and at the end of the page, "St. Andrews") on p. 2 and corrected one letter on p. 3. Two additional black ink marks on this copy of the outline were presumably made by Franklin. On the first page, a heavy line has been drawn down the center, stopping with the entry "Its plan and Utility." Since this topic concludes Part One, the logical explanation (first advanced by Bigelow, 1868, p. 52) is that Franklin drew this line before he began to write Part Two. And on the second page of the outline, a large heavy, closing half bracket comes after the entry "I am sent to England." The logical inference (again, first made by Bigelow, 1868, p. 53) is that Franklin made this mark after writing Part Three.

The original copyist of this outline (Henry Drinker, who was in 1781–82 clerking for Abel James in Philadelphia) added a heading to the outline: "Autographe très curieux de Bn. Franklin. 1ere [i.e., premiere] Esquisse memorandum de ses memoires." [Very interesting writing by Ben Franklin. First draft memorandum of his memoirs.] After Franklin's death, and after William Temple Franklin had given both the holograph of the *Autobiography* and this copy of the outline to Louis Guillaume Le Veillard, Le Veillard added the following heavily inked words to the heading: "Copie d'un Projet" [Copy of a draft] and "Les additions a l'encre rouge sont de la main de Franklin" [The additions in red ink are in Franklin's hand].

For a consideration of the six texts of the outline, and for detailed textual notes, see our *Genetic Text*, pp 196–202, 205–11. Source: Franklin's outline, Pierpont Morgan Library, New York.

The Outline of the *Autobiography*

Copie d'un [Autographe] Project très curieux de Bn. Franklin.—1ere. Esquisse memorandum de ses mémoires. Les additions à l'encre rouge sont de la main de Franklin.

My writing. Mrs.. Dogoods Letters—Differences arise between my Brother and me (his temper and mine) their Cause in general. His News Paper. The Prosecution he suffered. My Examination. Vote of Assembly. His Manner of evading it. Whereby I became free. My Attempt to get employ with other Printers. He prevents me. Our frequent pleadings before our Father. The final Breach. My Inducements to quit Boston. Manner of coming to a Resolution. My leaving him & going to New York. (return to eating Flesh.) thence to Pennsylvania, The Journey, and its Events on the Bay, at Amboy, the Road, meet with Dr. Brown. his Character. his great work. At Burlington. The Good Woman. On the River. My Arrival at Philada... First Meal and first Sleep. Money left. Employment. Lodging. First Acquaintance with my Afterwards Wife. with J. Ralph. with Keimer. their Characters. Osborne. Watson. The Governor takes Notice of me. the Occasion and Manner. his Character. Offers to set me up. My return to Boston. <y> Voyage and Accidents. Reception. My Father dislikes the proposal. I return to New York and Philada... Governor Burnet. J. Collins. the Money for Vernon. The Governors Deceit. Collins not finding Employment goes to Barbados much in my Debt. Ralph and I go to England. Disappointment of Governors Letters. Col. French his Friend. Cornwallis's Letters. Cabbin. Denham. Hamilton. Arrival in England. Get Employment. Ralph not. He is an Expence to me. Adventures in England. Write a Pamphlet and print 100. Schemes. Lyons. Dr. Pemberton. My Diligence and yet poor thro Ralph. My Landlady. her Character. Wygate. Wilkes. Cibber. Plays. Books I borrowed. Preachers I heard. Redmayne. At Watts's— Temperance. Ghost,. Conduct and Influence among the Men, persuaded by Mr Denham to return with him to Philada.. & be his Clerk. Our Voyage. and Arrival. My resolutions in Writing. My Sickness. His Death. Found D. R married. Go to work again with Keimer. Terms. His ill Usage of me. My Resentment. Saying of Decow. My Friends at Burlington. Agreement with H Meredith to set up in Partnership. Do so. Success with the Assembly. Hamiltons Friendship. Sewells History. Gazette. Paper Money. Webb. Writing Busy Body. Breintnal. Godfrey. his Character. Suit against us. Offer of my Friends Coleman and Grace. continue the Business and M. goes to Carolina. Pamphlet on Paper Money. Gazette from Keimer. Junto erected, its plan. Marry. Library erected. Manner of conducting the Project. Its plan and Utility. Children. Almanack. the Use I made of it. Great Industry. Constant Study. Fathers Remark and Advice upon Diligence. Carolina Partnership. Learn French and German.

Journey to Boston after 10 years. Affection of my Brother. His Death and leaving me [p. 2] his Son. Art of Virtue. Occasion. City Watch. amended. Post Office. Spotswood. Bradfords Behaviour. Clerk of Assembly. Lose one of my Sons. Project of subordinate Junto's. Write occasionally in the papers. Success in Business. Fire Companys. Engines. Go again to Boston in 1743. See Dr Spence. Whitefield. My Connection with him. His Generosity to me. my returns. Church Differences. My part in them. Propose a College. not then prosecuted. Propose and establish a Philosophical Society. War. Electricity. my first knowledge of it. Partnership with D Hall &c. Dispute in Assembly upon Defence. Project for it. Plain Truth. its Success. 10.000 Men raised and Disciplined. Lotteries. Battery built. New Castle. My Influence in the Council. Colours, Devices and Motto's.— Ladies. Military Watch. Quakers. chosen of the common council. Put in the Commission of the Peace. Logan fond of me. his Library. Appointed post Master General. Chosen Assembly Man. Commissioner to treat with Indians at Carlisle. ↑and at Easton.↓ Project and establish Academy. Pamphlet on it. Journey to Boston. At Albany. Plan of Union of the Colonies. Copy of it. Remarks upon it. It fails and how. (Journey to Boston in 1754.) Disputes about it in our Assembly. My part in them. New Governor. Disputes with him. His Character and Sayings to me. Chosen Alderman. Project of Hospital my Share in it. Its Success. Boxes. Made a Commissioner of the treasury My Commission to defend the Frontier Counties. Raise Men & build Forts. Militia Law of my drawing. Made Colonel. Parade of my Officers. Offence to Proprietor. Assistance to Boston Ambassadors— Journey with Shirley &c.. Meet with Braddock. Assistance to him. To the Officers of his Army. Furnish him with Forage. His Concessions to me and Character of me. Success of my Electrical Experiments. Medal sent me per Royal Society and Speech of President. Dennys Arrival & Courtship to me. his Character. My Service to the Army in the Affair of Quarters. Disputes about the Proprietors Taxes continued. Project for paving the City. I am sent to England.] Negociation there. Canada delenda est. My Pamphlet. Its reception and Effect. Projects drawn from me concerning the Conquest. Acquaintance made and their Services to me Mrs.. S.., Mr Small. Sir John P. Mr. Wood. Sargent Strahan and others. their Characters. Doctorate from Edinburg ↑St. Andrews↓ <F——d> [p.3] Doctorate from Oxford. Journey to Scotland. Lord Leicester. Mr. Prat.— DeGrey. Jackson. State of Affairs in England. Delays. Event. Journey into Holland and Flanders. Agency from Maryland. Sons Appointment. My Return. Allowance and thanks. Journey to Boston. John Penn Governor. My Conduct towards him. The Paxton Murders. My Pamphlet Rioters march to Philada... Governor retires to my House. My Conduct, <towards him. The Paxton Murders.> Sent out to the Insurgents—Turn them back. Little Thanks. Disputes revived. Resolutions against continuing under Proprietary Government. Another Pamphlet. Cool Thoughts. Sent again to England with Petition. Negociation there. Lord H. his Character. Agencies from New Jersey, Georgia, Massachusets. Journey into Germany 1766. Civilities received there. Gottingen Observations. Ditto into France in 1767. Ditto in 1769. Entertainment there at the Academy. Introduced to the King and the Mesdames. Mad. Victoria and Mrs. Lamagnon. Duc de Chaulnes, M Beaumont. Le Roy. Dali[t]bard. Nollet. See Journals. Holland. Reprint my papers and add many. Books presented to me <by> ↑from↓ many Authors. My Book translated into French. Lightning Kite. various Discoveries. My Manner of prosecuting that Study. King of Denmark invites me to Dinner. Recollect my Fathers Proverb. Stamp Act. My Opposition to it. Recommendation of J. Hughes. Amendment of it. Examination in Parliament. Reputation it gave me. Caress'd by Ministry. Charles Townsends Act. Opposition to it. Stoves and Chimney plates. ↑Armonica.↓ Accquaintance with Ambassadors. Russian Intimation. Writing in Newspapers. Glasses from Germany. Grant of Land in Nova Scotia. Sicknesses. Letters to America returned hither. the Consequences. Insurance Office. My Character. Costs me nothing to be civil to inferiors, a good deal to be submissive to superiors &c &c..

Farce of perpetl. Motion

Writing for Jersey Assembly. verte

[p. 4] Hutchinson's Letters. Temple. Suit in Chancery, Abuse before the Privy Council.—Lord Hillsborough's Character. & Conduct. Lord Dartmouth. Negotiation to prevent the War.—Return to America. Bishop of St. Asaph. Congress, Assembly. Committee of Safety. Chevaux de Frize.—Sent to Boston, to the Camp. To Canada. to <Gu> Lord Howe.— To France, Treaty, &c

Biographical Notes

ADAMS, MATTHEW (?1694–1753). This friend to the young BF wrote for the *New-England Courant* and later the *New-England Weekly Journal* and the *Boston News-Letter*. No record exists of the books he lent BF, but the *Courant* (July 2, 1722) itself boasted of being furnished with "a large and valuable collection" that included works of Milton, Shakespeare, and Swift.

> Elizabeth C. Cook, *Literary Influence in Colonial Newspapers* (New York, 1912), p. 20; C. Lennart Carlson, "John Adams, Matthew Adams, Mather Byles and the *New England Weekly Journal*," *American Literature*, 12 (1940), 347–48.

ALEXANDER, JAMES (1691–1756). The New Yorker who approved BF's Albany Plan was an aristocratic Scot who fled to America as a Jacobin in 1715 and who later held high public offices in New York and New Jersey. Mathematician, intellectual, and an original member of the American Philosophical Society, he was the actual editor of John Peter Zenger's *New York Weekly Journal*.

> P, 5: 336–38; Vincent Buranelli, "Peter Zenger's Editor," *American Quarterly*, 7 (1955), 174–81; Stanley Nider Katz, ed., *A Brief Narrative of the Case and Trial of John Peter Zenger* (1736) by James Alexander (Cambridge, Mass., 1963); *DAB*.

ALLEN, JOHN (c. 1685–1750). One of the committee supervising BF's printing money at Burlington in 1728, he was a member of the New Jersey legislature (1722–27), treasurer of West Jersey (1722–50) and became a Superior Court judge in 1736.

> Edwin R. Walker, *et. al.*, *History of Trenton*, 2 vols. (Princeton, 1929), 1: 75, 120.

ALLEN, WILLIAM (1704–1780). An early ally, WA supported BF for postmaster-general in 1753 but became a staunch enemy in the fight over proprietary privileges and referred to BF as the "Chief" of the "Factioneers," as "that Disturber of the Peace," and as "the grand Incendiary." Son-in-law of Andrew Hamilton and father-in-law of John Penn, he was Chief Justice (1750–74) but resigned when Pennsylvania moved towards Independence. He emigrated to England in 1776.

> P, 3: 296–97; Lewis Burd Walker, ed., *The Burd Papers: Extracts from Chief Justice William Allen's Letter Book* ([Pottsville, Pa.,], 1897), 10, 49, 57, 63; *DAB*.

AMHERST, JEFFREY (1717–1797). Succeeding Lord Loudoun as British commander-in-chief in North America, he defeated the French in a series of battles (1758–60) that ended their threat to the colonies. Offered the same command in 1776, he refused to fight against the Americans, but accepted command of the British land forces in England after France declared war.

P, 8: 328n; Valentine, 1: 18; *DAB*; *DNB*.

ANDREWS, JEDEDIAH (1674–1747). The Harvard-educated Andrews was the only Presbyterian minister in Philadelphia before Samuel Hemphill became his assistant in September, 1734. Others beside Franklin found his sermons less than inspiring. A poet in the *American Weekly Mercury* of June 12, 1729, complained that "The priest did creep / So dull and slowly that I fell asleep." After having Hemphill excommunicated for "liberalism," Andrews was himself briefly suspended in 1744 for a "disgraceful act."

P, 2: 27; Sprague, 3: 11; *Sibley's Harvard Graduates*, 4: 219–24.

ANNIS, THOMAS. Captain of the *London Hope*, the packet boat on which BF sailed to London, November 5, 1724, Annis contributed to Philadelphia civic affairs as late as November 1736.

PMHB, 58: 267.

BARD or BAIRD, PATRICK. This politically powerful Secretary of the Province and clerk of the Council (1723–26, 1743) was also Philadelphia Port Physician (from 1720) and registrar of the Vice-Admiralty Court (1738).

Keith, 2: 672, 687, 689.

BALTIMORE, CHARLES CALVERT, 5th BARON (1699–1751). The proprietor of Maryland, where he resided 1732–33, he was sued by the Penns in 1734 over a boundary dispute that was finally settled by the Mason-Dixon survey in 1767. BF printed the key documents in the suit. A Member of Parliament from 1734–1751, he was famous for his malapropisms.

Miller, p. 31; Sedgwick, 1: 518.

BASKET or BASKETT, JOHN (d. 1742). Master of the Stationers Company (1714–15) and printer of the Oxford Bible (1716–17), he was a creditor of Sir William Keith and in February 1726 supported his retaining the governorship.

Plomer, 22–23; Keith, 2: 920; *DNB*.

BEATTY, CHARLES CLINTON (c. 1715–1772). Chaplain also on the successful Forbes campaign (1757) for Fort Duquesne, he believed that Indians were descended from the Ten Tribes of Israel. The gullible Beatty was also duped by a frontiersman who told of Indians living "on the west side of the Mississippi" who were descended from medieval Welsh prince Madoc, a legendary explorer of America.

Sprague, 3: 119–23; *DAB*; Guy S. Klett, ed., *Journals of Charles Beatty* (Univ. Park, Pa., 1962); J.A. Leo Lemay, "The Tall Tales of a Colonial Frontiersman," *Western Pa. Historical Mag.*, 64 (1981), 33–46.

BENEZET, JOHN STEPHEN (1683–1751). Father of BF's good friend, the Quaker schoolmaster Anthony Benezet, JSB was a Huguenot merchant immigrating to London in 1715 and to Philadelphia in 1731 as a Quaker but turning Moravian in 1743 upon his retiring and moving to Germantown. Whitefield had been the family's friend when they lived in England.

George S. Brooks, *Friend Anthony Benezet* (Philadelphia, 1937), p. 96: P, 2: 285n.

BENGER, ELLIOTT (d. 1753). Though unnamed, he was the deputy postmaster-general whom BF succeeded. He himself purchased the office from his relative Alexander Spotswood, his predecessor, for the customary cost of £200 and earned about £150 a year.

P, 4: 134; 5: 18.

BOND, THOMAS (1712–1784). BF's "particular Friend" and family physician along with brother PHINEAS (1717–75) joined BF in founding the medical school, hospital, and American Philosophical Society.

E. H. Thomson, "Thomas Bond," *Journal of Medical Education*, 33 (1958), 614–24; P, 2: 240n; *DAB*.

BONNELL, JOHN DOD. Captain of the packet *Harriott* on Loudoun's abortive Louisburg campaign, he was wounded there. He later commanded an East India packet.

P, 7: 234; 9: 38.

BRADDOCK, EDWARD (1695–1755). Named to command British forces in North America in 1755, he was the victim of ill-made plans based on bad advice. He forced his troops on needlessly long marches without proper supplies, so that the surprise encounter with the French and Indians found them utterly exhausted. Although George Washington behaved heroically in the battle of the Monongahela, July 9, 1755, the English were defeated and Braddock fatally wounded. Said BF: "The General presum'd too much, and was too secure" (P, 6: 170).

Sargent; *DAB*; *DNB*.

BRADFORD, ANDREW (c. 1686–1742). Sole printer in Philadelphia until the advent of Samuel Keimer shortly before BF's arrival, he supported James Franklin's stand against the Massachusetts assembly in his *American Weekly Mercury* for February 26, 1723. He thus would have welcomed BF to Philadelphia. They later were spirited competitors, and BF succeeded him as local postmaster in 1737 because of his "Detaining the Ballance of his Accounts, and his Neglecting to render any Account for a long time" (P, 2: 276). AB had additional income from investments in iron works and real estate.

DeArmond; P, 2: 235, 275–81, 304–5; *DAB*.

BRADFORD, WILLIAM (1663–1752). BF's early counselor in New York, WB had served as apprentice to London's principal Quaker printer and came to Philadelphia in 1685 to be printer for the Quakers here. But in 1692, they tried him for libel because he published a pamphlet by George Keith critical of local magistrates. Acquitted by a jury, he went to New York in 1693 where he became that colony's official printer.

A.J. Wall, Jr., "William Bradford, Colonial Printer—a Tercentenary Review," *PAAS*, n.s. 73 (1963), 361–84; *P*, 1: 166n.

BREINTNALL, JOSEPH (d. 1746). Of all the Junto, he was BF's favorite. Co-author of the "Busy-Body" series and occasional poet, he shared BF's interest in science and corresponded with the Royal Society. When he drowned, March 16, 1746, some suspected suicide because his clothes were "found by the River" and because "he was remarkable for Deistical principles, & much distrest by his Circumstances" (F. B. Tolles, "Note on Joseph Breintall . . . ," *Philological Quarterly*, 21 [1942], 247–49).

Stephen Bloore, "Joseph Breintnall . . . ," *PMHB*, 59 (1935), 42–56; *P*, 1: 114n, 114, 134n, 344n; 2: 164n.

BRISSON, MATHURIN-JACQUES (1723–1806). In 1771, translating Joseph Priestley's *History of Electricity* (1767) into French, this disciple and successor of Abbé Nollet added his own footnotes disparaging BF's theories, but in 1785 he was convinced by Martin Van Marum of the correctness of Franklin's single-fluid (or electron) theory of electricity.

I. Bernard Cohen, pp. 386, 569.

BROCKDEN, CHARLES (1683–1769). After coming to Philadelphia in 1706, he was the leading drafter of legal documents. He was also recorder of deeds and proprietary records. BF did much job printing for him during 1732–39. This grandfather of the novelist Charles Brockden Brown was successively an Anglican, a Quaker, a Whitefield "New Light," and a Moravian.

Miller, pp. 457–61.

BROWNE, JOHN (1667–1737). A physician-innkeeper of Burlington, JB probably traveled in Europe in the course of medical training. He owned 230 acres near Burlington at his death. Franklin's obituary in the *Pennsylvania Gazette* (May 19, 1737) called JB a "Gentleman of singular Skill in the Profession of Surgery."

P, 2: 187n; Fred B. Rogers, "Dr. John Browne: Friend of Benjamin Franklin," *Bulletin of History of Medicine*, 30 (1956), 1–6.

BROWNELL, GEORGE (c. 1690–1738). BF's schoolmaster, citizen of Boston from 1713, taught dancing and sewing as well as writing and ciphering. In 1718 he opened the first licensed dancing school which flourished even after his death.

Robert Seybolt, *Private Schools of Colonial Boston* (Cambridge, Mass., 1935), pp. 12, 13, 89, 96.

BUFFON, GEORGES-LOUIS LECLERC, COMTE DE (1707–1788). In 1751 he suggested that BF's electrical experiments be translated into French. He was among the first to experiment with lightning rods; he translated Newton; and he devised the classification of animals. His thesis that America's humid climate caused the degeneration of plants, animals, and men was answered at length by Jefferson's *Notes on the State of Virginia*.

P, 3: 111n; Mottelay, p. 200; Antonello Gerbi, *The Dispute of the New World* (Pittsburgh, 1973).

BURNET, WILLIAM (1688–1729). Son of Bishop Gilbert Burnet and godson of King William and Queen Mary, he governed New York (1720–27) and Massachusetts (1728–29) as a steadfast champion of royal prerogatives. In this role he occasioned BF's first editorial, October 1729, in the *Pennsylvania Gazette*.

P, 1: 159n; *DAB*.

BUSTILL, SAMUEL (d. 1742?). A Burlington Friend, he was a leader in the assembly's struggles against governors of West Jersey, including its moves to issue the new money that brought BF and Keimer there in 1728.

Tanner, pp. 234, 699.

CANTON, JOHN (1718–1772). This "very ingenious" London schoolmaster was the first in England to repeat BF's electrical experiments. He went on to contribute independently to the study of electricity and later became BF's friend in the "Club of Honest Whigs," sharing interests in science, rational religion, and liberalism.

P, 4: 390n; Verner W. Crane, "The Club of Honest Whigs," *WMQ*, 3d s., 23 (1966), 210–33; I. Bernard Cohen, pp. 516–24; *DNB*.

CAVE, EDWARD (1691–1754). The printer of BF's *Experiments & Observations* (1751), EC published the influential *Gentleman's Magazine*.

C. Lennart Carlson, *The First Magazine* (Providence, 1938); P, 4: 126–27; *DNB*.

CHARLES, ROBERT (d. 1770). Joint Pa. agent with BF (1757–61), he had been secretary of the Provincial Council (1726–39), then emigrated to England where he was named agent for New York (1748) and also for Pennsylvania (1752). "He finally put an End to his Perplexities—by a Razor!" (P, 17: 171).

Nicholas Varga, "Robert Charles," *WMQ*, 17 (1961), 211–15.

CLAPHAM, WILLIAM (d. 1763). Successor to BF at Ford Allen, he later commanded Fort Augusta (1756–57). An ineffectual com-

mander, he was rumored to be a drunkard. He later settled near Fort Pitt, where he and his family were massacred in May, 1763.
P, 6: 383n; 10: 273–74n. Nolan, *General Benjamin Franklin*, p. 84n.

CLIFTON, JOHN (d. 1759). The Quaker apothecary credited by BF with placing the first street light in Philadelphia was disowned by the Society of Friends for marrying a woman whose husband was believed to be still living.
P, 7: 317.

CLINTON, GEORGE (c. 1686–1761). This mercenary governor of New York (1743–53) who called the Albany conference in 1751 was father of Sir Henry Clinton, British commander during part of the Revolution.
P, 4: 68n; *DAB*.

COLEMAN, WILLIAM (1704–1769). Helping to subsidize BF's career in 1728, he remained a lifelong friend despite opposing him politically. A merchant, he was a Supreme Court justice (1758–69). When he went to London for cancer surgery in 1768, BF nursed him.
P, 2: 406n; 15: 139, 174, 274n; 16: 57.

COLLINSON, PETER (1694–1768). Early patron and London agent for the Library Company, he was a merchant trading with America and a correspondent of scientists at home and abroad. BF wrote a memoir (February 8, 1770) testifying that his early work on electricity had been "encouraged by the friendly Reception he gave to the Letters I wrote to him upon it." (*P*, 17: 65–66).
Norman G. Brett-James, *Life of Peter Collinson* (London, 1926); *DNB*.

COOPER, JOSEPH (1691–1751). Another New Jersey politician whom BF met at Burlington, he was an assemblyman from Gloucester County and, with Isaac Pearson, was a Proprietary representative on the committee overseeing the new money. Franklin told John Jay that while he was at Burlington, Cooper "prevailed" upon him to reply on behalf of the New Jersey Assembly to a message from Governor Lewis Morris.
Edgar J. Fisher, *New Jersey as a Royal Province 1738–76* (New York, 1911), pp. 82–83; *New Jersey Archives*, 1st s., 12: 59n.

COPLEY, GODFREY (c. 1654–1709). BF was first to receive the Copley medal as a selectee of the president and council of the Royal Society. Previously it had been awarded by executors of the estate of GC who, though not a scientist, had been a member and a close friend of Sir Hans Sloane.
P, 5: 126n; Lyons, p. 138; *DNB*.

CROGHAN, GEORGE (d. 1782). An Irish immigrant trader and Indian expert, he assisted Washington, Braddock, Forbes and Bouquet in their western campaigns, and in 1756 was named Deputy Superintendent of Indian Affairs. He and Washington aided Orme in carrying the fatally wounded Braddock.

P, 5: 64n; Nicholas B. Wainwright, *George Croghan, Wilderness Diplomat* (Chapel Hill, 1959); *DAB*; *DNB*.

DALIBARD, THOMAS-FRANÇOIS (1703–1799). Translator of BF's *Experiments & Observations* into French (February, 1752), he was first to prove BF's theory that lightning was electrical (May 10, 1752).

P, 4: 302n; Mottelay, p. 200.

DECOW, ISAAC (d. 1750). When BF met this shrewd Huguenot-Quaker scion of one of the pioneering families of New Jersey, he was a proprietor of the Province as well as clerk of the Council, Treasurer, and Surveyor-general.

Tanner, pp. 312, 550, 695–99; *New Jersey Archives*, 1st s., 12: 2n.; *Pa. Gaz.*, March 19, 1750.

DELOR. Dalibard's teacher at the Sorbonne, Delor joined Dalibard in 1752 to test BF's theories on lightning, and later (1753) translated from the Italian into French a letter by Giambatista Beccaria answering Nollet's attacks on BF (1753).

P, 4: 424; 5: 395.

DENHAM, THOMAS (d. 1728). A Philadelphia merchant who left Bristol in 1715 after falling into "bad Company" and going bankrupt, he paid all debts seven years later. He lent BF passage money to return to Philadelphia in 1726 (he was half-owner of the ship) and forgave the debt in his will. At Philadelphia BF worked for him from October 1726 to March 1727/8; but by the time TD died (July 4, 1728), BF had already begun his own business.

Roach, 134–36; P, 1: 73.

DENNY, WILLIAM (1709–1765). Pennsylvania's mercenary governor (1756–59), antisocial, petulant, and mean, disgusted friend and foe, took bribes from the assembly to disobey the Proprietors. Through these and other corrupt means he was able to retire to a life of ease in London. BF thought him "half a Madman" (P, 6: 273).

Wainwright, *passim*; P, 6: 489–90n; 9: 136–37; 11: 271–77; 12: 426.

DUNBAR, THOMAS (d. 1767). The colonel who succeeded to Braddock's command in the field (1755) resigned after his much censured retreat and was appointed lieutenant-governor of Gibraltar.

P, 6: 28n; Sargent.

EGREMONT, CHARLES WYNDHAM, 2d EARL OF (1710–1763). Sir William Wyndham's son assumed the earldom from an uncle (1750), and in 1761 succeeded William Pitt as the secretary of state in charge of colonial affairs. With George Grenville (his brother-in-law) and Lord Halifax, he headed the British government in 1763.

P, 10: 325; Valentine; *DNB*.

ENNIS, JAMES (c. 1709–1774). He was official courier for the government of Pennsylvania. His daughter Sarah wed an elder brother of the painter Benjamin West.
Hinshaw, 2: 359, 517.

FAWKENER, EVERARD (1684–1758). London merchant, friend of Voltaire (who resided at his home when in England), he was joint postmaster-general of Great Britain and appointed BF to his postmastership in 1753. His widow wed Thomas Pownall.
P, 5: 334n; *DNB*.

FISHER, MARY FRANKLIN (1673–1758). Shortly after BF visited this first cousin at Wellingborough, she and her husband both died, leaving their property to him and five cousins. BF generously divided his share between two of them, "ancient Women and poor" (*P*, 8: 414).
P, 8: 224–25, 288–89, 302.

FOLGER, PETER (1617–1690). BF's maternal grandfather, a Baptist and native of Norwich, England, emigrated in 1635. Wedding an indentured servant of Puritan leader Hugh Peter, he settled on Nantucket (1664) as Indian interpreter and clerk of the court. He went to jail in 1676 rather than turn over court records to an incoming administration.
P, 1: liii, lvi; Anderson, *passim*.

FOSTER, JAMES (1697–1753). The preacher from whom Samuel Hemphill copied sermons was a leading London Baptist "freethinker" who, denying "mysteries in religion," urged every man to choose whatever religion seemed "most rational, and agreeable to the divine will." BF called his sermon against deism an "excellent Defence of Christianity" (*P*, 2: 120).
A. C. Underwood, *History of English Baptists* (London, 1947), p. 138; *DNB*.

FOTHERGILL, JOHN (1712–1780). BF's personal physician in London. He was also leader of English Quakers and reported regularly to Pennsylvania on all matters affecting their sect. Physician to the highest government officers, he provided timely intelligence and, during the Revolution, mediated between them and BF who said of him, "I can hardly conceive that a better man has ever existed" (Smyth, 9: 16).
Betsy Copping Corner & C. C. Booth, *Chain of Friendship* (Cambridge, Mass., 1971); *P*, e.g., 6: 7–8; 12: 328–29; *DNB*.

FRANCIS, TENCH (d. 1758). Appointed Pennsylvania's attorney-general (1741–55) only three years after his arrival from Maryland, he prepared the draft of the Academy's charter; approved April, 1752.
P, 5: 7; *DAB*.

FRANKLIN, ABIAH FOLGER (1667–1752). BF's mother was born on Nantucket, wed when 22 and her husband (a widower with six children under 11) was 35, then bore him ten of her own over the next 20 years. Widowed in 1745, she lived, said BF, "a good life" with her daughter Jane Mecom (1712–94) in Boston. She worried about BF being a Freemason and an Arminian (*P*, 2: 204). Her wish for him was "that you may be liked in all your postes" (*P*, 4: 199).

P, 1: liii, lvi; 2: 204; 3: 474; 4: 318; 7: 229–30; Anderson.

FRANKLIN, ANN SMITH (1696–1763). BF's sister-in-law at Newport, she was probably New England's first woman printer. When her husband James died (1735), she ran the business for 13 years until James, Jr. returned from his apprenticeship with BF. With her son, she began *The Newport Mercury* in 1758 and continued it after his death in 1762.

Howard M. Chapin, "Ann Franklin of Newport, Printer," *Bibliographical Essays: A Tribute to Wilberforce Eames* (Cambridge, Mass., 1924). Bradford F. Swan, "Franklin, Ann Smith," in James, 1: 662–63.

FRANKLIN, BENJAMIN (1650–1727). BF's favorite uncle, an unprosperous silk-dyer of London, emigrated in 1715 after losing his wife and nine of ten children. Until his son Samuel could afford to take him in, he lived with Josiah. Favorite brothers while apart, BF recalled their "mutual Disgusts and Misunderstandings" while under the same roof (*P*, 18: 185).

P, 1: li, lii, 3–6 (poems on BF); 18: 176.

FRANKLIN, DEBORAH READ (c. 1707–1774). BF's wife of 44 years, whose birthplace and birthdate are unknown, was second of seven children of carpenter and contractor John Read who came to Philadelphia in 1711. She wed potter John Rogers in August 1725, but he fled to the West Indies in December 1727. BF explains above the two reasons for their common-law (rather than legal) marriage on September 1, 1730. Because she refused to sail, BF was away from her for 25 of the 44 years of their marriage, yet their affection remained constant. After her death from a stroke, he said: "I have lately lost my old and faithful Companion; and I every day become more sensible of the greatness of the Loss; which cannot now be repair'd."

P, 1: lxii, 362–70 & later vols.; Edward M. Riley, "The Deborah Franklin Correspondence," *PAPS*, 95 (1951) 239–45; Leonard W. Labaree, "Franklin, Deborah Read" in James, 1: 663–64.

FRANKLIN, JAMES (1697–1735). Returning from London with a press and types in 1717, BF's brother set up a shop where he printed the *Boston Gazette* (December 1719–August 1720) and then published his own *New-England Courant* (1721–26). After the *Courant* failed (1727), he moved to Newport where he anticipated "Poor Richard's Almanac" with "Poor Robin's Almanac" (1728–35), became colony printer, and published the *Rhode-Island Gazette* (March

1732–September 1733). After his death, his son JAMES, JR. (c. 1730–62) was apprenticed to BF, and "was always dissatisfied and grumbling" (P, 3: 304). James, Jr., returned to Newport about 1748 to work for his mother, Ann Smith Franklin.

Clarence S. Brigham, "James Franklin and the Beginnings of Printing in Rhode Island," *PMHS*, 65 (1932–36), 536–44; P, 1: lvi, lix, 8, 47–48.

FRANKLIN, JOHN (1690–1756). BF's favorite and eldest brother followed his father's trade, making soap, moving to Newport in 1715 and there developing a clear, green soap stamped with a crown that helped support the family for many years. By 1744 he had returned to Boston, a partner in a new glassworks; and 10 years later BF appointed him postmaster, an office he enjoyed till his death.

J. R. Bartlett, ed., *Records of. . . Rhode Island* (Providence, 1859), 4: 183; P, 2: 420.

FRANKLIN, JOSIAH (1657–1745). BF's father, a silk-dyer on coming to Boston in 1683, settled nearly opposite the Old South Church where BF would be baptized. He was the "praecentor" or chant leader at Samuel Willard's South Church in Boston. By 1708, Josiah belonged to a private religious worship group which included Chief Justice Samuel Sewall. In July 1771, BF recalled his father as "a very wise man" (P, 18: 185).

Justin Winsor, ed., *Memorial History of Boston* (Boston, 1881); P, 1: lvi–lvii; 2: 229–32 (his letter to BF on genealogy); M. Halsey Thomas, ed., *Diary of Samuel Sewall* 2 v. (N.Y., 1973), 2: 874, 886, 921.

FRANKLIN, JOSIAH, JR. (1685–c.1715). BF's half-brother who ran away to sea, spent about nine years in the East Indies, then returned home for the memorable feast attended by 13 Franklin children and was never heard of again.

P, 9: 18.

FRANKLIN, THOMAS (fl. 1563–1573). BF's great-great-grandfather started out as a tailor's apprentice, but his master "kept such a stingy house, that he left him" for a blacksmith and thus became a blacksmith himself.

P, 2: 230.

FRANKLIN, THOMAS (1598–1682). BF's grandfather was also a blacksmith. He was once jailed a year-and-a-day for writing libelous verse, but by precept and example brought up his family in a religious way.

P, 2: 231.

FRANKLIN, THOMAS (1673–1702). BF's uncle whom he was said to resemble had been bred a blacksmith but became a teacher, scrivener, tobacco merchant, clerk of county court and of the archdeacon. He devised a method of flood control and, though some thought him a conjuror, all sorts of people sought his advice and

opinion. His genius extending to music also, he installed the chimes in Ecton church and built an organ for himself.
P, 8: 137, 161–62.

FRANKLIN, WILLIAM (c. 1731–1813). BF's illegitimate son (evidently by a prostitute) was brought up in BF's house and was his father's companion until 1762 when, having passed the bar and married an heiress, he was appointed Royal Governor of New Jersey. As Governor, he promoted agriculture and roads, deftly managed Indian relations and the more difficult assembly relations, warned the Ministry about taxation without representation, and even proposed a government-sponsored Continental Congress. He was at least forty and probably the most successful Royal Governor in the colonies when BF wrote Part One of the autobiography in 1771—ostensibly for him. As the revolution drew close, William Franklin's views were clearly Loyalist. In 1773, BF said he was "a thorough government man," and on September 7, 1774, BF wrote "you, who are a thorough courtier, see everything with government eyes" (P, 20: 437; Smyth, 6: 241). Remaining loyal, imprisoned with the outbreak of war then freed in an exchange of 1778, William Franklin became president of the Associated Loyalists in 1780 and sponsored guerilla raids on Connecticut and New Jersey. After the British banned the raids for the murder of Captain Joshua Huddy, WF lived in England on pension. In a post-war reconciliation, BF wrote: "Our Opinions are not in our town Power; they are form'd and govern'd much by Circumstances, that are often as inexplicable as they are irresistible." (Smyth, 9: 252). WF's own illegitimate son WILLIAM TEMPLE FRANKLIN (1762–1823) succeeded him as BF's companion and became BF's delinquent literary heir.
William H. Marboe, "Life of William Franklin," Ph.D. dissertation, University of Pennsylvania, 1962; P, e.g., 3: 474n; 8: 132; *PMHB*, 43 (1919), 253.

FRENCH, JOHN (d. 1728). Political henchman of Governor Keith at New Castle, Delaware, he held many offices: high sheriff, councilor in Indian affairs, commander of the fort, registrar of wills, speaker of the assembly, and also (when BF met him) justice of the Supreme Court (1722–28).
Governor's Register, 1674–1851. (Delaware Public Archives, 1926), pp. 9–10.

GODFREY, THOMAS (1704–1749). BF's lodger (1728–30) was a brilliant self-taught mathematician who supplemented his income from glazing (he did most of the glass work on Independence Hall) with an almanac. BF printed *Godfrey's Almanac* in 1729, 1730, and 1731, but when Godfrey—angered by BF's satire in the *Pennsylvania Gazette* (10 July 1732)—took his almanac to Andrew Bradford in late 1732, BF hastily compiled the first *Poor Richard's Almanac*. Godfrey

independently invented Hadley's quadrant. His son was the poet Thomas Godfrey (1736–63).
  Lemay, "Benjamin Franklin," pp. 211–12; *P*, 1: 190n; 3: 432; *DAB*.

GORDON, PATRICK (1664–1736). An army major who succeeded Keith as governor for ten uneventful years (1726–36), Gordon recommended Ferdinand John Paris as Pennsylvania's agent in London, thus launching a career culminating in the litigious contest of 1757. BF's friend Robert Charles was Gordon's son-in-law.
  P, 2: 159n.

GRACE, ROBERT (1709–1766). BF's early benefactor, who helped him finance his own business, was also his landlord for thirty-seven years. Scion of Irish aristocracy, Philadelphian by birth, he inherited his grandfather's estate at seventeen, and in 1740 married into a prosperous family of ironmasters. BF helped RG when he was being pressed by creditors in 1748 (*P*, 3: 329–30), and designed the "Franklin stove" for RG to manufacture. RG studied mineralogy abroad for three years, then returned to manage the successful Warwick Furnace, Chester County (1745–65).
  P, 1: 209n; 3: 50–51; Arthur C. Bining, *Pennsylvania Iron Manufacturing in Eighteenth Century* (Harrisburg, 1938), pp. 131–32, 144. Eddy, 2: 60–63; *Pa. Gaz.*, May 29, 1740.

GRANVILLE, JOHN CARTERET, FIRST EARL OF (1690–1763). President of the powerful Privy Council (1751–63) ruling on BF's case against the Proprietors, his second wife (m. 1744) was Thomas Penn's sister-in-law.
  P, 7: 249n; *DNB*.

HALIFAX, CHARLES MONTAGU, FIRST EARL OF (1661–1715). This patron of BF's uncle Thomas, probably known to him as clerk of the Archbishop of Northampton, was president of the Royal Society (1695–98).
  Lyons, p. 74.

HALL, DAVID (1714–1772). BF's partner, a Scots printer working in London, came to Philadelphia in July 1744 at BF's invitation for a three-year trial period prior to setting up under his sponsorship in the West Indies. But at the end of the term, BF kept him as full partner in Philadelphia. On January 1, 1748, a week before he married into Deborah Franklin's family, he bought BF's stock for £700 and paid him £500 a year from shop profits for the next 18 years, plus a share of the profits from the *Pennsylvania Gazette* till 1772.
  Miller, p. 453; *P*, 2: 409–10; 13: 87–107; *DAB*; Roach, p. 150.

HAMILTON, ANDREW (c. 1676–1741). A young Virginia lawyer who was left a sizeable fortune by his patron, AH rose to be speaker of the assembly, and earned lasting fame (and created the sobriquet of "the Philadelphia Lawyer") for his defense of John Peter Zenger in the landmark censorship case. BF revered him as "the Poor Man's Friend," and defended "His free Manner of treating Religious Subjects": "If he could not subscribe to the Creed of any particular Church, it was not for want of considering them All" (*P*, 2: 238). His son, James, became governor, and his daughter, Margaret, the wife of Chief Justice William Allen—one of BF's chief political antagonists.

Foster C. Nix, "Andrew Hamilton's Early Years in American Colonies," *WMQ*, 21 (1964), 390–407; Carter; *P*, 1: 333, 343; 2: 327–28; *DAB*.

HAMILTON, JAMES (c. 1710–1783). Son of Andrew Hamilton, he worked with BF in the Masons and in founding the Library, the College, and the American Philosophical Society. Governor twice (1748–1754, 1759–1763), his administrations were marked by assembly bickering. BF admired him as "a benevolent and upright . . . sensible Man" (*P*, 3: 283).

P, 3: 327n–328n.

HANBURY, JOHN (1700–1758). The wealthy merchant who greeted BF in London in 1757 headed a large, influential Quaker family whose great fortune was based in the colonial tobacco trade.

P, 7: 249n.

HARRY, DAVID (1708–1760). Resident of the "Welsh Barony" near Philadelphia, center of a large population of Welsh Quakers, he became the first printer in the Barbados (1730). He sold out to Keimer in a year and moved to South Carolina to farm for another seven years before returning to Philadelphia sometime before 1756.

Leah Townsend, *South Carolina Baptists* (Florence, 1935), pp. 62–63; *P*, 1: 113n; Hinshaw, 2: 371.

HEMPHILL, SAMUEL. An Irish Presbyterian minister, he was installed as Jedediah Andrew's assistant, September 23, 1734, and by April 1735 was charged with preaching subversive sermons, attracting a crowd of freethinkers, and plagiarizing. After April 26, 1735, when he was prohibited from preaching, BF began writing pamphlets in his defense, questioning the judgment of the commission which removed him (*P*, 2: 37–126).

Merton A. Christensen, "Franklin on the Hemphill Trial," *WMQ*, 3d s. 10 (1953), 422–40; *P*, 2: 27.

HOMES, ROBERT (1694–d. before 1743). Married in 1716 to BF's sister Mary (1694–1731), he captained a ship plying between Boston and Philadelpha, and died at sea.

Charles E. Banks, ed., "Diary of William Homes," *New England Historical & Genealogical Register*, 48 (1894), 448; *P*, 1: 171n.

HOPKINSON, THOMAS (1709–1751). Close friend of BF's in Junto activities, he was a magistrate in several sensitive courts, with a reputation for honesty and integrity, brilliant wit and bashfulness. He was first president of the American Philosophical Society. His

humorist son, Francis (1737–91), was an executor of BF's estate and was willed BF's scientific equipment.
  P, 4: 208; Elizabeth R. Waara, "Franklin's 'Ingenious Friend' and Scientific Heir," PAPS, 118 (1974), 317.

HOUSE, GEORGE (d. 1754?). The friend who sent BF his first customer in 1728 was a Quaker shoemaker and an original member of BF's Union Fire Company. He later served on the common council and as overseer of the poor (1746).
  P, 2: 153n; Hinshaw, 2: 377.

HUME, DAVID (1711–1776). The great philosopher and historian was secretary to General Henry Conway (1721–91) and Francis Conway, Marquis of Hertford (1719–49). In 1762 he ranked BF as a "Philosopher, and . . . Great Man of Letters," but in 1771, angered at his politics, called him "a very factious man" (Melvin H. Buxbaum, "Hume, Franklin and America," Enlightenment Essays, 3 [1972], 93–94).
  P, 9: 227–28n; 14: 147n; E. C. Mossner, Life of David Hume (Austin, 1954); DNB.

HUNTER, WILLIAM (d. 1761). Joint-deputy postmaster-general with BF, he was a fellow printer in Williamsburg, publisher of the Virginia Gazette. BF took charge of his natural son's education—"for I loved his Father truly" (P, 10: 317).
  P, 5: 18n; Douglas C. McMurtrie, Beginnings of Printing in Virginia (Lexington, Va., 1935), pp. 15–19.

ISTED, AMBROSE (1718–1781). Owner of "Franklin House," Ecton, when BF visited in 1758, he lived in the manor house visited by the artist Hogarth and by Bishop Percy who is said to have begun work on his collection of ballads there.
  P, 8: 136; Victoria History of Northamptonshire, 4 vols. (London, 1902), 4: 122–27.

JAMES, ABEL (1724–1790). For many years an official of the Quakers and of their political arm, the Friendly Association, he worked on Indian affairs with BF in the 1750s. As the Revolution approached, his mercantile business declined because he was identified with the Loyalists. But he served as financial adviser and executor for distressed Quakers like Grace Galloway, among whose effects he recovered BF's manuscript of Part One of the Autobiography.
  P, 8: 152n; Richard Bauman, For the Reputation of Truth (Baltimore, 1971), pp. 80, 113, 152, 240.

KEIMER, SAMUEL (c. 1688–1742). During his nine years as a printer in London, he was twice bankrupt and nine times jailed—once for six years. In Philadelphia (1722) he started a school for slaves, but by BF's arrival (1723) had set up as a printer and, two years after, was hired to reprint Sewel's History of Quakers. In 1728 he subcontracted

44½ sheets of the book to the new firm of BF and Meredith. In 1729, stung by the "Busy-Body" essays, he satirized BF as a combination of Diogenes and Don Quixote (*Pa. Gaz.*, March 13). After selling the newspaper to BF, he moved to Bridgetown, Barbados, where he started the first Caribbean newspaper in 1731.

> C. Lennart Carlson, "Samuel Keimer," *PMHB*, 61 (1937), 357–86; Miller, pp. 1–2; *P*, 1: 113n, 111–39 ("Busy-Body"); *DAB*: *DNB*.

KEITH, GEORGE (1638–1716). Master (1689) of the Quaker school in Philadelphia, he was the leader of Quakers violently opposed to being taxed to arm ships for fighting pirates. Convicted of contempt of court for refusing to pay (and urging his followers to refuse also), he went into exile in England (1692), and later (1702–4) served as an Anglican minister in America.

> DeArmond, pp. 4–5, 24, 33; *DAB*; *DNB*.

KEITH, WILLIAM (1680–1749). Scion of an old Scots barony, he was a popular customs inspector for the Southern colonies when named governor (1716) at the request of Philadelphia merchants who later turned on him when he issued more paper money (1722). He formed his own political party and, after being fired (1726) by the Proprietors as governor, was twice elected to the assembly. Andrew Hamilton described his politics: "he inveyed much against . . . rich men as Persons having a design of enslaving the Poor . . . he stirr'd up a very great uneasiness in the Minds of the Common People" (Pa. Hist. Soc. *Memoirs*, 2, pt. 2 [1830], 37–38). At the height of his new power he fled from debt to England (1728), there turning writer and consultant on colonial affairs until jailed for new debts (1734–35). He died in debtor's prison, November 18, 1749 (*Gent. Mag.*, 19 [Nov. 1749], 524). A granddaughter, Elizabeth Graeme (Fergusson), was briefly engaged to William Franklin

> Keith, 2: 698–700; *P*, 1: 126n; 2: 288n; 11: 137n; *DAB*.

KENNEDY, ARCHIBALD (1685–1763). The "Mr. Kennedy" who approved BF's Albany Plan was receiver general of New York and a leading intellectual and political theorist of the pre-Revolutionary period. His pamphlet *The Importance of Gaining and Preserving the Friendship of the Indians* (1751) prefigured BF's plan and called forth a key letter (*P*, 4: 117–21) from BF on Indian affairs, colonial politics, and population.

> Milton M. Klein, "Archibald Kennedy: Imperial Pamphleteer," in *The Colonial Legacy*, v. 2, ed. Lawrence H. Leder (New York: Harper & Row, 1971), pp. 75–105; *P*, 4: 117n; *DAB*.

KENNEDY, ARCHIBALD, JR. (d. 1794). Son of the above, he (though a fellow passenger) was the naval captain who dramatically prevented shipwreck off the Scilly Isles on BF's 1757 voyage. After acquiring extensive properties in New York and New Jersey, he (upon the death of a cousin) became the 11th Earl of Cassillis (1792).

> P, 14: 293 and n; *Burke's Peerage and Baronetage*, 105th ed. (London: Burke's Peerage Ltd., 1970), p. 35.

KINNERSLEY, EBENEZER (1711–1778). BF's chief collaborator on electrical experiments was a Baptist minister. BF's "Statement of Editorial Policy," *Pa. Gaz.*, July 24, 1740, prefaced EK's letter opposing The Great Awakening's emotionalism. Beginning in 1749, he lectured widely on the Franklinian system of electricity (including the hypothesis of the electrical nature of lightning). He headed the English School in BF's Academy (1753). When his superior, William Smith, Provost of the Academy and political enemy of Franklin, charged BF with taking credit for EK's experiments, Kinnersley refuted him in the *Pa. Gaz.*, November 30, 1758, but the charge was kept alive by BF's enemies even after his death; e.g., the Loyalist Jonathan Boucher, *View of the Causes & Consequences of the American Revolution* (London, 1797), p.438.

> Lemay, *Ebenezer Kinnersley*; P, 4: 192n; DAB.

LAWRENCE, THOMAS (1689–1754). BF's choice to lead the militia was a native of New York who had become a partner of BF's friend James Logan and served as a provincial councilor and trustee of the Academy.

> P, 2: 154.

LE ROY, JEAN-BAPTISTE (1720–1800). BF's friend, correspondent, and early scientific disciple, had only recently (1751) been elected to the French Academy of Sciences when he rebutted Nollet's attack on the Franklinian system of electricity. BF met him in Paris in 1767.

> P, 6: 99n; I. Bernard Cohen, p. 509.

LE VEILLARD, LOUIS (1733–1793). BF's next-door neighbor in Passy warmly urged him to complete his "Memoirs," and in November 1789 was sent a press-copy of the completed portion. William Temple Franklin exchanged the original, more complete manuscript for Le Veillard's copy, "as more convenient for the press." The original then remained in his family for over half a century. Mayor of Passy, he was guillotined, June 1793. According to Charles de Senarmont, BF said of him: "In a nation I love, this is the man I hold closest to my heart."

> Charles de Senarmont, "Notice Sur M. Le Veillard," Henry Stevens Papers, UCLA, MS 801, Box 46, f.21.

LOGAN, JAMES (1674–1751). Book collector, classicist, and mathematician, he came to Philadelphia as William Penn's secretary in 1699 and then for fifty years looked after the proprietors' business and political interests. After 1710 his own success in exporting furs enabled him to devote time to science, literature, and the classics. In 1730 he moved into a Philadelphia mansion, Stenton, where BF had free access to his 3000-volume library and to his stimulating conversation. BF "acknowledged his obligations to him in the beginning of his Career, and valued himself on his friendship" (*P*, 1: 191n).

Frederick B. Tolles, *James Logan and the Culture of Provincial America* (Boston, 1957); *P*, 2: 184; 3: 185n; Edwin Wolf, 2nd, *The Library of James Logan of Philadelphia* (Philadelphia, 1974); *DAB*; *DNB*.

LOUDOUN, JOHN CAMPBELL, FOURTH EARL OF (1705–1782). When he first succeeded Braddock in 1756 as commander-in-chief, BF thought him "very well fitted" for the post (*P*, 6: 472), yet a year later said, "His Lordship has on all Occasions treated me with the greatest Goodness, but I find frequently that strong Prejudices are infus'd into his Mind against our Province" (*P*, 7: 228). After the Louisburg debacle (ordered by Sir William Pitt), he was recalled, but regained his reputation in Continental wars.

Stanley M. Pargellis, *Lord Loudoun in North America* (New Haven, 1933); *P*, 7: 223–29; *DAB*; *DNB*.

LUTWIDGE, WALTER (d. 1761). It was Lutwidge, captain of the packet *General Wall*, who, "with an air of some little contempt, as to a Person ignorant of what every Body else knew," told BF on his 1757 trip to England that the cooks' greasy water accounted for the smooth wakes of two ships in the convoy, thus starting BF's interest in the surface tension of water (*P*, 20: 465). Four years after the trip with BF, Lutwidge "was mortally wounded by a nine Pound shot" (March 20, 1761) in a battle with a French privateer.

Pa. Gaz., May 21, 1761; *P*, 7: 234n.

LYONS, WILLIAM. BF's early guide in London's intellectual circles was a surgeon and author of *The Infallibility, Dignity, and Excellence of Humane Judgment* (London, 1719). BF treasured the copy of *Liberty and Necessity* (1725) that Lyons annotated.

P, 1: 57n; Smyth, 7: 412.

MACCLESFIELD, GEORGE PARKER, SECOND EARL OF (c. 1697–1764). The President of the Royal Society who presented BF the Copley Medal, he was instrumental in having England change from the Julian ("Old Style") to the Gregorian ("New Style") calendar in 1752.

P, 4: 448n; *DNB*.

MANDEVILLE, BERNARD (c. 1670–1733). Popularizing the view that man is motivated only by self-interest, this Dutch physician, Enlightenment philosopher, and important man-of-letters residing in

London was notorious for his satiric *Fable of the Bees; or Private Vices, Public Benefits* (1714), the third edition of which was presented by the Grand Jury of Middlesex in 1723. Mandeville thus epitomized avant-garde infamy when BF arrived in London in 1724.
P, 1: 5n; DNB.

MANSFIELD, WILLIAM MURRAY, BARON (1705–1793). The Chief Justice of the King's Bench (1756–88) who worked out the compromise between BF and the proprietors in the interests of colonial defense was moderate in everything but his insistence on Parliament's complete sovereignty over America.
William S. Hanna, *Benjamin Franklin and Pennsylvania Politics* (Stanford, 1964), pp. 140–41; P, 9: 207n; Valentine 2: 635–6; DNB.

MATHER, COTTON (1663–1728). Assistant to and successor of his father Increase as pastor of the Second Church in Boston (1685–1728), he was the greatest American Puritan writer, politician, and promoter of his time. Losing popularity by his defense of Salem witch trials, and losing official favor for asserting the power of the church over the state, he turned to and promoted such causes as inoculation against smallpox. Of his 450 books, at least three—*Bonifacius* ("Essays to Do Good") (1710), *Religious Societies* (1724), and *Manuductio ad Ministerium* (1726)—gave inspiration and models for BF's Junto. BF wrote CM's son Samuel about *Bonifacius*: "If I have been . . . a useful citizen, the public owes the advantage of it to that book" (Smyth, 9: 208).
Phyllis Franklin, *Show Thyself a Man* (Hague, 1969); P, 1: 255; DAB.

MAUGRIDGE, WILLIAM (d. 1766). BF's "solid, sensible" Junto friend was a ship-carpenter, and possibly BF's landlord in 1727–28. He left town in 1750 to take over the farm of relatives, the parents of Daniel Boone. To make ends meet, he twice mortgaged the farm through BF.
J. Bennett Nolan, "Benjamin Franklin's Mortgage on the Daniel Boone Farm," *PAPS*, 87 (1943–44), 394–97; Roach, pp. 137–38; P, 14: 135.

MEREDITH, HUGH (c. 1697–c. 1750). BF's partner, son of Simon Meredith, assemblyman from rural Chester County, withdrew from the business by April 1730, and went to Cape Fear, North Carolina, which he described in the *Pa. Gaz.*, May 6 and 15, 1731. By 1738 he had returned to Pennsylvania and by 1742 became a leader of "the country party" in local politics. In 1750, after BF several times loaned him money, he dropped from view.
Roach, pp. 140–41; Eddy, 2: 83–84; P, 1: 175, 216; 2: 234.

MICKLE, SAMUEL (1684–1765). The "croaker" who attempted to dishearten BF was an "elderly" forty-four in 1728, a Quaker merchant optimistic enough to have built a new stable only eight years earlier. A real-estate entrepreneur, he acquired at least 1250 rural acres, along with a desirable lot in the central city.

Hinshaw, 2: 395; *PMHB*, 4(1880): 417; 32(1908): 178; 34(1910): 238; 53(1929): 198.

MITCHELL, JOHN (d. 1768). The friend who introduced BF's electrical theories to the Royal Society was a naturalist, physician, and map-maker. BF used his map of "British and French Dominions in North America" (1755) in negotiating the peace in 1782–83. BF's last letter (to Thomas Jefferson, April 8, 1790) concerned the map, which continued in use for treaties and border adjustments down to 1932. JM lived in Virginia (1725–46) before moving to London.

Edmund Berkeley and Dorothy Smith Berkeley, *Dr. John Mitchell* (Chapel Hill, 1974).

MORRIS, JAMES (1707–1751). The Quaker who protested Fire Company contributions to defense belonged to a prominent Quaker family. His father Anthony once found a friend reading a book and exclaimed: "What! Art thee reading that Book? Why a Man might earn forty Shillings in the Time necessary to read it thro' " (Monaghan, p. 15). James Morris was an assemblyman, a trustee of the Loan Office, and a member of the Library Company.

P, 2: 153.

MORRIS, ROBERT HUNTER (c. 1700–1764). Governor of Pennsylvania (October 1754–August 1764), he was son of New Jersey governor Lewis Morris who had named him Chief Justice of that province in 1730. He was also, with Thomas Penn, a proprietor of New Jersey, and his reputation for being anti-Quaker and venal preceded him to Philadelphia. He warned Braddock that Pennsylvanians were not to be trusted, and told Ferdinando John Paris that BF had "nothing in view but to serve himself" (*P*, 7: 247n). His devious ways and provocative rulings led BF to brand him "a Knave . . . a Fool . . . a Liar; a Libeller &c." (*P*, 6: 212). Replaced, he returned to his lifelong post as Chief Justice in New Jersey.

James R. Hutson, "Franklin and Politics 1751–55," *PMHB*, 93 (1969), 335–59; *P*, 5: 528n; *DAB*.

NEWTON, ISAAC (1642–1727). One of BF's heroes, along with John Locke and Francis Bacon, this great scientist, best known for explaining the motions of celestial bodies, for theories of gravity, light and color, and physical laws, was president of the Royal Society from 1703–27, being succeeded by his friend Sir Hans Sloane.

P, 1: 54n; I. Bernard Cohen, *passim*; *DNB*.

NOLLET, ABBÉ JEAN-ANTOINE (1700–1770). BF's antagonist in debates on electricity was France's foremost scientist in the field and director of the Academy of Sciences. His Cartesian two-fluid theory of electricity was widely accepted when Franklin introduced his Newtonian single-fluid (i.e., electron) theory. Nollet's *Lettres sur L'Electricité* (1753) attacked BF's *Experiments and Observations* . . . (1751).

P, 4: 423–24; I. Bernard Cohen, pp. 505–11.

NORRIS, ISAAC (1701–1766). BF's companion at Carlisle and Albany was his political ally against the proprietors. He was grandson of Thomas Lloyd (patriarch of Philadelphia's Quaker aristocracy), son of Isaac Norris (1671–1735, Quaker leader), son-in-law of the learned James Logan, and father-in-law of John Dickinson. When elected to the assembly in 1734, he already had served as common councilor of Philadelphia, and was an alderman (1730–42). If he were the "new member" whose opposition BF feared, BF was uncannily correct in his judgment. He led the Quaker majority in the assembly (1734–66) and, as Speaker (1750–64), worked closely with BF until they disagreed on petitioning for a royal vs. proprietary provincial government. After James Logan's, his library was among Philadelphia's finest.

P, vols. 5–12; Tolles, pp. 97, 120, 162–163; Carter; Marie Elena Korey, *The Books of Isaac Norris . . . at Dickinson College* (Carlisle, Pa.: Dickinson College, 1975); *DAB*.

ONION, STEPHEN (d. 1754). Fellow passenger on BF's first voyage to England, he and Thomas Russell had come to Maryland about 1722, prospecting, leasing land, and finding ore for the Principio Iron Works. Employed by a syndicate of English investors, they returned to London (November 1724) to report their findings. Onion was named superintendent of the Works in 1726.

PMHB, 11 (1887), 63–68, 190–98, 288–95; Aubrey C. Land, *The Dulanys of Maryland* (Baltimore, 1955), p. 111.

ORME, ROBERT (d. 1790). Braddock's aide-de-camp was wounded with his chief, then returned to England and resigned his captain's commission in 1756. He died on June 17, 1790.

P, 6: 109; *Gentlemen's Magazine*, 60 (June, 1790), 577.

OSBORNE, CHARLES. BF says this friend of his youth became an eminent attorney in the West Indies where he died young. He could be the subject of an obituary in the *Gentleman's Magazine*, 19 (1749), 380: "——Osborne, Esq.: Barbadoes merchant worth 60,000 £ of the small pox."

F. H. Williams, "Pennsylvania Poets of the Provincial Period," *PMHB* 17 (1893), 30.

PALMER, JOHN (1612–1779). As Archdeacon of Northamptonshire (1665–79) he employed BF's uncle Thomas as clerk. A son of the same name established "A School for Poor Children" (1752), and a granddaughter provided information about uncle Thomas to BF in 1758.

P, 4: 122–27.

PALMER, SAMUEL (d. 1732). BF's first employer in London had a shop in Bartholomew Close from about 1723. He wrote portions of a "very bad" *History of Printing,* published *The Grub Street Journal,* and supervised a private press for the Royal Family in 1731, but went bankrupt before his death.
Plomer, pp. 228–29; *DNB.*

PARIS, FERDINAND JOHN (d. 1759). BF's legal antagonist in London had preceded him as agent in the 1730s, and been the Penn family's adviser on colonial affairs since the 1720s. Expert in technicalities of colonial laws, he penned instructions to the governors and replied to the assembly's messages. He died on December 16, 1759, only a few months after the hearing described in the final pages of Part Four.
P, 7: 247, 266n; *London Magazine,* 28 (Dec, 1759), 684.

PARSONS, WILLIAM (1701–1757). Member of the original Junto, this English-born shoemaker became Surveyor-general (1741–48). He was a member of the American Philosophical Society and librarian of the Library Company. Retiring because of ill health, he went to Easton as the proprietors' agent and there commanded the North-ampton militia in Indian wars. Though opposing him politically, BF still called him "Dear Friend," and at his death said he was "a wise Man, that often acted foolishly . . . in his Prosperity, always fret-ting!" (*P,* 8: 159).
P, 1: 359n; John W. Jordan, "William Parsons," *PMHB,* 33 (1909), 340–46.

PEARSON, ISAAC (d. 1749). A New Jersey assemblyman and "wet" Quaker, he was a friend of Governor Lewis Morris who would have made him a judge in 1740 but wished to spare him public abuse. He had a large silversmith and clockmaking business in Burlington, New Jersey.
"Papers of Lewis Morris," *New Jersey Historical Society Collections* (New York, 1852), 4: 83; Carl M. Williams, *Silversmiths of New Jersey, 1700–1825* (Philadelphia, 1949), pp. 35–41.

PEMBERTON, HENRY (1694–1771). The "Dr. Pemberton" BF met at Batson's was a physician and member of the Royal Society. A friend of Newton, he superintended publication of the *Principia* (3rd ed., 1726) and also published a memoir, *A View of Sir Isaac Newton* (1728).
P, 1: 57n; Cohen, pp. 209–14; *DNB.*

PENN, JOHN (1729–1795). Friendly to BF and to Pennsylvania, this nephew of Thomas Penn resided in Philadelphia from 1752 to 1755; and he was governor from 1763 to 1771, and from 1773 to 1776. He maneuvered to have delegates to the first Continental Congress elected by the assembly, thus giving them legitimacy. He remained in Philadelphia the rest of his life.

William R. Shepherd, *Proprietary Government of Pennsylvania* (New York, 1896), pp. 449n, 493, 494n, 571–75; *P*, 10: 401; *DAB*; *DNB*.

PENN, THOMAS (1702–1775). William Penn willed Pennsylvania to three sons. The eldest, John, died in 1746, willing his share to Thomas. The youngest, Richard, left administration of the province up to Thomas also. Thus Thomas made the policies which F. J. Paris then wrote as elaborate instructions to the governors (technically deputy governors). In 1754 Penn thought BF "as capable as any man in America to serve the Crown" (*P*, 5: 334n). But after the clash over taxes on proprietary lands, he refused to "have any conversation with [BF] on any pretence" (*P*, 7: 364n,) while BF conceived "a more cordial and thorough Contempt for him than I ever before felt for any Man living—" (*P*, 7: 362).

Howard M. Jenkins, *Family of William Penn* (Philadelphia, 1899); Wainwright, *passim*; *DAB*; *DNB*.

PENN, WILLIAM (1644–1718). Founder and proprietor of Pennsylvania, he twice visited the province (1682–84, 1699–1701). His charter of 1701 was Pennsylvania's constitution until 1776. BF parodied his pamphlet on titles of honor, *No Cross, No Crown* (1669), in the *New England Courant* (February 18, 1723).

P, 1: 51n; *DAB*; *DNB*.

PETERS, RICHARD (c. 1704–1776). An early friend of BF, sharing cultural interests, he was, as secretary of the Provincial Council, 1743 to 1762, the proprietors' chief correspondent. James Logan called him "the most learned man in Pennsylvania" (*Quaker History*, 57 [1968], 68), and Peters headed the Academy's board of trustees. But his friendship with BF ended when the latter attacked the proprietors. In 1757, Peters wrote: "I have a very high opinion of BF's virtue and uncorrupted honesty but party Zeal throws down all the pales of Truth and Candour and lays all the soul waste to Temptation without knowing or suspecting it" (*P*, 7: 133n). He left public service in 1762 to become pastor of Philadelphia's two Episcopal churches.

Hubertis Cummings, *Richard Peters* (Philadelphia, 1944); *DAB*.

PITT, WILLIAM (1708–1778). A brilliant orator and savage opponent, prime minister (1756–61), made Earl of Chatham in 1766, he championed the American colonies and worked with BF in 1774–75 to avoid war. In 1761, Americans were said to "almost idolize him" (*P*, 9: 403). He later called BF "an Honour not to the English Nation only but to Human Nature" (*P*, 21: 582).

P, 7: 375; Namier, 3: 290–99; *DNB*.

POTTS, STEPHEN (1704–1758). A Quaker bookbinder, member of the original Junto, he was BF's lodger (1731–37) until becoming doorkeeper of the assembly. Later, besides a bindery, he also ran a tavern (1748–58). BF said he was "a Wit, that seldom acted wisely . . . in the midst of his Poverty, ever laughing!" (P, 8: 159).

P, 2: 209; 8: 84; Eddy, 1: 38–43; 2: 107–8; Miller, pp. 1-li.

POWNALL, THOMAS (1722–1805). BF's close friend and political ally abroad was a professional administrator who came to New York as secretary to a governor who committed suicide there, leaving him to travel the colonies on his own. At Philadelphia, he began the alliance with BF that in 1756 alarmed the proprietors because of Pownall's influence in London and BF's in America (P, 6: 486n). After serving as secretary to Lord Loudoun (1756) and governor of Massachusetts (1757–60) he went home to England to write an influential book, *The Administration of the Colonies* (1764) and to defend the colonies as a Member of Parliament (1767–80).

John A. Schutz, *Thomas Pownall* (Glendale, 1951); P, 12: 428; Namier, 3: 316–18; Valentine, 2: 717; DAB; DNB.

PRATT, CHARLES, FIRST EARL CAMDEN (1714–1794). The "new" attorneys general who studied BF's complaint against the proprietors in 1757 had previously had a retainer from the Pennsylvania assembly, but was not therefore barred from working on the new case. In 1759 BF found him inclined to favor the assembly, "tho' the Nature of his Office requires him to be something of a Prerogative Man" (P, 8: 294–95). In the House of Lords he championed the colonies.

P, 8: 3n–4n; Namier 3: 322–24; Valentine, 2: 719–20; DNB.

QUINCY, JOSIAH (1710–1784). One of Massachusetts' wealthiest merchants, a member of assembly, and later a firm patriot, he retired in 1750 to Braintree. There, among other enterprises, he had an interest in John Franklin's glassworks, and there BF also owned property, so that they were not total strangers when Quincy solicited BF's assistance in 1755.

P, 6: 3n, 4–5; *Sibley's Harvard Graduates*, 8: 463–75.

RALPH, JAMES (c. 1705–1762). After BF left London in 1726, Ralph stayed on, writing poetry and plays, collaborating with Henry Fielding in political journalism, and becoming a skilled writer against the government, which in 1753 gave him a pension of £300 a year to stay out of politics. In 1757, at the request of the child Ralph had deserted 30 years earlier, BF found him in London, gave him editorial work, and, upon his death, bought books from his library to benefit his heirs.

Elizabeth R. McKinsey, "James Ralph . . . ," *PAPS*, 117 (1973), 59–78; P, 1: 58–59; 7: 274; 9: 404n; 10: 186n; DAB; DNB.

READ, JAMES (1718–1793). Husband of Deborah F's second cousin, he was BF's neighbor and rival bookseller. He unsuccessfully opposed BF as assembly clerk (1747), then moved to Reading, Pennsylvania, leaving debts BF tried to collect for London friends.

J. Bennett Nolan, *Printer Strahan's Book Account* (Reading, 1939); *P*, 3: 39n, 329–30, 377.

READ, JOHN (1677–1724). Deborah F's father came to Philadelphia from Birmingham by 1711. As a carpenter and building contractor, he was well off; but before dying, he mortgaged his property (1724), leaving his family in debt.

P, 1: 362–63.

READ, SARAH WHITE (1675–1761). Deborah F's mother, born in Birmingham, wed John Read there in 1701, then bore him seven children, of whom only three reached maturity. As a widow, she shared BF's shop, selling medicines. At her death, BF consoled his wife: "Your Comfort will be, that no Care was wanting on your Part towards her," and "I cannot charge myself with having ever fail'd in one Instance of Duty and Respect for her" (*P*, 10: 69).

P, 1: 362–63.

RIDDLESDEN, WILLIAM VANHAESDONCK (d. before 1733). The international confidence man for whom John Read foolishly stood security was transported to Maryland on Oct. 27, 1720, for "Robbing the Chappel at Whitehall." He fled to Philadelphia in 1721 where he bilked Read and others before leaving the colonies. In France in 1722 he passed counterfeit English banknotes. Back in England, using the alias William Cornwallis (posing as a descendant of the early Maryland settler Thomas Cornwallis), he wed "a Gentlewoman of considerable fortune in the County of Cambridge" and petitioned Lord Baltimore to confirm his rights to the Cornwallis lands in Maryland. Discovered to be Riddlesden, he was imprisoned (December 1723) by the King's Bench, but offered bail if he promised to transport himself back to America for seven years. In 1724, he forged land grants for at least eleven thousand acres in Delaware and New Jersey.

American Weekly Mercury, May 2, 1723; April 16, 1724; January 11, 1725/6; March 24, 1725/6; and Jan. 18, 1732/3; *The Archives of Maryland*, vols. 25, 34, 35, 36, and 38; *The Calvert Papers Number Two* (Baltimore: Md. Historical Soc., 1894), pp. 33–37; 43–44; Marion & Jack Kaminkow, *Original Lists of Emigrants in Bondage* (Baltimore: Magna Carta Book Co., 1967), pp. 134, 180–81.

ROBERTS, JAMES (1673?–1754). The printer who rejected Ralph's offer to write a weekly paper for him had an office in Warwick Lane and served as Master of the Stationers Company, 1729–31.

Plomer, p. 255.

ROGERS, JOHN (d. 1745?). Married (perhaps bigamously) on August 5, 1725, to Deborah F., he fled his debtors in December 1727. If he is the John Rogers who died in Antigua, August 1745, then BF himself avoided the charge of bigamy by not officially marrying Deborah in 1730.

V.L. Oliver, *Caribbeana*, 6 vols. (London, 1909–19), 1: 237.

ROSE, AQUILA (c. 1695–1723). A journeyman printer for Andrew Bradford, he was also clerk of the assembly and operated a ferry. He died June 24, 1723. His son, JOSEPH, after apprenticeship with BF (1730), became foreman of his shop and printed Aquila Rose's *Poems on Several Occasions* (1740).

P, 2: 239n; Miller, pp. 98–99; *DAB*.

RUSSELL, THOMAS. *See* ONION, STEPHEN.

SCULL, NICHOLAS II (1687–1761). One of the original Junto, a surveyor who wrote verses, he supervised the famous "Walking Purchase" of Indian lands that BF later called a fraud (P, 9: 222). He laid out Easton with William Parsons, succeeding him as surveyor-general (1748–61). His map of Philadelphia was the "most popular ever made of that section" (N. B. Wainwright, "Scull and Heap's Map . . . ," *PMHB*, 81 [1975], 69).

P, 9: 222n; N. B. Wainwright, "Nicholas Scull's Junto Verses," *PMHB*, 73 (1949), 82–84.

SHIPLEY, JONATHAN, BISHOP OF ST. ASAPH (1714–1788). One of BF's dearest English friends, his bishopric was perhaps lowest in the hierarchy, and he received no further advancement because of his outspoken support of American colonies ("the only great nursery of freemen left on the face of the earth").

P, 18: 136–37; Smyth, 10: 32; *TLS*, July 24, 1937, pp. 1–2; Valentine, 2: 787–88.

SHIRLEY, WILLIAM (1694–1771). As governor of Massachusetts (1741–57), he shared BF's hope for colonial union and exchanged ideas with BF in letters of 1754, published a dozen years later in the popular press for their bearing on the Stamp Act. In 1745 he led the splendidly successful expedition against Cape Breton, and in 1756 was named to succeed Braddock. Replaced as commander-in-chief by Lord Loudoun, he returned to London and later served as governor of the Bahamas (1759–67), before retiring to Roxbury, Massachusetts.

John Schutz, *William Shirley* . . . (Chapel Hill, 1961); P, 5: 441–67; Valentine, 2: 789; *DAB*; *DNB*.

SHOVELL, CLOWDISLEY (1650–1707). This hero of Queen Anne's fleet went down with his flagship, the *Association*, and three other ships on the rocks of the Scilly Islands the night of October 22, 1707. Two other ships escaped to tell the tale.

C. H. Firth, *Naval Songs and Ballads* (Naval Records Society, 1908), p. lxvii; *DNB*.

SLOANE, HANS (1660–1753). Irish-born botanist and physician of Queen Anne and George II, he succeeded Newton as president of the Royal Society (1727–41). His museum and library were the nucleus of the British Museum—which still has the asbestos purse he purchased from BF in June 1725.

P, 1: 54; E. St. John Brooks, *Sir Hans Sloane* (London, 1954); *DNB*.

SPANGENBERG, AUGUSTUS GOTTLIEB (1704–1792). BF met this Moravian Bishop at Bethlehem, which Spangenberg had made the Moravian center for America in 1744. An internationally known expert on colonial missions, he lived there, off and on until 1762, writing voluminously on religious affairs in Pennsylvania. He introduced the mysticism of Jacob Boehme and William Law to America.

P, 6: 362n; Clarke Garret, "The Spiritual Odyssey of Jacob Duché," *PAPS*, 119 (1975), 143–44.

SPENCER, ARCHIBALD (c. 1698–1760). BF met this physician and popular lecturer on electricity in Boston, June 1743, and doubtless the following year when he lectured in Philadelphia before settling in Fredericksburg, Virginia. Because of Dr. Spencer's influence with the widow Mary Washington, William Fairfax spoke to him about the future of young George Washington. Despite being infamous as a deist, he was ordained in 1749 and spent the rest of his life as an Anglican minister in Anne Arundel County, Maryland (1751–60).

J. A. Leo Lemay, "Franklin's Dr. Spence . . . ," *Md. Hist. Mag.*, 59 (1964), 199–216.

SPOTSWOOD, ALEXANDER (1676–1740). Earlier deputy postmaster (1730–40) for North America, he had been a military leader and acting governor of Virginia (1710–22). BF's obituary of him in the *Pa. Gaz.*, June 12, 1740, said his death was a great loss to "all who have at Heart the Interest and Glory of Great Britain" (P, 2: 287).

P, 2: 235n; *DAB*; *DNB*.

SYNG, PHILIP (1703–89). Member of the original Junto, this Irish-born silversmith worked with BF on many civic enterprises and in his electrical experiments.

P, 1: 209n–210n; *DAB*.

TAYLOR, ABRAHAM (c. 1703–1772). One of BF's companions in seeking cannon from New York, he was a merchant and provincial councilor as well as colonel of the militia. As Collector of Customs, he was said to be in league with the firm of Chief Justice William Allen and Co., which smuggled sugar, rum and molasses.

P, 3: 428n. Carl Bridenbaugh, *Cities in Revolt* (New York, 1968), p. 66.

TENNENT, GILBERT (1703–1764). Presbyterian preacher in New Brunswick, New Jersey (1726–43), he toured New England with Whitefield in 1740, then three years later formed Whitefield's converts into the new Presbyterian congregation at Philadelphia where he remained the rest of his life as a leader of Presbyterianism "New Light."

P, 2: 313n; *DAB*.

THOMAS, GEORGE (c. 1695–1774). Governor of Pennsylvania (1738–47) whose efforts at defense were obstructed by the Quaker-dominated assembly, he managed Indian affairs ably. He later served as governor of the Leeward Islands (1753–66), and was knighted on his retirement.

P, 2: 186n, 350n; *DAB*.

TIMOTHÉE, ELIZABETH (d. 1757). She was wife of Louis Timothée (d. 1738), emigrating from Holland in 1731. BF employed Louis as journeyman printer and librarian of the Library Company (1732–33), then sent him as partner to South Carolina. At his death, Elizabeth continued the business, buying out BF's share in six years.

Hennig Cohen, pp. 238–41. P, 1: 230n; 341n–42n; Richard Maxwell Brown, "Timothy, Elizabeth" in James, 3: 465–66.

VAUGHAN, BENJAMIN (1751–1835). BF's disciple, Vaughan was an independently wealthy son of a Jamaican merchant and Maine mother. A pupil of Joseph Priestley's, he studied law and medicine but practiced neither. In 1776–79 he edited BF's essays, assisted by BF himself. Private secretary to Lord Shelburne, he was his personal emissary to BF in the Paris peace talks (1782–83). After two years in revolutionary France and in Switzerland (1794–96) he came to the family estate in Maine, where he wrote voluminously and farmed experimentally till his death.

Francis W. Philbrick, "Some Early Editions & Editors of Franklin," *PAPS*, 97 (1953), 533–34; Smyth, 1: 180–81, 10: 32, 51; *DAB: DNB*.

VERNON, SAMUEL (1683–1737). The Rhode Island silversmith who entrusted BF to collect a debt had a son, THOMAS, whom BF later appointed postmaster of Newport (1754). BF also rescued a grandson from debt many years later, out of "Gratitude to his Grandfather who had been my Friend when I was very young."

Carl Van Doren, ed., *Benjamin Franklin's Autobiographical Writings* (New York, 1945), pp. 658–62; Henry N. Flynt and Martha G. Fales, *The Heritage Collection of Silver . . .* (Old Deerfield, Mass., 1968), p. 347.

WATSON, JOSEPH (d. 1728?). This poetical companion of BF's youth, a clerk of Charles Brockden's, later married Deborah Read's sister Frances. A passage BF deleted from the manuscript of the autobiography says that the Read family warmly welcomed back BF in 1726 because of Watson.

P, 4: 136.

WATSON, WILLIAM (1715–1787). The "celebrated Dr. Watson" who summarized BF's electrical experiments for the Royal Society was the leading English scientist in the field. He demonstrated that electricity was transmitted instantaneously through wires, water, earth, and a vacuum—in experiments that BF repeated the next year (1747) in Philadelphia.

P, 3: 457; Mottelay, pp. 175–76; Cohen, pp. 390–413, 441–52.

WATTS, JOHN (c. 1678–1763). One of the most important London printers in the first half of the eighteenth century, he trained such other eminent printers as William Strahan and BF's partner David Hall. "Watts' near Lincoln's Inn Fields" was in Wild Court, about nine blocks west of Palmer's in Bartholomew Close.

Plomer, p. 304.

WEBB, GEORGE (1708–1736?). Member of the original Junto who attended Oxford (1724–26), he bought his remaining time as an indentured servant from Keimer in 1728 with money from a "female friend." He may have been the George Webb who printed for the Virginia assembly in 1728 and who became South Carolina's first printer in 1731. BF printed his poem, *Batchelors-Hall* in 1731. He could be the same George Webb who took a law degree at the Middle Temple in 1734 and compiled a handbook for justices of the peace in Virginia in 1736.

Wroth, *Colonial Printer*, pp. 45–46; P, 1: 113; Hennig Cohen, p. 231; George Foster, ed., *Alumni Oxonienses . . . 1715–1886* (Oxford, 1888), 4: 1516; Miller no. 46.

WELFARE (WOHLFAHRT), MICHAEL (1687–1741). As Brother Agonius, he was a leader of the "Dunkers," or Seventh Day Baptist, community at Ephrata. BF reported in the *Pa. Gaz.* for September 25, 1734, that Welfare "appeared in full Market in the Habit of a Pilgrim, his hat of Linnen, his Beard at full Length, and a long Staff in his Hand. He declared himself sent by Almighty God, to denounce Vengeance against the Iniquity and Wickedness of the Inhabitants of this City and Province, without speedy Repentance." BF printed a sermon of his in 1737.

P, 1: 382n; Donald F. Durnbaugh, *The Brethren in Colonial America* (Elgin, Illinois, 1967); Miller nos. 145, 146.

WHITEFIELD, GEORGE (1714–1770). Inspiration for the "Great Awakening," this prodigiously popular Methodist preacher converted even the sailors who brought him to America in 1738. He returned to America six times between 1739 to 1770, promoting evangelical religion and his Georgia orphanage. BF printed both sides of the sometimes vicious controversies Whitefield ignited.

P, 2: 241n; Tyerman; John R. Williams, "The Strange Case of Dr. Franklin and Mr. Whitefield," *PMHB*, 102 (1978), 399–421; *DAB*; *DNB*.

WHITMARSH, THOMAS (d. 1733). The "excellent Workman" BF brought over from London to replace Meredith came as a journeyman

by April 1730, and the next year went to South Carolina as BF's partner. There he printed the *South Carolina Gazette* (1732–33).
P, 1: 205n; Hennig Cohen, pp. 230–33.

WIGATE (WYGATE), JOHN. BF kept in touch with this fellow worker long after leaving Watts' printing shop in 1726. "Please to remember me affectionately to my old Friend Wigate," he wrote in 1744.
P, 2: 412n.

WILCOX, JOHN (fl. 1721–1762). The London bookseller who lent BF books when he lived next door in Little Britain could have been the same "John Wilcox" who served as warden of the Stationer's Company in 1762.
Plomer, p. 313.

WILKS, ROBERT (1665?–1732). Irish actor-manager of Drury Lane Theatre, to whom James Ralph applied for a job, RW was one of three partners who dominated London theatrical life from 1710 to 1730.
Emmett L. Avery, ed., *The London Stage*, 1660–1800, pt. 2 (Carbondale, 1960), pp lxxxii–lxxxviii; *DNB*.

WOLFE, JAMES (1727–1759). Named major-general in January 1759, he commanded the campaign to capture Quebec, heroically dying on the Plains of Abraham in September at the moment of victory over Montcalm.
P, 8: 408n; *DNB*.

WRIGHT, EDWARD (d. 1761). The "Dr. Wright" then at Paris who reported BF's reputation there was a Scots physician and Fellow of the Royal Society who later wrote *Conjectures on the Course of Thunder* (Paris, 1756).
P, 7: 24n; *Gentleman's Magazine*, 31 (1761), 430.

WYNDHAM, WILLIAM (1687–1740). Once Chancellor of the Exchequer (1713–14), he acted as Tory leader in Parliament during the exile of Henry St. John, Viscount Bolingbroke. His son, Charles (1710–63) became second Earl of Egremont, a Whig leader who succeeded William Pitt as secretary of state responsible for America (1762–63).
P, 10: 115n, 325; Sedgwick, 2: 562–64; *DNB*.

YORKE, CHARLES (1722–1770). The solicitor-general at the time of BF's complaint against the proprietors became attorney-general in 1762 and lord chancellor in 1770. In 1759 BF called him "wholly and strongly tinctured with high Notions of . . . Prerogative" (*P*, 8: 295).
P, 8: 3n; Namier 3: 675–78; Valentine, 2: 955; *DNB*.

Backgrounds

EXCERPTS FROM FRANKLIN'S LETTERS
MENTIONING THE *AUTOBIOGRAPHY*

Unfortunately, Franklin rarely mentioned his *Autobiography* until the last years of his life, so that few references to it survive from the years before 1786. The most significant references to it by his friends are the letters from Abel James and from Benjamin Vaughan that Franklin included as an introduction to Part Two of the *Autobiography*.

The following excerpts from his letters constitute his most telling remarks about the *Autobiography*.

To Mathew Carey, August 10, 1786†

Sir:—The Memoirs you mention would be of little or no Use to your Scheme, as they contain only some Notes of my early Life, and finish in 1730. They were written to my Son, and intended only as Information to my Family. I have in hand a full Account of my Life which I propose to leave behind me; in the meantime I wish nothing of the kind may be publish'd, and shall be much oblig'd to the Proprietors of the Columbian Magazine if they will drop that Intention, for the present.

To the Duke de La Rochefoucauld, October 22, 1788††

*   *   *

Having now finish'd my Term of being President, and promising myself to engage no more in public Business, I hope to enjoy the small Remains of Life that are allow'd me, in the Repose I have so long wish'd for. I purpose to so employ it in compleating the personal History you mention. It is now brought down to my Fiftieth Year. What is to follow will be of more important Transactions: But it seems to me that what is done will be of more general Use to young Readers; as exemplifying strongly the Effect of prudent and imprudent Conduct in the Commencement of a Life of Business.

*   *   *

To Benjamin Vaughan, October 24, 1788*

* * * I am recovering from a long-continued gout, and am diligently employed in writing the History of my Life, to the doing of

† On August 9, 1786, Mathew Carey, publisher of the Philadelphia *Columbian Magazine*, wrote to Franklin saying that he would like to include a biography of him and asking his permission to read over the memoirs that he has heard Franklin wrote some time ago. Franklin replied the next day with this letter. Source: Smyth, 9: 533–34.
†† The two Frenchmen closest to Franklin

were Louis Le Veillard and the Duc de La Rochefoucauld. Both knew of his Autobiography and both urged Franklin to complete it. Source: Smyth, 9: 665.
* One of Franklin's close English friends was his disciple Benjamin Vaughan, who published an edition of Franklin's writings in 1779. Source: Smyth, 9: 675–76.

which the persuasions contained in your letter of January 31st, 1783, have not a little contributed. I am now in the year 1756, just before I was sent to England. To shorten the work, as well as for other reasons, I omit all facts and transactions, that may not have a tendency to benefit the young reader, by showing him from my example, and my success in emerging from poverty, and acquiring some degree of wealth, power, and reputation, the advantages of certain modes of conduct which I observed, and of avoiding the errors which were prejudicial to me. If a writer can judge properly of his own work, I fancy, on reading over what is already done, that the book will be found entertaining, interesting, and useful, more so than I expected when I began it. If my present state of health continues, I hope to finish it this winter. When done, you shall have a manuscript copy of it, that I may obtain from your judgment and friendship such remarks, as may contribute to its improvement.

*   *   *

To William Vaughan, December 9, 1788†

Dear Sir:—I received your kind Letter of Oct. 5. I am glad the little Papers I sent you were not unacceptable. Having done with public Business, I am now employing myself in a Work your good brother Benjamin once strongly recommended to me, which is writing the History of my own Life. This will contain a Number of Precepts of the kind you desire, and all exemplified by the Effects of their Practice in my own Affairs. Please to inform Benjamin of this, and that I have got as far as my fiftieth Year.

*   *   *

To Benjamin Vaughan, June 3, 1789††

My Dearest Friend,
I received your kind letter of March 4th, and wish I may be able to complete what you so earnestly desire, the Memoirs of my Life. But of late I am so interrupted by extreme pain, which obliges me to have recourse to opium, that, between the effects of both, I have but little time in which I can write any thing. My grandson, however, is copying what is done, which will be sent to you for your opinion by the next vessel; and not merely for your opinion, but for your advice; for I find it a difficult task to speak decently and properly of one's own

---

† William Vaughan, Benjamin Vaughan's brother, wrote Franklin on March 31, 1788, urging him to collect in book form his writings on the common conduct in life. In another letter of October 5, 1788, Vaughan reported that he repeatedly read with pleasure these little writings by Franklin. Source: Smyth, 9: 688.
†† Source: Smyth, 10: 32.

conduct; and I feel the want of a judicious friend to encourage me in scratching out.

* * *

To Benjamin Vaughan, November 2, 1789†

* * * What is already done, I now send you, with an earnest request that you and my good friend Dr. Price would be so good as to take the trouble of reading it, critically examining it, and giving me your candid opinion whether I had best publish or suppress it; and if the first, then what parts had better be expunged or altered. I shall rely upon your opinions, for I am now grown so old and feeble in mind, as well as body, that I cannot place any confidence in my own judgment. In the mean time, I desire and expect that you will not suffer any copy of it, or of any part of it, to be taken for any purpose whatever.

* * *

To M. Le Veillard, November 13, 1789††

Dear Friend:—This must be but a short Letter, for I have mislaid your last and must postpone answering them till I have found them; but to make you some Amends I send you what is done of the Memoirs, under this express Condition however, that you do not suffer any Copy to be taken of them, or of any Part of them, on any Account whatever, and that you will, with your excellent Friend the Duke de la Rochefoucault, read them over carefully, examine them critically, and send me your friendly, candid Opinion of the Parts you would advise me to correct or expunge; this in Case you should be of Opinion that they are generally proper to be published; and if you judge otherwise, that you would send me that Opinion as soon as possible, and prevent my taking farther Trouble in endeavouring to finish them.* * *

"AUTHENTIC MEMOIR OF DR. FRANKLYN"

Alfred Owen Aldridge, "The First Published Memoir of Franklin," *William and Mary Quarterly*, 24 (1967), 624–28, called attention to this sketch, pointed out that it was "the earliest known forerunner of the publication of Franklin's life story," and noted that it was "directly related" to the *Autobiography*. The sketch, evidently reflecting Franklin's anecdotes, must have been written by someone (like Richard Price) who was a close friend of Franklin and a sympathizer with the Americans. (By 1778, most Englishmen considered the American "patriots" as rebels or traitors.) This version of Franklin's early life focuses upon the difficulty of the journey to Philadelphia, upon the American Dream motif, and upon the consequences of an older man's help to a young one—all major motifs (although differing in details) in the *Autobiography*.

"Authentic Memoir of Dr. Franklyn"†

The Public have been already acquainted with the birth and parentage of this great philosopher and statesman; and all Europe has lately beheld, with astonishment, this venerable old man acting the part of a patriot, when perhaps he stands alone in the greatness of his cause and abilities. This memoir, therefore, only goes to show the accidental circumstance that first introduced him into life, and may well be reckoned in the catalogue of "great events from little causes."

Dr. Franklyn was bred a printer, and followed this profession for some time in Boston, but possessing too liberal a spirit at that time for the meridian of that city, he was obliged to quit it abruptly, and fly to Philadelphia. Being much narrowed in his circumstances, he was obliged to walk all the way to the last-mentioned place, where, being arrived just at the time that the congregation were going to morning service, young Franklyn mixed with the croud, and, perhaps partly for the benefit of getting a seat to sit down on, attended divine service.

Oppressed with too much fatigue, he had not been long there, when he fell asleep, and continued so, after the service was over, till the sexton, just going to lock the door, perceiving his situation, woke him. Franklyn on this immediately got up, *unknowing where to go, or what to do*.

At last a wealthy citizen of Philadelphia, seeing him a stranger, and perhaps seeing that perturbation of mind in his face which such a situation as his generally paints, he asked him, "Whether he was not a stranger? How long he had been in town, etc?" To these questions Franklyn gave such ingenious and modest answers, that the citizen asked him home to dinner with him; the consequence of which visit was, that liking his conversation, and above all, the openness of his manner, and the enterprise of his spirit, he made out an appointment for him in his own family, and there having the benefit of seeing and conversing with some of the principles of that city, he progressively laid the foundation of his present exalted situation.

ANECDOTES RECORDED BY JOHN JAY††

Franklin told anecdotes about his youth and early friends to a number of persons, including John Jay (1745–1829), who was in Paris in 1783 with

† Source: *London Chronicle*, October 1, 1778.

†† Source: Frank Monaghan, ed., *Some Con-* *versations of Dr. Franklin and Mr. Jay* (New Haven: Three Monks Press, 1936).

Franklin negotiating the peace treaty with Great Britain. A few anecdotes are identical to those recorded in the *Autobiography*; others embody similar themes; and some supplement the information in the *Autobiography*. In jotting down these bits of oral history, Jay used numerous abbreviations.

[Robert Hunter Morris]†

* * *

Robert Hunter Morris, the Son of the former, and who for about a Year was Govr of Pennsylvania, the Dr knew very well—It seems that the Dr was at New York on his Way to Boston when Morris arrived there from England. He asked the Dr. many Questions abt Pennsylvania, abt the Temper of the People, and whether he thought it difficult for him to pass his Time agreable among them—The Dr. told him nothing wd be more easy if he avoided Disputes with the Assembly—but replied he laughingly, *why wd you have me deprive myself of one of my greatest pleasures*—he was fond of disputing and thought he had Talents for it—However added he I will take your advice—on Franklin's Return from Boston to Pha he found the Govr and Assembly in warm altercations—the Dr was a member of the assembly, and was appointed to Draw up their answr—Morris after having sent a Message to the assembly, met Saml. Rhodes and asked him what he thought of it—Rhodes said he thought it very smart—ah sd Morris I thought so too when I had finished it—but tomorrow we shall see Benj. Franklin's answer and then I suspect we shall both change our Minds—Altho he knew that Franklin conducted the dispute agt him—yet they were always good friends, and frequently dined together &.—When the Dr's Son was many Years afterwards made Govr of Jersey, & was going to take upon him the Govt Morris came to meet him on the Road and behaved kindly & in a friendly Manner—He was a very good natured Man—had Talents & Learning but his Imagination was too strong & he was not deep in any Thing.

* * *

[Andrew Hamilton]† †

* * *

19 July 1783. Dr. Franklin says he was very well and long acquainted With andw Hamilton the Lawyer who distinguished himself on Zengers Tryal at New York. He was a Scotchman who came young

† Franklin told Jay of his meeting with Robert Hunter Morris in New York in the winter of 1754–55, and of their later easy relations, despite their official bickering. Franklin probably suppressed Morris's compliment concerning the brilliance of Franklin's replies to Morris's "smart" messages to the assembly in order not to seem to be praising himself. Cf. pp. 111–12 and 129–30 this edition.

†† Andrew Hamilton appears in the *Autobiography* as Franklin's patron. In this anecdote, he is a version of Franklin, rising, by "great application," from poverty and obscurity to fame and fortune. And "Mr. Brooke" predicts Hamilton's rise, just as Isaac Decow predicts Franklin's. Cf. p. 45 this edition.

into Pensylvania, some said he came a Servant—Mr Brooke who in those Days was an old Man told Dr Franklin that he had seen Hamilton who then lived at Lewis Town studying the Law in an Osnabrigs Shirt and Trowsers,[1] that he observed him often, and that from his great application he predicted that he wd one Day make a Figure in that Proffession—He was a Man of exceeding good Talents & ready Elocution.

Wm Allen then one of the most Wealthy Men in Pensa & afterwards Ch. Justice—married Hamilton's Daughter—That Event gave Hamilton more Weight & Consideration—he practiced generously, & took no Fees in the Cause of Zenger, the City of New York presented him with the Freedom of the City in a Gold Box with handsome Inscriptions—

He left a good Estate, made by laying out his Money as he acquired it in Lotts & Lands wh rose daily in Value.

His son was afterwards Govr of Pensylva—sustained a good Character, had a decent Share of Talents but not much improved.

* * *

[Writing for the New Jersey Assembly][†]

* * *

19 July 1783. Dr. Franklin told me that not long after the elder Lewis Morris (who was once chief Justice of N York) came to the Governmt of N Jersey, he involved himself in a Dispute with the Assembly of that Province. The Doctr (who was then a printer at Pha) went to Burlington while the Assembly was sitting there, & were engaged in the Dispute with their Govr—The House had referred his Message to a Committee, consisting of some of their principal Members, Jos. Cooper was one of them—but tho they were Men of good understanding & respectable, yet there was not one among them capable of writing a proper ansr to the Message—and Cooper who was acquaintd with the Dr prevailed upon him to undertake it—he did and went thro the Business much to their Satisfaction—In Consideration of the Aid he gave them in that way then & afterwards, they made him their Printer (This shews the then State of Literature in Jersey)

* * *

1. A heavy, coarse cotton, used for grain sacks and for clothing of the cheapest sort.
† This anecdote concerns Franklin's stay at Burlington, New Jersey, in April, 1740, when he wrote the address that the House of Representatives delivered to Governor Lewis Morris, April 28, 1740. The topic "Writing for Jersey Assembly" in BF's Outline (see p. 153) this edition) proves that he once meant to include this anecdote in the *Autobiography*.

[Quaker Attitude toward Warfare]†

* * *

March 1784. Doctr Franklin, who has lived long & much with Quakers, tells me that he thinks the far greater part of them approve of defensive tho not of offensive War. In the Course of the War wh ended in 1748—It was thought necessary to erect a Battery at Pha & a Lottery was made to defray part of ye Expence—at that Time the Doctr was of a fire Company of thirty Members, twenty two of whom were Quakers—they had sixty pounds of public or Company Stock—and the Dr proposed to lay it out in Lottery Tickets. it was their Custom in all Money Matters to give Notice or make the Motion a Week before its Determination—When the Dr moved his Proposition Anthy Morris a Quaker Member opposed it strenuously observing that the Friends cd not apply Money to Purposes of War & that if the Dr persisted in this motion, it wd be the Means of breaking up the Company—the Dr observed that the Minority must be bound by the Majority, & as the greater part of ye Co. were Quakers it wd be in their power to decide as they pleased. When the Day for ye Determination came, Any Morris was ye only Quaker who appd—the Doctr observing that Circumstance pressed for the Vote,—Morris sd he expected that other Members wd soon come it [in], & begd that the Vote might be deferred for an Hour—While that matter was in agitation, the Waiter called him out, Telling him that two Men below Stairs wanted to Speake to him—he found they were two Quaker Members of ye Company—They told him they came from six or seven others who were in a Home next Door but one—they came to inquire whether he was strong enough to carry his Mo. if not that on being sent for they wd attend & vote with him—but they wishd to avoid it if possible lest they shd give offence to certain of ye Friends who were more scrupulous on that Head—The Docr returned & agreed to Anthony Morris's Request for another Hour—the Hour elapsed and not a single Quaker appd— the Question was then put & carried.

While Govr Thomas was Govr of Pennsylvania shortly after the taking of Louisbourgh by an armamt from Boston, advice came to Pha that the Garrison was in great want of Gun powder—Govr Thomas communicated it to the Assembly & wanted them to afford Supplies—the Quaker Majority in ye Assembly wd not consent to supply any Gun powder—but they granted three thousand pounds to be laid out in Flour Wheat or other *Grain* for the use of the Garrison—Govr Thomas said that by *other Grain* was meant Gun Powder—he laid the Money out accordingly & nothing was sd about it—

* * *

† Cf. pp. 94–96 this edition.

Excerpts from Franklin's Writings on Wealth, The Art of Virtue, and Perfection

Franklin's major topics in the *Autobiography* include the American Dream, virtue, writing, religion, and pride. Because he wrote so much on these topics throughout his life, it would be possible to compile book-length anthologies on these subjects from his writings. What we have decided to do is to print a selection of his comments on three topics. First, since Franklin is often condemned as materialistic and since the rise from rags to riches is an aspect of the *Autobiography*, we include a selection of his comments and his actions on wealth. Second, since his "bold and arduous Project of arriving at moral Perfection" is frequently criticized, we print some of his other writings on "The Art of Virtue." And third, since one reason for the strictures on Franklin's project for moral perfection arises from our anachronistic ideas on the meaning of *perfection*, we print some of his other writings on perfection.

WEALTH

From *Poor Richard*, March, 1736†

[Although Poor Richard is generally stereotyped as an avaricious almanac-maker, excessively concerned with money, the actual sayings that Franklin wrote (or merely revised) for his *Poor Richard* almanacs sometimes reveal Franklin's own complex mind and sophisticated attitudes. Franklin, however, never lost sight of his primary audience—the common farmer of colonial America, or of his primary purpose—the selling of almanacs.]

Wealth is not his that has it, but his that enjoys it.

To Cadwallader Colden, Philadelphia, September 29, 1748††

[By 1740, just twelve years after opening his own printing shop in Philadelphia, Franklin had emerged as the most daring, innovative, skilled and successful printer in America. And he gave it up. On January 1, 1748, he

† Source: Poor Richard for March, 1736; P, 2: †† Source: P, 3: 317–18.
138.

formed a partnership with his shop foreman and retired before his forty-second birthday. He presented his reasons for retirement in a letter of September 29, 1748, to his friend Cadwallader Colden (1688–1776), philosopher, scientist and, later, Loyalist governor of New York.]

Sir

I received your Favour of the 12th Inst. which gave me the greater Pleasure, as 'twas so long since I had heard from you. I congratulate you on your Return to your beloved Retirement: I too am taking the proper Measures for obtaining Leisure to enjoy Life and my Friends more than heretofore, having put my Printing house under the Care of my Partner David Hall, absolutely left off Bookselling, and remov'd to a more quiet Part of the Town, where I am settling my old Accounts and hope soon to be quite a Master of my own Time, and no longer (as the Song has it) *at every one's Call but my own*. If Health continues, I hope to be able in another Year to visit the most distant Friend I have, without Inconvenience. With the same Views I have refus'd engaging further in publick Affairs; The Share I had in the late Association, &c. having given me a little present Run of Popularity, there was a pretty general Intention of chusing me a Representative for the City at the next Election of Assemblymen; but I have desired all my Friends who spoke to me about it, to discourage it, declaring that I should not serve if chosen. Thus you see I am in a fair Way of having no other Tasks than such as I shall like to give my self, and of enjoying what I look upon as a great Happiness, Leisure to read, study, make Experiments, and converse at large with such ingenious and worthy Men as are pleas'd to honour me with their Friendship or Acquaintance, on such Points as may produce something for the common Benefit of Mankind, uninterrupted by the little Cares and Fatigues of Business. Among other Pleasures I promise my self, that of Corresponding more frequently and fully with Dr. Colden is none of the least; I shall only wish that what must be so agreable to me, may not prove troublesome to you.

* * *

To Abiah Franklin, Philadelphia, April 12, 1750†

[In 1750 Franklin wrote his mother a letter of family news, joking about his expenses and telling her about the reputation he would prefer to have.]

* * *

As to your Grandchildren, Will.[1] is now 19 Years of Age, a tall proper Youth, and much of a Beau.[2] He acquir'd a Habit of Idleness on the

---

† Source: *P*, 3: 474–75.
1. William Franklin, BF's illegitimate son (see

biographical sketches).
2. Beau, i.e., a dandy and ladies' man.

Expedition, but begins of late to apply himself to Business, and I hope will become an industrious Man. He imagin'd his Father had got enough for him: But I have assur'd him that I intend to spend what little I have, my self; if it please God that I live long enough: And as he by no means wants Sense, he can see by my going on, that I am like to be as good as my Word.

Sally[3] grows a fine Girl, and is extreamly industrious with her Needle, and delights in her book. She is of a most affectionate Temper, and perfectly Dutiful and obliging, to her Parents and to all. Perhaps I flatter my self too much; but I have Hopes that she will prove an ingenious sensible notable and worthy Woman, like her Aunt Jenney.[4] She goes now to the Dancing School.

For my own Part, at present I pass my time agreably enough. I enjoy (thro' Mercy) a tolerable Share of Health; I read a great deal, ride a little, do a little Business for my self, more for others; retire when I can, and go [into] Company when I please; so the Years roll round, and the last will come; when I would rather have it said, *He lived usefully*, than, *He died rich*.

*　　*　　*

To William Strahan, Philadelphia, June 2, 1750†

[Franklin wrote to his friend Strahan (successful London printer of Samuel Johnson, David Hume, Adam Smith, and Edward Gibbon, among others) of his disgust with "the Pursuit of Wealth to no End."]

*　　*　　*

The Description you give of the Company and Manner of Living in Scotland, would almost tempt one to remove thither. Your Sentiments of the general Foible of Mankind, in the Pursuit of Wealth to no End, are express'd in a Manner that gave me great Pleasure in reading: They are extreamly just, at least they are perfectly agreable to mine. But London Citizens, they say, are ambitious of what they call *dying worth* a great Sum: The very Notion seems to me absurd; and just the same as if a Man should run in debt for 1000 Superfluities, to the End that when he should be stript of all, and imprison'd by his Creditors, it might be said, he *broke worth* a great Sum. I imagine that what we have above what we can use, is not properly *ours*, tho' we possess it; and that the rich Man who *must die*, was no more *worth* what he leaves, than the Debtor who *must pay*.

*　　*　　*

---

3. Sarah Franklin (Bache), BF's and Deborah's daughter.   4. Jane (Franklin) Mecom, BF's younger sister.
† Source: *P*, 3: 479.

To Peter Collinson, Philadelphia, November 5, 1756†

[Writing to Collinson, Franklin spoke of his contempt for the avariciousness of Pennsylvania's Proprietors.]

* * * I have some natural Dislike to Persons who so far *Love Money*, as to be *unjust* for its sake: I dispise their *Meanness*, (as it appears to me) in several late Instances, most cordially.* * *

[Benjamin Rush on Franklin]††

*   *   *

On the [16th] of Feb. I set out for Paris with letters of introduction from Dr. Franklin, to several of his philosophical friends. When I parted with the Doctor, he asked me "how I was provided with money for my jaunt." I told him I believed I had enough. "Perhaps not, you may be exposed to unexpected expenses. Here, said he, is a credit upon a Banker in Paris for two or three hundred guineas."*   *   *

A day or two after I arrived in London I called upon Dr. Franklin, and informed him that my expenses in Paris had so far exceeded my expectations that I had been obliged to avail myself of his kind offer, by drawing upon his Banker for 30 guineas. He seemed pleased and requested that I would pay them when convenient to his wife in Philadelphia. This I did, out of the first money I earned after my arrival. Mrs. Franklin for a while refused to receive it for the Doctor had not mentioned the debt to her in any of his letters. I take great pleasure in recording this delicate act of paternal friendship in Dr. Franklin. It attached me to him during the remainder of his life, and it has, since his death, disposed me to respect and love all the branches of his family.

*   *   *

To Jane Mecom, London, December 30, 1770*

*   *   *

[From the time that Franklin was appointed Joint Postmaster General of North America in 1755 until the Ministry took away the position in 1774 because he was "too much an American," Franklin frequently outraged the Ministry because, although he held a patronage position, he did not work for the Ministry's supposed interests. On the other hand, some jealous American patriots occasionally impugned his motives and his actions because he en-

† Source: *P*, 7: 14.
†† Source: George W. Corner, ed., *The Autobiography of Benjamin Rush* (Princeton:
Princeton Univ. Press, 1948), pp. 66, 74.
* Source: *P*, 17: 314–15.

joyed official patronage. When his favorite sister Jane Mecom expressed alarm about the latest rumor that he had been removed as Postmaster General, he explained his position to her and gave his "Rule" regarding the conflict of public and private interest.]

As to the Rumour you mention (which was, as Josiah tells me, that I had been depriv'd of my Place in the Post Office on Account of a letter I wrote to Philadelphia) it might have this Foundation, that some of the Ministry had been displeas'd at my Writing such Letters, and there were really some Thoughts among them of shewing that Displeasure in that manner. But I had some Friends too, who unrequested by me advis'd the contrary. And my Enemies were forc'd to content themselves with abusing me plentifully in the Newspapers, and endeavouring to provoke me to resign. In this they are not likely to succeed, I being deficient in that Christian Virtue of Resignation. If they would have my Office, they must take it——I have heard of some great Man, whose Rule it was with regard to Offices, *Never to ask for them*, and *never to refuse them*: To which I have always added in my own Practice, *Never to resign them*. As I told my Friends, I rose to that office thro' a long Course of Service in the inferior Degrees of it: Before my time, thro' bad Management, it never produced the Salary annex'd to it; and when I receivd it, no Salary was to be allow'd if the office did not produce it. During the first four Years it was so far from defraying itself, that it became £950 Sterling in debt to me and my Collegue. I had been chiefly instrumental in bringing it to its present flourishing State, and therefore thought I had some kind of Right to it. I had hitherto executed the Duties of it faithfully, and to the perfect Satisfaction of my Superiors, which I thought was all that should be expected of me on that Account. As to the Letters complain'd of, it was true I did write them, and they were written in Compliance with another Duty, that to my Country. A Duty quite Distinct from that of Postmaster. My Conduct in this respect was exactly similar with that I held on a similar Occasion but a few Years ago, when the then Ministry were ready to hug me for the Assistance I afforded them in repealing a former Revenue Act. My Sentiments were still the same, that no such Acts should be made here for America; or, if made should as soon as possible be repealed; and I thought it should not be expected of me, to change my Political Opinions every time his Majesty thought fit to change his Ministers. This was my Language on the Occasion; and I have lately heard, that tho I was thought much to blame, it being understood that every Man who holds an Office should act with the Ministry whether agreable or not to his own Judgment, yet in consideration of the goodness of my private Character (as they are pleas'd to compliment me) the office was not to be taken from me. Possibly they may still change their Minds, and remove me; but no Apprehension of that sort, will, I trust, make the least Alteration in my Political Conduct. My rule in which I have always found Satisfaction, is, Never to turn asside in Publick Affairs thro' Views of private Interest; but to go strait forward in doing what appears to me right at the time, leaving the Consequences with Providence. What in my younger Days enabled me more easily to walk upright, was, that I had a Trade; and that I could live upon a little; and thence (never having had views of making a Fortune) I was free from Avarice, and contented with the plentiful Supplies my business afforded me. And now it is still more easy for me to preserve my Freedom and Integrity, when I consider, that I am almost at the End of my Journey, and therefore need less to complete the Expence of it; and that what I now possess thro' the Blessing of God may with tolerable Oeconomy, be sufficient for me (great Misfortunes excepted) tho' I should add nothing more to it by any Office or Employment whatsoever.

* * *

To Thomas Cushing, London, June 10, 1771†

[Since some Royal and Proprietary officials (in direct violation of their instructions from England) had passed popular measures in order to win high salaries from colonial assemblies, and since other officials were kept in comparative poverty by the colonial assemblies for not approving popular measures or for enforcing unpopular laws, the Crown reacted in the pre-Revolutionary era by paying Royal officials directly from England. The Boston patriots rightly judged this action a threat to local self-rule. Franklin as the Massachusetts Agent tried in vain to prevent the change, but in reporting his failure he philosophized about the nature of avarice.]

* * *

I do not at present see the least likelihood of preventing the Grant of Salaries or Pensions from hence to the King's Officers in America, by any Application in Behalf of the People there. It is look'd on as a strange thing here to object to the King's paying his own Servants sent among us to do his Business; and they say we should seem to have much more Reason of Complaint if it were requir'd of us to pay them. And the more we urge the Impropriety of their not depending on us for their Support, the more Suspicion it breeds that we are desirous of influencing them to betray the Interests of their Master or of this Nation. Indeed if the Money is rais'd from us against our Wills, the Injustice becomes more evident than where it arises from hence. I do not think, however, that the Effect of these Salaries is likely to be so considerable, either in favour of Government here, or in our Prejudice, as may be generally apprehended. The Love of Money is not a

† Source: *P*, 18: 124–25.

Thing of certain Measure, so as that it may be easily filled and satisfied. Avarice is infinite, and where there is not good Oeconomy, no Salary, however large, will prevent Necessity. He that has a fixed, and what others may think a competent Income, is often as much to be byassed by the Expectation of more, as if he had already none at all. If the Colonies should resolve on giving handsome Presents to good Governors at or after their Departure, or to their Children after their Decease, I imagine it might produce even better Effects than our present annual Grants. But the Course probably will soon be, that the Chief Governor to whom the Salary is given, will have Leave to reside in England, a Lieutenant or Deputy will be left to do the Business and live on the Perquisites, which not being thought quite sufficient, his receiving Presents yearly will be wink'd at thro' the Interest of his Principal, and thus things will get into the old Train, only this Inconvenience remaining, that while by our Folly in consuming the Duty-Articles, the fixed Salary is raised on ourselves without our Consent, we must pay double for the same Service. However, tho' it may be a hopeless Task while the Duties continue sufficient to pay the Salaries, I shall on all proper Occasions make Representations against this new Mode; and if by the Duties falling short, the Treasury here should be call'd on to pay those Salaries, it is possible they may come to be seen in another Light than at present, and dropt as unnecessary.

* * *

To David Hartley, Passy, France, February 2, 1780†

[Franklin repeatedly risked his personal fortune (and his life) in support of what he deemed justice to America. When the Boston Port Bill was before Parliament in 1774, Franklin himself engaged to pay the 15,000 pounds for the tea destroyed by the Boston Tea Party in order to prevent the passage of the inflammatory Boston Port Bill. He thus risked his whole fortune—and was rejected.]

* * * I am as much for peace as ever I was, and as heartily desirous of seeing the War ended, as I was to prevent its Beginning; of which your Ministers know I gave a strong Proof before I left England, when, in order to an accommodation, I offer'd at my own Risque, without Orders for so doing, and without knowing whether I should be own'd in doing it, to pay the whole Damage of destroying the Tea at Boston, provided the Acts made against that Province were repealed. This offer was refused. I still think it would have been wise to have accepted it.

* * *

† Source: Smyth, 8: 5.

Benjamin Vaughan to Lord Shelburne, Dover, November 24, 1782†

[Benjamin Vaughan, Lord Shelburne's private secretary, acted as Shelburne's personal emissary in the Paris peace negotiations—no doubt because he was Franklin's friend and disciple. His letters to Shelburne record in detail his talks with the American peace commissioners, even when the discussions did not bear directly upon the peace negotiations. He thus reported Franklin's conversation concerning political equality among rich and poor (an advanced doctrine in the eighteenth century), as well as Franklin's shrewd appraisal of the underlying economic reasons for past historical actions and his surprisingly modern view of the causes of poverty and oppression.]

My lord,

I think it necessary to inform your lordship in a few words, that Dr. Franklin's opinions about *parliaments* are, that people should not be rejected as electors because they are *at present* ignorant; or because their ignorance *arises* from their being excluded. He thinks that a statesman should meliorate his people; and I suppose would put this, among other reasons for extending the privilege of Election, that it *would* meliorate them. When the act to lessen the number of voters, passed in Edward the 3d's time, it was followed by an act to reduce wages; & he thinks that probably one act was made with a view to the other. On the other hand when knowledge began to spread in England, it helped everything; for instance, the post office revenue increased beyond all conception, while the same revenue in Ireland continues still as contemptible, as to be worth only a few thousand pounds. He says, that with themselves in America, they find no inconvenience in every man's voting that is free; & that the qualifications of a representative are matters sufficiently well distinguished by them. He says that savages would do the same, taking their best men as they can find them, & others forming themselves in business under them.

Perhaps your lordship will think all this too theoretical. When I return, I hope to have the honor of communicating his *own* expressions. As an American, the Dr. would *choose* to give no opinion of a different cast; but I believe, by some more positions he added to it, that this is his own genuine opinion. He thinks that the lower people are as we see them, because oppressed; & then their situation in point of manners, becomes the reason for oppressing them. But he is full of the measure of raising the sentiments & habits of all, as a thing that is wanting to contribute to the real *sensible* happiness of *both* orders— the rich & the poor.

* * *

† Source: Benjamin Vaughan Papers, American Philosophical Society.

To Robert Morris, Passy, France, December 25, 1783†

[Franklin's basic attitude toward wealth was radical. In eighteenth-century fashion, he related wealth to the origin of society and the basic rights of man. He reasoned that all wealth in addition to that necessary for the basic requirements of subsistence, clothing, and shelter was created by arbitrary conventions of society—and thus that such wealth was at the disposal of society.]

All Property, indeed, except the Savage's temporary Cabin, his Bow, his Matchcoat, and other little Acquisitions, absolutely necessary for his Subsistence, seems to me to be the Creature of public Convention. Hence the Public has the Right of Regulating Descents, and all other Conveyances of Property, and even of limiting the Quantity and the Users of it. All the Property that is necessary to a Man, for the Conservation of the Individual and the Propagation of the Species, is his natural Right, which none can justly deprive him of: But all Property superfluous to such purposes is the Property of the Publick, who, by their Laws, have created it, and who may therefore by other Laws dispose of it, whenever the Welfare of the Publick shall demand such Disposition. He that does not like civil Society on these Terms, let him retire and live among Savages. He can have no right to the benefits of Society, who will not pay his Club towards the Support of it.

* * *

To Benjamin Webb, Passy, France, April 22, 1784††

[Nowhere is Franklin's personal generosity better seen than in this letter to his acquaintance Benjamin Webb.]

Dear Sir,

I received yours of the 15th Instant, and the Memorial it inclosed. The account they give of your situation grieves me. I send you herewith a Bill for Ten Louis d'ors. I do not pretend to *give* such a Sum; I only *lend* it to you. When you shall return to your Country with a good Character, you cannot fail of getting into some Business, that will in time enable you to pay all your Debts. In that Case, when you meet with another honest Man in similar Distress, you must pay me by lending this Sum to him; enjoining him to discharge the Debt by a like operation, when he shall be able, and shall meet with such another opportunity. I hope it may thus go thro' many hands, before it meets with a Knave that will stop its Progress. This is a trick of mine for doing a deal of good with a little money. I am not rich enough to afford *much* in good works, and so am obliged to be cunning and make the most of a *little*. With best wishes for the success of your Memorial, and your future prosperity, I am, dear Sir, your most obedient servant,

B. Franklin

To Benjamin Vaughan, Passy, France, July 26, 1784†

[Luxury was a standard intellectual topic throughout the eighteenth century. Writers from the time of Joseph Addison's "A Letter from Italy" (1701) to Edward Gibbon's *Decline and Fall of the Roman Empire* (1776–88) generally attacked it, but at least one masterpiece of literary as well as intellectual history appeared in its defense—Bernard Mandeville's *Fable of the Bees* (1714–29). In America, the great Quaker stylist and humanitarian John Woolman (1720–72), in his *Journal* (1774) and in his classic essays, attacked "superfluities" just as Thoreau was later to do in *Walden* (1854) and as the economist Thorstein Veblen was to do in his *Theory of the Leisure Class* (1899). Franklin's own complex attitudes toward luxury are set forth in his letter to Benjamin Vaughan, from which we quote only the conclusion.]

* * *

One reflection more, and I will end this long, rambling Letter. Almost all the Parts of our Bodies require some Expence. The Feet demand Shoes; the Legs, Stockings; the rest of the Body, Clothing; and the Belly, a good deal of Victuals. Our Eyes, tho' exceedingly useful, ask, when reasonable, only the cheap Assistance of Spectacles, which could not much impair our Finances. But *the Eyes of other People* are the Eyes that ruin us. If all but myself were blind, I should want neither fine Clothes, fine Houses, nor fine Furniture.

[Private Property Is a Creature of Society, November, 1789]††

[Franklin's last thoughts on the nature of wealth replied to a newspaper proposal in November, 1789 on Pennsylvania's new state constitution. The anonymous author urged a bicameral legislature: "The Upper should represent the Property; the Lower the Population of the State. The upper should be chosen by Freemen possessing in Lands and Houses one thousand Pounds; the Lower by all such as had resided four Years in the Country, and paid Taxes. The first should be chosen for four, the last for two years. They should in Authority be co-equal." In rebuttal, Franklin returned to the idea that wealth is created by the laws and customs of a society. Franklin probably intended to publish his reply and so he concluded with a supposed Biblical passage, which (although it echoes *Jeremiah*) is apparently his own creation.]

* * *

Several Questions may arise upon this Proposition. 1st. What is the Proportion of Freemen possessing Lands and Houses of one thousand

---

† Source: Smyth, 9: 248.   †† Source: Smyth, 10: 58–60.

Pounds' value, compared to that of Freemen whose Possessions are inferior? Are they as one to ten? Are they even as one to twenty? I should doubt whether they are as one to fifty. If this minority is to chuse a Body expressly to controul that which is to be chosen by the great Majority of the Freemen, what have this great Majority done to forfeit so great a Portion of their Right in Elections? Why is this Power of Controul, contrary to the spirit of all Democracies, to be vested in a Minority, instead of a Majority? Then is it intended, or is it not, that the Rich should have a Vote in the Choice of Members for the lower House, while those of inferior Property are deprived of the Right of voting for Members of the upper House? And why should the upper House, chosen by a Minority, have equal Power with the lower chosen by a Majority? Is it supposed that Wisdom is the necessary concomitant of Riches, and that one Man worth a thousand Pounds must have as much Wisdom as Twenty who have each only 999; and why is Property to be represented at all? Suppose one of our Indian Nations should now agree to form a civil Society; each Individual would bring into the Stock of the Society little more Property than his Gun and his Blanket, for at present he has no other. We know, that, when one of them has attempted to keep a few Swine, he has not been able to maintain a Property in them, his neighbours thinking they have a Right to kill and eat them whenever they want Provision, it being one of their Maxims that hunting is free for all; the accumulation therefore of Property in such a Society, and its Security to Individuals in every Society, must be an Effect of the Protection afforded to it by the joint Strength of the Society, in the Execution of its Laws. Private Property therefore is a Creature of Society, and is subject to the Calls of that Society, whenever its Necessities shall require it, even to its last Farthing; its Contributions therefore to the public Exigencies are not to be considered as conferring a Benefit on the Publick, entitling the Contributors to the Distinctions of Honour and Power, but as the Return of an Obligation previously received, or the Payment of a just Debt. The Combinations of Civil Society are not like those of a Set of Merchants, who club their Property in different Proportions for Building and Freighting a Ship, and may therefore have some Right to vote in the Disposition of the Voyage in a greater or less Degree according to their respective Contributions; but the important ends of Civil Society, and the personal Securities of Life and Liberty, these remain the same in every Member of the society; and the poorest continues to have an equal Claim to them with the most opulent, whatever Difference Time, Chance, or Industry may occasion in their Circumstances. On these Considerations, I am sorry to see the Signs this Paper I have been considering affords, of a Disposition among some of our People to commence an Aristocracy, by giving the Rich a predominancy in Government, a Choice peculiar to themselves in one half the Legislature to be proudly called the UPPER House, and the other Branch, chosen by the Majority of the People, degraded by the Denomination of the LOWER; and giving to this upper House a Permanency of four Years, and but two to the lower. I hope, therefore, that our Representatives in the Convention will not hastily go into these Innovations, but take the Advice of the Prophet, "*Stand in the old ways, view the ancient Paths, consider them well, and be not among those that are given to Change.*"

THE ART OF VIRTUE

Franklin's "project for achieving moral perfection" is the most appealing and successful presentation of his "Art of Virtue." He wrote numerous brief aphorisms on virtue in the Poor Richard almanacs, 1733–1758; and, in order to help his nephew Benjamin Mecom, he wrote a sententious version of the "Art of Virtue" ("A Letter from Father Abraham to his beloved Son"—*P*, 8: 123–31) for the initial issue of Mecom's *New England Magazine* (August, 1758). Plans for self-improvement are commonplaces of ethical writing, and Franklin must have read numerous ones, including those by Aristotle, Plutarch, Bacon, Descartes, Hobbes, Locke, Addison, Shaftesbury, Hutcheson, Wollaston, and Isaac Watts. Louis I. Bredvold, "The Invention of the Ethical Calculus" (in Richard Foster Jones, et al., *The Seventeenth Century* [Stanford: Stanford University Press, 1951], pp. 165–80) surveys some of Franklin's progenitors—and such plans for self-improvement continued to be written after Franklin's time, as the schemes by the French philosophes prove. Franklin's plan is closest to a piece which appeared in the popular periodical press of his day entitled "A Scheme for Regulating Human Conduct: Or, Directions for attaining to the Knowledge of Ourselves, and the World," *The Museum: Or, The Literary and Historical Register*, Aug. 16, 1746 (rpt. in *The London Chronicle*, March 20, 1758; and in the *Boston Weekly Advertiser*, June 12, 1758). But what makes Franklin's scheme memorable (while all the others are, comparatively, unknown) is the interplay between the persona, the subject, and the audience.

[Poor Richard on Self-Improvement, 1749]†

[Franklin adopted the following observation from Joseph Addison, *Spectator* no. 447, August 2, 1712, who, in turn, was reflecting Pythagoras.]

It was wise counsel given to a young man, *Pitch upon that course of life which is most excellent, and Custom will make it the most delightful.* But many pitch on no course of life at all, nor form any scheme of living, by which to attain any valuable end; but wander perpetually from one thing to another.

† Source: *P*, 3: 341.

To Lord Kames, May 3, 1760†

[Franklin's best description of his projected Art of Virtue is contained in a letter to Lord Kames.]

* * * I purpose, likewise, a little Work for the Benefit of Youth, to be call'd *The Art of Virtue*. From the Title I think you will hardly conjecture what the Nature of such a Book may be. I must therefore explain it a little. Many People lead bad Lives that would gladly lead good ones, but know not *how* to make the Change. They have frequently *resolv'd* and *endeavour'd* it; but in vain, because their Endeavours have not been properly conducted. To exhort People to be good, to be just, to be temperate, &c. without *shewing* them *how* they shall *become* so, seems like the ineffectual Charity mention'd by the Apostle, which consisted in saying to the Hungry, the Cold, and the Naked, *be ye fed, be ye warmed, be ye clothed*, without shewing them how they should get Food, Fire or Clothing. Most People have naturally *some* Virtues, but none have naturally *all* the Virtues. To *acquire* those that are wanting, and *secure* what we acquire as well as those we have naturally, is the Subject of *an Art*. It is as properly an Art, as Painting, Navigation, or Architecture. If a Man would become a Painter, Navigator, or Architect, it is not enough that he is *advised* to be one, that he is *convinc'd* by the Arguments of his Adviser that it would be for his Advantage to be one, and that he *resolves* to be one, but he must also be taught the Principles of the Art, be shewn all the Methods of Working, and how to acquire the *Habits* of using properly all the Instruments; and thus regularly and gradually he arrives by Practice at some Perfection in the Art. If he does not proceed thus, he is apt to meet with Difficulties that discourage him, and make him drop the Pursuit. My *Art of Virtue* has also its Instruments, and teaches the Manner of Using them. Christians are directed to have *Faith in Christ*, as the effectual Means of obtaining the Change they desire. It may, when sufficiently strong, be effectual with many. A full Opinion that a Teacher is infinitely wise, good, and powerful, and that he will certainly reward and punish the Obedient and Dis-obedient, must give great Weight to his Precepts, and make them much more attended to by his Disciples. But all Men cannot have Faith in Christ; and many have it in so weak a Degree, that it does not produce the Effect. Our *Art of Virtue* may therefore be of great Service to those who have not Faith, and come in Aid of the weak Faith of others. Such as are naturally well-disposed, and have been carefully educated, so that good Habits have been early established, and bad ones prevented, have less Need of this Art; but all may be more or less benefited by it. It is, in short, to be adapted for universal Use. I

† Source: *P*, 9: 104–5.

imagine what I have now been writing will seem to savour of great Presumption; I must therefore speedily finish my little Piece, and communicate the Manuscript to you, that you may judge whether it is possible to make good such Pretensions. I shall at the same time hope for the Benefit of your Corrections.

* * *

To Joseph Priestley, September 19, 1772†

[Franklin's *"Moral or Prudential Algebra"* attempts to devise a way of measuring values in order to have a rational basis for making decisions. It thus has affinities with the method and outlook of the "project for attaining moral Perfection." When Franklin recommended the system to his grand-nephew Jonathan Williams on April 8, 1779, he amusingly concluded: "By the way, if you do not learn it [*Moral Algebra*], I apprehend you will never be married" (Smyth, 7: 282).]

London Sept. 19. 1772

Dear Sir,

In the Affair of so much Importance to you, wherein you ask my Advice, I cannot for want of sufficient Premises, advise you *what* to determine, but if you please I will tell you *how*. When these difficult Cases occur, they are difficult chiefly because while we have them under Consideration all the Reasons *pro* and *con* are not present to the Mind at the same time; but sometimes one Set present themselves, and at other times another, the first being out of Sight. Hence the various Purposes or Inclinations that alternately prevail, and the Uncertainty that perplexes us. To get over this, my Way is, to divide half a Sheet of Paper by a Line into two Columns, writing over the one *Pro*, and over the other *Con*. Then during three or four Days Consideration I put down under the different Heads short Hints of the different Motives that at different Times occur to me for or against the Measure. When I have thus got them all together in one View, I endeavour to estimate their respective Weights; and where I find two, one on each side, that seem equal, I strike them both out: If I find a Reason *Pro* equal to some two Reasons *con*, I strike out the three. If I judge some two Reasons *con* equal to some three Reasons *pro*, I strike out the five; and thus proceeding I find at length where the Ballance lies; and if after a Day or two of farther Consideration nothing new that is of Importance occurs on either side, I come to a Determination accordingly. And tho' the Weight of Reasons cannot be taken with the Precision of Algebraic Quantities, yet when each is thus considered separately and comparatively, and the whole lies before me, I think I

† Source: Franklin to Joseph Priestley; *P*, 19: 299–300.

can judge better, and am less likely to make a rash Step; and in fact I have found great Advantage from this kind of Equation, in what may be called *Moral* or *Prudential Algebra*. Wishing sincerely that you may determine for the best, I am ever, my dear Friend, Yours most affectionately

B Franklin

PERFECTION

Franklin's "project of arriving at moral Perfection" has been misunderstood for several reasons, including the meaning of *perfection*. In the twentieth century, we think of *perfection* as a completed, finished state, rather than one in process. But in the eighteenth century, *perfect* did not necessarily imply an achieved condition, but could mean simply an approach to that condition. The words *perfecter* and *perfectest*, then in common use, give some idea of the comparative possibilities of the words *perfect* and *perfection*. Franklin frequently used them in this comparative manner. The following quotations illustrate both Franklin's use of the words *perfect* and *perfection*, and his reasons for believing one might arrive to some degree of human perfection. (In these quotations, the original italics have been ignored and italics have been supplied by the editors.)

Franklin's Epitaph, 1728†

The Body of
B. Franklin,
Printer;
Like the Cover of an old Book,
Its Contents torn out,
And stript of its Lettering and Gilding,
Lies here, Food for Worms.
But the Work shall not be wholly lost:
For it will, as he believ'd, appear once more,
In a new & *more perfect* Edition,
Corrected and amended
By the Author.
He was born Jan. 6. 1706
Died   17

[Franklin's Junto Query on Human Perfection, 1732]††

Qu. Can a Man arrive at *Perfection* in this Life as some Believe; or is it impossible as others believe?

A. Perhaps they differ in the meaning of the Word *Perfection*.

---

† Source: *P*, 1: 111.   †† Source: *P*, 1: 261–62.

I suppose the *Perfection* of any Thing to be only the greatest the Nature of that Thing is capable of;

Different Things have different *Degrees of Perfection*; and the same thing at different Times.

Thus an Horse is *more perfect* than an Oyster yet the Oyster may be a *perfect* Oyster as well as the Horse a *perfect* Horse.

And an Egg is not so *perfect* as a Chicken, nor a Chicken as a Hen; for the Hen has more Strength than the Chicken, and the C[hicken] more Life than the Egg: Yet it may be a *perfect* Egg, Chicken and Hen.

If they mean, a Man cannot in this Life be so *perfect* as an Angel, it is [written above: "may be"] true; for an Angel by being incorporeal is allow'd *some Perfections* we are at present incapable of, and less liable to *some Imperfections* that we are liable to.

If they mean a Man is not capable of being so *perfect* here as he is capable of being in Heaven, that may be true likewise. But that a Man is not capable of being so *perfect* here, as he is capable of being here; is not Sense; it is as if I should say, a Chicken in the State of a Chicken is not capable of being so *perfect* as a Chicken is capable of being in that State. In the above Sense if there may be a *perfect* Oyster, a *perfect* Horse, a *perfect* Ship, why not a *perfect* Man? that is as *perfect* as his present Nature and Circumstances admit?

[An Early Version of the Art of Virtue, 1758]†

* * * It is . . . necessary for every Person who desires to be a wise Man, to take particular Notice of his own Actions, and of his own Thoughts and Intentions which are the Original of his actions; with great Care and Circumspection; otherwise he can never arrive to that *Degree of Perfection* which constitutes the amiable Character he aspires after.* * *

[On Perfection in Human Institutions, 1770]††

[Franklin annotated a number of books and pamphlets in his library. Some of these private notes (where he was not adopting a *persona* and not attempting to appeal to a particular audience) reveal his opinions more starkly than his public writings. An Englishman, Matthew Wheelock, writing on the relations between England and the colonies used *perfection* in the usual twentieth-century meaning when he wrote "To expect perfection in human institutions is absurd." In an annotation, Franklin attacked Wheelock's position.]

Does this justify any and every Imperfection that can be invented and added to our Constitution? Why did you yourselves not leave our Constitutions as you found them? Why did you aim at making them

† Source: P, 8: 128.   †† Source: P, 17: 395–96.

according to your Ideas, *more perfect*, by taking away our Rights in order to subject us to Parliamentary Taxation?

[On Religious Tests for Citizenship, 1780]†

*   *   *

I am fully of your Opinion respecting religious Tests; but, tho' the People of Massachusetts have not in their new Constitution kept quite clear of them, yet, if we consider what that People were 100 Years ago, we must allow they have gone great Lengths in Liberality of Sentiment on religious Subjects; and we may hope for *greater Degrees of Perfection*, when their Constitution, some years hence, shall be revised.
* * *

† Source: Franklin to the Rev. Richard Price, Oct. 9, 1780; Smyth, 8: 153–54.

Criticism

Contemporary Opinions

Eighteenth-century opinions about Franklin were shaped mainly by political views. From the 1730s to the 1760s he led the popular party against the proprietary party; in England and America during the pre-Revolutionary period, he personified American resistance to English imperialism; in America and France during the Revolution, he was the most famous American rebel; and in America after the Revolution, he was an outspoken Federalist. Aside from politics, some people disliked Franklin because of his avowed deistic opinions and religious satires. And some persons (including John Adams and Ralph Izard) were jealous simply because he was so famous and so widely respected. In the latter part of his life, he was probably the best-known and most widely-respected scientist in the world. He was undoubtedly America's most famous writer. He had one of the most numerous and varied correspondences of any person in the eighteenth century and attracted such literary and philosophical disciples as Benjamin Vaughan and Jacques Barbeu-Dubourg.

DAVID HUME

David Hume (1711–1776), the great English philosopher, evidently met Franklin (probably through their mutual friend William Strahan) in London in 1758–59. Although Hume was ambivalent toward the colonies, he found Franklin congenial but (as Franklin certainly perceived) too much an American. Hume was familiar with several of Franklin's political and scientific papers, as well as some of his personal letters, when he paid him the following great compliment.

David Hume to Franklin, Edinburgh, May 10, 1762†

* * *

I am very sorry, that you intend soon to leave our Hemisphere. America has sent us many good things, Gold, Silver, Sugar, Tobacco, Indigo &c.: But you are the first Philosopher, and indeed the first Great Man of Letters for whom we are beholden to her: it is our own Fault, that we have not kept him: Whence it appears, that we do not

† Source: P, 10: 81–82.

agree with Solomon,[1] that Wisdom is above Gold: For we take care never to send back an ounce of the latter, which we once lay our Fingers upon. * * *

MATHER BYLES

Mather Byles (1701–1788), grandson of Increase Mather, nephew of Cotton Mather, Boston divine, and later a Loyalist, was perhaps Boston's most famous man of letters in the mid-eighteenth century. Byles splendidly testifies to the early reputation of Franklin's personal letters.

Mather Byles to Franklin, Boston, late 1765[†]

* * *

I have just been reading a beautiful Letter of yours, written Feb. 22. 1756, on the Death of your Brother, which is handed about among us in Manuscript Copies. I am charmed with the Easy and Gay Light in which you view our leaving this little Earth, as Birth among the Immortals: and as setting out on a Party of Pleasure a little before our Friends are ready. The Superstition with which we size and preserve little accidental Touches of your Pen, puts one in mind of the Care of the Virtuosi[1] to collect the Jugs and Galipots with the Paintings of Raphael.[2]

FRANKLIN IN THE COCKPIT

The *Pennsylvania Gazette* Report, 1774[††]

[In the early winter of 1772, a series of letters by Thomas Hutchinson (1711–1780), Royal Governor of Massachusetts, and by Andrew Oliver and others to Thomas Whately in London were presented to Franklin. Franklin wrote that the letters were given him in order to prove that the most odious anti-American measures taken by the Ministry in England "Took their Rise, not from Government here [England], but were projected, proposed to administration, solicited, and obtained by some of the most respectable people among the Americans themselves, as necessary Measures for the welfare of that Country" (Smyth, 6: 262–63). Franklin as Agent of the Massachusetts House of Representatives sent the letters to Thomas Cushing (1725–1788), Speaker of the House, in the idealistic belief that the resentments of the

---

1. Solomon, King of Israel, celebrated for his wisdom in the Bible.
† Source: *P*, 12: 424 (corrected from the original).
1. Virtuosi, precursors of museum curators, sometimes collected memorabilia.

2. Raphael (1483–1520), Italian Renaissance painter.
†† Source: *Pennsylvania Gazette*, April 20, 1774, evidently reprinted from a London newspaper dated January 31.

Massachusetts radicals against England would be lessened when they learned that the worst anti-American measures were "projected, advised, and called for by Men of Character among ourselves" (Smyth 6: 266).

Franklin hoped that the Hutchinson-Oliver letters would lessen the tension between America and England, but they did not. The Boston radicals merely found more scapegoats in Hutchinson, Oliver, and the other writers of the letters to Whately, while the English generally thought it objectionable that the letters had been surreptitiously obtained, sent to Boston, and published there. The identity of the person who obtained the letters has never been positively ascertained (Franklin could keep a secret), but Franklin, finding that two Englishmen were dueling about who sent the letters to America, announced in a London paper of December 25, 1773, "I alone am the person who obtained and transmitted to Boston the letters in question" (P, 20: 515).

As a result of the letters, the Massachusetts House of Assembly petitioned for the removal of Governor Hutchinson and Lieutenant Governor Oliver from office. Cushing sent the petition to Franklin on June 25, 1773 (P, 20: 243). Franklin forwarded the petition to Lord Dartmouth on August 21, 1773, telling him that since the Bostonians had "lately discovered as they think, the authors of their grievances to be some of their own people, their resentment against Britain is thence much abated" (P, 20: 373). The petition was presented to the Privy Council. On Saturday, January 8, 1774, Franklin was suddenly informed that the Privy Council would hear the petition on Tuesday, three days later, in the Cockpit (so-called because the location had formerly actually been used for fighting cocks). The following Monday afternoon, he received a notice saying that Israel Mauduit, Agent for the Governor and Lieutenant-Governor, "had obtained leave to be heard by Council" before the Privy Council. The next day, Tuesday, it developed that the Attorney General, Alexander Wedderburn, acting as counsel for Hutchinson and Oliver, wanted to know how the letters were obtained. To Franklin, the question seemed irrelevant, but it confirmed the rumors he had heard that the Ministry intended to seize this occasion to abuse him. He was also uncertain whether he would have to reply to such questions and so he decided to be represented by attorneys.

Three weeks later, on January 29, 1774, the Privy Council reconvened to hear the Massachusetts petition for the removal of Hutchinson and Oliver. Since news had just arrived in London of the Boston Tea Party, English public opinion was outraged. Franklin, as the Agent for the Massachusetts House, was identified with the Boston Tea Party, so that feeling against America and against Franklin was at a high point when he appeared before the Privy Council on January 29.

He was viciously attacked and—in the opinion of most of his English and Scottish friends—publicly disgraced. Alexander Wedderburn's speech was generally regarded as a masterpiece of oratory and invective. The Ministry was pleased with Wedderburn, an obsequious placeman, for the English establishment meant to punish Franklin, not only because he was the most famous American patriot in the world, but also because his recent clever hoaxes ("An Edict by the King of Prussia," "Rules by Which a Great Empire May be Reduced to a Small One") had succeeded in embarassing the Ministry.

Here follows the first notice of the Cockpit scene in Franklin's former newspaper, the *Pennsylvania Gazette*.]

On Saturday last the Privy Council met to hear the arguments for and against the petition of the Assembly of Boston (which was some time since presented by their Agent Dr. Franklin) "praying that his Majesty would be pleased to remove the Governor, &c." Serjeant Glynn, and Mr. Dunning, were counsel for the petition, and urged very strongly the expediency and necessity of granting the prayer[1] of it. Mr. Solicitor General was employed on the other side, and instead of answering the learned arguments of his brethren, or refuting the allegations of the petition, contented himself with pronouncing a most severe *Phillipic* on the celebrated American Philosopher, in which he loaded him with all the licensed scurrility of the bar, and decked his harrangue with the choicest flowers of Billingsgate.[2] The Doctor seemed to receive the thunder of his eloquence with philosophic tranquility, and sovereign contempt, whilst the approving smiles of those at the board clearly shewed, that the coarsest language can be grateful to the politest ears.

The King of Prussia, in one of his epistles, calls Dr. Franklin "ce nouveau *Promethee.*" Our correspondent says, that he could not help wishing (while the Solicitor General was pouring forth his tide of scurrility) that the American *Prometheus* could have called fire from Heaven to blast the unmannered railer.

Benjamin Vaughan's Account, 1779†

[Israel Mauduit, the agent for Hutchinson and Oliver, published Alexander Wedderburn's speech attacking Franklin but he suppressed "the grosser parts of the abuse" because (according to Franklin) they were "in their own eyes too foul to be seen on paper" (Smyth 6: 189–90). When Benjamin Vaughan published Franklin's *Political, Miscellaneous and Philosophical Pieces*, he mentioned that Mauduit "prudently omitted" Wedderburne's "most odious personal applications," but that he was now publishing them "as well as they could be collected" in order "to mark the politics of the times, and the nature of the censures passed in England upon Dr. Franklin's character."]

'The letters could not have come to Dr. Franklin,' said Mr. Wedderburn, 'by fair means. The writers did not give them to him; nor yet did the deceased correspondent, who from our intimacy would otherwise have told me of it: Nothing then will acquit Dr. Franklin of the charge of obtaining them by fraudulent or corrupt means, for the most malignant of purposes; unless he stole them, from the person who stole them. This argument is irrefragable.'——

'I hope, my lords, you will mark [and brand] the man, for the honour of this country, of Europe, and of mankind. Private correspondence has hitherto been held sacred, in times of the greatest party

1. the request of a complainant in a court of law.

2. foul and abusive language.

† Source: [Benjamin Vaughan, ed.] *Political, Miscellaneous and Philosophical Pieces* (London, 1779), pp. 340–41.

rage, not only in politics but religion.'——'He has forfeited all the respect of societies and of men. Into what companies will he hereafter go with an unembarrassed face, or the honest intrepidity of virtue. Men will watch him with a jealous eye; they will hide their papers from him, and lock up their escritoires. He will henceforth esteem it a libel to be called *a man of letters*; *homo* trium[1] *literarum!*

'But he not only took away the letters from one brother; but kept himself concealed till he nearly occasioned the murder of the other. It is impossible to read his account, expressive of the coolest and most deliberate malice, without horror.' [*Here he read the letter above; Dr. Franklin being all the time present.*]——'Amidst these tragical events, of one person nearly murdered, of another answerable for the issue, of a worthy governor hurt in his dearest interests, the fate of America in suspense; here is a man, who with the utmost insensibility of remorse, stands up and avows himself the author of all. I can compare it only to Zanga in Dr. Young's *Revenge*.[2]

> "Know then 'twas—I:
> "I forged the letter, I disposed the picture;
> "I hated, I despised, and I destroy."

I ask, my Lords, whether the revengeful temper attributed, by poetic fiction only, to the bloody African; is not surpassed by the coolness and apathy of the wily American?'

HOUSE OF LORDS, FEBRUARY 1, 1775

When Lord Chatham (1708–1778) presented his plan for settling the American disputes in the House of Lords on February 1, 1775, it was soundly defeated. The opposition began when Lord Sandwich (1718–1792), 1st lord of admiralty and an outspoken anti-American, seized the occasion to insult both Chatham and Franklin.

William Pitt, Lord Chatham, vs. John Montague, Lord Sandwich, on Franklin†

* * *

But Lord Sandwich rose, and in a petulant vehement Speech, oppos'd its being receiv'd at all, and gave his Opinion that it ought to be immediately REJECTED with the Contempt it deserv'd. That he could never believe it the Production of any British Peer. That it appear'd to him rather the Work of some American; and turning his Face towards me, who was leaning on the Bar, said, he fancied he had

---

1. i.e., FUR (or *thief*) [Vaughan's note].
2. Act Vth [Vaughan's note]. Edward Young's popular tragedy *The Revenge* (1721) was mod-

eled upon Shakespeare's *Othello*.
† Source: *P*, 21: 581, 582.

in his Eye the Person who drew it up, one of the bitterest and most mischievous Enemies this Country had ever known. This drew the Eyes of many Lords upon me: but as I had no Inducement to take it to myself, I kept my Countenance as immoveable as if my Features had been made of Wood.* * *

Lord Chatham, in his Reply to Lord Sandwich, took notice of his illiberal Insinuation that the Plan was not the Person's who propos'd it: declar'd that it was intirely his own, a Declaration he thought himself the more oblig'd to make, as many of their Lordships appear'd to have so mean an Opinion of it; for if it was so weak or so bad a Thing, it was proper in him to take care that no other Person should unjustly share in the Censure it deserved. That it had been heretofore reckon'd his Vice not to be apt to take Advice. But he made no Scruple to declare, that if he were the first Minister of this Country, and had the Care of Settling this momentous Business, he should not be asham'd of publickly calling to his Assistance a Person so perfectly acquainted with the whole of American Affairs as the Gentleman alluded to and injuriously reflected on, one, he was pleas'd to say, whom all Europe held in high Estimation for his Knowledge and Wisdom, and rank'd with our Boyles[1] and Newton;[2] who was an Honour not to the English Nation and but to Human Nature. I found it harder to stand this extravagant Compliment than the preceding equally extravagant Abuse, but kept as well as I could an unconcern'd Countenance, as not conceiving it to relate to me.

* * *

EDMUND BURKE

Edmund Burke (1729–1792), Whig leader in Parliament, found it extraordinary that the elderly Franklin (age 69, not "upwards of seventy," in 1775) set off on a dangerous ocean voyage to America in order to join a country on the verge of civil war.

Edmund Burke to Count Patrick D'Arcy, October 5, 1775†

* * *

What say you to your friend and brother Philosopher Franklin, who at upwards of seventy years of age, quits the Study of the Laws of

---

1. Robert Boyle (1627–91), British scientist and naturalist.
2. Isaac Newton (1642–1727), English mathematician and scientist; see this edition, p. 191.

† Source: Thomas W. Copeland, ed., *The Correspondence of Edmund Burke* 9v. (Cambridge: Cambridge Univ. Press, 1958–1970), 3: 228.

Nature, in order to give Laws to new Commonwealths; and has crossed the Atlantick ocean at that time of Life, not to seek repose, but to plunge into the midst of the most laborious and most arduous affairs that ever were. Few things more extraordinary have happened in the history of mankind. These rebels of ours are a singular sort of people—[1]

* * *

PETER OLIVER

Peter Oliver (1713–1791), Loyalist and Chief Justice of the Massachusetts Superior Court, had special reason to hate Franklin, for the Hutchinson letters which Franklin sent to the Boston patriot leaders included letters by Peter's brother Andrew Oliver (1706–1774), Lieutenant Governor of Massachusetts. The publication of the Hutchinson letters caused public demonstrations against Hutchinson and both Olivers. Peter Oliver's facts about Franklin are often wrong (e.g., he confuses the young Franklin with his brother James Franklin), but his animosity is obviously sincere.

Excerpt from *Origins & Progress of the American Rebellion*[†]

* * *

There was one Person more who might, *now*, be termed, the *instar omnium*[1] of Rebellion. The Features of whose Soul were so minutely expressed in the Lines of his Countenance, that a Gentleman, whose Acumen was so great as to strike out a Character from a very slight View of a Face, was introduced to his Company many Years since; and upon his being asked his Opinion of the Man, he replied, "that he was calculated to set a whole Kingdom in a Flame." This was his Opinion of Dr. *Benjamin Franklin.*

This Narrative hath been frequently interrupted by the Description of Characters; but it seemed necessary to describe, when the Persons introduced theirselves upon the Stage. Let this suffice for Apology. It is now Dr. *Franklyn's Turn* to sit for his Portrait; & I shall endeavor to sketch the Outlines: perhaps I may catch a Feature or two as I go on with the Narrative.

---

1. When Burke wrote Franklin on August 15, 1781, he addressed him as "Doctor Franklin the Philosopher; my friend, and the lover of his Species." And on February 28, 1782, informing Franklin of the vote in Parliament that ended the war in America, he said: *"I congratulate you, as the friend of America, I trust, as not the enemy of England, I am sure, as the friend of* mankind." Source: Copeland, 4: 364–65, 419. [Editors' Note.]

† Source: Douglass Adair & John A. Schultz, eds., *Peter Oliver's Origin & Progress of The American Rebellion* (San Marino, Ca.: Huntington Library, 1961), pp. 78–82.

1. Image of all, archetype.

Dr. *Benjamin Franklin* was a Native of *Boston* in the *Massachusetts Bay*. He was born in 1706, of very reputable Parents. His Father was a capital Tallow Chandler, & a worthy honest Man. His Brother also was a Man held in very good esteem. The Doctor himself was what is called a *Printers Devil* but, by a Climax in Reputation, he reversed the Phrase, & taught us to read it backward, as Witches do the Lords Prayer. He worked at the Business of the Press untill he went to *England*, & continued in *London* for about two Years, to perfect himself in the Art, & black as the Art was before, he made it much blacker, by forcing the Press often to speak the Thing that was not. He published a Libel in *Boston*, for which he was obliged to quit. He fled to *Rhode Island*,[2] the Asylum for those who had done what they ought not to have done—from thence he went to *Philadelphia*, & settled in the printing Business. The *Philadelphia* News Paper was published by him; & the Almanacks of *Poor Richard*, which he annually struck off, were interlaced with many usefull Observations in Agriculture & other Sciences.

Dr. *Franklin* (pardon the Expression) was cursed with a full Share of Understanding; he was a Man of Genius, but of so unprincipled an Heart, that the Merit of all his political & philosophical Disquisitions can never atone for the Mischiefs which he plunged Society into, by the Perversion of his Genius. He had such an Insight into human Nature, that he insinuated himself into various publick Departments in the Province of *Pennsilvania*, & at last arrived to the Office of one of the Post Masters in *America*, a Place worth 4 or £500. Sterling per Year. He was now released from the necessary Cares for a moderate Support; & was at Leisure to indulge in what might first strike his Fancy. He invented a Fire Stove, to warm Rooms in the northern Climates, & at the same Time to save Fuel; he succeeded: but, at the same Time, they were so destructive of Health that they fell into Disuse. He also invented a Chamber Urn contrived to make the Flame descend instead of rising from the Fire: upon which a young Clergyman of a poetical Turn, made the following Lines,[3] vizt.

> Like a *Newton*, sublimely he soar'd
> To a Summit before unattain'd,
> New Regions of Science explor'd,
> And the Palm of Philosophy gain'd.

———

> With a Spark that he caught from the Skies
> He display'd an unpararell'd Wonder,
> And we saw, with Delight & Surprize,
> That his Rod would defend us from Thunder.

———

2. Oliver confuses BF with his older brother James Franklin.
3. The poem by Jonathan Odell appeared originally in the *Gentleman's Magazine*, 47 (April, 1777), 188. See A. Owen Aldridge, "Charles Brockden Brown's Poem on Benjamin Franklin," *American Literature*, 38 (May, 1966), 230–35.

Oh! had he been Wise to pursue
The Track for his Talents design'd,
What a Tribute of Praise had been due
To the Teacher & Friend of Mankind?

But, to covet political Fame
Was in him a degrading Ambition,
A Spark that from *Lucifer* came,
And kindled the Blaze of Sedition.

Let Candor then write on his Urn,
Here lies the renowned Inventor,
Whose Flame to the Skies ought to burn,
But, inverted, descends to the Centre.

Agreeable to the Hint given in the above Lines, the Doctor had made
some new Experiments in Electricity, which drew the Attention of the
Literate, as well as of the great Vulgar & the Small. The Eclat, which
was spread from some new Phænomena he had discovered in this
Science, introduced him into some of the first Company in *England*,
whither he came, soon after he struck out these new Scenes. Men of
Science gave their Attention, and others, of no ignoble Degree, gaped
with a foolish Face of Praise; & it was this Circumstance, lucky for
him, but unlucky for *Great Britain* & her Colonies, which gave such a
Shock to Government, & brought on such Convulsions, as the english Constitution will not be cured of in one Century, if ever. By this
Introduction, he grew into Importance with the Leaders of the Opposition in *England*. They found him to be usefull to them, in their
Attempts, to subvert the Foundations of Government, & they caught
at every Circumstance that Chance threw in their Way. They knew
him to be as void of every Principle as theirselves, & each of them
play'd into the others Hands. The Doctor play'd his Card well, &
procured the Agency of some of the Colonies; & the lower House of
Massachusetts Assembly chose him for theirs. I have seen Letters from
him to the latter, inciting them to a Revolt, at the same Time when he
enjoyed the above lucrative Office from the Crown; but he was so
abandoned to an utter Insensibility of Virtue or Honor, that he would
not stick at any Villainy to gratifye his Pride.

When the Stamp Act was on the Tapis, he encouraged the passing
of it; & procured, for one of his Friends, the Appointment of a Stamp
Master. He procured the Government of *New Jersies* for his Son; who
hath behaved with a spirited Fidelity to his Sovereign to this Day. But
his unnatural Treatment of this Son will fix upon him an indelible
Reproach; for when the Son was about to imbark for his Government,
he was in Arrears £100 Sterling, & could not leave *England* without
discharging them. The Father refused to assist him, & a private

Gentleman, out of Compassion, lent him the Mony—[4] and this Son afterwards was harrassed for his Loyalty & kept in a Gaol as a Prisoner in *Connecticut*, where he suffered greatly his self & where he lost his Lady, through Hardships. All this he underwent, whilst his humane Father had the Control of the Congress, & never attempted his Release. This fixes a Character which a Savage would blush at. Whilst he was in *England*, he travelled from one manufacturing Town to another, spreading Sedition as he went, & prognosticating the Independance of *America*; & notwithstanding all the Civilities he met with here, & the Bounties of the Crown, he afterwards boasted, in an intercepted Letter to his american Friends, of humbling *this huckstering Nation*, as he politely & gratefully termed them. Surely! his patriotick Friends in *England* must have Souls callous to every virtuous Feeling, to support a Man, whose every Exertion tends to the Ruin of his Country.

After the Destruction of Lieut. Govr. *Hutchinson's* House in 1765, Dr. *Franklin* maintained a familiar literary Correspondence with him, & condemned the Opposition of the Faction to him. Yet this very Man, a Traitor to his Friend as well as to his Country, set another abandoned Man to filch, from a Gentleman's File of Letters, left in his Custody by a deceased Brother, a Number of confidential ones wrote by Mr. *Hutchinson* to that Brother, which did Honor to the Writer; & had they been attended to by Government, would in all Probability have put a Stop to the present Rebellion. This base Theft brought on a Duel between the Thief & the Proprietor of the Letters. The Latter nearly lost his Life, being unacquainted with the Sword; but fought upon the false Principle of Honor, because he must fight; & carried off those Marks in his Back which Swordsmen pronounced of the murderous Kind. Upon a hearing of the State of this Transaction, before the King and Council, Dr. *Franklin*, with the Effrontery of that Countenance where Virtue could never raise a Blush, took the Theft upon himself; & was discarded by every Man who felt any Regard to Propriety of Character. It may, with strict Justice, be said of the Doctor, what *Churchill* says of his Hero in the Duellist,

> ———of Virtue,
> Not one dull, dim Spark in his Soul,
> Vice, glorious Vice, possess'd the whole;
> And in her Service truly warm,
> He was in Sin, most Uniform.

Pride is Dr. *Franklin's* ruling Passion, & from this Source may be traced all the Actions of his Life. He had a Contempt of Religion, of Mankind, & even of those whom he had duped; & had he viewed the Subject in a moral Light, he would have contemned hisself. Had

4. Oliver's malicious rumor is, of course, false.

Churchill drawn his Character, instead of saying, as he did of his Hero,
And shove his Savior from the Wall. He would have changed his Phrase into—*and shove his Savior, God & All.*

He is now caressed at that perfidious Court, where it would have been Thought; further Instructions were not necessary; untill this Adept in the Science of Perfidy appeared, like a blazing Meteor, & has taught them, that all their former Knowledge was but the first Rudiments of their Grammar; & has qualified them for *Professors* in that Art which they were too well acquainted with before. This Hatred to the english Nation is so rivetted that it is no Breach of Charity to suppose, that when he makes his Exit:

Such, in those Moments as in all the past
Ye Gods! let Britain sink! will be his last.

* * *

RICHARD PRICE

Richard Price (1723–1791), dissenting minister, philosopher and theoretical actuary, was one of the two English friends whose opinion Franklin solicited during the process of composing the *Autobiography*. Price replied just a few days before he learned of Franklin's death.

Unfortunately, we possess only a shorthand draft of Price's letter. Nevertheless, Price's comments on Franklin's humor and moral purpose reveal the reactions that Franklin must have expected from those contemporary intellectuals and friends to whose judgment he submitted the manuscript—Benjamin Vaughan and Richard Price in England, and the Duc de La Rochefoucauld and Louis Le Veillard in France. Franklin must also have anticipated the criticism which his Christian (and especially his clerical) friends, such as the Reverends Price and Joseph Priestley, were sure to level—Franklin's lack of "faith in Christianity and the animating hopes of a resurrection to an endless life." Indeed, the revisions Franklin made during the course of composing the *Autobiography* often make it more religious. At any rate, Price's letter is the earliest reaction to the *Autobiography*, and his religious criticism anticipates the commonest eighteenth and nineteenth century strictures.

The letter has graciously been made available to us by Professor D. O. Thomas, whose wife Beryl Thomas deciphered the shorthand, and it is printed with the permission of Professor Bernard Peach.

Richard Price to Franklin, May, 1790†

(c. 30 May 1790)

My dear Friend,

I writ to you in March last and accompanied my letter with a discourse which I hope you have received. I cannot help taking the

---

† Source: Shorthand notes on the back and margins of Franklin's holograph letter to Price of April 30, 1789. American Philosophical Society.

opportunity which Mr. *Will*[iam's] return to America offers me to write again a line to you to return you my best thanks for that account of your life which with your permission Mr. Vaughan has allowed me to peruse and which indeed I have read with particular pleasure and satisfaction. Mr. Vaughan will probably send you some remarks but none have occurred to me that I can think worth communicating to you. Your life has been so distinguished that your account of it must, were it made public, excite much curiosity and be read with *eagerness*, and it is agreeable to look forward to the good it must do. It is writ with an agreeable sense of *pleasantry* and many parts of it convey the most important instruction by showing in a striking example how talents when tied to industry, prudence and integrity may elevate us from obscurity to the first consequence and *eminence*. I cannot however help wishing that the qualities and talents which produced this eminence had been aided by a faith in Christianity and the animating hopes of a resurrection to an endless life with which it inspires. Had this been the case such talents and qualities would I fancy have (been) raised to still greater eminence. But indeed is it not wonderful[1] that the nonsense that has been mistaken for Christianity and the liberality generally encountered with the profession of it should render many wise and upright men averse to them. Nor do I think that such will suffer in any other way than by losing in this life a satisfaction and an additional spur to eminence for a character which they might have derived from their bright views of the government of the world and those boundless hopes which true religion communicates. But I am afraid I have reason to apologize for writing thus to you. I have no doubt of the equal happiness hereafter of all equally virtuous men and honest inquirers, whether they have or have not been attended with a feeling of difficulties, whatever their faith has been and I wish I was myself better than I am by the faith I profess. A faith, however, in most instances only a preponderance (greater or less) in favour of particular points.

I have heard with great concern of your ill-health and wish it may not prevent you from going on with the account of your life. Having been a witness to and actively concerned in bringing about two of the most important revolutions that ever took place in the world, it is extremely desirable that your health and your life may be preserved to see it down to the present time. I cannot express to you the satisfaction that the proceedings in France continue to give me. They seem a prelude to happier times than any this world has yet seen. And the last determination, the account of which is just arrived here—that the right of declaring peace and war shall belong to the nation and not to the King, and that they renounce for ever all offensive wars—exhibits an example to the world which may produce the time when the aspirations (?) of Kings and the intrigues of courts will be no longer

1. astonishing.

capable of kindling the flame of war and delighting the rich.

I know what it is from my own experience how burdensome it is to have a multiplicity of letters to write. I would not therefore encumber you by desiring you to write to me. Should I by any means hear that you are tolerably well and going on with your important history and also that I retain a place in your favourable remembrance I shall be satisfied and happy. I continue to enjoy as much health as well as a man of a weak (?) constitution (at) my age can well expect. My spirits however often fail me and all business becomes more and more a burden to me. I am often thinking of withdrawing into some distant corner in order to spend the remainder of my life as much as possible in obscurity and quietness.

I am, my dear Friend, with the warmest affection and the greatest respect

Additional Note appended to the Draft

But indeed I cannot wonder that the liberality which (is) commonly encountered with regard (to) and the nonsense which is commonly mistaken for Christianity should render many wise and honest men averse to them

Nor do I think that such men will suffer in any other way than by a loss in this world of the satisfaction inspired (?) from the boundless hopes and bright views of the Divine Government. I have no doubt of the equal happiness hereafter of all equally honest and virtuous men

ANONYMOUS

Excerpt from *The Bee*, February 27, 1793†

* * *

Of all the literary men in my time, Benjamin Franklin occupied the first rank in respect to elegance, conjoined with philosophical accuracy, and depth of observation. Every subject he treated, assumed, under his hand, a new and more inviting appearance than any other person could ever give it. His magical touch converted the science of electricity into one of the most interesting amusements that was ever laid open to the minds of men. Politics, religion, science, in all its branches, which used to be dry and unamiable studies, he taught by apologues, fables, and tales, calculated not less to inform, than to amuse; and these are always constructed with an elegance of taste that is highly delightful. The miscellaneous philosophical works of Franklin, I consider as one of the most valuable presents that can be

† Source: *The Bee*, excerpt from "Critical Remarks on Some Celebrated English Authors," 13 (Feb. 27, 1793), 313.

put into the hands of youth. Read them my dear, ——with care. If you can lay them aside with indifference, you have not those dispositions of mind I have flattered myself you possess. In perusing them, you will find more amusement than in reading a romance, and be more improved than even in listening to some sermons. I know no book from which you can derive so much improvement and amusement.

* * *

JOHN ADAMS

It is ironic that the most interesting and detailed appreciation of Franklin by any contemporary was written by John Adams—who hated him. The ostensible cause of Adams's hatred was that Franklin was both too generous in his opinions of the French and too influenced by Vergennes and French official policy. The underlying cause, which was obvious to many of their contemporaries, was Adams's jealousy. Yet, for all his puritan provinciality and impossible vanity, Adams always tried "To do justice to his merits," even when he indiscreetly attacked Franklin before perfect strangers.

John Adams on Franklin, May 15, 1811†

Mr. Jefferson has said that Dr. Franklin was an honor to human nature. And so, indeed, he was. Had he been an ordinary man, I should never have taken the trouble to expose the turpitude of his intrigues, or to vindicate my reputation against his vilifications and calumnies. But the temple of human nature has two great apartments: the intellectual and the moral. If there is not a mutual friendship and strict alliance between these, degradation to the whole building must be the consequence. There may be blots on the disk of the most refulgent luminary, almost sufficient to eclipse it. And it is of great importance to the rising generation in this country that they be put upon their guard against being dazzled by the surrounding blaze into an idolatry to the spots. If the affable archangel[1] understood the standard of merit, that

Great or bright infers not excellence,[2]

Franklin's moral character can neither be applauded nor condemned, without discrimination and many limitations.

To all those talents and qualities for the foundation of a great and lasting character, which were held up to the view of the whole world by the university of Oxford, the Royal Society of London, and the Royal Academy of Sciences in Paris, were added, it is believed, more artificial modes of diffusing, celebrating, and exaggerating his reputation, than were ever before or since practised in favor of any individual.

† Source: Charles Francis Adams, ed., *The Works of John Adams* (Boston: Little, Brown, 1856), 1: 659–64, reprinting from the newspaper the *Boston Patriot*, May 15, 1811.

1. In Milton's *Paradise Lost*, bk. 7, l. 41, Raphael is called the "affable archangel."
2. *Paradise Lost*, bk. 8, ll. 90–91.

His reputation was more universal than that of Leibnitz or Newton, Frederick or Voltaire, and his character more beloved and esteemed than any or all of them. Newton had astonished perhaps forty or fifty men in Europe; for not more than that number, probably, at any one time had read him and understood him by his discoveries and demonstrations. And these being held in admiration in their respective countries as at the head of the philosophers, had spread among scientific people a mysterious wonder at the genius of this perhaps the greatest man that ever lived. But this fame was confined to men of letters. The common people knew little and cared nothing about such a recluse philosopher. Leibnitz's name was more confined still. Frederick was hated by more than half of Europe as much as Louis the Fourteenth was, and as Napoleon is. Voltaire, whose name was more universal than any of those before mentioned, was considered as a vain, profligate wit, and not much esteemed or beloved by anybody, though admired by all who knew his works. But Franklin's fame was universal. His name was familiar to government and people, to kings, courtiers, nobility, clergy, and philosophers, as well as plebeians, to such a degree that there was scarcely a peasant or a citizen, a *valet de chambre*, coachman or footman, a lady's chambermaid or a scullion in a kitchen, who was not familiar with it, and who did not consider him as a friend to human kind. When they spoke of him, they seemed to think he was to restore the golden age. They seemed enraptured enough to exclaim

Aspice, venturo lætentur ut omnia sæclo.[3]

To develop that complication of causes, which conspired to produce so singular a phenomenon, is far beyond my means or forces. Perhaps it can never be done without a complete history of the philosophy and politics of the eighteenth century. Such a work would be one of the most important that ever was written; much more interesting to this and future ages than the "Decline and Fall of the Roman Empire," splendid and useful as that is. La Harpe promised a history of the philosophy of the eighteenth century; but he died and left us only a few fragments. Without going back to Lord Herbert, to Hobbes, to Mandeville, or to a host of more obscure infidels, both in England, France, and Germany, it is enough to say that four of the finest writers that Great Britain ever produced, Shaftesbury, Bolingbroke, Hume, and Gibbon, whose labors were translated into all languages, and three of the most eloquent writers that ever lived in France, whose works were also translated into all languages, Voltaire, Rousseau, and Raynal, seem to have made it the study of their lives and the object of their most strenuous exertions, to render mankind in Europe discontented with their situation in life, and with the state of society, both in religion and government. Princes and courtiers as well as citizens and countrymen, clergy as well as laity, became infected.

3. "Behold, how all things exult in the age that is at hand!" Vergil, *Eclogue* 4, 1. 50.

The King of Prussia, the Empress Catherine, were open and undisguised. The Emperor Joseph the Second was suspected, and even the excellent and amiable King of France grew impatient and uneasy under the fatiguing ceremonies of the Catholic church. All these and many more were professed admirers of Mr. Franklin. He was considered as a citizen of the world, a friend to all men and an enemy to none. His rigorous taciturnity was very favorable to this singular felicity. He conversed only with individuals, and freely only with confidential friends. In company he was totally silent.

When the association of Encyclopedists[4] was formed, Mr. Franklin was considered as a friend and zealous promoter of that great enterprise, which engaged all their praises. When the society of economists[5] was commencing, he became one of them, and was solemnly ordained a knight of the order by the laying on the hands of Dr. Quesnay, the father and founder of that sect. This effectually secured the affections and the panegyrics of that numerous society of men of letters. He had been educated a printer, and had practised his art in Boston, Philadelphia, and London for many years, where he not only learned the full power of the press to exalt and to spread a man's fame, but acquired the intimacy and the correspondence of many men of that profession, with all their editors and many of their correspondents. This whole tribe became enamoured and proud of Mr. Franklin as a member of their body, and were consequently always ready and eager to publish and embellish any panegyric upon him that they could procure. Throughout his whole life he courted and was courted by the printers, editors, and correspondents of reviews, magazines, journals, and pamphleteers, and those little busy meddling scribblers that are always buzzing about the press in America, England, France, and Holland. These, together with some of the clerks in the Count de Vergennes's office of interpreters, (*bureau des interprètes*,) filled all the gazettes of Europe with incessant praises of Monsieur Franklin. If a collection could be made of all the Gazettes of Europe for the latter half of the eighteenth century, a greater number of panegyrical paragraphs upon *"le grand Franklin"* would appear, it is believed, than upon any other man that ever lived.

While he had the singular felicity to enjoy the entire esteem and affection of all the philosophers of every denomination, he was not less regarded by all the sects and denominations of Christians. The Catholics thought him almost a Catholic. The Church of England claimed him as one of them. The Presbyterians thought him half a Presbyterian, and the Friends believed him a wet Quaker.[6] The dissenting clergymen in England and America were among the most distinguished asserters and propagators of his renown. Indeed, all sects

---

4. The French intellectuals (led by Denis Diderot) who wrote *L'Encyclopédie*, 35 vols. (1751–80).
5. The French physiocrats, economic theorists, including François Quesnay and Pierre-Samuel du Pont de Nemours.
6. One not strict in the observances of the sect.

considered him, and I believe justly, a friend to unlimited toleration in matters of religion.

Nothing, perhaps, that ever occurred upon this earth was so well calculated to give any man an extensive and universal celebrity as the discovery of the efficacy of iron points and the invention of lightning-rods. The idea was one of the most sublime that ever entered a human imagination, that a mortal should disarm the clouds of heaven, and almost "snatch from his hand the sceptre and the rod." The ancients would have enrolled him with Bacchus and Ceres, Hercules and Minerva.[7] His *Paratonnères*[8] erected their heads in all parts of the world, on temples and palaces no less than on cottages of peasants and the habitations of ordinary citizens. These visible objects reminded all men of the name and character of their inventor; and, in the course of time, have not only tranquillized the minds, and dissipated the fears of the tender sex and their timorous children, but have almost annihilated that panic terror and supersititious horror which was once almost universal in violent storms of thunder and lightning. To condense all the rays of this glory to a focus, to sum it up in a single line, to impress it on every mind and transmit it to all posterity, a motto was devised for his picture, and soon became familiar to the memory of every school-boy who understood a word of Latin:—

"Eripuit cœlo fulmen sceptrumque tyrannis."[9]* * *

The few who think and see the progress and tendency of things, have long foreseen that resistance in some shape or other must be resorted to, some time or other. They have not been able to see any resource but in the common people; indeed, in republicanism, and that republicanism must be democracy; because the whole power of the aristocracy, as of the monarchies, aided by the church, must be wielded against them. Hence the popularity of all insurrections against the ordinary authority of government during the last century. Hence the popularity of Pascal Paoli,[1] the Polish insurrections, the American Revolution, and the present struggle in Spain and Portugal. When, where, and in what manner all this will end, God only knows. To this cause Mr. Franklin owed much of his popularity. He was considered to be in his heart no friend to kings, nobles, or prelates. He was thought a profound legislator, and a friend of democracy. He was thought to be the magician who had excited the ignorant Americans to resistance. His mysterious wand had separated the Colonies from Great Britain. He had framed and established all the American constitutions of government, especially all the best of them, *i.e.* the most

---

7. According to the doctrine of euhemerism, the classical gods were people who became famous for their contributions to culture: Bacchus supposedly discovered how to make wine; Ceres first cultivated wheat; Hercules was an individual of great strength who performed incredible feats; and Minerva discovered how to make cloth.

8. Lightning rods.

9. Anne-Robert-Jacques Turgot's famous epigram on Franklin: "he seized the lightning from the sky and the scepter from the tyrants."

1. Pasquale di Paoli (1725–1807), Corsican patriot.

democratical. His plans and his example were to abolish monarchy, aristocracy, and hierarchy throughout the world. Such opinions as these were entertained by the Duke de la Rochefoucauld, M. Turgot, M. Condorcet, and a thousand other men of learning and eminence in France, England, Holland, and all the rest of Europe.

Mr. Franklin, however, after all, and notwithstanding all his faults and errors, was a great and eminent benefactor to his country and mankind.

*   *   *

Franklin had a great genius, original, sagacious, and inventive, capable of discoveries in science no less than of improvements in the fine arts and the mechanic arts. He had a vast imagination, equal to the comprehension of the greatest objects, and capable of a steady and cool comprehension of them. He had wit at will. He had humor that, when he pleased, was delicate and delightful. He had a satire that was good-natured or caustic, Horace or Juvenal, Swift or Rabelais,[2] at his pleasure. He had talents for irony, allegory, and fable, that he could adapt with great skill to the promotion of moral and political truth. He was master of that infantine simplicity which the French call *naïveté* which never fails to charm, in Phædrus and La Fontaine,[3] from the cradle to the grave. Had he been blessed with the same advantages of scholastic education in his early youth, and pursued a course of studies as unembarrassed with occupations of public and private life, as Sir Isaac Newton, he might have emulated the first philosopher. Although I am not ignorant that most of his positions and hypotheses have been controverted, I cannot but think he has added much to the mass of natural knowledge, and contributed largely to the progress of the human mind, both by his own writings and by the controversies and experiments he has excited in all parts of Europe. He had abilities for investigating statistical questions, and in some parts of his life has written pamphlets and essays upon public topics with great ingenuity and success; but after my acquaintance with him, which commenced in congress in 1775, his excellence as a legislator, a politician, or a negotiator most certainly never appeared. No sentiment more weak and superficial was ever avowed by the most absurd philosopher than some of his, particularly one that he procured to be inserted in the first constitution of Pennsylvania, and for which he had such a fondness as to insert it in his will.[4] I call it weak, for so it must have been, or hypocritical; unless he meant by one satiric touch to ridicule his own republic, or throw it into everlasting contempt.

*   *   *

2. The classical satirists Horace (65–8 B.C.) and Juvenal (60–130? A.D.), and the English and French satirists Jonathan Swift (1667–1745) and François Rabelais (1494?–1553) are all touchstones for different kinds of satire.
3. The classical writer Phaedrus (15? B.C.–50 A.D.) and the French La Fontaine (1621–95) are famous for their seemingly simple fables.
4. Franklin wrote in his will "that in a democratical state there ought to be no offices of profit." (Smyth, 9: 501.)

Nineteenth-Century Opinions

Religion continued to be a key influence in creating nineteenth-century opinion, with Franklin's deism remaining objectionable to many commentators, even though a few ministers, like the Reverend Edward Everett Hale, were nevertheless devoted Franklinists. The increasingly popular role of the self-made man in American culture, together with the characterization of American society as materialistic and pragmatic, led a number of students to seek for the origin of these traits in Franklin—a position which could be supported by a slanted reading of Franklin's best-known writings, *The Way to Wealth* and the *Autobiography*. Naturally the Romantics and later writers, English and American, revolted against the supposedly typical nineteenth-century philistine American and against his supposed eighteenth-century progenitor. Resentment, too, of the wealth and power of the burgeoning United States caused some foreigners to revile "the Father of all the Yankees." In addition, old family animosities continued to influence a few writers, including Leigh Hunt and Charles Francis Adams. On the other hand, multi-volume editions of Franklin's works by Jared Sparks (ten volumes, 1836–40) and John Bigelow (ten volumes, 1887–89) and the major biography by James Parton (two volumes, 1864) made the writings and the life of a complex, multi-faceted, idealistic and artful Franklin widely available.

JOSEPH DENNIE

Joseph Dennie (1768–1812), a dominant man-of-letters in America's Early National Period, attacked Franklin in Dennie's influential Philadelphia magazine, *The Port Folio*. Lewis Leary, "Joseph Dennie on Benjamin Franklin," *Pennsylvania Magazine of History and Biography*, 72 (1948), 240–46, has pointed out that although Dennie's conservative politics demanded that Dennie oppose the supposedly "jacobin" Franklin, Dennie's aristocratic literary tastes reflected a common point of view. If Dennie, as we suppose, is referring to Franklin's "The Art of Procuring Pleasant Dreams" (Smyth, 10, 131–37) as being plagiarized from John Aubrey, he seems to us even further askew than Poe was in labeling Hawthorne a plagiarist.

From *The Port Folio*, 1801†

———— "For you
I tame my youth to philosophic cares,
And grow still paler by the midnight lamps."
Dr. Armstrong[1]

† Source: *The Port Folio*, 1 (February 14, 1801), 53–54.
Book 3, ll. 9–10, by Dr. John Armstrong (1709–79).
1. From *The Art of Preserving Health* (1744),

I remember, when I was a boy, somebody put into my hand, the life and essays of Dr. Franklin. At the time this man lived, and particularly when his *philosophy*, and his newspaper ethics and economics were diffused over the continent, it was the fashion for Vanity to "rejoice and be exceeding glad" in the possession of such a treasure. I have heard somewhere of a book, for the use of apprentices, servant maids, &c. entitled, "The *Only* Sure Guide to Love and Esteem." In like manner, it was thought that there was no other road to the temple of Riches, except that which run through—Dr. Franklin's works; and that, as quacks boast of an infallible cure for the itch, the Doctor could communicate a nostrum for the preservation of prudence, and the cure of poverty. Every miser read his precepts with rapture, and Franklin was pronounced not only wise, and good, and *patriotic*, and all that—but an *original writer!* Such a strange opinion as the last never could have been entertained, except in a country, from its newness, paucity of literary information, and the imperfection of its systems of education, puzzled to distinguish an original from a copy. For, the fact is, that "our Benjamin" was no more distinguished for the *originality* of his conceptions, than for the purity of his life, or the soundness of his religious doctrine. As a writer, he plundered his thoughts and his phrases from others—and, as a deist, he supported his religion with the *arts* of infidelity; with the rank garbage of Mandeville, Tindal, and Chubb;[2] with the *crumbs* which fell from those *poor* men's tables. It may be recollected, that, among other things which appear in his "Essays," there is a scheme for an "air bath," and hints for procuring quiet sleep, by rising in the night, and beating up your bed, and walking about your chamber, &c. This profound discovery was ushered into the world with the greatest pomp, copied into innumerable newspapers, and praised as a most ingenious invention. Every American, who had read or spelt through two or three almanacs, or two or three papers in the Spectator, talked of the doctor's genius, and *philosophy*, and simplicity in writing. Ignorance and Unskilfulness, as they are wont, naturally wondered at what bore the semblance of specious novelty. Like those children, described in *Shenstone's* Schoolmistress.[3]

"They in gaping wonderment abound,
"And think he was the greatest wight on ground."

Unfortunately for the Doctor's philosophy and invention, as they respect the discovery of the above opiate, both of them are as baseless

---

2. Mandeville, Tindal, and Chubb are all iconoclastic writers, and all sometimes categorized as deists. For Mandeville, see the biographical sketches (this edition, p. 189). Matthew Tindal (1657–1733) is best known for his *Christianity as old as the Creation* (1730);

and Thomas Chubb (1679–1747), for A *Discourse on Miracles* (1741).
3. From "The Schoolmistress" (1742), stanza 8, ll. 8–9, substituting "he was" for "she been," by William Shenstone (1714–63).

as his reputation. If a man, whose brain is laboring, with thought, or agitated by the spells of hypochrondria, or fired with the rays of Fancy, should rise from a sleepless couch, and patrol his chamber like a centinel, and then return to bed, he may still ask in vain for the poppies of Morpheus.[4] For the experience of almost every sedentary scholar will prove that there are moments, nay hours, when the billows of the brain will not, at bidding, subside. The soul of a man of genius is, often, broad awake at midnight hours, and to attempt to stupify it into sleep, by the above and similar tricks, is worthy of Franklin, and of Frenchmen, and of their philosophy. It becomes all three to treat the mind as they would a bit of wax or a lump of dough, and presumptuously strive to mould it into any and every fantastic shape. But this occassional *vigilance* of our mental faculties is an ordinance of the CREATOR OF MIND, and wisely intended as a hint, as a goad to the sluggishness of our grosser powers to arise to action. When sleeplessness is experienced, let a man leave his bed, and light his lamp, and read or write, or meditate, as was the custom of Mr. POPE,[5] and tire the body in that way, and not stalk about like the ghost of Banquo,[6] or stand at open windows, to terrify the owls, and to "make night hideous." This trick of Benjamin has been repeatedly tried, and he, who made the experiment, has a right to declare it fallacious. Strolling about one's chamber will not close the mental eye: all such schemes are a bubble, and it is a risible proof of the emptiness of modern philosophy, that its vain followers imagine mind may be managed upon mechanical principles; and, as an ingenius friend once expressed it, that we can throw off speculation from the soul, as a miller throws a sack of corn from his shoulder.

Thus much for the *truth* and *utility* of Franklin's scheme, to sleep at will. Now, "mark how a plain tale shall put down" all the glory of the *invention*. Americans are so little in the habit of literary research, and so arrogantly confident ours "is the first and most enlightened country in the world," that, without examination, they eulogize extravagantly every thing that is their own; and, as Dr. Benjamin had the double honour to be born in Boston, and print in Philadelphia, therefore he must be an Addison[7] in style, and a Bacon in philosophy.[8] I have heard and read encomiums by dozens, on the invention of the above scheme to cheat the senses into a slumber. But, even this receipt to procure drowsiness, though childish, trivial, and false, is not *new*. The doctor *stole* it from an old and obscure writer; and,

4. Poppies yield opium; Morpheus is the god of dreams.
5. Alexander Pope (1688–1744), the great English poet.
6. Banquo's ghost haunts Macbeth in Shakespeare's play.
7. Joseph Addison (1672–1719), major contributor to the *Spectator* (1711–12), the English periodical essays that Franklin used as a model for style.
8. Francis Bacon (1651–1627), scientist and philosopher, proponent of the inductive method.

As *saints* themselves will sometimes be,
Of gifts, that cost them nothing, free,[9]

he bountifully imparted it to the American world, and this same world, so liberally *"free"* to give, and so thoroughly "enlightened" to discern, discovered that he was a philosopher, who *could beat up a bed*, and walk about in his shirt, and stand at a window without catching cold, and then fall a sleep, and snore till morning. The proof of plagiarism may be found in AUBREY, a writer nearly obsolete. He published "Miscellanies,"[1] which, like the Noctes Atticae of Aulus Gellius,[2] are quoted frequently by the learned, more for the quaint and curious than for the true and useful. He is speaking, in his loose and rambling way, of Dr. Harvey,[3] the celebrated discoverer of the circulation of the blood. "He was very hotheaded, and his thoughts, working much, would oft times keep him from sleeping. His way was to rise out of his bed, and walk about his chamber, in his shirt, till he began to have a horror or shivering, and then return to bed, and sleep very comfortably." Here is the grand discovery, described in the words of an old, weak, and credulous writer, and what is curious, Franklin's boasted essay is almost a literal transcript of Aubrey's anecdote.

It is proposed to devote some future speculations to the subject of Dr. FRANKLIN. Something shall be said of his style, his economics, politics, philosophy, &c. As his style has been compared to Addison's, as his electricity is boasted of as his sole invention, as his strings of Proverbs have been called wit, and his beggarly maxims humour, it is time to have these things diligently scrutinized. The enquiry shall be fairly but faithfully pursued. From a diligent review of his character, conduct, and writings, the author of this article has acquired the right to affirm, that this pseudo philosopher has been a mischief to his country. He was the founder of that Grub-street sect, who have professedly attempted to degrade literature to the level of vulgar capacities, and debase the polished and current language of books, by the vile alloy of provincial idioms, and colloquial barbarism, the shame of grammar, and akin to any language, rather than English. He was one of our first Jacobins,[4] the first to lay his head in the lap of French harlotry; and prostrate the christianity and honour of his country to the deism and democracies of Paris. Above all, he was the author of that pitiful system of Economics, the adoption of which has degraded our national character. Far, very far, be it from the writer of this article, to attempt to vilify that clear sighted prudence, which at once discerns the remotest possibility of penury, and wisely guards itself against the evil. But there is a low and scoundrel appetite for

---

9. From *Hudibras* (1663–78), Pt. 1, canto 1, ll. 489–90, by Samuel Butler (1612–80).
1. *Miscellanies* (1696) by John Aubrey (1626–97).
2. The Latin grammarian Aulus Gellius (c.

A.D. 130–c. 180).
3. Dr. William Harvey (1578–1657).
4. Those who identified with the principles of the French Revolution.

small sums, acquired by base and pitiful means; and, whoever planted or cherished it, is worthy of no better title than the foul disgrace of the country.

Of economy there are two kinds, the liberal and the sordid. The first is perfectly consistent with the habits and generosity of a gentleman and a cavalier; it legitimates every expence, and is the lord high treasurer of every real delight, and the natural and necessary ally of tranquility, honour, and independence. I believe this species of economy was well understood by many of the *ancient gentlemen* of France, and that it is at home among the high minded Castilians,[5] the munificent, punctual, upright and fair dealing merchants of England, and many of the high and honourable among our own countrymen. Whether Dr. Franklin, his associates, or his *disciples* understood, or practiced this last species of economy is not a question, among men of "long views," of *"prisca* fides,"[6] and of habitual liberality.

FRANCIS, LORD JEFFREY

Francis, Lord Jeffrey (1773–1850), a founder of the *Edinburgh Review* (1802–1929), wrote a long appreciation of the writings and character of Franklin in a review of an unauthorized edition of Franklin's *Complete Works*, 3 vols. (London: Johnson, 1806). Although Jeffrey labors some pet theories (he begins by blaming America for its "singular want of literary enterprize" and claims that Franklin was able to achieve greatness because of his lack of education), he also introduces several key ideas in Franklin criticism—Franklin's common sense, the seeming effortlessness of his scientific theories and speculations, an appreciation of how Franklin's writings are adapted to the audience, the comparisons to Swift, and an appreciation of his private correspondence.

From the *Edinburgh Review*, 1806[†]

* * *

This self-taught American is the most rational, perhaps, of all philosophers. He never loses sight of common sense in any of his speculations; and when his philosophy does not consist entirely in its fair and vigorous application, it is always regulated and controuled by it in its application and result. No individual, perhaps, ever possessed a juster understanding, or was so seldom obstructed in the use of it by indolence, enthusiasm, or authority.* * *

5. Spanish from the province of Castile were generally thought to be the most aristocratic.
6. Vergil, *Aeneid*, book 9, l. 79, "old faith."

† Source: *Edinburgh Review*, 8 (1806), 328, 340–41, 344.

As a writer on morality and general literature, the merits of Dr Franklin cannot be estimated properly, without taking into consideration the peculiarities, that have been already alluded to, in his early history and situation. He never had the benefit of any academical instruction, nor of the society of men of letters;—his style was formed entirely by his own judgement and occasional reading; and most of his moral pieces were written while he was a tradesman, addressing himself to the tradesmen of his native city. We cannot expect, therefore, either that he should write with extraordinary elegance or grace; or that he should treat of the accomplishments, follies, and occupations of polite life. He had no great occasion, as a moralist, to expose the guilt and the folly of gaming or seduction; or to point a poignant and playful ridicule against the lighter immoralities of fashionable life. To the mechanics and traders of Boston and Philadelphia, such warnings were altogether unnecessary; and he endeavoured, therefore, with more appropriate eloquence, to impress upon them the importance of industry, sobriety, and economy, and to direct their wise and humble ambition to the attainment of useful knowledge and honourable independence. That morality, after all, is certainly the most valuable, which is adapted to the circumstances of the greater part of mankind; and that eloquence is the most meritorious, that is calculated to convince and persuade the multitude to virtue. Nothing can be more perfectly and beautifully adapted to its object, than most of Dr. Franklin's compositions of this sort. The tone of familiarity, of good-will, and homely jocularity—the plain and pointed illustrations—the short sentences, made up of short words—and the strong sense, clear information, and obvious conviction of the author himself, make most of his moral exhortations perfect models of popular eloquence; and afford the finest specimens of a style which has been but too little cultivated in a country, which numbers perhaps more than 100,000 readers among its tradesmen and artificers.

* * *

His account of his own life, down to the year 1730, has been in the hands of the public since 1790. It is written with great simplicity and liveliness, though it contains too many trifling details and anecdotes of obscure individuals. It affords a striking example of the irresistible force with which talents and industry bear upwards in society, as well as an impressive illustration of the substantial wisdom and good policy of invariable integrity and candour. We should think it a very useful reading for all young persons of unsteady principle, who have their fortunes to make or to mend in the world.* * *

CHARLES BROCKDEN BROWN

When Charles Brockden Brown (1771–1810), early American novelist, re-printed Francis Jeffrey's review (excerpt immediately above) in his Philadelphia *Literary Magazine*, he prefaced it with a brief comment endorsing Jeffrey's evaluation.

From *Literary Magazine*, 1806†

* * *

A just view of the character of Dr. Franklin has probably never been given by any of his countrymen. While living, the world was divided into passionate friends and rancorous enemies, and since his death a kind of political tincture still adheres to all our sentiments concerning him. Among his own countrymen, prejudice and passion, which used to be enlisted wholly on his side, has, in some respects, become hostile to him, and an impartial estimate of his merits can perhaps only be looked for among foreigners. The following portrait is taken from a foreign publication, and seems to be altogether dispassionate and equitable.* * *

JOHN FOSTER

John Foster (1770–1843), essayist and Baptist minister, was among the earliest writers to comment on Franklin's "love of the useful." And, like many other critics of Franklin—before and since—Foster found Franklin disturbingly unreligious. Although Foster's piece in *The Eclectic Review*, 9 (May, 1818), 433–50, ostensibly reviewed only William Temple Franklin's edition of *The Private Correspondence*, Foster evidently had read the *Autobiography* as well.

From *The Eclectic Review*, 1818††

* * *

And here it may be remarked, that his predominant passion appears to have been a love of the useful. The useful was to him the *summum bonum*, the supreme fair, the sublime and beautiful, which it may not perhaps be extravagant to believe he was in quest of every week for half a century, in whatever place, or study, or practical undertaking. No

† Source: *Literary Magazine*, 6 (November, 1806), 367.
†† Source: John Foster, *Critical Essays Con-*tributed to the Eclectic Review (London: Bell & Sons, 1877), 2: 417, 428–29.

department was too plain or humble for him to occupy himself in for this purpose; and in affairs of the most ambitious order this was still systematically his object. Whether in directing the constructing of chimneys or of constitutions, lecturing on the savings of candles or on the economy of national revenues, he was still intent on the same end, the question always being how to obtain the most of solid tangible advantage by the plainest and easiest means. There has rarely been a mortal, of high intelligence and flattering fame, on whom the pomps of life were so powerless. On him were completely thrown away the oratorical and poetical heroics about glory, of which heroics it was enough that he easily perceived the intention or effect to be, to explode all sober truth and substantial good, and to impel men, at the very best of the matter, through some career of vanity, but commonly through mischief, slaughter, and devastation, in mad pursuit of what amounts at last, if attained, to some certain quantity of noise, and empty show, and intoxicated transient elation.

* * * he constantly professes his firm belief in an Almighty Being, wise and good, and exercising a providential government over the world; and in a future state of conscious existence, rendered probably by the nature of the human soul, and by the analogies presented in the renovations and reproductions in other classes of being, and rendered necessary by the unsatisfactory state of allotment and retribution on earth. On the ground of such a faith, so sustained, he appears always to anticipate with complacency the appointed removal to another scene, confident that he should continue to experience in another life the goodness of that Being who had been so favourable to him in this, "though without the smallest conceit," he says, "of meriting such goodness." The merely philosophic language uniformly employed in his repeated anticipations of an immortal life, taken together with two or three profane passages in these letters (there are but few such passages), and with the manner in which he equivocates on the question respectfully pressed upon him by the worthy President of Yale College, respecting his opinion of Christ, leave no room to doubt that, whatever he did really think of the Divine Teacher, he substantially rejected Christianity—that he refused to acknowledge it in anything like the character of a peculiar economy for the illumination and redemption of a fallen and guilty race. Nothing, probably, that he believed, was believed on the authority of its declarations, and nothing that he assumed to hope after death, was expected on the ground of its redeeming efficacy and its promises. And this state of opinions it appears that he self-complacently maintained without variation, during the long course of his activities and speculations on the great scale; for in this letter to Dr. Stiles, of the date of 1790, he enclosed, as expressive of his latest opinions one written nearly forty years before, in answer to some religious admonitions addressed to him by George Whitefield. So that, throughout a period

much surpassing the average duration of the life of man, spent in a vigorous and very diversified exercise of an eminently acute and independent intellect, with all the lights of the world around him, he failed to attain the one grand simple apprehension how man is to be accepted with God. There is even cause to doubt whether he ever made the inquiry, with any real solicitude to meet impartially the claims of that religion which avows itself to be on evidence, a declaration of the mind of the Almighty on the momentous subject. On any question of physics, or mechanics, or policy, or temporal utility of any kind, or morals as detached from religion, he could bend the whole force of his spirit, and the result was often a gratifying proof of the greatness of that force; but the religion of Christ it would appear that he could pass by with an easy assumption that whatever might be the truth concerning it, he could perfectly well do without it. To us this appears a mournful and awful spectacle; and the more so from that entire unaffected tranquillity with which he regarded the whole concern in the conscious near approach of death. Some of the great Christian topics it was needless to busy himself about then, because he should soon learn the "truth with less trouble!"

*　*　*

JOHN KEATS

John Keats (1795–1821), writing a letter to his brother and sister-in-law, reveals that he knows only the Poor Richard caricature of Franklin—and he joins this caricature with an anti-American prejudice.

To George and Georgiana Keats, October 14–31, 1818†

* * * Dilke,[1] whom you know to be a Godwin perfectibility Man,[2] pleases himself with the idea that America will be the country to take up the human intellect where england leaves off—I differ there with him greatly—A country like the united states whose greatest Men are Franklins and Washingtons will never do that—They are great Men doubtless but how are they to be compared to those our countrey men Milton and the two Sidneys—The one is a philosophical Quaker full of mean and thrifty maxims the other sold the very Charger who had taken him through all his Battles Those American's are great but

† Source: Hyder Edward Rollins, ed., *Letters of John Keats, 1814–1821*, 2 vols. (Cambridge: Harvard Univ. Press, 1958), 1: 397–98.
1. Charles Wentworth Dilke (1789–1864), a close personal friend of Keats, later published many items about him in the *Athenaeum*.
2. William Godwin (1756–1836), English novelist and philosopher, advocated man's perfectibility.

they are not sublime Man—the humanity of the United States can never reach the sublime.

*   *   *

EDGAR ALLAN POE

In his splendidly annotated *Collected Works of Edgar Allan Poe*, Thomas Ollive Mabbott notes that "The Business Man" parodies Joseph C. Neal's *Charcoal Sketches* (1838), which humorously but sympathetically portrayed urban low life characters. No one previously has pointed out that Poe's story also burlesques Franklin's *Autobiography*, especially Part Two, the Art of Virtue. Poe's *reductio ad absurdam* of the Art of Virtue applies Franklin's practical advice on conduct and achievement to the efforts of a scoundrel who prides himself on being a methodical business man.

Poe's emphasis on method alludes to Franklin's chart for spending the hours of a day, to his list of thirteen virtues, and to his systematic scheme for attaining virtue. Of course, order or method is itself Franklin's third virtue, and Franklin wrote at length of his efforts to attain "Method," illustrating his acceptance of his comparative failure with the anecdote of the "speckled Ax" (See p. 73 this edition). Poe alludes to Franklin's running away from home at 16, to Franklin's love and use of proverbs, and to his project for cleaning streets. When the business man says that method characterized his actions as well as his accounts, Poe probably glances at Franklin's saying "I took care not only to be in *Reality* Industrious and frugal, but to avoid all *Appearances* of the Contrary," a moral that Franklin illustrated with his anecdote of bringing home his paper on a wheelbarrow (See p. 54 this edition). Like Franklin, Poe was proud of his feats of swimming, and he echoes Franklin's unusual but repeated metaphor "I went on swimmingly." The business man's "Day-book and Ledger" may allude to Franklin's "little Book in which I allotted a Page for each of the Virtues" (See p. 70 this edition). And the allusion to "the Scriptural injunction" ("Be fruitful and multiply") may glance at another piece by Franklin, "The Speech of Miss Polly Baker," or simply to Franklin's citing the Bible and to his well-known advocacy of philoprogenitiveness.

Poe's chart of the account of "Peter Proffit, Walking Advertiser" echoes Franklin's use of charts and anticipates Thoreau's similar satire in his first chapter "Economy" in *Walden*. At the same time, Poe's portrayal of modern man as nothing but a walking machine between two signs hauntingly embodies Franklin's supposed disregard of man's spiritual qualities. Indeed, Poe's image aptly anticipates Yeats's lines "An aged man is but a paltry thing / A tattered coat upon a stick, unless . . ." ("Sailing to Byzantium") and the main image of Eliot's "The Hollow Men." The epigraph "Method is the soul of Business" (which echoes the nineteenth-century saying "Punctuality is the soul of business") is Poe's creation, although it sounds like something from Poor Richard. Actually, its use of "soul" points to Poe's basic criticism. Poe implicitly argues that Franklin's supposed philosophy of man reduces him to nothing more than an entity for business or, in law, a corporation. But even Poe's scoundrelly caricature of a business man realizes the difference between real men and corporations, which (and Poe's story originally ended with these words) had "neither bodies to be kicked, nor souls to be damned."

Of course, the criticism, as Poe well knew, did not apply to the real Benjamin Franklin or even to a careful reading of the *Autobiography*. It was true, however, of a tendency within American society of the nineteenth (and twentieth) century, and it was true of numerous business men who imitated some aspects of Franklin and who were proud to do so.

The Business Man†

Method is the soul of business.—OLD SAYING

I AM a business man. I am a methodical man. Method is *the* thing, after all. But there are no people I more heartily despise, than your eccentric fools who prate about method without understanding it; attending strictly to its letter, and violating its spirit. These fellows are always doing the most out-of-the-way things in what they call an orderly manner. Now here—I conceive—is a positive paradox. True method appertains to the ordinary and the obvious alone, and cannot be applied to the *outré*. What definite idea can a body attach to such expressions as "methodical Jack o'Dandy," or "a systematical Will o' the Wisp"?

My notions upon this head might not have been so clear as they are, but for a fortunate accident which happened to me when I was a very little boy. A good-hearted old Irish nurse (whom I shall not forget in my will) took me up one day by the heels, when I was making more noise than was necessary, and, swinging me round two or three times, d——d my eyes for "a skreeking little spalpeen,"[1] and then knocked my head into a cocked hat against the bed-post. This, I say, decided my fate, and made my fortune. A bump arose at once on my sinciput, and turned out to be as pretty an organ of *order* as one shall see on a summer's day. Hence that positive appetite for system and regularity which has made me the distinguished man of business that I am.

If there is anything on earth I hate, it is a genius. Your geniuses are all arrant asses—the greater the genius the greater the ass—and to this rule there is no exception whatever. Especially, you cannot make a man of business out of a genius, any more than money out of a Jew, or the best nutmegs out of pine-knots. The creatures are always going off at a tangent into some fantastic employment, or ridiculous speculation, entirely at variance with the "fitness of things," and having no business whatever to be considered as a business at all. Thus you may tell these characters immediately by the nature of their occupations. If you ever perceive a man setting up as a merchant, or a manufacturer; or going into the cotton or tobacco trade, or any of those eccentric

pursuits; or getting to be a dry-goods dealer, or soap-boiler, or something of that kind; or pretending to be a lawyer, or a blacksmith, or a
physician—anything out of the usual way—you may set him down at
once as a genius, and then, according to the rule-of-three, he's an ass.

Now I am not in any respect a genius, but a regular business man.
My Day-book and Ledger will evince this in a minute. They are well
kept, though I say it myself; and, in my general habits of accuracy and
punctuality, I am not to be beat by a clock. Moreover, my occupations
have been always made to chime in with the ordinary habitudes of my
fellow men. Not that I feel the least indebted, upon this score, to my
exceedingly weak-minded parents, who, beyond doubt, would have
made an arrant genius of me at last, if my guardian angel had not
come, in good time, to the rescue. In biography the truth is everything, and in autobiography it is especially so—yet I scarcely hope to
be believed when I state, however solemnly, that my poor father put
me, when I was about fifteen years of age, into the counting-house of
what he termed "a respectable hardware and commission merchant
doing a capital bit of business!" A capital bit of fiddlestick! However,
the consequence of this folly was, that in two or three days, I had to be
sent home to my button-headed family in a high state of fever, and
with a most violent and dangerous pain in the sinciput, all round
about my organ of order. It was nearly a gone case with me then—just
touch-and-go for six weeks—the physicians giving me up and all that
sort of thing. But, although I suffered much, I was a thankful boy in
the main. I was saved from being a "respectable hardware and commission merchant, doing a capital bit of business," and I felt grateful to
the protuberance which had been the means of my salvation, as well as
to the kind-hearted female who had originally put these means within
my reach.

The most of boys run away from home at ten or twelve years of age,
but I waited till I was sixteen. I don't know that I should have gone,
even then, if I had not happened to hear my old mother talking about
setting me up on my own hook in the grocery way. The *grocery*
way!—only think of that! I resolved to be off forthwith, and try and
establish myself in some *decent* occupation, without dancing attendance any longer upon the caprices of these eccentric old people, and
running the risk of being made a genius of in the end. In this project I
succeeded perfectly well at the first effort, and by the time I was farily
eighteen, found myself doing an extensive and profitable business in
the Tailor's Walking-Advertisement line.

I was enabled to discharge the onerous duties of this profession, only
by that rigid adherence to system which formed the leading feature of
my mind. A scrupulous *method* characterised my actions, as well as
my accounts. In my case, it was method—not money—which made
the man: at least all of him that was not made by the tailor whom I
served. At nine, every morning, I called upon that individual for the

clothes of the day. Ten o'clock found me in some fashionable prom-
enade or other place of public amusement. The precise regularity with
which I turned my handsome person about, so as to bring successively
into view every portion of the suit upon my back, was the admiration
of all the knowing men in the trade. Noon never passed without my
bringing home a customer to the house of my employers, Messieurs
Cut and Comeagain. I say this proudly, but with tears in my eyes—for
the firm proved themselves the basest of ingrates. The little account
about which we quarreled and finally parted, cannot, in any item, be
thought overcharged, by gentlemen really conversant with the nature
of the business. Upon this point, however, I feel a degree of proud
satisfaction in permitting the reader to judge for himself. My bill ran
thus:

Messrs. Cut and Comeagain, Merchant Tailors.

	To Peter Proffit, Walking Advertiser,	Drs.
July 10.	To promenade, as usual, and customer brought home,	$00 25
July 11.	To do. do. do.	25
July 12.	To one lie, second class; damaged black cloth sold for invisible green,	25
July 13.	To one lie, first class, extra quality and size; recommending milled sattinet as broadcloth,	75
July 20.	To purchasing bran new paper shirt collar or dickey, to set off gray Petersham,	2
Aug. 15.	To wearing double-padded bobtail frock, (thermometer 106 in the shade,)	25
Aug. 16.	Standing on one leg three hours, to show off new-style strapped pants, at 12½ cts. per leg, per hour	37½
Aug. 17.	To promenade, as usual, and large customer brought (fat man,)	50
Aug. 18.	To do. do. (medium size,)	25
Aug. 19.	To do. do. (small man and bad pay,)	6
		$2 96½

The item chiefly disputed in this bill was the very moderate charge
of two pennies for the dickey. Upon my word of honor, this *was
not* an unreasonable price for that dickey. It was one of the cleanest
and prettiest little dickeys I ever saw; and I have good reason to believe
that it effected the sale of three Petershams. The elder partner of the
firm, however, would allow me only one penny of the charge, and
took it upon himself to show in what manner four of the same sized
conveniences could be got out of a sheet of foolscap. But it is needless
to say that I stood upon the *principle* of the thing. Business is business,
and should be done in a business way. There was no *system* whatever
in swindling me out of a penny—a clear fraud of fifty per cent.—no
method in any respect. I left, at once, the employment of Messieurs

Cut and Comeagain, and set up in the Eye-Sore line by myself—one of the most lucrative, respectable, and independent of the ordinary occupations.

My strict integrity, economy, and rigorous business habits, here again came into play. I found myself driving a flourishing trade, and soon became a marked man upon 'Change. The truth is, I never dabbled in flashy matters, but jogged on in the good old sober routine of the calling—a calling in which I should, no doubt, have remained to the present hour, but for a little accident which happened to me in the prosecution of one of the usual business operations of the profession. Whenever a rich old hunks, or prodigal heir, or bankrupt corporation, gets into the notion of putting up a palace, there is no such thing in the world as stopping either of them, and this every intelligent person knows. The fact in question is indeed the basis of the Eye-Sore trade. As soon, therefore, as a building-project is fairly afoot by one of these parties, we merchants secure a nice corner of the lot in contemplation, or a prime little situation just adjoining or right in front. This done, we wait until the palace is half-way up, and then we pay some tasty architect to run us up an ornamental mud hovel, right against it; or a Down-East or Dutch Pagoda, or a pig-sty, or any ingenious little bit of fancy work, either Esquimau, Kickapoo, or Hottentot. Of course, we can't afford to take these structures down under a bonus of five hundred per cent. upon the prime cost of our lot and plaster. *Can* we? I ask the question. I ask it of business men. It would be irrational to suppose that we can. And yet there was a rascally corporation which asked me to do this very thing—this *very thing*! I did not reply to their absurd proposition, of course; but I felt it a duty to go that same night, and lamp-black the whole of their palace. For this, the unreasonable villains clapped me into jail; and the gentlemen of the Eye-Sore trade could not well avoid cutting my connexion when I came out.

The Assault and Battery business, into which I was now forced to adventure for a livelihood, was somewhat ill-adapted to the delicate nature of my constitution; but I went to work in it with a good heart, and found my account, here as heretofore, in those stern habits of methodical accuracy which had been thumped into me by that delightful old nurse—I would indeed be the basest of men not to remember her well in my will. By observing, as I say, the strictest system in all my dealings, and keeping a well regulated set of books, I was enabled to get over many serious difficulties, and, in the end, to establish myself very decently in the profession. The truth is, that few individuals, in any line, did a snugger little business than I. I will just copy a page or so out of my Day-Book; and this will save me the necessity of blowing my own trumpet—a contemptible practice, of which no high-minded man will be guilty. Now, the Day-Book is a thing that don't lie.

"Jan. 1.—New Year's day. Met Snap in the street, groggy. Mem—he'll do. Met Gruff shortly afterwards, blind drunk. Mem—he'll answer, too. Enter both gentlemen in my Ledger, and opened a running account with each.

"Jan. 2.—Saw Snap at the Exchange, and went up and trod on his toe. Doubled his fist, and knocked me down. Good!—got up again. Some trifling difficulty with Bag, my attorney. I want the damages at a thousand, but he says that, for so simple a knockdown, we can't lay them at more than five hundred. Mem—must get rid of Bag—no *system* at all.

"Jan. 3.—Went to the theatre, to look for Gruff. Saw him sitting in a side box, in the second tier, between a fat lady and a lean one. Quizzed the whole party through an opera glass, till I saw the fat lady blush and whisper to G. Went round, then, into the box, and put my nose within reach of his hand. Wouldn't pull it—no go. Blew it, and tried again—no go. Sat down then, and winked at the lean lady, when I had the high satisfaction of finding him lift me up by the nape of the neck, and fling me over into the pit. Neck dislocated, and right leg capitally splintered. Went home in high glee, drank a bottle of champagne, and booked the young man for five thousand. Bag says it'll do.

"Feb. 15.—Compromised the case of Mr. Snap. Amount entered in Journal—fifty cents—which see.

"Feb. 16.—Cast by that villain, Gruff, who made me a present of five dollars. Costs of suit, four dollars and twenty five cents. Nett profit—see Journal—seventy-five cents."

Now, here is a clear gain, in a very brief period, of no less than one dollar and twenty five cents—this is in the mere cases of Snap and Gruff; and I solemnly assure the reader that these extracts are taken at random from my Day-Book.

It's an old saying, and a true one, however, that money is nothing in comparison with health. I found the exactions of the profession somewhat too much for my delicate state of body; and, discovering, at last, that I was knocked all out of shape, so that I didn't know very well what to make of the matter, and so that my friends, when they met me in the street, couldn't tell that I was Peter Proffit at all, it occurred to me that the best expedient I could adopt, was to alter my line of business. I turned my attention, therefore, to Mud-Dabbling, and continued it for some years.

The worst of this occupation, is, that too many people take a fancy to it, and the competition is in consequence excessive. Every ignoramus of a fellow who finds that he hasn't brains in sufficient quantity to make his way as a walking advertiser, or an eye-sore-prig, or a salt and batter man, thinks, of course, that he'll answer very well as a dabbler of mud. But there never was entertained a more erroneous idea than that it requires no brains to mud-dabble. Especially, there is nothing to be made in this way without *method*. I did only a retail business myself, but my old habits of *system* carried me swimmingly along. I selected my street-crossing, in the first place, with great deliberation, and I never put down a broom in any part of the town *but that*. I took care, too, to have a nice little puddle at hand, which I could get at in a minute. By these means I got to be well known as a man to be trusted; and this is one-half the battle, let me tell you, in trade. Nobody ever failed to pitch *me* a copper, and got over *my* crossing with a clean pair of pantaloons. And, as my business habits, in this respect, were sufficiently understood, I never met with any attempt at imposition. I wouldn't have put up with it, if I had. Never imposing upon any one myself, I suffered no one to play the possum with me. The frauds of the banks of course I couldn't help. Their suspension put me to ruinous inconvenience. These, however, are not individuals, but corporations; and corporations, it is very well known, have neither bodies to be kicked, nor souls to be damned.

I was making money at this business, when, in an evil moment, I was induced to merge it in the Cur-Spattering—a somewhat analogous, but, by no means, so respectable a profession. My location, to be sure, was an excellent one, being central, and I had capital blacking and brushes. My little dog, too, was quite fat and up to all varieties of snuff. He had been in the trade a long time, and, I may say, understood it. Our general routine was this:—Pompey, having rolled himself well in the mud, sat upon end at the shop door, until he observed a dandy approaching in bright boots. He then proceeded to meet him, and gave the Wellingtons a rub or two with his wool. Then the dandy swore very much, and looked about for a boot-black. There I was, full in his view, with blacking and brushes. It was only a minute's work, and then came a sixpence. This did moderately well for a time;—in fact, I was not avaricious, but my dog was. I allowed him a third of the profit, but he was advised to insist upon half. This I couldn't stand—so we quarreled and parted.

I next tried my hand at the Organ-Grinding for a while, and may say that I made out pretty well. It is a plain, straightforward business, and requires no particular abilities. You can get a music-mill for a mere song, and, to put it in order, you have but to open the works, and give them three or four smart raps with a hammer. It improves the tone of the thing, for business purposes, more than you can imagine. This done, you have only to stroll along, with the mill on your back, until you see tan-bark in the street, and a knocker wrapped up in buck skin. Then you stop and grind; looking as if you meant to stop and grind till doomsday. Presently a window opens, and somebody pitches you a sixpence, with a request to "Hush up and go on," &c. I am aware that some grinders have actually afforded to "go on" for this sum; but for my part, I found the necessary outlay of capital too great, to permit of my "going on" under a shilling.

At this occupation I did a good deal; but, somehow, I was not quite satisfied, and so finally abandoned it. The truth is, I labored under the disadvantage of having no monkey—and American streets are *so* muddy, and a Democratic rabble is *so* obtrusive, and so full of demnition mischievous little boys.

I was now out of employment for some months, but at length succeeded, by dint of great interest, in procuring a situation in the Sham-Post. The duties, here, are simple, and not altogether unprofitable. For example:—very early in the morning I had to make up my packet of sham letters. Upon the inside of each of these I had to scrawl a few lines—on any subject which occurred to me as sufficiently mysterious—signing all the epistles Tom Dobson, or Bobby Tompkins, or anything in that way. Having folded and sealed all, and stamped them with sham post-marks—New Orleans, Bengal, Botany Bay, or any other place a great way off—I set out, forthwith, upon my daily route, as if in a very great hurry. I always called at the big houses to deliver the letters, and receive the postage. Nobody hesitates at paying for a letter—especially for a double one—people are *such* fools—and it was no trouble to get round a corner before there was time to open the epistles. The worst of this profession was, that I had to walk so much and so fast; and so frequently to vary my route. Besides, I had serious scruples of conscience. I can't bear to hear innocent individuals abused—and the way the whole town took to cursing Tom Dobson and Bobby Tompkins, was really awful to hear. I washed my hands of the matter in disgust.

My eighth and last speculation has been in the Cat-Growing way. I have found this a most pleasant and lucrative business, and, really, no trouble at all. The country, it is well known, has become infested with cats—so much so of late, that a petition for relief, most numerously and respectably signed, was brought before the legislature at its last memorable session. The assembly, at this epoch, was unusually well-informed, and, having passed many other wise and wholesome enactments, it crowned all with the Cat-Act. In its original form, this law offered a premium for cat-*heads*, (four-pence a-piece) but the Senate succeeded in amending the main clause, so as to substitute the words *"tails"* for "heads." This amendment was so obviously proper, that the house concurred in it *nem. con.*

As soon as the Governor had signed the bill, I invested my whole estate in the purchase of Toms and Tabbies. At first, I could only afford to feed them upon mice (which are cheap) but they fulfilled the Scriptural injunction at so marvellous a rate, that I at length considered it my best policy to be liberal, and so indulged them in oysters and turtle. Their tails, at the legislative price, now bring me in a good income; for I have discovered a way, in which, by means of Macassar oil, I can force three crops in a year. It delights me to find, too, that the animals soon get accustomed to the thing, and would rather have the appendages cut off than otherwise. I consider myself, therefore, a made man, and am bargaining for a country seat on the Hudson.

EDGAR A. POE.

LEIGH HUNT

Leigh Hunt (1784–1859), essayist, and friend of Byron, Keats, and Shelley, was the grandson of Isaac Hunt (1742?–1809), a political enemy of Franklin in the 1770s. In his *Autobiography*, Hunt tells how as a youth he disliked his grandfather for inviting him to come to Philadelphia where "he would make a man of me." Hunt admits to an anti-American prejudice because of his grandfather: "As a nation, I can not get it out of my head, that the Americans are Englishmen with the poetry and romance taken out of them; and that there is one great counter built along their coast from north to south, behind which they are all standing like so many linendrapers." His view of Franklin is of a piece with his view of America. The opening "Partly on the same account" refers to his dislike for his grandfather.

From Hunt's *Autobiography*†

* * *

Partly on the same account, I acquired a dislike for my grandfather's friend Dr. Franklin, author of *Poor Richard's Almanack*: a heap, as it appeared to me, of "Scoundrel maxims."[1] I think I now appreciate Dr. Franklin as I ought; but although I can see the utility of such publications as his Almanack for a rising commercial state, and hold it useful as a memorandum to uncalculating persons like myself, who happen to live in an old one, I think it has no business either in commercial nations long established, or in others who do not found their happiness in that sort of power. Franklin, with all his abilities, is but at the head of those who think that man lives "by bread alone." He will commit none of the follies, none of the intolerances, the absence of which is necessary to the perfection of his system; and in setting his face against these, he discountenances a great number of things very inimical to higher speculations. But he was no more a fit representa-

---

† Source: Leigh Hunt, *Autobiography* (New York: Harper, 1850), I, 130–32.

1. Thomson's phrase, in the *Castle of Indolence*, speaking of a miserly money-getter:

> " 'A penny saved is a penny got;'
> Firm to this scoundrel maxim keepeth he,
> Ne of its rigor will he bate a jot,
> Till it hath quench'd his fire and banishèd
>   his pot."

The reader will not imagine that I suppose all money-makers to be of this description. Very gallant spirits are to be found, among them, who only take to this mode of activity for want of a better, and are as generous in disbursing as they are vigorous in acquiring. You may always know the common run, as in other instances, by the soreness with which they feel attacks on the body corporate.

For the assertion that Dr. Franklin cut off his son with a shilling, my only authority is family tradition. It is observable, however, that the friendliest of his biographers are not only forced to admit that he seemed a little too fond of money, but notice the mysterious secrecy in which his family history is involved. [Leigh Hunt's note.]

tive of what human nature largely requires, and may reasonably hope to attain to, than negative represents positive, or the clearing away a ground in the back-settlements, and setting to work upon it, represents the work in its completion. Something of the pettiness and materiality of his first occupation always stuck to him. He took nothing for a truth or a matter-of-fact that he could not handle, as it were, like his types: and yet, like all men of this kind, he was liable, when put out of the ordinary pale of his calculations, to fall into the greatest errors, and substitute the integrity of his reputation for that of whatsoever he chose to do. From never doing wrong in little things, he conceived that he could do no wrong in great; and, in the most deliberate act of his life, he showed he had grievously mistaken himself. He was, I allow, one of the *cardinal* great men of his time. He was Prudence. But he was not what he took himself for—all the other Virtues besides; and, inasmuch as he was deficient in those, he was deficient even in his favorite one. He was not Temperance; for, in the teeth of his capital recommendations of that virtue, he did not scruple to get burly and big with the enjoyments that he cared for. He was not Justice; for he knew not how to see fair play between his own wisdom and that of a thousand wants and aspirations, of which he knew nothing: and he cut off his son with a shilling, for differing with him in politics. Lastly, he was not Fortitude; for having few passions and no imagination, he knew not what it was to be severely tried; and if he had been there is every reason to conclude, from the way in which he treated his son, that his self-love would have been the part in which he felt the torture; that as his Justice was only arithmetic, so his Fortitude would have been nothing but stubbornness.

If Franklin had been the only great man of his time, he would merely have contributed to make the best of a bad system, and so hurt the world by prolonging it; but, luckily, there were the French and English philosophers besides, who saw farther than he did, and provided for higher wants. I feel grateful to him, for one, inasmuch as he extended the sphere of liberty, and helped to clear the earth of the weeds of sloth and ignorance, and the wild beasts of superstition; but when he comes to build final homes for us, I rejoice that wiser hands interfere. His line and rule are not every thing; they are not even a tenth part of it. Cocker's numbers are good; but those of Plato and Pythagoras have their merits too, or we should have been made of dry bones and tangents, and not had the fancies in our heads, and the hearts beating in our bosoms, that make us what we are. We should not even have known that Cocker's numbers were worth any thing; nor would Dr. Franklin himself have played on the harmonica, albeit he must have done it in a style very different from that of Milton or Cimarosa. Finally, the writer of this passage on the Doctor would not have ventured to give his opinion of so great a man in so explicit a manner. I should not have ventured to give it, had I not been backed by so many powerful interests of humanity, and had I not suffered in common, and more than in common, with the rest of the world, from a system which, under the guise of economy and social advantage, tends to double the love of wealth and the hostility of competition, to force the best things down to a level with the worst, and to reduce mankind to the simplest and most mechanical law of their nature, divested of its heart and soul—the law of being in motion. Most of the advantages of the present system of money-making, which may be called the great *lay* superstition of modern times, might be obtained by a fifth part of the labor, if more equally distributed. Yet all the advantages could not be so obtained; and the system is necessary as a portion of the movement of time and progress, and as the ultimate means of dispensing with its very self.

* * *

HERMAN MELVILLE

Herman Melville (1819–91), evidently read widely in Franklin, perhaps in Jared Sparks's edition, *The Works of Benjamin Franklin*, 10 v. (Boston: Hilliard, Gray & Co., 1836–40). Melville alludes to Franklin and his writings numerous times, and presents a detailed impression in his semi-historical novel *Israel Potter*.

From *Israel Potter*†

Chapter 8

WHICH HAS SOMETHING TO SAY ABOUT DR. FRANKLIN
AND THE LATIN QUARTER

THE first, both in point of time and merit, of American envoys was famous not less for the pastoral simplicity of his manners than for the politic grace of his mind. Viewed from a certain point, there was a touch of primeval orientalness in Benjamin Franklin. Neither is there wanting something like his scriptural parallel. The history of the patriarch Jacob is interesting not less from the unselfish devotion which we are bound to ascribe to him, than from the deep worldly wisdom and polished Italian tact, gleaming under an air of Arcadian unaffectedness. The diplomatist and the shepherd are blended; a union not without warrant; the apostolic serpent and dove. A tanned Machiavelli in tents.

Doubtless, too, notwithstanding his eminence as lord of the moving

† Source: *Israel Potter: His Fifty Years of Exile* (1855).

manor, Jacob's raiment was of homespun; the economic envoy's plain coat and hose, who has not heard of ?

Franklin all over is of a piece. He dressed his person as his periods; neat, trim, nothing superfluous, nothing deficient. In some of his works his style is only surpassed by the unimprovable sentences of Hobbes of Malmesbury,[1] the paragon of perspicuity. The mental habits of Hobbes and Franklin in several points, especially in one of some moment, assimilated. Indeed, making due allowance for soil and era, history presents few trios more akin, upon the whole, than Jacob, Hobbes, and Franklin; three labyrinth-minded, but plain-spoken Broadbrims,[2] at once politicians and philosophers; keen observers of the main chance; prudent courtiers; practical Magians in linsey-woolsey.

In keeping with his general habitudes, Doctor Franklin while at the French Court did not reside in the aristocratical faubourgs. He deemed his worsted hose and scientific tastes more adapted in a domestic way to the other side of the Seine, where the Latin Quarter, at once the haunt of erudition and economy, seemed peculiarly to invite the philosophical Poor Richard to its venerable retreats.

* * *

In this congenial vicinity of the Latin Quarter, and in an ancient building something like those alluded to, at a point midway between the Palais des Beaux Arts and the College of the Sorbonne, the venerable American envoy pitched his tent when not passing his time at his country retreat at Passy. The frugality of his manner of life did not lose him the good opinion even of the voluptuaries of the showiest of capitals, whose very iron railings are not free from gilt. Franklin was not less a lady's man, than a man's man, a wise man, and an old man. Not only did he enjoy the homage of the choicest Parisian literati, but at the age of seventy-two he was the caressed favourite of the highest born beauties of the Court; who through blind fashion having been originally attracted to him as a famous savant, were permanently retained as his admirers by his Plato-like graciousness of good humour. Having carefully weighed the world, Franklin could act any part in it. By nature turned to knowledge, his mind was often grave, but never serious. At times he had seriousness—extreme seriousness—for others, but never for himself. Tranquillity was to him instead of it. This philosophical levity of tranquillity, so to speak, is shown in his easy variety of pursuits. Printer, post-master, almanac maker, essayist, chemist, orator, tinker, statesman, humorist, philosopher, parlour man, political economist, professor of housewifery, ambassador, projector, maxim-monger, herb-doctor, wit: Jack of all trades, master of each and mastered by none—the type and genius

---

1. Thomas Hobbes (1588–1679), English philosopher, author of *Leviathan* (1651).
2. Although generally restricted to Quakers,

"Broadbrims" here suggests a combination of morality and worldliness.

of his land. Franklin was everything but a poet. But since a soul with many qualities, forming of itself a sort of handy index and pocket congress of all humanity, needs the contact of just as many different men, or subjects, in order to the exhibition of its totality; hence very little indeed of the sage's multifariousness will be portrayed in a simple narrative like the present. This casual private intercourse with Israel but served to manifest him in his far lesser lights; thrifty, domestic, dietarian, and, it may be, didactically waggish. There was much benevolent irony, innocent mischievousness, in the wise man. Seeking here to depict him in his less exalted habitudes, the narrator feels more as if he were playing with one of the sage's worsted hose, than reverentially handling the honoured hat which once oracularly sat upon his brow.

* * *

ANONYMOUS

An anonymous reviewer of John Bigelow's edition of the *Autobiography* attempted to account for the opposed attitudes toward Franklin and the *Autobiography*.

From *The Nation*, 1868†

* * * Of the memoirs themselves—which are Franklin himself —it is late in the day to be saying anything. It is not only late, but nothing, perhaps, would be harder. To criticise it thoroughly, is to go to the bottom of things—to answer jesting Pilate and to find the *summum bonum*. From the beginning of the world till now, mankind divides into two classes, of which you may say that one are natural-born lovers and believers, and the other are natural-born haters and despisers of this "Autobiography." Is religion the policing of society, or is it more? Is the ideal the only real, or is it a more or less hateful delusion? What is God? The men "diligent in business"—of clear heads due to good digestions consequent on sagacious feeding—who finally "stand before princes" according to the text, are these the children of whom Wisdom is justified, or are they servants, not heirs? In short, is this world the be-all and the end-all and is "the beautifull regularity of Philadelphia" the be-all and the end-all of this world, or is the teacher who makes it so to be reviled as a hog of Epicurus's sty?[1] It

† Source: "Bigelow's Franklin," *The Nation*, 7 (9 July 1868), 35.
1. Someone who believes only in the senses; a   degenerate follower of the materialism of the Greek philosopher Epicurus (341–270 B.C.).

is as men answer these questions that they extol or abase Poor Richard. In fact, there are disciples who incline toward acceptance of the general doctrines of which our Philadelphia philosopher has fairly enough been made the representative, who yet yield him only a qualified fealty, and have helped as much as some of his natural enemies to keep his fame down. It is not given to the mass of mankind, only to one here and there, they say, to be "earthly" without fulfilling the whole of the scripture which reads "earthly, sensual, devilish." The earthiness of Mr. Parton's "greatest of Americans,"[2] unaccompanied by his weight of brain, is the mud and mire in which the race has been stalled since Adam, and which it is the labor of prophets, priests, poets, the poor metaphysician, and other non-producers, to lighten and brighten; and it would bother all the saints—of Positivism, we were going to say—of M. Comte's[3] old age to "inform the clay" of more than a few of us if they had no more than a spark from Saint Franklin's easily accessible heavens.

Still, there is need of no quarrel between the disciples and the scoffers. Or, in the golden age, there will be no need. And Franklin will then get his due of praise as the most common-sensible of men in a world not ripe yet for pure common sense, and which, when it is ripe for that, as that is now known to us, will be ripe for something better. For "common sense" is in the nature of a means to an end, and how to attain that end perhaps Marcus Aurelius[4] and others will teach us better than our good-natured, strong-bodied, strong-headed Philadelphia *philosophe*. But even now there is no great need of quarrel. It ought to be quite possible, we suppose, for Mr. Bronson Alcott,[5] of Concord, to agree with Mr. Bigelow when he frames a wish for "the rising generation of Americans" that they may "study the lessons of humility, economy, industry, toleration, charity, and patriotism which are made so captivating in this 'Autobiography.' " The transcendentalist, when he sees the world sinking into base prosperity, and feeding fat under the shrines of the housekeeping gods, may comfort himself with the remarks of his own Saadi[6] concerning the relation between the manure and the roses. "The intelligent are aware," says Saadi, "that the zeal of devotion is made warmer by good fare, and the sincerity of piety rendered more serene in a nicety of vesture: for he that is poor is well-nigh being an infidel;" and it will be a sad day for loathed materialism when we all have walked with Poor Richard far enough to have got ahead of the world.

2. James Parton (1822–91), author of the major biography *Benjamin Franklin*, 2 vols. (1864).
3. Auguste Comte (1798–1857), French philosopher of positivism, which excludes metaphysics and revealed religion.
4. Marcus Aurelius (121–180 A.D.), Roman emperor, whose *Meditations* reflect the religious Stoic traditions.
5. Bronson Alcott (1799–1888), radical American transcendentalist.
6. Sadi (fl. 1200), Persian poet whose *Gulistan* or *Rose-Garden* was a favorite work among American transcendentalists.

MARK TWAIN

As a newspaperman, printer, humorist and writer, Twain followed in an American tradition begun by Franklin. Although this is his only sustained piece on Franklin, Twain shows by allusions throughout his writings that he, too, has read widely in Franklin. As Alan Gribben shows in his monumental study *Mark Twain's Library*, 2 vols. (Boston: G.K. Hall, 1980), pp. 241–43, Twain's attitude was strongly influenced by the great admiration for Franklin of Orion Clemens, Twain's beloved older brother, who even imitated the regimens Franklin imposed upon himself and who, dying young, was thought by Twain to have failed in his aspirations. Although Twain reveals in the following primarily humorous piece that he has chafed at Poor Richard's proverbs and at the example Franklin presents in the *Autobiography*, yet the portrait contains considerable irony, partially because it recalls his beloved deceased brother, partially because Twain appreciates Franklin both as a prototype of the self-made man and as a great genius, and partially because Twain sees himself as a latter-day Franklin.

The Late Benjamin Franklin†

[Never put off till to-morrow what you can do day after to-morrow just as well.—B.F.]

This party was one of those persons whom they call Philosophers. He was twins, being born simultaneously in two different houses in the city of Boston. These houses remain unto this day, and have signs upon them worded in accordance with the facts. The signs are considered well enough to have, though not necessary, because the inhabitants point out the two birth-places to the stranger anyhow, and sometimes as often as several times in the same day. The subject of this memoir was of a vicious disposition, and early prostituted his talents to the invention of maxims and aphorisms calculated to inflict suffering upon the rising generation of all subsequent ages. His simplest acts, also, were contrived with a view to their being held up for the emulation of boys forever—boys who might otherwise have been happy. It was in this spirit that he became the son of a soap-boiler; and probably for no other reason than that the efforts of all future boys who tried to be anything might be looked upon with suspicion unless they were the sons of soap-boilers. With a malevolence which is without parallel in history, he would work all day and then sit up nights and let on to be studying algebra by the light of a smouldering fire, so that all other boys might have to do that also or else have Benjamin Franklin thrown up to them. Not satisfied with these proceedings, he had a fashion of living wholly on bread and water, and studying astronomy at meal time—a thing which has brought affliction to millions of boys since, whose fathers had read Franklin's pernicious biography.

His maxims were full of animosity toward boys. Nowadays a boy cannot follow out a single natural instinct without tumbling over some of those everlasting aphorisms and hearing from Franklin on the spot. If he buys two cents' worth of peanuts, his father says, "Remember what Franklin has said, my son,—'A groat a day's a penny a year;' " and the comfort is all gone out of those peanuts. If he wants to spin his top when he is done work, his father quotes, "Procrastination is the thief of time." If he does a virtuous action, he never gets anything for it, because "Virtue is its own reward." And that boy is hounded to death and robbed of his natural rest, because Franklin said once in one of his inspired flights of malignity—

> Early to bed and early to rise
> Make a man healthy and wealthy and wise.

As if it were any object to a boy to be healthy and wealthy and wise on such terms. The sorrow that that maxim has cost me through my parents' experimenting on me with it, tongue cannot tell. The legitimate result is my present state of general debility, indigence, and mental aberration. My parents used to have me up before nine o'clock in the morning, sometimes, when I was a boy. If they had let me take my natural rest, where would I have been now? Keeping store, no doubt, and respected by all.

And what an adroit old adventurer the subject of this memoir was! In order to get a chance to fly his kite on Sunday, he used to hang a key on the string and let on to be fishing for lightning. And a guileless public would go home chirping about the "wisdom" and the "genius" of the hoary Sabbath-breaker. If anybody caught him playing "mumble-peg" by himself, after the age of sixty, he would immediately appear to be ciphering out how the grass grew—as if it was any of his business. My grandfather knew him well, and he says Franklin was always fixed—always ready. If a body, during his old age, happened on him unexpectedly when he was catching flies, or making mud pies, or sliding on a cellar-door, he would immediately look wise, and rip out a maxim, and walk off with his nose in the air and his cap turned wrong side before, trying to appear absent-minded and eccentric. He was a hard lot.

He invented a stove that would smoke your head off in four hours by the clock. One can see the almost devilish satisfaction he took in it, by his giving it his name.

He was always proud of telling how he entered Philadelphia, for the first time, with nothing in the world but two shillings in his pocket and four rolls of bread under his arm. But really, when you come to examine it critically, it was nothing. Anybody could have done it.

To the subject of this memoir belongs the honor of recommending the army to go back to bows and arrows in place of bayonets and muskets. He observed, with his customary force, that the bayonet was very well, under some circumstances, but that he doubted whether it could be used with accuracy at long range.

Benjamin Franklin did a great many notable things for his country, and made her young name to be honored in many lands as the mother of such a son. It is not the idea of this memoir to ignore that or cover it up. No; the simple idea of it is to snub those pretentious maxims of his, which he worked up with a great show of originality out of truisms that had become wearisome platitudes as early as the dispersion from Babel; and also to snub his stove, and his military inspirations, his unseemly endeavor to make himself conspicuous when he entered Philadelphia, and his flying his kite and fooling away his time in all sorts of such ways, when he ought to have been foraging for soap-fat, or constructing candles. I merely desired to do away with somewhat of the prevalent calamitous idea among heads of families that Franklin *acquired* his great genius by working for nothing, studying by moonlight, and getting up in the night instead of waiting till morning like a Christian, and that this programme, rigidly inflicted, will make a Franklin of every father's fool. It is time these gentlemen were finding out that these execrable eccentricities of instinct and conduct are only the *evidences* of genius, not the *creators* of it. I wish I had been the father of my parents long enough to make them comprehend this truth, and thus prepare them to let their son have an easier time of it. When I was a child I had to boil soap, notwithstanding my father was wealthy, and I had to get up early and study geometry at breakfast, and peddle my own poetry, and do everything just as Franklin did, in the solemn hope that I would be a Franklin some day. And here I am.

FREDERICK JACKSON TURNER

The great American historian Frederick Jackson Turner began a review of an important book about Franklin with a splendid appreciation of his reputation, image, and achievement.

From *The Dial*, May, 1887†

* * *

Of late the question has been asked, Who was the first great American? If we accept as necessary conditions of this title that the recipient must be preëminently the representative of the leading tendencies of the nation, original as it is original, and that he must have won and held the admiration of the world, whom can we find to

† Source: *The Dial*, 8 (May, 1887), 7–8.

fulfil the requirements before Benjamin Franklin, and who has better satisfied them? His greatness lay in his ability to apply to the world a shrewd understanding that disclosed in the ordinary things about him potent forces for helpfulness. His life is the story of American common-sense in its highest form, applied to business, to politics, to science, to diplomacy, to religion, to philanthropy. Surely this self-made man, the apostle of the practical and the useful, is by the verdict of his own country and of Europe entitled to the distinction of being the first great American. Probably the three men who would find the choicest niches in an American Pantheon would be Franklin, Washington, and Lincoln. They achieved their success not so much by brilliancy of the higher intellectual powers as by their personal character. This is generally recognized in the case of Washington and of Lincoln, and it will be apparent in that of Franklin if we consider the leading incidents in his political services. There is truth in the remark of Condorcet[1] that he was really an envoy not to the ministers of France, but to her people. He was welcomed by them not alone as the wise and simple searcher of nature's secrets; it was the Poor Richard wearing his fur cap among the powdered wigs, the shrewd humorist, the liberal in religion, the plain republican, that became the idol of the gay society of the Ancient Régime. Of such a man in such an age one can scarcely gain too full a knowledge.

*   *   *

WILLIAM DEAN HOWELLS

Although Howells never wrote at length on Franklin, he reviewed several books dealing with him (including Bigelow's edition of the *Autobiography* in 1868) and gave his characteristically thoughtful opinions in snippets over a course of more than forty years. In 1888, reviewing John Bach McMaster's *Life of Franklin*, he delivered a judiciously balanced opinion.

From "Editor's Study," April, 1888†

* * * One cannot very well mention autobiography without mentioning Franklin, whose fragment in that sort remains the chief literary work of his life, and the perpetual pleasure of whoever likes to meet a man face to face in literature.* * *

Franklin, who was in many if not most respects the greatest American of his time, has come down to ours with more reality than any of

---

1. The Marquis de Condorcet (1743–94), French philosopher, revolutionary, and BF's friend, made a speech (November 13, 1790) on Franklin after his death.
† Source: "Editor's Study," *Harper's*, 76 (April, 1888), 804–5.

his contemporaries, and this has by no means hurt him in the popular regard. It could not be shown by the most enthusiastic whitewasher that Franklin's personal conduct was exemplary, and Professor McMaster is not a whitewasher. He is not tempted to paint Franklin as a hero or a saint, and Franklin was assuredly neither. But he was a very great man, and the objects to which he dedicated himself with an unfailing mixture of motive were such as concerned the immediate comfort of men, and the advancement of knowledge in even greater degree than they promoted Franklin's own advantage. He tore the lightning from the clouds, and the sceptre from tyrants; he also invented the Franklin stove, and gave America her first postal system. He was a great natural philosopher, a patriotic statesman, a skilful diplomatist, a master of English prose; he was likewise the father of a natural son whose mother he abandoned to absolute oblivion; he was a rather blackguardly newspaper man, a pitiless business rival, a pretty selfish liberal politician, and at times (occasionally the wrong times) a trivial humorist. The sum of him was the intellectual giant who towers through history over his contemporaries, indifferent to fame, almost cynically incredulous of ideals and beliefs sacred to most of us, but instrumental in promoting the moral and material welfare of the race; a hater of folly, idleness, and unthrift; and finally, one of the most truthful men who ever lived. It would be hard to idolize him or to overvalue him.

[Howells returned to Franklin in July of 1888, in an essay concerned with Matthew Arnold's criticisms of America. Replying to Arnold's stricture that America lacked men of "distinction," Howells claimed that this very lack of an aristocratic tradition was the hallmark of American democratic success. And naturally this thought took him to the creation of the American democracy— an evolving civilization which Howells hoped would continue to become more democratic.]

From "Editor's Study," July, 1888†

* * * We spoke in a recent Study of the character of Franklin, and we think of him now as the most modern, the most American, among his contemporaries. Franklin had apparently none of the distinction which Mr. Arnold lately found lacking in us; he seems to have been a man who could no more impose upon the imagination of men used to abase themselves before birth, wealth, achievement, or mastery in any sort, as very many inferior men have done in all times, than Lincoln or Grant. But he was more modern, more American than any of his contemporaries in this, though some of them were of more democratic ideals than he. His simple and plebeian past made it impossible for a man of his common-sense to assume any superiority

† Source: "Editor's Study," *Harper's*, 77 (July, 1888), 316.

of bearing, and the unconscious hauteur which comes of aristocratic breeding, and expresses itself at its best in distinction, was equally impossible to him.* * *

[When Howells was reviewing Mark Twain's latest book, A *Connecticut Yankee at the Court of King Arthur* in January, 1890, he made some remarks about the traditions of American humor.]

From "Editor's Study," January, 1890†

* * *

This kind of humor, the American kind, the kind employed in the service of democracy, of humanity, began with us a long time ago; in fact Franklin may be said to have torn it with the lightning from the skies. Some time, some such critic as Mr. T. S. Perry[1] (if we ever have another such) will study its evolution in the century of our literature and civilization; but no one need deny himself meanwhile the pleasure we feel in Mr. Clemens's book as its highest development.
* * *

[In October, 1905, Howells reviewed a new autobiography which, in turn, led him to think of the origins and traditions of autobiography as a genre.]

From "Editor's Easy Chair," October, 1905††

* * *

Autobiography is almost as modern a thing in letters as music in the arts, and it is perhaps still more modern in its development. * * *

Why with the revival of learning this agreeable species of literature should have sprung up, and since flourished so vigorously, with such richness of flower and fruit, in almost every modern language, it would be curious to inquire, but such an inquiry would lead our wandering steps too far. It seems to have risen from that nascent sense of the importance of each to all which the antique world apparently ignored; and perhaps the wonder should be that we have not ourselves more abounded in it. Autobiography seems supremely the Christian contribution to the forms of literaturing. As the special charge and care of the Almighty, every anxious soul has doubtless had the impulse to record its aspirations and experiences; and many, we know, have done so, the weaker souls keeping to the narrative of their sins and sufferings, and the stronger souls involuntarily glancing, if only

---

† Source: "Editor's Study," *Harper's*, 80 (Jan., 1890), 321.

1. Thomas Sergeant Perry (1845–1928), American intellectual, had recently written

English Literature of the Eighteenth Century (1883).

†† Source: "Editor's Easy Chair," *Harper's*, 119 (Oct., 1905), 795–96.

askance, at the manners and customs of the provisional world they were born into. One of the most charming in this involuntary humanness is the brief, too brief, autobiography of the great Jonathan Edwards,[1] the mighty theologue who first gave our poor American provinciality world-standing, and did for us in one way almost as much as Franklin in another. Edwards's sketch of his own life is very slight, and Franklin's is more lamentably slight. Yet Franklin's is one of the greatest autobiographies in literature, and towers over other autobiographies as Franklin towered over other men. It is about as long as Goethe's autobiography,[2] and goes about as far as that in the story of the author's life. If either had gone farther, the record might have come to things of less real value to the reader, to impersonal things, to the things that history is made of; but in a region of literature rich in masterpieces they remain alike monumental, and exalt forever the memories of geniuses equally great; for the sage whose make was pure prose was not inferior to the sage whose make was of poetry and prose a good deal mixed.

* * *

1. Jonathan Edwards (1703–58), American theologian, whose "Personal Narrative" is a classic spiritual autobiography.

2. Goethe (1749–1832), the great German author of *Faust*, wrote an autobiography entitled *Dichtung und Wahrheit* (1831).

Twentieth-Century Opinions

In addition to numerous specialized studies, twentieth-century Franklin scholars brought out Smyth's edition of Franklin's writings (1907), the excellent biography by Carl Van Doren (1938), and the great edition of *The Papers of Benjamin Franklin* (in progress; 20 vols. to 1978). D. H. Lawrence (who seems to have read only the *Autobiography* and *The Way to Wealth*) published the classic attack on Franklin as a spiritual philistine in 1923. And, in opposition to the religionists who reviled Franklin from his own day to our time, the great German sociologist Max Weber, in his deservedly influential Marxist interpretation, introduced a new twist by portraying Franklin as a typical example of the Protestant ethic, although Weber continued one nineteenth-century criticism by finding that Franklin embodied American capitalism. Although the old prejudices persist (the descendants of Adams, Lee, et al, generally being succeeded by partisan scholars) and new neurotic scholars appear on the scene, there have been a number of sane and informed and even brilliant historical and critical studies of Franklin's prolific achievements in science, diplomacy, literature and life by Alfred Owen Aldridge, I. Bernard Cohen, Verner W. Crane, and Claude-Anne Lopez, among others.

MAX WEBER

Excerpt from *The Protestant Ethic and the Spirit of Capitalism*†

IN the title of this study is used the somewhat pretentious phrase, the *spirit* of capitalism. What is to be understood by it? The attempt to give anything like a definition of it brings out certain difficulties which are in the very nature of this type of investigation.

If any object can be found to which this term can be applied with any understandable meaning, it can only be an historical individual, i.e. a complex of elements associated in historical reality which we unite into a conceptual whole from the standpoint of their cultural significance.

Such an historical concept, however, since it refers in its content to a phenomenon significant for its unique individuality, cannot be defined according to the formula *genus proximum, differentia specifica*,[1] but it must be gradually put together out of the individual parts which are taken from historical reality to make it up. Thus the

† Source: Max Weber, *The Protestant Ethic and the Spirit of Capitalism*. Trans. Talcott Parsons. London: Allen & Unwin, 1930, pp. 47–56, 192–98. Except where otherwise speci-

fied, the notes are Weber's.
1. Classified according to genus and species. [Editors' Note.]

final and definitive concept cannot stand at the beginning of the investigation, but must come at the end. We must, in other words, work out in the course of the discussion, as its most important result, the best conceptual formulation of what we here understand by the spirit of capitalism, that is the best from the point of view which interests us here. This point of view (the one of which we shall speak later) is, further, by no means the only possible one from which the historical phenomena we are investigating can be analysed. Other standpoints would, for this as for every historical phenomenon, yield other characteristics as the essential ones. The result is that it is by no means necessary to understand by the spirit of capitalism only what it will come to mean to *us* for the purposes of our analysis. This is a necessary result of the nature of historical concepts which attempt for their methodological purposes not to grasp historical reality in abstract general formulæ, but in concrete genetic sets of relations which are inevitably of a specifically unique and individual character.[2]

Thus, if we try to determine the object, the analysis and historical explanation of which we are attempting, it cannot be in the form of a conceptual definition, but at least in the beginning only a provisional description of what is here meant by the spirit of capitalism. Such a description is, however, indispensable in order clearly to understand the object of the investigation. For this purpose we turn to a document of that spirit which contains what we are looking for in almost classical purity, and at the same time has the advantage of being free from all direct relationship to religion, being thus, for our purposes, free of preconceptions.

"Remember, that *time* is money. He that can earn ten shillings a day by his labour, and goes abroad, or sits idle, one half of that day, though he spends but sixpence during his diversion or idleness, ought not to reckon *that* the only expense; he has really spent, or rather thrown away, five shillings besides.

"Remember, that *credit* is money. If a man lets his money lie in my hands after it is due, he gives me the interest, or so much as I can make of it during that time. This amounts to a considerable sum where a man has good and large credit, and makes good use of it.

"Remember, that money is of the prolific, generating nature.

2. These passages represent a very brief summary of some aspects of Weber's methodological views. At about the same time that he wrote this essay he was engaged in a thorough criticism and revaluation of the methods of the Social Sciences, the result of which was a point of view in many ways different from the prevailing one, especially outside of Germany. In order thoroughly to understand the significance of this essay in its wider bearings on Weber's sociological work as a whole it is necessary to know what his methodological aims were. Most of his writings on this subject have been assembled since his death (in 1920) in the volume *Gesammelte Aufsäze zur Wissenschaftslehre.* A shorter exposition of the main position is contained in the opening chapters of *Wirtschaft und Gesellschaft, Grundriss der Sozialökonomik,* III.–TRANSLATOR'S NOTE.

Money can beget money, and its offspring can beget more, and so on. Five shillings turned is six, turned again it is seven and threepence, and so on, till it becomes a hundred pounds. The more there is of it, the more it produces every turning, so that the profits rise quicker and quicker. He that kills a breeding-sow, destroys all her offspring to the thousandth generation. He that murders a crown, destroys all that it might have produced, even scores of pounds."

"Remember this saying, *The good paymaster is lord of another man's purse.* He that is known to pay punctually and exactly to the time he promises, may at any time, and on any occasion, raise all the money his friends can spare. This is sometimes of great use. After industry and frugality, nothing contributes more to the raising of a young man in the world than punctuality and justice in all his dealings; therefore never keep borrowed money an hour beyond the time you promised, lest a disappointment shut up your friend's purse for ever.

"The most trifling actions that affect a man's credit are to be regarded. The sound of your hammer at five in the morning, or eight at night, heard by a creditor, makes him easy six months longer; but if he sees you at a billiard-table, or hears your voice at a tavern, when you should be at work, he sends for his money the next day; demands it, before he can receive it, in a lump.

"It shows, besides, that you are mindful of what you owe; it makes you appear a careful as well as an honest man, and that still increases your credit.

"Beware of thinking all your own that you possess, and of living accordingly. It is a mistake that many people who have credit fall into. To prevent this, keep an exact account for some time both of your expenses and your income. If you take the pains at first to mention particulars, it will have this good effect: you will discover how wonderfully small, trifling expenses mount up to large sums, and will discern what might have been, and may for the future be saved, without occasioning any great inconvenience."

"For six pounds a year you may have the use of one hundred pounds, provided you are a man of known prudence and honesty.

"He that spends a groat a day idly, spends idly above six pounds a year, which is the price for the use of one hundred pounds.

"He that wastes idly a groat's worth of his time per day, one day with another, wastes the privilege of using one hundred pounds each day.

"He that idly loses five shillings' worth of time, loses five shillings, and might as prudently throw five shillings into the sea.

"He that loses five shillings, not only loses that sum, but all the advantage that might be made by turning it in dealing, which by the time that a young man becomes old, will amount to a considerable sum of money."[3]

It is Benjamin Franklin who preaches to us in these sentences, the same which Ferdinand Kürnberger satirizes in his clever and malicious *Picture of American Culture*[4] as the supposed confession of faith of the Yankee. That it is the spirit of capitalism which here speaks in characteristic fashion, no one will doubt, however little we may wish to claim that everything which could be understood as pertaining to that spirit is contained in it. Let us pause a moment to consider this passage, the philosophy of which Kürnberger sums up in the words, "They make tallow out of cattle and money out of men". The peculiarity of this philosophy of avarice appears to be the ideal of the honest man of recognized credit, and above all the idea of a duty of the individual toward the increase of his capital, which is assumed as an end in itself. Truly what is here preached is not simply a means of making one's way in the world, but a peculiar ethic. The infraction of its rules is treated not as foolishness but as forgetfulness of duty. That is the essence of the matter. It is not mere business astuteness, that sort of thing is common enough, it is an ethos. *This* is the quality which interests us.

When Jacob Fugger, in speaking to a business associate who had retired and who wanted to persuade him to do the same, since he had made enough money and should let others have a chance, rejected that as pusillanimity and answered that "he (Fugger) thought otherwise, he wanted to make money as long as he could",[5] the spirit of his statement is evidently quite different from that of Franklin. What in the former case was an expression of commercial daring and a personal inclination morally neutral,[6] in the latter takes on the character of an ethically coloured maxim for the conduct of life. The concept spirit of

3. The final passage is from *Necessary Hints to Those That Would Be Rich* (written 1736, Works, Sparks edition, II, p. 80), the rest from *Advice to a Young Tradesman* (written 1748, Sparks edition, II, pp. 87 ff.). The italics in the text are Franklin's.

4. *Der Amerikamüde* (Frankfurt, 1855), well known to be an imaginative paraphrase of Lenau's impressions of America. As a work of art the book would to-day be somewhat difficult to enjoy, but it is incomparable as a document of the (now long since blurred-over) differences between the German and the American outlook, one may even say of the type of spiritual life which, in spite of everything, has remained common to all Germans, Catholic and Protestant alike, since the German mysticism of the Middle Ages, as against the Puritan capitalistic valuation of action.

5. Sombart has used this quotation as a motto for his section dealing with the genesis of capitalism (*Der moderne Kapitalismus*, first edition, I, p. 193. See also p. 390).

6. Which quite obviously does not mean either that Jacob Fugger was a morally indifferent or an irreligious man, or that Benjamin Franklin's ethic is completely covered by the above quotations. It scarcely required Brentano's quotations (*Die Anfänge des modernen Kapitalismus*, pp. 150 ff.) to protect this well-known philanthropist from the misunderstanding which Brentano seems to attribute to me. The problem is just the reverse: how could such a philanthropist come to write these particular sentences (the especially characteristic form of which Brentano has neglected to reproduce) in the manner of a moralist?

capitalism is here used in this specific sense,[7] it is the spirit of modern capitalism. For that we are here dealing only with Western European and American capitalism is obvious from the way in which the problem was stated. Capitalism existed in China, India, Babylon, in the classic world, and in the Middle Ages. But in all these cases, as we shall see, this particular ethos was lacking.

Now, all Franklin's moral attitudes are coloured with utilitarianism. Honesty is useful, because it assures credit; so are punctuality, industry, frugality, and that is the reason they are virtues. A logical deduction from this would be that where, for instance, the appearance of honesty serves the same purpose, that would suffice, and an unnecessary surplus of this virtue would evidently appear to Franklin's eyes as unproductive waste. And as a matter of fact, the story in his autobiography of his conversion to those virtues,[8] or the discussion of the value of a strict maintenance of the appearance of modesty, the assiduous belittlement of one's own deserts in order to gain general recognition later,[9] confirms this impression. According to Franklin, those virtues, like all others, are only in so far virtues as they are actually useful to the individual, and the surrogate of mere appearance is always sufficient when it accomplishes the end in view. It is a conclusion which is inevitable for strict utilitarianism. The impression of many Germans that the virtues professed by Americanism are pure hypocrisy seems to have been confirmed by this striking case. But in fact the matter is not by any means so simple. Benjamin Franklin's own character, as it appears in the really unusual

7. This is the basis of our difference from Sombart in stating the problem. Its very considerable practical significance will become clear later. In anticipation, however, let it be remarked that Sombart has by no means neglected this ethical aspect of the capitalistic entrepreneur. But in his view of the problem it appears as a result of capitalism, whereas for our purposes we must assume the opposite as an hypothesis. A final position can only be taken up at the end of the investigation. For Sombart's view see *op. cit.*, pp. 357, 380, etc. His reasoning here connects with the brilliant analysis given in Simmel's *Philosophie des Geldes* (final chapter). Of the polemics which he has brought forward against me in his *Bourgeois* I shall come to speak later. At this point any thorough discussion must be postponed.
8. "I grew convinced that truth, sincerity, and integrity in dealings between man and man were of the utmost importance to the felicity of life; and I formed written resolutions, which still remain in my journal book to practise them ever while I lived. Revelation had indeed no weight with me as such; but I entertained an opinion that, though certain actions might not be bad because they were forbidden by it, or good because it commanded them, yet probably these actions might be forbidden because they were bad for us, or commanded because they were beneficial to us in their own nature, all the circumstances of things considered." *Autobiography* (ed. F. W. Pine, Henry Holt, New York, 1916), p. 112. [See this edition, p. 46.]
9. "I therefore put myself as much as I could out of sight and started it"—that is the project of a library which he had initiated—"as a scheme of a *number of friends*, who had requested me to go about and propose it to such as they thought lovers of reading. In this way my affair went on smoothly, and I ever after practised it on such occasions; and from my frequent successes, can heartily recommend it. The present little sacrifice of your vanity will afterwards be amply repaid. If it remains awhile uncertain to whom the merit belongs, someone more vain than yourself will be encouraged to claim it, and then even envy will be disposed to do you justice by plucking those assumed feathers and restoring them to their right owner." *Autobiography*, p. 140. [See this edition, p. 64.]

candidness of his autobiography, belies that suspicion. The circumstance that he ascribes his recognition of the utility of virtue to a divine revelation which was intended to lead him in the path of righteousness, shows that something more than mere garnishing for purely egocentric motives is involved.

In fact, the *summum bonum* of this ethic, the earning of more and more money, combined with the strict avoidance of all spontaneous enjoyment of life, is above all completely devoid of any eudæmonistic, not to say hedonistic, admixture. It is thought of so purely as an end in itself, that from the point of view of the happiness of, or utility to, the single individual, it appears entirely transcendental and absolutely irrational.[1] Man is dominated by the making of money, by acquisition as the ultimate purpose of his life. Economic acquisition is no longer subordinated to man as the means for the satisfaction of his material needs. This reversal of what we should call the natural relationship, so irrational from a naïve point of view, is evidently as definitely a leading principle of capitalism as it is foreign to all peoples not under capitalistic influence. At the same time it expresses a type of feeling which is closely connected with certain religious ideas. If we thus ask, *why* should "money be made out of men", Benjamin Franklin himself, although he was a colourless deist, answers in his autobiography with a quotation from the Bible, which his strict Calvinistic father drummed into him again and again in his youth: "Seest thou a man diligent in his business? He shall stand before kings" (Prov. xxii. 29). The earning of money within the modern economic order is, so long as it is done legally, the result and the expression of virtue and proficiency in a calling; and this virtue and proficiency are, as it is now not difficult to see, the real Alpha and Omega of Franklin's ethic, as expressed in the passages we have quoted, as well as in all his works without exception.[2]

And in truth this peculiar idea, so familiar to us to-day, but in reality so little a matter of course, of one's duty in a calling, is what is most

---

1. Brentano (*op. cit.*, pp. 125, 127, note I) takes this remark as an occasion to criticize the later discussion of "that rationalization and discipline" to which worldly asceticism [This seemingly paradoxical term has been the best translation I could find for Weber's *innerweltliche Askese*, which means asceticism practised within the world as contrasted with *ausserweltliche Askese*, which withdraws from the world (for instance into a monastery). Their precise meaning will appear in the course of Weber's discussion. It is one of the prime points of his essay that asceticism does not need to flee from the world to be ascetic. I shall consistently employ the terms worldly and otherworldly to denote the contrast between the two kinds of asceticism.—TRANSLATOR'S NOTE.] has subjected men. That, he says, is a rationalization toward an irrational mode of life. He is, in fact, quite correct. A thing is never irrational in itself, but only from a particular rational point of view. For the unbeliever every religious way of life is irrational, for the hedonist every ascetic standard, no matter whether, measured with respect to its particular basic values, that opposing asceticism is a rationalization. If this essay makes any contribution at all, may it be to bring out the complexity of the only superficially simple concept of the rational.

2. In reply to Brentano's (*Die Anfänge des modernen Kapitalismus*, pp. 150 ff.) long and somewhat inaccurate apologia for Franklin, whose ethical qualities I am supposed to have misunderstood, I refer only to this statement, which should, in my opinion, have been sufficient to make that apologia superfluous.

characteristic of the social ethic of capitalistic culture, and is in a sense the fundamental basis of it. It is an obligation which the individual is supposed to feel and does feel towards the content of his professional[3] activity, no matter in what it consists, in particular no matter whether it appears on the surface as a utilization of his personal powers, or only of his material possessions (as capital).

Of course, this conception has not appeared only under capitalistic conditions. On the contrary, we shall later trace its origins back to a time previous to the advent of capitalism. Still less, naturally, do we maintain that a conscious acceptance of these ethical maxims on the part of the individuals, entrepreneurs or labourers, in modern capitalistic enterprises, is a condition of the further existence of present-day capitalism. The capitalistic economy of the present day is an immense cosmos into which the individual is born, and which presents itself to him, at least as an individual, as an unalterable order of things in which he must live. It forces the individual, in so far as he is involved in the system of market relationships, to conform to capitalistic rules of action. The manufacturer who in the long run acts counter to these norms, will just as inevitably be eliminated from the economic scene as the worker who cannot or will not adapt himself to them will be thrown into the streets without a job.

Thus the capitalism of to-day, which has come to dominate economic life, educates and selects the economic subjects which it needs through a process of economic survival of the fittest. But here one can easily see the limits of the concept of selection as a means of historical explanation. In order that a manner of life so well adapted to the peculiarities of capitalism could be selected at all, i.e. should come to dominate others, it had to originate somewhere, and not in isolated individuals alone, but as a way of life common to whole groups of men. This origin is what really needs explanation. Concerning the doctrine of the more naïve historical materialism, that such ideas originate as a reflection or superstructure of economic situations, we shall speak more in detail below. At this point it will suffice for our purpose to call attention to the fact that without doubt, in the country of Benjamin Franklin's birth (Massachusetts), the spirit of capitalism (in the sense we have attached to it) was present before the capitalistic order. There were complaints of a peculiarly calculating sort of profit-seeking in New England, as distinguished from other parts of America, as early as 1632. It is further undoubted that capitalism remained far less developed in some of the neighbouring colonies, the

---

3. The two terms profession and calling I have used in translation of the German *Beruf*, whichever seemed best to fit the particular context. Vocation does not carry the ethical connotation in which Weber is interested. It is especially to be remembered that profession in this sense is not contrasted with business, but it refers to a particular attitude toward one's occupation, no matter what that occupation may be. This should become abundantly clear from the whole of Weber's argument.—TRANSLATOR'S NOTE.

later Southern States of the United States of America, in spite of the
fact that these latter were founded by large capitalists for business
motives, while the New England colonies were founded by preachers
and seminary graduates with the help of small bourgeois, craftsmen
and yoemen, for religious reasons. In this case the causal relation is
certainly the reverse of that suggested by the materialistic standpoint.

But the origin and history of such ideas is much more complex than
the theorists of the superstructure suppose. The spirit of capitalism, in
the sense in which we are using the term, had to fight its way to
supremacy against a whole world of hostile forces. A state of mind
such as that expressed in the passages we have quoted from Franklin,
and which called forth the applause of a whole people, would both in
ancient times and in the Middle Ages[4] have been proscribed as the

4. I make use of this opportunity to insert a few
anti-critical remarks in advance of the main
argument. Sombart (*Bourgeois*) makes the un-
tenable statement that this ethic of Franklin is a
word-for-word repetition of some writings of
that great and versatile genius of the Renaissance, Leon Battista Alberti, who besides
theoretical treatises on Mathematics,
Sculpture, Painting, Architecture, and Love
(he was personally a woman-hater), wrote a
work in four books on household management
(*Della Famiglia*). (Unfortunately, I have not at
the time of writing been able to procure the
edition of Mancini, but only the older one of
Bonucci.) The passage from Franklin is printed
above word for word. Where then are corresponding passages to be found in Alberti's work,
especially the maxim "time is money", which
stands at the head, and the exhortations which
follow it? The only passage which, so far as I
know, bears the slightest resemblance to it is
found towards the end of the first book of *Della
Famiglia* (ed. Bonucci, II, p. 353), where Alberti speaks in very general terms of money as
the *nervus rerum* of the household, which must
hence be handled with special care, just as Cato
spoke in *De Re Rustica*. To treat Alberti, who
was very proud of his descent from one of the
most distinguished cavalier families of Florence
(*Nobilissimi Cavalieri, op. cit.*, pp. 213, 228,
247, etc.), as a man of mongrel blood who was
filled with envy for the noble families because
his illegitimate birth, which was not in the least
socially disqualifying, excluded him as a
bourgeois from association with the nobility, is
quite incorrect. It is true that the recommendation of large enterprises as alone worthy of a
nobileè onesta famiglia and a *libero è nobile
animo*, and as costing less labour is characteristic of Alberti (p. 209; compare *Del governo della
Famiglia*, IV, p. 55, as well as p. 116 in the
edition for the Pandolfini). Hence the best thing
is a putting-out business for wool and silk. Also
an ordered and painstaking regulation of his

household, i.e. the limiting of expenditure to
income. This is the *santa masserizia*, which is
thus primarily a principle of maintenance, a
given standard of life, and not of acquisition (as
no one should have understood better than
Sombart). Similarly, in the discussion of the
nature of money, his concern is with the management of consumption funds (money or *pos-
sessioni*), not with that of capital; all that is clear
from the expression of it which is put into the
mouth of Gianozzo. He recommends, as protection against the uncertainty of *fortuna*, early
habituation to continuous activity, which is also
(pp. 73–4) alone healthy in the long run, *in cose
magnifiche è ample*, and avoidance of laziness,
which always endangers the maintenance of
one's position in the world. Hence a careful
study of a suitable trade in case of a change of
fortune, but every *opera mercenaria* is unsuit-
able (op. cit., 1, p. 209). His idea of *tranquillita
dell' animo* and his strong tendency toward the
Epicurean λάθε βιώσας (*vivere a sè stesso*, p.
262); especially his dislike of any office (p. 258)
as a source of unrest, of making enemies, and of
becoming involved in dishonourable dealings;
the ideal of life in a country villa; his nourish-
ment of vanity through the thought of his ancestors; and his treatment of the honour of the
family (which on that account should keep its
fortune together in the Florentine manner and
not divide it up) as a decisive standard and
ideal—all these things would in the eyes of
every Puritan have been sinful idolatry of the
flesh, and in those of Benjamin Franklin the
expression of incomprehensible aristocratic
nonsense. Note, further, the very high opinion
of literary things (for the *industria* is applied
principally to literary and scientific work),
which is really most worthy of a man's efforts.
And the expression of the *masserizia*, in the
sense of "rational conduct of the household" as
the means of living independently of others and
avoiding destitution, is in general put only in
the mouth of the illiterate Gianozzo as of equal

value. Thus the origin of this concept, which comes (see below) from monastic ethics, is traced back to an old priest (p. 249).

Now compare all this with the ethic and manner of life of Benjamin Franklin, and especially of his Puritan ancestors; the works of the Renaissance *littérateur* addressing himself to the humanistic aristocracy, with Franklin's works addressed to the masses of the lower middle class (he especially mentions clerks) and with the tracts and sermons of the Puritans, in order to comprehend the depth of the difference. The economic rationalism of Alberti, everywhere supported by references to ancient authors, is most clearly related to the treatment of economic problems in the works of Xenophon (whom he did not know), of Cato, Varro, and Columella (all of whom he quotes), except that especially in Cato and Varro, *acquisition* as such stands in the foreground in a different way from that to be found in Alberti. Furthermore, the very occasional comments of Alberti on the use of the *fattori*, their division of labour and discipline, on the unreliability of the peasants, etc., really sound as if Cato's homely wisdom were taken from the field of the ancient slave-using household and applied to that of free labour in domestic industry and the metayer system. When Sombart (whose reference to the Stoic ethic is quite misleading) sees economic rationalism as "developed to its farthest conclusions" as early as Cato, he is, with a correct interpretation, not entirely wrong. It is possible to unite the *diligens pater familias* of the Romans with the ideal of the *massajo* of Alberti under the same category. It is above all characteristic for Cato that a landed estate is valued and judged as an object for the investment of consumption funds. The concept of *industria*, on the other hand, is differently coloured on account of Christian influence. And there is just the difference. In the conception of *industria*, which comes from monastic asceticism and which was developed by monastic writers, lies the seed of an *ethos* which was fully developed later in the Protestant worldly asceticism. Hence, as we shall often point out, the relationship of the two, which, however, is less close to the official Church doctrine of St. Thomas than to the Florentine and Siennese mendicant-moralists. In Cato and also in Alberti's own writings this *ethos* is lacking; for both it is a matter of worldly wisdom, not of ethic. In Franklin there is also a utilitarian strain. But the ethical quality of the sermon to young business men is impossible to mistake, and that is the characteristic thing. A lack of care in the handling of money means to him that one so to speak murders capital embryos, and hence it is an ethical defect.

An inner relationship of the two (Alberti and Franklin) exists in fact only in so far as Alberti, whom Sombart calls pious, but who actually, although he took the sacraments and held a Roman benefice, like so many humanists, did not himself (except for two quite colourless passages) in any way make use of religious motives as a justification of the manner of life he recommended, had not yet, Franklin on the other hand no longer, related his recommendation of economy to religious conceptions. Utilitarianism, in Alberti's preference for wool and silk manufacture, also the mercantilist social utilitarianism "that many people should be given employment" (see Alberti, *op. cit.*, p. 292), is in this field at least formally the sole justification for the one as for the other. Alberti's discussions of this subject form an excellent example of the sort of economic rationalism which really existed as a reflection of economic conditions, in the work of authors interested purely in "the thing for its own sake" everywhere and at all times; in the Chinese classicism and in Greece and Rome no less than in the Renaissance and the age of the Enlightenment. There is no doubt that just as in ancient times with Cato, Varro, and Columella, also here with Alberti and others of the same type, especially in the doctrine of *industria*, a sort of economic rationality is highly developed. But how can anyone believe that such a literary *theory* could develop into a revolutionary force at all comparable to the way in which a religious belief was able to set the sanctions of salvation and damnation on the fulfillment of a particular (in this case methodically rationalized) manner of life? What, as compared with it, a really religiously oriented rationalization of conduct looks like, may be seen, outside of the Puritans of all denominations, in the cases of the Jains, the Jews, certain ascetic sects of the Middle Ages, the Bohemian Brothers (an offshoot of the Hussite movement), the Skoptsi and Stundists in Russia, and numerous monastic orders, however much all these may differ from each other.

The essential point of the difference is (to anticipate) that an ethic based on religion places certain psychological sanctions (not of an economic character) on the maintenance of the attitude prescribed by it, sanctions which, so long as the religious belief remains alive, are highly effective, and which mere worldly wisdom like that of Alberti does not have at its disposal. Only in so far as these sanctions work, and, above all, in the direction in which they work, which is often very different from the doctrine of the theologians, does such an ethic gain an independent influence on the conduct of life and thus on the economic order. This is, to speak frankly, the point of this whole essay, which I had not expected to find so completely overlooked.

Later on I shall come to speak of the theologi-

lowest sort of avarice and as an attitude entirely lacking in self-respect. It is, in fact, still regularly thus looked upon by all those social groups which are least involved in or adapted to modern capitalistic conditions. This is not wholly because the instinct of acquisition was in those times unknown or undeveloped, as has often been said. Nor because the *auri sacra fames*, the greed for gold, was then, or now, less powerful outside of bourgeois capitalism than within its peculiar sphere, as the illusions of modern romanticists are wont to believe. The difference between the capitalistic and precapitalistic spirits is not to be found at this point. The greed of the Chinese Mandarin, the old Roman aristocrat, or the modern peasant, can stand up to any comparison. And the *auri sacra fames* of a Neapolitan cab-driver or *barcaiuolo*,[5] and certainly of Asiatic representatives of similar trades, as well as of the craftsmen of southern European or Asiatic countries, is, as anyone can find out for himself, very much more intense, and especially more unscrupulous than that of, say, an Englishman in similar circumstances.[6]

* * *

---

cal moralists of the late Middle Ages, who were relatively friendly to capital (especially Anthony of Florence and Bernhard of Siena), and whom Sombart has also seriously misinterpreted. In any case Alberti did not belong to that group. Only the concept of *industria* did he take from monastic lines of thought, no matter through what intermediate links. Alberti, Pandolfini, and their kind are representatives of that attitude which, in spite of all its outward obedience, was inwardly already emancipated from the tradition of the Church. With all its resemblance to the current Christian ethic, it was to a large extent of the antique pagan character, which Brentano thinks I have ignored in its significance for the development of modern economic thought (and also modern economic policy). That I do not deal with its influence here is quite true. It would be out of place in a study of the Protestant ethic and the spirit of capitalism. But, as will appear in a different connection, far from denying its significance, I have been and am for good reasons of the opinion that its sphere and direction of influence were entirely different from those of the Protestant ethic (of which the spiritual ancestry, of no small practical importance, lies in the sects and in the ethics of Wyclif and Hus). It was not the mode of life of the rising bourgeoisie which was influenced by this other attitude, but the policy of statesmen

and princes; and these two partly, but by no means always, convergent lines of development should for purposes of analysis be kept perfectly distinct. So far as Franklin is concerned, his tracts of advice to business men, at present used for school reading in America, belong in fact to a category of works which have influenced practical life, far more than Alberti's large book, which hardly became known outside of learned circles. But I have expressly denoted him as a man who stood beyond the direct influence of the Puritan view of life, which had paled considerably in the meantime, just as the whole English enlightenment, the relations of which to Puritanism have often been set forth.

5. Boatman [Editors' Note.]

6. Unfortunately Brentano (*op. cit.*) has thrown every kind of struggle for gain, whether peaceful or warlike, into one pot, and has then set up as the specific criterion of capitalistic (as contrasted, for instance, with feudal) profit-seeking, its acquisitiveness of *money* (instead of land). Any further differentiation, which alone could lead to a clear conception, he has not only refused to make, but has made against the concept of the spirit of (modern) capitalism which we have formed for our purposes, the (to me) incomprehensible objection that it already includes in its assumptions what is supposed to be proved.

D. H. LAWRENCE

Benjamin Franklin†

The Perfectibility of Man! Ah heaven, what a dreary theme! The perfectibility of the Ford car! The perfectibility of which man? I am many men. Which of them are you going to perfect? I am not a mechanical contrivance.

Education! Which of the various me's do you propose to educate, and which do you propose to suppress?

Anyhow, I defy you. I defy you, oh society, to educate me or to suppress me, according to your dummy standards.

The ideal man! And which is he, if you please? Benjamin Franklin or Abraham Lincoln? The ideal man! Roosevelt or Porfirio Díaz?

There are other men in me, besides this patient ass who sits here in a tweed jacket. What am I doing, playing the patient ass in a tweed jacket? Who am I talking to? Who are you, at the other end of this patience?

Who are you? How many selves have you? And which of these selves do you want to be?

Is Yale College going to educate the self that is in the dark of you, or Harvard College?

The ideal self! Oh, but I have a strange and fugitive self shut out and howling like a wolf or a coyote under the ideal windows. See his red eyes in the dark? This is the self who is coming into his own.

The perfectibility of man, dear God! When every man as long as he remains alive is in himself a multitude of conflicting men. Which of these do you choose to perfect, at the expense of every other?

Old Daddy Franklin will tell you. He'll rig him up for you, the pattern American. Oh, Franklin was the first down-right American. He knew what he was about, the sharp little man. He set up the first dummy American.

At the beginning of his career this cunning little Benjamin drew up for himself a creed that should "satisfy the professors of every religion, but shock none".

Now wasn't that a real American thing to do?

"That there is One God, who made all things."

(But Benjamin made Him.)

"That He governs the world by His Providence."

(Benjamin knowing all about Providence.)

"That He ought to be worshipped with adoration, prayer, and thanksgiving."

† Source: D. H. Lawrence, "Benjamin Franklin," in his *Studies in Classic American Literature* (London: Martin Secker, 1924), pp. 15–27.

(Which cost nothing.)

"But——" But me no buts, Benjamin, saith the Lord.

"But that the most acceptable service of God is doing good to men."

(God having no choice in the matter.)

"That the soul is immortal."

(You'll see why, in the next clause.)

"And that God will certainly reward virtue and punish vice, either here or hereafter."

Now if Mr. Andrew Carnegie, or any other millionaire, had wished to invent a God to suit his ends, he could not have done better. Benjamin did it for him in the eighteenth century. God is the supreme servant of men who want to get on, to *produce*. Providence. The provider. The heavenly storekeeper. The everlasting Wanamaker.[1]

And this is all the God the grandsons of the Pilgrim Fathers had left. Aloft on a pillar of dollars.

"That the soul is immortal."

The trite way Benjamin says it!

But man has a soul, though you can't locate it either in his purse or his pocket-book or his heart or his stomach or his head. The *wholeness* of a man is his soul. Not merely that nice little comfortable bit which Benjamin marks out.

It's a queer thing is a man's soul. It is the whole of him. Which means it is the unknown him, as well as the known. It seems to me just funny, professors and Benjamins fixing the functions of the soul. Why, the soul of man is a vast forest, and all Benjamin intended was a neat back garden. And we've all got to fit into his kitchen garden scheme of things. Hail Columbia!

The soul of man is a dark forest. The Hercynian Wood[2] that scared the Romans so, and out of which came the white-skinned hordes of the next civilization.

Who knows what will come out of the soul of man? The soul of man is a dark vast forest, with wild life in it. Think of Benjamin fencing it off!

Oh, but Benjamin fenced a little tract that he called the soul of man, and proceeded to get it into cultivation. Providence, forsooth! And they think that bit of barbed wire is going to keep us in pound for ever? More fools they.

This is Benjamin's barbed wire fence. He made himself a list of virtues, which he trotted inside like a grey nag in a paddock.

1

TEMPERANCE

Eat not to fulness; drink not to elevation.

1. Wanamaker's is the largest Philadelphia department store.   2. The classical name for the forests of middle Germany.

2
SILENCE

Speak not but what may benefit others or yourself; avoid trifling conversation.

3
ORDER

Let all your things have their places; let each part of your business have its time.

4
RESOLUTION

Resolve to perform what you ought; perform without fail what you resolve.

5
FRUGALITY

Make no expense but to do good to others or yourself—i.e., waste nothing.

6
INDUSTRY

Lose no time, be always employed in something useful; cut off all unnecessary action.

7
SINCERITY

Use no hurtful deceit; think innocently and justly, and, if you speak, speak accordingly.

8
JUSTICE

Wrong none by doing injuries, or omitting the benefits that are your duty.

9
MODERATION

Avoid extremes, forbear resenting injuries as much as you think they deserve.

10
CLEANLINESS

Tolerate no uncleanliness in body, clothes, or habitation.

11
TRANQUILLITY

Be not disturbed at trifles, or at accidents common or unavoidable.

12
CHASTITY

Rarely use venery but for health and offspring, never to dulness, weakness, or the injury of your own or another's peace or reputation.

13
HUMILITY

Imitate Jesus and Socrates.

A Quaker friend told Franklin that he, Benjamin, was generally considered proud, so Benjamin put in the Humility touch as an afterthought. The amusing part is the sort of humility it displays. "Imitate Jesus and Socrates," and mind you don't outshine either of these two. One can just imagine Socrates and Alcibiades roaring in their cups over Philadelphian Benjamin, and Jesus looking at him a little puzzled, and murmuring: "Aren't you wise in your own conceit, Ben?"

"Henceforth be masterless," retorts Ben. "Be ye each one his own master unto himself, and don't let even the Lord put His spoke in." "Each man his own master" is but a puffing up of masterlessness.

Well, the first of Americans practised this enticing list with assiduity, setting a national example. He had the virtues in columns, and gave himself good and bad marks according as he thought his behaviour deserved. Pity these conduct charts are lost to us. He only remarks that Order was his stumbling block. He could not learn to be neat and tidy.

Isn't it nice to have nothing worse to confess?

He was a little model, was Benjamin. Doctor Franklin. Snuff-coloured little man! Immortal soul and all!

The immortal soul part was a sort of cheap insurance policy.

Benjamin had no concern, really, with the immortal soul. He was too busy with social man.

1. He swept and lighted the streets of young Philadelphia.

2. He invented electrical appliances.

3. He was the centre of a moralizing club in Philadelphia, and he wrote the moral humorisms of Poor Richard.

4. He was a member of all the important councils of Philadelphia, and then of the American colonies.

5. He won the cause of American Independence at the French Court, and was the economic father of the United States.

Now what more can you want of a man? And yet he is *infra dig.*,[3] even in Philadelphia.

I admire him. I admire his sturdy courage first of all, then his sagacity, then his glimpsing into the thunders of electricity, then his common-sense humour. All the qualities of a great man, and never more than a great citizen. Middle-sized, sturdy, snuff-coloured Doctor Franklin, one of the soundest citizens that ever trod or "used venery".

I do not like him.

And, by the way, I always thought books of Venery were about hunting deer.

There is a certain earnest naïveté about him. Like a child. And like a little old man. He has again become as a little child, always as wise as his grandfather, or wiser.

Perhaps, as I say, the most complete citizen that ever "used venery".

Printer, philosopher, scientist, author and patriot, impeccable husband and citizen, why isn't he an archetype?

Pioneer, Oh Pioneers! Benjamin was one of the greatest pioneers of the United States. Yet we just can't do with him.

What's wrong with him then? Or what's wrong with us?

I can remember, when I was a little boy, my father used to buy a scrubby yearly almanac with the sun and moon and stars on the cover. And it used to prophesy bloodshed and famine. But also crammed in corners it had little anecdotes and humorisms, with a moral tag. And I used to have my little priggish laugh at the woman who counted her chickens before they were hatched and so forth, and I was convinced that honesty was the best policy, also a little priggishly. The author of these bits was Poor Richard, and Poor Richard was Benjamin Franklin, writing in Philadelphia well over a hundred years before.

And probably I haven't got over those Poor Richard tags yet. I rankle still with them. They are thorns in young flesh.

Because, although I still believe that honesty is the best policy, I dislike policy altogether; though it is just as well not to count your chickens before they are hatched, it's still more hateful to count them with gloating when they *are* hatched. It has taken me many years and countless smarts to get out of that barbed wire moral enclosure that Poor Richard rigged up. Here am I now in tatters and scratched to ribbons, sitting in the middle of Benjamin's America looking at the barbed wire, and the fat sheep crawling under the fence to get fat outside, and the watchdogs yelling at the gate lest by chance anyone should get out by the proper exit. Oh America! Oh Benjamin! And I just utter a long loud curse against Benjamin and the American corral.

Moral America! Most moral Benjamin. Sound, satisfied Ben!

3. Beneath dignity.

He had to go to the frontiers of his State to settle some disturbance among the Indians. On this occasion he writes:

"We found that they had made a great bonfire in the middle of the square; they were all drunk, men and women quarrelling and fighting. Their dark-coloured bodies, half-naked, seen only by the gloomy light of the bonfire, running after and beating one another with fire-brands, accompanied by their horrid yellings, formed a scene the most resembling our ideas of hell that could well be imagined. There was no appeasing the tumult, and we retired to our lodging. At midnight a number of them came thundering at our door, demanding more rum, of which we took no notice.

"The next day, sensible they had misbehaved in giving us that disturbance, they sent three of their counsellors to make their apology. The orator acknowledged the fault, but laid it upon the rum, and then endeavoured to excuse the rum by saying: The Great Spirit, who made all things, made everything for some use; and whatever he designed anything for, that use it should always be put to. Now, when he had made the rum, he said: "Let this be for the Indians to get drunk with." And it must be so.'

"And, indeed, if it be the design of Providence to extirpate these savages in order to make room for the cultivators of the earth, it seems not improbable that rum may be the appointed means. It has already annihilated all the tribes who formerly inhabited all the seacoast. . . ."

This, from the good doctor with such suave complacency, is a little disenchanting. Almost too good to be true.

But there you are! The barbed wire fence. "Extirpate these savages in order to make room for the cultivators of the earth." Oh, Benjamin Franklin! He even "used venery" as a cultivator of seed.

Cultivate the earth, ye gods! The Indians did that, as much as they needed. And they left off there. Who built Chicago? Who cultivated the earth until it spawned Pittsburgh, Pa?

The moral issue! Just look at it! Cultivation included. If it's a mere choice of Kultur or cultivation, I give it up.

Which brings us right back to our question, what's wrong with Benjamin, that we can't stand him? Or else, what's wrong with us, that we find fault with such a paragon?

Man is a moral animal. All right. I am a moral animal. And I'm going to remain such. I'm not going to be turned into a virtuous little automaton as Benjamin would have me. "This is good, that is bad. Turn the little handle and let the good tap flow," saith Benjamin, and all America with him. "But first of all extirpate those savages who are always turning on the bad tap."

I am a moral animal. But I am not a moral machine. I don't work with a little set of handles or levers. The Temperance-silence-order resolution- frugality- industry- sincerity- justice- moderation- cleanliness- tranquillity- chastity- humility keyboard is not going to get me going. I'm really not just an automatic piano with a moral Benjamin getting tunes out of me.

Here's my creed, against Benjamin's. This is what I believe:

"That I am I."

"That my soul is a dark forest."

"That my known self will never be more than a little clearing in the forest."

"That gods, strange gods, come forth from the forest into the clearing of my known self, and then go back."

"That I must have the courage to let them come and go."

"That I will never let mankind put anything over me, but that I will try always to recognize and submit to the gods in me and the gods in other men and women."

There is my creed. He who runs may read. He who prefers to crawl, or to go by gasoline, can call it rot.

Then for a "list". It is rather fun to play at Benjamin.

1
TEMPERANCE

Eat and carouse with Bacchus, or munch dry bread with Jesus, but don't sit down without one of the gods.

2
SILENCE

Be still when you have nothing to say; when genuine passion moves you, say what you've got to say, and say it hot.

3
ORDER

Know that you are responsible to the gods inside you and to the men in whom the gods are manifest. Recognize your superiors and your inferiors, according to the gods. This is the root of all order.

4
RESOLUTION

Resolve to abide by your own deepest promptings, and to sacrifice the smaller thing to the greater. Kill when you must, and be killed the same: the *must* coming from the gods inside you, or from the men in whom you recognize the Holy Ghost.

5
FRUGALITY

Demand nothing; accept what you see fit. Don't waste your pride or squander your emotion.

6
INDUSTRY

Lose no time with ideals; serve the Holy Ghost; never serve mankind.

7
SINCERITY

To be sincere is to remember that I am I, and that the other man is not me.

8
JUSTICE

The only justice is to follow the sincere intuition of the soul, angry or gentle. Anger is just, and pity is just, but judgment is never just.

9
MODERATION

Beware of absolutes. There are many gods.

10
CLEANLINESS

Don't be too clean. It improverishes the blood.

11
TRANQUILLITY

The soul has many motions, many gods come and go. Try and find your deepest issue, in every confusion, and abide by that. Obey the man in whom you recognize the Holy Ghost; command when your honour comes to command.

12
CHASTITY

Never "use" venery at all. Follow your passional impulse, if it be answered in the other being; but never have any motive in mind, neither offspring nor health nor even pleasure, nor even service. Only know that "venery" is of the great gods. An offering-up of yourself to the very great gods, the dark ones, and nothing else.

13

HUMILITY

See all men and women according to the Holy Ghost that is within them. Never yield before the barren.

There's my list. I have been trying dimly to realize it for a long time, and only America and old Benjamin have at last goaded me into trying to formulate it.

And now I, at least, know why I can't stand Benjamin. He tries to take away my wholeness and my dark forest, my freedom. For how can any man be free, without an illimitable background? And Benjamin tries to shove me into a barbed wire paddock and make me grow potatoes or Chicagoes.

And how can I be free, without gods that come and go? But Benjamin won't let anything exist except my useful fellow men, and I'm sick of them; as for his Godhead, his Providence, He is Head of nothing except a vast heavenly store that keeps every imaginable line of goods, from victrolas to cat-o'-nine tails.

And how can any man be free without a soul of his own, that he believes in and won't sell at any price? But Benjamin doesn't let me have a soul of my own. He says I am nothing but a servant of mankind—galley-slave I call it—and if I don't get my wages here below—that is, if Mr. Pierpont Morgan or Mr. Nosey Hebrew or the grand United States Government, the great US, US or SOMEOFUS, manages to scoop in my bit, along with their lump—why, never mind, I shall get my wages HEREAFTER.

Oh Benjamin! Oh Binjum! You do NOT suck me in any longer.

And why, oh why should the snuff-coloured little trap have wanted to take us all in? Why did he do it?

Out of sheer human cussedness, in the first place. We do all like to get things inside a barbed wire corral. Especially our fellow men. We love to round them up inside the barbed wire enclosure of FREEDOM, and make 'em work. "*Work, you free jewel, WORK!*" shouts the liberator, cracking his whip. Benjamin, I will not work. I do not choose to be a free democrat. I am absolutely a servant of my own Holy Ghost.

Sheer cussedness! But there was as well the salt of a subtler purpose. Benjamin was just in his eyeholes—to use an English vulgarism, meaning he was just delighted—when he was at Paris judiciously milking money out of the French monarchy for the overthrow of all monarchy. If you want to ride your horse to somewhere you must put a bit in his mouth. And Benjamin wanted to ride his horse so that it would upset the whole apple-cart of the old masters. He wanted the whole European apple-cart upset. So he had to put a strong bit in the mouth of his ass.

"Henceforth be masterless."

That is, he had to break-in the human ass completely, so that much more might be broken, in the long run. For the moment it was the British Government that had to have a hole knocked in it. The first real hole it ever had: the breach of the American rebellion.

Benjamin, in his sagacity, knew that the breaking of the old world was a long process. In the depths of his own under-consciousness he hated England, he hated Europe, he hated the whole corpus of the European being. He wanted to be American. But you can't change your nature and mode of consciousness like changing your shoes. It is a gradual shedding. Years must go by, and centuries must elapse before you have finished. Like a son escaping from the domination of his parents. The escape is not just one rupture. It is a long and half-secret process.

So with the American. He was a European when he first went over the Atlantic. He is in the main a recreant European still. From Benjamin Franklin to Woodrow Wilson may be a long stride, but it is a stride along the same road. There is no new road. The same old road, become dreary and futile. Theoretic and materialistic.

Why then did Benjamin set up this dummy of a perfect citizen as a pattern to America? Of course, he did it in perfect good faith, as far as he knew. He thought it simply was the true ideal. But what we *think* we do is not very important. We never really know what we are doing. Either we are materialistic instruments, like Benjamin, or we move in the gesture of creation, from our deepest self, usually unconscious. We are only the actors, we are never wholly the authors of our own deeds or works. IT is the author, the unknown inside us or outside us. The best we can do is to try to hold ourselves in unison with the deeps which are inside us. And the worst we can do is to try to have things our own way, when we run counter to IT, and in the long run get our knuckles rapped for our presumption.

So Benjamin contriving money out of the Court of France. He was contriving the first steps of the overthrow of all Europe, France included. You can never have a new thing without breaking an old. Europe happens to be the old thing. America, unless the people in America assert themselves too much in opposition to the inner gods, should be the new thing. The new thing is the death of the old. But you can't cut the throat of an epoch. You've got to steal the life from it through several centuries.

And Benjamin worked for this both directly and indirectly. Directly, at the Court of France, making a small but very dangerous hole in the side of England, through which hole Europe has by now almost bled to death. And indirectly in Philadelphia, setting up this unlovely, snuff-coloured little ideal, or automaton, of a pattern American. The pattern American, this dry, moral, utilitarian little democrat, has done more to ruin the old Europe than any Russian nihilist. He has done it by slow attrition, like a son who has stayed at home and obeyed his parents, all the while silently hating their authority, and silently, in his soul, destroying not only their authority but their whole existence. For the American spiritually stayed at home in Europe. The spiritual home of America was, and still is, Europe. This is the galling bondage, in spite of several billions of heaped-up gold. Your heaps of gold are only so many muck-heaps, America, and will remain so till you become a reality to yourselves.

All this Americanizing and mechanizing has been for the purpose of overthrowing the past. And now look at America, tangled in her own barbed wire, and mastered by her own machines. Absolutely got down by her own barbed wire of shalt-nots, and shut up fast in her own "productive" machines like millions of squirrels running in millions of cages. It is just a farce.

Now is your chance, Europe. Now let Hell loose and get your own back, and paddle your own canoe on a new sea, while clever America lies on her muck-heaps of gold, strangled in her own barbed wire of shalt-not ideals and shalt-not moralisms. While she goes out to work like millions of squirrels in millions of cages. Production!

Let Hell loose, and get your own back, Europe!

W. SOMERSET MAUGHAM

In 1940, W. Somerset Maugham wrote an essay on "The Classic Books of America" for *Saturday Evening Post*, beginning with praise for Franklin's *Autobiography*. In context, the first sentence below says that autobiographies are rarely ranked among literary classics—but Franklin's is an exception.

[The Classic Books of America]†

* * * The histories of literature contain few autobiographies; they contain none more consistently entertaining than Benjamin Franklin's. It is written plainly, as befitted its author, but in pleasant easy English, for Franklin, as we know, had studied under good masters; and it is interesting not only for its narrative but for the vivid and credible portrait which the author has succeeded in painting of himself. I cannot understand why in America Franklin is often spoken of with depreciation. Fault is found with his character; his precepts are condemned as mean and his ideals as ignoble. It is obvious that he was

† Source: Maugham's *Books and You* (New York: Doubleday, Doran & Co., 1940), pp. 81–82.

not a romanticist. He was shrewd and industrious. He was a good business man. He wished the good of his fellow-men, but was too clear-sighted to be deceived by them, and he used their failings with pawky humour to achieve the ends, sometimes selfish, it is true, but as often altruistic, that he had in view. He liked the good things of life, but accepted hardship with serenity. He had courage and generosity. He was a good companion, a man of witty and caustic conversation, and he liked his liquor; he was fond of women, and being no prude, took his pleasure of them. He was a man of prodigious versatility. He led a happy and a useful life. He achieved great things for his country, his state and the city in which he dwelt. To my thinking he is as truly the typical American as Doctor Johnson is the typical Englishman, and when I ask myself why it is that his countrymen are apt to grudge him their sympathy, I can only think of one explanation. He was entirely devoid of hokum.

*   *   *

CHARLES L. SANFORD

An American *Pilgrim's Progress*†

A conventional rhetoric of spirit antedating Columbus' voyages of discovery helped to invest the new Western world and the way West with a magnetic attraction over European imaginations. It functioned to give the otherwise sordid pursuit of material riches moral and spiritual sanction, without which most men seem disinclined to dare and do. This rhetoric revolved on the spiritual voyage or quest for personal salvation and reached its fullest literary expression in Dante's *Divine Comedy* and Bunyan's *Pilgrim's Progress*.

In the journey patterns of Scripture as well as in the language of medieval church symbolism, the spiritual quest had traditionally been known as a "journey toward light."[1] According to this interpretation, if the bower of light was Paradise or the Celestial City, the original source of the bright beam was God, symbolized by the life-giving sun. The sun in medieval popular thought represented God's truth and righteousness, illuminating the dark corners of sin with His saving radiance in its solar cycle from East to West. Medieval fable with its strange wonders and miraculous beings had the kingdom of earthly

---

† Source: *American Quarterly* 6 (1954), 297–310.
1. This is expounded in Helen F. Dunbar, *Symbolism* in *Medieval Thought and its Consummation in the Divine Comedy* (New Haven: Yale University Press, 1929), *passim*, and in Dorothy Donnelly, *The Golden Well: An Anatomy of Symbols* (London: Sheed and Ward, 1950), pp. 115–53.

desire located vaguely and variously in Abyssinia, in Cathay and Ophir, somewhere in the Far East, beyond the western seas. Medieval explorers sought out the warmest climes of the sun.[2] But Christians, for the most part, looked for the promised land in the other world of life-after-death while they huddled in misery in this world. Anticipating the future importance of the direction West, Dante, in a famous passage from the *Divine Comedy*, has Ulysses sailing through the straits of Gibraltar to reach the West, seeking, "the new experience/ Of the uninhabited world behind the sun."[3] Shouldering the dawn in the unknown western seas, Ulysses comes upon Mount Purgatory, where one begins the ascent to the Celestial City. Columbus, too, was saturated with medieval legend and thought literally that he had discovered "the terrestrial paradise."[4]

But God's divine light did not shine everywhere with equal brilliance. "Wheresoever the children of Israel dwelt," Genesis maintained, "*there* was light." In other words, His brightest beams were reserved for God's elect, the chosen people. The Reformed Churches of Europe, under the leadership of Martin Luther, in effect revived the old Hebraic conception of a chosen people and claimed that the light of the true gospel dwelt in their house.[5] Since the Reformation rose first in the west of Europe and spread westward from Germany to France, the Netherlands, and thus to England, it became almost commonplace for the favored ones to suppose that the succession to the moral and spiritual leadership of the world followed the solar cycle of the sun from East to West. Settlement of the New World by militant Protestants completed the identification of geographical westering with moral and spiritual progress and, with the secularization of millennial hopes, contributed to the eighteenth and nineteenth-century idea of progress.

Before and during the settlement of America, the English considered themselves the custodians of the apostolic succession.[6] Shakespeare's England was not only "this blessed plot, this earth, this realm"; it was also a bower of light, "this other Eden, demi-paradise, this fortress built by Nature" for a chosen people. On the eve of settlement, as Louis B. Wright has pointed out, Protestant theologians

2. For the relationship between medieval legend and early exploration see Don Cameron Allen, *The Legend of Noah* (Urbana: University of Illinois Press, 1949); A. R. Anderson, *Alexander's Gate, Gog and Magog and the Inclosed Nations* (Combridge: The Medieval Academy of America, 1932); Washington Irving, *Life and Voyages of Christopher Columbus* (New York: Thomas Y. Crowell, n.d.), Appendices XIX-XXVI; Leonard Olschki, "Ponce de Leon's Fountain of Youth: History of a Geographical Myth," *Hisp.-Am. Hist. Rev.*, XXI, no. 3 (August 1941), 361-85.

3. Dante, *The Divine Comedy, I, Hell*, trans. Dorothy L. Sayers (Penguin Classics), p. 236.
4. Hakluyt Society, *Select Documents Illustrating the Four Voyages of Columbus* (London: Hakluyt Society, 1933), II, 42, 30-50, *passim*.
5. Ernest Tuveson, *Millennium and Utopia* (Berkeley: University of California Press, 1950), pp. 27, 39.
6. Louis B. Wright, *Religion and Empire* (Chapel Hill: University of North Carolina Press, 1943), p. 91, *et sequitur*.

were frantically transferring the Ark of the Covenant from Abraham to the English. There were, undoubtedly, many laymen who cried with the Baptist Henry Nicholas, "We have it, we are the Congregation of Christ, we are Israel, lo here it is!" or with the Anglican William Crashaw, "The God of Israel is . . . the God of England."[7] But there were also many Englishmen who were not loath to see the succession pass westward to America, so long as it redounded to the power and glory of England. Indeed, the English were divinely appointed to establish themselves in the promised lands of the New World! Thus, Richard Hakluyt urged in his *Discourse of Western Planting* that the western discoveries had provided England a heaven-sent opportunity for the spread of the gospel, "whereunto the Princes of the refourmed Relligion are chefely bounde."[8] John White of Dorchester, author of *The Planters Plea*, considered England to be singled out for that work, "being of all the States that enjoy the libertie of the Religion Reformed" the most orthodox and sincere.[9] As early as 1583 Sir Humphrey Gilbert thought England's "full possession of those so ample and pleasant countreys . . . very probable by the revolution and course of Gods word and religion, which from the beginning hath moved from the East, towards, and at last unto the West, where it is like to end. . . ."[1]

The belief that the bounties of God followed the course of the sun westward brought numerous prophecies of a bright future for America and contributed, in part, to their fulfillment.[2] Sir William Alexander, who was to become proprietor of Nova Scotia, wrote in 1616:

> America to Europe may succeed;
> God may stones raise up to Abram's seed.

The poet John Donne predicted in 1622 that the Virginia Company would make England a bridge between the Old World and the New "to join all to that world that shall never grow old, the kingdom of Heaven." A few years later another Anglican poet, George Herbert, noted in his *Church Militant* that

> Religion stands tip-toe in our land
> Ready to pass to the American strand.

Whereupon, Dr. Twiss, "considering our English Plantations of late,

---

7. See especially the promotional sermons and colonizing tracts calendared in Alexander Brown, *The Genesis of the United States*, 2 vols. (Boston 1890), and many similar rhetorical pronouncements quoted in William Haller, *The Rise of Puritanism* (New York: Columbia University Press, 1938).

8. Quoted in Wright, *Religion and Empire*, p. 45.

9. Peter Force, comp., *Tracts and Other Papers, Relating principally to the Origin, Settle-*

ment, and Progress of the Colonies in North America . . ., 4 vols. (Washington, 1836–46), II, 3, 12.

1. Original Narratives Series, *Early English and French Voyages . . .*, ed. Henry S. Burrage (New York: Charles Scribner's Sons, 1906), p. 183.

2. Quotations in this paragraph are from Edward D. Neill, *The English Colonization of America . . .* (London, 1871), 177–178n.

and the opinion of many grave divines concerning the Gospel's fleeing westward," asked his fellow clergyman, Mede—"Why may not that be the place of the new Jerusalem?" His question was later echoed by American colonists who founded cities in the wilderness and led periodic religious revivals on the frontier.[3]

The image of a new Jerusalem in the western world accompanied dreams of empire and a higher civilization. Among the blessings which God had bestowed upon fallen reason, and whose great revival, according to seventeenth-century Chiliasts, was to usher in the last stage before the millennium, was culture and learning. "Learning, like the Sun," Thomas Burnet wrote in his *Archaeologiae* in 1692,[4]

> began to take its Course from the *East*, then turned *Westward*, where we have long rejoiced in its Light. Who knows whether, leaving these Seats, it may not yet take a further Progress? Or whether it will not be universally diffused, and enlighten all the World with its Rays?

The English Puritan divine, John Edwards, also traced the advance of culture and religion as a westward movement. In 1725 Jeremy Dummer, Massachusetts' agent in London, hoped, apropos of his collection of books for the new Yale library, that religion and polite learning would not rest in their westward progress until they took up their chief residence in America.[5] Two years later Bishop Berkeley summed up for posterity ideas which had been in circulation for more than a century. His famous poem beginning, "Westward the course of empire takes its way," restated the familiar solar analogy to conform to the imperial vision of eighteenth-century Englishmen.

Although Englishmen transplanted in America shared this dream of imperial grandeur, they assumed a rôle for themselves which eclipsed that of the mother country and unconsciously hastened the separation of the colonies. They believed that they were the chosen instruments of God appointed to carry out the Protestant mission in the New World, which was to set up a "city on the hill" as an example to Europe and the rest of the world of the true Reformation.[6] In this mission they regarded themselves as the heirs of all history, curiously

3. See, for instance, the *Letter-Book of Samuel Sewall* in *Coll. Mass. Hist. Soc.*, 6th ser., 2 vols. (Boston, 1886–88), I, 177; II, 156, 201. Sewall quoted both Twiss and Mede on this point and for many years sought to elucidate it by biblical prophecies.
4. Quoted by Tuveson, *Millennium and Utopia*, p. 166.
5. In his letter to Timothy Woodbridge, *Trans. Col. Soc. Mass.* (Boston, 1895-present), VI, 201–02.
6. Perry Miller, *The New England Mind: From*

Colony to Province (Cambridge: Harvard University Press, 1953), pp. 4–5; also his "Errand into the Wilderness," *Wm. and Mary Qtly*, 3rd ser., X (1953), 3–19. This belief was by no means confined to New England Puritans, however. For the importance of the religious impulse in the colonizing of Virginia see Perry Miller, "The Religious Impulse in the Founding of Virginia," *ibid.*, 3rd ser., V (1948), 492–522; VI (1949), 24–41; and the promotional sermons and tracts calendared in Alexander Brown, *The Genesis of the United States*.

unappreciated by Englishmen at home, for whose salvation they prayed. Their preëminence on the stage of history seemed guaranteed not only by the westward progression of religion and culture, but also by God's Providence in concealing America from European eyes until the time of the Reformation.[7] There was little doubt in their minds that the final drama of moral regeneration and universal salvation was to begin here, with them.

This sense of unique destiny bred a religious patriotism which unwittingly started the colonists down the long road to political independence. The inner logic of their position was revealed by Thomas Paine, who on the eve of the American Revolution acknowledged the design of Heaven, adding, "The Reformation was preceded by the discovery of America, as if the Almighty graciously meant to open a sanctuary to the persecuted in future years. . . ."[8] An incipient patriotism was also reflected, unconsciously to be sure, in the change in emphasis which many colonists, particularly New Englanders, gave to the conventional sun rhetoric. In the symbolic language of spirit they sometimes denied the sun its regular transit from East to West, and, instead, had it hovering or rising for the first time over them. As early as 1647 John Eliot, missionary to the Indians, was announcing "The Daybreaking if not the Sunrising of the Gospel . . . in New England."[9] "O New-England," Samuel Willard hymned in a sermon of 1704, "thou art a Land of Vision; and has been so for a long time. The Sun for one day stood over Gibeon, so has the Sun of the Gospel been standing over us for Fourscore years together."[1] The Sun of Righteousness, according to Jonathan Edwards, "shall *rise in the west*, contrary to the course of this world, or the course of things in the old heavens and earth."[2] Such language implied a break with the European past. It is not surprising that Thomas Jefferson proposed as a Seal of State for the new nation a representation of the children of Israel led by a pillar of light, or that the goddess of liberty on our coins is flanked by a rising sun.

The chosen people of the American colonies looked upon their mission in the wilderness not merely as the continuation of something old, but as the beginning of something new: they were to usher in the final stage of history. They had inherited a new world in a physical sense, and in order "to vindicate the most rigorous ideal of the Reformation" they felt it necessary, as Jonathan Edwards said, "to begin a new world in a spiritual respect." Moreover, they associated

7. This idea recurs frequently in colonial writing, but see especially Cotton Mather, *Magnalia Christi Americana . . .* 2 vols. (Hartford, 1820), I, 40–41; Jonathan Edwards, *Works*, 4 vols. (Boston, 1843), III, 314–15.
8. In his *Common Sense* (1776).
9. John Eliot, *The Daybreaking if not the Sun-*rising of the Gospel with the Indians in New England* (London, 1647).
1. Quoted by Perry Miller, *The New England Mind; From Colony to Province*, p. 178.
2. Jonathan Edwards, *op. cit.*, III, 316, 314–17. Italics are mine.

their drama of moral and spiritual regeneration with a special plot of virgin land untouched by mistakes of the past and where failure was inexcusable. By national covenant with the children of Israel, God had appointed a promised land in Canaan. John Cotton told his people that they were the heirs of the covenant promise and that New England was the appointed place.[3] Up and down the colonies, from Maine to Virginia, with a frequency suggesting that most colonists were, to a greater or less degree, touched by a sense of mission, colonists likened themselves to the tribes of Israel and called their country the "new Canaan," the "second Paradise," the "promised land," the "new heaven on earth." Not a few colonists, especially in New England, lived daily in agonized expectation of the Second Coming of Christ to America to inaugurate the millennium.[4] What the colonists did not realize was that, in tying their spiritual hopes to a plot of earth, they had already begun the process of what Carl Becker has called dismantling the celestial heaven in favor of an earthly one.

By the eighteenth century, piety had largely given way to moralism. But moralism continued to express a sense of mission and was intimately connected with the land. Just as the early frontier hardships had been held to be a test of the fitness of an Elect people in their incessant warfare against sin, so success in subduing the wilderness was tantamount to entering the kingdom of Heaven and seemed to demonstrate a direct causal relationship between moral effort and material reward. The opportunity for advancement afforded by the free lands of promise was contrasted to the static caste system of a Europe still fettered by feudalism. America's answer to Europe was now to rise in the economic scale by the application of industry, sobriety, and frugality, to improve upon the brutish state of nature, to carve out of the wilderness a pleasant land of rural villages, small shops, churches, and tilled fields—in short, to establish a superior civilization in which prosperity was the mark of special virtue. The process of moral regeneration was indeed a civilizing process, but, as opposed to the corrupt urban culture of Europe, the new American civilization was to have an agrarian basis, celebrating the simple virtues of the saw and the axe. The ultimate effect of the discovery of the new world was thus to substitute for the spiritual pilgrimage of Dante and Bunyan the "way West" as the way of salvation. It remained for an American Bunyan, Benjamin Franklin, to express the sense of this transformation in a moral fable which has gripped the imaginations of Americans ever since.

3. John Cotton, *God's Promise to his Plantations* (London, 1630), reprinted in *Old South Leaflets*, no. 53, pp. 1–15.
4. Ira V. Brown, "Watchers for the Second Coming: The Millenarian Tradition in America," *Miss. Valley Hist. Rev.*, XXXIX (1952), 441–58. Millennialism was more widespread in colonial America than Perry Miller is willing to grant.

II

It would be rather easy to show that Benjamin Franklin was the product of eighteenth-century urban culture extending from Europe to colonial Boston and Philadelphia, that Franklin's "Poor Richard" had an affinity with the *Compleat Tradesman* of Daniel Defoe's England, and that therefore Franklin's moral virtues were broadly middle-class rather than peculiarly American.[5] But such a view, whatever its merits, would overlook the fact that Americans, in response to a frontier environment and to a cyclical theory of history, have tended to emphasize the theme of moral regeneration in connection with the supposedly superior virtues of an agrarian civilization. The two most perceptive foreign observers of the nineteenth century, Alexis de Tocqueville and James Bryce, agreed in calling Americans as a whole the most moralistic and religious people in the world. The philosopher George Santayana once remarked that to be an American "is of itself almost a moral condition, an education, and a career," and in a similar tenor the expatriate Logan Pearsall Smith complained that Americans acted as if "America were more than a country, were a sort of cause."[6]

A. Whitney Griswold has shown that Franklin's thirst for moral perfection was a distillation of the Protestant business ethic taught by Puritan ministers in Franklin's hometown of Boston. Franklin himself acknowledged the influence of Cotton Mather's "Essays to Do Good." Though the colonial urban culture opened to Franklin the opportunities for advancement, gave him access to the scientific and philosophic ideas of the Enlightenment, and enlisted him in projects for civic improvement, his moral vision was colored by the presence of the frontier. The colonial city, after all, rested on rural foundations. Cosmopolitan though he was, Franklin dreamed of a great agrarian utopia in which to preserve America's "glorious public virtue."

As early as 1753, when he was preoccupied with problems of Indian defense, he proposed, as a means both of enriching himself and strengthening the British empire, to settle a wilderness colony on the banks of the Ohio. "What a glorious Thing it would be," he wrote on that occasion, "to settle in that fine Country a large strong Body of Religious and Industrious People!"[7] But his imperialistic vision of a greater England in the West reserved a special destiny for Americans which overshadowed the rôle of the mother country. He expressed this

5. This view is suggested by Stuart P. Sherman, "Franklin and the Age of Enlightenment," in *Americans* (New York: Charles Scribner's Sons, 1922), pp. 28–62; Carl and Jessica Bridenbaugh, *Rebels and Gentlemen: Philadelphia in the Age of Franklin* (New York: Reynal and Hitchcock, 1942), Ch. I; Gladys Meyer, *Free Trade in Ideas* (Morningside Heights: King's Crown Press, 1941); Vernon L. Parrington, *Main Currents in American Thought* (New York: Harcourt, Brace and Company, 1927), I, 166.

6. George Santayana, *Character and Opinion in the United States* (New York: Charles Scribner's Sons, 1920), p. 168; Logan Pearsall Smith, *Unforgotten Years* (Boston: Little, Brown and Company, 1939), p. 280.

7. *The Writings of Benjamin Franklin*, ed. Albert H. Smyth, 10 vols. (New York: MacMillan Company, 1905–07), III, 339.

incipient patriotism in the sun and light imagery common to the rhetoric of westward expansion. " 'Tis said the Arts delight to travel Westward," he once remarked.[8] He was long of the opinion "that the *foundations of the future grandeur and stability of the British empire lie in America.*"[9] He playfully attributed a cosmic significance to the work of spiritual pioneering: "by *clearing America* of Woods" Americans were "*Scouring* our Planet, . . . and so making this Side of our Globe reflect a brighter Light to the Eyes of the Inhabitants in *Mars* or *Venus. . . .*"[1] Franklin early identified the frontier with opportunity and tended to measure spiritual progress by progress in converting the wilderness into a paradise of material plenty.

A city-dweller, by profession a printer and tradesman, Franklin nevertheless located the true source of virtue in agricultural pursuits. "There seem to be but three ways for a nation to acquire wealth," he wrote, with an eye to the widening breach between England and the colonies. "The first is by *war*, as the Romans did, in plundering their conquered neighbors. This is *robbery*. The second by *commerce*, which is generally *cheating*. The third by *agriculture*, the only *honest way*, wherein man receives a real increase of the seed thrown into the ground, in a kind of continual miracle. . . ."[2] This was more than physiocratic doctrine; it was a program to keep a chosen people on the path of righteousness and prepare them for the moral and spiritual leadership of the earth. He made it clear that public morality was his special concern when he wrote after independence had been secured: "The vast Quantity of Forest Lands we have yet to clear, and put in order for Cultivation, will for a long time keep the Body of our Nation laborious and frugal."[3] He repeatedly contrasted the vices of Europe and England with the "glorious public virtue" of America and habitually bestowed upon American farmers the ennobling title of "Cultivators of the Earth." By an outstanding example of good works, by his *Almanacks* and *Autobiography*, by his proposed *Art of Virtue* and by other writings, Franklin constituted himself chief guardian of the national conscience.

It has been said that Franklin's ethics were those of a tradesman and that the eighteenth-century concept of tradesman was English in origin. Yet an English writer, D. H. Lawrence, has found Franklin's archetypal new-world quality essentially in his moralism, and Herbert Schneider has written that, as a moralist, Franklin was "a child of the New England frontier."[4] The truth is that the individualistic virtues of industry, frugality and sobriety taught, if not always practiced, by Franklin, were adaptable to both the tradesman and farmer. Like the

8. *Ibid.*, IV, 194.
9. *Ibid.*, IV, 4.
1. *Writings*, III, 72–73.
2. *Writings*, V, 202.
3. *Ibid.*, IX, 245.

4. D. H. Lawrence, *Studies in Classic American Literature* (New York: Thomas A. Seltzer, 1923), pp. 13–31; Herbert W. Schneider, *The Puritan Mind* (New York: Henry Holt and Company, 1930), p. 256.

middle-class tradesman, the pioneer farmer was a small entrepreneur and capitalist, a speculator in land, a "cultivator," as Veblen has said, "of the main chance as well as of the fertile soil." The career of Daniel Defoe, who died in obscurity and poverty, shows that Defoe spoke for a single class which was not yet able to break through the cramping restrictions of class and caste. Franklin spoke for a whole nation of middle-class *arrivistes*, but addressed himself particularly to the "Cultivators of the Earth" in opposition to the urban dwellers of the colonial city and of the European metropolis.

The American mission of moral regeneration derived its dynamism from the tension generated by the polarity between what the colonists considered an over-ripe stage of civilization in a Europe corrupted by feudal institutions and a simpler, agrarian society which more than made up in morals what it lacked in sophistication. American moralism implied a repudiation of European culture and of urbanism, though not a denial of the civilizing process. As the Revolution drew near, Franklin exaggerated the differences. From England he wrote to Joseph Galloway, who longed for a reconciliation, "When I consider the extream Corruption prevalent among all Orders of Men in this old rotten State, and the glorious publick Virtue so predominant in our rising Country, I cannot but apprehend more Mischief than Benefit from a closer Union."[5] Political and military necessity demanded a smiling compliance with the ways of the world in Paris, where, among the powdered heads, he wore his fur cap as a native emblem; but he also had private reservations about the state of French culture. Occasionally his moral obsessions led him to flirt with a primitivism akin to the sentimental cult of the noble savage. Returning from a tour of Ireland and Scotland, he wrote.[6]

> . . . if my Countrymen should ever wish for the honour of having among them a gentry enormously wealthy, let them sell their Farms and pay rack'd Rents; the Scale of the Landlords will rise, as that of the Tenants is depress'd, who will soon become poor, tattered, dirty, and abject in Spirit. Had I never been in the American colonies, but was to form my Judgment of Civil Society by what I have lately seen, I should never advise a Nation of Savages to admit of Civilization: For I assure you, that, in the Possession and Enjoyment of the various Comforts of Life, compar'd to these People every Indian is a Gentleman. . . .

In his identification of prosperity with virtue Franklin remembered that the covenant promise was with a whole people, not merely the few, and he wanted, as he said, "a general happy Mediocrity of fortune."

To be an American was to be a backtrailer to a more sophisticated society, in itself a moral condition. An aristocracy of wealth based on commerce and land speculation blossomed in the larger seaport towns of America. Rich Boston merchants thirsted after London, much as London aspired to Paris. Like Jefferson and many other Americans imbued with a sense of mission, Franklin did not want to see colonial urban centers emulate the class patterns of European society, and he, too, sometimes wished for an "ocean of fire" between the old world and the new. He transferred some of his animus against Europe to the coastal towns. "The People of the Trading Towns," he wrote at the end of the Revolution, "may be rich and luxurious, while the Country possesses all the Virtues, that tend to private Happiness and publick Prosperity. Those Towns are not much regarded by the Country; they are hardly considered as an essential Part of the States . . . we may hope the Luxury of a few Merchants on the Seacoast will not be the Ruin of America."[7] Franklin viewed with some alarm the social dislocations and misery caused by the new factory system in Europe. No more than Jefferson did he want to see Americans "twirling a distaff" in factories. Though he was the prophet of American technological efficiency, he did not anticipate industrialism. It may be supposed that his response to such urban problems as fire-fighting, poor street-lighting, pauperism, and improper sanitation was unconsciously motivated by a patriotic desire to avoid or mitigate the worst evils of urbanization.

Franklin's whole moral fiber was geared to raising a new man and a new society in the world of nations. Viewed in this light, his *Autobiography* is a great moral fable pursuing on a secular level the theme of John Bunyan's *Pilgrim's Progress.* There is little doubt of the serious intent underlying either the *Autobiography* or the creation of "Poor Richard," to impart moral instruction to the public. He wrote the *Autobiography,* as he said, to acquaint his posterity with the means of his success, "as they may find some of them suitable to their own situations, and therefore fit to be imitated."[8] After breaking off the work, a friend persuaded him to continue it on the grounds that it would be useful to millions and would "lead the youth to equal the industry and temperance of thy early youth."[9] Another friend urged its continuation "in conjunction with your Art of Virtue (which you design to publish) of improving the features of private character, and consequently of aiding all happiness, both public and domestic."[1] Franklin originated *Poor Richard's Almanack* to make money, but, more importantly, to convey "instruction among the common people." He filled the calendar spaces "with proverbial sentences, chiefly such as inculcated industry and frugality, as the means of

---

7. *Writings,* IX, 245–46, 248.
8. Benjamin Franklin, *Autobiography,* ed. Dixon Wecter (Rinehart Edn., 1948), p. 1. [See this edition, p. 1]

9. *Autobiography,* p. 71. [This edition, p. 58.]
1. *Ibid.,* p. 73. [This edition, p. 59.]

procuring wealth, and thereby securing virtue."[2] Of late it has been popular to say with Robert Spiller that "Poor Richard" was a humorous creation, never intended to be taken seriously. But Franklin's very humor was a vehicle for serious moral instruction and also expressed his sense of special destiny. Thus, his tall tales of sheep with tails so heavily laden with wool that they needed trailer-carts to carry them and of the whale which chased salmon up Niagara Falls, tales which anticipated the characteristic humor of the American frontier, were Franklin's way of whittling the urban sophisticate and European down to size and telling him, in effect, that things grew bigger and better in God's country.

The *Autobiography* is not simply a formless record of personal experience, or just a charming success story. Consciously or unconsciously, it is a work of imagination which, by incorporating the "race" consciousness of a people, achieves the level of folk myth. Franklin's biographer, Carl Van Doren, tell us that Franklin had no model for his kind of autobiography.[3] This is not quite true. As a report on Franklin's spiritual progress in the new heaven on earth, the *Autobiography* in its basic dramatic form parallels Bunyan's great allegory. Franklin merely substituted, to use the phrase of Carl Becker, the secular story with a happy ending for the Christian story with the happy ending. *Pilgrim's Progress* was a best seller in New England during the latter part of the seventeenth century.[4] It admirably fitted the situation of a people whose feet were planted on the path to worldly success, but whose heads were still filled with visions of the Celestial City. Franklin's first book was *Pilgrim's Progress*, and his favorite author was John Bunyan.[5] Franklin absorbed from the pages of *Pilgrim's Progress* lessons in artistry as well as confirmations for the new-world theme of moral regeneration. According to Franklin, Honest John was the first author whom he had met "who mixed narration and dialogue, a method of writing very engaging to the reader, who in the most interesting parts finds himself, as it were, brought into the company and present at the discourse."[6] Franklin regarded Defoe's works as imitations of Bunyan in this respect. Franklin also combined narrative and dialogue in his *Autobiography* in order to convey the felt immediacy of his experience, but in relating Bunyan's theme to the details of his new environment, he created an allegory of American middle-class superiority.

Franklin states his central organizing theme at the outset: his emergence "from the poverty and obscurity" in which he was born and

2. *Ibid.*, pp. 97–98. [This edition, p. 79.]
3. Carl Van Doren, *Benjamin Franklin* (New York: Viking Press, 1938), pp. 414–15.
4. See the book lists in Daniel Henchman's ms. account book in the Boston Public Library. Also Thomas G. Wright, *Literary Culture in*

Early New England, 1620–1730 (New Haven: Yale University Press, 1920), p. 123.
5. *Autobiography*, pp. 10, 21. [This edition, pp. 9, 18.]
6. *Autobiography*, p. 21. [This edition, p. 18.]

bred "to a state of affluence and some degree of reputation in the world."[7] He gives to this secular "rise" a moral and spiritual meaning discoverable in the special blessings of God. The boy entering Philadelphia with three loaves under his arm is obviously the prototype of Bunyan's Christian beginning his toilsome ascent to the Heavenly City. Franklin heightens the drama of his struggle upward against odds in his more worldly pilgrimage by reiterating the contrast between his humble beginnings and his improved station in life. Three times he halts his narrative at conspicuous points in order to recall to his readers the pathetic picture of his first arrival in Philadelphia. He frames the Philadelphia anecdote as carefully as if he were deliberately setting out to create an immortal legend. "I have been the more particular," he writes, "in this description of my journey, and shall be so of my first entry into the city, that you may in your mind compare such unlikely beginnings with the figure I have since made there."[8] He would have the reader believe that his future wife, Deborah Read, happened also to be present on that occasion to observe his unlikely beginnings.

Since his marriage is a marriage of convenience contributing to his rise in life, he associates the episode of the rolls with his courtship of Miss Read. Once established as an up-and-coming printer, he notes for the reader's convenience that he "made rather a more respectable appearance in the eyes of Miss Read than I had done when she first happened to see me *eating my roll* in the street."[9] Though his success story is a triumph of moral individualism and personal salvation, he identifies it with the rise of a whole people. His rise in life thus parallels the growth of Philadelphia. After he has bought out his partner Meredith, there is a building boom: "whereas I remembered well, that when I first walked about the streets of Philadelphia, *eating my roll*, I saw most of the houses in Walnut Street . . . with bills on to be let. . . ."[1] When, finally, he achieves world-wide fame by his electrical experiments, he confesses to being flattered by the honors heaped upon him: "for, *considering my low beginning*, they were great things to me."[2] By now he has no need to mention the symbolic rolls.

Franklin's confessed *errata* are analogous to Christian's bundle of sins and to the giant Despair, over which he must prevail in order to gain the Heavenly City. Carl Van Doren has said that Franklin owed his success to "natural gifts of which Poor Richard could not tell the secret."[3] But Franklin was not altogether without a sense of sin, and he believed that good works were the necessary means to personal salva-

7. *Ibid.*, p. 1. [This edition, p. 1.]
8. *Autobiography*, p. 23. [This edition, p. 20.]
9. *Ibid.*, p. 27. Italics are mine. [This edition, p. 22.]

1. *Ibid.*, p. 65. Italics are mine. [This edition, p. 53.]
2. *Autobiography*, p. 123. Italics are mine. [This edition, p. 101.]
3. Carl Van Doren, *Franklin*, p. 118.

tion, or success. Obversely, as his attitude towards charity in the *Autobiography* indicates, he felt that failure to rise in life was the result of moral turpitude. Accordingly, in one of the most famous passages of the *Autobiography*, about the year 1728, Franklin "conceived the bold and arduous project of arriving at moral perfection."[4] The important point is not that he failed, but that he tried and that the program of good works which he outlined here and elsewhere, in effect, completed the long process of dismantling the Celestial City. A tale by Nathaniel Hawthorne, "The Celestial Railroad," suggests an ironic inversion of Bunyan's original allegory. Franklin, in his pilgrimage towards the heavenly city, sends his baggage ahead by postal service and sets up signposts for other travelers. He fills the Slough of Despond with Philadelphia cobblestones and almanacs. He lights the Valley of the Shadow of Death with street lamps. He smites Apollyon with a thunderbolt. He throws a bridge over the River Styx.

In the spiritual drama of a chosen people lay the source of that economic romanticism, so frequently confused with materialism, by which so many Americans have assumed a God-given right to the fruits of an Edenic tree. As Franklin said, "The Divine Being seems to have manifested his Approbation . . . by the remarkable Prosperity with which He has been pleased to favour the whole Country."[5] Americans after Franklin would merely inherit the earth by presumption and without waiting for Divine Approbation. Franklin's motives for land speculation were not sordidly pecuniary, but included, as did his enthusiasm for science, a poetic conception of national destiny. Thus, he called his proposed colony on the Ohio the future "paradise on earth."[6] The outbreak of the Revolution ended his petition to the Crown for western lands, but Americans came into a larger inheritance. To a great degree the American passion for liberty was an extension of the passion to possess the earthly inheritance. This passion was not essentially economic, for Americans felt that they were enacting a spiritual pilgrimage in their westward trek towards light.

The spiritual longing of the colonists prepared the psychological foundations of the nineteenth-century concept of Manifest Destiny, which sanctioned American imperialism. Thus, Nathaniel Ames, Franklin's competitor in almanacs, predicted in 1758 that "As the celestial light of the gospel was directed here by the finger of God, . . . So arts and sciences will change the face of nature in their tour from hence over the Appalachian Mountains to the Western Ocean."[7] After Franklin's death Americans who were disappointed

4. *Autobiography*, p. 83. [This edition, p. 66.]
5. *Writings*, VIII, 614.
6. Quoted by Carl Van Doren, *Franklin*, p. 592.
7. In Moses Coit Tyler, *A History of American Literature, 1607–1765* (Ithaca: Cornell University Press, 1949), p. 372.

with the results of coastal civilization pursued their special destiny inland, continuing to read the promise of American life in the westward cycle of the sun. At the height of westward expansion in the nineteenth century, Fourth of July orators often recaptured the old millennial fervor and were typically lyrical in sun worship:[8]

> Christianity, rational philosophy, and constitutional liberty, like an ocean of light are rolling their resistless tide over the earth. . . . Doubtless there may be partial revulsions. But the great movement will . . . be progressive, till the millennial sun shall rise in all the effulgence of universal day.

Americans refashioned for their own use a conventional rhetoric of spirit which had antedated the voyages of Columbus. For the millions who went west in their new-world version of "Pilgrim's Progress," the classic anecdote was the story of the poor boy who came to Philadelphia with three rolls under his arms and rose to fame and fortune.

ROBERT FREEMAN SAYRE

The Worldly Franklin and the Provincial Critics†

Despite the passage of years, the portrait of Benjamin Franklin most prominently hung in the imaginations of many educated and emancipated Americans is still that etched by D. H. Lawrence and other writers and critics of the twenties and thirties like William Carlos Williams and Charles Angoff. Their essays, particularly Lawrence's, have had a wide circulation,[1] and they have put to flight the nineteenth-century conception of Franklin as a model of virtue and industry. The "wisdom" of Poor Richard is now classified as smug opportunism. Franklin's pluralism is now looked upon as cynically noncontroversial. Franklin retains his mythic status as an "original" American, a prototype of the race, but that type is now regarded as a little old-fashioned, moralistic, plodding, and rather tiresome.

It is not the function of this paper to defend the man. That has been ably and recently done by I. Bernard Cohen and Alfred Owen Ald-

8. The following quotations, typical of a great many in the literature of nineteenth-century westward expansion, is taken from Ralph H. Gabriel, *The Course of American Democratic Thought* (New York: Ronald Press, 1940), p. 36.
† Source: *Texas Studies in Literature and Language,* 4 (1963), 512–24.
1. *Studies in Classic American Literature* (New York, 1923, and Anchor Books, 1955) is also in Edmund Wilson (ed.), *The Shock of Recogni-*

tion (New York, 1943 and 1955), and abridged in Charles L. Sanford (ed.), *Benjamin Franklin and the American Character* (Boston, 1955). Angoff's criticism appeared in his *A Literary History of the American People* (New York and London, 1931), and is also abridged in Sanford. Williams' "Poor Richard" is in *In the American Grain* (Norfolk, Connecticut, 1925). References in this article will be to Williams' and Angoff's first editions and to the Anchor edition of Lawrence.

dridge,[2] and the publication of *The Papers of Benjamin Franklin* by the American Philosophical Society and Yale University will eventually confirm his own belief that "When a man's actions are just and honourable, the more they are known the more his reputation is increased and established."[3] Neither does this paper aim to glue back together the dull and admonitory Victorian Franklin so conclusively smashed by the Jazz Age. The essence of the Lawrence-Angoff attack was that Franklin protected himself from experience behind a wall of maxims and moral dogma, a just and necessary criticism of the man as they had been taught him. What is needed is a defense and reappraisal of the *Autobiography*, or the four memoirs to which we give that name. It is this self-portrait, after all, by which Franklin will always be known and which provided the material for most of the iconoclasm; so it is appropriate that on it we should launch our counterattack. The very nature of the *Autobiography* disproves the notion that Franklin held a static, moralistic attitude toward his experience. Its three main sections demonstrate that he was continually reassessing his early life and past in the terms and style of his present. It reflects the ceaseless adventure of his personality and his always fresh receptivity to new points of view. The time has come for new criticism of it.

I

The detractions of Lawrence, Williams, and Angoff all employ two techniques. First they blame Franklin for faults and vulgarities which are not his but those of men we are encouraged to believe are his ethical heirs. Secondly, they abstract portions of his work and damn the whole by the part. Williams quotes the whole of *Information to Those Who Would Remove to America*, then follows it with five pages of "Notes for A Commentary on Franklin." Lawrence and Angoff, whose interests are more explicit fixed on the *Autobiography*, quote most extensively from the portion dealing with the author's "Project of arriving at moral Perfection." Indeed, it is for this piece that the man and the self-portrait have suffered most, and it is here that reappraisals are most important, but first I shall deal with those aspersions in which Franklin is blamed for the sins of his supposed successors.

The attack on Franklin as moralistic and overly dedicated to the Goddess of "Getting Ahead" is, at bottom, not so much an attack on him as on the middle class. Thus Angoff corrects Carlyle for calling him the "father of all the Yankees" and says, "It would be more

2. Cohen, *Benjamin Franklin: His Contribution to the American Tradition* (Indianapolis, 1953); Aldridge, *Franklin and His French Contemporaries* (New York, 1957). Carl Van Doren's *Benjamin Franklin* (New York, 1945) is standard and Carl Becker's article in *The Dictionary of American Biography* is the best short estimate of Franklin in print.

3. Franklin, letter to Juliana Ritchie, Paris, January 19, 1777. Quoted from Carl Van Doren (ed.), *Benjamin Franklin's Autobiographical Writings* (New York, 1945), p. 426. All quotations of Franklin's letters are from this work.

accurate to call Franklin the father of all the Kiwanians."[4] Lawrence similarly berates him for inventing a God perfectly suited to the ends of Andrew Carnegie. "God is the supreme servant of men who want to get on, to *produce*. Providence. The provider. The heavenly storekeeper. The everlasting Wanamaker."[5] This is lively pamphleteering, but it is misdirected. About halfway through *Babbitt* Sinclair Lewis says that,

> If you had asked Babbitt what his religion was, he would have answered in sonorous Boosters' Club rhetoric, "My religion is to serve my fellow men, to honor my brother as myself, and to do my bit to make life happier for one and all."

This—a wretched degeneration of Franklin's "the most acceptable Service of God is doing Good to man"—is a far more accurate rendering of the public religion of the Kiwanians than anything that can be pejoratively extracted from Franklin. His religion, we can tell by his writings, was almost constantly on his mind. It impresses different people different ways, but it was not cunning, cocky, or selfish.

The failure of Angoff and Lawrence in understanding Franklin's statement of his creed in the famous letter to Ezra Stiles and in the opening of the third memoir is a failure of sophistication and humor. The eighty-four-year-old statesman was in his best form when he wrote President Stiles, and there is something benign in his replies to the minister's entreaties. If Yale College wants a portrait of him, then the artist "must not delay setting about it, or I may slip through his fingers." He states his beliefs simply and succinctly, holding them too privately to wish them publicized and too sacredly to wish any excitement made over them. If there is blasphemy about the long, careful, and yet easy sentence on the divinity of Jesus of Nazareth, it is a blasphemy invoked expressly to forestall the remark's being taken too seriously. To treat the creed as a hypocrite's, as Lawrence does, or to treat the letter as "flippant," as Angoff does, is to miss Franklin's sincere humility and grace. Like Stiles, these critics were comparatively provincial!

They were similarly obtuse before the Poor Richard aspect of Franklin. Carl Van Doren observed that the supposed "wisdom" of Poor Richard is hardly Franklin's. As well as the fact of the mask, it must also be remembered that the maxims are first and foremost folk sayings that go back hundreds of years.[6] Not all are in support of industry and thrift. They are crazily contradictory. Lawrence is again fighting symbol rather than fact:

4. Angoff, II, 304.
5. Lawrence, p. 20.
6. Robert E. Spiller, et al. (eds.), *Literary His-* *tory of the United States* (New York, 1946), pp. 105–106.

I can remember, when I was a little boy, my father used to buy a scrubby yearly almanac . . . And . . . crammed in corners it had little anecdotes and humorisms, with a moral tag. And I used to have my little priggish laugh at the woman who counted her chickens before they were hatched, and so forth, and I was convinced that honesty was the best policy, also a little priggishly. The author of these bits was Poor Richard, and Poor Richard was Benjamin Franklin, writing in Philadelphia well over a hundred years before.

And probably I haven't got over those Poor Richard tags yet. I rankle still with them. They are thorns in young flesh.[7]

He criticizes himself, not Franklin. Angoff, recognizing that the wisdom is of a "low order," argues that "one does not always have to be a vulgarian when talking to the man in the street. Consider Jesus and Socrates and Confucious and Lao-Tze. Consider Montaigne. Consider even Krylov."[8] This is flattering company for a seller of almanacs!

A fact that must constantly be attended in considering Franklin is the almost unequalled length of his active life and the multiplicity of his careers. The urbane letter to Stiles, for example, comes fifty-eight years after the first edition of the *Almanac*. Within these years are at least five complete careers: printer, civic leader, scientist, ambassador, patriot, and a whole host of sidelines and occasional interests. The scope of his achievement and the reach of his personality make the narrow specialist gasp. He was not a poet; but he was vastly creative. All this must be remembered in dealing with the *Autobiography*.

II

First of all, the modern critic of that work must recall that it was written in three (really four) different installments and that each reflects the place and time at which it was written. The memoirs are no more the same throughout than Franklin was the same when he wrote them. To realize this, each must be studied separately. I shall begin by taking up the first part, then the third and fourth sections, and finally the second one, since it, written at Passy, outside Paris, in 1784, provided Lawrence and Angoff with their most remarkable criticisms.

The first part, as is well known, was written in August, 1771, while Franklin was staying at the home of Bishop Shipley near Twyford in Hampshire. He at that time liked England, the Shipleys were good friends, and his life was comfortable. As Max Farrand has said, this memoir in every way indicates this repose and contentment.[9] Note the opening:

---

7. Lawrence, p. 24.
8. Angoff, II, 305.

9. *Meet Doctor Franklin* (Philadelphia, 1943), p. 31.

Dear Son,
I have ever had a Pleasure in obtaining any little Anecdotes of my
Ancestors. You may remember the Enquiries I made among the
Remains of my Relations when you were with me in England; and
the Journey I took for that purpose. Now imagining it may be
equally agreeable to you to know the Circumstances of *my* Life,
many of which you are yet unacquainted with; and expecting a
Weeks uninterrupted Leisure in my present Country Retirement, I
sit down to write them for you.[1]

This memoir is uniform in tone and masterfully organized. It adheres
to a fairly strict chronological order, yet is also held together by several
continuing themes—his ambition to be in business for himself, his
education in writing, his struggle to repay the debt to Vernon, his
regret over such "errata" as the effort to seduce his friend James
Ralph's mistress, and his uneven progress toward marriage with Deb-
bie Read. In some ways it is a short picaresque novel, with deceitful
villains like Governor Keith, braggadocios like Samuel Keimer, and
adventurous travels from Boston through New York and New Jersey to
Philadelphia, back to Boston, to London, and back to Philadelphia.
Franklin and the other "characters" occasionaly masquerade and
mistake one another or fail to distinguish between real and apparent
natures. The hero is a bright, yet over-proud and ambitious, young
man whose impatience to succeed makes him incompatible with his
brother and vulnerable to the empty promises of Governor Keith. The
narrator, on the other hand, is a skilled story teller and indulgent older
man who is now amused by the slips and falls of his younger self and
now ashamed and penitent. Moralistic commentary is actually very
small; there is much more in Defoe and a good deal more in
Richardson. Franklin moves too fast. Finding himself too involved in
a record of the life of his parents, he abruptly reins himself in:

By my rambling Digressions I perceive my self to be grown old. I
us'd to write more methodically. But one does not dress for private
Company as for a publick Ball. 'Tis perhaps only Negligence.

To return. I continu'd thus employ'd. (p. 8, this edition)

Because of the reference to "private Company," the opening "Dear
Son," and the occasional direct address to his son, many people persist
in believing this part of the *Autobiography* to differ markedly from the
other parts in being private and not intended for publication. It does
differ markedly, but this is not how. William Franklin was at this time
governor of New Jersey and about forty years old, considerably beyond
paternal counsel. Robert Spiller is right in calling the various signs of a

1. Max Farrand (ed.), *Benjamin Franklin's
Memoirs, Parallel Text Edition* (Berkeley,
1949), p. 2. All quotations are from the version
of the original manuscript. Succeeding references will be given in parentheses. [This edition, p. 1.]

letter literary devices, techniques by which Franklin established his particular relationship to his material.[2] He definitely designed it for publication, though not until after his death. Furthermore he enjoyed writing it, and he took in it, as he did with much of his writing, the opportunities it offered for self-examination and self-advertisement. The famous arrival in Philadelphia, "eating my Roll," is recognized to have enormous symbolic value, and the elder Franklin used it to its fullest advantage. He gives the exact itinerary of his walk through the town, the people he met, the things he did, the places he stopped, and the "Meeting House of the Quakers near the Market . . . the first House I was in or slept in, in Philadelphia." (p. 21) William Carlos Williams' comment that " 'He's sort of proud of his commonness, isn't he?' "[3] should be a truism, not an insight. He was not only proud of it—loving to "gratify my own Vanity" and being willing to "give it fair Quarter wherever I meet with it"; (p. 2) he also knew how to manipulate and display it so as to make it work for him. It put other people at their ease. It was a self-imposed check on his social ambitions and at the same time gave great interest to his success. It was the foundation of his most famous and effective public character, "Benjamin Franklin of Philadelphia, printer."

In the third and fourth sections of the *Autobiography* he is decidedly the Philadelphian. The ambassador has returned a national hero, has participated in the Constitutional Convention, and the memoirs show it. The account of General Braddock's campaign, the offhand remarks about working hours in London, and the impatience with Lord Loudon's delay of the ship Franklin sailed in to England in 1757 all reflect a post-Revolution Anglophobia which is entirely lacking from the first piece. This is in spite of the obvious fact that the first was written sooner after the events themselves occurred. Stylistically, the narrative control and the power of organization have been lost, or else they simply were not so available within the material, for the action is naturally that of a busier, more widely involved man. Yet the narrator is a more deceptively naive, more ultimately sophisticated man. He was back in Philadelphia when he wrote it, in August, 1788, and in one sense was an old Poor Richard. Practically every adventure is preceded or followed by a moral or principle: *"It is hard for an empty sack to stand upright."* "When Men are employ'd they are best contented." "Human Felicity is produc'd not so much by great Pieces of good Fortune that seldom happen, as by little Advantages that occur every Day." "The best public Measures are therefore seldom *adopted from previous Wisdom*, but *forc'd by the Occasion.*"

So much for the wise saws and modern instances!

This old man is rich in many ways. Rich in the helter-skelter clutter

2. "Franklin on the Art of Being Human," *Proceedings of the American Philosophical Soci-* *ety*, C (August, 1956), 313.
3. Williams, p. 153.

of a busy, eventful, refreshingly earthy, confoundingly practical, and still ordered and thoughtful life. It is gloriously undignified: fire ladders, dirty streets, smoky lamps, stoves, bags and buckets, waggons, munitions, bonds and subscriptions, pigs and chickens, schools, evangelists, and dull assemblies. Where the memoir written at Twyford in 1771 was like a picaresque novel, this one is like portions of *Gargantua and Pantagruel*.[4] Franklin has been called Rabelaisian for certain of his drinking songs and obscene hoaxes. He is much more like the other Rabelais of Renaissance energy, good-will, and boundless possibilities.

Mixed in with all this is a modest and shrewd politician. The earlier lessons about vanity and the manipulations of appearance and reality are now extended and employed in one project after another. While making his way as a printer, he had learned that it was necessary "not only to be in *Reality* Industrious & frugal, but to avoid all *Appearances* of the Contrary." (p. 54) In putting together the Philadelphia Public Library, he soon felt "the Impropriety of presenting one's self as the Proposer of any useful Project that might be suppos'd to raise one's Reputation in the smallest degree above that of one's Neighbours, when one has the need of their Assistance to accomplish that Project." (p. 64) This is policy of a most subtle sort. The projects undertaken were entirely in the public interest; people might have been expected to subdue their personal vanities and antagonisms. Franklin became attentive, however, both to how people *should* behave and also to how they *do* behave. Support for the public hospital from private subscription and from the Pennsylvania Assembly was obtained only after a system of matching public and private funds was devised. Then members of the Assembly "conceiv'd they might have the Credit of being charitable without the Expence." (p. 103) Pacifist Quakers, Franklin found, were not opposed to "the Defence of the Country . . . provided they were not requir'd to assist in it." (p. 94)

The actor in these projects became a master of compromise and held within himself an amazing combination of idealism, vision, and practicality. Of great interest is his receptivity to new ideas, to new possibilities, and to new roles for himself. Most autobiography is the account of an arrival, written by the figure who has arrived and who holds a fixed conception of himself. Compare, for example, Gibbon's picture of himself as the emerging author of *The Decline and Fall of the Roman Empire* in his *Memoirs of my Life and Writings*. Franklin, while in one sense always remaining "Benjamin Franklin of Philadelphia, printer," is also constantly becoming something else: from printer to public servant to scientist to ambassador and on to the patriot and retired philosophizer who is the author of the third and fourth sections of the *Autobiography*.

4. *Gargantua and Pantagruel* is the satirical masterpiece of Francois Rabelais (1494?–1553).

It is because of this flexibility and never-ending development of Franklin's character that I have been stressing the difference between the man writing and the man written about. The first memoir is a story of youthful adventure and self-discovery told by a sixty-five-year-old scientist, political journalist, and colonial representative. In a rare hour of country retirement he is recollecting and confessing his wilder days. The third and fourth are the work of an eighty-two-year-old national hero. Back at his remodeled Philadelphia residence he is reviewing the mass of the public projects of his thirties and forties and writing *memoirs* of a more conventional nature. In giving the account of his experience as a civic leader he is also composing a kind of handbook. It is full of the lessons he learned and of counsel for future committee men, militia officers, and good citizens.

III

The much abused second memoir requires an even closer attention to the place and time of its composition and to the differences between author and subject. Alfred Owen Aldridge's study of Franklin in France makes us more aware than ever of the great ambassador's uncanny sense for depicting himself both as he was and also as the various circles of his friends, his associates, and the public thought he was. The particular selections of his writings which were available there before his arrival in December, 1776, combined with his first appearance in plain clothes and marten-fur cap to crystallize him in the French imagination as the rural sage, the "philosophical Quaker."[5] A letter of Franklin's to Mary Stevenson Hewson, written from Paris on January 12, 1777, demonstrates his awareness of the effect he had created:

> My dear, dear Polly: Figure to yourself an old man, with grey hair appearing under a marten-fur cap, among the powdered heads of Paris. It is this odd figure that salutes you, with handfuls of blessings on you and your dear little ones.

This half-cultivated and half-imposed role of the rural philosopher was a pose, but it was not a deceitful pose. To think so is to be a little provincial and to rush to conclusions. Franklin's poses were chosen to reveal rather than to conceal: they were a means of presenting himself. The character of the philosophical Quaker, which could be abstracted from works so widely different as *The Way to Wealth*, his descriptions of the American Indians, and the reports of his electrical experiments, became another elaboration of "Benjamin Franklin of Philadelphia, printer."

At the same time the French experience developed in him a certain sophistication and gallantry few Americans are able to appreciate.

5. Aldridge, pp. 38–73.

Most are ignorant of it and continue to treat him as a moralistic pedant. On the other hand, if they knew the Franklin of the French bagatelles and hoaxes, the letters to Madame Helvetius and the chess games with Madame Brillon, they would respond with the Puritan horror of John and Abigail Adams! The delightful quality of moral pieces like "The Morals of Chess," "Remarks Concerning the Savages of North America," and "The Handsome and the Deformed Leg" is that they season and age—*mellow* might be most apt—moral instruction with a sunny humor. The Passy Franklin could remain quite serious, but he mixed the seriousness with the style and artfulness of play.[6] In this way he was both the rural philosopher in the plain Poor Richard sense and also the rural philosopher in a pastoral sense, a man who gave in simplicity the furthest and most natural expression of his worldiness and experience. The author of the second part of the *Autobiography* was a *naïf*.

The major portion of the second memoir and the part of it that is best known and most attacked is the description of the project for attaining moral perfection. This is the passage by which many well-intentioned readers make Franklin such an admonitory exemplar and it is largely because of this passage that Lawrence and Angoff found him so detestable. In reading it, however, one must forget the pious, bifocaled Doctor Franklin and concentrate on the sly and straightfaced ironies which attend the recollections of youthful presumption. The man who writes, in 1784, is very different from the conscientious young tradesman of 1728–1730:

> It was about this time that I conceiv'd the bold and arduous Project of arriving at moral Perfection. I wish'd to live without committing any Fault at any time; I would conquer all that either Natural Inclination, Custom, or Company might lead me into. As I knew, or thought I knew, what was right and wrong, I did not see why I might not *always* do the one and avoid the other. But I soon found I had undertaken a Task of more Difficulty than I had imagined. (p. 66)

At this point Franklin discusses the need of a method and his selection of the virtues to be acquired. "For the sake of Clearness," he decided "to use rather more Names with fewer Ideas annex'd to each, than a few Names with more Ideas; . . ." This would also have the advantage of allowing him to devote himself more completely to each virtue. "Temperance" might be more easily arrived at if it referred only to eating and drinking. Intemperance of other kinds could be resisted by "Moderation" and "Chastity."

6. See the discussion of play in Johan Huizinga's *Homo Ludens: A Study of the Play Element in Culture* (Boston, 1955), pp. 173–194. Herman Melville, a more penetrating critic of Franklin than Lawrence or Angoff, called him "didactically waggish," in introducing him in Paris in *Israel Potter*.

The final list of thirteen and the famous precepts that accompanied each ("Eat not to Dulness/ Drink not to Elevation." "Speak not but what may benefit others or yourself./ Avoid trifling Conversation." Etc.) are so familiar that they need not be repeated. It is more important to reread the story of the attempt to practice the virtues.

> My Intention being to acquire the *Habitude* of all these Virtues, I judg'd it would be well not to distract my Attention by attempting the whole at once, but to fix it on one of them at a time, . . . *Temperance* first, as it tends to procure that Coolness & Clearness of Head, which is so necessary where constant Vigilance was to be kept up, and Guard maintain'd, against the unremitting Attraction of ancient Habits, and the Force of perpetual Temptations. This being acquir'd & establish'd *Silence* would be more easy, . . . (p. 68)

It all fitted together, each virtue being ingeniously conceived to facilitate the acquisition of the next! To keep score he invented the childlike plan of the "little Book in which I allotted a Page for each of the Virtues." Only Franklin could have done it. By comparison Robinson Crusoe's balance sheet of the "Evil" and "Good" in being castaway on his island is primitive: Franklin's "moral algebra" is complete with red-ink lines, columns, mottos, dots, abbreviations, and headlines. Children are absorbed by it, even D. H. Lawrence! ("It is rather fun to play at Benjamin.")

> I made a little Book in which I allotted a Page for each of the virtues. I rul'd each Page with red Ink, so as to have seven Columns, one for each Day of the Week, marking each Column with a letter for the Day. I cross'd these Columns with thirteen red Lines, marking the Beginning of each Line with the first Letter of one of the Virtues, on which Line & in its proper Column I might mark by a little black Spot every Fault I found upon Examination to have been committed respecting that Virtue upon that Day. (p. 70)

The intricacy of "arriving at moral Perfection" makes it the most confounding of games, though the rules were still less difficult than the objective. The young man decided to "give a Week's strict Attention to each of the Virtues successively." If the "Temperance" line was kept clear of foul "Spots" during the first week, then he could turn ahead to "Silence," and so on, endeavoring all the while to prevent backsliding! Thirteen virtues, thirteen weeks: four courses a year. The beginning of the book was given over to bolstering mottos and prayers; the end contained the "Scheme of Employment for the Twenty-four Hours of a natural Day," which was brought into being by the requirements of the precept "Order." It, says Franklin, "gave me the most Trouble." No one but Franklin could have said so! None but the victims of his popularizers and mechanical disciples, however, could find it remarkable!

Now it is imprecise and invites misunderstanding to refer to this portion of the *Autobiography*, as a large number of Franklin critics and scholars have done, as his "Art of Virtue." He indeed refers to that never-written project here and reveals the "Design" of it in one paragraph of words for ambitious servants of power (p. 75), but this is not that book and its title does not have the same meaning for the twentieth century that it had for the eighteenth century.[7] If the modern meaning is in mind, one can only be glad he never wrote it. This part of the memoirs is something of a different kind. The author of this piece was parading himself as a *naïf*.

The role of the rural philosopher demanded a youthful experience like this, a "Project of arriving at moral Perfection." On the other hand, only the wiser, older man was aware just how "bold and arduous" it was. It is the combination of the apparently serious and conscientious youth and the gay, mellow gentleman of Passy that meet to produce this part of the *Autobiography*. Like the other sections, it is an exercise in self-examination and self-advertisement. As the first memoir was a picaresque tale of mistakes and travels told by an indulgent "father" and the third and fourth memoirs were accounts of public causes related by a civic leader and national hero, this is a *naïf* "Philosophical Quaker's" initiation into the trials of a moral life.

When Franklin has completed the chronicle of this project, he goes on to explain to "my Posterity . . . that to this little Artifice, with the Blessing of God, their Ancestor ow'd the constant Felicity of his Life down to his 79th Year." This is the high-flown recollection of a man plainly playing the role of the retired sage. It is the writer of memoirs who is speaking, the man who looks backwards and avails himself of the opportunity to distinguish the crises and decisive choices of his life. The list of thirteen virtues and his intricate system of practicing them is responsible for "that Evenness of Temper, & that Chearfulness in Conversation which makes his Company still sought for, & agreable even to his younger Acquaintance." (p. 74) This is as revealing a kind of acting as Robert Frost's pose as the octogenerian New England poet:

> I shall be telling this with a sigh
> Somewhere ages and ages hence:
> Two roads diverged in a wood, and I—
> I took the one less traveled by,
> And that has made all the difference.

The man who tells of this "bold and arduous Project of arriving at moral Perfection," then, is no dogmatist or facile believer in the possibilities of moral Perfection. It was a "bold and arduous Project."! Note the history of the young man's tribulations with it:

7. See Spiller, p. 309.

I was surpriz'd to find myself so much fuller of Faults than I had imagined, . . . To avoid the Trouble of renewing now & then my little Book, which by scraping out the Marks on the Paper of old Faults to make room for new Ones in a new Course, became full of Holes: I transferr'd my Tables & Precepts to the Ivory Leaves of a Memorandum Book, on which the Lines were drawn with red Ink that made a durable Stain, and on those Lines I mark'd my Faults with a black Lead Pencil, which Marks I could easily wipe out with a wet sponge. (p. 71)

Franklin is not telling sarcastic jokes on himself, but he is enjoying the natural ironies which the seventy-eight-year-old autobiographer watched quietly emerge in a detailed and truthful record of his youthful vanity. Lawrence's outbursts were the result of too flat and impoverished a reading: "The Perfectibility of Man! Ah heaven, what a dreary theme! The Perfectibility of the Ford car!" "I am a moral animal. But I am not a moral machine. I don't work with a little set of handles or levers." Franklin was not a moral machine either. Moral Perfection, instead, was a kind of game. Its very mechanic quality did not reduce its inventor to a slave of lines and squares ("that barbed-wire moral enclosure that Poor Richard rigged up"), it broke the more confining bonds of unconscious habit. And it broke them without morbid brooding and immobilizing self-consciousness. Faults and offences were black dots. They were committed and recorded and later wiped away. The "wet sponge" is no mighty symbol of foregiveness and should not be hyper-critically thought of as a travesty of such charity. Time brings second chances. In the rules Franklin prescribed for himself the cycle of time was arranged at thirteen weeks, a quarter of a year!

The gallant and naïf autobiographer described his Project with a thoroughness that is absorbing, meanwhile letting the ironies of its vanity and impossibility rise up where they might. There is as much education and moral instruction in them as in the pious, more traditional reading of the second memoir. Abel James and Benjamin Vaughan, in the letters that precede the Passy section, ask for serious and inspirational matter that will be a guide to youth. They are in a sense like Ezra Stiles in his letter requesting Franklin's opinion on Jesus of Nazareth: a little too holy. What Franklin returns is something that includes the instruction but also mellows it with the temperate wisdom of later experience. Too much of the game could result in "a kind of Foppery in Morals." In respect to "Humility" Franklin noted: "I cannot boast of much Success in acquiring the *Reality* of this Virtue; but I had a good deal with regard to the *Appearance* of it." He gave them more advice than they were capable of expecting. He was quite sincere, even in the midst of his ironies, but his gravity was not dreary; it was naïf. The Franklin of Passy had put aside moral Perfection ("but I always carried my little Book with me") and arrived at a worldly perfection of his humanity instead.

JOHN WILLIAM WARD

Who Was Benjamin Franklin?†

Benjamin Franklin bulks large in our national consciousness, sharing room with Washington and Jefferson and Lincoln. Yet it is hard to say precisely what it means to name Franklin one of our cultural heroes. He was, as one book about him has it, "many-sided." The sheer variety of his character has made it possible to praise him and damn him with equal vigor. At home, such dissimilar Yankees as the laconic Calvin Coolidge and the passionate Theodore Parker could each find reason to admire him. Abroad, David Hume could say that he was "the first great man of letters" for whom Europe was "beholden" to America. Yet D. H. Lawrence, brought up, he tells us, in the industrial wastelands of midland England on the pious saws of "Poor Richard," could only "utter a long, loud curse" against "this dry, moral, utilitarian little democrat."

Part of the difficulty in comprehending Franklin's meaning is due to the opposites he seems to have contained with complete serenity within his own personality. He was an eminently reasonable man who maintained a deep skepticism about the power of reason. He was a model of industriousness who, preaching the gospel of hard work, kept his shop only until it kept him and retired at forty-two. He was a cautious and prudent man who was a revolutionist. And, to name only one more seeming contradiction, he was one who had a keen eye for his own advantage and personal advancement who spent nearly all his adult life in the service of others. Small wonder that there have been various interpretations of so various a character.

The problem may seem no problem at all. Today, when we all know that the position of the observer determines the shape of reality, we observe the observer. If Franklin, seeing to it that the streets of Philadelphia are well lit and swept clean at a moderate price, that no fires rage, does not appeal to D. H. Lawrence, we tend not to think of Franklin. We think of Lawrence; we remember his atavistic urge to explore the dark and passionate underside of life and move on. Franklin contained in his own character so many divergent aspects that each observer can make the mistake of seeing one aspect as all and celebrate or despise Franklin accordingly. Mr. I. Bernard Cohen, who has written so well on so much of Franklin, has remarked that "an

† Source: *American Scholar,* 32 (Autumn, 1963), 541–53.

account of Franklin . . . is apt to be a personal testament of the commentator concerning the America he most admires." Or contemns.

Yet there still remains the obstinate fact that Franklin could mean so many things to so many men, that he was so many-sided, that he did contain opposites, that he was, in other words, so many different characters. One suspects that here is the single most important thing about Franklin. Rather than spend our energies trying to find some consistency in this protean, many-sided figure, trying to resolve who Franklin truly was, we might perhaps better accept his variety itself as our major problem and try to understand that. To insist on the importance of the question, "Who was Benjamin Franklin?" may finally be more conclusive than to agree upon an answer.

The place to begin to ask the question is with the *Memoirs*, with the *Autobiography* as we have come to call them, and the place to begin there is with the history of the text. Fascinating in and of itself, the history of the text gives us an initial lead into the question of the elusiveness of Franklin's personality.

The *Autobiography* was written in four parts. The first part, addressed by Franklin to his son, William, was begun during some few weeks in July and August, 1771, while Franklin was visiting with his friend, Jonathan Shipley, the Bishop of St. Asaph, in Hampshire, England. Franklin was then sixty-five years old. As he wrote the first part he also carefully made a list of topics he would subsequently treat. Somehow the manuscript and list fell into the hands of one Abel James who eleven years later wrote Franklin, returning to him the list of topics but not the first part of the manuscript, urging him to take up his story once again. This was in 1782, or possibly early in January, 1783. Franklin was in France as one of the peace commissioners. He wrote the second part in France in 1784, after the achievement of peace, indicating the beginning and the ending of this short second part in the manuscript itself.

In 1785, Franklin returned to America, promising to work on the manuscript during the voyage. Instead he wrote three of his utilitarian essays: on navigation, on how to avoid smoky streetlamp chimneys, and on his famous stove. He did not return to his life's story until 1788. Then, after retiring from the presidency of the state of Pennsylvania in the spring, Franklin, quite sick, made his will and put his house in order before turning again to his own history. This was in August, 1788. Franklin was eighty-three years old, in pain, and preparing for death. The third part is the longest part of the autobiography, less interesting than the first two, and for many years was thought to conclude the manuscript.

In 1789, Franklin had his grandson, Benjamin Franklin Bache, make two fair copies of Parts I, II and III in order to send them to friends abroad, Benjamin Vaughan in England and M. le Veillard in France. Then, sometime before his death in April, 1790, Franklin added the last and fourth part, some seven and one-half manuscript pages, which was not included, naturally, in the fair copies sent abroad. For the rest, Mr. Max Farrand, our authority on the history of the text:

> After [Franklin's] death, the publication of the autobiography was eagerly awaited, as its existence was widely known, but for nearly thirty years the reading public had to content itself with French translations of the first and second parts, which were again translated from the French into other languages, and even retranslated into English. When the authorized English publication finally appeared in 1818, it was not taken from the original manuscript but from a copy, as was the preceding French version of the first part. The copy, furthermore, did not include the fourth and last part, which also reached the public in a French translation in 1828.
> . . . the complete autobiography was not printed in English from the original manuscript until 1868, nearly eighty years after Franklin's death.

The story is, as I have said, interesting in and of itself. The tangled history of one of our most important texts has its own fascination, but it also provides us the first clue to our question. Surely it must strike any reader of the *Autobiography* as curious that a character who speaks so openly should at the same time seem so difficult to define. But the history of the text points the way to an answer. All we need do is ask why Franklin wrote his memoirs.

When the Quaker, Abel James, wrote Franklin, returning his list of topics and asking "kind, humane, and benevolent Ben Franklin" to continue his life's story, "a work which would be useful and entertaining not only to a few but to millions," Franklin sent the letter on to his friend, Benjamin Vaughan, asking for advice. Vaughan concurred. He too urged Franklin to publish the history of his life because he could think of no "more efficacious advertisement" of America than Franklin's history. "All that has happened to you," he reminded Franklin, "is also connected with the detail of the manners and situation of a rising people." Franklin included James's and Vaughan's letters in his manuscript to explain why he resumed his story. What had gone before had been written for his family; "what follows," he said in his "Memo," "was written . . . in compliance with the advice contained in these letters, and accordingly intended for the public. The affairs of the Revolution occasioned the interruption."

The point is obvious enough. When Franklin resumed his story, he did so in full self-consciousness that he was offering himself to the world as a representative type, the American. Intended for the public now, his story was to be an example for young Americans, as Abel James would have it, and an advertisement to the world, as Benjamin Vaughan would have it. We had just concluded a successful revolution; the eyes of all the world were upon us. Just as America had succeeded in creating itself a nation, Franklin set out to show how the American went about creating his own character. As Benjamin Vaughan said, Franklin's life would "give a noble rule and example of self-education" because of Franklin's "discovery that the thing is in many a man's private power." So what follows is no longer the simple annals of Franklin's life for the benefit of his son. Benjamin Franklin plays his proper role. He becomes "The American."

How well he filled the part that his public urged him to play, we can see by observing what he immediately proceeds to provide. In the pages that follow James's and Vaughan's letters, Franklin quickly treats four matters: the establishment of a lending library, that is, the means for satisfying the need for self-education; the importance of frugality and industriousness in one's calling; the social utility of religion; and, of course, the thirteen rules for ordering one's life. Here, in a neat package, were all the materials that went into the making of the self-made man. This is how one goes about making a success of one's self. If the sentiments of our Declaration were to provide prompt notes for European revolutions, then Franklin, as the American Democrat, acted them out. Family, class, religious orthodoxy, higher education: all these were secondary to character and common sense. The thing was in many a man's private power.

If we look back now at the first part, the opening section addressed by Franklin to his son, William, we can see a difference and a similarity. The difference is, of course, in the easy and personal tone, the more familiar manner, appropriate to a communication with one's son. It is in these early pages that Franklin talks more openly about his many *errata*, his "frequent intrigues with low women," and displays that rather cool and calculating attitude toward his wife. Rather plain dealing, one might think, at least one who did not know that William was a bastard son.

But the similarity between the two parts is more important. The message is the same, although addressed to a son, rather than to the world: how to go about making a success. "From the poverty and obscurity in which I was born and in which I passed my earliest years," writes the father to the son, "I have raised myself to a state of affluence and some degree of celebrity in the world." A son, especially, must have found that "some" hard to take. But the career is not simply anecdotal: "my posterity will perhaps be desirous of learning the means, which I employed, and which, thanks to Providence, so well succeeded with me. They may also deem them fit to be imitated." The story is exemplary, although how the example was to affect a son who was, in 1771, about forty years old and already Royal Governor of New Jersey is another matter.

The story has remained exemplary because it is the success story to beat all success stories: the runaway apprentice printer who rose to dine with kings; the penniless boy, walking down Market Street with two large rolls under his arms, who was to sit in Independence Hall and help create a new nation. But notice that the story does not deal with the success itself. That is presumed, of course, but the *Autobiography* never gets to the later and more important years because the *Autobiography* is not about success. It is abut the formation of the character that makes success possible. The subject of the *Autobiography* is the making of a character. Having lifted himself by his own bootstraps, Franklin described it that way: "I have raised myself." We were not to find the pat phrase until the early nineteenth century when the age of the common man made the style more common: "the self-made man." The character was for life, of course, and not for fiction where we usually expect to encounter the made-up, but that should not prevent us from looking a little more closely at the act of creation. We can look in two ways: first, by standing outside the *Autobiography* and assessing it by what we know from elsewhere; second, by reading the *Autobiography* itself more closely.

A good place to begin is with those years in France around the end of the Revolution. It is so delicious an episode in plain Ben's life. More importantly—as Franklin said, one can always find a principle to justify one's inclinations—it is in these very years at Passy that Franklin, in response to James's and Vaughan's letters, wrote those self-conscious pages of the second part of the *Autobiography*. Just as he wrote the lines, he played them. As Carl Van Doren has written, "the French were looking for a hero who should combine the reason and wit of Voltaire with the primitive virtues celebrated by Rousseau . . . . [Franklin] denied them nothing." This is the period of the simple Quaker dress, the fur cap and the spectacles. France went wild in its adulation and Franklin knew why. "Think how this must appear," he wrote a friend, "among the powdered heads of Paris."

But he was also moving with equal ease in that world, the world of the powdered heads of Paris, one of the most cosmopolitan, most preciously civilized societies in history. Although he was no Quaker, Franklin was willing to allow the French to think so. They called him *"le bon Quackeur."* The irony was unintentional, a matter of translation. But at the same time that he was filling the role of the simple backwoods democrat, the innocent abroad, he was also playing cavalier in the brilliant salon of Madame Helvétius, the widow of the French philosopher. Madame Helvétius is supposed to have been so beautiful that Fontenelle, the great popularizer of Newton, who lived to be one hundred years old, was said to have paid her the most famous

compliment of the age: "Ah, madame, if I were only eighty again!"
Madame Helvétius was sixty when Franklin knew her and the classic
anecdote of their acquaintance is that Madame Helvétius is said to
have reproached him for not coming to see her, for putting off his long
anticipated visit. Franklin replied, "Madame, I am waiting until the
nights are longer." There was also Madame Brillon, not a widow, who
once wrote to Franklin, "People have the audacity to criticize my
pleasant habit of sitting on your knee, and yours of always asking me
for what I always refuse."

Some, discovering this side of Franklin, have written him off simply
as a rather lively old lecher. Abigail Adams, good New England lady
that she was, was thoroughly shocked. She set Madame Helvétius
down as a "very bad woman." But Franklin, despite his public style,
was not so provincial. He appealed to Madame Brillon that he had
spent so many days with her that surely she could spend one night with
him. She mockingly called him a sophist. He then appealed to her
charity and argued that it was in the design of Providence that she
grant him his wish. If somehow a son of the Puritans, Franklin had
grown far beyond the reach of their sermonizing. Thomas Hooker had
thought, "It's a grievous thing to the loose person, he cannot have his
pleasures but he must have his guilt and gall with them." But Franklin
wrote Madame Brillon, "Reflect how many of our duties [Providence]
has ordained naturally to be pleasures; and that it has had the goodness
besides, to give the name of sin to several of them so that we might
enjoy them the more."

All this is delightful enough, and for more one need only turn to
Carl Van Doren's biography from which I have taken these anecdotes,
but what it points to is as important as it is entertaining. It points to
Franklin's great capacity to respond to the situation in which he found
himself and to play the expected role, to prepare a face to meet the
faces that he met. He could, in turn, be the homespun, rustic
philosopher or the mocking cavalier, the witty sophist. He knew what
was expected of him.

The discovery should not surprise any reader of the *Autobiography*.
Throughout it, Franklin insists always on the distinction between
appearance and reality, between what he is and what he seems to be.

> In order to secure my credit and character as a tradesman, I took
> care not only to be in *reality* industrious and frugal, but to avoid all
> *appearances* of the contrary. I dressed plain and was seen at no
> places of idle diversion. I never went out a fishing or shooting; a
> book, indeed, sometimes debauched me from my work, but that
> was seldom, snug, and gave no scandal; and to show that I was not
> above my business, I sometimes brought home the paper I pur-
> chased at the stores, thro' the streets on a wheelbarrow. Thus being
> esteemed an industrious, thriving young man, and paying duly for

what I bought, the merchants who imported stationery solicited my custom; others proposed supplying me with books, and I went on swimmingly.

Now, with this famous passage, one must be careful. However industrious and frugal Franklin may in fact have been, he knew that for the business of social success virtue counts for nothing without its public dress. In Franklin's world there has to be someone in the woods to hear the tree fall. Private virtue might bring one to stand before the King of kings, but if one wants to sit down and sup with the kings of this world, then one must help them see one's merit. There are always in this world, as Franklin pointed out, "a number of rich merchants, nobility, states, and princes who have need of honest instruments for the management of their affairs, and such being so rare [I] have endeavoured to convince young persons, that no qualities are so likely to make a poor man's fortune as those of probity and integrity."

Yet if one wants to secure one's credit in the world by means of one's character, then the character must be of a piece. There can be no false gesture; the part must be played well. When Franklin drew up his list of virtues they contained, he tells us, only twelve. But a Quaker friend "kindly" informed him that he was generally thought proud and overbearing and rather insolent; he proved it by examples. So Franklin added humility to his list; but, having risen in the world and content with the degree of celebrity he had achieved, he could not bring himself to be humble. "I cannot boast of much success in acquiring the *reality* of this virtue, but I had a good deal with regard to the *appearance* of it."

He repeats, at this point, what he had already written in the first part of his story. He forswears all "positive assertion." He drops from his vocabulary such words as "certainly" and "undoubtedly" and adopts a tentative manner. He remembers how he learned to speak softly, to put forward his opinions, not dogmatically, but by saying, " 'I imagine' a thing to be so or so, or 'It so appears to me at present.' " As he had put it to his son earlier, he discovered the Socratic method, "was charmed with it, adopted it, dropped my abrupt contradiction and positive argumentation, and put on the humble enquirer." For good reason: "this habit . . . has been of great advantage to me."

What saves all this in the *Autobiography* from being merely repellent is Franklin's self-awareness, his good humor in telling us about the part he is playing, the public clothes he is putting on to hide what his public will not openly buy. "In reality," he writes, drawing again the distinction from appearance, "there is perhaps no one of our natural passions so hard to subdue as *pride*; disguise it, struggle with it, beat it down, stifle it, mortify it as much as one pleases, it is still alive and will every now and then peep out and show itself. You will see it perhaps often in this history. For even if I could conceive that I had completely overcome it, I should probably be proud of my humility." Here, despite the difference in tone, Franklin speaks like that other and contrasting son of the Puritans, Jonathan Edwards, on the nature of true virtue. Man, if he could achieve virtue, would inevitably be proud of the achievement and so, at the moment of success, fall back into sin.

The difference is, of course, in the tone. The insight is the same but Franklin's skeptical and untroubled self-acceptance is far removed from Edwards' troubled and searching self-doubt. Franklin enjoys the game. Mocking himself, he quietly lures us, in his Yankee deadpan manner, with the very bait he has just described. After having told us that he early learned to "put on the humble enquirer" and to affect a self-depreciating pose, he quotes in his support the line from Alexander Pope, "To speak, though sure, with seeming diffidence." Pope, Franklin immediately goes on to say, "might have joined with this line that which he has coupled with another, I think less properly, 'For want of modesty is want of sense.' "

If you ask why *less properly*, I must repeat the lines,

> Immodest words admit of *no defence*,
> For want of modesty is want of sense.

Now is not the "want of sense" (where a man is so unfortunate as to want it) some apology for his "want of modesty"? and would not the lines stand more justly thus?

> Immodest words admit *but* this defense
> That want of modesty is want of sense.

This, however, I should submit to better judgements.

Having been so bold as to correct a couplet of the literary giant of the age, Franklin quietly retreats and defers to the judgment of those better able to say than he. Having just described the humble part he has decided to play, he immediately acts it out. If we get the point, we chuckle with him; if we miss the point, that only proves its worth.

But one of the functions of laughter is to dispel uneasiness and in Franklin's case the joke is not enough. Our uneasiness comes back when we stop to remember that he is, as his friends asked him to, writing his story as an efficacious advertisement. We must always ask whether Franklin's disarming candor in recounting how things went on so swimmingly may not be yet another role, still another part he is playing. Actually, even with Yale's sumptuous edition of Franklin's papers, we know little about Franklin's personal life in the early years, except through his own account. The little we do know suggests that his way to wealth and success was not the smooth and open path he would have us believe. This leads us, then, if we cannot answer finally the question who Franklin was, to a different question. What does it mean to say that a character so changeable, so elusive, somehow represents American culture? What is there in Franklin's style that makes him, as we say, characteristic?

At the outset in colonial America, with men like John Winthrop, there was always the assumption that one would be called to one's appropriate station in life and labor in it for one's own good and the good of society. Magistrates would be magistrates and printers would be printers. But in the world in which Franklin moved, the magistrates, like Governor Keith of Pennsylvania who sends Franklin off on a wild-goose chase to England, prove to be frauds while the plain, leather-aproned set went quietly about the work of making society possible at all, creating the institutions—the militia, the fire companies, the libraries, the hospitals, the public utilites—that made society habitable. The notion that underlay an orderly, hierarchical society failed to make sense of such a world. It proved impossible to keep people in their place.

One need only consider in retrospect how swiftly Franklin moved upward through the various levels of society to see the openness, the fluidity of his world. Simply because he is a young man with some books, Governor Burnet of New York asks to see him. While in New Jersey on a job printing money he meets and makes friends with all the leaders of that provincial society. In England, at the coffeehouses, he chats with Mandeville and meets the great Dr. Henry Pemberton who was seeing the third edition of Newton's *Principia* through the press. As Franklin said, diligent in his calling, he raised himself by some degree.

The Protestant doctrine of calling, of industriousness in the world, contained dynamite for the orderly, hierarchical, social structure it was originally meant to support. The unintended consequence showed itself within two generations. Those who were abstemious, frugal and hardworking made a success in the world. They rose. And society, rather than the static and closed order in which, in Winthrop's words, "some must be rich some poor, some high and eminent in power and dignitie; others meane and in subieccion," turned out to be dynamic, fluid and open.

If there is much of our national character implicit in Franklin's career, it is because, early in our history, he represents a response to the rapid social change that has remained about the only constant in American society. He was the self-made man, the jack-of-all-trades. He taught thirteen rules to sure success and purveyed do-it-yourself kits for those who, like himself, constituted a "rising" people. Franklin stands most clearly as an exemplary American because his life's story is a witness to the uncertainties about social status that have characterized our society, a society caught up in the constant process of change. The question, "Who was Benjamin Franklin?" is a critical question to ask of Franklin because it is the question to which Franklin himself is constantly seeking an answer. In a society in which there are no outward, easily discernible marks of social status, the question always is, as we put it in the title of reference works that are supposed to provide the answer, "Who's Who?"

Along with the uncertainties generated by rapid social mobility, there is another aspect to the difficulty we have in placing Franklin, an aspect that is more complex and harder to state, but just as important and equally characteristic. It takes us back again to the Puritans. In Puritan religious thought there was originally a dynamic equipoise between two opposite thrusts, the tension between an inward, mystical, personal experience of God's grace and the demands for an outward, sober, socially responsible ethic, the tension between faith and works, between the essence of religion and its outward show. Tremendous energy went into sustaining these polarities in the early years but, as the original piety waned, itself undermined by the worldly success that benefited from the doctrine of calling, the synthesis split in two and resulted in the eighteenth century in Jonathan Edwards and Benjamin Franklin, similar in so many ways, yet so radically unlike.

Franklin, making his own world as he makes his way through it, pragmatically rejects the old conundrum whether man does good works because he is saved, or is saved because he does good works. "Vicious actions are not hurtful because they are forbidden, but forbidden because they are hurtful," he decides, and then in an added phrase calmly throws out the God-centered universe of his forebears, "the nature of man alone considered."

Content with his success, blandly sure it must be in the design of Providence that printers hobnob with kings, Franklin simply passes by the problem of the relation between reality and appearance. In this world, appearance is sufficient. Humanely skeptical that the essence can ever be caught, Franklin decided to leave the question to be answered in the next world, if there proved to be one. For this world, a "tolerable character" was enough and he "valued it properly." The result was a commonsense utilitarianism which sometimes verges toward sheer crassness. But it worked. For this world, what others think of you is what is important. If Franklin, viewed from the perspective of Max Weber and students of the Protestant ethic, can seem to be the representative, *par excellence*, of the character who internalizes the imperatives of his society and steers his own course unaided through the world, from a slightly different perspective he also turns out to be the other-directed character David Riesman has described, constantly attuned to the expectations of those around him, responding swiftly to the changing situations that demand he play different roles.

We admire, I think, the lusty good sense of the man who triumphs in the world that he accepts, yet at the same time we are uneasy with the man who wears so many masks that we are never sure who is there behind them. Yet it is this, this very difficulty of deciding whether we admire Franklin or suspect him, that makes his character an archetype for our national experience. There are great advantages to be had in belonging to a culture without clearly defined classes, without an establishment, but there is, along with the advantages, a certain strain, a necessary uneasiness. In an open and pluralistic society we have difficulty "placing" people, as we say. Think how often in our kind of society when we meet someone for the first time how our second or third question is apt to be, "What do you do?" Never, "Who are you?" The social role is enough, but in our more reflective moments we realize not so, and in our most reflective moments we realize it will never do for our own selves. We may be able to, but we do not want to go through life as a doctor, lawyer or Indian chief. We want to be ourselves, as we say. And at the beginning of our national experience, Benjamin Franklin not only puts the question that still troubles us in our kind of society, "Who's Who?" He also raises the question that lies at the heart of the trouble: "Who am I?"

DAVID LEVIN

The Autobiography of Benjamin Franklin: The Puritan Experimenter in Life and Art†

It would be difficult to find a book that seems more widely understood, as a model of plain exposition of character, than *The Autobiography of Benjamin Franklin*. Everyone knows that this is the life of a self-made, self-educated man and that *Poor Richard's Almanac* was a best-seller. Everyone knows that the penniless sixteen-year-old boy who first walked down the streets of Philadelphia with his pockets bulging with shirts and stockings, and with two great puffy rolls under his arms, worked so diligently at his calling that for him the promise of Scripture was fulfilled, and he one day stood before kings. (He "stood before five," he wrote later, with characteristic precision, and sat down to dine with one.) We all know, too, that the Franklin stove and bifocals and the electrical experiments bear witness to Franklin's belief in life-long education, and that it was because of his ability to explain clearly and persuade painlessly—even delightfully—that his international reputation soared higher than his famous kite.

Too often, however, we forget a few simple truths about this great

† Source: *Yale Review*, 53 (Winter, 1964), 258–75.

man and his greatest works. We forget the chief purposes for which he wrote his autobiography, and the social system that led him to conceive such aims. Remembering his plainness, his clarity, we overlook the subtlety of his expression, his humor, and his qualifying statements. Above all, we forget that he was a writer, that he had a habit of creating characters. And so he takes us in. Some of us forget that Poor Richard is just as clearly Franklin's creation as is Mrs. Silence Dogood, the fictitious character through whom young Benjamin had published in his brother's newspaper in Boston; many of us forget that *The Way to Wealth,* Franklin's brilliantly successful collection of economic proverbs, is a humorous *tale* narrated by Poor Richard, who at first makes fun of himself and then reports the long speech made by another fictitious character named Father Abraham; and most of us overlook the crucial distinction, especially in the first half of Franklin's autobiography, between the *writer* of the book and the chief *character* he portrays.

Please understand that I do not mean to call Franklin's autobiography a work of fiction. I must insist, however, that we refuse to let its general fidelity to historical fact blind us to the author's function in creating the character who appears in the book. Franklin's first entry into Philadelphia may serve as an example. We are apt to consider the picture of that boy as a natural fact of history, as if no conceivable biographer could have omitted it. It merges in our experience with the myth that Horatio Alger exploited a century later, and with dozens of other pictures of successful men at the beginning of their careers: the country boy walking into the big city, the immigrant lad getting off the boat and stepping forth in search of his fortune. So grandly representative is this human experience that our current critical fashion would call it archetypal. But it was Franklin the writer who elected to describe this picture, and who made it memorable. He was not obliged to include it. He *chose* to make it represent an important moment in his life, and he chose to depict his young former self in particular detail. His dirty clothes, his bulging pockets, and the huge rolls constitute nearly the only details respecting his personal appearance in the entire book. He might have omitted them, and he might have ignored the whole incident.

If we try to imagine what our view of Franklin might have been had he not written his autobiography, we will recognize that the author's conception of himself has considerably more literary significance than one can find in a single descriptive passage. Though the honest autobiographer refuses to invent fictitious incidents, he *actually creates himself as a character*. He selects incidents and qualities for emphasis, and discards or suppresses others. He portrays himself in relation to some other character (whom he also "creates" in this book), but refrains from portraying himself in relation to some others whom he once knew. He decides on the meaning of his life and the purpose of his book, and he selects traits, incidents, and characters accordingly. Obviously he cannot record everything that happened unless he spews forth every feeling, impulse, twitch that ever entered his mind or affected his senses. Indeed, the very conception of a happening requires some selection, some ordering of experience, and a point of view from which to perceive that order. D. H. Lawrence did not understand Franklin's autobiography, but he saw that it recognized a kind of order, and a view of the self, which imposed a planned control on natural feelings. "The ideal self!" he cried scornfully in his critique of Franklin.

> Oh, but I have a strange and fugitive self shut out and howling like a wolf or a coyote under the ideal windows. See his red eyes in the dark? This is the self who is coming into his own.
> The perfectibility of man, dear God! When every man as long as he remains alive is in himself a multitude of conflicting men. Which of these do you choose to perfect, at the expense of every other?
> Old Daddy Franklin will tell you. He'll rig him up for you, the pattern American. Oh, Franklin was the first downright American.

As we shall see later on, this gross caricature of "the sharp little man" reflects some imperfections in Franklin's ability to communicate with ages beyond his own, and as we shall see even sooner, it reflects an inability or unwillingness in Lawrence and many others to read carefully. For the moment, however, let us content ourselves with two observations in support of Lawrence's limited perception. First, Franklin's autobiography represents that kind of art in which the author tries to understand himself, to evaluate himself, to see himself, in a sense, from outside; it is a *portrayal* of the self rather than simply an *expression* of current feeling or an outpouring of those multiple selves that Lawrence celebrates. Old Daddy Franklin did indeed know what he was about. But the second observation must limit the praise in the first. The very terms in which Franklin expresses his admirable self-awareness limit his communication in a way that obscures the identity of the author. The technique of humor, and the disarming candor about techniques of influence and persuasion—these occasionally make us wonder which of several selves Benjamin Franklin is.

Franklin's art is deceptive. At first there may seem to be none at all. The book, written at four different times from 1771 to 1790, the year Franklin died, is loosely constructed; it is almost conversational in manner. It begins, indeed, as a letter to Franklin's son. It is episodic, anecdotal. Clearly, however, its narrative order includes two major divisions: the first half of the book describes his education, as he strives for a secure position in the world and for a firm character; the second half concentrates on his career of *public* service, though the account breaks off well before the American Revolution.

That simple pattern itself illustrates the most important fact about

Franklin's autobiography. He not only creates an attractive image of himself but uses himself as a prototype of his age and his country. There are three essential ways in which he establishes this story of the self-made man securely in the broadest experience of his time. If we examine them with some care, we may understand his purposes and his achievement more clearly.

The first context is that of Puritanism, represented here by Franklin's admiration for John Bunyan's *Pilgrim's Progress* and Cotton Mather's *Essays To Do Good*. Although Franklin says that he was converted to Deism by some anti-Deistic tracts in his Presbyterian father's library, we cannot overestimate the importance of his Puritan heritage, and his own account gives it due credit. (I refer, of course, not to the gross distortion suggested by the word "puritanical," the joy-killing and fanatical, but to that firm tradition that required every Christian to venture into this world as a pilgrim, doing right for the glory of God.) It is to this tradition that we owe Franklin's great proverb "Leisure is time for doing something useful," his emphasis on diligence in one's calling, the moral preoccupation that colors his view of ordinary experience. We see the Puritan influence in his insistence on frugality, simplicity, and utility as standards of value; and we see it just as clearly in his acceptance of public duty, his constant effort to improve the community, his willingness at last to serve the local and international community without pay. When we remember that the Protestant ethic combines the profit motive with religious duty, we should remember that in Franklin's day (as in John Winthrop's before him) it also obliged one to use one's fortune, and one's own person, in public service.

The Puritan tradition, indeed, gave Franklin a more purely literary kind of model. By the time he was growing up there existed in both old and New England a fairly large body of personal literature that emphasized objective self-examination and the need to keep an objective record of divine Providence as it affected an individual life. One recorded one's daily life in order to evaluate one's conduct and also to find evidence of God's will in the pattern of events. It was the Puritan custom, moreover, to improve every opportunity to find moral instruction and signs of universal meaning in particular experience. Franklin himself describes and exemplifies this custom in an anecdote (not in the *Autobiography*, but in a letter) of a visit that he made in 1724 to the old Puritan minister Cotton Mather. As Franklin was leaving, he wrote later, Mather

> showed me a shorter way out of the house, through a narrow passage, which was crossed by a beam overhead. We were talking as I withdrew, he accompanying me behind, and I turning partly towards him when he said hastily, "STOOP, STOOP!" I did not understand him till I felt my head against the beam. He was a man that never missed any occasion of giving instruction, and upon this

he said to me: "You are young, and have the world before you; STOOP as you go through it, and you will miss many hard thumps." This advice, thus beat into my head, has frequently been of use to me, and I often think of it when I see pride mortified and misfortunes brought upon people by carrying their heads too high.

One of the most successful devices that Franklin uses in his autobiography is the kind of symbolic anecdote, or parable; what brings Franklin's practice closer to Puritan preaching than to the parables in the Bible is his careful addition of a conclusion that drives home the point—the application or use—for those who might otherwise misunderstand it.

Before turning from Puritanism to a second quality of eighteenth-century experience, we should pause for another minute over the name of John Bunyan. For the first half of Franklin's autobiography, as Charles Sanford has said, represents a kind of pilgrim's progress. As his pious contemporaries Jonathan Edwards and John Woolman published accounts of their growth in Christian grace, so Franklin, acknowledging the aid of Providence, narrates the progress of a chosen, or at least fortunate, and often undeserving young man through a series of perils (including the valley of the shadow of death) to a relatively safe moral haven, if not to the Heavenly City. Others, we must remember, do not fare so well. A number of his early associates fall into one pit or another, and although Franklin tries to show what he did to save himself, so that others might profit by his example, he makes it perfectly clear that on several occasions he was so foolish that he too would have gone down had he not been preserved by Providence—or plain good luck.

It is this sense of the perils facing a young man in the free society of the new capitalism that brings me to the second of my three kinds of representativeness. Whether he was a Puritan or not, the young indentured servant, the young apprentice, the young artisan or farmer of Franklin's time had to walk a perilous way in the world. And if, like a great many Americans, he was leaving his childhood community as well as the restraints and comforts of his childhood religious faith, when he came forth to make his way in the world, he faced those dangers with very little help from outside himself. He had precious little help in the experience of others, for often his experience was new for the entire society. The mistakes he made did not entitle him to the protection of bankruptcy laws or of the less grand comforts of our welfare state. They sent him to a debtor's prison, or subjected him to the permanent authority of a creditor. Franklin described plain economic fact as well as moral truth when he said, "It is hard for an empty sack to stand upright."

Thus one of Franklin's major purposes in the *Autobiography* was to instruct the young, not only by good example but by warning. Especially in his account of his youth, he presents himself repeatedly as the relatively innocent or ignorant young man in conflict with those who would take advantage of him. Much of the sharp dealing that annoys D. H. Lawrence and others occurs in this kind of situation. Franklin's older brother, exploiting and sometimes beating the young apprentice, tries to circumvent a court ruling against his newspaper by freeing young Benjamin and making him nominal owner of the paper; Benjamin takes advantage of the opportunity by going off to Philadelphia to strike out on his own. Samuel Keimer uses Franklin to train other printers so that Franklin's services may then be dispensed with; but Franklin plans to set up his own shop, and when he does, he prospers as Keimer fails.

As in the fiction of Daniel Defoe, whom Franklin admired, and Samuel Richardson, whom he was among the first American printers to publish, Franklin's *Autobiography* indicates clearly that the relations between the sexes concealed some of the chief dangers to the young freeman's liberty. Luckily, he concedes, he escaped the worst consequences of occasional encounters with "low women"; but in a society that frankly recognized marriage as an economic contract he was almost entrapped by a clever pair of parents who seem to have counted on hoodwinking the young lad because he had to bargain for himself in a matter that required cooler heads. Franklin's account of the episode is priceless:

> Mrs. Godfrey [his landlady] projected a match for me with a relation's daughter, took opportunities of bringing us often together, till a serious courtship on my part ensued, the girl being in herself very deserving. The old folks encouraged me by continued invitations to supper and by leaving us together, till at length it was time to explain. Mrs. Godfrey managed our little treaty. I let her know that I expected as much money with their daughter as would pay off my remaining debt for the printing house, which I believe was not then above a hundred pounds. She brought me word they had no such sum to spare. I said they might mortgage their house in the Loan Office. The answer to this after some days was that they did not approve the match; that on enquiry of Bradford [another printer] they had been informed the printing business was not a profitable one, the types would soon be worn out and more wanted; that Samuel Keimer and D. Harry had failed one after the other, and I should probably soon follow them; and therefore I was forbidden the house, and the daughter shut up. Whether this was a real change of sentiment or only artifice, on a supposition of our being too far engaged in affection to retract and therefore that we should steal a marriage, which would leave them at liberty to give or withhold what they pleased, I know not. But I suspected the motive, resented it, and went no more. Mrs. Godfrey brought me afterwards some more favourable accounts of their disposition and would have drawn me on again, but I declared absolutely my resolution to have nothing more to do with that family.

This anecdote is not among the most popular with modern readers. It should be noticed, however, that people who owned their house outright did not ordinarily leave their daughter alone with a young man until they had some assurance of his economic eligibility for marriage, and that these parents were not worried about Franklin's ability to provide for their daughter until he demanded the usual dowry. We should notice, too, that the young Franklin who is described in this anecdote seems at last to have obeyed his own feelings of resentment rather than the economic interest that might have been served by allowing the girl's parents to re-open negotiations.

But although he always prospers, the innocent young man is not infallibly wise. Although he is never so roguish as Moll Flanders, his confession appears to be remarkably candid. He concedes that he was greatly deceived by the Governor of Pennsylvania, who sent him as a very young man to England, along with supposed letters of recommendation and letters of credit that never arrived. (That, by the way, was probably the greatest peril of Franklin's young life, and he confesses that he walked into it despite his father's clear warning.) He admits freely to motives and perceptions that we, along with most of his contemporaries, prefer to conceal. He thanks heaven for vanity, "along with the other comforts of life," and admits that it is useful to cultivate not only the reality but the *appearance* of industry and humility. It was effective, he says, to carry his own paper stock through the streets in a wheelbarrow, so that people could see how hard he was willing to work. A book, he confesses, "sometimes debauch'd me from my work, but that was seldom, snug, and gave no scandal."

This apparent honesty leads us to the heart of the book. My third kind of representativeness, the most important of all, can be summed up in a single statement that appears near the end of the *Autobiography*. "This," Franklin wrote, "is an age of experiments." It *was* an age of experiments, an age of empirical enlightenment, when every freeman might, if wary and lucky, learn by experience and test for himself. Franklin's greatest achievement in this book is that of characterizing himself repeatedly as a man of inquiry. He creates for us a convincing image of the inquiring man, self-educated, testing for himself, in morality, in business, in religion, in science. On almost every page we see some evidence of his willingness to learn. He contrives to reveal the vast range of his interests—from the pure science of electricity, to the effect of lading on the speed of merchant ships, to street-lighting and street-cleaning, to the value of learning modern romance languages before trying to learn Latin—all these he contrives to reveal in anecdotes of questioning and discovery. And in anecdote after anecdote, the plain questioning of Benjamin Franklin in action applies an experimental test to theories and assumptions. As a young journeyman printer in England, he demonstrates to his fellow

342 • *David Levin*

workmen that the customary beer is not necessary to the maintenance of strength; he drinks water, and carries more type than they can carry. Young Franklin and a friend agree that the one who dies first will prove the possibility of communicating from beyond the grave by getting in touch with the other who remains alive; but, Old Franklin the narrator reports, "he never fulfilled his promise." As a military commander at the start of the Seven Years' War with France, Franklin hears the zealous Presbyterian chaplain's complaint that the men do not attend religious services; he solves the problem by persuading the chaplain himself to serve out the men's daily rum ration just *after* prayers. ". . . and never," the narrator comments, "were prayers more generally and more punctually attended—so that I thought this method preferable to the punishments inflicted by some military laws for non-attendance on divine service."

Especially in the narrative of the early years, this wide-eyed freshness of perception is perfectly compatible with the young man's shrewdness, and it is nowhere more delightful than in his depiction of some of the other chief characters in the book. One of the most remarkable qualities in the book is the author's almost total lack of rancor. His brother James, Samuel Keimer, Governor Keith, and General Edward Braddock—all these people may be said to have injured him; yet he presents them all with the charitable curiosity of a man who was once interested in learning from his experience with them something about human nature. I refer here not to the kind of curiosity that can be so easily caricatured, the ingenious Yankee's humor that leads him to tell us how he measured reports of the distance at which the revivalist George Whitefield's voice might be heard. What I mean to admire is the humorous *discovery* of another person's strange faults. Consider the economy of this portrayal of Samuel Keimer, whose faults are balanced against those of the young Franklin:

Keimer and I lived on a pretty good familiar footing and agreed tolerably well, for he suspected nothing of my setting up [for myself]. He retained a great deal of his old enthusiasm and loved argumentation. We therefore had many disputations. I used to work him so with my Socratic method and had trappaned him [that is, tricked him] so often by questions apparently so distant from any point we had in hand, and yet by degrees leading to the point and bringing him into difficulties and contradictions, that at last he grew ridiculously cautious and would hardly answer the most common question without asking first, "What do you intend to infer by that?" However, it gave him so high an opinion of my abilities in the confuting way that he seriously proposed my being his colleague in a project he had of setting up a new sect. He was to preach the doctrines, and I was to confound all opponents. When he came to explain with me upon the doctrines, I found several conundrums which I objected to, unless I might have my way a little, too, and introduce some of mine. Keimer wore his beard at full length, because somewhere in the Mosaic Law it is said, "Thou shalt not mar the corners of thy beard." He likewise kept the seventh day Sabbath, and these two points were essentials with him. I disliked both but agreed to admit them upon condition of his adopting the doctrine of not using animal food. "I doubt," says he, "my constitution will bear it." I assured him it would and that he would be the better for it. He was usually a great glutton, and I wished to give myself some diversion in half-starving him. He consented to try the practice if I would keep him company; I did so, and we held it for three months. Our provisions were purchased, cooked, and brought to us regularly by a woman in the neighbourhod who had from me a list of forty dishes to be prepared for us at different times, in which there entered neither fish, flesh, nor fowl. This whim suited me better at this time from the cheapness of it, not costing us above eighteen pence sterling each per week. I have since kept several Lents most strictly, leaving the common diet for that, and that for common, without the least inconvenience, so that I think there is little in the advice of making those changes by easy gradations. I went on pleasantly, but poor Keimer suffered grievously, tired of the project, longed for the flesh pots of Egypt, and ordered a roast pig. He invited me and two women friends to dine with him, but it being brought too soon upon table, he could not resist the temptation and ate it all up before we came.

Franklin's acute awareness that Keimer is a ridiculously pretentious, affected character does not prevent him from expressing some unsentimental sympathy for his former victim, or from hinting broadly that he himself now disapproves of giving himself diversion at the expense of others—although he might relish the chance to repeat the same experiment. We must remember, in reading this anecdote, that Franklin has previously told us of his decision some years later to abandon the Socratic method, because it had sometimes won him victories that neither he nor his cause deserved. And we must notice that his rational skepticism, his testing by experience, extends even to reason itself.

In an age of reason Franklin was not afraid to admit the limits of reason nor did he hesitate in his autobiography to illustrate those limits by recounting an experience in which young Franklin himself is the only target of his humor. He used this device on several occasions, but one of them is astonishing in its brilliance, for it not only establishes the author's attitude toward himself but phrases the issue in the key terms of eighteenth-century psychology. The battle in young Franklin is a battle between principle and inclination. The anecdote appears immediately before the vegetarian experiment with Keimer. During a calm on his voyage back from Boston to Philadelphia, Franklin says,

our crew employed themselves catching cod, and hauled up a great number. Till then I had stuck to my resolution to eat nothing that had had life; and on this occasion I considered . . . the taking every fish as a kind of unprovoked murder, since none of them had or ever could do us any injury that might justify this massacre. All this seemed very reasonable. But I had formerly been a great lover of fish, and when this came hot out of the frying pan, it smelled admirably well. I balanced some time between principle and inclination, till I recollected that when the fish were opened, I saw smaller fish taken out of their stomachs. "Then," thought I, "if you eat one another, I don't see why we mayn't eat you." So I dined upon cod very heartily and have since continued to eat as other people, returning only now and then occasionally to a vegetable diet. So convenient a thing it is to be a *reasonable creature*, since it enables one to find or make a reason for everything one has a mind to do.

Franklin gives us, then, the picture of a relatively innocent, unsophisticated, sometimes foolish young man who confounds or at least survives more sophisticated rivals. Consistently, the young man starts at the level of testing, and he often stumbles onto an important truth. We see his folly and his discoveries through the ironically humorous detachment of a candid old man, whose criticism of the young character's rivals is tempered by the same kind of affectionate tolerance that allows him to see the humor of his own mistakes. The wise old writer expects people to act selfishly, but retains his affection for them. He leads us always to consider major questions in terms of simple practical experience, as when he tells us that he soon gave up converting people to belief in Deism because the result seemed often to be that they thus became less virtuous than before. Deism, he said, might be true, but it did not seem to be very useful. Because he assumed that at best people will usually act according to their conception of their own true interest, because all his experience seemed to confirm this hypothesis, and because metaphysical reasoning often turned out to be erroneous, he concentrated on demonstrating the usefulness of virtue.

It is right here, just at the heart of his most impressive achievement as an autobiographer, that Franklin seems to have made his one great error in communication. Many people, first of all, simply misunderstand him; he did not take sufficient account of the carelessness of readers. Many are completely taken in by the deceptive picture. So effective has Franklin been in demonstrating the usefulness of virtue through repeated anecdotes from his own educational experience, so insistent on effectiveness as a test of what is good in his own life, that many readers simply believe he has no other basis for deciding what is good. They simply conclude that the man who would say, "Honesty is the best *policy*" will be *dis*honest if ever dishonesty becomes the best policy. Readers wonder what the man who tells them candidly that he profited by *appearing* to be humble hopes to gain by *appearing* to be candid.

If I were to follow Franklin and judge chiefly by the results, I would give up trying to clarify the misunderstanding, for I am sure that many readers will refuse to follow me beyond this point. Yet it seems to me important to understand Franklin's intention as clearly as possible, if only to measure properly the degree of his miscalculation or his inadequacy. Let us examine one other brief passage from the *Autobiography*, a statement describing Franklin's own effort to propagate a new set of religious beliefs, to establish a new sect which he proposed, characteristically, to call The Society of the Free and Easy. "In this piece [a book to be called *The Art of Virtue*] it was my design to explain and enforce this doctrine: That vicious actions are not hurtful because they are forbidden, but forbidden because they are hurtful, *the nature of man alone considered*; that it was therefore everyone's interest to be virtuous who wished to be happy *even in this world.*"

I have stressed the qualifying phrases in this statement in order to emphasize the nature of Franklin's faith: *the nature of man alone considered*; everyone who wished to be happy *even in this world*. This doctrine of enlightened self-interest represents an important reversal—almost an exact reversal—of a sentence written by a sixteenth-century English Puritan named William Perkins, who in propounding the absolute sovereignty of God had declared: "A thing is not first of all reasonable and just, and then afterwards willed by God; it is first of all willed by God, and thereupon becomes reasonable and just." Yet Franklin's reversal does *not* say that discovering what is apparently to our interest is the only way of *defining* virtue. He, every bit as much as the Calvinist, believes that virtues must be defined by some absolute standard. Vicious actions, he says, *are forbidden*—by the benevolent authority of a wise God and by the universal assent, as he understood it, of wise men throughout history. But some actions *are* inherently vicious, whether or not they seem profitable.

Franklin's faith, then, professes that a true understanding of one's interest even in this world will lead one to virtue. Since the obvious existence of viciousness and folly in every society demonstrates that men do not yet practice the virtues on which most philosophers *have* agreed, finding a way to increase the practice of virtue—the number of virtuous actions—is a sufficiently valuable task to need no elaborate justification. And so the same Franklin who in the year of his death refused to dogmatize on the question of Jesus Christ's divinity because he expected soon to "have an opportunity of knowing the truth with less trouble," contented himself with questions of moral practice. His faith told him that the best way to serve God was to do good to one's fellow men, and he reasoned that just as all wise men preferred benevolent acts to flattery, so the infinitely wise God would not care very much to be flattered, but would prefer to have men *act* benevolently. He denied, however, that any man could ever *deserve* a heavenly, infinite reward for finite actions. He knew perfectly well the implications of his faith, but he saw no reason to worry very much about whether it was absolutely correct. For all his experience indicated that whether or not virtue and interest do coincide, no other argument but that of self-interest will persuade men to act virtuously, and even that argument will not always persuade them.

It is in this context that we must read Franklin's account of the thirteen-week course he gave himself in the Art of Virtue. D. H. Lawrence and other critics have overlooked the humorous self-criticism with which Franklin introduces the account. "It was about this time," Franklin says, "that I conceived the bold and arduous project of arriving at moral perfection. As I knew, or thought I knew, what was right and wrong, I did not see why I might not *always* do the one and avoid the other. But I soon found I had undertaken a task of more difficulty than I had imagined. While my attention was taken up and care employed against one fault, I was often surprized by another." Franklin, you will remember, listed the chief instrumental virtues under thirteen headings and at first devoted a week to concentrating especially on the habit of practicing one of the thirteen virtues. He made himself a chart, and in the daily period that he allotted to meditating the question "What good have I done today?" he entered a black mark for each action that could be considered a violation of the precepts. He worked to achieve a clear page. At thirteen weeks for each completed "course," he was able, he says, to go through four courses in a year. As he was surprised, at first, to find himself so full of faults, so he was pleased to find that he was able to decrease the number of his faulty actions. He endeavors to persuade us by pointing out that this improvement of conduct made him happier and helped him to prosper. But he makes perfectly clear the relative nature of his progress. He compares his method of attacking one problem at a time to weeding a garden, a task that is never really completed. He tells us not only that he later advanced to taking one course each year (with four weeks for each virtue), but also that he bought a book with ivory pages, so that he could erase the black marks at the end of one term and begin the course anew. The task was endless. Wondering about D. H. Lawrence's reading of Franklin, we may echo his own uncomprehending words: The perfectibility of man, indeed!

In trying to clarify Franklin's beliefs, I have not meant to absolve him of all responsibility for the widespread misunderstanding of his work. As I have already suggested, he invites difficulty by deliberately appearing to be more simple than he is, by choosing the role of the inquisitive, experimental freeman. By daring to reduce metaphysical questions to the terms of practical experience, he sometimes seems to dismiss them entirely, and he draws our attention away from the books that he has read. Thus, although he alludes to the most influential philosophical and psychological treaties of his age, and although he certainly read widely in every kind of learning that attracted his remarkably curious mind, he does not give this theoretical groundwork any important place in the narrative of his life. He mentions that he read John Locke at a certain point, and the Earl of Shaftesbury, and he says that this sort of education is extremely valuable. But in the narrative itself he is plain Benjamin Franklin, asking questions prompted by the situation. Even as he recounts, much later in the book, his successful correspondence with some of the leading scientists of England and the Continent, he underemphasizes his learning and portrays himself as a fortunate and plain, if skillful and talented, amateur.

This effect is reinforced by another quality of Franklin's literary skill, the device of humorous understatement. I have already cited one or two examples, as in his statement about answering the question of the divinity of Jesus. Similarly, he refers to the discovery that an effective preacher was plagiarizing famous English sermons as "an unlucky occurrence," and he says that he preferred good sermons by others to bad ones of the minister's own manufacture. He repeatedly notices ridiculous incongruity by putting an apt word in a startlingly subordinate place and thus shocking us into a fresh, irreverent look at a subject that we may well have regarded in a conventional way. So he says that for some time he had been regularly absent from Presbyterian church services, "Sunday being my studying day"; and he remarks that enormous multitudes of people admired and respected the revivalist George Whitefield, "notwithstanding his common abuse of them by assuring them they were naturally 'half beasts and half devils.'" This is the method that Henry Thoreau later used in *Walden* when he declared that the new railroads and highways, which were then called internal improvements, were all external and superficial; it is the method Samuel Clemens employed through his narrator Huckleberry Finn, who says that at mealtime the widow Douglas began by lowering her head and grumbling over the victuals, "though there warn't really anything the matter with them." The device is often delightfully effective in negative argument, in revealing ludicrous inconsistency. But because it depends on an appeal to simple self-reliance, and often to a hard-headed practicality, it is not conducive to the exposition of positive, complex theory. The particular form of Franklin's wit, his decision to portray himself as an inquisitive empiricist, the very success of his effort to exemplify moral values in accounts of practical experience, his doctrine of enlightened self-interest, and the fine simplicity of his exposition—all these combine to make him seem philosophically more naïve, and practically more materialistic, than he is.

Yet this is a great book, and despite the limitations implicit in his

348 • *David Levin*

pedagogical method, the breadth and richness of Franklin's character do come through to the reasonably careful reader. One chief means, of course, is the urbane yet warm tone of the wise old narrator, who begins by conceding that one of his reasons for writing an autobiographical statement to his son is simply the desire of an old man to talk about himself. We should also notice that although his emotional life is clearly beyond the bounds of his narrative purpose, he expresses an unmistakable affection, even in retrospect, for his parents, his brother, and his wife. His judgment is nowhere firmer or more admirable than in his account of the self-satisfied young Benjamin's return to taunt brother James, his former master, with the signs of the Philadelphia journeyman's prosperity. His record of his wife's life-long usefulness to him is not in the least incompatible with genuine affection for her. And in one brief paragraph citing as an argument for smallpox vaccination the death of his own son, "a fine boy of four years old," he reveals that his serenity could be rippled by the memory of an old grief.

We must remember, finally, that Franklin was one of the most beloved men of his time. The first American who was called the father of his country, he had no reason to feel anxious about the quality of what our own public relations men would call his "image." He had retired at the age of 42 to devote the rest of his long life to public service and scientific study; he was known internationally as a faithful patriot who had for decades defended the popular cause in almost every political controversy; he had been a great success at the French court, and he was a member of the Royal Society in England. With these sides of his character known so well, he had no reason to expect that his instructive *Autobiography* would be taken as the complete record of his character, or of his range as a writer. The polished *Bagatelles* that he had written in France; the brilliant ironic essays that he had published in England during the years just before the Revolution; the state papers that he had written in all seriousness as an agent of the Congress—all these formed a part of his public character before he completed his work on the *Autobiography*. He could not foresee that, in a romantic age in which many writers believed capitalism and practical science were overwhelming the human spirit, a novelist like D. H. Lawrence would make him a symbol of acquisitive smugness; nor could he foresee that F. Scott Fitzgerald, lamenting in *The Great Gatsby* the betrayal of the great American dream, would couple Ben Franklin's kind of daily schedule with a Hopalong Cassidy book, and would imply that in the 1920's anyone who followed Franklin's advice would have to be a stock-waterer or a bootlegger.

What Franklin represented in his day, and what we should see in his greatest book, was something much more complex than this stereotype. He was deceptively simple, to be sure; but his life and his character testified to the promise of experience, the value of education, the possibility of uniting fruitful public service with simple self-reliance, the profitable conduct of a useful business enterprise, and the free pursuit of knowledge in both pure and practical science. His book remains an admirable work of art, and its author still speaks truth to us as an admirable representative of the Enlightenment.

J. A. LEO LEMAY

Franklin's *Autobiography* and the American Dream†

*   *   *

Franklin's *Autobiography* is the first great book in American literature, and, in some ways, it remains the most important single book. One cannot claim for it the structural perfection of, say, Henry James's *Ambassadors* or Nathaniel Hawthorne's *Scarlet Letter*, nor does it possess the grandiloquent language of Melville, Whitman, or Faulkner. But Franklin's *Autobiography* contains those "short quick probings at the very axis of reality,"[1] which, in Melville's opinion, were a touchstone of literary greatness. The youthful Franklin lapsed from his vegetarian diet after observing that big fish ate smaller fish (and after seeing and smelling the fresh fish sizzling hot in the pan), and so he ate the fish; and the old man who was writing the *Autobiography* ironically commented on the young man's justification: "So convenient a thing it is to be a *reasonable creature*, since it enables one to find or make a Reason for every thing one has a mind to do" (p. 28). Franklin's profound skepticism concerning reason, his implied positions on eighteenth-century theological and psychological debates on voluntarism, and his pessimism concerning the vanity and selfishness of mankind are important themes of the *Autobiography* (and of that quotation), present for those who read it carefully.

But few people read the *Autobiography* for its satire on the nature of man, or for its important contributions to the key questions of ethical and moral philosophy which racked eighteenth-century thought, or for its ridicule of various religions and religious doctrines. It is not because of these themes that the book has been an important influence upon such disparate current Americans as the Chinese-born Nobel Prize winner in physics in 1957, Chen Ning Yang, and the Georgia-

---

† Source: Excerpted from a paper read at a Clark Library Seminar on October 9, 1976, and published as *The Renaissance Man in the Eighteenth Century* (Los Angeles: William Andrews Clark Memorial Library, 1978), pp. 21–33, 41–44.

1. Herman Melville, "Hawthorne and His Mosses," in Walter Blair, Theodore Hornberger, and Randall Stewart, eds., *The Literature of the United States: An Anthology and a History*, 2 vols. (Chicago: Scott, Foresman & Co., 1953), I: 1005.

born Democratic nominee for president in 1976, Jimmy Carter.[2] No, these themes add a depth to its greatness, a richness and complexity to its thought, a texture and subtlety to its language and content that is generally unseen and unappreciated, although friends of Franklin with whom he corresponded about aspects of the book, like Joseph Priestley and Henry Home, Lord Kames, or those who read it in manuscript at his request, like Richard Price and the Duke de La Rochefoucauld, would have appreciated its subtleties.[3] But everyone knows, or thinks he knows, one major theme and subject of the *Autobiography*. Everyone can say why the book has been enormously popular and why it is among the classics of American literature.

It is because Franklin gave us the definitive formulation of the American Dream. What is the American Dream? The simplest possible answer, as well as the most common general impression, is expressed by the standard cliché, the rise from rags to riches. This theme was certainly not new to Franklin's *Autobiography* or even to American literature, though Franklin is often commonly supposed to be the progenitor of the Horatio Alger success story of nineteenth-century American popular literature.[4] Actually the Horatio Alger stories are later versions of popular Renaissance and seventeenth-century ballads and chapbooks such as *The Honour of a London Prentice* and *Sir Richard Whittington's Advancement*. Such ballads usually portray the rise of the hero by a sudden stroke of good fortune, or by knightly feats of heroic courage.[5] Franklin's version of the rise is different from the Horatio Alger model but similar to the motif as presented in miniature in the numerous promotion tracts of America, such as John Hammond's *Leah and Rachel*, which stress the possible rise of the common man by industry and frugality.[6] On this basic level of the American Dream motif, the *Autobiography* combines the kinds

2. See Jeremy Bernstein, *Encyclopedia Britannica*, 15th ed., s.v. "Yang, Chen Ning"; and Hugh Sidey's article on Carter's reading, "The Presidency," *Time*, 6 September 1976, p. 15.

3. Franklin to Priestley on moral algebra, 19 September 1772, in Albert Henry Smyth, ed., *The Writings of Benjamin Franklin*, 10 vols. (1907; reprint ed., New York: Haskell House, 1970), 5: 437–38; Franklin to Kames, 3 May 1760, in *The Papers of Benjamin Franklin*, ed. Leonard W. Labaree, William B. Willcox, et al. (New Haven: Yale University Press, 1959—) 9: 104–5; *Autobiography*, this edition, p. 241–43. Franklin to La Rochefoucauld, in Smyth, 9: 665.

4. Dixon Wecter, *The Hero in America: A Chronical of Hero-Worship* (New York: Charles Scribner's Sons, 1941), p. 61.

5. For *The Honour of a London Prentice*, see Donald Wing, *Short-Title Catalogue of Books Printed . . . 1641–1700*, H 2592, and *The Na-*

tional Union Catalog: Pre-1956 Imprints, 253: 502, NH 0500961; John Ashton, *Chap-Books of the Eighteenth Century* (1882; reprint ed., New York: B. Blom. 1966), pp. 227–29; William Chappell and Joseph Woodfall Ebsworth, eds., *The Roxburghe Ballads*, 9 vols. (Hertford: Ballad Society, 1871–99), 7: 587–91; and Claude M. Simpson. *The British Broadside Ballad and Its Music* (New Brunswick: Rutgers University Press, 1966), p. 13. For *Sir Richard Whittington's Advancement*, see *London's Glory and Whittington's Renown*, Wing, L2930, and the British Museum, *General Catalogue of Printed Books . . . to 1955*, vol. 256, cols. 1086–89; and William Chappell, *The Ballad Literature and Popular Music of the Olden Time*, 2 vols. (1859; reprint ed., New York: Dover, 1965), 2: 515–17.

6. See the discussion of *Leah and Rachal* in J. A. Leo Lemay, *Men of Letters in Colonial Maryland* (Knoxville: University of Tennessee Press, 1972), pp. 38–42.

of popular appeal present in the old ballads with the view of life in America as possibility. The idea of possibility is the constant message of the promotion tracts and echoes the archetypal ideas of the West, both as the terrestial paradise and as the culmination of the progress of civilization.[7]

But the *Autobiography*, as every reader knows, is not primarily about Franklin's economic rise. At best, this is a minor subject. When he refers to it, he generally does so for a number of immediate reasons, nearly all of which are as important as the fact of his wealth. For example, Franklin tells that Deborah Franklin purchased "a China Bowl with a Spoon of Silver" for him "without my Knowledge." He relates this anecdote partly for the sake of its ironic quality ("she thought *her* Husband deserv'd a Silver Spoon and China Bowl as well as any of his Neighbours" [p. 65]), partly for its testimony of the rewards of Industry and Frugality (it follows a passage praising Deborah as a helpmate), and, of course, partly as a testimony of the beginning of their wealth. Although Franklin writes of his early poverty a number of times, he rarely mentions his later wealth. It might be said that in twice telling of his retirement from private business, Franklin indirectly boasts of his financial success. But the sentence structure on both occasions demonstrates that the major subject is public business, not private wealth.[8] The rags to riches definition of the American Dream is a minor aspect of the American Dream theme in Franklin's *Autobiography*. Those readers who are unhappy with the *Autobiography* because it is primarily a practical lesson in how to become rich, themselves emphasize the demeaning message that they decry.

A second and more important aspect of the American Dream theme in the *Autobiography* is the rise from impotence to importance, from

7. Charles Sumner, "Prophetic Voices About America: A Monograph," *Atlantic Monthly* 20 (September 1867): 275–306, gathers together a number of authors from the ancients to the mid-nineteenth century who use one or both of these motifs. On the West as terrestrial paradise, see William H. Tillinghast. "The Geographical Knowledge of the Ancients Considered in Relation to the Discovery of America," in Justin Winsor, ed., *Narrative and Critical History of America*, 8 vols. (Boston: Houghton Mifflin & Co., 1884–89), 1: 1–58; and Loren Baritz, "The Idea of the West," *American Historical Review* 66 (1960–61): 618–40. On the *translatio* idea (the theory of the westward movement of civilization), see Rexmond C. Cochrane, "Bishop Berkeley and the Progress of Arts and Learning: Notes on a Literary Convention," *Huntington Library Quarterly* 17 (1953–54): 229–49; Aubrey L. Williams, *Pope's Dunciad: A Study of Its Meaning* (London: Methuen & Co., 1955), pp. 42–48; Lewis P. Simpson, ed., *The*

Federalist Literary Mind (Baton Rouge: Louisiana State University Press, 1962), pp. 31–41; Lemay, *Men of Letters*, pp. xi, 131–32, 191, 257, 296, 299, 303, 307, 311; William D. Andrews, "William Smith and the Rising Glory of America," *Early American Literature* 8 (1973): 33–43; and Kenneth Silverman, *A Cultural History of the American Revolution* (New York: Thomas Y. Crowell, 1976), pp. 9–11 and see the index. Although he gives no indication of being aware of the intellectual and historical backgrounds of these motifs, Paul W. Conner, in *Poor Richard's Politicks: Benjamin Franklin and His New American Order* (New York: Oxford University Press, 1965), gathers together many of Franklin's allusions to these typical promotion tract topics in his subchapter "Muses in a Cook's Shop," pp. 96–107.
8. *Autobiography*, this edition, pp. 100. Future references to this edition will be given in the text.

dependence to independence, from helplessness to power. Franklin carefully parallelled this motif with the rags to riches motif in the opening of the *Autobiography*: "Having emerg'd from the Poverty and Obscurity in which I was born and bred, to a State of Affluence and some Degree of Reputation in the World . . ." (p. 1). The *Autobiography* relates in great detail the story of Franklin's rise from "Obscurity" to "some Degree of Reputation in the World."

This aspect of the American Dream motif gives the book much of its allegorical meaning and its archetypal power. Readers frequently observe that the story of Franklin's rise has its counterpart in the rise of the United States. Franklin was conscious of this. In the later eighteenth century he was the most famous man in the Western world. Even John Adams, in an attack on Franklin written thirty years after his death, conceded: "His reputation was more universal than that of Leibnitz or Newton, Frederick or Voltaire, and his character more beloved and esteemed than any or all of them."[9] And Franklin was famous *as an American*.[1] He frequently wrote about America, was familiar with all the eighteenth-century ideas about America, and knew that his *Autobiography* would be read, at least by some Englishmen and Europeans, as a book about America. As Benjamin Vaughan pointed out in a letter urging Franklin to go on with the *Autobiography*: "All that has happened to you is also connected with the detail of the manners and situation of a *rising* people" (p. 59.) And critical articles, such as that by James M. Cox, show that the book has frequently been read as an allegory of the rise to power and to independence of the United States.[2]

A more fundamental reason for the book's power and popularity lies in the archetypal appeal of the individual's rise from helplessness to power, from dependence to independence. In that normal development that every human being experiences from nebulousness to identity, from infancy to maturity, we all recapitulate the archetypal experience of the American Dream.[3] That is why the American Dream has been and is so important to so many people, as well as to American literature. That explains the appeal of the myth of the log-cabin birth of our American presidents and the popularity of the role of the self-made man. The American Dream, on this archetypal level, embodies a universal experience. *But* what is the identity, the strength, the power, or the independence that we adults enjoy? Aye, there's the rub. To an infant, the adult's power seems unlimited. To a

9. Adams, *Works*, 1: 660.
1. See, for example, the popular 1777 French medallion of Franklin, which bears the inscription "B Franklin Americain," in Charles Coleman Sellers, *Benjamin Franklin in Portraiture* (New Haven: Yale University Press, 1962), pp. 344–46 and pl. 10.
2. James M. Cox, "Autobiography and America," *Virginia Quarterly Review* 47 (1971): 256–62.
3. As far as I know, I first suggested this line of thought; see my "Benjamin Franklin," in *Major Writers of Early American Literature*, ed. Everett Emerson (Madison: University of Wisconsin Press, 1972), pp. 240–41.

child or adolescent, it seems a goal that cannot be too quickly achieved. But the achieved status is no great shakes, as every suicide bears ample witness. And we all recognize the lamentable truth of what Poor Richard said: "9 Men in 10 are suicides."[4] Who could not feel disenchanted with life? It is not only every person who ever reads a newspaper or has many dealings with the public; it is every person who goes through infancy and childhood anticipating that glorious state of adult freedom and independence, and who achieves it—as, of course, we all have. How many qualifications there are, how little real independence, how constraining nearly all occupations, how confining the roles we must act, and how unpleasant all the innumerable forces that are so glumly summed up under the forbidding heading of *the realities of life*. Who could not feel disenchanted with the American Dream?

A third aspect of the American Dream as it appears in Franklin's *Autobiography* is a philosophy of individualism: it holds that the world can be affected and changed by individuals. The American Dream is a dream of possibility—not just of wealth or of prestige or of power but of the manifold possibilities that human existence can hold for the incredible variety of people of the most assorted talents and drives. Generalized, the American Dream is the hope for a better world, a new world, free of the ills of the old, existing world. And for the individual, it is the hope for a new beginning for any of the numerous things that this incredible variety of human beings may want to do.[5] Although these desires can be as varied as the different people who exist, they have one thing in common. Before anyone can achieve any measure of competence, much less extraordinary success, in any field, it is necessary to believe in the possibility of accomplishment. Franklin graphically expressed a common-sense attitude in a woodcut (America's first political cartoon) which portrays a Conestoga wagon struck in the mud, with the wagoner beside it praying to Hercules. Under it, Franklin printed the opening of Cato's well-known speech in Sallust. In effect, Hercules tells the wagoner to get up, whip up the horses, put his shoulder to the wheel, and push.[6]

Before we apply to the American Dream the common sense of today, we should appreciate its eighteenth-century significance. The fictive world of Franklin's *Autobiography* portrays the first completely modern world that I know in Western literature: nonfeudal, nonaristocratic, and nonreligious. One has only to compare it with the fictive world of Jonathan Edwards's autobiography or Henry Fielding's *Tom*

4. *Poor Richard*, October 1749, in *P*, 3: 346.
5. See my remarks toward a definition of the American Dream in *Men of Letters*, pp. 6–7, 41–42, 59.
6. *P*, 3: xiv and 190. The quotation is from Sallust, *The War with Catiline*, chap. 52, sec.

29. The Loeb Library translation is "Not by vows nor womanish entreaties is the help of the gods secured" (John C. Rolfe, trans., *Sallust*, rev. ed. [Cambridge: Harvard University Press, 1931], p. 107).

Jones to realize that Franklin's world, like Edwards's and Fielding's, was indeed a world of his imagination, although that imaginative world, as portrayed in the *Autobiography*, suspiciously corresponded to an ideal democratic world as imagined by European philosophers and men of letters. Franklin's *persona*—that runaway apprentice whose appetite for work and study is nearly boundless, that trusting youth flattered and gulled by Governor Keith, that impecunious young adult who spent his money supporting his friend Ralph and his friend's mistress—that youth is the first citizen in literature who lives in a democratic, secular, mobile society.[7] The *persona* has the opportunity of choosing (or, to put it another way, faces the problem of choosing) what he is going to *do* in life and what he is going to *be* in life. Will he be a tallow chandler and soap maker like his father and his older brother John? A cutler like his cousin Samuel? Or a printer like his older brother James? Or will he satisfy his craving for adventure and run off to sea like his older brother Josiah?[8] These choices—presented in poignant terms early in the *Autobiography* and presented against the background of his father's not being able to afford to keep even Benjamin, "the Tithe of his Sons" (p. 6), in school so that he could become a minister—these choices actually function as a series of paradigms for the underlying philosophical questions of the role of man in society. But their primary function in the *Autobiography* is to demonstrate that man does have choice in the New World, that man can create himself. This is the primary message of Franklin's American Dream, just as it had been the fundamental message of the American Dream in the promotion tracts of the seventeenth and eighteenth centuries and in the writings of the European intellectuals.

Most sentences in Franklin's *Autobiography* are unrevised, but that sentence at the opening of the *Autobiography* in which he presented the American Dream motif caused him trouble, and he carefully reworked it. The finished sentence coordinates two participial phrases: one concerns Franklin's rise both from rags to riches and from obscurity to fame; the other tells us that Franklin generally had a happy life; but the main clause says that Franklin will inform us *how* he was able to accomplish these. "Having emerg'd from the Poverty and Obscurity in which I was born and bred, to a State of Affluence and some Degree of Reputation in the World, and having gone so far thro' Life with a considerable Share of Felicity, the conducing Means I made use of, which, with the Blessing of God, so well succeeded, my Posterity may like to know, as they may find some of them suitable to their own Situations, and therefore fit to be imitated" (p. 1) Franklin sees *the means* that a person can use in order to create himself, to shape

7. For some remarks on the democratic and modern background of Franklin's *Autobiography*, see Paul Ilie, "Franklin and Villarroel: Social Consciousness in Two Autobiographies," *Eighteenth-Century Studies* 7 (1973–74); 321–42.

8. *Autobiography*. This edition, pp. 6, 8–10. *P*, 4: lii, lvi–lix.

his life into whatever form that he may choose, as the primary subject of his book—insofar as it is a book about the American Dream.

Some readers (notably D. H. Lawrence) have mistaken Franklin's means as his ends.[9] That famous chart of the day, and that infamous list of virtues to be acquired, are not the ends that Franklin aims at; they are merely the means of discipline that will allow the ends to be achieved.[1] Franklin's own ultimate values are there in the book as well, for it is a book about values even more than it is a book about the means to achievement, but that is another, and larger, subject, and I have time only to sketch out some of the implications of this one.

With consummate literary artistry, Franklin embodied his portrait of the American Dream not only in that youth seeking to find a calling, a trade, but also in that scene which long ago became the dominant visual scene in all American literature, Franklin's entry into Philadelphia.[2] Franklin prepares the reader for the scene by saying: "I have been the more particular in this Description of my Journey, and shall be so of my first Entry into that City, that you may in your Mind compare such unlikely Beginnings with the Figure I have since made there" (p. 20). We all recall Franklin's entrance into Philadelphia: dirty, tired, hungry, practically penniless, his "Pockets . . . stuff'd out with Shirts and Stockings," buying his three great puffy rolls of bread. That image echoes throughout the *Autobiography* and resounds throughout American literature. Near the end of the *Autobiography*, it is contrasted with the Franklin who, in 1756, was escorted on a journey out of town by the officers of his regiment: "They drew their Swords, and rode with them naked all the way" (p. 129). Franklin writes that the display was foolish and embarrassing and that it ultimately did him considerable political disservice. And Franklin ironically points out the absurdities of such ceremonies: "The first Time I review'd my Regiment, they accompanied me to my House, and would salute me with some Rounds fired before my Door, which shook down and broke several Glasses of my Electrical Apparatus. And my new Honour prov'd not much less brittle; for all our Commissions were soon after broke by a Repeal of the Law in England" (pp. 128–29). My point in citing this passage is partly to show that the American Dream motif provides one of the elements that unify the book, but mainly to show how Franklin himself undercuts the value of the public honors paid to him, even as he tells us of those honors. Such complexities are found in every aspect of Franklin's presentation of the American Dream, even while Franklin nonetheless demonstrates that he is, in Matthew Arnold's words, "a man who was the very

9. D. H. Lawrence, "Benjamin Franklin," in his *Studies in Classic American Literature* (New York: T. Seltzer, 1923), pp. 13–31.
1. See especially Herbert W. Schneider, "The Significance of Benjamin Franklin's Moral Philosophy," Columbia University. Department of Philosophy, *Studies in the History of Ideas* 2 (1925): 293–312.
2. I echo my earlier claim in "Franklin and the *Autobiography*: An Essay on Recent Scholarship," *Eighteenth-Century Studies* 1 (1967–68): 200–201.

incarnation of sanity and clear sense."[3] Amidst all of Franklin's complexities and his radical skepticism, no one ever doubts his uncommon possession in the highest degree of common sense.[4]

This third aspect of the American Dream, which holds that the world can be affected by individuals, goes much beyond the common sense enshrined in Franklin's wagoner cartoon and in such sayings as "God helps those who help themselves."[5] For there is something most uncommon implied in the American Dream. It posits the achievement of extraordinary goals, a distinction in some endeavor, whether football or physics, politics or scholarship, a distinction not to be achieved by ordinary application or by ordinary ability. And common sense, though hardly so common as the phrase would have it, is still nothing extraordinary. This third motif of the American Dream believes in the possibility of extraordinary achievement. When Franklin tells of his early grand scheme to promulgate the Art of Virtue (which, in his own mind, amounted to a new and better religion), he succinctly expresses a philosophy of belief in the individual, a philosophy that allows for the extraordinary accomplishments of mankind: "And I was not discourag'd by the seeming Magnitude of the Undertaking, as I have always thought that one Man of tolerable Abilities may work great Changes, and accomplish great Affairs among Mankind, if he first forms a good Plan, and, cutting off all Amusements or other Employments that would divert his Attention, makes the Execution of that same Plan his sole Study and Business" (pp. 78–79).

A fourth aspect of the American Dream is, like the third, an underlying implication of the first two themes. Philosophically, it subsumes the earlier three motifs I have mentioned. The fourth theme takes a position on the age-old dialectic of free will versus determinism; or, to put this opposition in its degenerate present guise, between those people who think that what they do (whether voting in an election, teaching in a classroom, or answering questions from behind the reference desk) might make a difference and those who think it does not. Obviously Franklin is to be placed with those who believe in the possible efficacy of action. But Franklin is nothing if not a complex man and a complex thinker. Several long passages in his writings—as well as his only philosophical treatise—argue just the opposite.[6] Even in that consummate and full statement of the Ameri-

3. Matthew Arnold, *Culture and Anarchy*, in *The Complete Prose Works of Matthew Arnold*, ed. R. H. Super (Ann Arbor: University of Michigan Press, 1960–), 5: 110.

4. On the general topic of common sense in the *Autobiography*, see the discerning essay by John Griffith, "Franklin's Sanity and the Man behind the Masks," in Lemay, ed., *The Oldest Revolutionary: Essays on Benjamin Franklin*

(Philadelphia: University of Pennsylvania Press, 1976), pp. 123–38.

5. Franklin's form was "God helps them that help themselves," in *Poor Richard*, June 1736 (*P*, 2: 140), and in "The Way to Wealth" (*P*, 7: 341).

6. For Franklin's *Dissertation on Liberty and Necessity, Pleasure and Pain*, see *P*, 1: 55–71.

can Dream, the *Autobiography*, he has discordant notes.

At one point, he says that his early mistakes had "something of *Necessity* in them." That is, the world is not governed solely by free will: experience, knowledge, and background—or the lack of them—may determine, indeed predestine, the actions of an individual. Franklin speaks of his conviction as a youth that "*Truth, Sincerity and Integrity* in Dealings between Man and Man, were of the utmost importance to the Felicity of Life" (p. 46). He goes on: "And this Persuasion, with the kind hand of Providence, or some guardian Angel, or accidental favourable Circumstances and Situations, or all together, preserved me . . . without any *wilful* gross Immorality or Injustice that might have been expected from my Want of Religion. I say *wilful*, because the Instances I have mentioned, had something of *Necessity* in them, from my Youth, Inexperience, and the Knavery of others" (p. 46).

In addition to the species of necessity which arises from inexperience and from trusting in humanity, Franklin also mentions the Marxian version of predestinarianism, economics. Because Franklin's father could not afford to keep him in school, he took the boy home at ten to teach him his own trade, and so Franklin writes: "there was all Appearance that I was destin'd to . . . be a Tallow Chandler" (pp. 8–9). As I have suggested, Franklin's painful series of constricting choices concerning what he was going to be in life is played out against a backdrop of free will versus determinism, and necessity nearly carries the outcome. As Poor Richard said, "There have been as great Souls unknown to fame as any of the most famous."[7] But the necessitarian notes are deliberately minor. Franklin's classic statement of the American Dream rests firmly upon the belief in man's free will, but Franklin is not blind to the realities of economics, education, innocence, or evil. To regard his version of the American Dream as in any way simple is to misread the man—and the book.

A fifth and final aspect of the American Dream is, like the last two, a concomitant of the first two, as well as a precondition of their existence. It is a philosophy of hope, even of optimism. Belief in individualism and in free will, like the prospect of a rise from rags to riches or from impotence to importance, demands that the individual have hope. And so the *Autobiography* is deliberately optimistic about mankind and about the future. Nor is Franklin content with the implication. He gives a practical example of the result of an opposite point of view in his character sketch of the croaker, Samuel Mickle. It opens: "There are Croakers in every Country always boding its Ruin." Franklin tells of Samuel Mickle's prediction of bankruptcy for Franklin and for Philadelphia. Franklin testifies that Mickle's speech "left me half-melancholy. Had I known him before I engag'd in this

7. *P*, 1: 355.

Business, probably I never should have done it." And he concludes the sketch by telling that Mickle refused "for many Years to buy a House . . . because all was going to Destruction, and at last I had the Pleasure of seeing him give five times as much for one as he might have bought it for when he first began his Croaking" (p. 47).[8]

What makes this sketch particularly interesting to me is that Franklin falsifies the conclusion for the sake of the moral. One gathers from Franklin's sketch that Mickle hesitated for years before buying a house. No one knows anything about the personality of Samuel Mickle, who may well have been a pessimist. We do know that he was a real estate operator who bought and sold numerous properties.[9] Franklin certainly knew it, although for the sake of showing the impractical results of a philosophy of pessimism, he falsifies the facts. And we all know that, though the facts may be false, Franklin is right. It is better to be optimistic than pessimistic, better to be hopeful than hopeless. But we may not be able to be. Franklin knew too that men are at the mercy of their personalities, their world views, as well as of their ability, background, finances, health, and age. To his Loyalist son, Franklin wrote after the Revolution: "Our Opinions are not in our own Power; they are form'd and govern'd much by Circumstances, that are often as inexplicable as they are irresistible."[1]

When Franklin's old friend Hugh Roberts wrote him of the deaths of two of their former fellow members of the Junto, Franklin wrote back: "Parsons, even in his Prosperity, always fretting! Potts, in the midst of his Poverty, ever laughing! It seems, then, that Happiness in this Life rather depends on Internals than Externals; and that, besides the natural Effects of Wisdom and Virtue, Vice and Folly, there is such a Thing as being of a happy or an unhappy Constitution."[2]

Franklin himself seems to have been blessed with a happy constitution, but it is better never to be too certain of Franklin. He was capable of enormous self-discipline and had the common sense to know that it is better to be happy than miserable. Poor Richard advised hosts: "If you wou'd have Guests merry with your cheer, / Be so your self, or so at least appear."[3] Since a dominant theme of the Autobiography is the American Dream, and since this theme holds that it is desirable and beneficial to have hope, even optimism, Franklin's Autobiography is an optimistic work. But that is too partial a view of life to satisfy Franklin. He tells us in the Autobiography that at age twenty-one, when he began to recover from a severe illness, he regretted that he had not died: "I suffered a good deal, gave up the Point in my own

8. Compare Benjamin Franklin's account of his brother's starting a newspaper (Autobiography, p. 15), which implicitly makes the same point. Franklin deliberately does not tell the reader that his brother's newspaper failed.

9. See the biographical sketch, this edition, pp. 190–91.
1. Smyth, 9: 252.
2. P, 8: 159–60.
3. P, 1: 358.

mind, and was rather disappointed when I found my Self recovering; regretting in some degree that I must now some time or other have all that disagreable Work to do over again" (p. 41). This pessimism surprises no Franklinist, for his writings contain numerous similar passages. I'll cite just one more. In his only straightforward philosophical treatise, he defined life as suffering and death as the absence of pain: "We are first mov'd by *Pain*, and the whole succeeding Course of our Lives is but one continu'd Series of Action with a View to be freed from it."[4]

In the *Autobiography* Franklin balances optimism against the realities of life, and this tension in the *persona* is presented by an authorial voice that calls attention to the wishful, self-deceiving nature of the *persona*, and of man, who sees only what his vanity allows him to see. And Franklin had other good reasons to make the foolish vanity of man a major subject of the *Autobiography*, for the vanity of the autobiographer, as Franklin well knew, was the greatest literary pitfall of the genre. But the ways that Franklin dealt with this is another major theme of the book, and I have already outstayed my time.

I hope, though, to have shown that even dealing with its most obvious theme, the American Dream, the *Autobiography* possesses unity and complexity. Franklin deliberately creates a certain kind of fictive world, embodies that world in some unforgettable scenes, creates and sustains one character who is among the most memorable in American literature, and writes vivid truths that strike us with a shock of recognition. For these, among other reasons, I believe that the *Autobiography* is a major literary achievement, more complex, and in many ways, more artful, than a beautifully constructed novel like *The Rise of Silas Lapham*, which, of course, is much indebted to Franklin's *Autobiography*. Even so, Franklin would, I believe, have a much greater reputation as a literary artist if he had not written his masterpiece. We ordinary mortals want to turn against him, for what excuse does it leave us? Howells, in *The Rise of Silas Lapham*, gives that usual businessman's apology for financial failure: I was not a cheat; I was honest; therefore I failed. Its comforting implication is that all men who make fortunes are dishonest. Franklin maintains that cheats fail and honest men rise. We can say (what is partially true) that Franklin's book is written for young people, but that offers us little solace. And I can maintain that it portrays a fictive world of Franklin's imagination, and that offers us a little solace. But the Franklin portrayed in the *Autobiography* allows us older people little comfort for our comparative failure. That's part of the reason why we want to disbelieve him. The laws of physics, the moral wisdom of the an-

4. P, 1: 64.

cients, and our own visions of reality say that everything rises but to fall.[5] The Franklin of the *Autobiography*, however, displays himself behind that sturdy peasant's face and that old man's heavy figure, nimbly, magically dancing to his own complex music, while permaently suspended in the heights above us.

5. Sallust, *The War with Jugurtha*, chap. 2, sec. 3, in Rolfe, trans., *Salust*, p. 135.

Bibliography

KEY EDITIONS OF FRANKLIN'S AUTOBIOGRAPHY

I. The Two Anticipatory Publications

1. [Stuber, Dr. Henry.] "History of the Life and Character of Benjamin Franklin," *Universal Asylum and Columbian Magazine,* 4 (May, 1790), 268–72; (June), 332–39; 5 (July, 1790), 4–9; (Sept.), 139–45; (Oct.), 211–16; (Nov.), 283–87; 6 (Feb., 1791), 68–70; (March), 131–34; (May), 297–300; and (June), 363–66. Ford. p. 401. For his account in May, June, and July, 1790, Stuber relied upon a copy of the unrevised Part One of the *Autobiography.* For his later additions (Sept., 1790 to June, 1791), he used Mathew Carey's condensation (No. 2, below) of the entire *Autobiography,* as well as other sources. Stuber added a few valuable notes which have been retained by most annotated editions.

2. [Carey, Mathew.] "Memoirs of the late Benjamin Franklin," *American Museum,* 8 (July, 1790), 12–20; (Nov.), 210–12. Ford, p. 399. Carey's first installment condenses all four parts of the original holograph manuscript and includes BF's note on the name "Franklin." In the concluding installment, Carey expanded the remaining portions of BF's Outline and briefly sketched the rest of Franklin's life.

II. Editions

1. [Gibelin, Jacques, tr.] *Mémoires de la vie privée de Benjamin Franklin, écrits par lui-même, et adressés a son fils.* Paris: Chez Buisson, 1791. Ford, no. 383. The first edition of Franklin's *Autobiography* freely translates a faulty transcription of the unrevised Part One only.

2. *Works of the late Doctor Benjamin Franklin: Consisting of His Life Written by Himself, together with Essays, Humorous, Moral, & Literary.* 2v. London: G. G. J. and J. Robinson, 1793. Ford, no. 437. This anonymous retranslation of Gibelin's translation was published in July in vol. one. It first began publication in the Robinsons' *Lady's Magazine,* January, 1793. Influenced by Mathew Carey's redaction (no. 1, 2, above) and supplemented by Henry Stuber's account (no. I. 1, above), this edition was the best-known and most frequently reprinted version until Bigelow's 1868 edition (no. 9, below).

3. [Stevens, Alexander, tr.] *The Private Life of the Late Benjamin Franklin.* London: J. Parsons, 1793. Ford, no. 386. Another retranslation of the Gibelin translation. Like the Robinson edition (no. 2, above), it first appeared in July.

4. Castéra, Jean Henry, tr. *Vie de Benjamin Franklin, Écrits par lui-même, suivie de ses OEuvres.* 2v. Paris: Chez F. Buisson, 1798. Ford, no. 448. Part One retranslates back into French the Robinsons' English retranslation (no. 2, above) of Gibelin's translation (no. 1, above).

Castéra first prints (vol. 2, pp. 388–412) a fragment of Part Two of the *Autobiography* in a book, from the periodical *La Decade Philosophique, Littéraire et Politique,* 30 pluviôse, An VI, No. 15 [Feb. 18, 1798], pp. 345–58. Although Castéra (2: 388) notes that this portion of the *Autobiography* has been extracted at Philadelphia from a manuscript loaned to the citizen Delessert, it is in fact from the French translation made about 1791 by Louis Le Veillard. (Compare Le Veillard, as printed in Farrand's *Parallel Text Edition* [no. 12, below], pp. 211–233, with Castéra, 2: 388–412.)

5. Franklin, William Temple, ed. *Memoirs of the Life and Writings of Benjamin Franklin.* 3v. London: Henry Colburn, 1817–18. Ford, no. 561. Volume One, the *Life,* appeared in 1818, constituting the first appearance in English of Part Two of the *Autobiography* and the first appearance of Part Three. Although Franklin's grandson, former secretary, and literary heir had possessed the original holograph of the *Autobiography,* he had traded it for a copy that contained only the first three parts. Unfortunately, William Temple Franklin revised the original in accordance with his own genteel literary judgment and occasionally preferred to follow Buisson's translation or the Robinson retranslation (nos. 1 and 2, above). Although he added only a few annotations to the *Autobiography,* they are uniquely valuable.

6. Duane, William, ed. *The Works of Dr. Benjamin Franklin, in Philosophy, Politics and Morals*. 6v. Philadelphia: William Duane, 1808–18. Ford, no. 568. Volume one, the *Memoirs*, appeared in 1818. Since Duane married the widow of Benjamin Franklin Bache (BF's other grandson), Duane had access to the materials left in Philadelphia by William Temple Franklin. Duane reprinted William Temple Franklin's text and added a few important notes.

7. [Renouard, Augustine Charles, tr.] *Mémoires sur la vie de Benjamin Franklin, écrits par lui-même. Traduction nouvelle*. 2v. Paris: Jules Renouard, 1828. Ford, no. 403. Although mainly a translation of William Temple Franklin's edition, Renouard first published Part Four of the *Autobiography* (2: 1–9). This translation is different from and superior to Le Veillard's. (CF. Le Veillard, as printed in Farrand's *Parallel Text Edition* [no. 12, below], pp. 411–17, with Renouard, 2: 1–9.)

8. Sparks, Jared, ed. *The Works of Benjamin Franklin*. 10v. Boston: Hilliard, Gray & Co., 1836–40. Ford, no. 588. Volume one (1840) contains the *Autobiography*. Sparks used W. T. Franklin's text and prepared the first thorough annotations. Separate reprints of Sparks' edition as *The Life of Benjamin Franklin* began to appear in 1844.

9. Bigelow, John, ed. *Autobiography of Benjamin Franklin*. Philadelphia: Lippincott, 1868. Ford, no. 423. Bigelow revised Sparks' edition from the original holograph (which he had purchased in France), printed Part Four for the first time in English, and added a series of valuable notes, as well as an account of the original holograph's misadventures. Bigelow also first published Franklin's Outline of the *Autobiography*.

10. Smyth, Albert Henry, ed. *The Writings of Benjamin Franklin*. 10v. New York: Macmillan, 1905–7. Smyth printed Bigelow's text and added a few notes.

11. [Rogers, Bruce, typographer.] *The Autobiography of Benjamin Franklin*. Boston: Houghton, Mifflin, & Co., 1906. This beautifully printed and illustrated edition was set from Bigelow's edition. It contains a snippet in facsimile of the original holograph (from p. 99) and a good facsimile of the Outline between pp. 182 and 183.

12. Farrand, Max, ed. *Benjamin Franklin's Memoirs: Parallel Text Edition*. Berkeley: University of California Press, 1949. This edition (actually completed after Farrand's death by Godfrey Davies and other members of the Huntington Library staff) prints in parallel columns four texts: *1*, the holograph original (but the text is actually mainly transcribed from a corrected version of Bigelow); *2*, William Temple Franklin's edition (no. *5*, above); *3*, Louis Guillaume Le Veillard's French translation based upon both a copy of the manuscript and the original holograph; and *4*, Buisson's edition (no. *1*, above). Unfortunately, it has no index.

13. Labaree, Leonard W., Ralph L. Ketcham, Helen C. Boatfield, and Helene H. Fineman, eds. *The Autobiography of Benjamin Franklin*. New Haven: Yale University Press, 1964. This splendidly annotated edition reprints Farrand's version of the holograph (from no. 12) as "corrected" from a photocopy of the manuscript. The edition contains a facsimile of p. 28 of the original holograph, lovely drawings of the three places where Franklin was living while composing the *Autobiography*, and a color reproduction of David Martin's portrait of Franklin.

14. Lemay, J. A. Leo and P. M. Zall, eds. *The Autobiography of Benjamin Franklin: A Genetic Text*. Knoxville: University of Tennessee Press, 1981. The *Genetic Text* attempts to follow the genesis of the original manuscript. It prints all materials in the holograph, showing cancellations, interlineations, and columnar additions as such. Lemay and Zall also elaborately edit all the documents that Franklin intended to print in the *Autobiography*, as well as his Outline.

ABBREVIATIONS AND BIBLIOGRAPHY FOR THE ANNOTATIONS AND THE BIOGRAPHICAL NOTES

Adams. *see* Butterfield.

Allinson, Edward P. and Boies Penrose. *Philadelphia 1681–1887: A History of Municipal Development*. Philadelphia: Allen, Lane, & Scott, 1887.

Anderson, Florence B. *A Grandfather for Benjamin Franklin*. Boston: Meador Publishing Co., 1940.

Axtell, James L., ed. *Educational Writings of John Locke*. Cambridge: University Press, 1968.

Bezanson, Anne, et al. *Prices in Colonial Pennsylvania*. Philadelphia: University of Pennsylvania Press, 1935.

Bibliography • 363

BF=Benjamin Franklin.

Boyd, Julian P., ed. *The Papers of Thomas Jefferson*. Princeton: Princeton University Press, 1950–.

Breslaw, Elaine G. "A Dismal Tragedy: Drs. Alexander and John Hamilton Comment on Braddock's Defeat." *Md. Historical Magazine*, 75 (1980), 118–44.

Butterfield, Lyman H., ed. *The Adams Papers. The Diary and Autobiography of John Adams*. 4 vols. Cambridge, Mass.: Harvard University Press, 1961.

Cabanis, Pierre J. G. *Oeuvres Posthumes*. Paris: Bossange frères, 1823–25. In *Oeuvres complètes de Cabanis*.

Carter, Katherine. "Isaac Norris II's Attack on Andrew Hamilton." *PMHB*, 104 (1980), 139–61.

Cohen, Hennig. *South Carolina Gazette*. Columbia, S. C.: University of South Carolina Press, 1953.

Cohen, I. Bernard. *Franklin and Newton*. Philadelphia: American Philosophical Society, 1956.

Cummings, Hubertis. *Richard Peters, Provincial Secretary and Cleric*. Philadelphia: University of Pennsylvania Press, 1944.

DAB=Allen Johnson and Dumas Malone, eds. *Dictionary of American Biography*. 20 vols. New York: Scribner's, 1928–37.

Davis, Richard Beale, ed. *The Colonial Virginia Satirist*. Philadelphia: *Transactions of the American Philosophical Society*, n.s., 57, pt. 1, 1967.

DeArmond, Anna J. *Andrew Bradford*. Newark, De.: University of Delaware Press, 1949.

DNB=Sir Leslie Stephen and Sir Sidney Lee, eds. *Dictionary of National Biography*. 63 vols. London: Smith, Elder, 1885–1901. Rpt. in 22 vols. London: Smith, Elder, 1908–9.

Dexter, Franklin Bowditch, ed. *Literary Diary of Ezra Stiles*. 3 vols. New York: Scribners, 1901.

Eddy, George Simpson, ed. *Account Books Kept by Benjamin Franklin*. 2 vols. New York: Columbia University Press, 1928–29.

Evans, Charles. *American Bibliography. A Chronological Dictionary . . . [through] 1800*. 14 vols. Chicago, Worcester, 1903–59.

Fisher, Joshua Francis. *Some Account of the Early Poets and Poetry of Pennsylvania*. Philadelphia: Memoirs of the Historical Society of Pennsylvania, v. 2, pt. 2, 1830.

Fitzpatrick, John C., ed. *The Writings of George Washington*. 39 vols. Washington: Government Printing Office, 1931–44.

Ford, Paul Leicester. *Franklin Bibliography. A List of Books written by, or relating to Benjamin Franklin*. Brooklyn, N. Y.: [no. pub.], 1889.

Franklin, Benjamin (Uncle of BF). "A short account of the Family of Thomas Franklin of Ecton in Northamptonshire, 21 June 1717." MS., Yale University Library.

Gipson, Lawrence H. *British Empire before the American Revolution*. 15 vols. New York: Knopf, 1939–70.

Hanna, William S. *Benjamin Franklin and Pennsylvania Politics*. Palo Alto: Stanford University Press, 1964.

Hinshaw, William Wade. *Encyclopedia of American Quaker Genealogy*. 7 vols. Ann Arbor: Edwards Brothers, 1936–65.

Howe, Ellic. *The London Compositor*. London: Bibliographical Society, 1947.

Hutson, James H. *Pennsylvania Politics 1746–1770*. Princeton: Princeton University Press, 1972.

James, Edward T., ed., *Notable American Women 1607–1950: A Biographical Dictionary*. 3 vols. Cambridge, Mass.: Harvard University Press, 1971.

Keith, Charles P. *Chronicles of Pennsylvania, 1688–1748*. 2 vols. Philadelphia: Patterson & White, 1917.

Korty, Margaret Barton. *Benjamin Franklin and Eighteenth Century American Libraries*. Philadelphia: *Transactions of the American Philosophical Society*, n.s., 55, pt. 9, 1955.

Lemay, J. A. Leo. "Benjamin Franklin." In *Major Writers of Early American Literature*. Everett H. Emerson, ed. Madison: University of Wisconsin Press, 1972, pp. 205–243.

Lemay, J. A. Leo. *Ebenezer Kinnersley: Franklin's Friend*. Philadelphia: University of Pennsylvania Press, 1964.

Lemay, J.A. Leo. "Franklin's 'Dr. Spence': The Reverend Archibald Spencer (1698?–1760), M.D." *Maryland Historical Magazine,* 59 (1964), 199–216.

Lemay, J. A. Leo. "Franklin's Suppressed 'Busy-Body.' " *American Literature,* 38 (1965), 307–11.

Lester, Richard A. "Currency Issues to Overcome Depression in Pennsylvania, 1723 and 1729." *Journal of Political Economy,* 46 (1938), 324–75.

Lewis, Janette Seaton. "A Turn of Thinking: The Long Shadow of *The Spectator* in Franklin's *Autobiography.*" *Early American Literature,* 13 (1978/9), 268–77.

Lillywhite, Bryant. *London Signs: a Reference Book of London Signs from Earliest Times to About the Mid-Nineteenth Century.* London: Allen and Unwin, 1972.

Lillywhite, Bryant. *London Coffee Houses; a Reference Book.* London: Allen & Unwin, 1963.

Lyons, Henry. *The Royal Society 1660–1940.* Cambridge: The University Press, 1944.

Maury, Ann. *Memoirs of a Huguenot Family.* New York: Putnam's, 1852.

Miller, C. William. *Benjamin Franklin's Philadelphia Printing.* Philadelphia: American Philosophical Society, 1974.

Monaghan, Frank, ed. *Some Conversations of Dr. Franklin and Mr. Jay.* New Haven: Three Monks Press, 1936.

Mottelay, Paul F. *Bibliographical History of Electricity and Magnetism.* London: C. Griffin, 1922.

Namier, Lewis, and John Brooke. *The House of Commons 1754–1790.* 3 vols. New York: Oxford University Press, 1964.

Newman, Eric P. *Bicentennial Edition of The Early Paper Money of America.* Racine, WI.: Western Publishing Co., 1976.

Nolan, J. Bennett. *Benjamin Franklin in Scotland and Ireland.* Philadelphia: University of Pennsylvania Press, 1938.

Nolan, J. Bennett. *General Benjamin Franklin.* Philadelphia: University of Pennsylvania Press, 1936.

P=*The Papers of Benjamin Franklin,* ed. by Leonard W. Labaree, William B. Willcox, et al. New Haven: Yale University Press, 1959—.

Pa. Gaz. =*Pennsylvania Gazette.*

PAPS =*Proceedings of the American Philosophical Society.*

Pa. Archives =*Pennsylvania Archives: Selected and Arranged from Original Documents . . .* , ed. Samuel Hazard et al. 138 vols. in 9 series. Harrisburg and Philadelphia: [various publishers], 1852–1935.

Pennsylvania Colonial Records=*Minutes of the Provincial Council of Pennsylvania.* 16 vols. Philadelphia: J. Stevens & Co., 1838–53.

Plomer, Henry R. *A Dictionary of Printers and Booksellers . . . in England, Scotland and Ireland from 1668 to 1725.* Oxford: University Press, 1922.

PMHB =*Pennsylvania Magazine of History and Biography.*

Roach, Hannah B. "Benjamin Franklin Slept Here." *PMHB,* 84 (1960), 127–74.

Sargent, Winthrop. *The History of An Expedition Against Fort DuQuesne in 1755.* Philadelphia: Lippincott for the Historical Society of Pennsylvania, 1856.

Sedgwick, Romney. *The House of Commons 1715–1754.* 2 vols. New York: Oxford University Press, 1970.

Shipton-Mooney=Shipton, Clifford K. and James E. Mooney. *National Index of American Imprints Through 1800: The Short-Title Evans.* 2 vols. Worcester, Mass.: American Antiquarian Society, 1969.

Sibley's Harvard Graduates=Sibley, John Langdon, and Clifford K. Shipton, *Biographical Sketches of Those Who Attended Harvard College.* 17 vols. Boston: Massachusetts Historical Society, 1873–1975.

Smyth, Albert H., ed. *The Writings of Benjamin Franklin.* 10 vols. New York: Macmillan, 1905–7.

Sparks, Jared, ed. *The Works of Benjamin Franklin.* 10 vols. Boston: Tappan & Whittemore, 1836–40.

Sprague, William Buell. *Annals of the American Pulpit.* 9 vols. New York: R. Carter and Brothers, 1857–69.

Stearns, Raymond Phineas. *Science in the British Colonies of America.* Urbana: University of Illinois Press, 1970.

Stock, Leo Francis, ed. *Proceedings and Debates of the British Parliaments Respecting North America.* 5 vols. Washington, D. C.: Carnegie Institution, 1924–41.

Tanner, Edwin P. *The Province of New Jersey 1664–1738*. New York: Columbia University Press, 1908.

Tilley, Morris Palmer. *A Dictionary of the Proverbs in England in the Sixteenth and Seventeenth Centuries*. Ann Arbor: University of Michigan Press, 1950.

Tolles, Frederick B. *James Logan and the Culture of Provincial America*. Boston: Little, Brown, 1957.

Tolles, Frederick B. *Meeting House and Counting House*. Chapel Hill: University of North Carolina Press, 1948.

Tourtellot, Arthur Bernon. "The Early Reading of Benjamin Franklin." *Harvard Library Bulletin*, 23 (1975), 5–41.

Tyerman, Luke. *Life of George Whitefield*. 2 vols. London: Hodder & Stoughton, 1876–77.

Valentine, Alan. *The British Establishment 1760–1784*. 2 vols. Norman: University of Oklahoma Press, 1970.

Van Doren, Carl. *Benjamin Franklin's Autobiographical Writings*. New York: Viking, 1945.

Wainwright, Nicholas B. "Governor William Denny in Pennsylvania." *PMHB*, 81 (1957), 170–98.

Webb, Edward Alfred. *Records of St. Bartholomew Priory*. 2 vols. London: Oxford University Press, 1921.

Wheatley, Henry B., and Peter Cunningham. *London Past and Present*. 3 vols. London: Murray, 1891.

Wilson, F. P., ed. *The Oxford Dictionary of English Proverbs*. Third Edition. Oxford: Clarendon Press, 1970.

Wing, Donald. *Short-Title Catalogue of Books Printed in England, Scotland, Ireland, Wales, and British America . . .1641–1700*. 3 vols. New York: Index Society, 1945–51.

WMQ=*William and Mary Quarterly*.

Wolf, Edwin, 2nd. "The First Books and Printed Catalogues of the Library Company." *PMHB*, 78 (1954), 45–70.

Wolf, Edwin, 2nd. "The Reconstruction of Benjamin Franklin's Library." *Papers of the Bibliographical Society of America*, 56 (1962), 1–16.

Wroth, Lawrence C. "Benjamin Franklin: The Printer at Work." *Journal of the Franklin Institute*, 234 (1942), 105–32.

Wroth, Lawrence C. *The Colonial Printer*. Portland, ME.: Southworth-Anthoesen Press, 1938.

WTF=Franklin, William Temple. *Memoirs of the Life and Writings of Benjamin Franklin*. 3 vols. London: H. Colburn, 1817–18. All references are to vol. 1.

Zall, Paul M. *Comical Spirit of Seventy-Six*. San Marino, CA: Huntington Library, 1976.

A SELECTIVE, ANNOTATED BIBLIOGRAPHY OF TWENTIETH-CENTURY CRITICISM

1905

Weber, Max. *The Protestant Ethic and the Spirit of Capitalism*, trans. by Talcott Parsons. London: Allen & Unwin, 1930. (First edition published as *Die protestantische Ethik Und der Geist des Kapitalismus* in *Archiv Für Sozialwissenschaft und Sozialpolitik*, vols. 20 & 21 for 1904–5; revised and enlarged edition in 1920.) In perhaps the most influe ial twentieth-century comment on Franklin, Weber uses two examples from BF to define "The spirit of capitalism . . . in almost classical purity" (p. 48), and argues that BF's ethic is identical with "the Puritan worldly asceticism, only without the religious basis" (p. 180).

1923

Lawrence, D. H. "Benjamin Franklin" In his *Studies in Classic American Literature*, New York: T. Seltzer, 1923, pp. 13–31. In the most memorable attack on BF, Lawrence accuses him (and America) of lacking spirituality; objects to BF's proverbs he read as a child (they "rankle still"); claims that BF secretly hated England, Europe, and monarchy; condemns BF (and Woodrow Wilson!) for being "theoretic and materialistic"; and fulminates against BF's supposedly preaching chastity while practicing venery.

1925

Schneider, Herbert W. "The Significance of Benjamin Franklin's Moral Philosophy." In Columbia Univ., Dept. of Philosophy, *Studies in the History of Ideas*, vol. 2 (1925), 291–312. Schneider distinguishes between an ethics of means (i.e., instrumental virtues) and one of ends (i.e., intrinsic, ultimate values), claiming that both are proper subjects of the study of ethics but that agreement concerning the instrumental virtues is more possible than agreement concerning ideals. He argues that Franklin's Art of Virtue presents an ethics of means ("more illuminating than the formal and psychological analysis found in recent philosophy"), which is basically more useful than an ethics of ends. Schneider thus not only justifies viewing Franklin as an ethical philosopher, but even maintains that Franklin was philosophically astute in divorcing his utilitarian ethics from traditional disciplines in philosophy, for Franklin perceived that moral distinctions have no basis in the absolute but must be relative to a human point of view.

1940

Maugham, W. Somerset. "The Classic Books of America." *Saturday Evening Post*, 212 (Jan. 6, 1940), 29, 64–66, at 64. Reprinted, slightly revised, in Maugham's *Books and You* (New York: Doubleday, Doran & Co., 1940), pp. 81–82. Maugham judges no autobiography "more consistently interesting," calls BF "the typical American," and says the reason "why in America Franklin is often spoken of with depreciation" is that he "was entirely devoid of hokum."

1941

Pritchett, V. S. [Review of Franklin's *Autobiography*.] *New Statesman and Nation*, 22 (Sept. 27, 1941), 309. Pritchett labels Lawrence's criticism "a typical misfire," for "before Franklin's irony, urbanity and benevolence, Lawrence cuts an absurd figure." Viewing BF in the tradition of Puritan autobiography, Pritchett believes that Franklin's distinctive qualities are "the variety of his interests and the originality of his mind," and that "Use, Method and Order" were only the immense stimulus for his genius, whereas the Romantic Lawrence thought them his "dreary objectives."

1942

Spiller, Robert E. "Benjamin Franklin: Student of Life." *Journal of the Franklin Institute*, 233 (1942), 309–29. Seeing BF as a pragmatist, Spiller reads his scheme of moral perfection as merely a working guide for the youthful Franklin, not an ideal of perfection, and argues that BF applied experimental methods to conduct as well as to nature, reflecting (and creating) a pragmatism which distinguishes American character.

1946

Wright, Louis B. "Franklin's Legacy to the Gilded Age." *Virginia Quarterly Review*, 22 (1946), 268–79. Wright demonstrates that in late nineteenth-century popular culture, BF appears as the patron saint of the gospel of wealth.

1953

Stourzh, Gerald. "Reason and Power in Benjamin Franklin's Political Thought." *American Political Science Review*, 47 (1953), 1092–1115. Stourzh subtly analyzes seven key topics in BF's thought: the Great Chain of Being, the idea of progress, the belief in reason, the passion of pride, the nature of politics, the basis of his belief in democracy, and power versus equality.

1954

Sanford, Charles L. "An American Pilgrim's Progress." *American Quarterly*, 4 (1954), 297–310. Sanford charts the transformation, in early America, of the *translatio religii* motif (which anticipated the coming of the Second Millenium in America) into the American Dream (which anticipated the individual's moral regeneration accompanying his material improvement). Thus he finds that Franklin's *Autobiography* is a secular, American, eighteenth-century version of the religious story of Christian in John Bunyan's *Pilgrim's Progress*. Sanford further argues that BF's tale of moral individualism and personal salvation allegorizes the motif of the Rising Glory of America.

1956

Spiller, Robert E. "Franklin on the Art of Being Human." *Proceedings of the American Philosophical Society*, 100 (1956), 304–15. Spiller attempts to account for the different attitudes toward Franklin expressed by 1) BF's contemporaries; 2) the Romantics; 3) the Victorians; 4) such early twentieth-century figures as Max Weber and D. H. Lawrence; and 5) recent writers. After examining the Art of Virtue in comparison to similar plans, Spiller discusses the derivation and tradition of BF's individual virtues, claims that Franklin was a major literary artist, and argues that his pragmatic, scientific spirit is relevant today.

1957

Miles, Richard D. "The American Image of Benjamin Franklin." *American Quarterly*, 9 (1957), 117–43. Miles chronologically surveys American attitudes toward Franklin from eighteenth-century political enemies to specialized scholars of the 20th century. He finds that BF's dominant image is the self-made man, but notes two others. One popular attitude portrays BF as a "Poor Richard," i.e., as an embodiment of the ascetic-material qualities of industry, frugality, and thrift (a caricature especially liked by creative writers); the other sees BF as the embodiment of Americanism, a jingoistic approach popular in the late 19th and early 20th centuries.

1958

Bier, Jesse. "Franklin's *Autobiography*: Benchmark of American Literature." *Western Humanities Review*, 12 (1958), 57–65. Bier believes the *Autobiography* is "the most significant book in American literature" because it "holds in solution" the four major themes in American literature: the relation between the individual and society, the opposition between democracy and aristocracy, the tension between appearance and reality, and the values of Romantic Idealism (BF's belief in "the almost infinite possibilities of self-improvement") versus Pragmatic Realism (BF's utilitarianism).

1962

Shear, Walter. "Franklin's Self-Portrait." *Midwest Quarterly*, 4 (1962), 71–86. Shear finds the *Autobiography* "flat" because BF records the actions of his younger self with detachment. Franklin abstractly investigates, in himself, a "chief philosophic problem of the age, self interest." The *Autobiography* records that the young Franklin gradually came to identify his self-interest with the public good and shows that the discovery of one's true interest "demands a partial submission of the self to the dictates of the systematic reason."

1963

Sayre, Robert Freeman. "The Worldly Franklin and the Provincial Critics." *Texas Studies in Literature & Language*, 4 (1963), 512–24. Sayre argues that

Franklin's critics (like D. H. Lawrence, William Carlos Williams, and Charles Angoff) who attack him for middle-class virtues ignore the facts in order to make BF a symbol. These critics reveal their own provinciality in failing to appreciate Franklin's sophistication and humor. Sayre stresses BF's literary art, pointing out the dramatic interplay between the old Franklin as author and the young Franklin as subject. He also maintains that the different times of composition (1771, 1784, and 1788–90) influenced both Franklin's roles as narrator (printer, philosophical Quaker, and projector) and his attitudes.

Ward, John William. "Who was Benjamin Franklin?" *American Scholar*, 32 (1963), 541–53. Ward argues that Parts One and Two of the *Autobiography* are not about success but about the "formation of character that makes success possible," and that the example was intended for young Americans but also for Europeans—as an idea of what it meant to be an American. Ward claims that Franklin's self-aware and ironic tone is especially suitable for such subjects as reality and identity in a mobile and secular society. "Franklin stands most clearly as an exemplary American because his life's story is a witness to the uncertainties about social status that have characterized our society, a society caught up in the constant process of change."

1964

Granger, Bruce Ingham. *Benjamin Franklin: An American Man of Letters*. Ithaca, N.Y.: Cornell Univ. Press, 1964. On pages 209–38, Granger relates the *Autobiography* to the past traditions of biography, spiritual autobiography, and conduct book, then briefly discusses its intended audience as well as the topical and chronological structure.

Levin, David. "The Autobiography of Benjamin Franklin: The Puritan Experimenter in Life and Art." *Yale Review*, 53 (1964), 258–75. Levin distinguishes between Franklin as author and as character, and argues that Parts One and Two describe BF's education whereas Parts Three and Four chronicle his public career. Levin believes that Franklin grounded the book in three dominant experiences of his time: Puritanism, the difficulties and dangers of youth in eighteenth-century society, and experimental, scientific inquiry. Thus, although Levin points out both Franklin's faith in virtue and his attacks on the limits of reason, he emphasizes that Franklin rationally, skeptically, and empirically examined and tested society's customs.

Sayre, Robert F. *The Examined Self: Benjamin Franklin, Henry Adams, Henry James.* Princeton: Princeton Univ. Press, 1964. In a revision (which omits the detailed responses to critics) of his 1963 essay, Sayre (pp. 12–43) argues that the *Autobiography* mirrors BF's "pluralism and his unending versatility" in its three personae: printer (in Part One), naive philosophical Quaker (in Part Two), and projector and doer of good (in Part Three).

1965

Cawelti, John G. *Apostles of the Self-Made Man*. Chicago: University of Chicago Press, 1965, pp. 9–24. Cawelti believes that Franklin, "more than any other individual, . . . exemplified in his own person and articulated in his writings a new hero, different in character from traditional military, religious, and aristocratic conceptions of human excellence and virtue" (p. 9). He finds that the essence of Franklin's new conception of social order was "the belief that the individual's place in society should be defined by his ability to perform useful actions and not by his rank in a traditional hierarchy" (p. 12). He claims that the *Autobiography* has too often been read as an elaboration of *The Way to Wealth*, even though it presents "a broad and humane ideal of self-improvement" (p. 16), "based on the industrious pursuit of a profession, the cultivation of the moral and intellectual virtues, and the assumption of a responsible role in the general progress of society" (p. 23).

Lynen, John F. *The Design of the Present: Essays on Time and Form in American Literature*. New Haven: Yale Univ. Press, 1965. Lynen (pp. 119–52) examines the philosophic subtlety of BF's values, along with BF's views of reality and of identity. *Inter alia*, he argues that BF's main role in the *Autobiography* is that of the sage offering lessons for the reader's instruction.

1966

Bushman, Richard L. "On the Uses of Psychology: Conflict and Conciliation in Benjamin Franklin." *History and Theory*, 5 (1966), 225–40. Bushman finds that the underlying pattern in Franklin's *Autobiography* (and character) conforms to the syndrome of emotions that an infant experiences when his breast-feeding is interrupted by the eruption of his teeth.

1967

Aldridge, Alfred Owen, "The First Published Memoir of Franklin." *William & Mary Quarterly*, 3rd ser., 24 (1967), 624–28. Aldridge reprints a notice of Franklin's early life from the *London Chronicle*, October 1, 1778, which is similar to the *Autobiography*.
————. "Form and Substance in Franklin's *Autobiography*." In *Essays on American Literature in Honor of Jay B. Hubbell*. Ed. Clarence Gohdes. Durham: Duke University Press, 1967, pp. 47–62. Aldridge argues that BF's *Autobiography* is, in form, a "virtual disaster" because of its different times of composition, resulting in different tones and in several repetitions. He claims that its only unity is psychological—a unity arising from the delight and satisfaction that Franklin felt in writing the work. Aldridge discusses the style ("an exquisite balance between reflection and anecdote"), the functions of the anecdotes, the parallel development of Franklin and America, and the *Autobiography* within the eighteenth-century English and European autobiographical traditions.
Ross, Morton L. "Form and Moral Balance in Franklin's *Autobiography*." *Ariel*, 7, no. 3 (July, 1967), 38–52. Countering critics' complaints of BF's concern with industry and frugality, Ross asserts a "moral balance" between the first half of the *Autobiography* where those virtues and self-advertisement are stressed and the second half where Franklin emphasizes self-effacement and a "responsible use of wealth and leisure." Ross also touches on some characteristics of the "voice."

1968

Lemay, J. A. Leo. "Franklin and the *Autobiography*: An Essay on Recent Scholarship." *Eighteenth-Century Studies*, 1 (1968), 185–211. In the course of reviewing a decade of Franklin scholarship, Lemay discusses the *Autobiography's* intimate tone, its dominant visual image, and the project of achieving "moral Perfection."
Shea, Daniel B., Jr. *Spiritual Autobiography in Early America*. Princeton: Princeton Univ. Press, 1968. Shea (pp. 234–48) points out that several motifs in the *Autobiography* are common in eighteenth-century English literature and society (including the ambitious apprentice). Finding a utilitarian and Newtonian habit of mind throughout, Shea also claims that Franklin wrote for two audiences—sophisticated literary contemporaries and plain-minded readers. Thus when Franklin takes up the project for attaining moral perfection, Shea believes that BF offers the method, not the achievement, as exemplary, but that, although irony is indeed present, Franklin seriously presents a "hope of triumph over nature and limitation."

1969

Ketcham, Ralph L. "Benjamin Franklin: *Autobiography*." In *Landmarks of American Writing*. Ed. Hennig Cohen. New York: Basic Books, 1969, pp. 20–31. Viewing the story of BF's rise from obscurity and poverty to reputation and wealth as profoundly revolutionary in the eighteenth century, Ketcham finds that the diction (homely and vernacular), the purpose (showing the common man the way to prosperity), and such details as the Junto episode—all imply a democratic American society fundamentally different from the hierarchical European one.
Minter, David L. *The Interpreted Design as a Structural Principle in American Prose*. New Haven: Yale Univ. Press, 1969. Minter points out (pp. 77–85) that the *Autobiography* is a "surrogate for" BF's Art of Virtue.
Sappenfield, James A. "*The Autobiography of Benjamin Franklin*: The Structure of Success." *Wisconsin Studies in Literature*, 6 (1969), 90–99. Sappenfield

examines BF's use of characters in the first part of the *Autobiography* as the basis for the "dramatic structure" of the theme of "The American Dream of success by dint of industry, frugality and ingenuity."

1970

Ohmann, Carol. *"The Autobiography of Malcolm X:* A Revolutionary Use of the Franklin Tradition." *American Quarterly*, 22 (1970), 131–49. Ohmann finds that BF and Malcolm X both tell about self-made men who neither analyze nor explore the self. Although both measure achievement against the standards of an acquisitive society, only Malcolm X grows spiritually, thus aligning his story with the earlier traditions of spiritual autobiography.

1971

Cox, James M. "Autobiography and America." *Virginia Quarterly Review*, 47 (1971), 252–77. Cox relates four key autobiographies (Franklin's, Thoreau's *Walden*, Henry Adams' *Education*; and Gertrude Stein's) to the development of American civilization. He finds Franklin's *Autobiography* to be a conscious paradigm of the American Revolution and a step toward the liberation of the modern self.

Griffith, John. "The Rhetoric of Franklin's '*Autobiography*.' "*Criticism*, 13 (1971), 77–94. Griffith believes that the rhetorical unity of the *Autobiography* derives from the dramatic interplay between two points of view: "one (on which the younger Franklin moves) being past, external, and rather distant; the other (on which the mature Franklin the 'speaker,' moves) being a primarily internal or mental one, present and directly accessible to the reader's understanding."

Tatham, Campbell. "Benjamin Franklin, Cotton Mather, and the Outward State." *Early American Literature*, 6 (1971), 223–33. Tatham examines BF's attitudes toward Puritanism in the *Autobiography* and finds him hostile toward (a narrowly defined) Puritanism.

1972

England, A. B. "Some Thematic Patterns in Franklin's *Autobiography*." *Eighteenth-Century Studies*, 5 (1972), 421–30. Taking the central theme of the *Autobiography* as the conflict between order and chaos, England gives examples of this conflict in its form, character sketches, anecdotes, imagery, style, and BF's personality.

Lemay, J. A. Leo. "Benjamin Franklin." In *Major Writers of Early American Literature*. Ed. Everett H. Emerson. Madison: Univ. of Wisconsin Press, 1972, pp. 205–43. After discussing the *Autobiography*'s fictions and its American Dream theme (explaining its appeal as an "archetypal recapitulation of the development of every individual"), Lemay argues that the main persona is Franklin as the friend of mankind, *amicus humani generis*.

Miller, Ross. "Autobiography as Fact and Fiction: Franklin, Adams, Malcolm X." *Centennial Review*, 16 (1972), 221–32. Miller sets forth a number of themes and subjects which he believes characterize autobiography as a genre: the problem of vanity; the autobiographer's story as a microcosm of that historical period; the autobiography as "sensuous history"; the autobiographer's persona as representative of an occupation, profession, or type; the autobiographer as creator of (or, at least, as one who imposes a pattern on) his life; the genre as "an attempt to make history into a novel" (thus making Franklin's *Autobiography* the literary ancestor of such "new journalism" as Truman Capote's *In Cold Blood*); and the autobiography as a psychological investigation of the limits of self-knowledge.

1973

McLaughlin, John H. "His Brother's Keeper: Franklin's Sibling Rivalry." *South Atlantic Bulletin*, 38, no. 4 (1973), 62–69. McLaughlin attributes BF's drive for wealth and learning to his childhood disappointments and to his rivalry with his brother James.

Sappenfield, James A. A *Sweet Instruction: Franklin's Journalism as a Literary Appren-*
ticeship. Carbondale: Southern Illinois Univ. Press, 1973. In a chapter on the
Autobiography (pp. 178–214), Sappenfield argues that the work has only two
divisions—Part One comprising one unified "half" and Parts Two, Three, and
Four comprising a "second" half. Sappenfield discusses at length the functions
of the character sketches.

1974

Ilie, Paul. "Franklin and Villarroel: Social Consciousness in Two Autobiographies."
Eighteenth-Century Studies, 7 (1974), 321–42. Contrasting the social ethic of
Diego de Torres Villarroel with that of Franklin as "embodying the ideas of their
respective countries," Ilie finds aristocracy and moral idealism characteristically
Spanish, and democracy and ethical pragmatism characteristically American.

1975

Buxbaum, Melvin H. *Benjamin Franklin and the Zealous Presbyterians.* University
Park: Pennsylvania State Univ. Press, 1975. In a chapter on the *Autobiography*
(pp. 7–46), Buxbaum stresses BF's supposed Anglophilism, his promotion of
America, and the *Autobiography* as apologia and as refutation of public and
private criticisms of Franklin.
Larson, David M. "Franklin on the Nature of Man and the Possibility of Virtue." *Early*
American Literature, 10 (1975), 111–20. Larson argues that BF bases his "moral
theory upon consensus rather than metaphysics" and that he rejects "the
theoretical extremes of Hobbesian pessimism and Shaftesburian optimism."

1976

Cooley, Thomas. *Educated Lives: The Rise of Modern Autobiography in America.*
Columbus: Ohio State University Press, 1976. Cooley argues that BF and
Thoreau adhered to the same psychology and theories of identity, both believing
that character can only develop, not basically change. Therefore their stories
basically concern "fulfilling the self's innate capacities."
Griffith, John. "Franklin's Sanity and the Man behind the Masks." In *The Oldest*
Revolutionary: Essays on Benjamin Franklin. Ed. J. A. Leo Lemay. Philadelphia: Univ. of Pennsylvania Press, 1976, pp. 123–38. Griffith finds that a
recurring theme in Franklin criticism is the search for a role that underlies and
subsumes the numerous roles that Franklin acted. He believes that Franklin was
extraordinarily aware "of the social process by which self-awareness is formed"
and that his appeal is based upon his extraordinary common sense—a sanity so
balanced that his writings seem to give the reader a glimpse of a lost paradise.
Parker, David L. "From Sound Believer to Practical Preparationist: Some Puritan
Harmonics in Franklin's Autobiography." In *The Oldest Revolutionary.* Ed. J.
A. Leo Lemay. Philadelphia: Univ. of Pennsylvania Press, 1976, pp. 67–75.
Parker shows how BF's plan for "moral perfection" echoes the pattern of the
puritan stages of conversion and how BF's view of human nature (which is
similar to the puritan view) underlies his accommodating virtue to self-interest.
Thorpe, James. *The Autobiography of Benjamin Franklin.* San Marino, CA.: Huntington Library, 1976. This brief pamphlet, containing many illustrations,
pleasantly introduces Franklin and the holograph manuscript of his *Autobiog-*
raphy.
Weintraub, Karl J. "The Puritan Ethic and Benjamin Franklin." *Journal of Religion,*
56 (1976), 223–37. Weintraub, following Max Weber, believes that Franklin
has "the Puritan personality without the Puritan motivation and the Puritan
objective." Weintraub argues that Franklin, "a tepid Deist all his life," secular-
ized the Puritan ethic, thus helping "to shape a way of life and a pragmatic
utilitarian ethic." He also criticizes BF for retaining a trace of religion: "Franklin
is not Voltaire, who saw no meaning written into the universe. And in that sense
Franklin had not fully gone toward secularization."
Zall, P[aul] M. "The Manuscript and Early Printed Texts of Franklin's Autobiography." *Huntington Library Quarterly,* 39 (1976), 385–402. A brief version of

the introduction to the Lemay-Zall *Genetic Text* (1981) showing that the first printing of Franklin's *Autobiography* (Paris: Buisson, 1791) was based upon a surreptitious copy of the unrevised version of Franklin's manuscript of Part One.

Zall, P[aul] M. "A Portrait of the Autobiographer as an Old Artificer." In *The Oldest Revolutionary*. Ed. J. A. Leo Lemay. Philadelphia: Univ. of Pennsylvania Press, 1976, pp. 53–65. Discussing implications of such manuscript revisions as the seven instances of the errata trope (which were evidently added after most of Part One was written), Zall suggests that BF was fabricating a plot about moral development.

1977

Gilmore, Michael T. *The Middle Way: Puritanism and Ideology in American Romantic Fiction*. New Brunswick, N.J.: Rutgers University Press, 1977. Gilmore (pp. 47–64) finds key character sketches to be cautionary doubles of BF, thinks that sea and water are associated with BF's rebellion against his father, argues that the number of virtues recall the thirteen colonies as well as Christ and the apostles, and finds that Franklin preached the puritan social ethic as a secular gospel. He claims that Franklin stopped writing because his private life after 1757 betrayed the book's social and moral philosophy and charges that the Franklinian philosophy denies man's deepest spiritual needs.

Perkins, Jean A. "The Ironic Mode in Autobiography: Franklin and Rousseau." In Ronald C. Rosbottom, ed., *Studies in Eighteenth-Century Culture*, 6 (Univ. Of Wisconsin Press, 1977), pp. 215–28. Arguing that the eighteenth-century fashion of seeking causes or origins along with the new stylistic fictional techniques transformed autobiography, Perkins shows how BF and Rousseau, in stressing childhood and youth as keys to their adult selves, employed an ironic tone to manipulate aesthetic distance.

1978

Bell, Robert H. "Benjamin Franklin's 'Perfect Character,' " *Eighteenth-Century Life*, 5, ii (Winter, 1978), 13–25. Bell criticizes D. H. Lawrence for missing the irony in BF's attempt to achieve a "Perfect Character," but finds BF's basic self "insufficiently complex" because he "yielded to the autobiographer's strongest temptation: to make external, retrospective assessments of himself at the expence of an internal, authentically realized presentation of character." He also finds the book lacks unity, being "episodic, like a picaresque novel, with little pretense of exploring the relationship of one segment to another," and observes that although religious issues pervade the *Autobiography*, BF "invariably banters with the rigorous theological core of the old faith."

Dawson, Hugh J. "Franklin's 'Memoirs' in 1784: The Design of the *Autobiography*. Part I and II," *Early American Literature*, 12 (1978), 286–93. Arguing from Franklin's reordering of topics in the Outline of the *Autobiography*, Dawson maintains that Franklin attempted to complete the *Autobiography* both thematically and structurally when he wrote Part Two in 1784.

Fiering, Norman S. "Benjamin Franklin and the Way to Virtue." *American Quarterly*, 30 (1978), 199–223. Fiering argues that Franklin's approach to virtue was not Puritan (which is characterized by scrupulosity, "that intense self-examination that worries primarily about purity of intention") but Aristotelian (which stresses the contribution that habit makes to virtue and was common among eighteenth-century thinkers, especially the British associationists, who believed in a mechanistic model of behavior, whereby the slow, incremental inculation of habits modified external behavior). He classifies Franklin's thirteen virtues: four (order, frugality, industry, and cleanliness) are bourgeoise; three (silence, chastity, and humility) are Christian (as much Roman Catholic as Puritan); one (sincerity or honesty) is unclassifiable; and the remaining five are the traditional classical virtues. And Fiering points out that in eighteenth-century ethics, BF's virtues would be classified as "duties to self, as distinguished from duties to God and duties to other men."

Lemay, J. A. Leo. "Benjamin Franklin, Universal Genius." In *The Renaissance Man in the Eighteenth Century*. Los Angeles: William Andrews Clark Memorial Library, 1978, pp. 1–44. Lemay dichotomizes BF's public presentation of the American Dream motif into *1*, the rise from rags to riches; and *2*, the rise from impotence to importance, with the latter theme giving the book much of its allegorical meaning (BF's development parallels the rising independence of the American colonies) and its archetypal power (BF's rise parallels every individual's development from helplessness and nebulousness to the adult's comparative power and identity). He also sketches three of BF's underlying philosophic implications of the American Dream: *1*, a philosophy of individualism; *2*, a philosophy of Free Will; and *3*, a deliberate espousal of hope, even of optimism. And Lemay argues that the *Autobiography*'s fictive world is "the first completely modern world . . . in Western literature: nonfeudal, nonaristocratic, and non-religious."

Whitfield, Stephen J. "Three Masters of Impression Management: Benjamin Franklin, Booker T. Washington, and Malcolm X as Autobiographers." *South Atlantic Quarterly*, 77 (1978), 399–417. In Whitfield's comparison, the three men were all "shaped by paternal surrogates" (p. 406); all revealed a "protean flair for switching personae" (especially Malcolm X, p. 404); and all demonstrate that "the national fascination with human malleability seems to be holding constant" (p. 417).

1979

Couser, A. Thomas. "Deism and Prophecy: Benjamin Franklin's *Autobiography*," in Couser's *American Autobiography* (Amherst: University of Massachusetts Press, 1979), 41–50 and 204. In chapter 4, "Deism and Prophecy," Couser deals with the implications for autobiography caused by the shift from belief in Puritanism (and Quakerism) to deism. He finds that Franklin's "sense of delight" in his "succession of roles" and his belief in the "value and consequence" of the individual distinguish his autobiography "from the spiritual autobiographies preceding it" (p. 45). The "overall pattern" in BF's *Autobiography* is "a gradual but dramatic extension of the scope of his interest, knowledge, and influence" (p. 46). He calls the latter part of the *Autobiography* "increasingly dull and drained of individuality" (p. 50).

Lewis, Janette Seaton. "A Turn of Thinking: The Long Shadow of *The Spectator* in Franklin's *Autobiography*." *Early American Literature*, 13 (1978/9), 268–77. Lewis argues that BF's *Autobiography* reveals the occasional influence of *The Spectator* "in subject matter, attitude, method, intent, style, and tone."

Perkins, Jean A. "Contexts of Autobiography in the Eighteenth Century: France and America." *Enlightenment Studies in Honour of Lester G. Crocker*, eds. Alfred J. Bingham, Jr., and Virgil W. Topazio (Oxford: The Voltaire Foundation, 1979), pp. 231–41. Perkins believes that Franklin and Rousseau both reflect the historical situation of their countries. "America was a new land and pragmatic solutions pursued with rationality and a spirit of compromise could succeed," whereas "France was going through the agonies of a mortal illness which could only be cured by a monstrous upheaval."

Porter, Roger J. "Unspeakable Practices, Writable Acts: Franklin's *Autobiography*." *Hudson Review*, 32 (1979), 229–38. Although Franklin had "abundant capacity for vanity, aggression and luxuriant pleasure," he deliberately stressed control, order and discipline in the *Autobiography*. Porter also finds BF reluctant to explore the self; instead BF reveals an ironist's pleasure in "mock self-effacement," undercutting "himself even as he applauds himself."

1980

Dawson, Hugh J. "Fathers and Sons: Franklin's 'Memoirs' as Myth and Metaphor." *Early American Literature*, 14 (Winter, 1979/80), 269–92. Dawson argues that the underlying psychological reason BF wrote his *Memoirs* was to justify and to reconcile himself with the values and personality of his father, Josiah. Dawson points out passages in the *Autobiography* where he believes Franklin displays "his guilty ambivalence at having disobeyed his father in the process of surpassing him" (p. 285).

Spengemann, William C. *The Forms of Autobiography*. New Haven: Yale University Press, 1980, pp. 51–61. Spengemann believes that BF's Autobiography belongs in the religious tradition of John Bunyan and Augustine.

1981

Bailey, Tom. "Benjamin Franklin's *Autobiography*: The Self and Society in a New World," *Midwest Quarterly*, 22 (1981), 93–104. Bailey finds the *Autobiography* advocates "a radical, generous displaying of selfishness for cultural goals," giving examples, on the one hand, of Franklin's downplaying the pleasure he felt at displaying his swimming feats in London, and, on the other, of his downplaying the anguish he felt at the death of his son Francis.

1982

Banes, Ruth A. "The Exemplary Self: Autobiography in Eighteenth Century America," *Biography*, 5 (1982), 226–39. Banes examines the autobiographies of John Woolman, John Adams, Thomas Jefferson, and Benjamin Franklin to prove that "the exemplary self was the prevailing autobiographical persona during the eighteenth and nineteenth centuries." She finds that all four authors use "apologetic openings, parable form, and the purposes of Divine Providence."

Beidler, Philip D. "The 'Author' of Franklin's *Autobiography*." *Early American Literature* 16 (1981/2): 257–69. Beidler argues that BF's *Autobiography* reveals a "fundamentally Augustinian view of the relationship between human imperfection and of our utter presumptuousness in ever attempting a final pronouncement on anything." He further claims that Franklin's "apparently 'modern' rhetorical self-consciousness is in fact a direct response to much older imperatives of religion."

Bercovitch, Sacvan. "The Ritual of American Autobiography: Edwards, Franklin, Thoreau." *Revue Francaise d'Etudes Americaines* 7 (1982): 139–50. Bercovitch believes that the autobiographies of Edwards, Franklin, and Thoreau perpetuate and conserve American traditions of their day. Franklin, rooted in colonial conditions, draws on the libertarian heritage and conserves the civic traditions of a nation in upheavel.

Davis, Elizabeth. "Events in the Life and in the Text: Franklin and the Style of American Autogiography." *Revue Francaise d'Etudes Americaines* 7 (1982): 187–97. Davis argues that Franklin's repeated statements about the value of self-effacement "often invite, teasingly, mistrust." She believes that Franklin and other American autobiographers insist upon an unknowable secret self.

Lemay, J. A. Leo. "Poe's 'The Business Man': Its Contexts and Satire of Franklin's *Autobiography*," *Poe Studies* 15 (1982), 29–37. Lemay finds that Poe burlesques antebellum American materialism, the business ethic, and the idea of the self-made man through references to the *Autobiography*.

Authors

Aldridge, Alfred Owen. 1967 (2)
Bailey, Tom. 1981
Banes, Ruth A. 1982
Beidler, Philip D. 1982
Bell, Robert H. 1978
Bercovitch, Sacvan. 1982
Bier, Jesse. 1958
Buxbaum, Melvin H. 1975
Bushman, Richard L. 1966
Cawelti, John G. 1965
Cooley, Thomas. 1976
Couser, A. Thomas. 1979
Cox, James M. 1971
Davis, Elizabeth. 1982
Dawson, Hugh J. 1978; 1980
England, A. B. 1972
Fiering, Norman S. 1978
Gilmore, Michael T. 1977
Granger, Bruce Ingham. 1964
Griffith, John. 1971; 1976
Ilie, Paul. 1974
Ketcham, Ralph L. 1969
Larson, David M. 1975
Lawrence, D. H. 1923
Lemay, J. A. Leo. 1968; 1972; 1982
Lewis, Janette Seaton. 1978
Levin, David. 1964
Lynen, John F. 1965

McLaughlin, John H. 1973
Maugham, W. Somerset. 1940
Miles, Richard D. 1957
Miller, Ross. 1972
Minter, David L. 1969
Ohmann, Carol. 1970
Parker, David L. 1976
Perkins, Jean A. 1977; 1979
Porter, Roger J. 1979
Pritchett, V. S. 1941
Ross, Morton L. 1967
Sanford, Charles L. 1954
Sappenfield, James A. 1969; 1973
Sayre, Robert F. 1963; 1964
Schneider, Herbert W. 1925
Shea, Daniel B., Jr. 1968
Shear, Walter. 1962
Spengemann, William C. 1980
Spiller, Robert E. 1942; 1956
Stourzh, Gerald. 1953
Tatham, Campbell. 1971
Thorpe, James. 1976
Ward, John William. 1963
Weber, Max. 1905
Weintraub, Karl J. 1976
Whitfield, Stephen J. 1978
Wright, Louis B. 1946
Zall, P[aul] M. 1976 (2)

Index

Public affairs (*cont'd*)
85–86; BF occupied with, after retirement,
100; proposes civic improvements, 102–8;
Fothergill promotes, 106; best public
measures forced by occasion, 110; BF pens
Assembly message, 112; serves as provincial
commissioner, 123; builds frontier forts,
124–27; accepts agency to England, 135,
142–46. *See also* Academy; Albany Plan of
Union; Association; Defense; Fire
protection; Library Co.; Pennsylvania
Hospital; Post office.
Punning: Grave loves, 48; BF breaks habit of,
68. *See also* Riggite.
Pythagoras: on daily self-examination, 68;
"Golden Verses," 68

Quadrant, Godfrey invents, 48
Quakers: meetinghouse the scene of BF's first
sleep in Phila., 21; Franklin and Meredith
print history, 49; pacifism, 93, 94–97; permit
subterfuges, 96; control of Assembly, 94, 95,
97; quit power rather than principle, 97;
blackened by Morris, 112; exempted from
militia, 123; mentioned, 128
Quincy, Josiah: seeks aid for Mass., 113; BF
dictates address for, 113; thanks Assembly,
113; identified, 195
Quire book of letters, BF's, not extant, 114

Ralph, James: with BF in Phila., 29–31; as poet,
30–31, 35; Pope ridicules, 31, 135; with BF
to England, 31; with BF in London, 32, 35;
advised no actor, 33; proposes weekly paper,
33; borrows from BF, 33, 36, 40; *Liberty and
Necessity* dedicated to, 34; teaches school in
Berkshire, 35; uses BF's name, 35; his
mistress, 35–36; refuses to repay BF, 36;
relations with, in London, 40; BF converts to
deism, 45–46; Denny reports his later
success, 135; identified, 195
Rationalism, BF's early, 46. *See also* Reason,
Religion.
Rationalizing, BF on, 28
Read, Deborah. *See* Franklin, Deborah Read.
Read, James, warns BF to resign clerkship, 93;
identified, 195–96
Read, John: BF sees Deborah at door of, 20;
lodges with, 22; ruined by Riddlesden, 33;
identified, 196
Read, Sarah White: discourages BF's courtship
of Deborah, 29; acknowledges mistake, 56;
identified, 196
Reading, BF's: as child, 9; as boy, 10, 12, 13;
with Collins, 11, 26; father's religious books,
9; borrows from booksellers' apprentices, 10;
with Phila. friends, 22; BF's collection, 26;
arrangements for, in London, 34; two days a
week, 43; conversation improved by, 45; sole
diversion, 54, 64; moral virtues vary in, 67;
in daily schedule, 69. *See also* Authors;
Education.

Reading, general: M. Adams' library, 10;
Collins' library, 26; Burnet's library, 26;
improves knowledge, 40, 45, 57; of Junto
members, 48, 57, 63; contributes to
colonists' defense of privileges, 57; few
readers in Phila., 63; becomes fashionable,
63; makes Americans better instructed than
others, 57, 74. *See also* Library Co. of Phila.
Reason: convenience of, 28; versus
"inclination," 28. *See also* Rationalizing.
Reasonable creature, man as, 28
Reasoning, error in metaphysical, 46
Receiver General, Proprietors'. *See* Hockley,
Richard.
Religion: of BF's ancestors, 4–5; Folger on
liberty of conscience, 6; BF prefers studying
to church, 12, 66; influence of Shaftesbury
and Collins, 13; BF pointed at, as atheist, 17;
of Dr. Browne, 19; of Keimer, 22, 28–29,
43, 45; Keimer's projected sect, 28; BF keeps
Lents, 29; of BF's Phila. friends, 29; *Liberty
and Necessity* on, 34, 46; BF's early views
on, 46; BF's upbringing, 45, 65; BF's deistic
creed, 2, 45, 65, 78; BF's attitude toward
sects, 65; utility of, 65; prefers private liturgy,
66; address to *Powerful Goodness* in chart of
day, 69; quits the congregation, 82; BF
suggests minister dole out rum, 126. *See also*
Deism; Dunkers; Great Awakening;
Hemphill; Metempsychosis; Moravians;
Necessity; Quakers; Presbyterianism;
Providence; Roman Catholicism;
Whitefield.
Residences, BF's: at Crooked Billet, 21; with
Bradford, 22; with Read, 22; in Little Britain,
33, 34; in Duke Street, 37; near Market
Street, 47; near Jersey Market, 104; in
lodging Mr. Charles provided (Craven
Street), 142
Resolution: as virtue, 67, 68; value of 78–79
Revolution, American. *See* American
Revolution.
Rhode Island: commissioners at Albany
Congress, 109; French troops in, 120. *See
also* Newport.
Richardson, Samuel, mixes narration and
dialogue, 18
Riddlesden, William: rascal, 33; identified, 196
Riggite, BF esteemed a, 37. *See also* Punning.
Roberts, James: 33; identified, 196
Rogers, John: weds Deborah Read, 41; thought
to be a bigamist, 56; identified, 196–97
Roman Catholicism: Franklin family's zeal
against, 4; BF's landlandy converted to, 38;
of maiden lady in garret, 38
Roscommon, Wentworth, Dillon, Earl of
Essay on Translated Verse, quoted, 14;
comment on, 14
Rose, Aquila: death, 17; Keimer's elegy on, 22;
BF takes his son apprentice, 54; identified,
197
Rose, Joseph, BF takes as apprentice, 54